FIBONACCI NUMBERS in NATURE

MANY FLOWERS EXHIBIT
A FIBONACCI NUMBER
OF PETALS

PUSSY WILLOW
13 BUDS
GENERATED
IN 5 CIRCLES
OF GROWTH
RATIO: 5/13

COSMO
8

IRIS
3

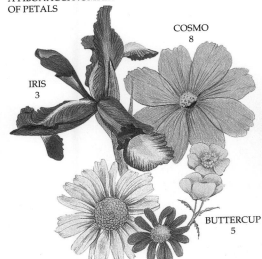

13 ROWS

8 ROWS

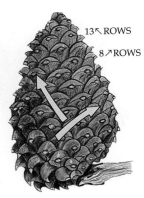

BUTTERCUP
5

DAISIES
21 AND 13

5

4

3

2

1

BRACTS SPIRAL
AROUND A PINECONE
AND PETALS SPIRAL
AROUND AN ARTICHOKE
IN FIBONACCI NUMBERS
OF ROWS

8 ROWS

5 ROWS

ARRANGEMENT OF BUDS
ON A BRANCH
TENDS TO BE
CHARACTERIZED
BY FIBONACCI RATIOS

1 2 3 5 8 13 21 34 55 89 144...

Mathematics for Elementary School Teachers

The Prindle, Weber & Schmidt Series in Mathematics

Althoen and Bumcrot, Introduction to Discrete Mathematics
Bean, Sharp, and Sharp, Precalculus
Boye, Kavanaugh, and Williams, Elementary Algebra
Boye, Kavanaugh, and Williams, Intermediate Algebra
Burden and Faires, Numerical Analysis, Fifth Edition
Cass and O'Connor, Fundamentals with Elements of Algebra
Cullen, Linear Algebra and Differential Equations, Second Edition
Dick and Patton, Calculus, Volume I & Volume II
Dick and Patton, Technology in Calculus: A Sourcebook of Activities
Eves, In Mathematical Circles
Eves, Mathematical Circles Squared
Eves, Return to Mathematical Circles
Faires and Burden, Numerical Methods
Fletcher, Hoyle, and Patty, Foundations of Discrete Mathematics
Fletcher and Patty, Foundations of Higher Mathematics, Second Edition
Fraser, Intermediate Algebra: An Early Functions Approach
Gantner and Gantner, Trigonometry
Geltner and Peterson, Geometry for College Students, Second Edition
Gilbert and Gilbert, Elements of Modern Algebra, Third Edition
Gobran, Beginning Algebra, Fifth Edition
Gobran, Intermediate Algebra, Fourth Edition
Gordon, Calculus and the Computer
Hall, Beginning Algebra
Hall, Intermediate Algebra
Hall, Algebra for College Students, Second Edition
Hall, College Algebra with Applications, Third Edition
Hartfiel and Hobbs, Elementary Linear Algebra
Huff and Peterson, College Algebra Activities for the TI-81 Graphics Calculator
Humi and Miller, Boundary-Value Problems and Partial Differential Equations
Kaufmann, Elementary Algebra for College Students, Fourth Edition
Kaufmann, Intermediate Algebra for College Students, Fourth Edition
Kaufmann, Elementary and Intermediate Algebra: A Combined Approach
Kaufmann, Algebra for College Students, Fourth Edition
Kaufmann, Algebra with Trigonometry for College Students, Third Edition
Kaufmann, College Algebra, Second Edition
Kaufmann, Trigonometry
Kaufmann, College Algebra and Trigonometry, Second Edition
Kaufmann, Precalculus, Second Edition
Kennedy and Green, Prealgebra for College Students
Laufer, Discrete Mathematics and Applied Modern Algebra
Lavoie, Discovering Mathematics
Nicholson, Elementary Linear Algebra with Applications, Second Edition
Nicholson, Introduction to Abstract Algebra
Pence, Calculus Activities for Graphic Calculators
Pence, Calculus Activities for the TI-81 Graphic Calculator
Plybon, An Introduction to Applied Numerical Analysis

Powers, Elementary Differential Equations
Powers, Elementary Differential Equations with Boundary-Value Problems
Proga, Arithmetic and Algebra, Third Edition
Proga, Basic Mathematics, Third Edition
Rice and Strange, Plane Trigonometry, Sixth Edition
Rogers, Haney, and Laird, Fundamentals of Business Mathematics
Schelin and Bange, Mathematical Analysis for Business and Economics, Second Edition
Sgroi and Sgroi, Mathematics for Elementary School Teachers
Swokowski and Cole, Fundamentals of College Algebra, Eighth Edition
Swokowski and Cole, Fundamentals of Algebra and Trigonometry, Eighth Edition
Swokowski and Cole, Fundamentals of Trigonometry, Eighth Edition
Swokowski and Cole, Algebra and Trigonometry with Analytic Geometry, Eighth Edition
Swokowski, Precalculus: Functions and Graphs, Sixth Edition
Swokowski, Calculus, Fifth Edition
Swokowski, Calculus, Fifth Edition, Late Trigonometry Version
Swokowski, Calculus of a Single Variable
Tan, Applied Finite Mathematics, Third Edition
Tan, Calculus for the Managerial, Life, and Social Sciences, Second Edition
Tan, Applied Calculus, Second Edition
Tan, College Mathematics, Second Edition
Trim, Applied Partial Differential Equations
Venit and Bishop, Elementary Linear Algebra, Alternate Second Edition
Venit and Bishop, Elementary Linear Algebra, Third Edition
Wiggins, Problem Solver for Finite Mathematics and Calculus
Willard, Calculus and Its Applications, Second Edition
Wood and Capell, Arithmetic
Wood and Capell, Intermediate Algebra
Wood, Capell, and Hall, Developmental Mathematics, Fourth Edition
Zill, Calculus, Third Edition
Zill, A First Course in Differential Equations, Fifth Edition
Zill and Cullen, Differential Equations with Boundary-Value Problems, Third Edition
Zill and Cullen, Advanced Engineering Mathematics

The Prindle, Weber & Schmidt Series in Advanced Mathematics

Brabenec, Introduction to Real Analysis
Ehrlich, Fundamental Concepts of Abstract Algebra
Eves, Foundations and Fundamental Concepts of Mathematics, Third Edition
Keisler, Elementary Calculus: An Infinitesimal Approach, Second Edition
Kirkwood, An Introduction to Real Analysis
Patty, Foundations of Topology
Ruckle, Modern Analysis: Measure Theory and Functional Analysis with Applications
Sieradski, An Introduction to Topology and Homotopy

Mathematics for Elementary School Teachers

Problem-Solving Investigations

Richard J. Sgroi
Laura Shannon Sgroi
State University of New York-New Paltz

PWS-KENT Publishing Company
Boston

PWS-KENT
Publishing Company

20 Park Plaza
Boston, Massachusetts 02116

To the memory of Professor Marc Belth:
mentor, friend, and inspiration

and

To our children,
Allison, Elizabeth, and Kathryn

Acquisitions Editor: Tim Anderson
Production Editors: S. London and Patricia Adams
Developmental Editor: Barbara Lovenvirth
Manufacturing Coordinator: Marcia Locke
Cover and Interior Designer: S. London
Cover Photographer: Greg Bowl Studio. Lens courtesy of C. Bennett Scopes, Inc.
Interior Illustrators: Artscribe; TI-81 Graphics Calculators: Scientific Illustrators
Typesetter: TSI Graphics
Endpaper and Cover Printer: New England Book Components, Inc.
Text Printer/Binder: R. R. Donnelley & Sons Company

PWS-KENT Publishing Company is a division of Wadsworth, Inc.

Library of Congress Cataloging-in-Publication Data

Sgroi, Richard J.
  Mathematics for elementary school teachers : problem-solving investigations / Richard J. Sgroi, Laura Shannon Sgroi.
    p.   cm.—(The Prindle, Weber & Schmidt series in mathematics)
  Includes index.
  ISBN 0-534-93255-X
    1. Mathematics—Study and teaching (Elementary) I. Sgroi, Richard J. II. Title. III. Series.
  QA135.5.S456   1993
  372.7—dc20   92-37211
                                                                                    CIP

Photography Credits: Ch. 1 opener, © Greg Bowl Studio; Ch. 2 opener, © Nienhuis Montessori USA; Ch. 3 opener, © Steve Dunwell/The Image Bank; Ch. 4 opener, © Flip Chalfant/The Image Bank; Ch. 5 opener, © Joe Sohm/Panoramic Images, Chicago 1992; Ch. 6 opener, © Greg Bowl Studio; Ch. 7 opener, © John P. Kelly/The Image Bank; Ch. 8 opener, © Greg Bowl Studio; Ch. 9 opener, © Accu-Weather, Inc.; Ch. 10, © Gary Gladstone/The Image Bank; Ch. 11 opener, © Greg Bowl Studio; Ch. 12, © Gary Gay/The Image Bank; Ch. 13 opener, © Co Rentmeester/The Image Bank.

Pg. 680, Fig. 13.22, reproduced by courtesy of the Director and University Librarian, the John Rylands Library of Manchester; **Pg. 681**, Figs. 13.23a and 13.23b, used with permission of The Metropolitan Museum of Art, Harris Brisbane Dick Fund.

Front and Back Endpapers: Trudi H. Garland © Dale Seymour Publications, Menlo Park, CA.

 This book is printed on recycled, acid-free paper.

Printed in the United States of America.
1 2 3 4 5 6 7 8 9 10—97 96 95 94 93

Contents

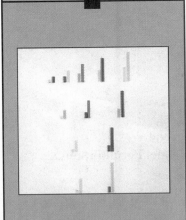

Preface

As we approach the turn of the century, many exciting changes are taking place in the field of mathematics education. A number of these changes are influenced by modifications in the world economy, which places greater and greater emphasis on mathematical skills. These changes are also necessitated by continuing technological innovations, which are constantly producing more powerful, affordable, and accessible calculators and computers.

NCTM Standards

The professional organization of mathematics educators from the United States and Canada, the National Council of Teachers of Mathematics (NCTM), has taken an active role in helping the mathematics education community achieve greater parity between mathematics as taught in schools and that which is likely to be useful to working professionals in the early part of the twenty-first century. As a step toward achieving this goal, the NCTM has issued a document, *The Curriculum and Evaluation Standards for School Mathematics* (1989), or as it is commonly referred to, *The Standards*. In this document, the educators identify certain curricular strands that merit increased attention, such as problem solving, or decreased attention, such as memorization of rules. *The Standards* also recommend employing specific pedagogical strategies, such as active learning, the use of manipulatives, writing to learn, and group activities. (Excerpts from *The Standards* are included in Appendix B.)

Because we as authors and educators recognize the importance of *The Standards* and agree with their goals, many of NCTM's suggestions are incorporated throughout this text. The recommendations contained within *The Standards* have influenced our selection of topics and the manner in which they are presented. Each chapter emphasizes problem solving, the meaning behind various algorithms or procedures, careful concept development, and the use of physical models.

Pedagogy and Features

Because of the importance of problem-solving skills to today's students, problem solving has not been relegated to a single chapter; we do not view it as a discrete topic. Rather, we view problem solving as the focus of this text and the focus of elementary school mathematics. Our combined teaching experience (which spans all educational levels, from kindergarten through graduate students) has led us to conclude that the ability to solve problems is acquired slowly. We present problems in a variety of contexts and for a variety of purposes, enabling the student to begin to understand that mathematics is a way of thinking about and understanding the world.

Problem-solving **Investigations**, found in each section of each chapter, are key to the presentations of concepts. Many of these investigations employ purposeful problem-solving strategies and use the four-step plan for solving problems introduced by George Polya in his book *How to Solve It* (1985). Beginning with the first section in Chapter 1, Polya's four-step plan is continually referred to and expanded upon throughout the text. Numerous problems and exercises can be found in the **Assessments** at the end of each section and chapter, providing the student with opportunities to practice and reinforce the use of Polya's four steps.

Other features in this text are also the result of recommendations contained in *The Standards*. There is evidence to suggest that students who study and work through math assignments in a group format are more successful than students who work in isolation. At the end of each section and chapter, we include the **Cooperative Activity**. These contain two parts: *Individual Accountability* and *Group Goal*. The student is first asked to make some contribution to the group effort. In some of the activities, the tasks are the same for all members of the group; in others, each group member works on a different aspect of the activity. Each student then brings to the group his or her findings and results, sharing strategies and refining plans based on comparing the methods used. The group is then given a problem to solve collaboratively, using the skills developed in the individual component of the activity.

Following each section and chapter, **In Other Words** offer students the opportunity to refine their thinking and understanding by writing explanations of selected mathematical concepts. Reflecting on a concept and then writing an explanation will help engage students in the mathematical communication process while structuring and strengthening their reasoning abilities.

At the end of each chapter, a **Vocabulary** of key terms reinforces and reminds the student of important issues discussed in the chapter. A **Review** is also provided at the end of each chapter. These reviews contain additional exercises and problems for the entire chapter.

Each chapter opener serves as an informal visual introduction to the concepts presented in the chapter. Students are asked to examine the photograph shown and answer questions about what they observe, using problem-solving and estimation skills. The photographs selected for the openers are repeated in color in the Contents, enabling students to obtain another perspective if they so desire.

Endpapers in color depict the Fibonacci Sequence of Numbers (front) and the Golden Proportion (back). Each of these charts provides information helpful to students and is related to text discussion. The Fibonacci sequence can be found in the *Appendix A—Spreadsheets*, **Investigation 2**, and the Golden Ratio is discussed in Chapter 11.

Calculator Use and Estimation Skills

One of the assumptions made in *The Standards* is that all students will have a calculator. Therefore, throughout this text, access to a calculator is assumed, and specific applications and instructions for efficient use of the calculator are included where appropriate. We do not indicate when to use a calculator, leaving this determination to the student. Knowing when to utilize a calculator and when to perform the work mentally or with paper and pencil is a judgment the student will learn to make while working through this text. Acquiring this ability will necessitate and reinforce the development and strengthening of students' estimation skills. Calculator keystroke sequences are introduced and used wherever appropriate.

Alternative Models and Visuals

This text recognizes that students learn in a variety of ways. For this reason, we offer many alternative models and algorithms that can be used to view and interpret a particular problem situation. In addition, this text contains well over 2000 illustrations that serve to pictorially represent arithmetic, algebraic, and geometric concepts and problems.

Laminated Card and Problem Solving

In writing this book, we struggled with the traditional example–solution techinique in which authors present a problem for the student and then immediately solve it. We believe an important part of the problem-solving process is to allow the student to reflect before he or she acts. When teaching problem solving in a classroom setting, there are many opportunities to give your students time to ponder the problem, to offer a hint to steer them in the right direction, and to further extend the problem. This subtle interplay is not possible within the framework of a textbook. In order to give students the opportunity to first attempt to solve the **Investigations** on their own, we designed the **Laminated Card**, which is included with this text. We suggest that the students use this card to cover the solutions to each investigation and make a serious effort to solve the problems before checking the solution. A symbol ⊞ appears in the margin at the start of each investigation as a reminder to the student to first use the card. Both the simulated geoboard and graph paper that appear on this card will be useful in the solutions of some of the problems, especially in Chapters 10–13, which deal with geometry. This card is laminated to allow the student to reuse it as often as needed, with a felt-tipped pen provided for this purpose.

Number Theory

We have purposely chosen to introduce and use number theory topics in contexts where relevant. We made this decision because we strongly feel that, taken out of context, some number theory rules and properties tend to be memorized rather than understood. When we place number theory in the contexts where it is most frequently used, students can develop a better understanding of its meaning and purpose.

Manipulatives

Also packaged with this text as an aid to both students and instructors are **Manipulatives transparencies** for hands-on use with the exercises found throughout the text. These **Manipulatives** will also be extremely useful with the *Student Activity Book* designed to be used with this text, and for any classroom activities chosen by instructors.

Philosophy of Standards and Authors

Just as important as the specific recommendations contained within *The Standards* is the basic philosophy that the document promotes. This philosophy, embraced by the text, adheres to the belief that learning mathematics is a task that can be accomplished by almost anyone who is willing to apply effort, perseverance, and diligence and who brings a questioning mind to the study of mathematics. If students, as they work through this text, find themselves asking why something is so, or where a particular concept came from and is leading to, or if there is an alternative explanation or method, then they are on their way to becoming learners of mathematics. It is necessary to become a learner of mathematics before one can become a teacher of mathematics.

Supplements

For Instructors

Instructor's Manual—contains complete solutions to all exercises found in the text and for all chapter reviews. Each chapter opens with an introduction to the material being covered, as well as a discussion of the chapter opening photograph in the text. Each section begins with the section objectives, followed by teaching suggestions for classroom activities, and a discussion of the cooperative group activities found in the Assessments. Related readings for each of the chapters are recommended. Transparency Masters of selected illustrations from the text are also included in the manual.

EXPTest—a computerized test bank for the IBM PC and compatibles, consisting of open-ended, multiple-choice, and true/false questions. Test items can be edited, rearranged, and expanded on according to need. Users may also add test items to the disk. A demo disk is available.

ExamBuilder—a computerized test bank for the Macintosh. Features and questions are identical to EXPTest. A demo disk is available.

For Students

Student Activity Book by Victoria Garrison—contains activities designed to accompany each chapter of the text. Each section will open with an "In Our World" activity motivating the student to see the applications of each chapter topic to the real world. The activities require selected materials, including cut-out manipulatives found at the back of the Activity Book, and actual manipulatives provided with the text. Each section will also contain pages entitled "Check Your Understanding," which the instructor can collect to monitor the students' progress. This manual enables students to use and reinforce skills acquired in each text chapter, and to build their expertise and confidence. Answers to the activities are provided. (Answers to "*Check Your Understanding*" are found in the Instructor's Manual.)

Problem-Solving Strategies by Robert Matulis—this workbook provides students with strategies for using the problem-solving skills they are learning. Chapters 1–13 follow the chapter sequence of the text, and each section contains problems utilizing Polya's Four Steps. Students are asked to try each problem before using the hints and suggestions provided by the author. Students are encouraged to use the laminated card from the text as they work on these problems. A final chapter entitled *True Problems* offers miscellaneous problems from all the earlier chapters without indicating which of the chapters are the source, allowing the students to make this determination.

Acknowledgments

This book has grown out of a firm desire to improve mathematics education for both students and teachers. We believe that students must come through the courses taught for preservice elementary school teachers with a feeling of accomplishment, understanding, and self-confidence. Their mathematical reasoning and problem-solving abilities must be strong, and their understanding of mathematics must go beyond rules and formulas. Only then will pedagogy make sense and methods of teaching mathematics have a firm foundation.

We must acknowledge many people who have assisted us in this endeavor. We greatly appreciate all of the efforts on the part of those at PWS-KENT. Many people worked on our project in the editorial and production departments. In particular, we recognize (in alphabetical order), Patty Adams, Tim Anderson, Susan London, and Barbara Lovenvirth. We would also like to thank Sally Stickney for her many long hours of impeccable copy editing. Her comments and suggestions were insightful and always well-taken.

Many reviewers helped to mold and shape our manuscript into a viable textbook. We greatly appreciate all of the efforts of the following reviewers.

Mary K. Alter
University of Maryland

Tom Bassarear
Keene State College

Janet J. Brougher
University of Oregon

Max Coleman
Sam Houston State University

Philip Downum
SUNY College at Oswego

Cynthia Fleck
Wright State University

Charlotte K. Lewis
University of New Orleans

Robert S. Matulis
Millersville University

Myron Morford
Edinboro University of Pennsylvania

Barbara J. Shabell
California State Polytechnic University-Pomona

Joe K. Smith
Northern Kentucky University

Judith Wells
Illinois State University

We also wish to thank Linda and Robert Gerver for reviewing the assessments and the solutions, Victoria Garrison for all of her hard work in developing a student resource book that has vision and purpose, and Robert Matulis for developing the problem-solving supplement to this textbook.

Finally, we wish to recognize our mentor, the late Professor Marc Belth, to whom this book is dedicated. His influence and guidance have helped shape our philosophy of education.

L. S. S.
R. J. S.

To the Student: Addressing Math Anxiety

One impediment to learning mathematics is the phenomenon commonly referred to as "math anxiety." This phrase (which first appeared in *Ms. Magazine* in 1976) describes the feelings of distress, lack of confidence, dread, and even panic that some students encounter when confronted with learning or using mathematics. These feelings most typically occur when a student has a poor background in mathematics or associates a particular trauma with mathematics or learning mathematics.

Researchers have found that levels of math anxiety often correspond inversely with levels of math achievement, that is, the lower the achievement level, the higher the anxiety level. Because mathematics has historically been viewed as a "male-oriented" subject, it is not surprising that math anxiety is found disproportionately in female students. This finding increases the need to address this phenomenon, since the majority of students entering the field of elementary education are women. Researchers have learned that math anxiety is eased in a positive and supportive classroom environment and that students who experience math anxiety prefer to study and work on math assignments in a group. In a supportive setting, students feel more comfortable asking questions for clarification because their peer group both understands and accepts the feelings math anxiety can produce.

Others who experience math anxiety have learned to use certain relaxation techniques, such as concentrating on a peaceful scene, breathing deeply for a few minutes, or taking a walk prior to math class or before sitting down to do math assignments. Students also report that it is helpful to leave the assignment for a little while and do something else if they are feeling anxious. On returning to the assignment, they feel more relaxed and able to focus on the work at hand. You may wish to try some of these techniques. You may also want to consider keeping two notebooks: one in class and one at home. Each evening, transcribe your class notes to your notebook at home. Rewriting the class notes in your own language personalizes the mathematics and gives you an opportunity to explain a concept in your own words.

For those of you who have experienced math anxiety, it may be of some comfort to know that as future teachers you have the opportunity to break the cycle that leads to avoidance of mathematics and therefore poor performance. Knowing from your own experience how debilitating math anxiety can be will help you better understand the importance of increasing your students' confidence and sense of competence.

We hope that this text, with its emphasis on math as a sense-making endeavor, its attention to understanding concepts behind the procedures, its step-by-step investigations of problems throughout, and its concern with illustrating and creating models of various abstract concepts will help you to think of yourself as capable of learning, and eventually teaching, mathematics.

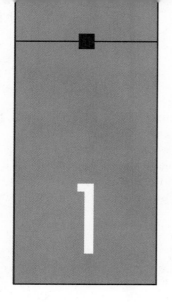

1

Mathematical **C**onnections: **V**isual, **V**erbal, and **S**ymbolic **P**atterns

Examine the photograph at the right.

Describe what you see.

Look for regularities. What aspects of the photograph are the same? What aspects are different?

What does this photograph resemble?

What do these resemblances have in common?

What would a mathematical description of this photograph contain?

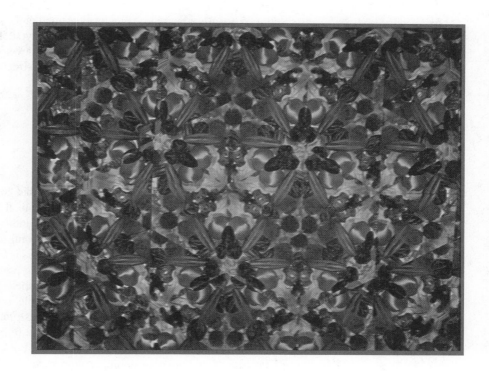

Introduction

It is often assumed that elementary school mathematics is concerned solely with operations on numbers. However, mathematics, even at the elementary school level, involves much more than simply finding sums, differences, products, and quotients. It is a way of looking at the world. When mathematicians view the world around them, they look for order and regularity, or the absence of order and regularity. In this chapter, we will explore visual, verbal, and symbolic patterns. As regularities surface, you will begin making connections between the known and the unknown, which is one of the first steps in the problem-solving process.

1.1 Patterns

One of the most important skills you need to develop to teach mathematics is the skill of solving problems. In this text, problem-solving skills and strategies will be explored as the need arises within particular contexts.

Patterns and Regularities

A problem can be viewed as any situation in which neither the solution nor the method of solution is readily apparent. Your level of mathematical experience will influence whether or not a particular situation is a problem to you. The basic framework we will use to structure investigations of problems is that developed by George Polya in his book *How to Solve It.** Polya outlines the following structure for problem solving:

1. Understand the problem
2. Devise a plan
3. Carry out the plan
4. Look back

These steps may appear to be simple and applicable to many problem-solving situations, mathematical or not. In fact, many strategies that are used for solving nonmathematical problems can also be used to solve mathematical ones. Once you understand a problem by having a clear picture of what is given and by knowing what you need to find, you must develop a plan of attack. As this text unfolds, you will learn a variety of such plans. One of the first problem-solving strategies is **looking for a pattern**.

In its simplest sense, recognizing and continuing a pattern involves finding regularity and repeating it. Being able to recognize and repeat a pattern helps structure what otherwise would seem to be unstructured. For example, knowing the way library books are arranged gives you the ability to understand the structure of the library and allows you to efficiently locate books and materials. Without fully understanding the alphabetical and numerical patterns that are used in shelving books, your search would be haphazard, unfocused, and time-consuming. Another example can be found in meteorology. Meteorologists often speak of weather patterns. Their knowledge of certain regularities

*Polya, George. *How to Solve It: A New Aspect of Mathematical Method*, 2d. Princeton, N.J.: Princeton University Press, 1957.

in the factors that influence the weather allows them to forecast weather conditions. Without the ability to recognize these regularities, meteorologists could not make these predictions.

Patterns can be identified in various settings. They can be visual, as in a graphic design; auditory, as in a rhythm; or symbolic, as in our number system. Examine the wallpaper border in Figure 1.1. Recognizing the inherent regularity allows you to predict what the unseen portion of this border should look like. You do not need to unroll the entire border to figure out what comes next. Now examine the border in Figure 1.2. The regularity in this border is both visual and numerical. You could predict what the rest of the border would look like either by sketching the repeated design or by counting the number of flowers and recognizing the 1 4 9 4 1 4 9 4 pattern.

Figure 1.1

Figure 1.2

Looking for a pattern is a strategy that you can consciously employ when attempting to solve problems. For instance, if you know that a certain traffic signal always follows the pattern of yellow, red, left turn, green, then you can predict how many light changes need to occur before you can make a left turn. But this strategy is not always conscious. For example, a child playing with a stacking toy composed of colored plastic "doughnuts" of various sizes learns that there is a pattern in the arrangement. The only way that all of the doughnuts can fit on the tapered spindle is if they are stacked in order from largest to smallest. The child does not consciously look for a pattern. Instead, through trial and error, the child realizes that to fit all of the doughnuts onto the spindle, the largest must be used first, followed by successively smaller ones. By interacting with the toy, the child discovers the pattern. Experiences such as this lead the child to believe that the world is governed by regularities, and understanding these regularities leads the child to a better understanding of the world.

Investigation 1

Examine the pattern illustrated below.

(a) Predict the next term.

(b) What would the ninth term be?

Understand the Problem: What is given? The arrow appears in five different orientations. What is unknown? You are asked to find the next term and the ninth term in the sequence.

Devise a Plan: Look for regularities. Identify the orientations of the arrows with north, south, east, and west.

Carry Out the Plan: The arrow is shown pointing north, east, south, west, and north, in that order. Each subsequent orientation is a clockwise turn to the next compass heading. If this pattern continues, the sixth arrow would illustrate a clockwise turn and be positioned facing east, as shown here:

To simplify the problem, use the letters N, E, S, and W to represent the compass headings. Thus, the pattern could be represented as

$$N \ E \ S \ W \ N \ E \ S \ W \ N \ E \ S \ W \dots$$

The ninth term in our simplified pattern is N. Therefore, the ninth term in the arrow pattern should appear as

Look Back: You might have solved this problem in another way. Notice the basic repeating unit consists of four symbols:

Therefore, you know the fourth, eighth, and twelfth terms will be

These terms are always followed by this arrow:

This information can be used to predict the fifth, ninth, and thirteenth terms, which also leads us to the solution to part (b). Can you determine the orientation of the 900th term?

When you are looking for a pattern that governs the arrangement of library books, you pay attention to the call number on the spine of the book. When a meteorologist is looking for weather patterns, he or she considers wind velocity and direction, movement of air masses, barometric pressure, and temperature. When we are looking for regularities in mathematics, we sometimes study the visual characteristics of shape and size. Examine the triangles in Figure 1.3. An obvious regularity is that triangles *A, C, D,* and *F* are identical. A simple way to verify this would be to cut out the triangles and superimpose them on each other. The different positions of these triangles do not change the fact that they are the same size and the same shape. Figures that are the same **congruent**   size and the same shape are said to be **congruent**.

Figure 1.3

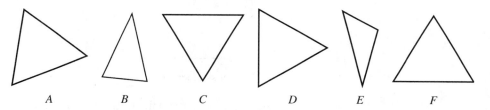

A	*B*	*C*	*D*	*E*	*F*

Congruency is an important concept to people who work in graphic design. The lettering on a sign often must be regular and consistent. It is usually important that each time a particular letter appears it be congruent to other images of that letter. This concept is crucial in other areas as well. A person responsible for cutting out pattern pieces to form a garment must ensure that all of the left sleeves, for instance, are congruent.

In addition to congruency between figures, a single figure can have congruent parts contained within it. Consider the six-sided figure, called a *hexagon*, in Figure 1.4. Each of the six triangles that form the hexagon are congruent to one another. You could demonstrate this by folding the hexagon along the dashed lines shown in Figure 1.4. Each triangle would exactly cover another, verifying their congruency.

Figure 1.4

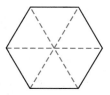

A figure that can be folded in such a way that one half completely covers the other **line symmetry**   half is said to have **line symmetry**. Children can have fun creating figures with line symmetry. Ask them to fold a sheet of paper in half and cut out half the outline of a shape such as a fir tree, a snowflake, or a heart, as shown in Figure 1.5. When the design is opened up, the fold in the paper represents the line of symmetry that divides the two congruent halves. If the line of symmetry is vertical, the figure is said to have *vertical line symmetry*. If the line of symmetry is horizontal, the figure is said to have *horizontal line symmetry*. Some shapes contain many lines of symmetry, whereas others have no lines of symmetry (see Figure 1.6).

Figure 1.5   Fold and cut out each pattern.

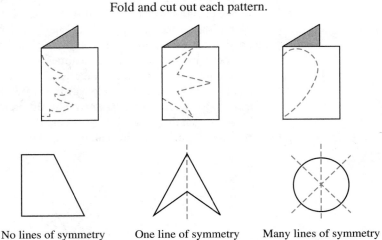

Figure 1.6

No lines of symmetry   One line of symmetry   Many lines of symmetry

In addition to being symmetrical about a line of symmetry, a figure can also be symmetrical about a point. A figure that is symmetrical about a point is said to have **rotational symmetry**   **rotational symmetry**. Since the shape in Figure 1.7 can be rotated around a central point until it appears identical to the original image, it has rotational symmetry. Obviously, every shape can be rotated one complete turn to match the original image. This does not mean that every shape has rotational symmetry. A shape is considered to have rotational symmetry only if it matches the original figure after a rotation of less than one complete turn.

Figure 1.7

Investigation 2

Identify the shapes that appear to be congruent in the following group.

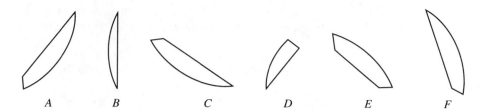

A B C D E F

Since cutting out these shapes would damage the book, instead place a piece of tracing paper over each of the shapes. Trace its outline. Match this outline to the other shapes, turning the tracing paper where necessary. Shapes A, C, and F are congruent. Congruency is commonly stated using the symbol $\cong$. The symbol is read as "is congruent to." Therefore, a correct statement of the solution would be $A \cong C$, $A \cong F$, $C \cong A$, $C \cong F$, $F \cong A$, $F \cong C$ (shapes A, C, and F are congruent to one another).

Investigation 3

Identify each of the following figures as having line symmetry, rotational symmetry, or no symmetry (asymmetry).

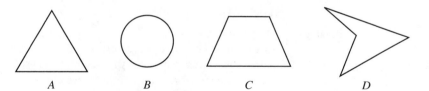

A B C D

Shape A is a special type of triangle in which all sides are equal. Line symmetry can be demonstrated by folding it in half three different ways, as illustrated here.

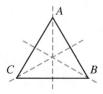

This shape also has rotational symmetry. Imagine this shape cut out and held in place by a straight pin through its center. It could be rotated so that point A is moved to the position of point B or point C, and it would still appear exactly the same.

Shape *B* has both line and rotational symmetry. Unlike shape *A*, it has an infinite number of lines of symmetry, a few of which are illustrated here.

Shape *C* can be folded only along one line of symmetry to achieve two congruent halves, as shown here. The only rotation that would result in an identical figure is a complete rotation (one full turn). Therefore, shape *C* does not have rotational symmetry.

Shape *D* has neither line nor rotational symmetry. This shape is said to be asymmetrical.

Analogies

analogy When trying to explain something unfamiliar, teachers often use an analogy. An **analogy** explains the unfamiliar in terms of the familiar by drawing attention to one or more characteristics that situations that seem otherwise unlike share. An example of an analogy can be seen when children first learn to play the flute. When they begin, they are instructed to blow into the flute as if it were a soda bottle. Although flutes are not soda bottles, the method of making a sound with a soda bottle is analogous to the method of making a sound with a flute.

Employing an analogy is a strategy that can be used when attempting to solve a problem. It utilizes prior knowledge about a known situation and applies it to an unknown situation that appears to be similar. For example, which is the best solution to this verbal analogy?

HAM is related to HUM as PAT is related to _____.

(a) PUM   (b) PAM   (c) HAT   (d) PUT   (e) HUT

Focus on the relationship between HAM and HUM. Recognize that they both begin with the letter H and end with the letter M. The only difference between them is that the vowel A in HAT has been changed to the vowel U in HUM. We need to transfer these similarities and differences to the word PAT and then examine the five choices to determine which is consistent with these relationships.

- Choice (a)   PUM begins with the same letter as PAT but does not end with the same letter as PAT. This choice contradicts one of the initial similarities.

- Choice (b)   PAM also does not end with the same letter as PAT; in addition, the vowel A does not change to the vowel U.
- Choice (c)   HAT can be eliminated because it does not begin with P.
- Choice (e)   HUT can also be eliminated because it does not begin with P.
- Choice (d)   PUT is the correct solution. It begins and ends with the same letters as does PAT. In addition, the vowel A has been changed to the vowel U.

distracters   In multiple-choice problems, the incorrect choices are referred to as **distracters**. Distracters are well-planned options that represent the most common errors that could be made in a particular situation. Many times, when answering multiple-choice questions, students ignore the choices and first solve the problem. If their answer matches one of the options, they are confident that it is correct. This method of solving a multiple-choice question often leads to incorrect solutions because of the presence of distracters. Notice how the above problem was solved. The given information was examined, and assumptions were made about the relationships between HAM and HUM. Then each individual choice was examined in light of the assumptions made. If the choice contradicted the given information, that is, the choice was inconsistent with what was initially assumed to be true, then the choice was deleted as a possible solution. This technique of making initial assumptions from the given information and then verifying whether or not a solution is consistent with the assumptions is called the technique of **looking for a contradiction**. It is a helpful strategy in many problem-solving situations throughout mathematics. It is particularly useful in multiple-choice questions.

Investigation 4

Select the best solution from the choices below.

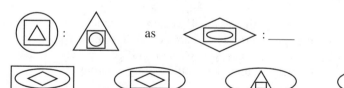

(a)   (b)   (c)   (d)   (e)

Understand the Problem: What is given? You are given a pictorial relationship between two figures.
What is unknown? You must determine how that relationship can translate to a second set of figures.

Devise a Plan: The first pair consists of only circles, triangles, and squares. In the first figure, the triangle is inside the square, which is inside the circle. The second figure reverses this order; the circle is inside the square, which is inside the triangle. Assume that this relationship defines the analogy. Then compare the third figure with each of the five choices, eliminating those that contradict the assumptions.

Carry Out the Plan:

- Choice (a)

- Choice (d)

- Choice (c)

- Choice (e)

- Choice (b)

Choices (a) and (d) contain only a rectangle, an oval, and a diamond shape, as does the third figure. They contradict the assumed relationship, however, since the order of an oval inside a rectangle inside a diamond is not reversed.

Choices (c) and (e) are inconsistent with the assumed relationship. They contain shapes other than an oval, a rectangle, and a diamond.

Choice (b) is consistent with the assumed relationship.

By the process of elimination, since choice (b) was the only choice that does not contradict the assumed pattern, it should be the correct solution.

Look Back: Choice (b) contains only an oval, a rectangle, and a diamond. These shapes are drawn in the reverse order of those in the third figure in the statement of the analogy. The relationship between the first two figures is the same as the relationship between the third figure and choice (b).

Investigation 5

Groups of figures can have similar characteristics. In this investigation, you are to find the characteristics that are common to those figures in Group A but are not present in Group B. Once you have identified the characteristics, select the shape from the Choices column that would belong to Group A.

| *Group A* | *Group B* | *Choices* |
| | | (a)   (b)   (c)   (d) |

Understand the Problem: What is given? Four figures in Group A share one or more common characteristics. These characteristics are not shared by the figures in Group B. What is unknown? You must determine the choice(s) that would belong to Group A, the one(s) that share the same characteristics as those figures in Group A.

Devise a Plan: Focus on a particular attribute.

Carry Out the Plan: The shapes in Group A are composed solely of straight sides. Those in Group B contain at least one curved side. Therefore, in order to be a member of Group A, the figure must have only straight sides. Choice (a) is the only option that is consistent with this assumption.

Look Back: Is it possible that another choice could belong to Group A? Is the solution that you have found unique? Another characteristic shared by all of the figures in Group A but none of the figures in Group B is that of line symmetry. If this is the identifying characteristic, then it could be argued that choices (a), (b), and (c) are all appropriate since all contain line symmetry.

Assessments for Section 1.1

1. Identify the next term.

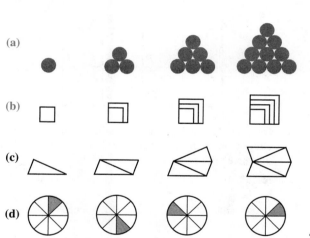

2. Identify the tenth term.

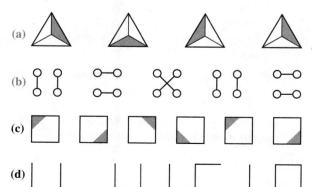

3. Identify the indicated term.

(a)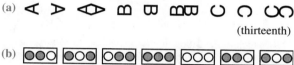

(thirteenth)

(b)

(fifteenth)

(c)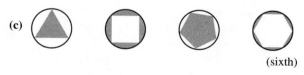

(sixth)

(d)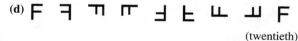

(twentieth)

4. Create a pattern that repeats every six terms. Identify the thirteenth term.

5. Create a pattern in which the third, sixth, ninth, and twelfth terms are 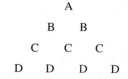 .

6. Continue the following pattern. Identify the eighth line.

```
        A
     B     B
   C    C    C
  D   D   D   D
```

7. Sometimes there are a number of possibilities for the terms in a pattern. Consider the following pattern:

Austin   Boston   Cincinnati   Detroit   Erie   Fresno

Identify three possibilities for the next term.

8. Create a pattern that has a range of possibilities for each term.

9. Here are some unusual patterns. Find the next three terms in each.

(a) O T T F F S S

(b) J F M A M J J A

10. Use the clock face below to find the next three terms.

12 5 10 3 8 1

Explain how the pattern is formed.

11. Which of the following figures appear to be congruent?

   (a)   (b)   (c)   (d)   (e)

12. Which of the following figures appear to be congruent?

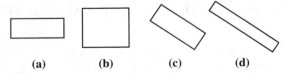

   (a)   (b)   (c)   (d)

13. Draw a figure congruent to the figure pictured here. Explain your method. How can you verify congruency?

14. Identify sets of congruent triangles in the figure below.

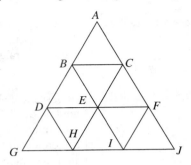

15. Identify sets of congruent squares in the figure below.

A	B	C	D	E
F	G	H	I	J
K	L	M	N	O
P	Q	R	S	T
U	V	W	X	Y

16. On a piece of graph paper, draw three congruent rectangles. Draw four smaller congruent rectangels within each. Do this three different ways.

17. (a) Identify all capital letters of the alphabet that have a horizontal line of symmetry.

(b) Identify all capital letters of the alphabet that have a vertical line of symmetry.

(c) Identify all capital letters of the alphabet that are both horizontally and vertically symmetric.

(d) Identify all capital letters of the alphabet that are rotationally symmetric.

(e) Identify all capital letters of the alphabet that are asymmetric.

18. In how many ways can a sandwich made on square pieces of bread be cut so that the two halves are congruent? Sketch the lines of symmetry.

19. Identify the types of symmetry (horizontal, vertical, diagonal, rotational) illustrated by each of the following logos.

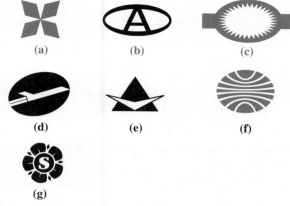

(a)   (b)   (c)

(d)   (e)   (f)

(g)

20. Identify the types of symmetry illustrated by each of the following figures. Indicate lines of symmetry where appropriate.

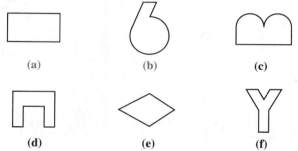

(a)   (b)   (c)

(d)   (e)   (f)

21. A palindrome is a word, verse, sentence, or number that reads the same forward and backward. (For our purposes, we will consider only single-word palindromes.) For example, RADAR is a palindrome. Some palindromes have a vertical line of symmetry. TOOT is a palindrome with a vertical line of symmetry, whereas NOON is not.

(a) List three palindromes that, when written with capital letters, have a vertical line of symmetry.

(b) Find a palindrome that, when written with capital letters, has a horizontal line of symmetry.

For Problems 22–31, select the best solution from the choices given.

22. WISH : WASH   as   TIME : _____
(a) TAME   (b) TASH   (c) TISH   (d) LATE
(e) TEAM

23.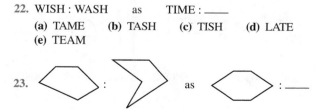

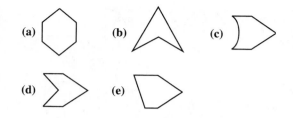

(a)   (b)   (c)

(d)   (e)

24.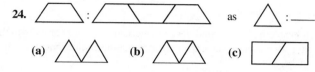

(a)   (b)   (c)

(d)   (e)

25.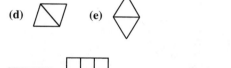

(a)   (b)   (c)

(d)   (e)

26. ZOO : OZ   as   ODD : _____
(a) STRANGE   (b) DO   (c) DAD
(d) DOD   (e) DD

27. AFTER : OFTEN   as   TIMID : _____
(a) TAMER   (b) TIMER   (c) LIMIT
(d) SHY   (e) DIMMER

28.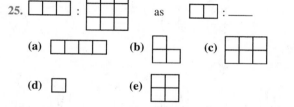

(a)   (b)   (c)

(d)   (e)

29.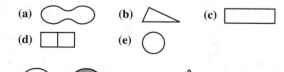

(a)   (b)   (c)

(d)   (e)

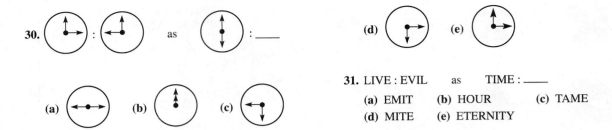

31. LIVE : EVIL   as   TIME : ____
(a) EMIT   (b) HOUR   (c) TAME
(d) MITE   (e) ETERNITY

In Problems 32–41, find the characteristics that are common to the figures in Group A but are not present in Group B. Once you have identified the characteristics, select the choice that would belong to Group A.

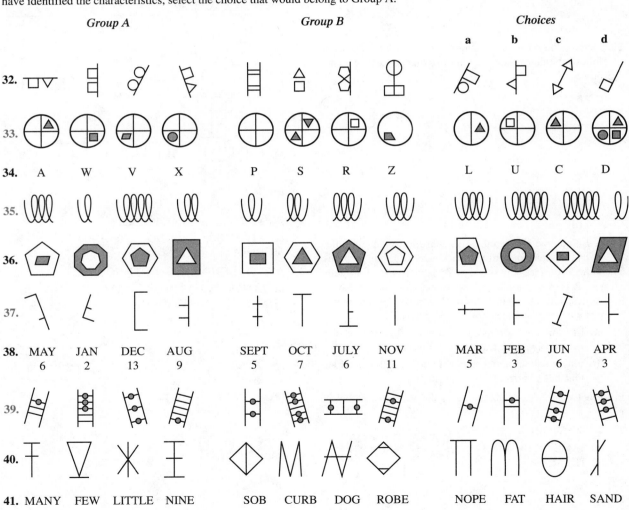

In Other Words

42. Define a pattern. Define an analogy. Describe the characteristics that the two share.

43. Explain the relationship between congruency and line symmetry.

44. Briefly discuss three patterns that provide regularity to your world.

45. What mathematical concepts might be illustrated to kindergarten children during a lesson involving paper folding and cutting? Explain your answer.

46. Explain why many patchwork quilt designs have both rotational symmetry and line symmetry.

Cooperative Activity

The final activity in this problem section and in all problem sections will be a cooperative group activity. Typically, successful cooperative group activities are characterized by two components:

Individual Accountability: Each group member is given an individual task to carry out. Each individual member is held responsible for completing that task.

Group Goal: The tasks that were performed individually are now presented to the group, which consists of two, three, or four members. The groups will typically expand on or synthesize the tasks that were begun individually.

47. Groups of four

Individual Accountability: Each group member is to develop or find examples of patterns in printed sources. The member will explain the pattern portrayed.

Group Goal: The group will examine the patterns brought in by each member. The group will attempt to develop criteria by which patterns can be sorted. For example, a pattern may be in the form A B A B A B . . . , or A A B A A B . . . . Alternately, the pattern might be a cumulative one in which terms get successively greater or larger. In addition, the pattern may be in the form of an analogy, such as A : B as C : D.

1.2 Identifying Relationships: The Study of Sets

set
element

members

In mathematics a collection or a group of objects is commonly known as a **set**. Each object in the set is called an **element** of that set. An analogy can be made between members belonging to an organization and elements belonging to a set. For this reason, elements of a set are sometimes referred to as its **members**.

Representing Sets

You may recall from page 12 the group of capital letters that had both horizontal and vertical symmetry. This group can be referred to as a set, and it can be identified in a variety of ways.

- One way to identify this set is through a description such as "the group of capital letters having both horizontal and vertical symmetry."

- A second way to identify the set is by listing its elements in the following way:

$$\{H, I, O, X\}$$

  Notice that the members of the set are separated by commas and enclosed within braces. The order in which they are listed is irrelevant. The letter H is an element of this set. This is symbolized by the statement: $H \in \{H, I, O, X\}$. The letter Q is not a member of this set, as shown in the statement $Q \notin \{H, I, O, X\}$.

Venn diagram

- A third way to represent a set is through the use of a **Venn diagram**. Venn diagrams are pictorial illustrations of a set and its relationships to other sets. The diagram is often drawn as circular regions representing individuals sets that are enclosed by a

universal set

large rectangle. The large rectangle represents the **universal set**, which contains all of the elements under consideration in the given situation. A *U* is sometimes placed in the upper right-hand corner of the rectangle, or if the exact elements of the universal set are known, the label of that set is used. The Venn diagram for the set containing the capital letters of the alphabet that have both vertical and horizontal symmetry is shown in Figure 1.8.

Figure 1.8

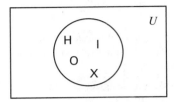

Empty Sets

To simplify statements about a set, a capital letter is often used to name the set. For example, assume that set *B* consists of the set of even numbers between 0 and 10. This is symbolized by *B* = {2, 4, 6, 8}. If a set contains no elements, such as the set of even

empty set numbers between 6 and 8, it is called an **empty set**. This is symbolized by { }, or ∅. This is not to be confused with the set {0}, which is the set containing the element zero.

Subsets

Sometimes there is a special relationship between sets. When every element of a first

subset set is a member of a second set, the first set is called a **subset** of the second set. Subsets can fall into three categories: a proper subset, the set itself, and the empty set.

Examine a new set, *C*. Say that *C* = {2, 4}. Notice that all of the elements of *C* are

proper subset also elements of set *B* above. Set *C* is considered a **proper subset** of set *B*. A set *C* is a proper subset of a set *B* if all of the elements in *C* are contained in *B*, but there are some elements in *B* that are not contained in *C*. The elements 2 and 4 of set *C* are both contained in set *B*, but set *B* contains some elements that are not in set *C*. This relationship can be symbolized by using the notation ⊂ and writing *C* ⊂ *B*. A Venn diagram that illustrates this relationship is shown in Figure 1.9.

Figure 1.9

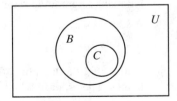

The second type of subset is the set itself. The set *B* is considered to be a subset of itself. The elements 2, 4, 6, and 8 are all contained in *B*, so set *B* cannot be considered a proper subset of itself. Because every element in the set {2, 4, 6, 8} is contained in *B*, set *B* is simply a subset of itself. This can be symbolized by using the notation ⊆ and writing *B* ⊆ *B*. The third type of subset is the empty set, { } or ∅, which is considered to be a subset of every set.

The following example will help illustrate these three categories of subsets. Suppose that set T consists of the six possible toppings available for a taco from the following list: lettuce, cheese, guacamole, olives, tomatoes, and taco sauce.

1. You could choose from one to five toppings in various combinations, forming a variety of proper subsets. Remember, all the elements of a proper subset (here, your choices of from one to five of the taco toppings) must be contained within the set (here, the six topping choices), yet the set must contain some elements not within the proper subset. A choice of just lettuce would be a proper subset here, as would a choice of cheese, guacamole, olives, tomatoes, and taco sauce. As long as at least one or more of the elements of the set of six toppings (and it doesn't matter which one or ones) are not in your choice of toppings, then you have formed a proper subset.

2. You could choose all of the six toppings, in which case you would be choosing the second type of subset, the set itself, which by definition contains all the elements of the original set.

3. Or you could choose no toppings, which would here illustrate the empty set, which contains no elements of the set and is considered a subset of every set.

Investigation 6

Given that $W = \{$North, South, East, West$\}$, list all the subsets of W.

Because the empty set and the set W itself are always subsets of every set, they can be listed first. Then list all of the possible subsets containing one element, two elements, and finally, three elements.

Empty set	$\varnothing$
Subset	{North, South, East, West}
Proper subsets	{North}, {South}, {East}, {West}
	{North, South}, {North, East}
	{North, West}, {South, East}
	{South, West}, {East, West}
	{North, South, East}, {North, South, West}
	{North, East, West}, {South, East, West}

Notice that the order of the elements does not matter. The set {North, South, East} is the same set as {East, North, South}.

Disjoint Sets

disjoint sets

Sets can be unrelated. If two sets have no elements in common, they are said to be **disjoint sets.** For example {1, 2, 3} and {r, s, t, u} are disjoint sets. Because disjoint sets share no elements, the Venn diagram looks like the one in Figure 1.10.

Figure 1.10

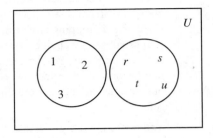

The Intersection of Sets

Let set H consist of all capital letters that are horizontally symmetric and set V be the set containing all capital letters that are vertically symmetric. These are both proper subsets of the set A containing all capital letters of the alphabet. Sets A, H, and V are listed below.

A = {A, B, C, D, E, F, G, H, I, J, K, L, M, N, O, P, Q, R, S, T, U, V, W, X, Y, Z}

H = {B, C, D, E, H, I, K, O, X}

V = {A, H, I, M, O, T, U, V, W, X, Y}

intersection

Because sets H and V share the elements {H, I, O, X}, the Venn diagram depicting the relationship between these two sets must illustrate that the two sets overlap, as shown in Figure 1.11. The shaded region is called the **intersection** of H and V. The intersection of two sets, H and V, is a new set containing the elements that are common to both H and V. The intersection of sets H and V is symbolized by $H \cap V$. $H \cap V$ = {H, I, O, X}.

Figure 1.11

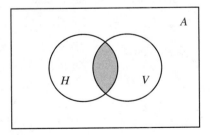

The Union of Sets

union

The set containing all letters that have horizontal and/or vertical symmetry can be formed by combining sets H and V. This is called the **union** of the two sets. The union of sets H and V is a new set containing all of the elements of H and all of the elements of V. If an element appears in both sets, it is listed only once. The union of H and V is symbolized by $H \cup V$. $H \cup V$ = {A, B, C, D, E, H, I, K, M, O, T, U, V, W, X, Y}. The Venn diagram illustrating $H \cup V$ is shown in Figure 1.12.

Figure 1.12

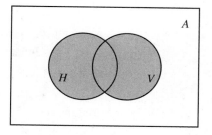

The Difference of Sets

Let $S = H \cup V$. Set S is the set of all capital letters having either horizontal or vertical symmetry, or both. Notice that set S is a proper subset of set A. The set of all letters of the alphabet having neither horizontal nor vertical symmetry is the set that contains those elements of set A that are not in the subset S. This set is known as the **difference** of sets A and S, and is symbolized by $A - S$. The Venn diagrams depicting this difference are shown in Figure 1.13.

difference

Figure 1.13

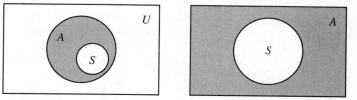

Notice that set S must be shown as a subset of set A. The shaded region, the difference, is the area inside A that is not inside S. Had the two sets not been related as subsets, the Venn diagram illustrating $A - S$, would be represented as in Figure 1.14.

Figure 1.14

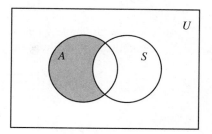

Investigation 7

A set S contains the names of students who serve on the Student Association Senate. Set C contains the names of those student members who serve on the Curriculum committee. Set A contains the names of those students who are on the Academic Affairs committee. When you are scheduling a Student Association Senate meeting, it is important to know the union, intersection, and difference of these sets in order to schedule the senate meetings when the greatest number of students can attend.

Let

$S = \{$Akiko, Mohammed, Lisa, Julianne, Robert, Linda, Allison, Donald, Jose, Mike$\}$

$C = \{$Mohammed, Lisa, Julianne$\}$

$A = \{$Robert, Julianne, Linda$\}$

Find (a) $C \cup A$ (b) $C \cap A$ (c) $S - C$ (d) $S - A$ (e) $S - (C \cup A)$ (f) $S - (C \cap A)$
Describe the resulting sets.

Understand the Problem: You are given three sets that describe the membership of three groups. You are asked to represent the union, intersection, and difference of these sets in order to arrive at some conclusion about when meetings should be called to avoid scheduling conflicts.

Devise a Plan: Use Venn diagrams to illustrate the individual situations.

Carry Out the Plan: **(a)** $C \cup A = \{$Mohammed, Lisa, Julianne, Robert, Linda$\}$. This set consists of those students who are on either the Curriculum committee, the Academic Affairs committee, or both. The Venn diagram looks as follows:

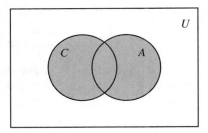

(b) $C \cap A = \{$Julianne$\}$. This set consists of the student who is on both the Curriculum committee and the Academic Affairs committee. The Venn Diagram looks like this:

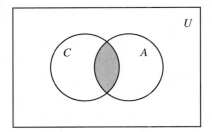

(c) $S - C = \{$Akiko, Robert, Linda, Allison, Donald, Jose, Mike$\}$. This set contains those Student Association Senate members who are not on the Curriculum committee. The Venn diagram appears on page 21.

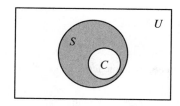

(d) $S - A$ = {Akiko, Mohammed, Lisa, Allison, Donald, Jose, Mike}. This set contains those Student Association Senate members who are not on the Academic Affairs committee. The Venn diagram follows:

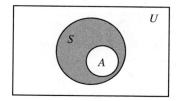

(e) $S - (C \cup A)$ = {Akiko, Allison, Donald, Jose, Mike}. This set contains those Student Association Senate members who are on neither the Curriculum committee nor the Academic Affairs committee. The appropriate Venn diagram is shown below:

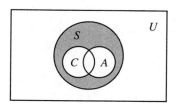

(f) $S - (C \cap A)$ = {Akiko, Mohammed, Lisa, Robert, Linda, Allison, Donald, Jose, Mike}. This set contains those Student Association Senate members who are not members of both the Curriculum committee and the Academic Affairs committee. The Venn diagram is illustrated here:

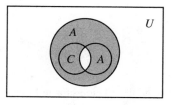

Look Back: Because the intersection of all three sets is not the empty set (Julianne belongs to all three groups), the committee meetings should be scheduled for days and times when they do not conflict with one another so that Julianne can attend all the meetings.

Assessments for Section 1.2

1. List the elements of each set described below.
   (a) The set of all states beginning with the letter A
   (b) The set of primary colors
   (c) The set of items that might be found in a wallet
   (d) The set of sizes in which a sweater might be made
   (e) The set of items that might be found in a picnic basket

2. Use a phrase to describe each of the following sets.
   (a) $G = \{$math, language arts, physical education, social studies, science, art, music, technology$\}$
   (b) $J = \{$winter, spring, summer, fall$\}$
   (c) $L = \{$"My dog ate it," "My mom washed it with my jeans," "I left it on the table"$\}$
   (d) $B = \{$train, boat, plane$\}$
   (e) $T = \{$street, avenue, road, boulevard, lane, drive$\}$

3. List all of the subsets for each set given.
   (a) $P = \{a, b, c\}$
   (b) $S = \{100, 200, 300, 400\}$
   (c) $V = \{7\}$
   (d) $Q = \{$white, black$\}$

4. Describe three possible subsets for each of the following sets.
   (a) Set S contains the states in the United States.
   (b) Set T contains the major league baseball teams.
   (c) Set R contains students attending Lincoln High School.

5. Given $A = \{2, 4, 6, 8, 10\}$, $B = \{6, 8, 10, 12, 14\}$, and $C = \{0, 2, 4, 6, 8, 10, 12, 14, 16, 18\}$, find
   (a) $A \cup B$
   (b) $A \cup C$
   (c) $B \cup C$
   (d) $A \cap B$
   (e) $A \cap C$
   (f) $B \cap C$
   (g) $C - A$
   (h) $C - B$

6. Draw Venn diagrams to illustrate the relationships in Problem 5 (a) through (h).

7. Set A contains the states in the continental United States that border the Atlantic Ocean, the Pacific Ocean, or the Gulf of Mexico; set B contains the states in the continental United States that border Canada or the Great Lakes on the north; and set C contains the states that were the 13 original colonies. Find
   (a) $A \cup B$
   (b) $A \cup C$
   (c) $B \cup C$
   (d) $A \cap B$
   (e) $A \cap C$
   (f) $B \cap C$
   (g) $C - A$
   (h) $C - B$

8. Draw Venn diagrams to illustrate the relationships in Problem 7 (a) through (h).

9. Given $A = \{a, b, c, d, e, f, g, h, i, j\}$, $B = \{b, d, h, j\}$, $C = \{h, i, j, l, m, n,\}$, and $D = \{c, f, h, m, p\}$, find
   (a) $(A \cup B) \cap C$
   (b) $(A - B) \cup C$
   (c) $A \cup (B \cap C)$
   (d) $D \cap (B \cup A)$
   (e) $(A \cap B) \cup C$

10. Draw Venn diagrams to illustrate the relationships in Problem 9 (a) through (e).

11. List sets A, B, and C whose intersection and union are given here.
    (a) $(A \cap B) \cup C = \{a, b, c\}$
    (b) $(A \cup B) \cup C = \{d, e, f, g\}$
    (c) $(A \cup B) \cap C = \{r, s, t, u\}$
    (d) $(A \cap B) \cap C = \varnothing$
    (e) $(A - B) \cap C = C$

12. To get an education degree at a certain college, students must be competent in at least one of the following programming languages: LOGO, BASIC, or Pascal. Some students study only one language; others take two languages; and a few become proficient in all three languages. The following Venn diagram illustrates this situation. Circle L represents those students who study LOGO, circle B represents those students who study BASIC, and circle P represents those students who study Pascal. The overlapping circles separate the interior into seven different regions (labeled 1–7). Keep in mind that these numbers are labels and do not indicate the number of elements in the sets represented by the regions. Identify the group of students defined by each region.

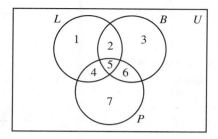

13. Many people own a variety of electronic equipment. A survey is taken of 500 people at a shopping center. The following Venn diagram represents their responses. Circle *C* represents those who own a compact disc player (CD). Circle *S* represents those who have a stereo system. Circle *V* represents those who own a video cassette recorder (VCR). Identify the equipment owned by the members belonging to each of the seven regions.

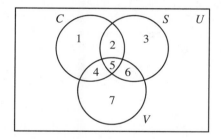

14. Draw a Venn diagram to illustrate the following situation. Be sure to label and identify all of the regions. Three different medications, *A*, *B*, and *C*, can be prescribed as a cure for a certain illness. Some people require two of the medications, whereas others need only one. Doctors do not prescribe medicine *A* and medicine *C* together because they interact.

In Other Words

15. Explain the conditions under which the intersection of two sets is one of the sets itself.

16. Explain the conditions under which the union of two sets is one of the sets itself.

17. Describe a possible context for the following Venn diagram.

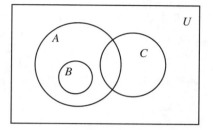

18. Describe how concepts of set theory might be useful to the owner of a restaurant.

19. How does the study of sets relate to the ideas contained in Section 1.1?

Cooperative Activity

20. **Groups of three**

Individual Accountability: Each group member is to identify four introductory-level courses from the course catalog at your college for one of the following three disciplines: mathematics, English, foreign languages. List the prerequisites for each course.

Group Goal: For each discipline, draw a Venn diagram that illustrates the prerequisites in each department. Reach some generalizations about the prerequisites in each department.

1.3   Elementary Logic

Elementary logic is a branch of mathematics that addresses the way we reason. Every day we encounter situations in which we must determine if a statement is true or false. Sometimes we must make these assessments immediately (It is true that I cannot cross the street now since a bus is rapidly approaching), whereas at other times we have the opportunity to wait and see what a situation will bring before determining the truth of any statement about it (If it rains on Friday, then I will not go shopping). In this section, we will take a closer look at the way reasoning is based on the laws of elementary logic.

As in many English sentences, a mathematical sentence often presents a fact or an idea that can be judged as either true or false. For example, the statements "Miami is the capital of the United States," "$3 \times 8 = 11$," and "Oxygen is necessary for human survival" can all be viewed in terms of whether they are true or false. These statements are, respectively, false, false, and true.

Sometimes it is difficult to test whether or not a sentence is true or false without getting additional information. For example, the sentences "She is my friend," "It does not work," and "$X - 9 = 1$" all contain some uncertainty. In the first statement, you must first determine to whom "she" refers. In the second, the pronoun "it" must be replaced by a more specific term. In the equation, a numerical value for the variable X must be given before the validity of the statement can be tested. These types of mathematical **open sentences** sentences are called **open sentences**. When examining an open sentence to test whether **domain** it is true or false, it is necessary to have some replacement set, called a **domain**, that will be used in place of the variable. For example, in the equation $X - 9 = 1$, the replacement set $\{8, 9, 10, 11\}$ might be examined. Each of the elements in the subset $\{8, 9, 11\}$ makes the statement false. The element 10 is the only replacement in the **solution set** domain that makes the statement true. The set $\{10\}$ is said to be the **solution set** of the open sentence $X - 9 = 1$.

As shown here, sentences can be partitioned into two groups: those that can be judged as either true or false based on the information they contain, and those that cannot be judged as either true or false without additional information. Where truth cannot be immediately ascertained, as in open sentences, the replacement set must be exam**closed sentence (statement)** ined for one or more variables. If a sentence can be determined to be true or false, then it is called a **closed sentence**, or a **statement**.

Investigation 8

Read the following passage. Classify each sentence as open or closed. In the open sentences, identify the variable. In the closed sentences, determine whether they are true or false.

> Washington, D.C., is the capital of the United States. I enjoy visiting Washington, D.C. It is located 250 kilometers from my home. The Empire State Building is a tourist attraction in Washington, D.C. The White House is located on Pennsylvania Avenue.

1. Washington, D.C., is the capital of the United States. (closed sentence, true statement)

2. I enjoy visiting Washington, D. C. (open sentence, variable is "I")

3. It is located 250 kilometers from my home. (open sentence, variables are "it" and "my home")

4. The Empire State Building is a tourist attraction in Washington, D.C. (closed sentence, false statement)

5. The White House is located on Pennsylvania Avenue. (closed sentence, true statement)

truth value

negation

    The **truth value** of a statement is either true or false. A closed sentence cannot be simultaneously true and false. If you have already determined the truth value of a particular statement, it follows that the **negation** of that statement must have the opposite truth value. A negation of a statement is formed by using the word *not,* as shown here.

True statement: The White House is located on Pennsylvania Avenue.

Negation (false statement): The White House is not located on Pennsylvania Avenue.

                           It is not true that the White House is located on Pennsylvania Avenue.

In elementary logic, it is more convenient to use a symbol to represent a statement. The lowercase letters p and q are often used to replace simple English sentences. For example,

    Let p represent the sentence "July 4th is Independence Day in the United States."

The negation of p would read "July 4th is not Independence Day in the United States" and is symbolized by $\sim p$. The symbol $\sim p$ is read as "not p." Knowledge of a statement and its negation allows you to examine all possible truth values of that statement. The

truth table

list of possibilities is displayed in a **truth table** as shown below.

    Let p represent a sentence.

    Let $\sim p$ represent the negation of that sentence.

If p is true, then $\sim p$ must be false. Conversely, if p is false, then $\sim p$ must be true. These truth values can be organized into a table:

p	$\sim p$
T	F
F	T

This is a truth table in its simplest form. Truth tables can also be used to examine the set of possible truth values for a complicated logic statement. Keep in mind that negations are statements themselves and thus can be negated. The statement $\sim p$, representing "July 4th is not Independence Day in the United States" can be negated and read as "It is not true that July 4th is not Independence Day in the United States." This statement would be symbolized by $\sim(\sim p)$, and the truth table representing it would be formed as follows:

p	$\sim p$	$\sim(\sim p)$
T	F	T
F	T	F

Conjunction

Just as in an English sentence, a mathematical sentence can contain one or more parts. In English, this type of sentence is called a compound sentence, and the parts of the

conjunction

sentence are joined by the part of speech called a conjunction. In logic, a **conjunction** is a compound sentence that contains one or more simple sentences joined together by the word *and*. If p and q represent two sentences, we symbolize the conjunction p *and* q by $p \wedge q$. Examine the following example.

p: It is snowing today.

q: I do not drive in the snow.

$p \wedge q$: It is snowing today and I do not drive in the snow.

The truth value of a conjunction is accepted as true if and only if both simple sentences are true. If either or both are false, the truth value of the entire conjunction is false. For example, suppose that it is true that it is snowing today. If it is not true that I do not drive in the snow, the compound sentence must be false. Now suppose that it is not snowing today. Whether or not it is true that I do not drive in the snow, the compound sentence must be false, since it is not snowing today. Only if it is true that it is snowing today, and it is true that I do not drive in the snow, can the truth value of the compound sentence be considered true. The set of possible truth values is illustrated in the following truth table:

p	q	$p \wedge q$
T	T	T
T	F	F
F	T	F
F	F	F

Notice that this truth table has four rows. For each of the two truth values of p, there are two possible truth values of q. Therefore, the table must contain 2×2, or 4, rows in order to be complete.

Investigation 9

Given

p: X is an even number.

q: X contains the digit 1.

Compare all possible truth values for the compound statements $p \wedge q$, $\sim(p \wedge q)$, and $\sim p \wedge \sim q$. What observations can you make?

Understand the Problem: You are given two simple statements and asked to determine the truth of a variety of logic relationships.

Devise a Plan: Construct a truth table.

Carry Out the Plan:

p	q	$\sim p$	$\sim q$	$p \wedge q$	$\sim(p \wedge q)$	$\sim p \wedge \sim q$
T	T	F	F	T	F	F
T	F	F	T	F	T	F
F	T	T	F	F	T	F
F	F	T	T	F	T	T

Look Back: Obviously, the negation of a conjunction, shown as $\sim(p \wedge q)$, does not always have the same truth value as the conjunction of the individual negations, shown as $\sim p \wedge \sim q$. Let's follow through the second row of the truth table using $X = 8$ and determine the meaning of each entry as it applies to the statements "X is an even number" and "X contains the digit 1."

p	q	$\sim p$	$\sim q$	$p \wedge q$	$\sim(p \wedge q)$	$\sim p \wedge \sim q$
T	F	F	T	F	T	F

It is true that 8 is an even number.

It is false that 8 contains the digit 1.

It is false that 8 is not an even number.

It is true that 8 does not contain the digit 1.

It is false that 8 is an even number and 8 contains the digit 1.

It is true that it is not the case that 8 is an even number and 8 contains the digit 1.

It is false that 8 is not an even number and 8 does not contain the digit 1.

Disjunction

Examine the following sentences:

> I'll go to the movies or I'll go shopping.
>
> He will have pie or he will have ice cream for dessert.
>
> It will rain on Saturday or Sunday.
>
> The baby will be male or female.
>
> $Y = 7$ or $Y = -7$.

disjunction   In each sentence, two simple statements are connected by the word *or.* In elementary logic, the connective *or* defines a compound statement called a **disjunction**. The disjunction "p or q" is symbolized by $p \vee q$.

For example,

   p: You take the local train to the museum.

   q: You take the express train to the museum.

p ∨ *q*: You take the local train to the museum or you take the express train to the museum.

Unlike a conjunction, which is true only when both statements are true, a disjunction is true when either statement is true or when both statements are true. The truth table for this disjunctive statement would be as follows:

p	*q*	*p* ∨ *q*
T	T	T
T	F	T
F	T	T
F	F	F

You begin your trip by taking the local train and then transferring to the express train. It is true that you arrive at the museum.
You take only the local train to arrive at the museum.
You take only the express train to arrive at the museum.
You take neither train and do not get to the museum by train.

If you have been reading carefully, you will have noticed that in all but one of the examples given at the beginning of our discussion of disjunction it is possible for both statements to be simultaneously true. For example, he might have both pie and ice cream for dessert; or it might rain on both Saturday and Sunday. These are said to illustrate the **inclusive "or."** However, in the sentence that states the baby will be male or female, only one of the statements can be true. This example illustrates the **exclusive "or."** For the purposes of clarity in this textbook, we will use only the inclusive "or."

inclusive "or"
exclusive "or"

Investigation 10

Let   *p*:   *X* is an even number.

                                       q: *X* contains the digit 1.

Compare all possible truth values for the compound statements *p* ∨ *q*, ~ (*p* ∨ *q*), and ~*p* ∨ ~*q*. What observations can you make?

Understand the Problem: You are given two simple statements and asked to determine the truth value of a variety of logic relationships.

Devise a Plan: Construct a truth table.

Carry Out the Plan:

p	*q*	~*p*	~*q*	*p* ∨ *q*	~(*p* ∨ *q*)	~*p* ∨ ~*q*
T	T	F	F	T	F	F
T	F	F	T	T	F	T
F	T	T	F	T	F	T
F	F	T	T	F	T	T

Look Back: Obviously, the negation of a disjunction, shown as ~($p \vee q$), does not always have the same truth value as the disjunction of the individual negations, shown as ~$P \vee$ ~q. Let's follow through the second row of the truth table using $X = 8$ and determine the meaning of each entry as it applies to the statements "X is an even number" and "X contains the digit 1."

p	q	~p	~q	$p \vee q$	~($p \vee q$)	~$p \vee$ ~q
T	F	F	T	T	F	T

It is true that 8 is an even number. ⟶

It is false that 8 contains the digit 1. ⟶

It is false that 8 is not an even number. ⟶

It is true that 8 does not contain the digit 1. ⟶

It is true that 8 is an even number or
8 contains the digit 1. ⟶

It is false that it is not the case that 8 is an even number
or 8 contains the digit 1. ⟶

It is true that 8 is not an even number or
8 does not contain the digit 1. ⟶

You have already seen the usefulness of looking for analogous situations when solving problems. Such an analogy can be made between the nature of conjunctive and disjunctive statements and set theory. Examine the following statements:

$$p:\ X > 10$$

$$q:\ X < 15$$

Let the replacement set for X be {8, 9, 10, 11, 12, 13, 14, 15, 16}. Notice that the subset {11, 12, 13, 14, 15, 16} is the solution set that makes p a true statement. The subset {8, 9, 10, 11, 12, 13, 14} is the solution set that makes q a true statement. The conjunction of p and q, $p \wedge q$, is a true statement only when p and q are simultaneously true. Notice that p and q are both true when the solution set for X consists of 11, 12, 13, or 14. In this case, $p \wedge q$ is a true statement when $X \in$ {11, 12, 13, 14}.

The disjunction of p with q, $p \vee q$, is a true statement when p is true, q is true, or both p and q are true. Examine the elements that make p a true statement and the elements that make q a true statement. If we are concerned with the truth of at least one of these statements, then $p \vee q$ is a true statement when $X \in$ {8, 9, 10, 11, 12, 13, 14, 15, 16}. These results may seem familiar to you.

Examine the following statements: Let Z equal the set of values that make p a true statement: {11, 12, 13, 14, 15, 16}. Let Y equal the set of values that make q a true statement: {8, 9, 10, 11, 12, 13, 14}.

$$Z \cap Y = \{11, 12, 13, 14\}$$

$$Z \cup Y = \{8, 9, 10, 11, 12, 13, 14, 15, 16\}$$

Compare the solution set that makes ($p \wedge q$) a true statement with ($Z \cap Y$). Compare the solution set that makes ($p \vee q$) a true statement with ($Z \cup Y$). Notice that the conjunction acts like the intersection of the solution sets, and the disjunction acts like the union of the solution sets. This relationship exemplifies one of the recommendations made by the National Council of Teachers of Mathematics in their *Curriculum and Evaluation Standards for School Mathematics*:

> The fourth curriculum standard . . . is titled Mathematical Connections. This label emphasizes our belief that although it is often necessary to teach specific concepts and procedures, mathematics must be approached as a whole. Concepts, procedures, and intellectual processes are interrelated. In a significant sense, "the whole is greater than the sum of its parts." Thus, the curriculum should include deliberate attempts, through specific instructional activities, to connect ideas and procedures both among different mathematical topics, and with other content areas. (1989, p. 11)

As prospective teachers of mathematics, it is imperative that you organize your own knowledge in ways that allow you to make connections within the discipline of mathematics as well as between mathematics and other disciplines.

The Conditional

The outcomes of many real-life situations are often based on implications. For example, consider the following statements:

> If it is raining, then I will carry an umbrella.

> If you exercise, then you will become stronger.

> If there are more than 20 people in the elevator, then the doors will not close.

conditional

In each case, two ideas are conditionally connected with the words *if* and *then*. In elementary logic, a **conditional** is a compound sentence that is formed by joining two statements using the connectives *if* and *then*. When p and q both represent sentences, the conditional statement "if p then q" is symbolized by $p \rightarrow q$. This is sometimes read as "p implies q," and for that reason, the conditional statement is often referred to as an

implication

implication. In the first conditional presented above, let p represent the sentence "It is raining" and q represent the sentence "I will carry an umbrella." Then $p \rightarrow q$ can be read as "If it is raining, then I will carry an umbrella," or "It is raining implies that I will carry an umbrella."

hypothesis
conclusion

In the conditional, the statement that usually follows the word *if* is called the **hypothesis**. The **conclusion** is a consequence of the *if* statement and usually follows the word *then*. The following example should help you understand the truth value of a conditional.

An insurance agent tells a client, "If a smoke alarm is installed in your home, then your home owner's insurance premium will decrease."

> Let p: A smoke alarm is installed in your home.

> Let q: Your home owner's insurance will decrease.

Examine all of the possible combinations of truth values for p and q.

1. ***p* is true and *q* is true:** *p* is true means that a smoke alarm is installed in your home. *q* is true means that your premium does decrease. The insurance agent's statement to the client appears to be true. Therefore, a *true* value is assigned to $p \rightarrow q$.

2. ***p* is true and *q* is false:** *p* is true means that a smoke alarm is installed in your home. *q* is false means that your insurance premium does not decrease. Here it appears that the insurance agent's statement is false. Therefore, a *false* value is assigned to $p \rightarrow q$.

3. ***p* is false and *q* is true:** *p* is false means that a smoke alarm is not installed in your home. *q* is true means that your insurance premium does decrease. We are trying to determine the truth of the insurance agent's statement. Because a smoke alarm was not installed, we cannot infer that the agent was not telling the truth. Therefore, a *true* value is assigned to this conditional.

4. ***p* is false and *q* is false:** *p* is false means that a smoke alarm is not installed in your home. *q* is false means that your insurance premium does not decrease. For the same reason as in case 3, we cannot infer that the agent was not telling the truth. Therefore, a *true* value is assigned to this conditional also.

It may help you to understand cases 3 and 4 by making an analogy to a premise of our criminal justice system: that one is innocent until proven guilty. In case 3 and 4, we cannot claim these implications to be false since, in both cases, the smoke alarm was never installed. Because the hypothesis is false, we have no way of determining if the insurance agent was being truthful or not. Therefore, we assume the conditional is true, since it cannot be shown to be false. The truth table for the conditional follows:

p	q	$p \rightarrow q$
T	T	T
T	F	F
F	T	T
F	F	T

Investigation 11

Construct a truth table that depicts the values of $q \rightarrow p$, $(\sim p) \rightarrow (\sim q)$, and $(\sim q) \rightarrow (\sim p)$.

p	q	$\sim p$	$\sim q$	$p \rightarrow q$	$q \rightarrow p$	$(\sim p) \rightarrow (\sim q)$	$(\sim q) \rightarrow (\sim p)$
T	T	F	F	T	T	T	T
T	F	F	T	F	T	T	F
F	T	T	F	T	F	F	T
F	F	T	T	T	T	T	T

converse, inverse, contrapositive

For ease of reference, the conditional statements in the last columns are given the names **converse** $(q \rightarrow p)$, **inverse** $(\sim p \rightarrow \sim q)$, and **contrapositive** $(\sim q \rightarrow \sim p)$. Students (and teachers) of logic are often surprised by the facts that the converse of a true statement can be either true or false and that the converse of a false statement is always true. When we are using logic to reason, we usually start with a true conditional statement.

This truth table depicts another interesting characteristic. Notice that the entries under the conditional (fifth column) and the contrapositive (last column) are identical. When compound sentences have identical entries in a truth table, they are said to be **logically equivalent**.

logically equivalent

Examine the conditional statement $q \rightarrow p$, which we have here called the converse. The contrapositive of $q \rightarrow p$ is $\sim p \rightarrow \sim q$, which we have here called the inverse. The converse and the inverse are also equivalent statements. You can verify this fact by referring to their column entries in the truth table (column 6 and column 7).

Investigation 12

Let p: The student hands in the assignment.

Let q: The teacher grades the assignment.

Write as both symbols and compound sentences the conditional, the converse, the inverse, and the contrapositive.

1. Conditional, $p \rightarrow q$:   If the student hands in the assignment, then the teacher grades the assignment.

2. Converse, $q \rightarrow p$:   If the teacher grades the assignment, then the student hands in the assignment.

3. Inverse, $\sim p \rightarrow \sim q$:   If the student does not hand in the assignment, then the teacher does not grade the assignment.

4. Contrapositive, $\sim q \rightarrow \sim p$:   If the teacher does not grade the assignment, then the student does not hand in the assignment.

In this chapter, you were introduced to the use of the problem-solving strategy of contradiction (see p. 9). You will now see how this strategy can be employed in conjunction with the laws of elementary logic.

Investigation 13

Assume that X is a whole number greater than or equal to 3 ($\{4, 5, 6, \ldots\}$). Show that if X^2 leaves a remainder of 1 when divided by 8, then X is an odd number greater than or equal to 3.

Understand the Problem: What is given? You are told that X represents a whole number that is greater than or equal to 3. In addition, you know that when X^2 is divided by 8, there is a remainder of 1.

What is unknown? You must determine a method of proving that X must be an odd number.

Devise a Plan: Use the laws of logic to better understand the problem statements and the consequences of their truth values.

Carry Out the Plan: Rather than try to prove this statement true for *every* odd number greater than or equal to 3, it may be easier to prove a logically equivalent statement true. Examine the following statements:

Let p: X^2 leaves a remainder of 1 when divided by 8.

Let q: X is an odd number greater than or equal to 3.

The conditional, $p \rightarrow q$, states that if X^2 leaves a remainder of 1 when divided by 8, then X is an odd number greater than or equal to 3. Remember that this statement is logically equivalent to the contrapositive $\sim q \rightarrow \sim p$, which states that if X is not an odd number greater than or equal to 3, then X^2 does not leave a remainder of 1 when divided by 8. If this contrapositive statement can be proven true, then the original conditional must also be accepted as true. The proof follows.

If X is not an odd number greater than or equal to 3, and we assume from the beginning that X is a whole number greater than or equal to 3, then X must be an even number greater than or equal to 3. Every even number greater than or equal to 3 can be written in the form $2N$ where N is a whole number greater than or equal to 2. We need to show that if $2N$ is squared and then divided by 8, it does not leave a remainder of 1. Any number that does leave a remainder of 1 when divided by 8 can be expressed as $8Y + 1$, where Y is a whole number greater than 0. Therefore, we must show that

$$(2N)^2 \neq 8Y + 1$$

Because $(2N)^2 = 4N^2$, and $4N^2 = 2(2N^2)$, then $(2N)^2$ has a factor of 2 and is therefore an even number. Now examine the number represented by $8Y$. Because $8Y = 2(4Y)$, $8Y$ represents an even number. It follows that $8Y + 1$ will represent an odd number (one more than an even number is an odd number).

We have come to the end of the proof. Because $(2N)^2$ represents an even number and $8Y + 1$ represents an odd number, $(2N)^2 \neq 8Y + 1$. We have shown that the contrapositive is a true statement, so its logical equivalent, the original conditional, must also be a true statement. Therefore, if X^2 leaves a remainder of 1 when divided by 8, then X is an odd number greater than or equal to 3.

Look Back: Try testing some values for X. Keep in mind that choosing a variety of values for X does not constitute a proof. Rather, by using numbers you will better understand the steps needed in the proof.

The Biconditional

Recall that the conditional $p \rightarrow q$ is false when p is true and q is false, and is true for all other combinations of truth values for p and q. Compare these results with the conditional $q \rightarrow p$ in the table below:

p	q	$p \rightarrow q$	$q \rightarrow p$
T	T	T	T
T	F	F	T
F	T	T	F
F	F	T	T

The conditionals $p \rightarrow q$ and $q \rightarrow p$ have the same truth values when p and q are *both* true or *both* false. In logic, a new compound sentence can be formed by combining the conditionals $p \rightarrow q$ and $q \rightarrow p$ as a conjunction. This compound sentence is called a **biconditional** and is symbolically represented as $(p \rightarrow q) \wedge (q \rightarrow p)$. Examine the truth table for the biconditional:

biconditional

p	q	$p \rightarrow q$	$q \rightarrow p$	$(p \rightarrow q) \wedge (q \rightarrow p)$
T	T	T	T	T
T	F	F	T	F
F	T	T	F	F
F	F	T	T	T

The biconditional, read as "if p then q, and if q then p" or, more commonly, "p if and only if q" can also be symbolized as $p \leftrightarrow q$.

Validity

valid argument

In logic, a **valid argument** is a proposition in which the conclusion necessarily follows from the statement or statements of the hypothesis. For example,

> All people who live in San Francisco live in California.
>
> Allison Meghan lives in San Francisco.
>
> Therefore, Allison Meghan lives in California.

The statement "All people who live in San Francisco live in California" is an alternate way of saying the conditional "If a person lives in San Francisco, then the person lives in California." Examine the Venn diagram in Figure 1.15, which depicts the relationship between the set of people who live in California and the set of people who live in San Francisco.

Figure 1.15

The set of Californians contains people who live in San Diego, Sacramento, Los Angeles, San Francisco, and other localities in the state. The set containing those people living in San Francisco is a subset of the larger set of Californians. The statement "Allison Meghan lives in San Francisco" tells us that Allison Meghan is an element of the set of people who live in San Francisco. This element is pictured as a dot contained within the set of San Franciscans. But notice that if the element is contained within the set of San Franciscans, it is necessarily contained within the set of Californians. The Venn diagram supports the conclusion drawn from the hypotheses above.

Now examine the following situation:

> All flights to Chicago will be delayed if the airport in Chicago is fogged in.
>
> Flight 702 to Chicago will be delayed.
>
> The airport in Chicago is fogged in.

Although it is true that flight 702 is an element of the set of all flights to Chicago, it does not necessarily follow that since flight 702 was delayed, the Chicago airport was fogged in. Flight 702 could have been delayed for mechanical reasons or any number of other reasons. Therefore, the conclusion that the Chicago airport is fogged in is an invalid one.

Law of Detachment

law of detachment (modus ponens)

Three laws in logic can be used to determine the validity of a compound statement. The first law is called the **law of detachment**, or **modus ponens**. This law can be best understood by examining the following statements, which are individually and collectively true.

> If the test is Friday, then I will study for the test tonight.
>
> The test is Friday.

> Let p: The test is Friday
>
> Let q: I will study for the test tonight.

Suppose that both p and q are true. We can symbolically represent the situation as

$$(p \rightarrow q) \wedge p$$

We are told that this conjunction is a true statement. Can anything be directly implied from this knowledge? Examine the following truth table:

p	q	$p \rightarrow q$	$(p \rightarrow q) \wedge p$
T	T	T	T
T	F	F	F
F	T	T	F
F	F	T	F

Notice from this table that the only time $p \rightarrow q$ and p are true is when q is also true.

Therefore, the following conditional can be written as

$$[(p \rightarrow q) \wedge p] \rightarrow q$$

A complete truth table including the truth values of the law of detachment follows:

p	q	$p \rightarrow q$	$(p \rightarrow q) \wedge p$	$[(p \rightarrow q) \wedge p] \rightarrow q)$
T	T	T	T	T
T	F	F	F	T
F	T	T	F	T
F	F	T	F	T

This is the statement of the law of detachment. It can be interpreted as, "if it is true that p implies q, and p is true, then it must follow that q is true."

Investigation 14

Assume the following statements to be true.

If Polya's four problem-solving steps are applied to a problem, then the problem is easier to solve.

Polya's four problem-solving steps are applied to a problem.

What conclusion can you draw from these statements? Justify your reasoning.

Let p: Polya's four problem-solving steps are applied to a problem.

Let q: The problem is easier to solve.

Since $[(p \rightarrow q) \wedge p]$ is true, by the law of detachment, q must also be true. Therefore, we can conclude that the problem is easier to solve using Polya's four problem-solving steps.

Law of Modus Tollens

Suppose in Investigation 14 that the problem was not easier to solve. In logical terms, $\sim q$ is a true statement. Does this also necessitate that Polya's four problem-solving steps were not applied (in logical terms, $\sim p$)? Once again, we assume the truth of the conditional $p \rightarrow q$. Examine the following table. What conclusion can you draw?

p	$\sim p$	q	$\sim q$	$p \rightarrow q$	$(p \rightarrow q) \wedge \sim q$
T	F	T	F	T	F
T	F	F	T	F	F
F	T	T	F	T	F
F	T	F	T	T	T

The only instance in which the conjunction $(p \rightarrow q) \wedge \sim q$ is true is when both $\sim p$ and $\sim q$ are true. Therefore, if the problem was not easier to solve, it necessitates that Polya's four problem-solving steps were not applied. In symbolic logic this is shown as

$$[(p \rightarrow q) \wedge \sim q] \rightarrow \sim p$$

Adding this last statement to the truth table, we get the following values:

p	$\sim p$	q	$\sim q$	$p \rightarrow q$	$p \rightarrow q \wedge \sim q$	$[(p \rightarrow q) \wedge \sim q] \rightarrow \sim p$
T	F	T	F	T	F	T
T	F	F	T	F	F	T
F	T	T	F	T	F	T
F	T	F	T	T	T	T

law of modus tollens   This is called the **law of modus tollens**. It is interpreted as, "if p implies q is true, and q is false (or $\sim q$ is true), then p is false (or $\sim p$ is true)."

Law of Syllogism

Each of the two laws just presented involve single conditional statements. Often many conditional statements must be examined before a conclusion can be reached. Consider the following two conditionals, which we will accept as true.

If I drink caffeinated coffee, I get a headache.

If I get a headache, I am unable to concentrate on my work.

To determine the logical conclusion from these two conditionals, we will represent the statements symbolically:

Let p: I drink caffeinated coffee.

Let q: I get a headache.

Let r: I am unable to concentrate on my work.

The assumption that both conditionals are true leads us to the notion that $[(p \rightarrow q) \wedge (q \rightarrow r)]$ is true. Examine the following truth table. Notice that it contains eight rows since p, q, and r all have two possible truth values ($2 \times 2 \times 2 = 8$). What can be concluded from the table?

p	q	r	$p \rightarrow q$	$q \rightarrow r$	$(p \rightarrow q) \wedge (q \rightarrow r)$
T	T	T	T	T	T
T	T	F	T	F	F
T	F	T	F	T	F
T	F	F	F	T	F
F	T	T	T	T	T
F	T	F	T	F	F
F	F	T	T	T	T
F	F	F	T	T	T

Generate the truth values of a new conditional, $p \rightarrow r$. Examine the conditional $[(p \rightarrow q) \wedge (q \rightarrow r)] \rightarrow (p \rightarrow r)$. Notice that it is true in all cases.

p	q	r	$p \rightarrow q$	$q \rightarrow r$	$(p \rightarrow q) \wedge (q \rightarrow r)$	$p \rightarrow r$	$[(p \rightarrow q) \wedge (q \rightarrow r)] \rightarrow (p \rightarrow r)$
T	T	T	T	T	T	T	T
T	T	F	T	F	F	F	T
T	F	T	F	T	F	T	T
T	F	F	F	T	F	F	T
F	T	T	T	T	T	T	T
F	T	F	T	F	F	T	T
F	F	T	T	T	T	T	T
F	F	F	T	T	T	T	T

law of syllogism (chain rule) The conditional statement $[(p \rightarrow q) \wedge (q \rightarrow r)] \rightarrow (p{\rightarrow}r)$ is known as the **law of syllogism**, or the **chain rule**. The following statements can consequently be made.

Hypotheses: If I drink caffeinated coffee, I get a headache.

If I get a headache, I am unable to concentrate on my work.

Conclusion: If I drink caffeinated coffee, I am unable to concentrate on my work.

Therefore, if you are told that two conditionals are true—one $p \rightarrow q$, and the other $q \rightarrow r$—it follows that $p \rightarrow r$ must also be true.

tautology In logic, when the truth values of a compound sentence are always true, the compound sentence is called a **tautology**. The three laws just presented all resulted in a tautology.

Assessments for Section 1.3

1. In each of the following statements, let p represent "There are tickets available for the concert" and let q represent "The concert is not sold out." Represent each of the following statements in symbolic form.

   (a) The concert is sold out.

   (b) There are no tickets available for the concert.

   (c) If there are tickets available for the concert, then the concert is not sold out.

   (d) If there are no tickets available for the concert, then the concert is sold out.

   (e) There are tickets available for the concert and the concert is not sold out.

   (f) The concert is not sold out if and only if there are tickets available for the concert.

2. In each of the following statements let p represent "The child is sick today," let q represent "The child is not in school today," and let r represent "The child is seen by a doctor." Represent each of the following statements in symbolic form.

   (a) The child is not seen by a doctor.

   (b) The child is in school today.

   (c) The child is sick today and the child is not in school today.

   (d) If the child is sick today, then the child is seen by a doctor.

   (e) If the child is in school today, then the child is not sick today.

   (f) If the child is sick today and the child is not in school today, then the child is seen by a doctor.

   (g) The child is seen by a doctor if and only if the child is sick today and the child is not in school today.

3. In each of the following statements, let p represent $X > 7$ and let q represent $X < 10$. Represent each of the following in symbolic form.

(a) $X > 7$ and $X < 10$

(b) $X < 10$ or $X > 7$

(c) If $X < 10$, then $X > 7$

(d) $X \leq 7$

(e) $X \geq 10$

(f) If $X \geq 10$, then $X > 7$

(g) If $X \leq 7$, then $X < 10$

(h) If $X < 10$ and $X > 7$, then $X \ngeq 10$

(i) If $X > 7$ or $X \geq 10$, then $X \nleq 7$

4. In each of the following statements, let p represent $X > 5$, q represent $X = 7$, and r represent $X < 15$. Represent each of the following in symbolic form.

(a) $X > 5$ and $X = 7$

(b) $5 < X < 15$

(c) $X \leq 5$

(d) $X \neq 7$

(e) If $X > 5$ and $X < 15$, then $X = 7$

(f) If $X > 5$, then $X = 7$ and $X > 5$

(g) If $X > 5$, then $X = 7$ and $X \neq 7$

(h) $X = 7$ if and only if $X > 5$ and $X < 15$

5. In each of the following logic statements, let p represent "You can ride the A train" and let q represent "You have a token." Interpret the symbols with words.

(a) $\sim p$

(b) $\sim q$

(c) $p \wedge q$

(d) $q \rightarrow p$

(e) $\sim p \rightarrow \sim q$

(f) $\sim q \rightarrow \sim p$

6. In each of the following logic statements, let p represent "You purchase a computer," let q represent "You purchase word processing software," and let r represent "You do not hire a typist for your paper." Interpret the symbols with words.

(a) $\sim r$

(b) $\sim q \wedge p$

(c) $p \wedge q$

(d) $p \rightarrow r$

(e) $\sim p \rightarrow \sim q$

(f) $\sim q \rightarrow \sim p$

(g) $(p \wedge q) \rightarrow r$

7. Let p: The house is dark.
Let q: There are no lights on in the house.
Let r: There is no one in the house.

Express in both words and symbols the laws of (a) detachment, (b) modus tollens, and (c) syllogism.

8. Let p: It is Friday evening.
Let q: The phone answering machine is on.
Let r: He is at the airport.

Express in both words and symbols the laws of (a) detachment, (b) modus tollens, and (c) syllogism.

9. Let p: $3X - 4 = 11$
Let q: $3X = 15$
Let r: $X = 5$

Express in both words and symbols the laws of (a) detachment (b) modus tollens, and (c) syllogism.

10. Construct a truth table for each of the following logic statements.

(a) $\sim p \rightarrow q$

(b) $p \rightarrow \sim q$

(c) $p \wedge \sim q$

(d) $(p \wedge \sim q) \vee (q \wedge \sim p)$

(e) $(p \rightarrow q) \leftrightarrow (\sim q \rightarrow \sim p)$

(f) $(p \rightarrow \sim q) \leftrightarrow (\sim p \vee \sim q)$

11. Assume p is true, q is false, and r is true. What is the value of the following statement?

$$[(p \vee q) \wedge (p \vee r)] \leftrightarrow [p \vee (q \wedge r)]$$

12. Construct a truth table for the following compound sentence. What conclusion can you draw?

$$[(p \vee q) \wedge \sim q] \rightarrow p$$

13. Define a statement for p and a statement for q. Express the law of detachment in words using your statements p and q.

14. Discuss the validity of each conclusion written below the line.

(a) All women are females.

Faith is a woman.
Faith is a female.

(b) All pianos have keys.

Some pianos are electric.
Some electric pianos have keys.

(c) People who live in the town of Rhinebeck live in Dutchess County.

Elizabeth lives in the town of Rhinebeck.
Elizabeth lives in Dutchess County.

15. Discuss the validity of each conclusion written below the line.

(a) All seniors must take the competency exam.

Kathryn is a freshman.

Kathryn does not take the competency exam.

(b) If the road is covered with ice, then school will be canceled.

School is not canceled.

The road was not covered with ice.

(c) Anna left the message or Mark left the message.

Mark did not leave the message.

Anna left the message.

16. Draw a conclusion from each of the following sets of statements.

(a) I will write the report or I will type the report.
It is not true that I will write the report.

(b) If Erin calls Allison, then Allison calls Susie.
If Allison calls Susie, then Susie calls Kathleen.

(c) If Mike can use his mom's car, then he will go to the movies.
If Mike has already seen the movie that is presently playing, then he will not go to the movies.
Mike has already seen the movie or Mike does not know what the movie is about.
Mike can use his mom's car.

17. Draw a conclusion from each of the following sets of statements.

(a) If Danielle is absent from school, she must be ill.
If Danille is ill, she will go to the doctor's office.
Danielle is absent from school or Danielle is healthy.
If Danielle is healthy, she will take the math test today.
Danielle does not take the math test today.

(b) If Laura goes shopping, then she will cash a check.
If there is no money in Laura's checking account, then Laura will not cash a check.
Laura will go shopping and out to dinner.

(c) Rich has seat #10l or Betsy has seat #102.
If Betsy has seat #102, then Jessie has seat #103.
If Jessie has seat #103, then Sara has seat #104.
Sara does not have seat #104.

(d) Gene will teach seventh grade or Gene will teach eighth grade.

If Gene teaches seventh grade, he will be assigned to the Sunset Road School.
Gene will carpool with Chris if he is assigned to the Sunset Road School.
If Gene teaches eighth grade, he will have his daughter Briana in his class.
Gene does not carpool with Chris.

(e) I can turn on the answering machine or I can wait at home for the call.
If my parents need my help, then I cannot wait at home for the call.
If my parents do not need my help, then I can watch TV.
I cannot watch TV.

In Other Words

18. Explain the difference between an open sentence and a closed sentence.

19. Give a real-world example of a statement that contains a conjunction and one that contains a disjunction.

20. Explain the meaning of logical equivalence.

21. A teacher believes that if a student studies, the student will do well in school. However, the teacher also believes that if a student does not do well in school, it is not necessarily because the student does not study. How can the logic illuminate this argument?

22. Are valid arguments always true? Explain your answer.

Cooperative Activity

23. Groups of four

Individual Accountability: Each group member should construct a set of statements similar to those contained in Problems 16 and 17. The member should then represent the situation symbolically.

Group Goal: Each group member will present his or her written statement to the group minus the final conclusion. The group must supply the conclusion, represent the entire set of statements symbolically, and support the conclusion reached by referring to the laws of logic.

Vocabulary for Chapter 1

analogy	law of detachment (modus ponens)
biconditional	law of modus tollens
closed sentence (statement)	law of syllogism (chain rule)
conclusion	line symmetry
conditional	logically equivalent
congruent	looking for a contradiction
conjunction	looking for a pattern
contrapositive	members
converse	negation
difference	open sentences
disjoint sets	proper subset
disjunction	rotational symmetry
distracters	set
domain	solution set
element	subset
employing an analogy	tautology
empty set	truth table
exclusive "or"	truth value
hypothesis	union
implication	universal set
inclusive "or"	valid argument
intersection	Venn diagram
inverse	

Review for Chapter 1

1. Find the pattern and then identify the next term.

(a)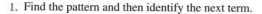

(d)

(b)

(e)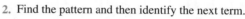

2. Find the pattern and then identify the next term.

(a)

(c)

(b)   A   D   G   J   M

(c)

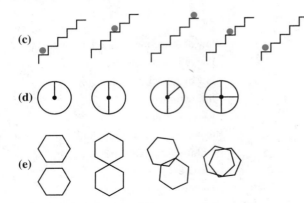

(d)

(e)

3. Find the pattern and then identify the indicated term.

(a) Eighth term

(b) Sixth term

(c) Seventh term

$$ ||| \quad \#\# \quad \#\# \quad \equiv \quad \#\# \quad \#\# \ldots $$

(d) Next term

ANNA...   NOON...   OTTO...

(e) Fifth term

January 7...   February 8...   March 5...   April 5...

4. Find the pattern and then identify the indicated term.

(a) Fifteenth term

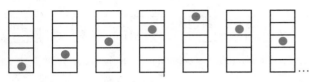

(b) Eleventh term

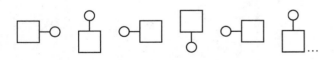

(c) Tenth term

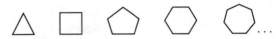

(d) Fourteenth term

(e) Ninth term

5. Identify sets of shapes that appear to be congruent in each figure.

(a)

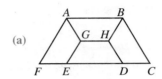

(b)

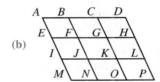

(c)

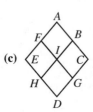

(d)

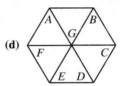

(e)

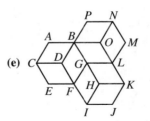

6. A calculator LED display contains seven segments, as shown below. Each of the single digits can be displayed by appropriate line segments. Identify those calculator digits that are symmetrical.

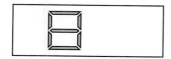

7. (a) On a sheet of paper draw four congruent squares. Draw two smaller congruent triangles inside each square.

   (b) On a sheet of paper draw two congruent squares. Draw four smaller congruent triangles inside each square.

   (c) In parts (a) and (b), identify the types of symmetry illustrated. Trace the lines of symmetry where appropriate.

8. Identify the types of symmetry in each of the following logos.

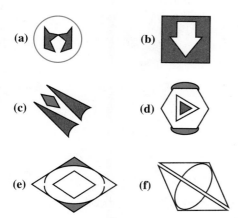

9. Create your own logos that have (a) line symmetry, (b) rotational symmetry, and (c) both line and rotational symmetry.

10. Sketch at least two solutions to the following problem. How can a pizza be sliced into eight pieces such that four of the slices are congruent to one another, and the remaining four slices are congruent to one another?

11. With one line a circle can be divided into two regions.

Two lines can create four regions.

Three lines can create seven regions.

What is the maximum number of regions that can be created by (a) four lines, (b) five lines, and (c) six lines?

12. Select the best solution for each from the choices below.

   (a) IN : OUT   as   PIN : ____
       PUT   ON   CUT   PUN   POUT

   (b) SLIP : SLIDE   as   TRIP : ____
       TRIBE   TRIED   TRAP   SLIP   SLID

   (c) THREE : TREE   as   FOUR : ____
       WHEAT   FLOWER   FLEE   FOUR   FOR

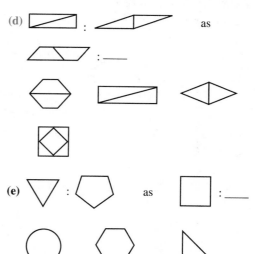

13. Select the best solution from each of the following choices.

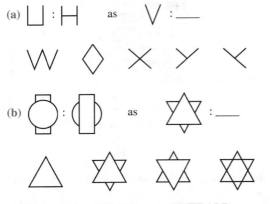

(a) $\sqcup$: $\vdash$ as $\vee$: ____

(b)   as   ⛤ : ____

(c) DIAMOND : NOMAD   as   EMERALD : ____
     WANDERER   DREAM   ALARM   ARMOR
     GYPSY

(d) I : VII   as   III : ____
     IIIII   X   IIV   IX   XI

14. Find the characteristics that are common to those figures in Group A but are not present in Group B. Identify the figure in Group C that belongs to Group A.

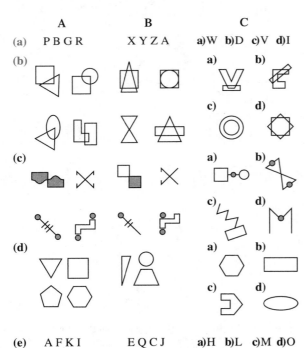

	A	B	C
(a)	P B G R	X Y Z A	a)W b)D c)V d)I

(b)

(c)

(d)

| (e) | A F K I | E Q C J | a)H b)L c)M d)O |

15. Given:
   $A = \{15, 25, 35, 45, 55, 65\}$
   $B = \{10, 20, 30, 40, 50, 60\}$
   $C = \{5, 10, 15, 20, 25, 30, 35, 40, 45, 50, 55, 60, 65\}$
   Find:
   (a) $A \cup B$
   (b) $A \cup C$
   (c) $B \cup C$
   (d) $A \cap B$
   (e) $A \cap C$
   (f) $B \cap C$
   (g) $C - A$
   (h) $C - B$

16. Draw Venn diagrams to illustrate the sets listed in Problem 15 (a) through (h).

17. Given:
   $A = \{R, T, W, G, B, D\}$
   $B = \{L, M, T, G, R, S, I\}$
   $C = \{B, C, D, E, F, G\}$
   Find:
   (a) $A \cup B$
   (b) $A \cup C$
   (c) $B \cup C$
   (d) $A \cap B$
   (e) $A \cap C$
   (f) $B \cap C$
   (g) $C - A$
   (h) $C - B$

18. List all the subsets of the set $\{\$, \#, *, \&\}$.

19. In each case, determine sets A, B, and C that can be illustrated by the following Venn diagrams.

(a)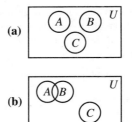

(b)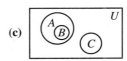

(c)

(d)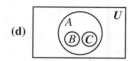

20. At a particular health club, the following options are each priced separately: Nautilus equipment, pool, aerobics class. Members may choose to pay for one, two, or all three options. Draw a Venn diagram to illustrate this situation.

21. Classify each of the following inclusive "or" statements or exclusive "or" statements.

   (a) Jack is 5 feet tall or Jack is 6 feet tall.

   (b) She is wearing red or she is wearing blue.

   (c) The party begins at 2:00 or the party begins at 3:00.

   (d) I will go sledding or I will go skiing.

   (e) She is in Dr. Peterson's biology class or she is in Dr. Gerver's math class.

22. Write the converse, inverse, and contrapositive of each statement below.

   (a) $p \rightarrow \sim q$ **(b)** $q \rightarrow p$

   (c) $(p \vee q) \rightarrow q$ **(d)** $p \rightarrow (p \wedge q)$

23. For each of the following conditionals, state in words the inverse, converse, and contrapositive.

   (a) If he leaves a message on her answering machine, then she calls him back.

   (b) If you use a mouthwash, then people talk to you.

   (c) If you teach elementary school courses, then you like working with young children.

   (d) If $x = 7$, then $3x - 2 = 19$.

24. Construct a truth table for the following compound sentence.

$$\sim(p \wedge q) \rightarrow \sim[(\sim q) \vee (\sim p)]$$

25. What conclusions can you draw from the following statements? Justify your conclusions.

   (a) If the number has more than eight digits, then it cannot be displayed on my calculator.
The number is 246829856.

   (b) If the airplane ticket is nonrefundable, then I cannot switch to the 3:30 P.M. flight.
If I cannot switch to the 3:30 P.M. flight, then I will stay at the hotel.
The airline ticket is refundable.

   (c) If Jesse goes to the movies with Ally, they will need a ride to the Red Hook theater.
Jesse and Ally do not need a ride to the theater.

   (d) Maria will buy a foreign car or Liz will buy a domestic car.
If Liz buys a domestic car, then her car will be equipped with antilock brakes.
If Liz's car is equipped with antilock brakes, then her insurance will be decreased by 10%.
Liz's insurance was not decreased by 10%.

   (e) If Kathryn does not answer her phone, she must have already left for the play.
If Kathryn has already left for the play, then she will pick up Geoffrey first.
Kathryn answers her phone or she doesn't answer her phone.
If Kathryn answers her phone, she will know to pick up Keith first.
Kathryn does not pick up Keith first.

   (f) Trudy will take a cruise or Trudy will rent a beach house.
If Trudy takes a cruise, then she will go to Alaska.
Kathleen and Bill will vacation with Trudy if she goes to Alaska.
If Trudy rents a beach house, Jean and Ray will vacation with her.
Kathleen and Bill do not vacation with Trudy.

In Other Words

26. Explain the relationships between set theory and logic. Cite particular examples.

27. List three problem-solving strategies that have been introduced in this chapter. Discuss their similarities and differences.

28. What is the difference between the inclusive "or" and the exclusive "or" statements?

29. We defined a proper subset in Section 1.2. What might you imagine the definition of an improper subset to be?

30. Select one of the three laws of logic outlined in Section 1.3. Describe a context in which that law of logic is illustrated. Define statements p and q (and r if necessary).

Cooperative Activity

31. Groups of three
In the Cooperative Activity of Section 1.2, you were asked to research some courses in your college course catalog. This activity will build on your findings.

Individual Accountability: Each group member is assigned one of the laws of logic. The group member must study this law and develop sets of statements that can be used to illustrate the law (define p and q [and r if necessary]). The member is to write up an explanation of the law, including examples. A copy of the write-up is to be given to each other group member. All group members are responsible for reviewing the write-ups before the group convenes.

Group Goal: The group is to discuss the laws and clarify any points that are unclear. The group must then select a particular department of the college whose course offerings are listed in the schedule of classes. As a group, the members must define statements referring to course offerings and use these statements to illustrate the laws of logic. For example, suppose that Math 105 is a prerequisite for Math 106. A conditional statement that could be written about these courses is, "If you pass Math 105, then you can take Math 106."

2

Numeration and **P**lace **V**alue

Examine the photograph at the right.

Describe what you see.

How many individual beads are there?

How might you determine how many individual beads there are?

What relationships exist among the sets of beads?

How might you determine what these relationships are?

What would a mathematical description of this photograph contain?

Introduction

One of the obvious aspects of mathematics that is regular, consistent, and bound by patterns is the way we count. For example, consider a car odometer as it records mileage. As the mileage increases, each column in the odometer follows a specific and predictable pattern. As any individuial column passes the digit 9, it forces the column to its left to increase by 1. Understanding this regularity is basic to understanding the relationship between a number and a quantity. You can appreciate the difficulty of grasping this relationship by listening to young children just learning to count. They often say ". . . twenty-seven, twenty-eight, twenty-nine, twenty-ten. . . . " These children recognize that there is a pattern in our number system and they attempt to apply this knowledge as best they can. Pattern recognition is an important problem-solving strategy and is one of the basic characteristics of numeration. In this chapter, we will explore various numeration systems, both ancient and modern. We will also introduce you to the structure underlying our system of numeration, or the patterns we follow when we count. Finally, we will discuss using calculators, both for the insight they can offer into our number system and for their uses as an instructional tool for understanding numbers and the uses of numbers.

2.1 Numeration Systems

This section begins by discussing three early numeration systems: the Egyptian, the Roman, and the Hindu-Arabic (which we still use today). You might be wondering why it is important for young children to be introduced to numeration systems they may never use or even encounter outside a mathematics class. First of all, studying ancient numeration systems gives a historical perspective to mathematics. Many children, and indeed many adults, may understand some of the different ways that language has evolved through the ages but may think of mathematics as some monolithic system that has remained unchanged since its origins. They need to realize that mathematics, too, has evolved from primitive beginnings to its current level of sophistication. Second, students need to recognize that different cultures throughout the ages have used different number systems. Again, this emphasizes the point that mathematics, like language, has been used in different ways throughout history depending on the needs and capabilities of particular cultures. And finally, studying ancient and diverse systems of numeration offers a contrast to the system of numeration we use today. After our discussion of ancient numeration systems, we move on to the structures and patterns important to our numeration system.

Archaeological findings have led us to believe that early humans used counting in the most practical sense. A notch (/) or a mark in the sand, on a piece of wood, or on a stone represented a single unit. Three notches might stand for three people, three animals, or three things. Each mark or tally was the direct representation of the unit to be

one-to-one correspondence   counted. It appears that early civilizations recognized the concept of **one-to-one correspondence**, that is, one mark for one item.

Egyptian Numeration System

Using a system that involves one-to-one correspondence would necessitate 45 marks to represent 45 objects. Obviously, such a system is lengthy and cumbersome. Perhaps this is why the ancient Egyptians (about 3400 B.C.) introduced symbols that stood for groups of objects. Figure 2.1 contains some of the symbols and values from this Egyptian grouping system.

Figure 2.1

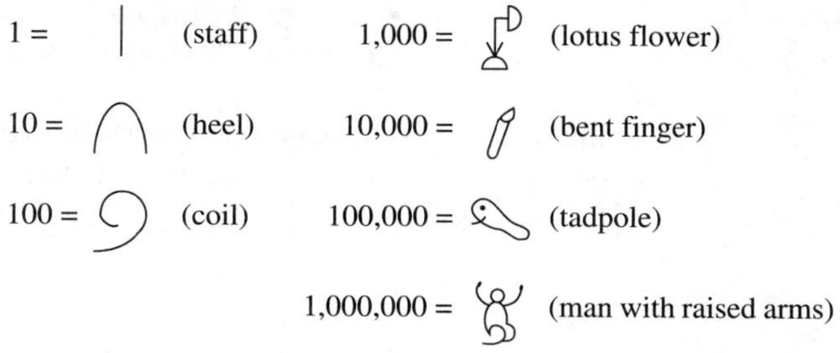

1 = | (staff)   1,000 = (lotus flower)

10 = (heel)   10,000 = (bent finger)

100 = (coil)   100,000 = (tadpole)

1,000,000 = (man with raised arms)

The set of symbols

uses three of the symbols for 1, five of the symbols for 10, and six of the symbols for 100. The total value is found by adding the individual values of each symbol. Therefore, the quantity

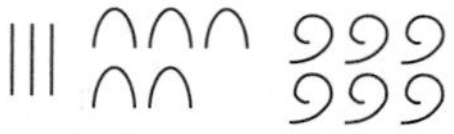

represents 3 + 50 + 600, or 653.

Investigation 1

Represent the quantities 24, 673, and 15,508 using the Egyptian symbols shown in Figure 2.1.

A person who has grown up using our number system might assume that the order in which the symbols appear in the Egyptian numeration system is unchangeable. However, this is not the case. Although the order was never scrambled, archaeologists have found tablets and scrolls with the symbols arranged from least to greatest and alternately from greatest to least. The custom appeared to be to arrange numbers from least to greatest rather than from greatest to least. Each of these quantities has been represented in both ways, as follows.

	Least to Greatest	*Greatest to Least*
24	ⅠⅠⅠⅠ∩∩	∩∩ⅠⅠⅠⅠ
673	ⅠⅠⅠ ∩∩∩∩∩ 999 / ∩∩∩ 999	999 ∩∩∩∩∩ / 999 ∩∩∩ ⅠⅠⅠ
15,508	ⅠⅠⅠⅠ 999 ...	... 99 ⅠⅠⅠⅠ

In the Egyptian system, the number of symbols used is not necessarily related to the quantity they represent, since it is not a system of one-to-one correspondence. Although the four symbols

$$∩∩∩∩$$

represent forty units, the single symbol,

$$9$$

represents 100 units. Therefore, when comparing quantities it is the *value* of the symbols rather than the *number* of symbols that is significant.

Investigation 2

Which set of symbols represents a greater quantity?

ⅠⅮⅩ   ⅠⅠⅠⅠⅠ ∩∩∩∩∩ 99999 / ⅠⅠⅠⅠ ∩∩∩∩ 9999

The set of symbols on the left represents 1 + 1000, or 1001. The set of symbols on the right represents 9 + 90 + 900, or 999. Therefore, the set of symbols on the left represents a greater quantity than the set of symbols on the right. This can be shown by writing

ⅠⅮⅩ > ⅠⅠⅠⅠⅠ ∩∩∩∩∩ 99999 / ⅠⅠⅠⅠ ∩∩∩∩ 9999

and is read as "one thousand one is greater than nine hundred ninety-nine." Alternately,

$$\text{IIIII } \wedge\wedge\wedge\wedge\wedge\ 99999 \ < \ | \ \text{P}$$
$$\text{IIII } \wedge\wedge\wedge\wedge\ 9999$$

is read as "nine hundred ninety-nine is less than one thousand one."

Roman Numeration System

As you can see from Figure 2.1 and Investigations 1 and 2, the Egyptian system was based on the number 10. Symbols for multiples of 10 appear to have been widely used. All other values were additive repetitions of these symbols. Many years later (500 B.C. to A.D. 100), the Romans utilized a numeration system that was somewhat similar to that of the Egyptians. Symbols were used for multiples of 10, along with some intermediate symbols for numbers such as 5, 50, and 500. As in the Egyptian system, the value of a set of Roman symbols was found by adding the individual values of the symbols used in the representation. Some of the basic symbols are shown here:

I	1
V	5
X	10
L	50
C	100
D	500
M	1000

Early examples of Roman numerals were written with the largest valued symbols at the left. The year 1985 would have been represented as MDCCCCLXXXV. However, to simplify the representation of numbers such as 4, 9, 40, 90, 400, and 900, the value was shown in a subtractive manner. Rather than representing the quantity 4 as IIII, the Romans instead used its equivalent, one less than 5. This was symbolized as IV. Here the smaller valued symbol is placed to the left of the symbol with the larger value. The smaller value is subtracted from the larger value. The subtraction held true only in the following instances: IV (4), IX (9), XL (40), XC (90), CD (400), and CM (900). The year 1999 would be represented as MCMXCIX, since

$$M \ + \quad CM \quad + \quad XC \quad + \quad IX \ = 1999$$
$$1000 + (1000 - 100) + (100 - 10) + (10 - 1) = 1999$$
$$1000 + \quad 900 \quad + \quad 90 \quad + \quad 9 \ = 1999$$

Larger quantities would be represented in a multiplicative manner. For instance, 23,000 would be interpreted as 23 times 1000. A bar was placed over the symbols to indicate that the total value was to be multiplied by 1000. Therefore, 23,000 would be represented by $\overline{\text{XXIII}}$.

Investigation 3

Express 999,000 in Roman numerals.

Consider 999,000 = 999 times 1000.

$$999,000 = 999 \text{ times } 1000$$

999,000 can be written as $\overline{\text{CMXCIX}}$ ⌐ ⌐ 999 can be written as CMXCIX

Investigation 4

Which set of symbols represents the greater value?

CMIV

MCVI

$$CMIV = CM + IV = (1000 - 100) + (5 - 1) = 900 + 4 = 904$$

$$MCVI = M + C + V + I = 1000 + 100 + 5 + 1 = 1151$$

Therefore, CMIV < MCVI. Alternately, MCVI > CMIV.

Hindu-Arabic Numeration System

place

It is generally believed that the Hindus invented the numeration system we use today and that the Arabs introduced it into Europe. Unlike the Egyptian and Roman systems, the values in the Hindu-Arabic system are not a function of the individual symbol alone but rather a function of the symbol in conjunction with its **place**. For example, in the Roman system, 3 is represented by III, 30 by XXX, and 300 by CCC. In each instance, three symbols are used. The total value is determined by the value of each of the symbols.

place value system

In the Hindu-Arabic system, three is represented by 3, thirty by 30, and three hundred by 300. The same symbol, 3, is used each time. What differs is its placement. Depending on where the 3 is placed, it can have a value of 3 ones, 3 tens, 3 hundreds, and so on. It is for this reason that our system of numeration is said to be a **place value system**. The value of a digit is determined by its place.

Investigation 5

Write five million, nine hundred thirteen thousand, six hundred five using Hindu-Arabic symbols.

The place values can be viewed in the following way:

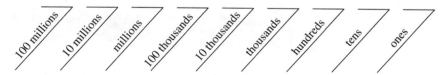

Therefore, five million, nine hundred thirteen thousand, six hundred five would be represented as 5,913,605. Notice that the placement of the commas when the number is written in words corresponds to the placement of the commas when the number is written in symbols.

The following table illustrates the names and values of large numbers.

Name	Symbol	Value
One thousand	1,000	One thousand ones
One million	1,000,000	One thousand thousands
One billion	1,000,000,000	One thousand millions
One trillion	1,000,000,000,000	One thousand billions
One quadrillion	1,000,000,000,000,000	One thousand trillions
One quintillion	1,000,000,000,000,000,000	One thousand quadrillions

These place value names are not universal. In Great Britain, one billion is equivalent to one million millions, instead of one thousand millions as in the United States. When economic reports are quoted in the media, it is necessary to know whether these numbers are from a U.S. source or a British source since a British billion is one thousand times as large as a U.S. billion.

Place Value Models

Place value numeration systems are based on a grouping principle. This principle allows for greater efficiency when dealing with large quantities of items. Without symbols standing for groups of items, a representation of the quantity two thousand, seven hundred nine would require two thousand, seven hundred nine symbols.

To better understand the concept of place value, examine what might happen when an apple grower packs apples for shipping. Suppose 24 apples can be placed in a crate. Now, instead of having to account for each apple individually, the apple grower can refer to the number of crates. When removing the crates from the orchard, perhaps 50 crates can be placed on a pallet for easy shipping. The apple grower can now refer to the number of pallets rather than the number of crates or individual apples. If a particular shipment consists of eight pallets, the "eight" refers to large groups of apples, not individual apples. The shipment pictured in Figure 2.2 might be recorded as $\boxed{8\,|\,2\,|\,0}$. This means eight pallets, two crates, and no single apples. Notice that this would not be the same shipment as one recorded by $\boxed{2\,|\,8\,|\,0}$.

Figure 2.2

Place value numeration systems are analogous to this example since a number can refer to individual items or groups of items depending on its placement. When introducing the concept of place value to children, an activity known as chip trading is a useful example. This activity illustrates the concept of one particular item having a value of, or representing, more than one individual item.

Three different colored chips, perhaps red, white, and blue, are needed, along with a spinner or a number cube showing the numbers 1, 2, and 3. An activity board as shown in Figure 2.3, is also used.

Figure 2.3

Red	White	Blue

The number appearing on the spinner or number cube represents the number of blue chips that can be placed on the board. Whenever three blue chips accumulate, they must be traded in for one white chip. Likewise, when three white chips accumulate, they must be traded in for one red chip. Students work in pairs, alternating turns, until one player accumulates three red chips, which ends the activity. Examine the sequence for one student, which is shown in Figure 2.4.

Figure 2.4 *Spinner Outcome*   *Board*   *Trades*

2

Red	White	Blue
		●
		●

2

Red	White	Blue
		●
		●
		●
		●

→

Red	White	Blue
	●	●

Figure 2.4 (continued)   *Spinner Outcome*   *Board*   *Trades*

3

Red	White	Blue
	•	•
		•
		•
		•

→

Red	White	Blue
	•	•
	•	

1

Red	White	Blue
	•	•
	•	•

3

Red	White	Blue
	•	•
	•	•
		•
		•
		•

→

Red	White	Blue
	•	•
	•	•
	•	

↓

Red	White	Blue
•		•
		•

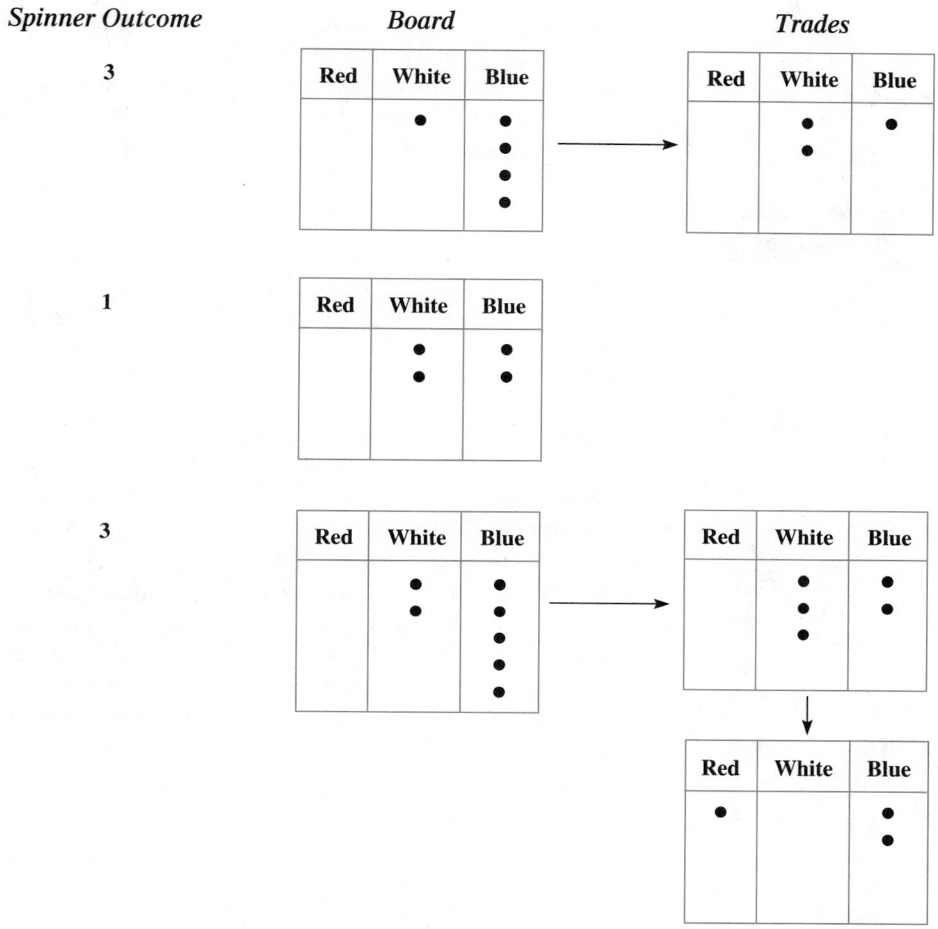

The function of this activity is to give students practice in trading for equivalences. They soon come to realize that three white chips are equivalent to one red chip. This will prepare them for formal instruction in our numeration system, where 10 ones are equivalent to 1 ten, and 10 tens are equivalent to one hundred.

Investigation 6

Here is a chip-trading activity in which 5 blues are needed to trade for 1 white, and 5 whites are needed to trade for 1 red. What is the value, in blue chips, of (a) 2 whites; (b) 1 red; (c) 1 red, 1 white, and 1 blue; (d) 2 reds and 1 blue?

(a) Since 5 blues are equivalent to 1 white, 10 blues would be equivalent to 2 whites. Therefore, the value of 2 whites is 10 blue chips.

(b) One red is equivalent to 5 whites. Each white has a value of 5 blue chips. Therefore, 1 red is equivalent to 25 blue chips.

(c) One red (25 blues) and 1 white (5 blues) and 1 blue are equivalent to 31 blues.

(d) Two reds (50 blues) and 1 blue have a value of 51 blue chips.

Investigation 7

Let 1 red be equivalent to 10 whites, and 1 white have a value of 10 blues. What is the value of 1 red, 3 whites, and 6 blues?

Since 1 red is equivalent to 10 whites, and each white has a value of 10 blues, 1 red is equivalent to 100 blues. And since 1 white is equivalent to 10 blues, 3 whites are equivalent to 30 blues. Therefore, the total value of 1 red (100 blues), 3 whites (30 blues), and 6 blues is 136 blue chips.

Investigation 7 models the Hindu-Arabic numeration system because it is based on the number 10. Instead of saying 1 white is equivalent to 10 blues, we say that 1 ten is equivalent to 10 ones. Instead of 1 red being equivalent to 10 whites, we say that 100 is equivalent to 10 tens. *One*, *ten*, and *hundred* are names of places in our place value system. Some of the larger place names are shown in the table on page 53. As you move from right to left in the table, each subsequent place has a value 10 times greater than the place to its right. Using exponents is a shorthand way to show repeated multiplication by 10:

$$1 = 10^0$$
$$1 \times 10 = 10^1$$
$$1 \times 10 \times 10 = 10^2$$
$$1 \times 10 \times 10 \times 10 = 10^3$$
$$1 \times 10 \times 10 \times 10 \times 10 = 10^4$$
$$1 \times 10 \times 10 \times 10 \times 10 \times 10 = 10^5$$

In general, 10^n represents

$$\underbrace{1 \times 10 \times 10 \times 10 \times \cdots \times 10}_{n \text{ tens}} \qquad n = \{0, 1, 2, 3, 4, \ldots\}$$

This notation can help make sense of the value given to each color in the chip-trading activity of Investigation 7. The value of a blue chip can be symbolized by 10^0, or 1. The value of a white chip can be symbolized by 10^1, or 10. The value of a red chip can be symbolized by 10^2, or 100. Therefore, the single red chip, three white chips, and six blue chips from Investigation 7 can be represented as follows.

$$136 = \quad 1 \text{ red } + 3 \text{ white} + 6 \text{ blue}$$
$$136 = 1 \times 10^2 + 3 \times 10^1 + 6 \times 10^0$$
$$136 = 1 \times 100 + 3 \times 10 \ + 6 \times 1$$
$$136 = \underbrace{\ 100 \ + \ 30 \ + \ 6\ }$$
$$136$$

exponential notation
expanded notation

When a number is expressed using exponents, as in the second line, the number is said to be written in **exponential notation**. When a number is expressed in expanded form, as in the third line, it is said to be written in **expanded notation**.

Investigation 8

Write the number 2367 in exponential and expanded notation.

$$2367 = (2 \times 10^3) \ + (3 \times 10^2) + (6 \times 10^1) + (7 \times 10^0)$$
$$2367 = (2 \times 1000) + (3 \times 100) + (6 \times 10) \ + (7 \times 1)$$
$$2367 = \quad 2000 \quad + \quad 300 \quad + \quad 60 \quad + \quad 7$$

base ten

Because our number system is based on 10, it is called a **base ten** numeration system. Ten digits are used in our system: 0, 1, 2, 3, 4, 5, 6, 7, 8, and 9. Other base systems are analogous to our base ten system. In Investigation 6, you worked with a base five system. Only five digits are used in a base five system: 0, 1, 2, 3, and 4. Recall that each time five chips accumulated, they were traded in for one chip of a different color. At no time were five chips of the same color allowed to be on the activity board. In part (c) of Investigation 6, you were asked to find the value in blue chips of 1 red chip, 1 white chip, and 1 blue chip. You were told that 5 blue chips are equivalent to 1 white chip, and that 5 white chips are equivalent to 1 red chip. These values are shown in the following display:

1 red	1 white	1 blue
25 blue	5 blue	1 blue
1×5^2	1×5^1	1×5^0
25	5	1

Compare the various base systems with the chip-trading activity models. Do you see any similarities? In all cases, the value of the blue chip was always 1, the value of the white chip was equal to the base, and the value of the red chip was equal to the square of the base (base × base). This pattern is present in any base system. In a base three chip-trading activity, one red would be equivalent to nine blues (3 × 3), one white would be equivalent to three blues (the value of the base), and again blue would have a value of one unit.

Although the base ten system is widely used in our culture, we do employ other base systems. A variation of base sixty can be seen in the way we record the passing of time.

Examine the following notation: 2:25:55. The time represented here is 2 hours, 25 minutes, and 55 seconds. If the time represented here were to be written only in seconds, a conversion could be made similar to the expanded notation illustrated for other bases:

$$(2 \times 60^2) \ + (25 \times 60^1) + (55 \times 60^0)$$
$$(2 \times 3600) + (25 \times 60) \ + (55 \times 1)$$
$$7200 \quad + \quad 1500 \quad + \quad 55 \quad = 8755 \text{ seconds}$$

Powers-of-Ten Blocks

A manipulative material commonly used to illustrate place value to elementary school children is a set of blocks called powers-of-ten blocks. These are illustrated in Figure 2.5. Notice that the ten block is 10 times the size of the unit block, the hundred block is 10 times the size of the ten block, and the thousand block is 10 times the size of the hundred block. This is in contrast to the model used in the chip-trading activity. In that place value model, all of the chips were the same size. The value of each chip was arbitrarily assigned by the rules of the activity. The only way you could know that three blues were equivalent to one white was if you were told this. Powers-of-ten blocks, on the other hand, bear an obvious and visible relationship to each other. Ten units are physically equivalent to one 10, and so on.

Figure 2.5

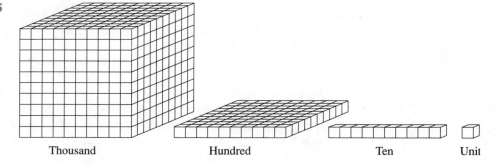

Thousand   Hundred   Ten   Unit

Assessments for Section 2.1

1. Write each of the following numbers in Egyptian symbols, Roman symbols, and Hindu-Arabic symbols.

   (a) Twenty thousand, four hundred fifteen

   (b) Five hundred ninety-five

   (c) Thirteen thousand, seven hundred eleven

   (d) Sixty-six

   (e) Nine thousand, three hundred twenty

2. Write each of the following in Egyptian symbols, Roman symbols, and Hindu-Arabic symbols.

   (a) $(4 \times 10^5) + (3 \times 10^4) + (5 \times 10^3) + (2 \times 10^2) + (1 \times 10^1) + (6 \times 10^0)$

   (b) $(9 \times 10^5) + (2 \times 10^3) + (3 \times 10^0)$

   (c) (8×10^4)

3. Use the symbols < or > to indicate which number is greater.

   (a) DL   or   DXV

   (b) 2011   or   2101

   (c) |||9⌐⌐ or |999⌐⌐

(d) ∩∩∩∩∩ℰℰ or 99999🜊🜊

(e) DCCCVIII or CMIX

4. Write each of the following numbers using Hindu-Arabic symbols.

   (a) Twenty-five thousand, twenty-five

   (b) Six hundred seventeen million, thirty-three thousand, two hundred

   (c) Seventy thousand, nine hundred nineteen

   (d) One hundred six thousand, eight hundred seventy-two

   (e) Three million, five

5. Write each of the following symbols in words.

   (a) DCCXCVII

   (b) ‖‖‖∩∩999🜊

   (c) |🜊ℰ

   (d) MCMXCII

   (e) 7,011,605

6. Write each of the following numbers in words.

   (a) 20,010,006

   (b) 34,708,296,015

   (c) 130,293,751,873,125

   (d) 11,001,801

   (e) 5,022,006,022

7. Examine the following hieroglyphic that was found on an ancient Egyptian papyrus. Offer a possible interpretaton.

   | 9999🜊🜊 |
   ‖ 999🜊🜊🜊🜊🜊 ‖

   ‖‖‖99🜊ℰ ‖‖‖‖

   ‖‖‖999🜊🜊🜊ℰ ⟁

8. A certain number written in Egyptian symbols contains 10 symbols of four different types. The value of the number is less than 3000. List three possible such numbers and their Egyptian equivalents.

9. How many different Roman numerals can be made with the X, V, I, and C if each symbol is repeated only once? List the base ten equivalents of the numerals found.

10. A certain numerical value is symbolized by 4 Hindu-Arabic digits, 10 Roman symbols, or 14 Egyptian symbols. Name one such number.

11. Determine the base ten value of each chip-trading board.

	Board			*Base*
(a)	Red	White	Blue	**Base two**
	●	●	●	

	Red	White	Blue	**Base three**
(b)	●	●	●	
	●		●	

	Red	White	Blue	**Base four**
(c)	●	●	●	
		●	●	
		●		

	Red	White	Blue	**Base five**
(d)	●	●	●	
	●	●		
	●	●		
	●			

	Red	White	Blue	**Base six**
(e)	●	●	●	
	●	●	●	
	●		●	
			●	

12. In each case, sketch a chip-trading board that would illustrate the following base ten values.
    (a) 24 on a base three board
    (b) 15 on a base five board
    (c) 9 on a base two board
    (d) 43 on a base four board

13. In each case, sketch a chip-trading board that would illustrate the following base ten values.
    (a) 79 on a base five board
    (b) 206 on a base ten board
    (c) 10 on a base three board
    (d) 50 on a base four board

14. Define the equivalences in a base N chip-trading game to be as follows:

    $$N \text{ blues} = 1 \text{ white}$$
    $$N \text{ whites} = 1 \text{ red}$$
    $$N \text{ reds} = 1 \text{ green}$$

    For each value of N, sketch a chip-trading board that has a value equivalent to the value of 67 blue chips.
    (a) $N = 3$ (b) $N = 4$ (c) $N = 6$
    (d) $N = 8$ (e) $N = 10$

15. Write each of the following base ten numbers in both exponential and expanded notations.
    (a) 2075 (b) 306 (c) 1515 (d) 7631 (e) 899

16. Write each of the following numbers in both exponential and expanded notations.
    (a) Three thousand, forty-two
    (b) Eighteen thousand, one
    (c) Three million, four hundred fifty-two thousand, fifteen
    (d) Five hundred sixty thousand, four hundred
    (e) Eighty-one thousand eighty-one

17. What is the value of each of the following expressions?
    (a) $3000 + 60 + 2$
    (b) $5000 + 700 + 80 + 8$
    (c) $6000 + 60$
    (d) $(8 \times 10^3) + (6 \times 10^2)$
    (e) $(9 \times 10^3) + (3 \times 10^2) + (2 \times 10^1)$

18. What is the value of each of the following expressions?
    (a) $400 + 90 + 3$
    (b) $10{,}000 + 800 + 70 + 1$
    (c) $(7 \times 10^4) + (4 \times 10^3) + (2 \times 10^2) + (5 \times 10^1)$
    (d) $(3 \times 10^4) + (0 \times 10^3) + (0 \times 10^2) + (3 \times 10^1)$
    (e) (6×10^5)

19. What is the tenth term of this sequence?

    $$(15 \times 10^6), (16 \times 10^7), (17 \times 10^8)$$

    How is this sequence generated?

20. What is the eighth term of the following sequence?

    $$(18 \times 10^0), (19 \times 10^1), (20 \times 10^2), (21 \times 10^3)$$

    How is this sequence generated?

21. The digit in the tens place of a three-digit number is three more than the digit in the hundreds place. The digit in the ones place is one less than the digit in the tens place. The sum of the digits is 8. What is this number?

22. The sum of the digits of a four-digit number is 16. The digit in the ones place is three times the digit in the thousands place. The digit in the tens place is four times the digit in the thousands place. The digit in the hundreds place is eight less than the digit in the tens place. What is this number?

23. Determine a palindromic six-digit number, the sum of whose digits equals 12.

In Other Words

24. Why is the Egyptian system not considered a place value system?

25. Explain the subtractive aspect of the Roman numeral system.

26. Is there a numeral 7 in the base seven system? Illustrate your reasoning by drawing an analogy to the base ten system.

27. How is a powers-of-ten block representation of 123 different from a base ten chip-trading board containing one red, two white, and three blue chips?

28. Examine the following set of numbers: 6, 16, and 29. Ascribe three different meanings to this set of numbers.

Cooperative Activity

29. Groups of three

Individual Accountability: This is a research activity. Each group member is to research a different numeration system (other than the Hindu-Arabic system). Some sources are listed here:

Boyer, Carl. *A History of Mathematics.* Princeton, N.J.: Princeton University Press, 1985.

Eves, Howard. *An Introduction to the History of Mathematics.* New York: Holt, Rinehart and Winston, 1964.

Kline, Morris. *Mathematics in Western Culture.* London: Oxford University Press, 1953.

Examine the system you choose to research in light of its similarities to and differences from the Hindu-Arabic system.

Group Goal: Compare the systems found. Are they place value systems? What limitations do they have? How do they compare with our base ten system? Why do you think that they fell into disuse?

2.2   The Calculator as an Instructional Tool

In 1989 the National Council of Teachers of Mathematics published the *Curriculum and Evaluation Standards for School Mathematics.* In it, recommendations were made for changes in the way mathematics is taught and studied. Of particular interest are the statements made concerning the role of technology in the mathematics classroom:

> Because technology is changing mathematics and its uses, we believe that appropriate calculators should be available to all students at all times. . . . Contrary to the fears of many, the availability of calculators and computers has expanded students' capability of performing calculations. There is no evidence to suggest that the availability of calculators makes students dependent on them for simple calculations. Students should be able to decide when they need to calculate and whether they require an exact or approximate answer. (p. 8)

As a preservice teacher, you need to know how to use a calculator for both personal and educational purposes. You should be aware of the fact that all calculators do not work in the same way. As you go through this text, some of the calculator instructions may need to be slightly altered to conform to the specifications of your particular calculator.

The most appropriate calculator for the early elementary grades is a basic four-function calculator (+, −, ×, ÷) with large keys, color coded to delineate between number keys and function keys. It is helpful to have a solar- or light-powered calculator to avoid the effort and expense of replacing batteries.

calculator keystroke sequence

The order in which calculator keys are pressed affects the final display. A sequence of calculator number and operation keys stated in a particular order is called a **calculator keystroke sequence**. The positions and labels on the keys vary with each calculator. Be sure you have read and understood the instuctions and can use your calculator correctly before you attempt to teach with it.

Unless otherwise indicated, a basic four-function calculator, as shown in Figure 2.6, will be used throughout this text. As we progress, calculator keystroke sequences will be introduced and used in the context of the skills being taught. All keystroke sequences will begin with the key $\boxed{\text{AC}}$. The function of this key is included on all calculators, although the label of the key may vary. The $\boxed{\text{AC}}$ (all clear) key clears everything that has been displayed or stored in the calculator. Some calculators link the function of this key with another key and delineate this combination of keys with the use of a slash (/).

Figure 2.6

The Calculator Constant Arithmetic Feature

constant arithmetic feature

A useful capability of many simple calculators is the ability to repeatedly add, subtract, multiply, and divide by a constant amount. This is called the **constant arithmetic feature**. It is particularly useful for teaching children, since it illustrates many patterns and regularities in our number system. To determine if your calculator has this feature, enter the following keystroke sequences and compare your display to that given here.

Constant Addition

In the first sequence, a 2 was repeatedly added five times, resulting in a display of 10. In the second, a 2 was repeatedly added five times to 3, resulting in a display of 13.

Some calculators require that the ⊞ key be pressed twice to activate the constant arithmetic feature.

Constant Subtraction

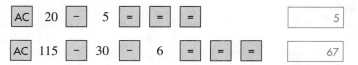

In the first sequence, a 5 was repeatedly subtracted three times from 20, resulting in a display of 5. In the second, the calculator first computes 115 – 30. The answer, 85, was displayed and became the number from which 6 was repeatedly subtracted three times. The result was 67.

Constant Multiplication

In the first sequence, a 3 was multiplied by itself four times [$3 \times (3 \times 3 \times 3 \times 3)$] resulting in the display 243. This number can also be written as 3^5. In the second sequence, 4 is multipled by 5, resulting in 20. Subsequent $\boxed{=}$ keystrokes multiply the number in the display by 4. Notice that the constant feature for multiplication differs from the constant features of addition and subtraction. In multiplication, it is the number *before* the operation key that acts as the repeated constant, rather than the number *after* the operation key, as in addition and subtraction.

Some calculators have a key labeled $\boxed{y^x}$. This key provides the same result as the constant multiplication feature. The following calculator keystroke sequences are equivalent. They each result in a display of 243.

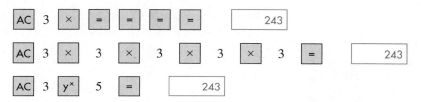

In the third sequence, 3 is raised to the fifth power. The constant multiplication by 3 is internal and only the final result is displayed. Students should learn to use the second calculator sequence to help them develop an understanding of the function of exponents. Once they understand how exponents work, students can use the $\boxed{y^x}$ if it is available on their calculator.

Constant Division

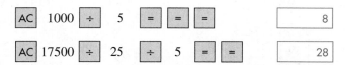

In the first sequence, 1000 is divided by 5 three times, resulting in a display of 8. In the second, 17500 is first divided by 25, resulting in 700. This answer is then divided by 5 twice. The final display is 28. In constant division, as in constant addition and subtraction, it is the number *after* the last operation key that acts as the repeated constant.

Some calculators do not operate as we have just discussed, but they still have the constant arithmetic feature capability. These calculators require using a key that is usually labeled $\boxed{K}$. The constant arithmetic number and operation are stored together in this key. To activate the feature, the $\boxed{K}$ key, rather than the $\boxed{=}$ key, is pressed repeatedly.

Investigation 9

If m and n are both counting numbers greater than 0 ({1, 2, 3, 4 . . .}), and m is greater than n, what is the relationship between m^n and n^m?

Understand the Problem: What is given? You are told that two numbers, m and n, are counting numbers and that m is greater than n.
What is unknown? You are asked to explore the relationship between m^n and n^m.

Devise a Plan: Sometimes when you are solving problems it helps to use a technique called **making a list**. When making a list, you examine a few specific cases in order to determine if any patterns exist.

Carry Out the Plan: Examine the following list:

m n m^n	Constant Arithmetic Keystroke Sequence	n^m	Constant Arithmetic Keystroke Sequence	Comparison
2 1 $2^1 = 2$	[AC] [2] [=]	$1^2 = 1$	[AC] [1] [=]	$m^n > n^m$
3 2 $3^2 = 9$	[AC] [3] [×] [=]	$2^3 = 8$	[AC] [2] [×] [=] [=]	$m^n > n^m$
4 3 $4^3 = 64$	[AC] [4] [×] [=] [=]	$3^4 = 81$	[AC] [3] [×] [=] [=] [=]	$m^n < n^m$
5 4 $5^4 = 625$	[AC] [5] [×] [=] [=] [=]	$4^5 = 1024$	[AC] [4] [×] [=] [=] [=] [=]	$m^n < n^m$
6 5 $6^5 = 7776$	[AC] [6] [×] [=] [=] [=] [=]	$5^6 = 15625$	[AC] [5] [×] [=] [=] [=] [=] [=]	$m^n < n^m$

A pattern begins to develop in the above list after the first two cases. The larger exponent is the critical factor in determining the size of the outcome. It appears that $m^n < n^m$. But would this still be the case if m and n were not consecutive? Let $m = 10$ and $n = 6$.

$m^n = 10^6 =$ [AC] [10] [×] [=] [=] [=] [=] [=]   1000000

$n^m = 6^{10} =$ [AC] [6] [×] [=] [=] [=] [=] [=] [=] [=] [=] [=]   60466176

Clearly, m^n is still less than n^m, since 1,000,000 is less than 60,466,176. Based on the information contained in the list, there appears to be a regularity in the results. This leads us to conclude that if m and n are both counting numbers greater than or equal to 3, and m is greater than n, then m^n is less than n^m.

Look Back: Test a few different values for m and n using your calculator. For example, is $3^{25} > 25^3$, or is $25^3 > 3^{25}$?

Investigating Place Value Using a Calculator

A calculator can help students explore the place value of certain digits within a number. The students can experiment to determine ways of increasing or decreasing the value of a number, as shown in Investigation 10.

Investigation 10

Enter the number 12795 into your calculator. Using any of the four operations (+, −, ×, ÷), change the number to 17295.

The required change involves both the hundreds place and the thousands place. Since the thousands place needs to be increased by 5000 and the hundreds place needs to be decreased by 500, the following keystroke sequence can be used:

$$\boxed{\text{AC}}\; 12795 \;\boxed{+}\; 5000 \;\boxed{-}\; 500 \;\boxed{=}\qquad \boxed{17295}$$

Since the initial number is being increased by 5000 and then decreased by 500, the overall effect is an increase of 4500. Therefore, the following keystroke sequence is also equivalent:

$$\boxed{\text{AC}}\; 12795 \;\boxed{+}\; 4500 \;\boxed{=}\qquad \boxed{17295}$$

Other Base Equivalences

In Section 2.1 of this chapter, we introduced the concept of bases. Numbers in the base ten system can easily be understood by writing them in expanded notation with 10 as a base. But a quantity represented by a specific base ten number can also be presented in other base systems. This process can be carried out more efficiently with a calculator than by hand. The calculator helps remove any computational stumbling blocks and allows you to focus on the process involved in changing from a base ten number to another base equivalent. Investigations 11 and 12 will lead you through the steps involved.

Investigation 11

Write 245 in base five notation.

Understand the Problem: What is given? You are given the base ten number two hundred forty-five (245).

What is unknown? You must determine the base five equivalent of 245.

Devise a Plan: Look for an analogy with the base ten system.

Carry Out the Plan: The only allowable digits in the base five system are 0, 1, 2, 3, and 4. In order to write the base five equivalent of 245, first examine the values of each place in the base five system.

5^4	5^3	5^2	5^1	5^0
625	125	25	5	1

The 5^4 place has a base ten value of 625. This is larger than 245. Therefore, there will be no digits in this place. The 5^3 place has a value of 125. This is the first base five place value that is less than or equal to 245. This will be the starting point for the conversion.

   In order to determine which digit (0, 1, 2, 3, or 4) belongs in the 5^3 place, you need to know how many 125s there are in 245. To figure this out, use the following keystroke sequence:

$$\boxed{AC} \quad 245 \quad \boxed{-} \quad 125 \quad \boxed{=} \quad 120$$

After subtracting 125 once, the number in the display falls below the value of 5^3. This indicates that the digit 1 must be entered in the 5^3 place:

$$\frac{1}{5^3} \quad \frac{}{5^2} \quad \frac{}{5^1} \quad \frac{}{5^0}$$

Now it is necessary to determine the number of 25s in the remaining quantity, 120.

$$\boxed{AC} \quad 120 \quad \boxed{-} \quad 25 \quad \boxed{=} \quad \boxed{=} \quad \boxed{=} \quad \boxed{=}$$

$$\boxed{95} \quad \boxed{70} \quad \boxed{45} \quad \boxed{20}$$

Since there were four 25s in 120, symbolized by the four equal signs in the above keystroke sequence, the digit 4 must go in the 5^2 place.

$$\frac{1}{5^3} \quad \frac{4}{5^2} \quad \frac{}{5^1} \quad \frac{}{5^0}$$

The same pattern is followed to determine the digits in the next two places.
   The base five equivalent of 245 is written as

$$1440_{\text{five}}$$

Notice that it is necessary to use the subscript "five" after the final digit to distinguish the number from 1440.

Look Back: You can check the accuracy of this answer by working backward from the base five equivalent to the base ten number. This process is shown in Investigation 12.

Investigation 12

Write 2533_{six} in base ten notation.

Understand the Problem: You are given a base six number and asked to express it in its base ten equivalent.

Devise a Plan: Look for an analogy with the base ten system.

Carry Out the Plan: Examine the base six place values for each digit in the number above.

	2	5	3	3
Place values	6^3	6^2	6^1	6^0
	216	36	6	1

To use a calculator efficiently to solve this problem, you must understand the function of the memory. The memory allows values from the display to be stored out of view and re-called when needed. In addition, the memory can be increased or decreased at any time without the result appearing in the display. This is accomplished through the use of three keys: M+, M−, and MR.

M+ adds the value in the display to the memory.

The initial memory value is 0. If a displayed number is the first entry into the memory, pressing M+ will merely store the displayed value in memory.

M− subtracts the value in the display from that in the memory.

MR or MRC recalls the value in the memory to the display.

Finding the base ten equivalent of 2533_{six} can be accomplished using the following keystroke sequence:

AC 2 × 216 = M+ 5 × 36 = M+ 3 × 6 = M+ 3 × 1 = M+ MR

The display should read 633. The base ten equivalent of 2533_{six} is 633. The y^x key can also be used here to determine the value of a number raised to an exponent. Rather than entering 216 for 6^3, the calculator can do this computation for you by entering 6 y^x 3. The following keystroke sequence uses the exponent key to determine the base ten equivalent.

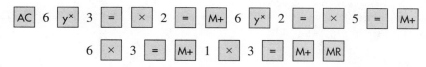

Look Back: You can check the accuracy of this base ten equivalent by writing it in base six using the method outlined in Investigation 11.

Operations in bases other than ten can be performed in ways that are similar to base ten arithmetic operations. We will explore operations in other bases in Section 3.2 when we discuss adding and subtracting whole numbers using step-by-step procedures called algorithms.

Assessments for Section 2.2

1. Will the following keystroke sequences eventually result in the display shown? Predict your answer and then verify it with a calculator.

   Keystroke Sequence   *Display*

   (a)    11

   (b) AC 5 + = = = = ...   120

   (c) AC 7 + 5 = = = = ...   33

   (d)    724

   (e) AC 5 × 2 = = ...   250

2. Will the following keystroke sequences eventually result in the display shown? Predict your answer and then verify it with a calculator.

   Keystroke Sequence   *Display*

   (a) 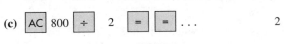 ... 654

   (b) AC 93 − 6 = = = = ... 15

   (c)  ... 2

   (d) AC 125 ÷ 5 = = ... 1

   (e) AC 73 − 8 = = ... 1

3. Write a possible keystroke sequence that would result in the following series of displays.
   (a) 11   16   21   26   31

   (b) 6   18   54   162   486
   (c) 91   84   77   70   63
   (d) 7   10   13   16   19
   (e) 13   17   21   25   29

4. Write a possible keystroke sequence that would result in the following series of displays.
   (a) 16   32   64   128   256
   (b) 297   287   277   267   257
   (c) 20   80   320   1280   5120
   (d) 320   160   80   40   20
   (e) 14   25   36   47   58

5. Using the digits 2, 3, 4, and 5 only once, determine the greatest final display for each.

   (a) AC ___ ___ × ___ ___ =

   (b)

   (c) AC ___ × ___ = ___ − ___ + ___ =

   (d)

   (e) AC ___ − ___ = ___ × ___ = ___ + ___ =

6. Using the digits 6, 7, 8, and 9 only once, determine the order of digits that will result in the greatest answer.

   (a) AC ___ ___ × ___ ___ =

   (b) AC ___ ___ + ___ ___ =

   (c)

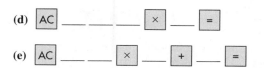

(d) AC ___ ___ ___ × ___ =

(e) AC ___ ___ × ___ + ___ =

7. Which of the following keystroke sequences will eventually display 59?

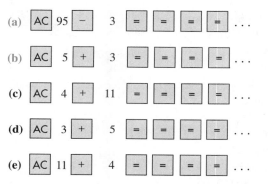

(a) AC 95 − 3 = = = = . . .

(b) AC 5 + 3 = = = = . . .

(c) AC 4 + 11 = = = = . . .

(d) AC 3 + 5 = = = = . . .

(e) AC 11 + 4 = = = = . . .

8. Construct a table for counting number values of N from $N = 1$ to 10 comparing the value of 3^N and $2^{(N + 1)}$. What conclusions can you draw?

9. Open this textbook randomly to any page. Using your calculator, multiply the two facing page numbers. Do this 10 times, making a list of the products you obtain.

   (a) Draw some conclusions about the ones digit in each of the products.

   (b) Why or why not could you ever get the product 2025?

   (c) Why or why not could you ever get the product 3453?

10. How might you make the display of your calculator show the number 58 using only the keys 1 , 0 , + , − , and = ? What is the fewest number of keys with which you can do this?

11. Use your calculator to complete the following list. Look for a pattern in the result.

$$35^2 = 1225$$
$$45^2 = \underline{\qquad}$$
$$55^2 = \underline{\qquad}$$
$$65^2 = \underline{\qquad}$$

   Use the pattern found to predict 95^2. Test your prediction.

12. Use your calculator to complete and extend the following list. Explain the pattern you find.

$$99 \times 12 = \underline{\qquad}$$
$$99 \times 23 = \underline{\qquad}$$
$$99 \times 34 = \underline{\qquad}$$
$$99 \times 45 = \underline{\qquad}$$
$$99 \times 56 = \underline{\qquad}$$

   Without using a calculator, predict 99×89. Verify your result with a calculator.

13. Use your calculator to complete and extend the following list. Explain the pattern you find.

$$9 \times \quad 9 + 7 = \underline{\qquad}$$
$$9 \times \quad 98 + 6 = \underline{\qquad}$$
$$9 \times \quad 987 + 5 = \underline{\qquad}$$
$$9 \times 9876 + 4 = \underline{\qquad}$$

   Without using a calculator, predict $9 \times 9{,}876{,}543 + 1$. Verify your result with a calculator.

14. Which of the following keystroke sequences will eventually display 60?

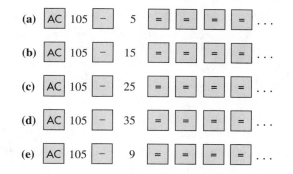

(a) AC 105 − 5 = = = = . . .

(b) AC 105 − 15 = = = = . . .

(c) AC 105 − 25 = = = = . . .

(d) AC 105 − 35 = = = = . . .

(e) AC 105 − 9 = = = = . . .

15. Write a calculator keystroke sequence for each of the following commands.

   (a) Enter 321. Make the 2 become a 7.

   (b) Enter 1095. Make the 9 become a 4.

   (c) Enter 5715. Make the 71 become 00.

   (d) Enter 8463. Make the display read 4863.

   (e) Enter 10825. Make the display read 18025.

16. Write a calculator keystroke sequence for each of the following commands.

   (a) Enter 974. Make the display show 489.

   (b) Enter 2525. Make the display show 5252.

   (c) Enter 1234. Make the display show 4321.

   (d) Enter 6289. Make the display show 6829.

   (e) Enter 1000001. Make the display show 123321.

17. Without using a calculator, determine the final display for each of the following calculator keystroke sequences.

(a) 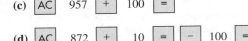 | AC | 295 | – | 60 | = |

(b) | AC | 1291 | + | 500 | = |

(c) | AC | 957 | + | 100 | = |

(d) | AC | 872 | + | 10 | = | | – | 100 | = |

(e) | AC | 2654 | + | 2 | = | | – | 200 | = |

18. Use your calculator to write the base five equivalent of each of the following base ten numbers.

(a) 647

(b) 391

(c) 2684

(d) 10,575

(e) 3298

19. Use your calculator to write the equivalent of the indicated base for each of the following base 10 numbers.

(a) 72 (base two)

(b) 111 (base three)

(c) 834 (base four)

(d) 955 (base six)

(e) 100,001 (base seven)

20. Use your calculator to convert each base ten number to its equivalent in the indicated base.

(a) Convert 101 to base eight.

(b) Convert 45 to base two.

(c) Convert 679 to base nine.

(d) Convert 8314 to base seven.

(e) Convert 977 to base six.

21. (a) Without using a calculator, determine the final display for the following calculator keystroke sequence. Then verify your result using a calculator.

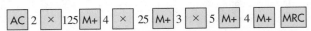 | AC | 2 | × | 125 | M+ | 4 | × | 25 | M+ | 3 | × | 5 | M+ | 4 | M+ | MRC |

(b) Explain what the keystroke sequence and final display in part (a) represent.

22. (a) Without using a calculator, determine the final display for the following calculator keystroke sequence. Then verify your result using a calculator.

 | AC | 7 | × | 512 | M+ | 6 | × | 64 | M+ | 4 | M+ | MRC |

(b) Explain what the keystroke sequence and final display in part (a) represent.

23. Write the base ten equivalent for each of the following numbers.

(a) 205_{six}

(b) 314_{five}

(c) 1001101_{two}

(d) 2818_{nine}

(e) 13756_{eight}

24. Write the base ten equivalent for each of the following numbers.

(a) 111_{three}

(b) 634_{seven}

(c) 112211_{three}

(d) 333_{four}

(e) 100110011_{two}

25. A number is written in base three. The sum of the digits is 10_{three}. List two such base three numbers and give their base ten equivalents.

26. A number is written in base five. The sum of its four digits is 9_{ten}. List two such base five numbers and give their base ten equivalents.

27. A number is written in base two. The sum of its digits is 20_{three}. List two possible base two numbers and their base ten equivalents.

28. Assume the following set of allowable digits in base 12: $\{0, 1, 2, 3, 4, 5, 6, 7, 8, 9, T, E\}$ where T represents 10_{ten} and E represents 11_{ten}. Determine the base ten equivalent of each of the following.

(a) ETE_{twelve} (b) $T00T_{twelve}$ (c) $T0E_{twelve}$

(d) 456_{twelve} (e) $E000T_{twelve}$

In Other Words

29. What is the basis for interpreting any number of a given base?

30. You have been introduced to three different tools for representing a quantity: a chip-trading activity, powers-of-ten blocks, and calculators. Compare and contrast these three tools.

31. What role does the digit 0 play in the Hindu-Arabic numeration system?

32. Invent a set of symbols that might be used in a base twenty system. Explain how you would represent your age in this system.

33. Explain the process of determining base ten equivalents of a number written in any base.

Cooperative Activity

34. Groups of two

Calculators can be useful in discovering patterns present in a sequence. In this activity, you will use a calculator to determine patterns as well as to create patterns in a variety of sequences.

Individual Accountability: Each group member is to complete the following exercises before meeting with his or her partner.

A. Determine the next term in each sequence. Explain the pattern you find.

(a) 1, 4, 9, 16, 25, —

(b) 1, 8, 27, 64, —

(c) 1, 2, 4, 7, 11, 16, —

(d) 89, 76, 65, 56, 49, —

(e) 160, 135, 110, 85, —

B. Create a sequence of the following forms. Explain your pattern.

(a) —, 18, —, —, 63, —

(b) 28, —, —, 20, —

(c) 9, —, 17, 51, 41, —

Group Goal: Before beginning the group sequences, compare the results from the individual part of this exercise. Are the answers unique? Why, or why not?

Each pair of students is to develop five sequences. These sequences are to be exchanged with those of another pair of students. Each pair of students attempts to discover the pattern and continue the sequences given to them.

Vocabulary for Chapter 2

base ten
calculator keystroke sequence
constant arithmetic feature
expanded notation
exponential notation

making a list
one-to-one correspondence
place
place value system

Review for Chapter 2

1. Write each of the following numbers using Egyptian, Roman, and Hindu-Arabic symbols.

(a) Sixteen thousand, nine

(b) Four thousand, three hundred thirty-eight

(c) Eight hundred twenty-seven

(d) Fifty-nine

(e) One thousand, thirty-four

2. Arrange each set in ascending numerical order.

(a) MCI   CMI   CMIX   MCIX   CMXI   MCXI

(b)

3. Are the following statements true or false?

(a) DLX > DXL

(b) LXXIV < XC

(c)

(d)

(e) = MMCMXX

4. Write each of the following in words.

(a) CMXXI

(b)

(c) 12,904,301

(d) 2,868,925,000

(e) 3,000,000,000,002

5. A certain calculator has an eight-digit display. What is the largest number that can be displayed in its entirety on this calculator? Express the number in Hindu-Arabic symbols and in words.

6. Determine the base ten value of each of the following chip-trading boards.

(a)

Red	White	Blue
●	●	●
	●	

Base three

(b)

Red	White	Blue
●	●	●
●	●	●
	●	
	●	

Base five

(c)

Red	White	Blue
●	●	●
●	●	
●		

Base four

7. The following spinner is used in a base three chip-trading game in which three blues equal one white and three whites equal one red

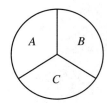

Each letter on the spinner is to be interpreted as follows: A = one blue; B = two blues; C = three blues. What is the total base ten value of the following sets of spins? How can each set be represented by the smallest number of red, white, and blue chips?

(a) $A\ B\ B\ C\ C\ C\ A\ A\ A\ B\ C\ B\ C\ A$

(b) $C\ C\ A\ A\ C\ B\ B\ B\ C\ A\ A\ C\ C\ A$

8. Examine the following chip equivalences.

Five blues = one white   Five reds = one green

Five whites = one red   Five greens = one orange

In each case below, sketch a chip-trading board that would use the least number of chips to illustrate the given base ten number.

(a) 50
(b) 125
(c) 73
(d) 891
(e) 1000

9. Express each number below in both exponential and expanded notations.

(a) 821
(b) 2543
(c) 1,408,215
(d) 12,806,000
(e) 1,437,000,001

10. What is the value of each of the following?

(a) $(8 \times 10^4) + (4 \times 10^3) + (2 \times 10^2) + (1 \times 10^1) + (3 \times 10^0)$
(b) $(6 \times 10^6) + (4 \times 10^4) + (2 \times 10^2) + (9 \times 10^0)$
(c) $(5 \times 10^3) + (2 \times 10^1)$
(d) $(4 \times 10^8) + (6 \times 10^5) + (2 \times 10^3) + (3 \times 10^0)$
(e) (5×10^8)

11. Without using a calculator, determine the result of each of the following keystroke sequences. Then verify your answer on a calculator.

(a) AC   7 + = = = =

(b) AC   8 × = =

(c) AC   100 − 3 = = = = =

(d) AC   2000 − 10 = =

(e) AC   54 − 6 = = = = =

12. Without using a calculator, determine the result of each of the following keystroke sequences. Then verify your answer on a calculator.

(a) [AC] 2 [×] 8 [=] [=] [=]

(b) [AC] 7 [+] 9 [=] [=] [=] [=]

(c) [AC] 600 [÷] 5 [=] [=]

(d) [AC] 10 [×] 2 [=] [=] [+] 10 [=] [=]

(e) [AC] 50 [−] 10 [=] [=] [=] [=]

     [+] 10 [=] [=] [=] [=]

13. Which of the following calculator keystroke sequences will eventually display 120?

(a) [AC] 2 [+] [=] [=] [=] ...

(b) [AC] 3 [+] [=] [=] [=] ...

(c) [AC] 4 [+] [=] [=] [=] ...

(d) [AC] 5 [+] [=] [=] [=] ...

(e) [AC] 6 [+] [=] [=] [=] ...

(f) [AC] 7 [+] [=] [=] [=] ...

(g) [AC] 8 [+] [=] [=] [=] ...

14. Which of the following keystroke sequences will eventually display 63?

(a) [AC] 90 [−] 3 [=] [=] [=] ...

(b) [AC] 90 [−] 2 [=] [=] [=] ...

(c) [AC] 90 [−] 9 [=] [=] [=] ...

(d) [AC] 90 [−] 6 [=] [=] [=] ...

(e) [AC] 90 [−] 13 [=] [=] [=] ...

15. Write the calculator keystroke sequence for each of the following numbers that illustrates the use of the constant arithmetic feature.

(a) 3^4

(b) 2^6

(c) 9^3

(d) 6^7

(e) 7^4

16. Construct a table for counting number values of N from $N = 1$ to 7 for $N^{(N+1)}$ and $(N+1)^N$. For what values of N is

$$N^{(N+1)} > (N+1)^N$$

17. Use the digits [5], [6], [7], and [8] and the function keys [+], [×], and [−] only once to write a calculator keystroke sequence that will yield the following displays. (You may use as many [=] as you wish.)

(a) 39   (b) 60   (c) 64   (d) 50   (e) 31

18. Using only the keys [0], [1], [+], [−], and [=], have your calculator display today's date in the form month, day, year (e.g., January 8, 1993 = 10893).

19. Fill in the blank box with <, >, or =.

(a) 42_{five} ☐ 34_{six}

(b) 117_{eight} ☐ 87_{eleven}

(c) 29 ☐ 2222_{three}

(d) 333_{four} ☐ 205_{six}

(e) 1011_{two} ☐ 11

20. Determine the missing operation keys in each of the following calculator keystroke sequences.

(a) [AC] 5 ☐ 4 ☐ 6 [=] | 14 |

(b) [AC] 900 ☐ 3 ☐ 100 [=] | 400 |

(c) AC 20 ☐ 20 ☐ 20 = ☐ 420

(d) AC 9 ☐ 8 ☐ 7 ☐ 6 = ☐ 16

(e) AC 102 ☐ 103 ☐ 104 ☐ 101 = ☐ 0

21. Change one of the operation keys from ☐ + to ☐ ÷ so that the display is 4. (Assume that your calculator follows the order of the operations stated from left to right.)

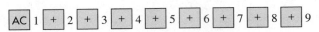

AC 1 + 2 + 3 + 4 + 5 + 6 + 7 + 8 + 9

22. Determine the missing number that will make the following calculator sequence display 46656.

AC ☐ × ☐ = ☐ =

23. Determine the base five equivalents of each of the following.
   (a) 44   **(b)** 44_{six} **(c)** 44_{seven}
   (d) 44_{eight} **(e)** 44_{nine}

24. Write the calculator keystroke sequence (which uses the memory keys) that will display the base ten equivalent of 5301_{six}.

25. A math test consists of 25 questions. Each correct answer is worth five points. For each wrong answer, a student loses four points. A student loses three points if the answer is left blank.
   (a) Make a list of some possible scores on the exam. Indicate the number correct, incorrect, and left blank that would determine such scores.
   (b) Suppose a student scored a total of 64 points. How many questions were correct, incorrect, and left blank?

26. Most calculators are not capable of displaying the exact answer for numbers of the type x^z, where z is large. Looking for a pattern will allow you to determine some information about the resulting value. In each of the following, use your calculator to help you predict the ones place digit of the answer.
   (a) 4^{101} **(b)** 6^{29} **(c)** 7^{84} **(d)** 8^{70} **(e)** 9^{45}

27. $X_{\text{ten}} = 123_a = 102_b = 212_c$. Determine the value of X. (X can contain more than one digit.)

In Other Words

28. Explain the process of writing the base A equivalent of a base ten number.

29. The Roman numeration system has been described as being multiplicative. Is the Hindu-Arabic base ten system also multiplicative? Explain your answer.

30. Explain how powers-of-ten blocks can be used to show the difference between 345 and 354. Can another commonly available model be used for the same purpose? Explain your answer.

31. Explain how our system of recording time can be viewed as a base sixty numeration system.

32. How might the appearance of an analog clock change if our system of recording time was a base ten system?

Cooperative Activity

33. Groups of two

Individual Accountability: Prior to meeting with your class partner, practice the following activity with another person.

Arrange 17 pennies in a horizontal line. First one person, and then the other, removes anywhere from one to three pennies. The object of the activity is to force the other person to take the final penny.

Try to discover a strategy that will allow you to always win. Does it matter who goes first? Write a description of your winning strategy.

Group Goal: Engage in this activity with your partner. Whose strategy is more successful? Why? Write a description of a strategy that will allow you to win when there are 26 pennies and anywhere from one to four pennies may be removed at a time.

3

Whole Number Relationships: Addition and Subtraction

Examine the photograph at the right.

Describe what you see.

How might you estimate the number of cars?

How might you determine the actual number of cars?

How might you determine the actual number of white cars?

How might you classify the cars in the picture?

What would a mathematical description of this photograph contain?

Introduction

Two of the most basic operations that children perform with objects are combination and separation. These two physical activities, putting together and taking apart, are tangible examples of the more abstract mathematical operations of addition and subtraction. Children begin applying these processes of combining and separating to objects in their environment. Later on, formal schooling will teach them to associate the set of symbols $2 + 4 = 6$ to the physical joining of two items and four items, resulting in a set of six items.

This chapter will follow the same progression from tangible examples to abstract concepts. In the first section, we examine concrete models and properties of addition and subtraction. In the second section, we extend our investigation into the symbolic representation of addition and subtraction using a process called algorithms. We discuss different strategies for estimating sums and differences using both algorithms and powers-of-ten blocks (which we introduced in Chapter 2). Alternative algorithms and adding and subtracting in other bases are also covered in this section. Throughout the chapter, common errors and pitfalls students are prone to and the applicability of calculators are addressed as they become pertinent to the discussion.

3.1 Models and Properties of Whole Number Addition and Subtraction

Our number system is composed of many subsets. The set containing the elements $\{1, 2, 3, 4, \ldots\}$ is called the set of **natural numbers**, or counting numbers. The set of natural numbers combined with the set $\{0\}$ forms the set $\{0, 1, 2, 3, 4, \ldots\}$, which is called the set of **whole numbers**. Much of the early elementary school mathematics curriculum investigates operations on the set of whole numbers.

natural numbers

whole numbers

Addition of Whole Numbers

set model of whole number addition

The **set model of whole number addition** is the model that is most frequently used at the elementary school level. In this model, two or more sets are combined to form a new set. The focus of the set model for addition is not on the actual elements themselves, but rather on the number of elements in each set. Therefore, whether the combination involves five cats and six dogs, five oranges and six pears, or five computers and six calculators, the symbolic notation will always be $5 + 6$. The set model for the combination of five elements in one set with six elements in another set is shown in Figure 3.1.

Figure 3.1

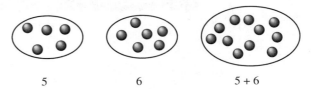

$$5 \qquad\qquad 6 \qquad\qquad 5 + 6$$

Therefore, if A and B are two disjoint, countable sets, the new set formed by combining A with B, symbolized by $A \cup B$, is defined as the elements in A combined with the elements in B (see Figure 3.2). It is important to remember the requirement that the two sets be disjoint. Recall that disjoint sets are sets that have no elements in common. The intersection of two disjoint sets is the empty set.

Figure 3.2

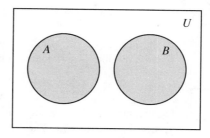

Consider the following situation. Let set A be defined as the members of Committee 1 and consist of Mark, Anna, Elizabeth, Margaret, and Joanne. Let set B be defined as the members of Committee 2 and consist of Margaret, Joanne, Tim, Amerigo, Roberto, and Julianne. If a new Committee 3 is formed $(A \cup B)$ that is composed of the members of both Committees 1 and 2, this new committee consists of Mark, Anna, Elizabeth, Margaret, Joanne, Tim, Amerigo, Roberto, and Julianne. Here, set A (with five members) was combined with set B (with six members) and resulted in a new set with nine members. This example is not a model of the operation of addition. The only way this example could accurately model the operation of addition would be if the membership on each committee was exclusive, that is, if no one on Committee 1 was also on Committee 2. Whenever two sets are both disjoint and countable, the number of elements in the union of these two sets will be the number of elements in the combination of the sets. This leads us to the definition of whole number addition.

Definition: Let A and B be two disjoint and countable sets, with the number of elements in A symbolized by $n(A) = a$, and the number of elements in B symbolized by $n(B) = b$. Then,

$$a + b = n(A) + n(B) = n(A \cup B)$$

Terminology: **sum, addends** The **sum** of a and b is the number of elements in set A combined with the number of elements in set B, where a and b are called **addends**.

number line model of whole number addition Rather than viewing addition as the combination of sets, the **number line model of whole number addition** involves directed movement along a path. This path is represented as a number line (see Figure 3.3). The basic number line illustrates the set of whole numbers beginning with zero, and increases as you move to the right. Each whole number is represented as a tick mark on the number line. The segments between each equally spaced tick mark are called **units**. In Figure 3.3, the distance between the tick marks representing 1 and 2, respectively, is one unit. The distance between the tick marks representing 1 and 4, respectively, is three units.

units

Figure 3.3

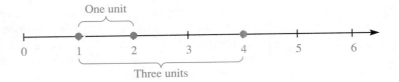

Use the number line model of addition to illustrate and find the sum of 2 and 4.

Draw a number line starting with 0 at the left and increase in increments of one unit as you move to the right. The first addend, 2, can be illustrated as the directed distance from points 0 to 2, respectively. Now, beginning at the tick mark representing the number 2, move four units to the right. This directed distance represents the addition of a line segment that is four units long to one that is two units long. The resulting line segment is six units long and is represented by the single line segment from 0 to 6.

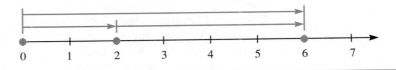

Addition Properties of Whole Numbers

Certain consistencies characterize the operation of addition of whole numbers. These consistencies, referred to as properties, form the basis of the ways in which we add.

1. The Closure Property of Whole Number Addition.   The sum of two whole numbers is itself a whole number. A set with this property is said to be *closed* under addition. The **closure property** of whole number addition can easily be seen on the number line. The sum of any two numbers on the number line must also be found on the number line; that is, the sum of any two whole numbers is itself an element of the set of whole numbers.

closure property

    The test for closure can be applied to subsets of the set of whole numbers. The set $\{0\}$ is closed under addition since $0 + 0$ is an element of the set. The set $\{2, 4, 6, 8, \ldots\}$, representing the set of even numbers, is also closed under addition since the sum of any two even numbers is itself an even number. The set $\{1, 3, 5, 7, \ldots\}$, representing the set of odd numbers, is not closed under addition. The sum of two odd numbers is an even number. Thus, the individual sums of $1 + 3$, $5 + 5$, and $7 + 11$ are all numbers that are not contained in the set of odd numbers. Another example of a set that is not closed under addition is the set $\{0, 1\}$. We leave it to you to determine why.

2. The Commutative Property of Whole Number Addition.   The order of the addends may be changed without changing the sum; that is, if a and b are both whole numbers,

commutative property $a + b = b + a$. This **commutative property** is evident in both the set and number line models of whole number addition. In the set model of addition, the resulting set is the same regardless of the order in which the sets are combined. The set containing three red marbles combined with the set containing four blue marbles yields a set containing seven marbles regardless of whether the four blue marbles are combined with the three red marbles or the three red marbles are combined with the four blue marbles. In the number line model of whole number addition, the order of the addends does not alter the directed distance that represents the sum, as illustrated in Figure 3.4.

Figure 3.4

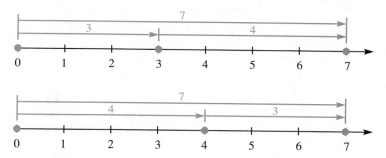

3. The Associative Property of Whole Number Addition.   When combining more than two addends, the way in which the addends are grouped does not affect the sum; that is, if a, **associative property** b, and c are whole numbers, then $(a + b) + c = a + (b + c)$. This **associative property** can be seen in Figure 3.5 using the set model of addition.

Figure 3.5

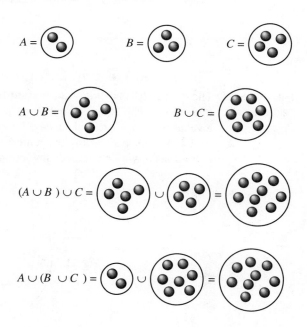

4. The Identity Property of Whole Number Addition.   There exists a whole number 0 that, when added to any whole number, does not change the value of that number. Zero is called the **additive identity element** since, for any whole number a,

additive identity element

$$a + 0 = 0 + a = a$$

Investigation 2

Use the properties of whole number addition to simplify the work required to find the following sum:

$$48 + 74 + 22 + 126$$

Grouping addends together that will yield "nice" numbers (multiples of 10) might be helpful in an addition problem. The commutative property assures you that the order of the addends can be changed without changing the sum. Rearrange the addends to make the addition process easier:

$$48 + 22 + 74 + 126 =$$

The associative property allows you to group the addends together and find the individual sums. This will not change the final result:

$$(48 + 22) + (74 + 126) =$$
$$70 \quad + \quad 200 \quad = 270$$

Subtraction of Whole Numbers

set model of whole number subtraction

The **set model of whole number subtraction** involves the removal of a subset from a given set. The action of removing is traditionally known on the elementary school level as the process of "take away." Figure 3.6 shows the set model view of subtraction for $7 - 5$. This leads us to the set model definition of whole number subtraction. Other definitions of whole number subtraction using different models will follow.

Figure 3.6

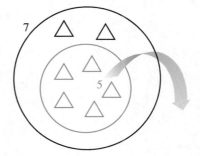

Definition: Let A and B be two sets, with the number of elements in A symbolized by $a = n(A)$, the number of elements in B symbolized by $b = n(B)$, and B, a subset of A, symbolized by

$B \subseteq A$. Then,

$$a - b = n(A) - n(B) = n(A - B)$$

Terminology:
difference, minuend
subtrahend

The **difference** of a and b, symbolized by $a - b$ and read as "a minus b," is the number of elements remaining in A after subset B is removed. The **minuend** is the term given to a, and the **subtrahend** is the term given to b.

As in addition, subtraction of whole numbers can be illustrated on a number line. Recall that in this model, operations on numbers are viewed as directed movements along a path. Examine Figure 3.7. The directed line segment that represents the minuend, in this case 7, begins at 0 and ends seven units to the right. Because this is a subtraction problem, the minus sign in conjunction with the subtrahend is illustrated by a directed line segment to the left, beginning at 7 and covering a distance of five units. The difference, $7 - 5$, is 2 units, as shown in Figure 3.7. This illustration is directly related to the take away model.

Figure 3.7

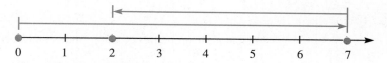

missing addends model

Another view of whole number subtraction is the **missing addends model**. This model relates addition to subtraction by viewing the difference as a missing addend in a related addition problem (see Figure 3.8). This alternative views subtraction as the process in which students are asked what must be added to 5 to arrive at 8. For example, if Frank is 163 centimeters tall and Angela is 171 centimeters tall, the answer to the question "How much taller than Frank is Angela?" can be symbolized by $163 + ? = 171$. Beginning at 163, the student would count up to get to 171. The missing addend is the difference between Angela's height and Frank's height. Notice how the missing addend model of subtraction emphasizes the relationship between addition and subtraction. Such a relationship is known as an **inverse relationship** and is illustrated by the following generalization:

inverse relationship

If $a + b = c$, then $c - b = a$ and $c - a = b$.

If $c - b = a$, then $c = a + b$.

If $c - a = b$, then $c = a + b$.

These conditional statements can be combined to form the following biconditional:

$$a + b = c \text{ if and only if } c - b = a \text{ and } c - a = b$$

Figure 3.8

$$8 - 5 = ? \quad \rightarrow \quad 5 + ? = 8$$

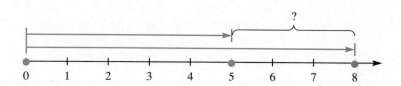

You need to be aware that subtraction occurs within various contexts. The physical removal of a certain number of objects from a given set of objects necessitates that the number of elements in the set to be removed be less than or equal to the number of elements in the given set. In the set model of whole number subtraction, it is true that a larger quantity cannot be subtracted from a smaller quantity. But this is not the case within a number line model. Teachers should be wary of making statements such as, "You can never subtract a larger number from a smaller number." An example of just such an operation would be the numerical representation of a daytime temperature of 7 degrees Celsius dropping 15 degrees overnight. The nighttime low would be 8 degrees below 0. Here a larger number has been subtracted from a smaller number, making the set model inappropriate. However, for the purposes of this chapter, the number line model will be used only to represent whole number subtraction in which the subtrahend is less than or equal to the minuend.

Investigation 3

Which of the properties of whole number addition are also true for subtraction?

1. Closure Property. Recall that the set of whole numbers is defined as $\{0, 1, 2, 3, 4, \ldots\}$. Although it is true that the sum of any two whole numbers is a unique whole number itself, it is not true that the difference between any two whole numbers is in the set of whole numbers. This can be illustrated by any example in which the subtrahend is greater than the minuend, resulting in a difference less than 0. Therefore, the set of whole numbers is not closed under subtraction.

2. Commutative Property. The commutative property of whole number addition states that the order of the addends may be changed without changing the sum. However, it is not the case that $a - b = b - a$ (unless $a = b$), so the commutative property does not hold for subtraction. The reason subtraction is not commutative will become clearer when we discuss integers in Chapter 5.

3. Associative Property. The associative property of addition assures that the way in which addends are grouped does not affect the sum. The associative property does not hold for subtraction, but will be better understood when the set of integers is studied. For now, we will use the following example to show that the associative property does not work with subtraction:

$$(15 - 3) - 1 = 12 - 1 = 11 \qquad 15 - (3 - 1) = 15 - 2 = 13$$

4. Additive Identity Property. Recall the identity property of whole number addition: $a + 0 = 0 + a = a$. This does not hold for subtraction since 0 as a subtrahend (subtracting 0) and 0 as a minuend (subtracting from 0) are not synonymous $(a - 0 \neq 0 - a)$.

Assessments for Section 3.1

1. Let set A contain the set of whole numbers that are less than 9, set B contain the set of even whole numbers less than 9, and set C contain the set of whole numbers that are greater than 3 and less than 13. Find

   (a) $n(A)$ (b) $n(B)$ (c) $n(C)$

   (d) $n(A - B)$ (e) $n(A \cup B)$ (f) $n(A \cap B)$

   (g) $n(A \cup C)$ (h) $n(A \cap B)$

2. Let set A contain whole numbers between 10 and 20, set B contain even whole numbers between 10 and 20, and set C contain whole numbers greater than 2 but less than 20. Find

   (a) $n(A)$ (b) $n(B)$

   (c) $n(C)$ (d) $n[A \cup (B \cap C)]$

   (e) $n[(A \cup B) \cap C]$ (f) $n(A \cup B \cup C)$

   (g) $n[A - (B \cap C)]$ (h) $n[(A \cup B) - (B \cap C)]$

   (i) $n[(C - B) - A]$

3. In each case, the elements of sets C and D are the numbers displayed on the calculator after each is pressed. Determine whether or not sets C and D are disjoint. Discuss your reasoning.

   Set C

   (a) `AC` 8 + 3 = = = = =

   (b) `AC` 4 × 3 = = = = =

   (c) `AC` 50 - 8 = = = = =

   (d) `AC` 1024 ÷ 4 = = = = =

   (e) `AC` 3 × = = = = = =

   Set D

   (a) `AC` 35 - 7 = = = = =

   (b) `AC` 64 ÷ 2 = = = =

   (c) `AC` 5 + = = = = = = =

   (d) `AC` 4 × = = = = =

   (e) `AC` 10 × = = = = = =

4. In Problem 3, for those sets that are disjoint, find $n(C)$, $n(D)$, and $n(C \cup D)$.

5. Express each sum using a number line model.

   (a) $20 + 5$ (b) $8 + 11$ (c) $0 + 4$

   (d) $8 + 9$ (e) $5 + 0$

6. Identify which of the following sets are closed under whole number addition. Explain your reasoning.

   (a) $\{0, 1\}$ (b) $\{1\}$

   (c) $\{5, 10, 15, 20, \ldots\}$ (d) $\{1, 2, 3\}$

   (e) The set formed by the displays of

   `AC` 8 + = = = = ...

7. Identify the property illustrated in each of the following:

   (a) $4 + 5 = 5 + 4$

   (b) $x + y + z = y + z + x$

   (c) $2 + (8 + 9) = (2 + 8) + 9$

   (d) $w + 0 = w$

   (e) $(6 + 5) + (2 + 8) = 6 + (5 + 2) + 8$

8. Use the properties of addition to simplify the process of finding each sum. State the property used in each step.

   (a) $37 + 64 + 83 + 91 + 86 + 9$

   (b) $27 + 46 + 33 + 94 + 11$

(c) $245 + 81 + 93 + 55 + 29 + 7$

(d) $1091 + 2635 + 1039 + 5405$

(e) $867 + 243 + 915 + 283 + 497 + 885 + 27$

9. Perform the following subtractions using the take away set model.

(a) $8 - 2$

(b) $16 - 3$

(c) $5 - 0$

(d) $9 - 7$

(e) $12 - 11$

10. Illustrate each of the following subtractions using the take away number line model.

(a) $4 - 1$

(b) $8 - 5$

(c) $9 - 7$

(d) $11 - 5$

(e) $6 - 2$

11. Illustrate each of the following subtractions using the missing addend number line model.

(a) $3 - 1$

(b) $9 - 4$

(c) $9 - 7$

(d) $13 - 8$

(e) $5 - 5$

12. Illustrate each of the following keystroke sequences on a number line.

(a) [AC] [9] [+] [4] [=]

(b) [AC] [6] [−] [3] [=]

(c) [AC] [11] [+] [4] [−] [2] [=]

(d) [AC] [8] [−] [5] [+] [6] [=]

(e) [AC] [10] [+] [5] [+] [2] [−] [17] [=]

13. Give a possible whole number example for the subtrahend and the minuend in each case.

(a) The difference is 0.

(b) The difference is odd.

(c) The difference is even.

(d) The difference is less than 0.

(e) The difference is twice the subtrahend.

14. Use the concept of forming "nice numbers" to mentally compute the sum

$$1 + 2 + 3 + 4 + 5 + 6 + 7 + 8 + 9$$

Explain how the "nice numbers" are formed.

15. Using the numbers from 1 to 9 inclusive, place each number in one of the boxes of this "magic" square so that each row, column, and diagonal have a sum of 15. (*Hint*: Refer to Problem 14.)

16. (a) What is the sum of the numbers from 1 to 10 inclusive?

(b) What is the sum of the numbers from 1 to 100 inclusive?

(c) What is the sum of the numbers from 1 to 1000 inclusive?

17. Have your calculator display 1559 using only the keys 1, 0

.

18. Have your calculator display 1559 using only the keys 1, 0

.

19. (a) What is the pattern in the following triangle?

(b) What would the eighth row be?

20. Two two-digit whole numbers have a difference of 34 and a sum of 60. Find these two numbers.

21. Two three-digit whole numbers have a difference of 211 and a sum of 585. Find these two numbers.

22. A sequence is known as an **arithmetic sequence** if each term (after the first term) is determined by adding the same number to the term that precedes it. For example, the sequence 13, 22, 31, 40, 49 is an arithmetic sequence since

each term after 13 is determined by adding 9 to the term that precedes it. The difference between any two consecutive terms in an arithmetic sequence is the same. It is easy to find the nth term, a_n, of an arithmetic sequence when the first term, a_1, and the common difference, d, are known. In general, $a_n = a_1 + (n - 1)d$. Use this general expression to find the indicated term in each sequence.

(a) 18, 41, 64, 87, 110 (fortieth term)

(b) 11, 27, 43, 59, 75 (fiftieth term)

(c) 125, 138, 151, 164 (nineteenth term)

(d) 1258, 1583, 1908, 2233 (eleventh term)

(e) 2874, 6846, 10,818, 14,790 (ninth term)

23. The sum of a countable number of consecutive terms of an arithmetic sequence is given as

$$S = \frac{n}{2}(a_1 + a_n)$$

where n is the number of terms, a_1 is the first term, and a_n is the nth term. Use this general expression to find the sum of the given sequences.

(a) 15, 62, 109, 156, 203, 250

(b) 25, 44, 63, 82, 101, 120, 139, 158, 177, 196, 215

(c) 63, 80, 97, 114 . . . (fourteen terms)

(d) 31, 52, 73, 94, 115 . . . (twelve terms)

(e) $a_1 = 26$, $d = 33$, $n = 8$

(f) $a_1 = 11$, $d = 15$, $n = 13$

(g) $a_5 = 82$, $d = 14$, $n = 5$

(h) $a_4 = 151$, $d = 39$, $n = 4$

24. In Problem 15, you examined a 3 by 3 "magic" square. The digits 1 through 9 inclusive were used only once so that the sum in any column, row, and diagonal equaled 15.

(a) What is the sum of the numbers from 1 to 9 inclusive? What relationship might this sum have to the "magic" sum required along any column, row, and diagonal?

(b) In a 4 by 4 "magic" square, the numbers 1 through 16 inclusive are used. The desired sum along any column or row is 34. What is the sum of the numbers from 1 to 16 inclusive? What relationship might this sum have to the "magic" sum of 34 in a 4 by 4 "magic" square?

(c) What possible generalization can be made about the relationship of the sum of the numbers used in an N by N magic square and the "magic" sum desired along each column, row, and diagonal?

(d) Use your generalization from part (c) to determine the "magic" sum along any column, row, and diagonal for a 9 by 9 magic square.

25. The following sequence is known as the Lucas sequence. It is named after a nineteenth-century mathematician.

$$1, 3, 4, 7, 11, 18, 29, 47, \ldots$$

(a) Is this an arithmetic sequence with a common difference between terms? Explain your answer.

(b) How is each term of the Lucas sequence generated?

(c) Examine the differences between each of the terms. What do you observe?

In Other Words

26. Explain the missing addend model of subtraction. How does it relate to the concept of inverse operations?

27. Compare and contrast the two number line models of subtraction.

28. Compare and contrast the missing addend number line model of subtraction with the set model of subtraction.

29. Write a word problem that would require using the missing addend model of subtraction for $12 + \underline{\quad} = 15$.

30. Write a word problem that would require using the take away model of subtraction for $15 - 12$.

Cooperative Activity

31. Groups of three

Assume that you have a piece of wood 5 cm long. It is possible to measure lengths of 1, 2, 3, 4, and 5 cm without moving the wood by placing only two markings on it. For example, if the "ruler" had a mark at 2 cm and a mark at 4 cm, all the measures could be found as follows:

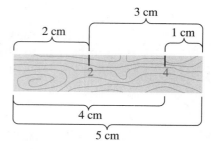

Individual Accountability: Where would you place four marks on an 11 cm length of wood in order that every length from 1 to 11 cm could be measured without moving the "ruler"? Write an explanation of your findings.

Group Goal: Share the discoveries that you made individually. Together, answer the following question: Where would you place four marks on a 13 cm length of wood in order that every length from 1 to 13 cm could be measured without moving the "ruler"?

3.2 Algorithms for Whole Number Addition and Subtraction

algorithm

An **algorithm** is an organized step-by-step process that is used to reach a particular goal. The term *algorithm* is derived from the name of the Persian mathematician al-Khowârizmî, who wrote an account of the Hindu system of numeration in approximately A.D. 825.

In the past, it was believed that children should be taught only one algorithm for each of the four basic mathematic operations. By doing this, it was thought, the risk of confusion would be minimized. Recently, such organizations as the National Council of Teachers of Mathematics have advocated introducing students to a variety of methods to be used to solve problems set in realistic contexts. It is no longer considered sufficient for a student to be able to accurately compute 345 + 23 according to a single standard algorithm. Rather, students should be able to recognize the setting in which 345 + 23 is an appropriate mathematical interpretation, estimate a reasonable answer, and know several methods that can be used to arrive at the correct sum. The low cost and the accessibility of calculators, combined with changing demands of the workplace, which students eventually enter, has forced a reexamination of the role of computation in the elementary schools. Along with traditional algorithms, students today should be able to compare, analyze, and discuss alternative paper-and-pencil algorithms, mental computation, and appropriate calculator procedures.

Estimating Sums and Differences

Although estimating is part of the elementary school curriculum, estimation skills are often taught without a context. Because of this, elementary school students do not realize the many situations in which estimation is useful. For example, many people use mathematics and estimation in the context of consumerism and data analysis. We mentally verify that we have enough money to pay for our groceries; we approximate the tip on a restaurant bill; we estimate the miles per gallon of gasoline our car gets; we determine what grade we need on the next test in order to get an A in the course; and we estimate home-run distances and football yardages.

The widespread use of calculators has increased the importance of estimation. It is very easy to make an error in keystroke sequencing. Unless the calculator user has estimated a reasonable result, a grossly incorrect answer can go unnoticed. It is impossible to check a keystroke sequence once it has been entered since there is no tangible record that can be reexamined.

To develop strong estimation skills, you need to become familiar with some specific estimation techniques.

1. Forming Multiples of Ten.   In this estimation strategy, you review the entire list of addends and attempt to group certain of those addends together forming tens or multiples of tens.

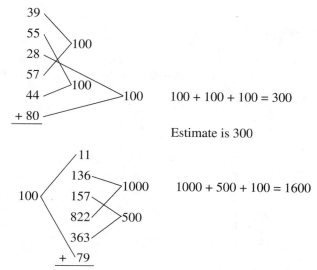

100 + 100 + 100 = 300

Estimate is 300

1000 + 500 + 100 = 1600

Estimate is 1600

2. Rounding. There are many ways that rounding can be used as an estimation technique. The simplest version requires that each number be rounded to its greatest place. For example, in the number 7629, the greatest place is the thousands place. Examine the digit immediately to the right of the greatest place. If it is 5 or greater, the digit in the greatest place is increased by one and followed by zeros. If it is less than 5, the digit in the greatest place remains unchanged and is followed by zeros. Therefore, since 6, the digit to the right of the greatest place in 7629, is greater than 5, the 7 is increased to 8 and followed by zeros. This number rounded to its greatest place is 8000. Examine the following addition and subtraction illustrations.

457	rounds to	500
216	rounds to	200
34	rounds to	30
+ 9722	rounds to	10,000

The estimated sum is 10,730.

2058	rounds to	2000
− 759	rounds to	800

The estimated difference is 1200.

3. Front-End Estimation. This is a refinement of the rounding technique. It is a two-step procedure that groups the largest place value digits together and then combines this sum with an estimate of the remaining amounts.

1256	1 thousand + 5 thousand + 4 thousand = 10 thousand
208	256, 208, and 627 can be grouped to form an estimate of 1000
5966	966 can be rounded to 1000
+ 4627	

The estimated sum is 10,000 + 1000 + 1000 = 12,000.

Investigation 4

Use the three estimation techniques outlined above to arrive at an estimate of the total monthly budget for the Shannon family. Here are their expenses:

Rent	$858
Food	415
Utilities	135
Car loan	279
Car expenses	185
Miscellaneous	60

 1. Forming Multiples of Ten.

$$858$$
$$415$$
$$\quad\; 700$$
$$135$$
$$1000$$
$$279$$
$$\quad\; 300$$
$$185$$
$$+\; 60$$

$$1000 + 700 + 300 = 2000$$

Estimate $2000

2. Rounding to the Largest Place Value.

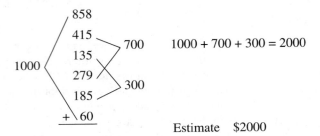

858	rounds to	900		
415	rounds to	400	1000	$1000 + 900 + 60 = 1960$
135	rounds to	100		
279	rounds to	300	900	
185	rounds to	200		
+ 60	rounds to	60		

Estimate $1960

3. Front-End Estimation.

$$858$$
$$415$$
$$135$$
$$279$$
$$185$$
$$+\; 60$$

$800 + 400 + 100 + 200 + 100 = 1600$

$58 + 35$ is approximately 100

$85 + 15$ is precisely 100

$79 + 60$ is approximately 150

Estimate $1600 + 100 + 100 + 150 = \$1950$

The following calculator keystroke sequence can be used to find the actual sum:

AC 858 + 415 + 135 + 279 + 185 + 60 =

The display should read 1932. The monthly budget for the Shannon family is $1932.

Investigation 5

A census indicated that 10 years ago the population of a particular town was 13,484. Currently, the population is 8,952. What was the approximate decrease in population?

The rules for rounding to the greatest place would result in the following:

13,484	rounds to	10,000
− 8,952	rounds to	9,000

The estimate of the difference is 1,000.

Common sense tells you that this estimate is far too inaccurate. A more precise estimate is needed. Here is a better version of the use of rounding as an estimation technique. In this case, the numbers are rounded to the nearest thousand:

13,484	rounds to	13,000
− 8,952	rounds to	9,000

The estimate of the difference is 4,000.

An even more precise estimate can be obtained by rounding to the nearest hundred:

13,484	rounds to	13,500
− 8,952	rounds to	9,000

The estimate of the difference is 4,500.

The necessary precision of the estimate will vary according to the context.

Investigation 6

Assume that you have a $3000 credit limit on your charge card account. You carried over a balance of $567.90 from the previous month. At the beginning of the month, you charged the following amounts: $723.99, $85.00, $1295.50, and $23.80. Can you charge a purchase for the amount of $550 without going over your limit?

Since this situation calls for an accurate estimate, the front-end estimation technique will be useful here.

$$\begin{array}{r} \$\ 567.90 \\ 723.99 \\ 85.00 \\ 1295.50 \\ 23.80 \end{array}$$

$500 + 700 + 1200 = 2400$

$67.90 + 23.99$ is approximately 100

$85.00 + 23.80$ is approximately 100

95.50 is approximately 100

$2400 + 100 + 100 + 100 = 2700$

An estimate of the charge card balance to date is $2700. Therefore, an additional purchase of $550 will cause the balance to exceed the $3000 limit.

Powers-of-Ten Blocks

In addition to developing skills of estimation, but before students are taught paper-and-pencil algorithms, they need to be exposed to concrete experiences. Many elementary school teachers use manipulative materials to accomplish this aim. Powers-of-ten blocks are often used to provide a tangible representation of numbers. A standard set is illustrated in Figure 3.9.

Figure 3.9

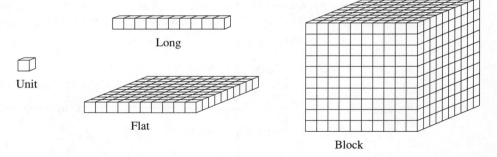

Notice that a long (representing one 10) is equal in size to 10 units. Similarly, a flat (representing one 100) is equal in size to 10 longs, and a block (representing one 1000) is equal in size to 10 flats. The number 14 could be shown using 14 units, or 1 long and 4 units. This physical trading for equivalences illustrates the symbolic regrouping that occurs in the standard addition algorithm.

Investigation 7

Illustrate the sum of 595 and 428 using powers-of-ten blocks.

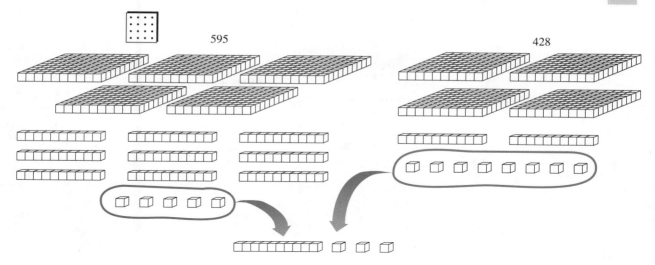

595   428

The 13 units can be traded for 1 long and 3 units, as shown above.

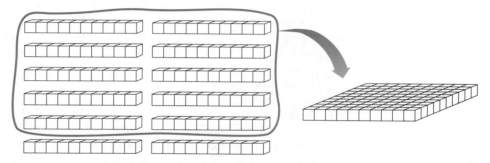

The 11 longs combined with the 1 long from above result in 12 longs, which can be traded for 1 flat and 2 longs.

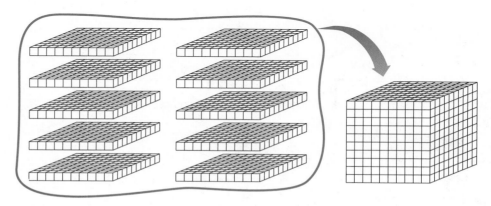

The 9 flats combined with the 1 flat from above can be traded for 1 block.

Therefore, the sum of 595 and 428 is 1023, which is represented by

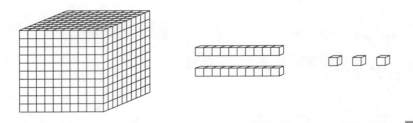

The operation of whole number addition illustrated in Investigation 7 can be symbolized in the following way:

$$\begin{array}{r} {\scriptstyle 1\ 1} \\ 595 \\ + \ 428 \\ \hline 1023 \end{array}$$

standard regrouping algorithm of whole number addition

Notice how this symbolic procedure, known as the **standard regrouping algorithm of whole number addition**, mirrors the process used with the powers-of-ten blocks. Concretely, 13 units were traded for 1 long and 3 units. Symbolically, 5 ones and 8 ones were added, resulting in a sum of 13 ones. Three ones remained in the ones column, whereas 10 ones were regrouped into 1 ten, which was placed in the tens column.

In Investigation 7, 12 longs were traded for 1 flat and 2 longs. Symbolically, when 1 ten, 9 tens, and 2 tens were added, resulting in the sum of 12 tens, 2 tens remained in the tens column, whereas 10 tens were regrouped into 100. This 1 hundred was then written in the hundreds column. Finally, 4 hundreds plus 5 hundreds plus 1 hundred resulted in 10 hundreds, or 1 thousand (one block). The symbolic result of 1023 is equivalent to the concrete result of 1 block, no flats, 2 longs, and 3 units.

Once students have a strong concept of number, they can tackle problems that strengthen their thinking and computational skills.

Investigation 8

 Illustrate 123 − 75 using powers-of-ten blocks.

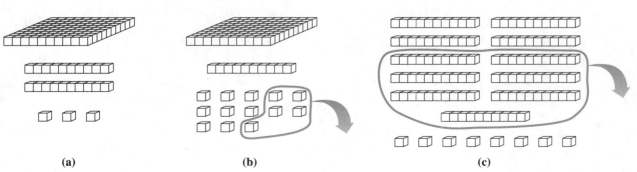

(a)　　　　　　　　(b)　　　　　　　　(c)

Since 5 units cannot be taken away from 3 units (a), 1 long must be traded for 10 units (b). Five units taken from 13 units leaves 8 units. Since 7 longs cannot be taken from 1 long, a flat must be traded for 10 longs (c). Seven longs taken from 11 longs leaves 4 longs. Therefore, the difference between 123 and 75 is 48 and is illustrated below.

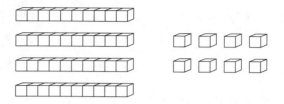

The operation of whole number subtraction illustrated in Investigation 8 can be symbolized in the following way:

$$\begin{array}{r} \overset{0}{\cancel{1}} \ \overset{11}{\cancel{2}} \ {}^{1}3 \\ -\quad 7\ \ 5 \\ \hline 4\ \ 8 \end{array}$$

decomposition algorithm for whole number subtraction

Notice how this symbolic procedure, known as the **decomposition algorithm for whole number subtraction**, mirrors the process followed with the powers-of-ten blocks. Concretely, 1 long was decomposed into 10 units, leaving 1 long and 13 units. Symbolically, in order to subtract 5 ones from 3 ones, the 2 in the tens column of 123 was decomposed into 1 ten and 10 ones. We used a slash (/) to indicate that such a decomposition had taken place. The 10 ones were then added to the 3 ones, resulting in 13 ones. Then, 13 – 5 yielded 8 ones.

In Investigation 8, 1 flat was decomposed into 10 longs, leaving no flats and 11 longs. Symbolically, we illustrated this decomposition by crossing out the 1 in the hundreds place, reducing it by 1, and adding the 10 tens to the 1 ten in the tens place. Now, 11 tens minus 7 tens equals 4 tens. The final symbolic result of 48 is equivalent to the concrete result of 4 longs and 8 units.

Investigation 9

Five darts are tossed at the target shown on page 94. All five darts hit the target and score. Which of the following total scores are possible: 72, 83, 52, 53, 43?

Understand the Problem: What is given? Five darts have hit the target shown. What is unknown? Which of the five scores could possibly be obtained.

Devise a Plan: Since all five darts contribute to the final score, the least sum possible is attained when each of the darts hits the 9-point ring (9 + 9 + 9 + 9 + 9), resulting in a score of 45. The greatest score possible is attained when each of the darts hits the 15-point center (15 + 15 + 15 + 15 + 15), resulting in a score of 75. Therefore, any possible scores must fall within the range of 45 to 75 inclusive. The problem-solving strategy of contradiction allows you to compare each of the possible choices with this given information. Any choice that contradicts what is known to be true about the solution can thus be eliminated.

Carry Out the Plan:
trial and error   Because they fall outside the possible range, both 43 and 83 can be eliminated. Examine the three remaining choices: 52, 53, and 72. One strategy you might use here is **trial and error**. The method of trial and error would require you to add up various combinations of any five of the possible scores to attain 52, 53, or 72. For example, you might try 15 + 13 + 11 + 9 + 9 = 57, or one of the following combinations:

$$15 + 13 + 11 + 11 + 9 = 59$$
$$15 + 15 + 15 + 11 + 11 = 67$$
$$15 + 15 + 15 + 15 + 13 = 73$$

Even with the help of a calculator, this process can be tedious and time-consuming.

solve a simpler problem   To make finding the answer easier, we can use the problem-solving strategy of **solve a simpler problem**. Suppose that only two darts were tossed. The possible point values would be

18	(9 + 9)	22	(11 + 11)	26	(13 + 13)	30	(15 + 15)
20	(9 + 11)	22	(9 + 13)	24	(9 + 15)		
24	(11 + 13)	26	(11 + 15)	28	(13 + 15)		

An interesting piece of information can be found here. All of the point values on the target are odd numbers, and all of the sums of the two odd numbers are even numbers. It is possible to generalize that the sum of two odd numbers is an even number.

We can continue to use the strategy of solving a simpler problem. What about the sum of three odd numbers, four odd numbers, and five odd numbers? It can be shown that the sum of an even number of odd numbers will always be even, and the sum of an odd number of odd numbers will always be odd. This leads us to the solution of the original problem. Since only one of the remaining scores, 53, is odd, and an odd number of darts were thrown, 53 is the only possible score.

Look Back: Verify that a person could actually score 53 points with five darts. The score of 53 can be obtained in a number of ways.

$$15 + 11 + 9 + 9 + 9 = 53$$
$$11 + 11 + 11 + 11 + 9 = 53$$
$$13 + 13 + 9 + 9 + 9 = 53$$

Alternative Algorithms

Because most people learn only one method of addition and subtraction in elementary school, they often believe that only one method exists. On the contrary, several methods, or algorithms, can be used to arrive at the answer in each of the four basic arithmetic operations. Three alternative algorithms for whole number addition, and two for whole number subtraction, are presented here.

Whole Number Addition

expanded notation algorithm

1. Expanded Notation Algorithm.   The algorithm highlights place values and can be used to understand the process of regrouping. Examine the following problem: A book was printed in two volumes. Volume I contains 336 pages, and Volume II contains 389 pages. What is the total number of pages in both volumes?

$$
\begin{array}{rcrcrcr}
336 & = & 300 & + & 30 & + & 6 \\
+\,389 & = & 300 & + & 80 & + & 9 \\
\hline
& & 600 & + & 110 & + & 15 \\
& & 600 & + & 100 + 10 + & & 10 + 5 = 700 + 20 + 5 = 725 \text{ pages}
\end{array}
$$

In the expanded notation algorithm, students align place values and find individual sums. The final answer is the total of the individual sums.

lattice addition algorithm

2. Lattice Addition Algorithm.   In this alternative algorithm, the regrouping is done as a separate step. This avoids the need to add, then regroup, add, then regroup, and so on. First, all the addition is done, then all the regrouping. Examine the following problem: Alice is saving to buy a car. Her bank account balance is $3429. What will her new balance be after she deposits $785?

The new balance will be $4214.

First, the sum of each individual column is placed in the lattice. To regroup to the appropriate place, the digits along each diagonal are added.

partial sums algorithm

3. **Partial Sums Algorithm.** This algorithm is a more efficient version of the expanded notation algorithm. Each place value will be summed separately providing the partial sums. Examine the following problem: The odometer on Alan's exercise bike reads 126. He plans to cycle 35 miles over the next week. What will the odometer read at the end of the week?

$$
\begin{array}{r}
1 \quad 2 \quad 6 \\
+ \qquad 3 \quad 5 \\
\hline
1 \quad 1 \qquad (6 + 5 = 11) \\
5 \quad 0 \qquad (20 + 30 = 50) \\
1 \quad 0 \quad 0 \qquad (100 + 0 = 100) \\
\hline
1 \quad 6 \quad 1 \qquad \text{The odometer will read 161.}
\end{array}
$$

Whole Number Subtraction

equal addends

1. **Equal Addends.** This algorithm is sometimes taught as a standard algorithm in elementary school. Many people maintain that it is a simpler algorithm than the decomposition model, which was illustrated in Investigation 8 with powers-of-ten blocks. The equal addends algorithm is based on the concept that if an equal amount is added to both the minuend and the subtrahend, the difference between them remains unchanged. Remember that subtraction is the process of determining the difference between two quantities.

Consider this problem: The distance between Boston, Massachusetts, and Memphis, Tennessee, is approximately 1384 miles. If 795 miles are traveled during the first two days of a trip, how many miles remain?

$$
\begin{array}{r}
1 \quad 3 \quad 8 \quad {}^{1}4 \\
- \qquad 7 \quad 9 \quad 5 \\
{}^{10} \\
\hline
9
\end{array}
$$
Since 5 ones cannot be subtracted from 4 ones, make the 4 ones 14 ones, and compensate by increasing the 9 tens in the subtrahend to 10 tens as shown. Notice that the difference between the numbers is unchanged, since the minuend was increased by 10 ones, and the subtrahend was increased by 1 ten.

$$
\begin{array}{r}
1 \quad 3 \quad {}^{1}8 \quad {}^{1}4 \\
- \qquad 7 \quad 9 \quad 5 \\
{}^{8} \quad {}^{10} \\
\hline
5 \quad 8 \quad 9
\end{array}
$$
Since 10 tens cannot be subtracted from 8 tens, make the 8 tens 18 tens and compensate by increasing the 7 hundreds in the subtrahend to 8 hundreds. Finally, 8 hundreds can be subtracted from 13 hundreds, resulting in a difference of 589.

There are 589 miles remaining.

counting up

2. **Counting Up.** This alternative algorithm models the process used to count back change. Examine the following problem: A plot of land requires 762 feet of fencing to fully enclose it. If 183 feet of fence has already been put in, how much fencing remains to be installed?

	7	6	2	Look at the subtrahend. Count up to the next highest ten
−	1	8	3	and record the number.
			7	(183 to 190)
		1	0	Count up to the next highest hundred (190 to 200).
	5	0	0	Count up to the value of the greatest place (200 to 700).
+		6	2	Count up to the minuend (700 to 762).
	5	7	9	Find the sum of all these differences.

There are 579 feet of fence that remain to be installed.

Investigation 10

The cargo section of a certain airplane can accommodate 2150 pounds. The following packages are scheduled to be put on the plane:

#1	732 pounds
#2	58 pounds
#3	116 pounds
#4	612 pounds
#5	280 pounds
#6	377 pounds
#7	409 pounds

Will the combined weight of these packages exceed the 2150-pound limit? If some of the packages must be removed to stay within the weight limit, how close can you get to 2150?

Understand the Problem: You are given the weights of seven packages. This airplane has a 2150-pound limit on cargo. You must determine which, if any, of the packages must be removed from the plane in order to stay as close to the limit as possible without going over it.

Devise a Plan: Use estimation, and then trial and error if it is necessary to remove any packages.

Carry Out the Plan: Estimate the sum of the package weights. Initially, simply rounding the numbers to the greatest place may be sufficient to determine if the weight exceeds the limit.

$$700 + 60 + 100 + 600 + 300 + 400 + 400$$

$$1000 \quad + \quad 1000 \quad + \quad 560 = 2560$$

Since 2560 > 2150, one or more packages must be eliminated. At this point a precise sum is required. It will be quicker and easier to find the sum if you use a calculator. The following keystroke sequence can be used to find the accurate sum and the amount by which it exceeds 2150.

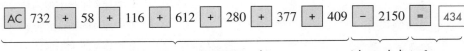

Finds the sum of the seven weights (2584 pounds)   Subtracts the limit   Overage

The combined weight is 434 pounds over the limit.

Look at the weights. Using trial and error, you may hypothesize that deleting packages #2 and #7 (58 pounds and 409 pounds) would bring the weight in under the limit. The following keystroke sequence can be used to find the accurate sum and the overage:

The combined weight is 33 pounds under the limit. Notice that a display of −33 indicates that the sum is 33 pounds less than the limit of 2150 pounds.

Look Back: Since airlines charge per pound of cargo, it would be to their advantage to get as close to 2150 pounds as possible. Examine the original seven packages to determine if deleting other packages will bring you closer to 2150. One attempt would be to delete packages #2 and #6 (58 pounds and 377 pounds). The following keystroke sequence will verify this trial:

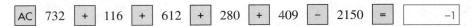

Since this solution brings the total weight to 1 pound less than the limit, it is the best possible solution.

———■———————

In Chapter 1 we introduced basic set theory. In that chapter, you saw how sets are formed, listed, and described, and how they relate to one another. Sets were portrayed in two different ways: through written descriptions and diagrammatic representations. The descriptions took the form of a list of the actual elements, or a definition of the nature of the set. Venn diagrams were used to picture or illustrate the sets. The study of sets forms the basis for understanding operations on numbers. You have already seen how the set model can be used to explain whole number operations. In later chapters, the set model will be used once again to illustrate work with fractions and integers.

Many problems can be solved by developing an analogy between the problem situaton and various sets. Venn diagrams, for example, can be useful in illustrating situations in which relationships between and among groups must be established. Investigation 11 shows how to incorporate set theory into a strategy for solving problems.

Investigation 11

There are 90 two-bedroom units in the Oaks Glen townhouse complex. Seventy-five of these units have air conditioning, 43 have fireplaces, and 11 have neither air conditioning nor fireplaces.

(a) How many units have both air conditioning and a fireplace?

(b) How many units have only air conditioning?

(c) How many units have only a fireplace?

Understand the Problem: You are given specific information about units in a townhouse complex and asked to deduce the number of units containing air conditioning and/or fireplaces.

Devise a Plan: Represent this situation using sets. Illustrate the sets with a Venn diagram.

Carry Out the Plan: **(a)** This problem can be solved by drawing on your knowledge of set theory. Let's view the entire townhouse complex as a single set, T. Then $n(T) = 90$, since the complex can be partitioned into 90 units. The units can be grouped in the following way:

Set A = Apartments with air conditioning $n(A) = 75$ (given information)

Set F = Apartments with fireplaces $n(F) = 43$ (given information)

Set N = Apartments with neither $n(N) = 11$ (given information)

You may have noticed that these three numbers, 75, 43, and 11, have a sum greater than 90. What does that imply? Some apartments in the complex must have both air conditioning and a fireplace. Identify this set as set B.

Set B = Apartments with both air conditioning and a fireplace $n(B) = ?$

Picture the relationships presented here in a Venn diagram.

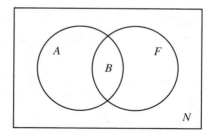

Four regions can be easily identified, representing the sets that have already been defined. The number of elements in set B, $A - B$, and $F - B$ remain to be found.

Notice that the elements of set N do not belong to other sets in the diagram, and that sets A and F intersect. The intersection of these two sets is the set that represents apartments with both air conditioning and a fireplace. We have symbolized this group as set B. Therefore,

$$B = A \cap F$$

Since $n(T) = 90$ and $n(N) = 11$, then $n(T) - n(N) = 90 - 11 = 79$. This number represents the number of apartments that have either air conditioning or a fireplace, or both. In set notation, this is symbolized as

$$n(A \cup F) = 79$$

Since $n(A) + n(F) = 75 + 43 = 118$, the difference between 118 and 79 represents those apartments that have been counted as belonging to both the air conditioning group and the fireplace group. Symbolically, this can be represented as

$$n(A) + n(F) - n(A \cup F) = n(A \cap F) = n(B)$$

$$118 \quad - \quad 79 \quad = \quad 39$$

Therefore, 39 units have both air conditioning and a fireplace.

(b) With the information from part (a) at hand, the rest of the problem begins to fall into place. Examine the following Venn diagram with the number of elements indicated in the sets.

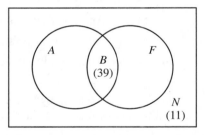

The units that have only air conditioning can be represented symbolically by $A - B$. Since all of the elements of B are in set A, the number of units that have only air conditioning, $n(A - B)$, is determined as follows:

$$n(A - B) = n(A) - n(B) = 43 - 39 = 4$$

Four units have only air conditioning.

(c) The units that have only a fireplace can be represented symbolically by $(F - B)$. Since all of the elements of B are in set F, the number of units that have only a fireplace, $n(F - B)$, is determined as follows:

$$n(F - B) = n(F) - n(B) = 75 - 39 = 36$$

Thirty-six units have only a fireplace.

Look Back: Drawing diagrams to solve problems such as these is a helpful problem-solving strategy. Using a set model allows you to visualize the mathematical connections between and among various interrelated parts. Set notation helped you make sense out of a real-world situation. Examine the numbers you found. Do they make sense when used in conjunction with the given information?

Addition and Subtraction in Other Bases

The methods of addition and subtraction in other bases are analogous to those in base ten. We will explore them briefly here.

Addition

To find the sum of 136_{seven} and 125_{seven}, we can view the individual place values separately in terms of powers-of-seven blocks, as shown in Figure 3.10.

Figure 3.10

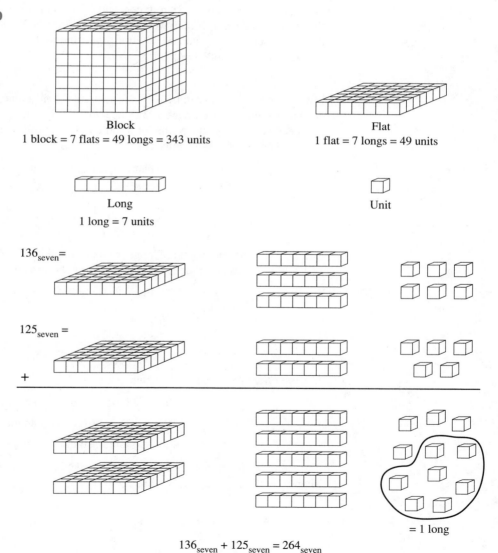

Block
1 block = 7 flats = 49 longs = 343 units

Flat
1 flat = 7 longs = 49 units

Long
1 long = 7 units

Unit

$136_{\text{seven}} =$

$125_{\text{seven}} =$

$+$

$= 1$ long

$$136_{\text{seven}} + 125_{\text{seven}} = 264_{\text{seven}}$$

These blocks give us a pictorial representation of the addition process. Now examine the same sum using the lattice addition and the standard addition methods.

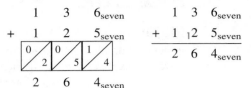

Perhaps the best real-world situation in which addition in other bases is used is in the context of adding elapsed times. For example, suppose that the first portion of a marathon took a runner 2 hours, 13 minutes, and 23 seconds to complete, and the second portion took 3 hours, 58 minutes, and 45 seconds to complete. These two elapsed times can be added as if they were base sixty numerals. We leave it to you to use either the lattice addition or standard addition algorithm to determine the combined time of 6 hours, 12 minutes, and 8 seconds.

Subtraction

Powers-of-five blocks can be used to illustrate the difference of 321_{five} and 133_{five}, as shown in Figure 3.11 on page 103. Since you cannot remove three units from one unit, it is necessary to take apart one long and combine those five units with the one unit of 321_{five}. Then subtract the units.

Flat	Long	Unit
3	1	6
− 1	3	3
		3

Since you cannot remove three longs from one long, it is necessary to take apart one flat and combine those five longs with the one long. Now subtract.

Flat	Long	Unit
2	6	6
− 1	3	3
1	3	3_{five}

It is important to note the following:

$$3 \text{ flats} + 2 \text{ longs} + 1 \text{ unit } = 86 \text{ units}$$
$$3 \text{ flats} + 1 \text{ long } + 6 \text{ units} = 86 \text{ units}$$
$$2 \text{ flats} + 6 \text{ longs} + 6 \text{ units} = 86 \text{ units}$$

The value of the minuend has not been changed at any point throughout this process. Therefore, $321_{\text{five}} - 133_{\text{five}} = 133_{\text{five}}$.

Figure 3.11

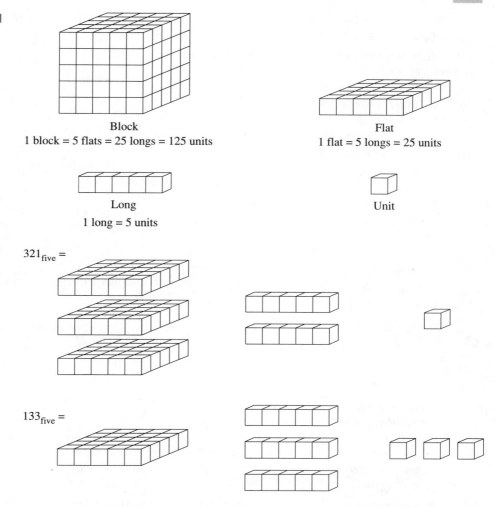

Block
1 block = 5 flats = 25 longs = 125 units

Flat
1 flat = 5 longs = 25 units

Long
1 long = 5 units

Unit

$321_{\text{five}} =$

$133_{\text{five}} =$

The standard subtraction algorithm can be used as well. Keep in mind that regrouping is done with powers of five, not ten.

$$\begin{array}{c} 321_{\text{five}} \\ -\,133_{\text{five}} \end{array} \quad \rightarrow \quad \begin{array}{c} 316 \\ -\,133 \\ \hline 3 \end{array} \quad \rightarrow \quad \begin{array}{c} 266 \\ -\,133 \\ \hline 133_{\text{five}} \end{array}$$

Notice the similarities between this algorithm and the block operations.

Assessments for Section 3.2

1. Estimate the following sums by forming multiples of ten. Check the accuracy of each estimate with a calculator.

(a) $29 + 36 + 55 + 72 + 44 + 45$

(b) $56 + 79 + 21 + 48 + 32 + 11$

(c) $173 + 268 + 591 + 326 + 78 + 34$

(d) $201 + 428 + 505 + 297 + 368$

(e) $178 + 391 + 58 + 72 + 150$

2. Estimate the following sums using the rounding technique. Check the accuracy of each estimate with a calculator.

   (a) $358 + 29 + 426 + 897 + 111$

   (b) $120 + 35 + 750 + 68 + 399$

   (c) $289 + 51 + 163 + 307 + 86$

   (d) $127 + 251 + 290 + 486 + 305$

   (e) $74 + 187 + 403 + 712 + 63$

3. Estimate the following sums using front-end estimation. Check the accuracy of each estimate with a calculator.

   (a) $2613 + 592 + 157 + 4031 + 6259$

   (b) $308 + 1972 + 586 + 6247 + 7815$

   (c) $3175 + 28 + 289 + 4613 + 501$

   (d) $406 + 2931 + 758 + 5613 + 87$

   (e) $234 + 789 + 6262 + 1583 + 4715$

4. Estimate the following differences using the rounding technique. Check the accuracy of each estimate using a calculator.

   (a) $2817 - 358$

   (b) $4215 - 1680$

   (c) $13,482 - 5307$

   (d) $62,548 - 29,074$

   (e) $40,311 - 11,893$

5. Write a word problem to correspond to the following diagram. Then compute the sum using each of the following algorithms.

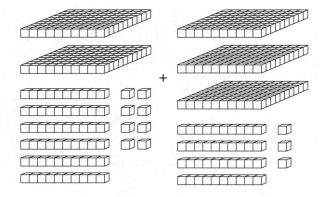

   (a) Lattice addition

   (b) Expanded notation

   (c) Partial sums

   (d) Standard regrouping

6. Illustrate the following example with powers-of-ten blocks. Then compute the difference using each of the algorithms below.

$$383$$
$$-\ \ 95$$

   (a) Equal addends

   (b) Counting up

   (c) Standard decomposition

7. Find the following sums using the expanded notation algorithm.

   (a) $263 + 1894$

   (b) $1742 + 695$

   (c) $218 + 475 + 654$

   (d) $1348 + 795 + 2662$

   (e) $748 + 529 + 68$

8. Find the following sums using the lattice addition algorithm.

   (a) $384 + 297$

   (b) $1617 + 263 + 489$

   (c) $148 + 298 + 775$

   (d) $2654 + 1789$

   (e) $15,831 + 29,624$

9. Find the following sums using the partial sums algorithm.

   (a) $324 + 789$

   (b) $677 + 342$

   (c) $709 + 845$

   (d) $438 + 985$

   (e) $783 + 258$

10. Find the following differences using the equal addends algorithm.

    (a) $7213 - 2675$

    (b) $2391 - 1585$

    (c) $5312 - 1755$

    (d) $4003 - 2739$

    (e) $6034 - 3888$

11. Find the following differences using the counting up algorithm.

    (a) $1583 - 1296$

    (b) $743 - 165$

    (c) $1314 - 925$

    (d) $786 - 349$

    (e) $2314 - 866$

12. Mentally choose three numbers from each set below that add up to approximately 150. With a calculator, check the sum of the three numbers. Indicate how much greater or less the sum is than 150.

Numbers	Sum	Difference from 150
(a) 26 39 85 72 16 53	?	?
(b) 48 25 67 43 21 35	?	?
(c) 35 17 20 72 56 51	?	?
(d) 53 34 68 31 22 6	?	?
(e) 28 44 75 16 48 55	?	?
(f) 21 63 73 49 42 24	?	?
(g) 92 39 53 61 71 49	?	?
(h) 18 64 80 82 47 28	?	?
(i) 42 68 24 26 38 58	?	?

13. Determine the next three terms in each sequence.

    (a) 0, 1, 3, 6, 10, 15, 21

    (b) 0, 1, 1, 2, 3, 5, 8

    (c) 50, 42, 45, 37, 40, 32

    (d) 27, 72, 74, 47, 49, 94

    (e) 17, 18, 21, 22, 25, 26, 29

14. Determine the values of the digits A, B, C, and D in the following four terms of this arithmetic sequence:

    $A3B$, $A6C$, ADA, $31D$, 346

15. Determine the values of the digits A, B, C, and D in the following five terms of this arithmetic sequence:

    $1AA7$, $1BBA$, $14CC$, $1D4D$, 1859

16. Determine the values of the digits B, C, and D in the following lattice addition example:

    6 D B 2
    9 C 3 D

    C / 0 / C / 0 /
    C D / 6 / 0 / B

    D B 0 B

17. A traveling salesperson left Asheville, North Carolina. On the way, she stopped in four cities. Her fifth and final stop was in Charleston, South Carolina. When she left Asheville, her odometer read 29,765. When she arrived in Charleston, her odometer read 30,299. Use the following map to identify her itinerary. Explain how you approached the solution to this problem.

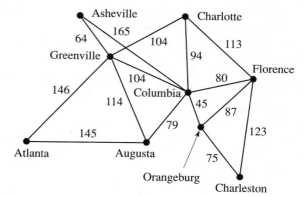

18. Write an expression equal to 2 using only four nines. Do this in more than one way.

19. Write an expression equal to 5 using only five fives. Do this in more than one way.

20. It is easy to identify even and odd base ten numbers.

    (a) Determine a way to identify even and odd base ten equivalents of numbers in base six.

    (b) Determine a way to identify even and odd base ten equivalents of numbers in base three.

21. If $A = 1$ penny, $B = 2$ pennies, $C = 3$ pennies, and so on, the "cost" of CAT would be 24¢. List as many words as you can that "cost" close to $1.00.

22. You are finding the sum of five numbers.

    (a) Mistakenly, you transpose (switch) the tens digit with the ones digit in one of those numbers. What effect will this transposition have on the sum?

    (b) Mistakenly, you transpose the hundreds digit with the tens digit in one of those numbers. What effect will this transposition have on the sum?

    (c) How can knowing transposition effects help you when you are balancing your checking account?

23. Identify and explain the errors made by a student in the following addition examples.

    (a)   ⁴26
        + 18
        ————
          71

    (b)   26
        + 18
        ————
        314

    (c)   26
        + 18
        ————
          35

24. Identify and explain the errors made by a student in the following subtraction examples.

    (a)   26
        − 18
        ————
          12

    (b) 2 ¹6
        − 1 8
        ————
          1 8

    (c)   26
        − 18
        ————
        114

25. Write a problem whose solution lies in the shaded region in each of the following Venn diagrams.

(a)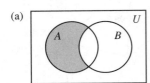

(b)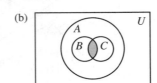

(c)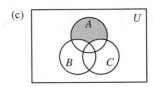

(d)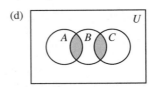

(e)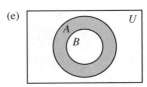

(f)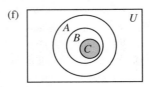

26. There are 40 applicants for a certain job.

(a) All of the applicants have knowledge in at least one of the following areas: word processing or data-base operations. Twenty-six of the applicants know word processing. Eighteen of the applicants know data-base operations. Only applicants who have knowledge of both word processing and data-base operations will be called back for a second interview. How many applicants will be called back for a second inteview?

(b) All of the applicants had to take a mathematics skills examination and a verbal skills examination. If 32 applicants passed the mathematics exam, 35 passed the verbal exam, and 30 passed both exams, how many applicants failed both the math and verbal exams?

(c) Eighteen of the applicants are male. Twenty-five applicants are willing to relocate, and 16 of these are male. How many females are not willing to relocate?

27. At a certain amusement park, three options are available. Visitors can go to the water slides, the indoor arcade, and the golf course. On a given day, the following numbers of people took advantage of the options:

> Water slides: 54
> Indoor arcade: 52
> Golf: 48
> Water slides and golf: 27
> Water slides and indoor arcade: 15
> Golf and indoor arcade: 16
> All three options: 9
> None of the three options: 13

(a) How many people chose only the water slide option?

(b) How many people chose only the golf option?

(c) How many people chose only the arcade option?

(d) How many people chose only the combination of water slide and golf?

(e) How many people chose only the combination of water slide and arcade?

(f) How many people chose only the combination of golf and arcade?

(g) How many visitors were at the park on this day?

28. Determine the sum in each indicated base.

(a) $1001_{two} + 1111_{two}$ (b) $212_{three} + 2202_{three}$

(c) $651_{seven} + 234_{seven}$ (d) $3406_{seven} + 6043_{seven}$

29. Determine the difference in each indicated base.

(a) $11011_{two} - 1101_{two}$ (b) $2122_{three} - 1002_{three}$

(c) $6215_{seven} - 4534_{seven}$ (d) $1716_{eight} - 745_{eight}$

In Other Words

30. Why must two sets be disjoint to be used to model whole number addition?

31. Explain why estimation has recently become an important topic in elementary school curriculum.

32. Explain front-end estimation.

33. Why does lattice addition work?

34. Explain the connection between the counting up alternative algorithm and the missing addend model.

Cooperative Activity

35. Groups of four

Individual Accountability: Each member of the group chooses one of the following categories:

1. Base four addition

2. Base four subtraction

3. Base five addition

4. Base five subtraction

Each member is responsible for making up and solving two numerical examples for his or her respective category: one that involves regrouping, and one that does not. This activity should be done entirely in the respective bases.

Group Goal: All group members present their examples to each other. As a group, solve the following examples within the indicated base to determine the missing digits.

$$2A88_{nine} + 31B6_{nine} = ABBA_{nine}$$
$$71CD_{nine} - 1536_{nine} = 54DC_{nine}$$

Vocabulary for Chapter 3

addends	minuend
additive identity property	missing addends model
algorithm	natural numbers
arithmetic sequence	number line model of addition
associative property	partial sums algorithm
closure property	set model of whole number addition
commutative property	set model of whole number subtraction
counting up	solve a simpler problem
decomposition algorithm	subtrahend
difference	sum
equal addends	trial and error
expanded notation algorithm	units
inverse relationship	whole numbers
lattice addition algorithm	

Review for Chapter 3

1. Write a number sentence illustrated by each of the following operation models.

(a)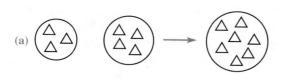

(b)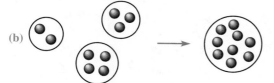

(c)

(d)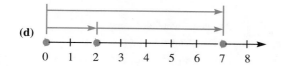

(e)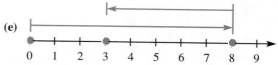

2. Let set R contain all odd whole numbers less than 17. Let set S contain all whole numbers less than 17. Let set T contain all numbers displayed after the $\boxed{=}$ key is pressed in the following keystroke sequence:

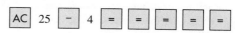

Find

(a) $n(R)$

(b) $n(S)$

(c) $n(T)$

(d) $n(S - R)$

(e) $n(R \cap S)$

(f) $n(R \cap T)$

(g) $n(S \cap T)$

(h) $n(S \cup T)$

(i) $n[(R \cap S) \cup (R \cap T)]$

(j) $n[(S \cap T) \cup (R \cap S)]$

(k) $n[(R \cup S) \cap (R \cup T)]$

3. Let set A contain all numbers displayed after the $=$ key is pressed in the following keystroke sequence:

$$\boxed{AC}\ 27\ \boxed{-}\ 5\ \boxed{=}\ \boxed{=}\ \boxed{=}\ \boxed{=}\ \boxed{=}$$

Let set B contain all even numbers greater than or equal to 2 and less than or equal to 26. Let set C contain all numbers displayed after the $=$ key is pressed in the following keystroke sequence:

$$\boxed{AC}\ 1\ \boxed{+}\ 3\ \boxed{=}\ \boxed{=}\ \boxed{=}\ \boxed{=}\ \boxed{=}\ \boxed{=}\ \boxed{=}\ \boxed{=}$$

Find

(a) $n(A)$

(b) $n(B)$

(c) $n(C)$

(d) $n(A \cup B)$

(e) $n(B \cap C)$

(f) $n(A \cap C)$

(g) $n(B \cup C)$

(h) $n(A \cap B)$

(i) $n[(A \cap B) \cup (A \cap C)]$

(j) $n[(B \cup C) \cap (A \cup B)]$

(k) $n(A \cup B \cup C)$

4. Write three calculator keystroke sequences that each use the constant arithmetic feature and whose displays form three sets, C, D, and E, that are not disjoint. Does $n(C) + n(D) + n(E) = n(C \cup D \cup E)$? Explain your answer.

5. Write three calculator keystroke sequences that each use the constant arithmetic feature and whose displays form three sets, F, G, and H, that are disjoint. Does $n(F) + n(G) + n(H) = n(F \cup G \cup H)$? Explain your answer.

6. In each case, create sets A and B such that

(a) $n(A) = 5$ $n(B) = 8$ $n(A \cup B) = 8$

(b) $n(A) = 3$ $n(B) = 3$ $n(A \cup B) = 6$

(c) $n(A) = 6$ $n(B) = 4$ $n(A \cup B) = 7$

(d) $n(A) = 7$ $n(B) = 6$ $n(A \cup B) = 13$

(e) $n(A) = 5$ $n(B) = 2$ $n(A - B) = 3$

7. Set $X = \{*, \Delta, \odot\}$ with the following addition rules:

$$* + * = \odot \qquad \Delta + * = * \qquad * + \odot = *$$
$$\Delta + \Delta = \odot \qquad \odot + * = \Delta \qquad * + \Delta = \Delta$$
$$\odot + \odot = \odot \qquad \Delta + \odot = \Delta \qquad \odot + \Delta = *$$

Verify whether or not the closure, commutative, and associative properties hold. State your reasoning.

8. Set $R = \{\text{fe, fi, fo, fum}\}$ with the following rules:

fe + fe = fum   fe + fi = fo   fe + fo = fo   fe + fum = fi

fi + fe = fo   fi + fo = fum   fi + fum = fum   fi + fi = fe

fo + fe = fo   fo + fi = fum   fo + fo = fi   fo + fum = fe

fum + fe = fi   fum + fi = fum   fum + fo = fe   fum + fum = fo

Verify whether or not the closure, commutative, and associative properties hold. State your reasoning.

9. Express each of the following sums and differences using a set model and a number line model.

(a) $6 + 2$

(b) $3 + 4$

(c) $8 + 1$

(d) $9 + 5$

(e) $4 + 0$

(f) $8 - 4$

(g) $6 - 1$

(h) $10 - 9$

(i) $9 - 9$

(j) $4 - 0$

10. Identify the whole number addition properties evident in each step.

$$(35 + 63) + 148\ + 262\ + (90 + 32)$$
$$(35 + 63) + 262\ + 148\ + (90 + 32)\ \text{(a)} \underline{\quad}$$
$$35 + (63 + 262) + 148\ + (90 + 32)\ \text{(b)} \underline{\quad}$$
$$35 +\quad 325\quad + 148\ + (32 + 90)\ \text{(c)} \underline{\quad}$$
$$35 +\quad 325\quad + (148 + 32) + 90\ \ \text{(d)} \underline{\quad}$$
$$35 +\quad 325\quad +\ 180 + 90$$
$$360 + 270$$
$$630$$

11. State a possible whole number example for each of the following when given information about the sum or difference.

(a) Minuend, subtrahend, when difference is 100

(b) Minuend, subtrahend, when difference is 1

(c) $\boxed{AC}$ minuend $\boxed{-}$ subtrahend $\boxed{-}$ subtrahend

$\boxed{=}$ subtrahend, when difference is 0

(d) Addend #1, addend #2, when sum is 0

(e) Addend #1, addend #2, addend #3, when sum is even

(f) Addend #1, addend #2, addend #3, when sum is odd

12. Estimate the following sums by forming multiples of ten.

    (a) 638 + 386 + 3827 + 129

    (b) 1458 + 384 + 283 + 238

    (c) 29 + 284 + 222 + 876

13. Estimate the following sums by rounding.

    (a) 259 + 539 + 243

    (b) 1573 + 7639 + 2875

    (c) 16 + 158 + 3854

14. Estimate the following sums using front-end estimation.

    (a) 756 + 285 + 908 + 861

    (b) 1860 + 4763 + 2850

    (c) 1656 + 687 + 45

15. Estimate the following differences by rounding.

    (a) 1543 − 987

    (b) 876 − 592

    (c) 14,356 − 7645

16. Set each of the following problems in a context that would accept an estimate as a reasonable solution.

    (a) 45 − 27

    (b) 862 + 97 + 274

    (c) 1375 − 284

    (d) 98 + 23 + 76 + 87 + 89

17. Without using a calculator, estimate the missing addend in each problem that would put the sum in the given range. Then check the accuracy of your estimate using a calculator.

    (a) 8643 + _____ =   range: 9600 to 9650

    (b) 12,723 + _____ =   range: 15,150 to 15,350

    (c) 384 + _____ =   range: 730 to 800

    (d) 3783 + _____ =   range: 23,400 to 23,860

    (e) 679 + 8543 + _____ =   range: 9800 to 10,000

18. Without using a calculator, estimate the missing subtrahend or minuend in each problem that would put the difference in the given range. Then check the accuracy of your estimate using a calculator.

    (a) 954 − _____ =   range: 250 to 300

    (b) 1278 − _____ =   range: 900 to 925

    (c) _____ − 850 =   range: 1000 to 1100

    (d) _____ − 3654 =   range: 7600 to 8000

    (e) _____ − 922 =   range: 989 to 1022

19. Arrange the numbers 5, 10, 15, 20, 25, 30, 35, 40, and 45 in the following grid so that each row, column, and diagonal all sum to 75. Each number is used only once, and all numbers are used.

20. Using each of the digits 2, 3, 5, 6, and 8 only once, arrange them so that they form the greatest sum, the least sum, the greatest difference, and the least whole number difference.

21. With unmarked containers that hold 3 liters, 5 liters, and 8 liters, and an unlimited supply of water, show how it is possible to measure exactly 4 liters of water. Solve this problem in at least two ways.

22. Assuming that three and only three darts hit the target illustrated below, what different scores are possible?

23. Find each of the following sums and differences using at least two different alternative algorithms.

    (a) 1345 + 2587

    (b) 826 − 58

    (c) 9846 − 987

    (d) 933 + 922 + 236

    (e) 872 + 78

24. The housing authority has guaranteed a certain elevator safe to carry 1500 pounds. If the following people want to ride the elevator to the fifth floor, how should it be done to transport the people on the fewest trips?

Person:	A	B	C	D	E	F	G	H	I	J
Weight:	93	115	244	108	187	157	192	123	155	206

Person:	K	L	M	N	O	P	Q	R
Weight:	85	116	273	114	105	185	243	293

25. Determine the values of A, B, and C in the four terms of the following arithmetic sequence:

$$A\,B4,\ B03,\ B3C,\ BA1$$

26. The sum of a three-digit number, X, and a two-digit number, Y, is equal to a three-digit number, Z, whose digits are in the reverse order of those in X. The difference between X and Y is 285. Find X and Y.

27. You are given the following true statements:

$X + Y$ is even or Y is odd.

If Y is odd, then X is even.

If X is even, then the digit 2 is in its ones place.

X does not have the digit 2 in its ones place.

What conclusion can you draw about the sum of X and Y?

28. Make a list of the numbers from 1 to 15. In a second column, make a list of the square of each of these numbers. Describe the relationship between the sum of any two consecutive numbers in the first list and the difference of the corresponding two consecutive squares in the second list.

29. The sum of the first four of five consecutive numbers is 44 more than the fifth number. What are the numbers?

30. Ten less than the sum of three consecutive numbers is twice the third number. What are the numbers?

31. You are given the following set of consecutive three-digit numbers:

$ABC, ABD, ABB, EFF, EFG, EFH$

The sum of these numbers is a four-digit number represented by $GCBC$. Determine the value of A, B, C, D, E, F, G, and H.

32. The sum of the ages of Ally and Erin is 30. The sum of the ages of Erin and Sara is 28. Ally's age and Sara's age sum to 34. What are the three ages?

33. An advertising agency conducted a survey with businesses using overnight express mail carriers. Businesses were asked whether they used some or all of carriers A, B, and C. The results were as follows:

> 35 had used carrier A
> 35 had used carrier B
> 23 had used carrier C
> 9 had used carriers A and B
> 10 had used carriers A and C
> 5 had used carriers B and C
> 3 had used carriers A, B, and C

How many businesses were surveyed?

In Other Words

34. What does it mean for whole numbers to be closed under addition but not closed under subtraction?

35. Discuss the advantages and disadvantages of the three estimation techniques of whole number addition.

36. Describe how regrouping can be illustrated using powers-of-ten blocks.

37. How can the expanded notation algorithm be viewed as a precursor to understanding the process of regrouping?

38. How might the concept of directed distance be placed in a real-life context to illustrate the operations of addition and subtraction?

Cooperative Activity

39. Groups of four

Individual Accountability: Each student is to examine the following alternative subtraction algorithm as illustrated in examples A, B, and C. Apply the algorithm to examples D, E, and F.

A	B	C
$15 \rightarrow \quad 15$	$203 \rightarrow \quad 203$	$15{,}683 \rightarrow \quad 15{,}683$
$- \ 6 \quad + \ 93$	$- \ 152 \quad + \ 847$	$- \ 14{,}320 \quad + \ 85{,}679$
$\overline{ 108}$	$\overline{ 1050}$	$\overline{ 101{,}362}$
$+ \hookleftarrow 1$	$+ \hookleftarrow 1$	$+ \hookleftarrow 1$
9	51	1363

D	E	F
$652 - 298$	$1001 - 391$	$1952 - 1527$

Group Goal: Now that you have determined *how* this subtraction alternative algorithm works, as a group determine *why* it works. To focus your investigation, answer the following questions.

(a) Does the algorithm work when a number is subtracted from itself?

(b) What role does the movement of the 1 from the leftmost column to the ones column play? Will this digit always be a 1?

(c) This algorithm is called the "nines complement" method of subtraction. Do you think an eights complement method of subtraction would be possible? Why or why not?

4

Whole Number Relationships: Multiplication and Division

Examine the photograph at the right.

Describe what you see.

How might you estimate the number of individual pieces inthe quilt?

How might you determine the actual number of individual pieces in the quilt?

What patterns can you describe in the photograph?

What would a mathematical description of the photograph contain?

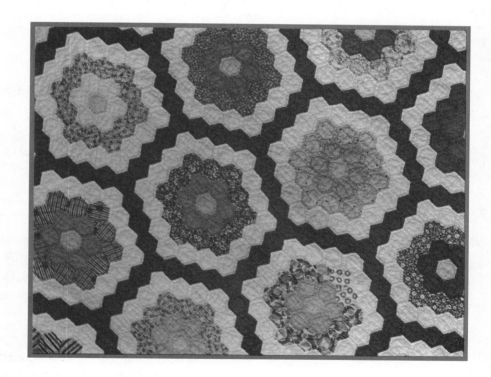

Introduction

Throughout the three preceding chapters, you have been introduced to many problem-solving strategies. Finding a pattern, employing an analogy, looking for a contradiction, solving a simpler problem, making a list, and trial and error were presented as tools to help you make sense of problem situations. In this chapter, we will continue our search for patterns and regularities, here looking for those that are inherent in the various multiplication and division algorithms.

As in Chapter 3, we will consider concrete models and properties of operations, but in this chapter our focus will be on multiplication and division rather than addition and subtraction. These models and properties of whole number multiplication and division are covered in Section 4.1. Section 4.2 moves into a discussion of the various algorithms available for whole number multiplication and division, offering a variety of techniques for estimating and then actually finding products and quotients. Multiplication and division in other bases are also examined. In Section 4.3, number theory concepts that pertain to multiplication and division, such as prime factorization, exponents, and tests for divisibility, are addressed. Finally, Section 4.4 prepares you to use the knowledge you have gained about whole number operations and problem-solving strategies to start making connections within the set of whole numbers and between the whole number system and other mathematical systems. Topics such as relations, functions, clock arithmetic, and modular arithmetic are discussed and related to what you have learned so far.

4.1 Models and Properties of Whole Number Multiplication and Division

In today's complex society, it is useful to know alternative approaches to solving problems, to have the ability to estimate answers, to know when and how to use appropriate technology, and to use mathematics as a tool for solving real-life problems. Because many real-life situations involve problem-solving processes that employ multiplication and division, the models and properties of these two operations will be the focus of this section. Models of these two operations will be introduced to serve as a foundation for the algorithms that follow in Section 4.2.

Multiplication Models of Whole Numbers

set model of whole number multiplication

number line model of whole number multiplication

There are many multiplication models. Both the **set model of whole number multiplication** and the **number line model of whole number multiplication** are based on recognizing a pattern of repeated addition. Consider the following example: A photo album can contain four photos per page. What is the maximum number of photos that can be contained on six pages?

The solution can be illustrated using the set model shown in Figure 4.1. In this model, six addends represent the number of photos on each of six pages. Since the addends are all the same, $4 + 4 + 4 + 4 + 4 + 4$ can be viewed as six groups of four and symbolized as 6×4. Here the number 4 is being multiplied by the number 6 since there are six groups (pages) each containing four photos. The number that you multiply by is

Figure 4.1

multiplier, multiplicand

called **multiplier**, and the number that is being multiplied is called the **multiplicand**. When viewing multiplication by the set model, the multiplier is the number of equal sets, and the multiplicand is the number of elements in each set. This leads us to the definition of whole number multiplication.

Definition: Given any whole number a of equal sets, each containing b elements,

$$ab = \underbrace{b + b + b + \cdots + b}_{a \text{ sets}}$$

Terminology: The solution to every multiplication example is called the **product**. The product, ab, is
product, factors   read as "a times b" where both a and b are called **factors**. The product of a and b can be symbolized by ab, $a \cdot b$, and $a \times b$.

The number line model can be used to express the repeated addition illustrated above. The number line model of 6×4 is shown in Figure 4.2.

Figure 4.2

An alternative to viewing multiplication as repeated addition is to view multiplica-
array   tion as an array. An **array** is a rectangular arrangement of objects consisting of rows and columns. The product of 3 and 4 can be viewed as an array in the following context: A garden is planted in three horizontal rows. Each row contains four rose bushes. How many rose bushes are in the garden?

Using the problem-solving strategy of **drawing a diagram**, this situation can be illustrated as in Figure 4.3. There are three rows of four bushes each, or 12 rose bushes in all.

Figure 4.3

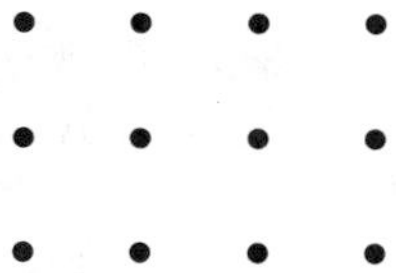

```
•   •   •   •

•   •   •   •

•   •   •   •
```

Cartesian product model of   Another model of multiplication is called the **Cartesian product model of multi-
multiplication   plication**, or **cross-product model**. Consider the following example: An airport park-
cross-product model   ing lot consists of three levels, A, B, and C. Each level is separated into three color-coded sections: blue, green, and red. How many different parking locations can be identified in this lot?

tree diagram   To answer this question, you can draw either a special type of diagram called a **tree diagram** (Figure 4.4a) or an array illustration (Figure 4.4b). In Figure 4.4a you can identify every possible combination of parking levels with color-coded sections by reading the tree diagram from left to right along the "branches." In Figure 4.4b, the various identifications are represented in each cell of the array as a pair. In both of these illustrations of the Cartesian product model, two pieces of information are communicated. You can readily see the identity of each possible combination as well as the total number of combinations. These pairs are listed here: {(A, blue), (A, red), (A, green), (B, blue), (B, red), (B, green), (C, blue), (C, red), (C, green)}. Notice that nine pairs are possible.

Figure 4.4

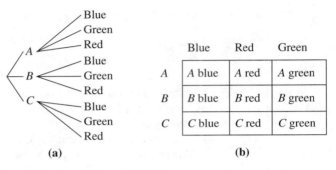

(a)   (b)

The Cartesian product definition of multiplication can be symbolized as follows:

Definition: Let A and B be two countable, nonempty sets, with $a = n(A)$ and $b = n(B)$. Then, $ab = n(A) \times n(B) = n(A \times B)$ where the set symbolized by $(A \times B)$ is the set containing all of the possible pairs formed by joining (in this order) one element of A with one element of B.

Multiplication Properties of Whole Numbers

Certain consistencies, or properties, characterize the operation of whole number multiplication. These are discussed below.

1. The Closure Property of Whole Number Multiplication. The product of two whole numbers is a unique whole number. A set with this property is said to be *closed* under multiplication.

2. The Commutative Property of Whole Number Multiplication. The order of the factors may be changed without changing the product; that is, if a and b are both whole numbers, $a \cdot b = b \cdot a$.

Investigation 1

Illustrate the commutative property of multiplication for 2×3 using (1) the repeated addition model, (2) the array model, and (3) the Cartesian product model.

1. The repeated addition model of 2×3 is illustrated by $3 + 3$, or 6. The repeated addition model of 3×2 is illustrated by $2 + 2 + 2$, or 6. Clearly, $3 + 3 = 2 + 2 + 2$. Therefore, $2 \times 3 = 3 \times 2$.

2.

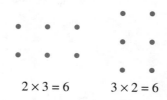

$$2 \times 3 = 6 \qquad 3 \times 2 = 6$$

3. Let $A = \{\text{vanilla, chocolate, strawberry}\}$ and $B = \{\text{cone, cup}\}$; $n(A) = 3$ and $n(B) = 2$.

	Cone	Cup
Vanilla	Vanilla cone	Vanilla cup
Chocolate	Chocolate cone	Chocolate cup
Strawberry	Strawberry cone	Strawberry cup

$$n(A \times B) = 6$$

	Vanilla	Chocolate	Strawberry
Cone	Cone vanilla	Cone chocolate	Cone strawberry
Cup	Cup vanilla	Cup vanilla	Cup strawberry

$$n(B \times A) = 6$$

---

3. The Associative Property of Whole Number Multiplication.   When multiplying more than two numbers, the way in which those numbers are grouped does not affect the product; that is, if a, b, and c are whole numbers, $(a \cdot b) \cdot c = a \cdot (b \cdot c)$. For example, $(4 \times 6) \times 5 = 4 \times (6 \times 5) = 120$.

4. The Identity Property of Whole Number Multiplication.   There exists a unique whole number, 1, such that for any whole number x, $x \cdot 1 = 1 \cdot x = x$. The number 1 is called the **multiplicative identity element**.

> **multiplicative identity element**

The word *unique* is very important in this definition. It means that there is one and only one number with that property. But how can you be sure that no other whole number exists with that same property? A standard proof for verifying uniqueness is given here.

We accept that 1 is the multiplicative identity element since for any whole number x, $x \cdot 1 = x$. Let's assume that another multiplicative identity element exists. Call it m. Then, for any whole number x, $x \cdot m = x$. Examine these two mathematical statements:

$$x \cdot 1 = x \qquad \text{and} \qquad x \cdot m = x$$

Since x can be any whole number, let $x = m$ in the first statement:

$$x \cdot 1 = x$$
$$m \cdot 1 = m$$

Since x can be any whole number, let $x = 1$ in the second statement:

$$x \cdot m = x$$
$$1 \cdot m = 1$$

Now examine the two new statements: $m \cdot 1 = m$ and $1 \cdot m = 1$. We have seen that by the commutative property, $m \cdot 1 = 1 \cdot m$. Thus, these two statements can be written in this form:

$$m \cdot 1 = m$$
$$m \cdot 1 = 1$$

Since $m \cdot 1$ equals both m and 1, it must be true that $m = 1$.

What have we proven? We assumed that another multiplicative identity existed and called it m. But now we determine that the only value m can have is 1. Therefore, there is a *unique* multiplicative identity, namely, 1.

5. The Zero Property of Whole Number Multiplication.   For any whole number x, $x \cdot 0 = 0 \cdot x = 0$.

6. The Distributive Property of Whole Number Multiplication over Addition.   For any whole numbers a, b, and c, $a \cdot (b + c) = a \cdot b + a \cdot c$, and $(a + b) \cdot c = a \cdot c + b \cdot c$. This property can be most clearly illustrated using the array model of multiplication. For example, imagine that you are laying square floor tiles in a hallway. Since the front of the hallway is near the entrance, you wish to lay black tiles there. The remainder of the hallway will be tiled in white, as shown in Figure 4.5.

Figure 4.5

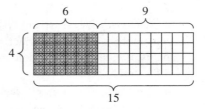

The black section is 4 tiles by 6 tiles, or 24 black tiles in all. The white section is 4 tiles by 9 tiles, or 36 white tiles in all. The total number of tiles used can be determined in two ways. You could find the sum of the number of black tiles and the number of white tiles used. This method would lead to the answer of 24 + 36, or 60 tiles. Alternately, you could view the entire hallway as one array measuring 4 tiles by 15 tiles. The product of 4 and 15 is also 60. This can be symbolized in the following fashion:

$$(4 \cdot 6) + (4 \cdot 9) = 4 \cdot (6 + 9)$$
$$24 + 36 = 4 \cdot 15$$
$$60 = 60$$

This property can also be extended to subtraction:

$$a(b - c) = ab - ac \qquad \text{and} \qquad (a - b)c = ac - bc$$

Investigation 2

Use the distributive property to simplify the process of finding the product of 8 and 35.

You can find the product of 8 and 35 in several ways, two of which are given here.

1. Rewrite 35 as the sum of 25 and 10:

$$8 \cdot 35 = 8 \cdot (25 + 10)$$

By the distributive property,

$$8 \cdot (25 + 10) = 8 \cdot 25 + 8 \cdot 10$$
$$= 200 + 80$$
$$= 280$$

2. Rewrite 35 as the difference of 50 and 15:

$$8 \cdot 35 = 8 \cdot (50 - 15)$$

By the distributive property,

$$8 \cdot (50 - 15) = 8 \cdot 50 - 8 \cdot 15$$
$$= 400 - 120$$
$$= 280$$

You can see how judicious use of the distributive property makes it possible to do this multiplication mentally in a variety of ways.

Investigation 3

Use a calculator to find the product of 628,971 and 352,888.

Enter the following calculator keystroke sequence:

On most eight-digit-display calculators, this keystroke sequence will not display the correct product. A variety of things can happen, depending on the type of calculator. Most four-function calculators will output an E somewhere in the display. The E indicates that an error has been made. In this case, it is an overflow error. The product contained more numbers than the display could show. But this problem can be done with a calculator using the knowledge of the properties of whole number multiplication.

$$628{,}971 = 628{,}000 + 971$$

$$352{,}888 = 352{,}000 + 888$$

Therefore, $628{,}971 \times 352{,}888 =$

$$(628000 + 971) \times (352000 + 888)$$

You must now apply a special case of the distributive property. You will distribute each of the numbers in the first parentheses over each of the numbers in the second parentheses, as shown here:

$$(628000 + 971) \times (352000 + 888) =$$

$$(628000 \times 352000) + (628000 \times 888) + (971 \times 352000) + (971 \times 888)$$

Examine each of these products separately.

Attempting to enter $628{,}000 \times 352{,}000$ into the calculator will once again yield an error message. Each of these numbers is a multiple of 1000.

$$628{,}000 = 628 \times 1000$$

$$352{,}000 = 352 \times 1000$$

$$(628{,}000 \times 352{,}000) = (628 \times 1000) \times (352 \times 1000)$$

$$= (628 \times 1000) \times (1000 \times 352) \quad \text{by the commutative property}$$

$$= 628 \times (1000 \times 1000) \times 352 \quad \text{by the associative property}$$

$$= 628 \times 352 \times (1000 \times 1000) \quad \text{by the commutative property}$$

$$= (628 \times 352) \times (1000 \times 1000) \quad \text{by the associative property}$$

Now you can find the product of 628 and 352 using the calculator:

| AC | 628 | × | 352 | = | 221056 |

This number must be multiplied by (1000×1000), or $1{,}000{,}000$. It is neither necessary nor even possible to use a calculator to find this product. It is easy to see that

$$221{,}056 \times 1{,}000{,}000 = 221{,}056{,}000{,}000 \quad \text{This number is read as two hundred twenty-one billion, fifty-six million.}$$

This line of reasoning can be followed for each of the three remaining products:

$$(628{,}000 \times 888) = (628 \times 888) \times 1000 = 557{,}664{,}000$$

$$(971 \times 352{,}000) = (971 \times 352) \times 1000 = 341{,}792{,}000$$

$$(971 \times 888) \quad \text{Using the calculator, the product is 862,248.}$$

To find the final product, you must find the sum of these partial products:

$$221,056,000,000$$
$$557,664,000$$
$$341,792,000$$
$$+ \quad\quad 862,248$$
$$\overline{221,956,318,248}$$

Although it is possible to model this procedure using a calculator to find the sum of these partial products, it is probably easier to add these four partial products using paper and pencil.

Investigation 4

A manufacturer has 18 congruent wooden disks and 76 identical metal chimes that can be used to make two types of wind chimes (see below). Type *A* requires 5 chimes attached to the disk, whereas type *B* requires 3 chimes. Using all of the chimes, how many of each type can be made?

A   B

Understand the Problem: What is given? Since each wind chime requires one wooden disk, a total of 18 wind chimes will be manufactured. Each type *A* wind chime requires 5 chimes and a disk. Each type *B* wind chime requires 3 chimes and a disk. There are 76 chimes, all of which must be used.

What is unknown? You are asked to determine the number of type *A* and type *B* wind chimes that can be made.

Devise a Plan: In order to establish a relationship among the number of disks, the number of chimes, and the number of each type produced, we will use the problem-solving strategies of **using a variable** and **making a chart**. A **variable** is used in mathematics to represent a number. It is called a variable since its value varies depending on the situation.

variable

> Let *a* represent the number of type *A* chimes that can be produced.
>
> Let *b* represent the number of type *B* chimes that can be produced.

It follows that the total number of wind chimes produced, 18, is represented by *a* + *b*. In addition, we know that for every type *A* chime, 5 chimes are needed, and for every type

B chime, 3 chimes are needed. Therefore, the total number of chimes to be used, 76, can be represented by the expression $5 \cdot a + 3 \cdot b$. We will use these variable expressions to explore some possible combinations.

Carry Out the Plan: The information can be organized in a chart as follows. We will select possible values of *a* and *b* and compare the outcomes with the given information.

a	*b*	*a + b*	$5 \cdot a$	$3 \cdot b$	$5 \cdot a + 3 \cdot b$
0	18	18	0	54	$0 + 54 = 54$
18	0	18	90	0	$90 + 0 = 90$
9	9	18	45	27	$45 + 27 = 72$
10	8	18	50	24	$50 + 24 = 74$
11	7	18	55	21	$55 + 21 = 76$

Look Back: Notice that the last line of the chart contains the information we seek. If 11 type *A* wind chimes and 7 type *B* wind chimes are made, all 76 chimes will be used to make the 18 wind chimes.

■

Division of Whole Numbers

Students need to understand the *concept* of division before they are introduced to any division algorithms. The process of division can be thought of in at least two ways: either as the process of partitioning (equal sharing) or as the process of repeated subtraction through a variety of models.

set model of whole number division   The **set model of whole number division** can be illustrated as the process of partitioning, or equal sharing. Consider the following situation: Eighteen cookies must be equally shared among six children. How many cookies does each child receive?

In this case, we know that six equal sets of cookies need to be formed, but we do not know how many cookies will be in each of the six sets. You can help children solve this problem by giving them 18 counters to symbolize the cookies and half of an egg carton (six receptacles). The children drop one counter in each of the six receptacles and continue in this manner until all of the counters are gone. The children then see that each of six children would receive three cookies. Had there been 20 cookies to be shared, the children would have realized that two cookies would have been left over. This would be an appropriate opportunity for the teacher to introduce the concept of a remainder and its relationship to the partition model of division.

You can view the division process as a method of partitioning a set into equal, disjoint subsets, with the union of these subsets being the original set. This leads us to a definition of whole number division.

Definition: Given set *S* containing a countable number of elements *b*, where $b = n(S)$, and a desired number, *x*, of equal, disjoint subsets into which *S* is to be partitioned. If P_1, P_2, P_3, ..., P_x represent the *x* subsets and $(x \neq 0)$, then $b \div x = n(P_d) + r$ where *d* is any number from 1 to *x*, and *r* represents the remainder, which is any number from 0 to $x - 1$.

Terminology:
quotient, dividend
divisor

The solution to every division problem is called the **quotient**. The number being divided is called the **dividend**. The number that it is divided by is called the **divisor**. In the definition above, b is the dividend and x is the divisor. Whole number division can be expressed as $b \div x$ or b/x.

Two facts critical to division must be recognized. First, division is not closed on the set of whole numbers. This can be seen in the counterexample of $10 \div 4$. The quotient, 2.5 is not a whole number. Second, zero is excluded as a divisor in all definitions of division. This can be readily seen by recognizing the inverse relationship between multiplication and division. If a and b are any whole numbers, with $b \neq 0$, and $a \div b = c$, then $b \cdot c = a$ for some whole number c. If 0 were not excluded from this definition, then $a \div 0 = c$ would imply that $0 \cdot c = a$. The zero property of multiplication states that 0 times any number is equal to zero. Therefore, $0 \cdot c = 0 = a$. This contradicts the given information that a could be any whole number. It is for this reason that division by 0 is said to be undefined.

Sometimes elementary school students will insist that any number divided by 0 equals 0, and others will say that any number divided by 0 is equal to that number itself. Examine each of the cases below.

$$a \div b = c$$

Let $a = 3$ and $b = 0$.　　　　Let $a = 3$ and $b = 0$.

If $3 \div 0 = 0$, then　　　　If $3 \div 0 = 3$, then

0×0 must equal 3　　　　3×0 must equal 3.

Clearly, neither of these statements is true.

number line model of whole
number division

The **number line model of whole number division** can be illustrated within the context of repeated subtraction, as shown in Investigation 5.

Investigation 5

A bottle of vitamin C contains 150 capsules. During the cold season, David takes seven capsules a day. How many days will elapse before David has to purchase another bottle?

Examine the following segment of a number line. The symbol ⋀ indicates that, because of space limitations, a portion of the number line does not appear. You should still think of this number line as being continuous from 0 to 150.

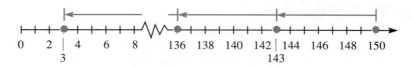

Beginning at 150, move to the left in groups of seven. Each move symbolizes one day. You can see that to continue this procedure would be tedious, since the numbers are fairly large. Repeated subtraction on the number line can be simulated by using the constant subtraction feature of the calculator in the following way:

Each press of the equal key represents one day's worth of vitamin C. The repeated subtraction of 7 is representative of a movement to the left on the number line. It is important to keep track of the number of times the equal key is pressed and to watch the display carefully. Three possibilities exist.

1. The display eventually reads 0. This means that the bottle contained some number of a full day's supply. In other words, 7 would divide 150 without a remainder. Whenever a number x divides another number y without a remainder, it is symbolized as $x \mid y$ and is read "x divides y."

2. A number that is less than 7 but greater than 0 is displayed. This means only a partial supply of vitamin C remains on the final day. This number represents the remainder when 150 is divided by 7. Since in this case there is a remainder, you could not say that $7 \mid 150$, but rather $7 \nmid 150$, which is read "7 does not divide 150."

3. A negative number is displayed. Different types of calculators vary in the way negative numbers are displayed. For the purposes of this text, it is assumed that the calculator displays the negative sign directly to the left of the numeral. If a negative number is displayed, it means that too many 7s were subtracted from 150. In the context of this problem, it means that David would have been taking vitamin C capsules that weren't there.

The calculator keystroke displayed above requires that the equal key be pressed 21 times. This results in a display of $\boxed{3}$. This means that David had a 21-day supply of vitamin C capsules, with three capsules remaining. The accuracy of this quotient can be verified with the following calculator keystroke sequence.

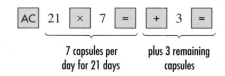

7 capsules per   plus 3 remaining
day for 21 days   capsules

The display should be 150.

Investigation 6

Describe a situation that would use the following calculator keystroke sequence:

Several possible interpretations of this keystroke sequence exist. One possibility is offered here. A certain school received a shipment of 5 cartons, each containing 36 boxes of crayons. These were to be shared equally among 3 kindergarten classes. If each class uses up 6 boxes of crayons per month, how many months will the crayons last?

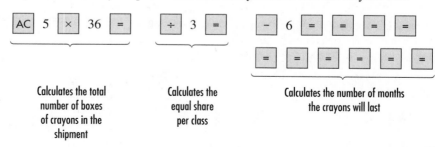

Calculates the total number of boxes of crayons in the shipment

Calculates the equal share per class

Calculates the number of months the crayons will last

The whole number properties that we defined for addition, subtraction, and multiplication are left for you to examine as they relate to division. Questions involving division will appear in the assessments section that follows.

Assessments for Section 4.1

1. Illustrate each product using the set model, number line model, array model, and Cartesian product model.
   (a) 3×5 (b) 8×6 (c) 2×7

2. Determine which of the following sets are closed under multiplication.
   (a) $\{1\}$
   (b) $\{0\}$
   (c) $\{0, 1\}$
   (d) $\{0, 1, 2\}$
   (e) The set of all even whole numbers
   (f) The set of all odd whole numbers
   (g) $\{0, 1, 2, 3, 4, 5, 6, 7, 8, 9\}$
   (h) $\{0, 5, 10, 15, 20, 25, 30, 35, \ldots\}$
   (i) $\{0, 5, 10, 15, 20, 25, 30, 35\}$
   (j) The set of all whole numbers, x, that can be written in the form $x \mid 10$

3. Supply a real-life context to illustrate each of the following properties.
   (a) The commutative property of multiplication for 5 and 6
   (b) The associative property of multiplication for 7, 14, and 21
   (c) The distributive property of multiplication over addition for $3 \times (2 + 7)$

4. Rewrite each of the following expressions in simpler form, using the distributive property of multiplication over addition.

   (a) 79×3
   (b) 203×5
   (c) 16×35
   (d) 27×48
   (e) 241×120

5. Determine whether each of the following statements is true or false.
   (a) $68 \div 0 = 0$
   (b) $5 \mid 111$
   (c) There is a commutative property of division.
   (d) There is an associative property of division.
   (e) If $4 \mid 20$, then 4 is a factor of 20.
   (f) Since $0 \times 0 = 0$, then zero is a multiplicative identity element over the set of whole numbers.

6. Determine the value of X for which each of the following statements is undefined.
   (a) $23 \div X$
   (b) $100 \div (X - 1)$
   (c) $X \div (X - 5)$
   (d) $(X + 3) \div (X - 3)$
   (e) $X^2 \div (2X - 4)$

7. Use a calculator to find the product of 78,345 and 84,299. (Use the method described in Investigation 3).

8. Use a calculator to find the product of 95,301 and 49,999. Can you think of an alternative method to the one explained in Investigation 3?

9. Is it possible to have a division problem in which the dividend, the divisor, and the quotient are the same number? Explain your answer.

10. Write a problem that illustrates the set model of whole number division for each expression.

    (a) $24 \div 6$ (b) $120 \div 15$ (c) $36 \div 12$

11. Write a problem that illustrates the number line model of whole number division for each expression.

    (a) $24 \div 6$ (b) $120 \div 15$ (c) $36 \div 12$

12. Write a problem that would use the given calculator sequence in (a)–(d).

    (a) | AC | 125 | × | 2 | = | = | = |

    (b) | AC | 300 | ÷ | 5 | = | = |

    (c) | AC | 1000 | ÷ | 100 | = | × | 7 | = |

    (d) | AC | 60 | × | 5 | = | ÷ | 20 | = |

13. Examine each of the following statements. If the statement is false, give a numerical example to illustrate your reasoning.

    (a) *Closure property of whole number division:* The quotient of two whole numbers is itself a whole number.

    (b) *Commutative property of whole number division:* $A \div B = B \div A$

    (c) *Associative property of whole number division:* $(A \div B) \div C = A \div (B \div C)$

    (d) *Identity property of whole number division:* There exists a unique whole number X such that for any whole number Y, $Y \div X = X \div Y$.

14. Examine each of the following statements. If the statement is false, give a numerical example to illustrate your reasoning.

    (a) *Distributive property of whole number multiplication over addition:* $(X + Y) \cdot Z = X \cdot Z + Y \cdot Z$

    (b) *Distributive property of whole number addition over multiplication:* $A + (B \cdot C) = (A + B) \cdot (A + C)$

    (c) *Distributive property of whole number multiplication over subtraction:* $R \cdot (S - T) = R \cdot S - R \cdot T$

    (d) *Distributive property of whole number multiplication over division:*
    $A \cdot (B \div C) = (A \cdot B) \div (A \cdot C)$ $[C \neq 0]$

    (e) *Distributive property of whole number division over addition:* $(B + C) \div E = (B \div E) + (C \div E)$ $[E \neq 0]$

    (f) *Distributive property of whole number division over addition:* $E \div (A + B) = (E \div A) + (E \div B)$

15. A certain number of marbles is partitioned into three bags, with each bag containing the same number of marbles. Bag A is partitioned into two equal bags. Bag B is partitioned into three equal bags. Bag C is partitioned into five equal bags. What is the smallest original number of marbles that this partitioning could have been accomplished with?

16. A *geometric sequence* is a sequence in which each term is determined by multiplying the previous term by a fixed number. In general, if $x_1, x_2, x_3, \ldots, x_k, x_{k+1}, \ldots, x_n$ is a geometric sequence, the quotient of each term with its preceding term, $(k + 1)/x_k$ is the same number. Use this information to determine the indicated term in each of the following geometric sequences.

    (a) 9, 117, 1521, 19,773   (seventh term)

    (b) 3, 21, 147, 1029, 7203   (ninth term)

    (c) 15, 45, 135, 405, 1215   (tenth term)

    (d) $\dfrac{x_{k+1}}{x_k} = 11, x_1 = 6$ (seventh term)

    (e) $\dfrac{x_{k+1}}{x_k} = 7, x_1 = 7$ (fifth term)

    (f) $\dfrac{x_{k+1}}{x_k} = 8, x_5 = 24{,}576$ (first term)

    (g) $\dfrac{x_{k+1}}{x_k} = 3, x_7 = 9477$ (second term)

    (h) $x_5 = 8750, x_4 = 1750$ (first term)

    (i) $x_4 = 4608, x_3 = 576$ (first and fifth terms)

17. In a geometric sequence, let r represent the common quotient found by dividing any term by its preceding term $(r = x_{k+1}/x_k)$, and let x_1 represent the first term of the sequence. The sum of the first n terms of a geometric sequence is given by

    $$\text{Sum} = \frac{x_1(r^n - 1)}{r - 1} \quad \text{(where } r \neq 1)$$

    Determine the sum of the given number of terms of each of the following geometric sequences.

    (a) 12, 48, 192, 768   (six terms)

    (b) 5, 10, 20, 40, 80   (twenty terms)

    (c) 6, 54, 486, 4374   (six terms)

    (d) $x_3 = 300, x_4 = 1500$ (five terms)

    (e) $x_3 = 3703, x_4 = 85{,}169$ (five terms)

18. The parents of a particularly obstreperous child offer you a choice of payment for two hours of babysitting: they will pay you either a flat fee of $1000, or a nickel for the first five minutes, a dime for the second five minutes, twenty cents for the third five minutes, and continue to double the amount for each additional five minutes. Which form of payment should you choose? Why?

19. An "assemble-your-own" furniture supplier makes book-cases in only one size. The bookcase can be packaged with 5 shelves, 4 shelves, or 3 shelves. If 19 bookcases and 79 shelves are ready to be packaged, how many of each type of bookcase (5-shelf, 4-shelf, or 3-shelf) can be shipped to the store?

20. The sum of seven consecutive numbers is 623. What are the seven numbers?

In Other Words

21. Describe the difference between the array model of multi-plication and the repeated addition model of multiplication.

22. Explain why the set of whole numbers is not closed under division but is closed under multiplication.

23. Why is the number line model most appropriate for illus-trating the repeated subtraction definition of division?

24. On page 120, the set model of division was defined as $b \div x = n(P_d) + r$ where d is any number from 1 to x, and r repre-sents the remainder, which is any number from 0 to $x - 1$. Explain the significance of the subscript d in P_d. What does its presence imply?

25. Is there an identity element for whole number division? Explain your answer.

Cooperative Activity

The Scottish mathematician John Napier (1550–1617) is cred-ited with inventing an interesting device for use when multiply-ing. This device has come to be known as Napier's rods or Napier's bones. In this activity, you will construct and use the rods as you discover the process involved.

26. Groups of two

Individual Accountability: Each partner is to construct a set of rods, all of the same size, for the numbers 0 through 9. A sam-ple rod illustrating the five times table is shown here:

Investigate how these rods are used to multiply 7×35.

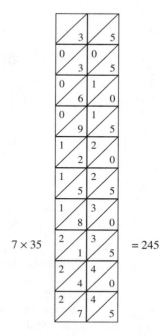

7×35 = 245

Group Goal: Share your conclusions with your partner. Together, explore how the rods might be used to find the products of 23×45, 57×123, and 375×198.

4.2 Algorithms for Whole Number Multiplication and Division

When elementary school students are first introduced to the traditional multiplication and division algorithms, they often become overwhelmed by the steps involved. The algorithmic procedures become ends in themselves. Often, students pay attention only to correctly completing the steps. As a teacher, it will be your job to see that students understand that the *meaning* of the procedure and the *context* in which it would appropriately be used are not overshadowed by mechanics. In this section, we present estimation techniques and alternative algorithms. We will stress the meaning of the algorithms of multiplication and division, which should help you better understand the significance of the products and quotients found.

Estimating Products and Quotients

The estimation techniques used for addition and subtraction can easily be modified for use in multiplication and division.

1. Rounding to Multiples of Ten. Consider the following example: A school auditorium has 52 rows. Each row contains 28 seats. Estimate the seating capacity of this auditorium.

A quick means of estimating this product is to round each factor to the nearest multiple of ten. It will then be possible to mentally multiply the leading digits and annex the appropriate number of zeros according to the rules of multiplication involving multiples of ten.

$$52 \;\rightarrow 50$$
$$\underline{\times 28} \;\rightarrow \underline{30}$$

$$
\begin{aligned}
50 \times 30 &= (5 \times 10) \times (3 \times 10) \\
&= (5 \times 10) \times (10 \times 3) && \text{by the commutative property} \\
&= 5 \times (10 \times 10) \times 3 && \text{by the associative property} \\
&= 5 \times 3 \times (10 \times 10) && \text{by the commutative property} \\
&= (5 \times 3) \times (10 \times 10) && \text{by the associative property} \\
&= 15 \times 100 \\
&= 1500
\end{aligned}
$$

You can easily perform these steps mentally. The product of 52 and 28 is approximately 1500. Therefore, the estimated seating capacity of the auditorium is approximately 1500 seats.

2. Rounding with Compensation. In the preceding example, one factor was rounded *up* to a multiple of ten whereas the other factor was rounded *down* to a multiple of ten. The resulting estimate of 1500 was quite accurate, since the actual seating capacity of the auditorium would be 1456. If, however, both factors are rounded up, or both factors are rounded down, the estimated product might be less accurate. In that case, you should compensate by adjusting the estimated product. Examine the following examples.

Case 1. A printer must put together 275 copies of a document that contains 87 pages. Approximately how many pages are necessary to complete the job?

In this situation, both 275 and 87 are rounded up as follows:

$$275 \rightarrow 300$$
$$\underline{\times\ 87} \rightarrow \underline{\ 90} \qquad (3 \times 9) \times (100 \times 10) = 27{,}000$$

Since both numbers were rounded up, we must adjust the estimated product. When attempting to adjust an estimate, focus on the larger of the two factors. Rounding 275 to 300 resulted in an additional 25 groups of 90 being added to the estimate. This can be seen by examining the distributive property as follows:

$$300 \times 90$$
$$(275 + 25) \times 90$$
$$(275 \times 90) + (25 \times 90)$$

The second of these two products represents the overage in the estimate of 27,000. This product itself can be estimated and deducted from the initial estimate. Since 25×90 is approximately 30×90, or 2700, the initial estimate of 27,000 should be decreased by approximately 3000. The revised estimate for the total number of pages is 24,000. This favorably compares to the actual product of 23,925.

Case 2. A certain employer contributes \$72 to the dental insurance plan for each of the 824 people she employs. What is the approximate total dental insurance contribution of the employer?

Notice that both 72 and 824 will be rounded down. This will result in an estimate that is considerably less than the actual amount. Compensation can be made as follows:

$$824 \rightarrow 800$$
$$\underline{\times\ 72} \rightarrow \underline{\ 70} \qquad (8 \times 7) \times (100 \times 10) = 56{,}000$$

Again, focus on the larger of the two factors. Rounding 824 to 800 resulted in a loss of 24 groups of 70 from the initial estimate. Since 24×70 is approximately 20×70, or 1400, the initial estimate should be increased by 1400. The revised estimate for the total contribution is 57,400.

The larger the factors involved, the greater will be the possible margin between the estimate and the actual answer. For example, when finding an estimate for the product of 1234 and 643, you might round both numbers down to 1000 and 600. Using this technique, the estimate would be 600,000, which doesn't come close to the actual product of 793,462. In cases such as this, you may need to use several steps of compensation before you reach an acceptable estimate. Remember, however, that if an accurate product is required with numbers of this magnitude, you should probably use a calculator.

To estimate quotients, you must understand the pattern found when the divisor and dividend are both multiples of ten. Use your calculator to uncover the regularity in the following examples.

$$560,000 \div 7000$$
$$56,000 \div 700$$
$$5600 \div 70$$
$$560 \div 7$$

Notice that in each case the quotient is 80. Beginning with the first line, and in each subsequent line, both the dividend and the divisor were divided by 10. Since this division occurred in both the dividend and the divisor, the quotient remained unchanged. When estimating quotients, first round both the dividend and the divisor to a multiple of ten. Determine the greatest power of 10 (10, 100, 1000, etc.) that divides both the dividend and the divisor. This power can be found by counting the number of zeros in each number. In the example above, 10,000 divides 560,000 but not 7000. The greatest power of 10 that divides both this dividend and divisor is 1000. Dividing by 1000 results in a quotient that has three fewer trailing zeros. Therefore, it remains only to divide 560 by 7, resulting in the estimated quotient of 80.

Investigation 7

The jackpot in a state lottery is $1,200,000. The single winner receives 20 equal payments spread out over 20 years. What is the approximate amount of each payment?

Both the dividend and the divisor are already multiples of ten. The greatest power of ten that divides both numbers is 10.

$$1,200,000 \div 20$$
$$120,000 \div 2$$

The quotient is 60,000. The winner will receive 20 annual payments of $60,000. This estimate is in fact a precise answer, because the dividend and the divisor were already multiples of ten, and no rounding was necessary.

Investigation 8

Sunnydale Elementary School, which has an enrollment of 411 students, is saving to build a jungle gym in its playground. The total cost of the project will be $1800. Each student is being asked to contribute 10 pennies per week. Given that the school year is 42 weeks, can this fund raising be accomplished in a single school year?

The solution to this problem will involve estimating both multiplication and division. Begin by estimating the contribution per student. Ten pennies per week for 42 weeks is 420 pennies. Estimating division by 100 (100 pennies = 1 dollar) results in a per-student contribution of approximately $4. Since this school has 411 students, the student population can be rounded to 400 to arrive at a total school contribution of $1600. Since this estimate is very close to the projected cost, you may want to use the following keystroke sequence to arrive at the precise amount.

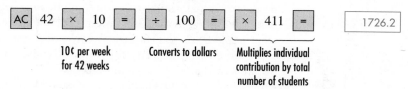

| AC | 42 | × | 10 | = | ÷ | 100 | = | × | 411 | = | | 1726.2 |

10¢ per week for 42 weeks   Converts to dollars   Multiplies individual contribution by total number of students

The display should read 1726.2. Notice that the calculator has dropped the final zero after the decimal point. This fund raising cannot be accomplished in one school year. Therefore the school may decide to increase the individual contribution, solicit funds from the community, or choose a less expensive jungle gym.

Procedures for Multiplying and Dividing

This section offers a variety of ways to find products and quotients. Some will be familiar to you and others will be new. Each algorithm is set within a context to underscore why students must understand the need for a particular operation.

Whole Number Multiplication

partial products method of whole number multiplication

1. Partial Products. The **partial products method of whole number multiplication** is based on an understanding of expanded notation and the distributive property of multiplication over addition.

Consider the following problem: The Jones family pays $750 per month in rent. What is their yearly rent expenditure?

An initial estimate would lead to an approximate yearly expenditure of $8000 ($800 \times 10$). The partial products method illustrates that 750 times 12 is equivalent to

$$750 \times (10 + 2) = (750 \times 10) + (750 \times 2)$$
$$= 7500 + 1500$$
$$= 9000$$

This expanded version of the partial products method of multiplication can be expressed alternately as follows:

$$
\begin{array}{r}
750 \\
\times\ \ 12 \\
\hline
1500 = 2 \times 750 \\
+ 7500 = 10 \times 750 \\
\hline
9000
\end{array}
$$

This illustration of the meaning behind the partial products method shows why students should be encouraged to write the final zero in the partial product of 7500 and not simply leave a space or write X. It is important that they realize that 7500 is obtained by multiplying 750 by 10, not 750 by 1.

lattice method of whole number multiplication

2. Lattice Multiplication. Recall the lattice method of addition introduced in Chapter 3, in which a grid was used to record the partial sums. The **lattice method of whole number multiplication** is very similar to this and has advantages over the standard partial products method, as illustrated in the following example. Assume that a certain business is budgeted to use 235 kilowatt hours of electricity per day. Based on this budget, what would be the total electricity consumption in one year?

Before performing any algorithm, it is advisable to get into the habit of estimating the answer. Here a rough estimate is 200×350, or 70,000 kilowatt hours. In the actual expression, 235×365, both factors contain three digits. A three by three lattice is necessary (the dimensions of the lattice depend on the number of digits in each factor).

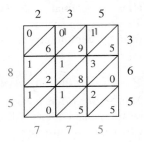

The business is budgeted for 85,775 kilowatt hours of electricity per year. This is somewhat close to our estimate of 70,000 kilowatt hours.

Notice the characteristics of the lattice method of multiplication. The cells in the lattice can be filled in any order. Individual partial products can be easily checked for correctness by examining the entries in each box. After all of the partial products have been inserted, then they are added. This contrasts with the standard partial products algorithm, in which the student needs to constantly multiply and then regroup. Finally, the lattice offers a simple organization of the digits. There is no danger of misaligning columns. Here are two other examples of lattice multiplication:

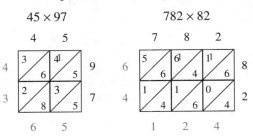

Russian peasant method of whole number multiplication

3. Russian Peasant Method. The **Russian peasant method of whole number multiplication** allows you to multiply multidigit numbers without knowing the times tables. Recall Problem 7 from Section 2.1. That problem illustrated an Egyptian method of multiplication that was based on repeated doubling of a quantity. The Russian peasant method is very similar.

Study the following example to determine the pattern: A ferry can accommodate a maximum of 34 automobiles. If the ferry is capable of 16 trips per day, how many automobiles can be transported in one day?

A good estimate of the total number of cars would be 600 (30 × 20). Using the Russian peasant method, two columns are set up as follows.

$$
\begin{array}{cc}
\cancel{34} & \cancel{16} \\
17 & 32 \\
\cancel{8} & \cancel{64} \\
\cancel{4} & \cancel{128} \\
\cancel{2} & \cancel{256} \\
1 & + 512 \\
\hline
 & 544
\end{array}
$$

Notice that the numbers on the left are repeatedly halved. When an odd number is halved (as in the case of 17), only the whole number portion of the quotient is recorded. The numbers on the right are repeatedly doubled. This process continues until the entry in the left-hand column is 1. Then any right-hand entry paired with an even number on the left is discarded. The remaining numbers in the right-hand column are added. This is the product of the two original numbers. Therefore, the ferry can transport up to 544 cars per day. For a discussion of why this method works, see *Projects to Enrich School Mathematics: Level 1*, National Council of Teachers of Mathematics (1974).

Whole Number Division

Egyptian method of whole number division

1. The Egyptian Method. The **Egyptian method of whole number division** is similar to the Egyptian method of whole number multiplication. The Egyptians relied heavily on a method called "duplation." Here, each line is the double of the line that precedes it. Recall from Chapter 2 that the Egyptians had a non–place value system that used a variety of symbols to represent number. Perhaps the doubling method was used because it was easy to draw duplicates (or doubles) of the symbols. Of course, this is just speculation. The Egyptian division method appears in many ancient scrolls. A somewhat casual translation of the directions to divide 192 by 16 would be "Make thou the operation on 16 for the finding of 192." In effect, this can be read as "What number times 16 is 192?" Examine the following problem: A cable car to a scenic overlook can hold a maximum of 16 people. How many trips are necessary to transport a tour of 192 people?

Set up two columns beginning with 16 (the divisor) and 1. This indicates a starting point of one group of 16. Repeatedly double both column entries. Stop when the next entry in the left-hand column would be greater than the "dividend."

$$
\begin{array}{ccc}
 & 16 & 1 \\
 & 32 & 2 \\
\sqrt{} & 64 & 4 \\
\sqrt{} & \underline{128} & \underline{8} \\
 & 192 & 12
\end{array}
$$

This method requires you to find a combination of the numbers in the left-hand column that add to the desired dividend. The doubling process is terminated at 128 since twice 128 would yield a number greater than 192. The sum of the numbers in the right-hand column that are associated with the desired combination in the left-hand column equals 12. Therefore, there are 12 groups of 16 in 192. Twelve trips will be necessary to transport the entire tour of 192 people.

subtractive method of whole number division

2. The Subtractive Method. The **subtractive method of whole number division** algorithm, although similar to the standard method of division, has as its primary advantage greater flexibility in finding partial quotients. Examine the following problem: The distance between two cities is 2703 miles. At an average speed of 50 miles per hour, approximately how many hours of driving time would the trip take?

An estimate of 60 hours is reasonable since $3000 \div 50 = 60$. The subtractive algorithm allows for repeated subtraction of groups of the divisor.

```
50 | 2703 | 10
     - 500
     2203  | 10
     - 500
     1703  | 10
     - 500
     1203  | 10
     - 500
      703  | 10
     - 500
      203  | 4
     - 200 |+
        3  | 54
```

This trip would take approximately 54 hours of driving time.

Had it been recognized that there are 50 groups of 50 in 2704, the scaffold would have appeared simpler, as shown here:

```
50 | 2703 | 50
     - 2500
      203  | 4
     - 200 |+
        3  | 54
```

Although this method is lengthy and somewhat impractical, it is useful to show students the process of division in this way so that they do not believe in some mystical operation called "guzinta."

standard algorithm method of whole number division

3. Standard Algorithm. The **standard algorithm method of whole number division** is a more efficient and compact version of the scaffold method. It is illustrated in the following example: A fruit-shipping company can pack 48 apples to a case. How many cases of apples need to be shipped for a 1296 apple order?

A quick estimate requires asking how many 50s there are in 1300. There are approximately 25 groups of 50 in 1300.

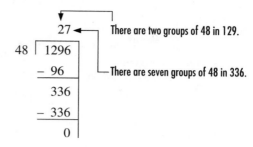

$$\begin{array}{r} 27 \\ 48 \overline{\smash{\big)}\ 1296} \\ -\ 96 \\ \hline 336 \\ -\ 336 \\ \hline 0 \end{array}$$

There are two groups of 48 in 129.

There are seven groups of 48 in 336.

Investigation 9

Three friends are at a sleep-over party. They decide to share a bowl of candy the following morning. During the night, one of the friends divides the candy into three equal shares, giving the one extra piece to her cat. She then hides her share and goes back to sleep. Later that night, another of the friends again divides what is left of the candy into three equal shares, giving the one extra piece to the cat. She also hides her share and then returns to sleep. The third friend later awakens and does the same thing. The next morning, the friends divide what is left of the candy into three equal shares, again giving the one extra piece to the cat. What is the fewest number of pieces of candy that originally could have been in the bowl?

Understand the Problem: What is given? A certain amount of candy is divided into three equal shares with one piece remaining. One share is then removed. This process is repeated three more times.
What is unknown? You must determine the fewest number of candies that can accomplish this process.

Devise a Plan: You can attempt to solve this problem by randomly choosing a number that can be divided by three with one remainder. To get a better understanding of this problem, make a chart.

Carry Out the Plan: Assume, for example, that the bowl initially contained 46 pieces of candy.

46

Friend 1:	15	15	15	+1 (cat)
Friend 2:	10	10	10	+0 (cat)

This trial clearly does not work since there is a contradiction with the given information: There is no leftover candy for the second friend to give the cat.
Try the number 64.

64

Friend 1:	21	21	21	+1 (cat)
Friend 2:	14	14	14	+0 (cat)

Again this contradicts the given information. There is no leftover candy for the second friend to give the cat.

Let's try again with 79.

79

Friend 1:	26	26	26	+1 (cat)
Friend 2:	17	17	17	+1 (cat)
Friend 3:	11	11	11	+1 (cat)
Next morning:	7	7	7	+1 (cat)

Seventy-nine appears to be the solution to the problem.

Look Back:

working backwards

But how can you be sure that 79 is the smallest number of candies that could have been in the bowl? It is possible to use the strategy of trial and error and continue choosing numbers less than 79. It may be more efficient, though, to utilize the strategy of **working backwards**. This strategy focuses on a possible solution and then works regressively through the problem to see if the solution fulfills the requirements of the problem statement.

When the friends divide the remaining candies in the morning, the smallest individual share could be one piece of candy. Again, we will make a chart, but this time working backwards from a possible solution.

Next morning: 1   1   1   +1 (cat)

Friend 3: At this step, it is necessary to divide the total of four candies into two shares since the four represents the two shares that were split up the next morning. Consequently, each friend's share must be equal to two candies, and the cat must be given one candy. At this stage, seven candies must have been involved.

2   2   2   +1 (cat)

Friend 2: Here it is necessary to divide the total of seven candies into two equal shares. This cannot be done since 2 does not divide 7. The conclusion that must be drawn is that the final share was not one piece of candy. However, subsequent trials should not be random trials since it would be possible to skip the solution that yields the fewest number of candies. You should now try consecutive whole numbers from 2 to 6 to make sure that there is not a number less than 7 that satisfies the conditions of the problem. It is left to you to continue with this strategy of working backwards.

Multiplication and Division in Other Bases

Perhaps when you were in elementary school, you constructed multiplication tables. The following is such a table for multiplication in base six.

×	0	1	2	3	4	5
0	0	0	0	0	0	0
1	0	1	2	3	4	5
2	0	2	4	10	12	14
3	0	3	10	13	20	23
4	0	4	12	20	24	32
5	0	5	14	23	32	41

Use this table to determine the product of 355_{six} and 423_{six}. For multiplication in other bases, perhaps the clearest method is the lattice method of multiplication, in which the partial products are written in individual cells.

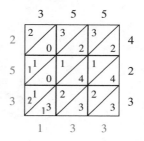

The product is read 253133_{six}. It is left to you to verify this product by using the standard partial products algorithm.

You have already seen that multiplication and division are inverse operations on base ten whole numbers. This relationship can be extended to numbers in other bases. For example, examine the base six multiplication chart that shows that $5_{six} \times 4_{six} = 32_{six}$. It therefore follows that $32_{six} \div 4_{six} = 5_{six}$. We will use the subtractive method to illustrate this division example.

$$32_{six}$$
$$\underline{-4_{six}} \quad 1$$
$$24_{six}$$
$$\underline{-4_{six}} \quad 1$$
$$20_{six}$$
$$\underline{-4_{six}} \quad 1$$
$$12_{six}$$
$$\underline{-4_{six}} \quad 1$$
$$4_{six}$$
$$\underline{-4_{six}} \quad 1$$
$$0 \quad 5_{six} = \text{Total}$$

Now we will extend this process to illustrate 1544_{six} divided by 13_{six}. We will use the facts that $10_{six} \times 13_{six} = 130_{six}$ and that $5_{six} \times 13_{six} = 113_{six}$ to facilitate this division process.

$$
\begin{array}{r|l}
13_{six} \quad 1544_{six} & \\
-\ 130 & 10 \\
\hline
1414 & \\
-\ 130 & 10 \\
\hline
1244 & \\
-\ 130 & 10 \\
\hline
1114 & \\
-\ 130 & 10 \\
\hline
544 & \\
-\ 130 & 10 \\
\hline
414 & \\
-\ 130 & 10 \\
\hline
244 & \\
-\ 113 & 10 \\
\hline
114 & \\
-\ 113 & 5 \\
\hline
1 & 115_6 = \text{Total}
\end{array}
$$

The quotient is 115_{six} with a remainder of 1_{six}.

Assessments for Section 4.2

1. Estimate each product. Justify the appropriateness of the method of estimation you choose.
   (a) 257×360
   (b) 8145×728
   (c) 92×126
   (d) 51×828
   (e) $10,865 \times 2917$

2. Estimate each quotient. Justify the appropriateness of the method of estimation you choose.
   (a) $294 \div 14$
   (b) $165 \div 11$
   (c) $6023 \div 317$
   (d) $18,360 \div 1080$
   (e) $252 \div 28$

3. Estimate the value of the missing term. Use a calculator to check the accuracy of your estimate.
   (a) $89 \times \underline{\quad} = 4984$
   (b) $\underline{\quad} \times 36 = 5724$
   (c) $\underline{\quad} \times 197 = 19,306$
   (d) $24 \times \underline{\quad} = 16,752$
   (e) $897 \times \underline{\quad} = 46,644$

4. Estimate the value of the missing term. Use a calculator to check the accuracy of your estimate.
   (a) $11,928 \div \underline{\quad} = 568$
   (b) $4810 \div \underline{\quad} = 65$
   (c) $\underline{\quad} \div 54 = 369$
   (d) $\underline{\quad} \div 25 = 711$
   (e) $\underline{\quad} \div \underline{\quad} = 154$

5. Estimate the product. Then multiply using the partial products algorithm.

   (a) 362×17 (b) 531×129

6. Estimate the product. Then solve the problem using the lattice algorithm.

   (a) 428×193 (b) 724×56

7. Estimate the product. Then solve the problem using the Russian peasant algorithm.

   (a) 27×34 (b) 59×16

8. Estimate the quotient. Then solve the problem using the Egyptian algorithm.

   (a) $253 \div 23$ (b) $465 \div 31$

9. Estimate the quotient. Then solve the problem using the subtractive algorithm.

   (a) $42 \overline{)21{,}252}$ (b) $79 \overline{)4424}$

10. Tim purchased two tickets to a raffle. The tickets were numbered consecutively. The product of the ticket numbers is 65,792. The sum of the ticket numbers is 513. What are Tim's ticket numbers?

11. At Manta Ray High School, all lockers have four-digit identification numbers. On the right-hand side of the main hall, the identification numbers are consecutive even numbers. The product of two adjacent locker identification numbers is 2,088,024. The sum of the two adjacent locker numbers is 2890. On one of the lockers, a digit is repeated three times. On the other locker, a digit is repeated twice. What are the locker numbers in question?

12. Tickets are numbered as follows:

   A1 B4 C2 D8 E4 F16 G8 H32 . . .

   What number is on the ticket that begins with the letter S?

13. Determine the missing digits.

   (a)
   ```
        3 _ 7
      × 9 _ _
      2 _ 1 6
      3 _ _
    2 _ 4 3
    _ _ 0 1 _ 6
   ```
   (b)
   ```
        4 _ _ 4
      ×   _ _
      3 _ _ 9 8
    2 _ 8 _ 4
    2 _ _ 0 3 8
   ```

14. Use the digits 2, 3, 4, 5, and 6 only once to determine the indicated solution in

   $$(\underline{\quad} \div \underline{\quad}) + [(\underline{\quad} \div \underline{\quad}) \times \underline{\quad}] = 12$$

15. A pencil manufacturer has 632,675,280 pencils in stock. They are to be packed in boxes of 40 pencils each. How many boxes will be needed? Will there be any pencils left

over? Determine the solution to this problem in at least two different ways.

16. At the beginning of a trip, Ned's odometer read 56,715. At the end of the trip, the odometer read 58,235. Ned's car gets approximately 16 miles per gallon. If gas cost Ned about $1.39 per gallon, what was his gas expense for this trip?

17. Suppose that the $\boxed{7}$ key does not operate on your calculator.

   (a) How can you find the product of 273 and 13?

   (b) Can you do this in more than one way?

18. Suppose that both the $\boxed{4}$ and $\boxed{9}$ keys do not operate on your calculator.

   (a) How can you find the quotient of 3038 and 49?

   (b) Can you do this problem in more than one way?

19. Determine the values of A, B, C, and D in the following lattice multiplication of $A87 \times BC$:

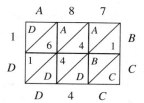

20. The digits 0, 1, 2, 3, 4, 5, 6, 7, 8, and 9 are to be used only once to form three, three-digit numbers. The second three-digit number must be twice the first three-digit number. The third three-digit number must be three times the first three-digit number. Find two sets of three such three-digit numbers.

21. A garage contains a number of bicycles, tricycles, and wagons. The total number of wheels on all the "vehicles" is 44. How many of each type of vehicle are there?

22. A copy machine produces 80 copies per minute. It takes 5 seconds to fold each copy, and 25 seconds to stuff, seal, address, and stamp each envelope. Assuming that the copies are made first and then one person works alone on the rest of the job, how long would the entire process take for 200 single-page copies of a letter?

23. A mail-order fruit company ships three sizes of gift packages: X, Y, and Z. The weight of one Y package is equivalent to the weight of four X packages. Twenty Z packages are equivalent to the weight of one Y package. How many X packages are equivalent to the weight of one Z package?

24. Suppose that a mathematical operation $\otimes$ exists. Each of the following statements containing the $\otimes$ operation are true.

$$5 \otimes 3 = 122$$
$$6 \otimes 2 = 34$$
$$1 \otimes 1 = 0$$
$$7 \otimes 2 = 47$$
$$2 \otimes 5 = 27$$
$$3 \otimes 4 = 77$$
$$10 \otimes 9 = 999,999,991$$

Determine a definition of the operation $\otimes$. What would be the result of $4 \otimes 4$? Would this operation be closed on the set of whole numbers? Explain your answer.

25. Determine the value of each of the following terms:

$$9 \times 1 + 2 \qquad 9 \times 12 + 3$$
$$9 \times 123 + 4 \qquad 9 \times 1234 + 5$$

Write a similar expression that would be equivalent to 11,111,111.

26. Determine the product in the indicated base.
    (a) $123_{four} \times 331_{four}$ (b) $1001_{two} \times 110_{two}$
    (c) $43_{five} \times 41_{five}$ (d) $801_{nine} \times 67_{nine}$

27. Use your solutions in Problem 26 to rewrite each multiplication as a division. Use the subtractive method of division to verify that your solutions in Problem 26 are correct.

In Other Words

28. Describe the role compensation plays in estimation.

29. Define a partial product. Discuss the similarities between partial sums and partial products.

30. How is it that adding along the diagonal in lattice multiplication yields the correct final product?

31. Is there a relationship between the partial products multiplication algorithm and the lattice multiplication algorithm? If so, describe the relationship.

32. Write a formal, generalizable definition of the concept of a remainder in division.

Cooperative Activity

33. **Groups of two:** (a closer look at the Russian peasant method)

Individual Accountability: Use the Russian peasant method of multiplication to individually determine the following products:

$$8 \times 10 \qquad 23 \times 45 \qquad 36 \times 839 \qquad 250 \times 58$$

Be prepared to explain to your partner how you arrived at your answer.

Group Goal: Compare your method and solutions to the above four examples with your partner. Together, develop a justification for this method. Use the following questions to focus your investigation.

1. Is the same product obtained if the order of the multiplier and multiplicand is reversed?

2. The expression 23×45 is sometimes interpreted as "23 groups of 45." How does this language relate to the Russian peasant method?

3. Why is the remainder dropped when, for instance, half of 11 is recorded as 5?

4. Under what circumstances will the remainder be dropped?

5. Do you see any connection between the Egyptian method of multiplication and the Russian peasant method?

4.3   # Number Theory in the Context of Multiplication and Division: Primes, Composites, and Divisibility

Recall that in the whole number product $a \cdot b$, both a and b are whole number factors of ab. In this text, the set of factors of whole numbers considered will be limited to whole number factors. We will now present a method that can be used to visually represent the factors of a whole number.

Obtain a package of small self-adhesive post-it notes. You may have to trim a rectangular pad to form squares (do not trim off the adhesive end). Number a sheet of lined paper along the left-hand margin with the numbers from 1 to 25. These numbers represent the number of adhesive notes you will use to form a square or rectangle at any given time.

For example, let's use four of the square post-its. How many different rectangular arrangements are possible with these four squares? Examine Figure 4.6.

Figure 4.6

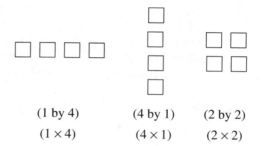

(1 by 4)   (4 by 1)   (2 by 2)

(1×4) (4×1) (2×2)

Three arrangements are possible: (1×4), (4×1), and (2×2). List these three arrangements next to the number 4 in your chart. Continue in this manner for all of the numbers from 1 to 25. Can you make any generalizations about the nature of the numbers that are listed?

You have found the factors of each number from 1 to 25 using a geometric or array model of multiplication. This model views each number as the area of rectangular regions of different dimensions. For example, in Figure 4.6 each area is four squares. The dimensions of the rectangles formed by these four squares are not unique.

Examine the set of dimensions that are listed next to each of the numbers from 1 to 25. Notice the similarities among the dimensions listed next to the numbers 2, 3, 5, 7, 11, 13, 17, 19, and 23. These rectangular regions could be formed in only two ways. For example, a rectangle made up of 23 squares could have only the dimensions 1 by 23, or 23 by 1. No other whole number dimensions would make up such a rectangle. This is another way of saying that these numbers, 2, 3, 5, 7, 11, 13, 17, 19, and 23, have only two distinct factors: themselves and 1. Numbers having this characteristic are called

prime number

prime numbers. A **prime number** is a number that has two and only two unique factors: itself and 1.

But should the number 1 be considered prime? Clearly, from the activity with the post-its (Figure 4.6), you can see that only one rectangle could be formed. The dimensions of that rectangle represent the factors of the number. One has a single factor. By definition, a prime has two unique factors. Therefore, 1 is not considered a prime number.

Prime Factorization

Numbers that can be represented by more than two possible arrays have more than two

composite numbers

factors. These numbers are called **composite numbers**. Every composite number can be expressed as a multiplicative composition of prime factors. This composition, which

prime factorization

is expressed as a product of primes, is called the **prime factorization** of a composite number. An easy, visual way of determining the prime factors of any composite number is to use a factor tree diagram. Follow the steps illustrated below to determine the prime factorization of 24.

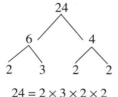

$$24 = 2 \times 3 \times 2 \times 2$$

Find any two factors whose product is the number itself. Here, 6 and 4 are both factors of 24. Neither of these two factors is prime. Therefore, repeat the process by expressing each of these factors as a product. Since the factors that now appear in the tree diagram are prime numbers, the process is complete.

The commutative property of multiplication allows this factorization to be rewritten as $24 = 2 \times 2 \times 2 \times 3$. It is standard procedure to write the product of primes in ascending order. A simpler, more compact way of expressing this factorization is by using exponents. Since $2^3 = 2 \times 2 \times 2$, the prime factorization can be written as $24 = 2^3 \times 3$.

The factor tree for 24 could also have looked like this:

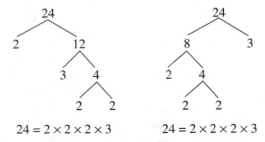

$$24 = 2 \times 2 \times 2 \times 3 \qquad 24 = 2 \times 2 \times 2 \times 3$$

Even though the factor trees appear to be different, notice that the prime factorization is not. The prime factorization of every composite number is unique. In other words, each number has only one prime factorization.

The prime factorization of a composite number can be used to determine all of the factors of that number. Consider once again the prime factorization of 24:

$$24 = 2 \times 2 \times 2 \times 3$$

Obviously, 1 is a factor of every number and will be included in the set of factors. Examine the various ways in which this factorization can be represented by using the commutative and associative properties.

Product	*Factor*
$(2) \times (2 \times 2 \times 3)$	2
$(2 \times 2 \times 2) \times (3)$	3
$(2 \times 2) \times (2 \times 3)$	4
$(2 \times 2) \times (2 \times 3)$	6
$(2 \times 2 \times 2) \times 3$	8
$(2) \times (2 \times 2 \times 3)$	12
$(2 \times 2 \times 2 \times 3)$	24

Notice the pattern in this process. Initially, single primes (2, 3) are recognized as factors. Then "product pairs" of primes (2×2, 2×3), followed by "product triples" ($2 \times 2 \times 2$, $2 \times 2 \times 3$) are listed. Finally, "product quadruples" of primes ($2 \times 2 \times 2 \times 3$) are recognized. In this case, the product quadruple yields the number itself. In some cases, it will be necessary to list product quintuples, sextuples, and beyond.

Investigation 10

The Martinsons are having a dinner party. Eighteen people will be at the party. A rental company rents tables of different sizes. What size tables could the Martinsons consider renting provided that they want to seat the same number of people at each table?

 Understand the Problem: You are told that 18 people will be attending a dinner party and that the hosts want the guests to be seated at tables each containing the same number of people. You must determine the possible arrangements.

Devise a Plan: Use the strategy of making a chart.

Carry Out the Plan: The Martinsons need to determine all of the factors of 18. This can be accomplished as follows:

$$18 = 2 \times 3 \times 3$$

The product groupings that will yield the factors are

Product	Factor
$(2) \times (3 \times 3)$	2
$(2 \times 3) \times (3)$	3
$(2 \times 3) \times (3)$	6
$(2) \times (3 \times 3)$	9
$(2 \times 3 \times 3)$	18

The set of factors of 18 is $\{1, 2, 3, 6, 9, 18\}$. Knowing these factors, the Martinsons can now plan the table arrangements. They can order any of the following number of tables:

1 table, which will seat 18 people, since $1 \times 18 = 18$

2 tables, each seating 9 people, since $2 \times 9 = 18$

3 tables, each seating 6 people, since $3 \times 6 = 18$

6 tables, each seating 3 people, since $6 \times 3 = 18$

9 tables, each seating 2 people, since $9 \times 2 = 18$

18 tables, each seating 1 person, since $18 \times 1 = 18$

Look Back: Since there are six factors of 18, six arrangements are possible.

What if the prime factorization of a number is not available to you? What if you wish to test whether or not a number is prime or composite? Using a calculator to test for divisibility by every whole number less than the number in question is tedious and time-consuming. Let's investigate this situation by examining the factors of 24 and 80.

You already know that 24 and 80 are both composite numbers. Examine the list of product pairs which form each of these numbers.

24	80
1×24	1×80
2×12	2×40
3×8	4×40
4×6	5×16
6×4	8×10
8×3	10×8
12×2	16×5
24×1	20×4
	40×2
	80×1

Notice that halfway down each list, the order of the product pair reverses. Where does this change occur? Under the heading of 24, the reversal occurs between the factors of 4 and 6. Under the heading of 80, the reversal occurs between the factors of 8 and 10. It is no coincidence that the square root of 24 falls between 4 and 6 ($\sqrt{24} \approx 4.89897$), and the square root of 80 falls between 8 and 10 ($\sqrt{80} \approx 8.94427$). This suggests that when building lists of product pairs, it is only necessary to test for divisibility up to the square root of the number.

Now, let's apply this knowledge to test whether or not a number is prime. Suppose that you wish to determine if 283 is a prime number. It will be necessary to test only prime divisors since every composite number is itself a product of primes. Examine the following table and look for patterns. Where does the "switching point" occur?

Prime Factor	Keystroke	Calculator Display	Approximation
2	$283 \div 2$	141.5	$2 \times 141 \approx 283$
3	$283 \div 3$	94.333333	$3 \times 94 \approx 283$
5	$283 \div 5$	56.6	$5 \times 56 \approx 283$
7	$283 \div 7$	40.428571	$7 \times 40 \approx 283$
11	$283 \div 11$	25.727272	$11 \times 25 \approx 283$
13	$283 \div 13$	21.76923	$13 \times 21 \approx 283$
17	$283 \div 17$	16.647057	$17 \times 16 \approx 283$

Let's stop at this point to examine the factors of the approximation product in the last column above. Notice that as the first factor increased (2, 3, 5, 7, 11, . . .), the second factor decreased (141, 94, 56, 40, 25, . . .), with the larger of the two factors remaining to the right of the multiplication symbol until the last row of the table. Here the pattern begins to reverse itself. This switching point occurs between the prime factors of 13 and 17. Notice that the square root of 283 is approximately 16.82260, which falls between the prime factors of 13 and 17. Once again, this suggests that it was only necessary to test the prime factors up to the square root of the number in question. Since 283 has no prime factors that are less than $\sqrt{283}$, we conclude that 283 must be a prime number.

Therefore, we can make the following generalization when testing the factors of a number:

Rule: To test whether or not a number X is prime, it is necessary to test only for divisibility by those primes that are less than $\sqrt{X}$.

Finally, it is important to recognize that if two numbers have a common factor, both their sum and difference will share the common factor. To explain this, suppose that x and y are both whole numbers, each of which has a factor of z. The number x can be written as the product of z and some whole number $r (x = z \cdot r)$. Similarly, y can be written as the product of z and some whole number $s (y = z \cdot s)$. The sum of x and y can be expressed as

$$x + y = z \cdot r + z \cdot s$$

And by the distributive property,

$$x + y = z \cdot (r + s)$$

Clearly, z is a factor of the sum of x and y.

For the difference between x and y to be a whole number, it is necessary to first stipulate that $x \geq y$. Using the expressions for x and y from above, the difference between x and y can be written as

$$x - y = z \cdot r - z \cdot s$$

And by the distributive property,

$$x - y = z \cdot (r - s)$$

Again, it is clear that z is a factor of the difference.

In general, if x, y, and z are whole numbers, and $z \mid x$ and $z \mid y$, then $z \mid (x + y)$ and $z \mid (x - y)$.

Exponents

The prime factorization of a composite number is often expressed using exponents. An exponent can take a variety of forms. It does not necessarily have to be a whole number. For the purposes of this section, however, we will examine the characteristics of exponents that are whole numbers. In any number expressed using an exponent of the form **base, power, exponent** a^M, a is called the **base**, and M is the **power**, or **exponent**.

Examine the following product:

$$a \cdot a \cdot a \cdot a \cdot a \cdot a = a^6$$

By the associative property of multiplication, this product can be expressed in a variety of forms, some of which are listed here:

$$a \cdot (a \cdot a \cdot a \cdot a \cdot a) = a^1 \cdot a^5 = a^6$$
$$(a \cdot a) \cdot (a \cdot a \cdot a \cdot a) = a^2 \cdot a^4 = a^6$$
$$(a \cdot a \cdot a) \cdot (a \cdot a \cdot a) = a^3 \cdot a^3 = a^6$$
$$(a \cdot a \cdot a \cdot a) \cdot (a \cdot a) = a^4 \cdot a^2 = a^6$$
$$(a \cdot a \cdot a \cdot a \cdot a) \cdot a = a^5 \cdot a^1 = a^6$$

Notice the exponential form of a^6 written after the first set of equal signs. What generalization can be made about the relationship between these exponents and the exponent 6? In each of the cases presented above, the sum of the exponents is equal to 6. Does this hold only for product pairs? Examine the following grouping of a^6.

$$a^6 = a \cdot a \cdot a \cdot a \cdot a \cdot a = (a \cdot a) \cdot (a \cdot a) \cdot (a \cdot a) = a^2 \cdot a^2 \cdot a^2$$

Once again, the sum of the exponents in the product triple $(2 + 2 + 2)$ is equal to 6. In general, the following rule applies when multiplying exponents with like bases:

Rule: Let X and Y be whole numbers. Then

$$a^X \cdot a^Y = a^{X+Y}$$

For example, $a^3 \cdot a^2 = a^{3+2} = a^5$.

This rule does not apply when the bases are different. Examine the following:

$$a \cdot a \cdot a \cdot a \cdot b \cdot b \cdot b \cdot b \cdot b \cdot b = (a \cdot a \cdot a \cdot a) \cdot (b \cdot b \cdot b \cdot b \cdot b \cdot b) = a^4 \cdot b^6$$

Each base is expressed separately using exponents. There is a special case, however, in which all bases are raised to the same exponent or power. For example,

$$
\begin{aligned}
a^3 \cdot b^3 = a \cdot a \cdot a \cdot b \cdot b \cdot b &= (a \cdot a \cdot a) \cdot (b \cdot b \cdot b) \quad \text{by the associative property} \\
&= a \cdot a \cdot (a \cdot b) \cdot b \cdot b \quad \text{by the associative property} \\
&= a \cdot a \cdot b \cdot b \cdot (a \cdot b) \quad \text{by the commutative property} \\
&= a \cdot (a \cdot b) \cdot b \cdot (a \cdot b) \quad \text{by the associative property} \\
&= a \cdot b \cdot (a \cdot b) \cdot (a \cdot b) \quad \text{by the commutative property} \\
&= (a \cdot b) \cdot (a \cdot b) \cdot (a \cdot b) \quad \text{by the associative property} \\
&= (a \cdot b)^3
\end{aligned}
$$

The following rule will apply when two different bases are raised to the same power:

Rule: Let a and b be whole numbers, and c any whole number not equal to zero. Then

$$a^c \cdot b^c = (a \cdot b)^c$$

For example,
$$5^3 \cdot 2^3 = 125 \cdot 8 = 1000 = (5 \cdot 2)^3 = 10^3$$
$$5^3 \cdot 2^3 = 125 \cdot 8 = 1000 = (10)^3 = (5 \cdot 2)^3$$

Numbers expressed as a base raised to a certain power can themselves be raised to an exponent. Consider the following example:

$$(2^3)^4 = (2^3) \cdot (2^3) \cdot (2^3) \cdot (2^3)$$
$$= 2^{3+3+3+3}$$
$$= 2^{12}$$

Notice that the single exponent in the final statement is the product of the two exponents in the original statement. This leads us to the following generalization:

Rule: Let a be any whole number. Let b and c be any nonzero whole numbers. Then

$$(a^b)^c = a^{bc}$$

Finally, examine $125 \div 25$. Clearly, the quotient is 5. Both the dividend and the divisor can be expressed as numbers raised to a power, as shown here:

$$125 \div 25 = 5^3 \div 5^2 = 5^1$$

Notice that the quotient is the same base as both the dividend and the divisor and that the exponent of the quotient is the difference between the exponent of the dividend and the exponent of the divisor. This leads us to the following generalization:

Rules: Let a be a nonzero whole number. Let b and c be whole numbers with $b > c$. Then

$$a^b \div a^c = a^{b-c}$$

Notice that the rule excluded the case where $b = c$. This requires special attention. In the case where $b = c$, the rule can be applied with the following interesting result:

$$a^b \div a^c = a^{b-c} = a^0 = 1 \qquad \text{(by definition)}$$

This is intuitive, since any number divided by itself is equal to 1.

Investigation 11

The prime factorization of 50 is $2 \times 5 \times 5$, or $2^1 \times 5^2$. How many factors does 50 have?

The factors of 50 can be found by grouping product pairs, triples, and so on, and then counting the number of factors listed.

$$50 = 2 \times 5 \times 5$$
$$= 2 \times 5 \times 5$$
$$= 2 \times 5 \times 5$$
$$= (2 \times 5) \times 5$$
$$= 2 \times (5 \times 5)$$

Fifty has six factors: $\{1, 2, 5, 10, 25, 50\}$. This answer could have been found in another way. Examine each of the factors expressed as a product of primes.

Factor	Expressed as a Product of Primes Using Exponents
1	$2^0 \times 5^0$
2	$2^1 \times 5^0$
5	$2^0 \times 5^1$
10	$2^1 \times 5^1$
25	$2^0 \times 5^2$
50	$2^1 \times 5^2$

Notice there are two forms in which 2 is the base $(2^0, 2^1)$, and three forms in which 5 is the base $(5^0, 5^1, 5^2)$. It is not a coincidence that the total number of factors of 50 is six (2×3). Knowing this enables you to determine the number of factors that will be generated before you actually do so. For example, since the prime factorization of 360 is $2^3 \times 3^2 \times 5^1$, we can determine that there will be 24 factors. Each of the factors of 360 can be expressed as a product of the primes 2, 3, and 5 using exponents. There will be four forms in which 2 is the base $(2^0, 2^1, 2^2, 2^3)$, three forms in which 3 is the base $(3^0, 3^1, 3^2)$, and two forms in which 5 is the base $(5^0, 5^1)$. The fact that there are 24 factors is determined by finding the product of 4, 3, and 2.

Rule: In general, if a number is written as a product of x primes $p_1, p_2, p_3, \ldots, p_x$, in the form $p_1^a, p_2^b, p_3^c, \ldots, p_x^z$, then the total number of factors possible is $(a + 1) \times (b + 1) \times (c + 1) \times \cdots \times (z + 1)$.

Divisibility

It is often important to be able to easily determine whether or not a certain number is a divisor (factor) of another number. Recall that a number A is said to divide B (symbolized by $A \mid B$) if there is a whole number C such that $B = A \times C$. If such a number C can be found, B is said to be *divisible* by A. A variety of "tests" can be used to mentally determine whether a number is divisible by each of the numbers 2 through 12. The statement and explanation of each of these tests is presented here. Similar divisibility tests are grouped together.

1. Test for Divisibility by 2. A number is divisible by 2 if and only if the digit in the ones place is 0, 2, 4, 6, or 8; that is, if the number itself is even. In Section 1.3, you learned about the biconditional "if and only if." Remember that when statements include this phrase, the relationship must also hold when the order of the statement is reversed. For example, a number is divisible by 2 if it is an even number. Correspondingly, if a number is an even number, then it is divisible by 2.

The proof of this test relies on the rule that if $a \mid x$ and $a \mid y$, then $a \mid (x + y)$. Let ABC represent a three-digit number. Then

$$ABC = 100A + 10B + C$$

It is clear that $2 \mid (100A)$, since $100A = 2 \times (50A)$. In addition, $2 \mid (10B)$, since $10B = 2 \times (5B)$. Therefore, ABC can be expressed as $2(50A) + 2(5B) + C$. If C can be expressed as $2N$, where N is a whole number, then it can be concluded that $2 \mid ABC$. It follows therefore that if C is an even number, 2 will divide ABC.

2. Test for Divisibility by 4. Two tests can be used to determine if a number is divisible by 4.

   (a) A number is divisible by 4 if and only if it is divisible by 2 twice. Any whole number N that is divisible by 4 would have a prime factorization that has at least two 2s in it. ($N = 2 \times 2 \times \cdots$). If the number is even, then it obviously has at least one factor of 2. Divide the number by 2 and determine the quotient. If this quotient is even, then it is also divisible by 2. Clearly, the original number was divisible by 2 twice. For example, 352 is divisible by 4 since it is even (divisible by 2), and the quotient of 352 and 2, 176, is also even (divisible by 2). Three hundred fifty-two is divisible by 2 twice. Therefore, it is divisible by 4.

   (b) A number is divisible by 4 if and only if its last two digits form a number that is divisible by 4. Examine 352, which has already been shown to be divisible by 4.

$$352 = 3 \times 100 + 52$$

   Clearly, 4 divides 100; therefore, 4 will divide 3×100. Fifty-two is divisible by 4 since it is divisible by 2 twice. The sum of two numbers that are both divisible by 4 yields a number divisible by 4.

   The number 6714 is not divisible by 4:

$$6714 = 67 \times 100 + 14$$

Four divides 67×100, but 4 does not divide 14.

3. Test for Divisibility by 3. A number is divisible by 3 if and only if the sum of its digits is divisible by 3. This warrants an explanation. Examine the case of the number 7335 (which is divisible by 3) and the number 2168 (which is not divisible by 3).

$$7335 = 7 \cdot 10^3 + 3 \cdot 10^2 + 3 \cdot 10^1 + 5 \cdot 10^0 \qquad 2168 = 2 \cdot 10^3 + 1 \cdot 10^2 + 6 \cdot 10^1 + 8 \cdot 10^0$$
$$= 7 \cdot 1000 + 3 \cdot 100 + 3 \cdot 10 + 5 \cdot 1 \qquad\qquad = 2 \cdot 1000 + 1 \cdot 100 + 6 \cdot 10 + 8 \cdot 1$$

Neither of these expansions clearly show whether or not the number is divisible by 3. Therefore, we will use the fact that any number containing only 9s as digits is divisible by 3 to complete this explanation.

$$7335 = 7 \cdot 1000 + 3 \cdot 100 + 3 \cdot 10 + 5 \cdot 1$$
$$7335 = 7 \cdot (999 + 1) + 3 \cdot (99 + 1) + 3 \cdot (9 + 1) + 5$$
$$= (7 \cdot 999) + 7 \cdot 1 + (3 \cdot 99) + 3 \cdot 1 + (3 \cdot 9) + 3 \cdot 1 + 5 \quad \text{by the distributive property}$$
$$= \underbrace{(7 \cdot 999) + (3 \cdot 99) + (3 \cdot 9)}_{\text{Known divisible by 3}} + \underbrace{7 + 3 + 3 + 5}_{\text{Sum of the digits of 7335}} \quad \text{by the commutative property}$$

Since 7335 is divisible by 3, the partial sums above must each be divisible by 3. Therefore, the sum of the digits must be divisible by 3 ($7 + 3 + 3 + 5 = 18$ and $3 \mid 18$). It is easy to tell whether a number is divisible by 3 just by finding the sum of its digits. If 3 divides that sum, then the number is divisible by 3. Now examine what happens with 2168 when tested for divisibility by 3.

$$2168 = 2 \cdot 1000 + 1 \cdot 100 + 6 \cdot 10 + 8 \cdot 1$$

$$2168 = 2 \cdot (999 + 1) + 1 \cdot (99 + 1) + 6 \cdot (9 + 1) + 8$$

$$= (2 \cdot 999) + 2 \cdot 1 + (1 \cdot 99) + 1 \cdot 1 + (6 \cdot 9) + 6 \cdot 1 + 8 \quad \text{by the distributive property}$$

$$= \underbrace{(2 \cdot 999) + (1 \cdot 99) + (6 \cdot 9)}_{\text{Known divisible by 3}} + \underbrace{2 + 1 + 6 + 8}_{\text{Sum of the digits of 2168}} \quad \text{by the commutative property}$$

For 2168 to be divisible by 3, each of these partial sums must be divisible by 3. But $2 + 1 + 6 + 8 = 17$, which is not divisible by 3. Therefore, 3 does not divide 2168.

4. Test for Divisibility by 9.   A number is divisible by 9 if and only if the sum of its digits is divisible by 9. The same reasoning that is used for the test for divisibility by 3 is applied here. Since $7 + 3 + 3 + 5 = 18$, and 18 is divisible by 9, 7335 is also divisible by 9.

5. Test for Divisibility by 5.   A number is divisible by 5 if and only if the digit in the units place is a 0 or a 5, or in other words, is divisible by 5. Examine the set of multiples of 5: $\{5, 10, 15, 20, 25, \dots \}$. All multiples of 5 have a 0 or a 5 in the ones place.

6. Test for Divisibility by 10.   A number is divisible by 10 if and only if there is a 0 in the ones place. Examine the set of multiples of 10: $\{10, 20, 30, 40, 50, 60, 70, \dots \}$. Notice that all multiples of 10 have a 0 in the ones place.

7. Test for Divisibility by 8.   There are two tests for divisibility by 8.

(a) A number is divisible by 8 if and only if it is divisible by 2 three times. If a number n is divisible by 2 three times, then its prime factorization must have the following form:

$$n = 2 \times 2 \times 2 \times a^b \times c^d \dots$$

where a and c are primes, and b and d are whole numbers. Notice that the product $2 \times 2 \times 2$ is equal to 8. Therefore, testing for divisibility by 2 three times will result in testing for divisibility by 8. For example, 992 is divisible by 8 since

$$992 \div 2 = 496 \text{ (even)}$$

$$496 \div 2 = 248 \text{ (even)}$$

Since the second quotient (248) is an even number, it too is divisible by 2. Therefore, 992 is divisible by 2 three times; that is, it is divisible by 8. The actual quotient of 992 and 8 could have been determined by dividing 248 by 2. The result, 124, is also the result attained when 992 is divided by 8.

(b) A number is divisible by 8 if and only if the last three digits form a number divisible by 8. To understand this divisibility test, it is important to recognize that $8 \mid 1000$. This can easily be seen by examining the prime factorization of 1000, as shown here:

$$1000 = \underbrace{2 \times 2 \times 2}_{8} \times 5 \times 5 \times 5$$

To test whether 19,488 is divisible by 8, it is necessary to write it in the following form:

$$19{,}488 = (19 \times 1000) + 488$$

Since $8 \mid 1000$, it also divides any multiple of 1000. It simply remains to determine if $8 \mid 488$ ($488 \div 8 = 61$). Both addends are divisible by 8 (19,000 and 488). The sum, 19,488, is also divisible by 8.

8. Test for Divisibility by 6.   A number is divisible by 6 if and only if it is divisible by 2 and 3. To test for divisibility by 6, it is necessary to apply the tests for divisibility by both 2 and 3; that is, the number must be even, and the sum of the digits must be divisible by 3. For example, 552 is divisible by 6 since it is even and the sum of its digits, 12, is divisible by 3.

9. Test for Divisibility by 12.   A number is divisible by 12 if and only if it is divisible by 4 and 3. To test for divisibility by 12, it is necessary to apply both the tests for divisibility by 4 and 3; that is, the sum of the digits must be divisible by 3, and the last two digits of the number must be divisible by 4. The number 948 is divisible by 12 since the sum of the digits, 21, is divisible by 3, and the last two digits, 48, form a number divisible by 4.

The tests for divisibility by 7, 11, and 15 will be left to you in the assessments at the end of this section.

Investigation 12

Determine the digits A and B in the number $260{,}A8B$ such that this six-digit number is divisible by 5, 8, and 9. Is your answer unique?

Understand the Problem: You are given a six-digit number. The hundreds place digit and the ones place digit are unknown. In addition, you are told that the number is divisible by 5, 8, and 9. You are asked to find the missing values and determine if more than one set of values for A and B are possible.

Devise a Plan: Use the method of contradiction to narrow down the possible choices.

Carry Out the Plan: There are 10 possible digits for A and 10 possible digits for B. For a number to be divisible by 5, it must have a 0 or 5 in the ones place. Any other digit in the ones place contradicts the given information about divisibility by 5. The range of possibilities is now narrowed down to

$$260{,}A80 \quad \text{and} \quad 260{,}A85$$

Every number divisible by 8 must be even. Any possibilities of the form $260,A85$ would contradict this requirement, since $260,A85$ is an odd number for all values of A. Therefore, the solution must have the form $260,A80$. In addition to being an even number, the last three digits must form a number that is divisible by 8. Examine the set of possibilities:

$$\{080, 180, 280, 380, 480, 580, 680, 780, 880, 980\}$$

Of these possibilities, only 080, 280, 480, 680, and 880 are divisible by 8. The other choices contradict the initial stipulation. The final set of possibilities is now

$$\{260{,}080, \quad 260{,}280, \quad 260{,}480, \quad 260{,}680, \quad 260{,}880\}$$

It remains to test for divisibility by 9. In order for a number to be divisible by 9, the sum of its digits must be divisible by 9.

$$
\begin{array}{lll}
260{,}080 & 2+6+0+0+8+0=16 & 9\nmid 16 \\
260{,}280 & 2+6+0+2+8+0=18 & 9\mid 18 \\
260{,}480 & 2+6+0+4+8+0=20 & 9\nmid 20 \\
260{,}680 & 2+6+0+6+8+0=22 & 9\nmid 22 \\
260{,}880 & 2+6+0+8+8+0=24 & 9\nmid 24 \\
\end{array}
$$

Look Back: The uniqueness question in this investigation forces you to review your work and focus on whether a different solution is possible. Since the number is divisible by 5, 8, and 9, it must be divisible by $5 \times 8 \times 9$, or 360. You can use your calculator to divide 260,000 by 360. The quotient is approximately 722. This can be used as the starting point in the following list.

$$360 \times 722 = 259{,}920$$
$$360 \times 723 = 260{,}280$$
$$360 \times 724 = 260{,}640$$
$$360 \times 725 = 261{,}000$$

Again we see that 260,280 ($A = 2$ and $B = 0$) appears as a possible solution. Indeed, it is the only solution that fits the desired form of the six-digit number.

Investigation 13

What is the remainder when 7^{50} is divided by 5?

Understand the Problem: Since you are asked to find the remainder when 7^{50} is divided by 5, you must determine a whole number c such that $5 \cdot b + c = 7^{50}$ (where b is a whole number).

Devise a Plan: Even the best calculator will not display an exact value of 7^{50}. You must therefore make a list and look for any patterns that might develop.

Carry Out the Plan: Keep in mind that if a number is divisible by 5 it ends in a 0 or a 5. Therefore, the remainder when dividing by 5 is the difference between the ones digit in the original number and 0 or 5 (whichever yields the smaller positive value). For example, 3678 is not divisible by 5. But 3675 is the first number less than or equal to 3678 that is divisible by 5. The remainder when 3678 is divided by 5 is therefore equal to 3 ($8 - 5 = 3$).

X	7^X	First Number $\leq 7^X$ That Is Divisible by 5	Remainder when $7^X \div 5$
1	$7^1 = 7$	5	2
2	$7^2 = 49$	45	4
3	$7^3 = 343$	340	3
4	$7^4 = 2401$	2400	1
5	$7^5 = 16,807$	16,805	2
6	$7^6 = 117,649$	117,645	4
7	$7^7 = 823,543$	823,540	3

It appears that the remainders begin to repeat. Make another list in order to establish a relationship between the exponent and the remainder.

Exponent	Remainder
1	2
2	4
3	3
4	1
5	2
6	4
7	3
8	1

It appears that exponents that are multiples of 4 will yield a remainder of 1. The closest number to 50 that is a multiple of 4 is 48. Continue the pattern from there.

Exponent	Remainder
48	1
49	2
50	4

There will be a remainder of 4 when 7^{50} is divided by 5.

Look Back: Obviously, this answer must be unique. Suppose that $X = a \cdot b + c$, and $X = a \cdot b + d$ where $c \neq d$. Then

$$a \cdot b + c = a \cdot b + d \qquad \text{which implies} \qquad c = d$$

This contradicts our assumption that c and d are different remainders. Therefore, the remainder of 4 is the only possible solution.

Investigation 14

A certain three-digit whole number is divisible by both 4 and 7. Each of its digits is different, and the sum of its digits is 15. Find one such number.

Understand the Problem: You are told that both 4 and 7 are factors of a certain three-digit number. You are asked to find a number that meets the condition that all of the digits are different and that the sum of its digits is 15.

Devise a Plan: Use a diagram to depict this situation.

Carry Out the Plan: This situation can be illustrated in several ways, one of which is shown here. In order to better understand the given information, examine the sets of numbers whose intersection will contain the final result.

First of all, we will be working with the set of whole numbers: $W = \{0, 1, 2, 3, 4, \ldots\}$. Any sets we will subsequently identify will all be subsets of W. Since the number we are looking for is a three-digit number, we must identify the set of three-digit whole numbers: $D = \{100, 101, 102, \ldots, 999\}$. Set D contains two sets that we need to identify: the set F of three-digit multiples of 4 and the sets of three-digit multiples of 7. Since the number in question must be divisible by *both* 4 and 7, it will lie in the intersection of set F and set S. Examine the Venn diagram here, which shows the relationship of sets $W, D, F,$ and S.

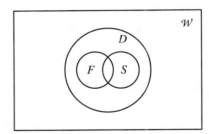

The problem also states that the sum of the digits of the number in question is equal to 15. Although a set of numbers whose digits add to 15 does exist, determining these numbers without the aid of a computer would be very tedious. Rather, knowing that the sum of the digits is 15 also tells you that the number is divisible by 3. Let T be the set of three-digit multiples of 3. Now the picture of the information looks as follows:

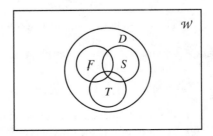

The solution lies within the intersection of multiples of 3, multiples of 4, multiples of 7, and three-digit whole numbers.

Being multiples of 3, 4, and 7, these numbers all must be divisible by $3 \times 4 \times 7$, or 84. Some three-digit multiples of 84 are {168, 252, 336, ... }. The search space has now been narrowed down significantly. What other clues does the given information yield?

Since the sum of the digits is 15, an odd number, examine the possible combinations of three odd and/or even digits that would yield an odd number as a sum. Making a list would be a helpful strategy at this point.

Digits	Sum
3 odds	odd
2 even, 1 odd	odd
1 even, 2 odd	even
3 evens	even

The solution must contain either three odd digits, or two even digits and an odd digit. But the solution must be a multiple of 4, which means that the final digit must be even. The only two arrangements that will work are *even odd even* and *odd even even*. With this information, you can systematically eliminate many of the multiples of 84. (You may remember that an easy way to generate the multiples of 84 is by using the constant feature of your calculator.) The set of three-digit multiples of 84 is {168, 252, 336, 420, 504, 588, 672, 756, 840, 924}. Only 168, 252, 504, 588, 672, 756, and 924 match the pattern. The solution to this problem is not unique. The set {168, 672, 924} contains elements that are three-digit numbers divisible by 4 and 7, whose sum is equal to 15.

Look Back: The elements of the sets were the focus of the problem. As each set was analyzed, a new set that narrowed the search space of the solution was determined. Notice how seemingly unorganized data were organized with the help of a set model to arrive at a solution.

Could this problem have been solved in another way? If you know that the number is divisible by both 4 and 7, then you know it is divisible by 28. Use a calculator to generate the set of multiples of 28. Examine this set for the number that meets the conditions set out in the problem statement.

Assessments for Section 4.3

1. Fill in the blanks with "is a factor of," "is a multiple of," "divides," "is divisible by," "is not a factor of," "is not a multiple of," "does not divide," or "is not divisible by." Identify all possible phrases that correctly complete the statement. In some cases, there may be more than one answer.

(a) 6 _____ 36

(b) 111 _____ 3

(c) 1206 _____ 9

(d) 5 _____ 103

(e) 27 _____ 27

(f) 6224 _____ 8

(g) 4 _____ 25

(h) 10 _____ 1000

(i) 3 _____ 27,015

(j) 129 _____ 2

2. How many different rectangular arrangements are possible with 36 congruent squares? Identify each of the rectangular arrangements. What are the factors of 36?

3. How many different rectangular arrangements are possible with 42 congruent squares? Identify each of the rectangular arrangements. What are the factors of 42?

4. Find the prime factorization of each of the following numbers.

(a) 60   (b) 144   (c) 3500

(d) 1540   (e) 1800

5. Identify each of the numbers whose prime factorization is listed below. Write each prime factorization in exponential form.

(a) $2 \times 2 \times 3 \times 5 \times 5$

(b) $2 \times 3 \times 3 \times 3 \times 3 \times 7 \times 7$

(c) $5 \times 5 \times 5 \times 11$

(d) $2 \times 3 \times 5 \times 7$

(e) $2 \times 3 \times 3 \times 5 \times 5 \times 5 \times 7 \times 7 \times 7$

6. Identify the value of the letters in each of the following factor tree diagrams.

(a)
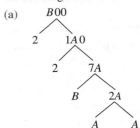

(b)
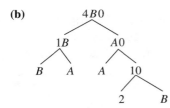

(c)
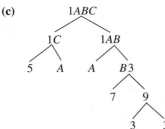

7. List the set of factors for each of the following numbers.

(a) 30   (b) 19   (c) 72   (d) 45   (e) 48

8. Identify the number whose prime factorization is given below.

(a) $2^4 \cdot 3^2 \cdot 5$ (b) $2^2 \cdot 3^3 \cdot 5^2$

(c) $3^2 \cdot 5^2 \cdot 7$ (d) $5^2 \cdot 7^3 \cdot 11$

(e) $2 \cdot 3^2 \cdot 5^3 \cdot 13$

9. Simplify each of the following terms using the rules of exponents outlined in Section 4.3.

(a) $Y^5 \cdot Y^3$ (b) $A^5 \cdot A^2 \cdot A^7$

(c) $(B^3)^3$ (d) $(R \cdot S)^2$

(e) $(A^3 \cdot B^3)$ (f) $X^8 \div X^4$

(g) $(m^2 \cdot m^3 \cdot m^4)^5$ (h) $(y^9 \cdot y^3)^0$ $[y \neq 0]$

10. Find the value of each of the following exponential expressions.

(a) $3^3 \cdot 3^2$ (b) $2^2 \cdot 2^5 \cdot 2^3$

(c) $(5^2 \cdot 5)^3$ (d) $4^6 \div 4^5$

(e) $(9^8 \cdot 9^7 \cdot 9^4)^0$

11. Use the tests for divisibility to determine if the following numbers are divisible by 2, 3, 4, 5, 6, 8, 9, or 10.

(a) 87,560   (b) 125,263   (c) 599,300

(d) 17,100   (e) 16,674   (f) 5763

(g) 230,544   (h) 37,421   (i) 721,721

(j) 46,295

12. A test for divisibility by 7 is given here for 5824.

Drop the ones digit from the number.	582
Double the dropped number and subtract it from the truncated number.	− 8
	574

If this number is divisible by 7, then the original number is also divisible by 7. You can either repeat the process for 574 (57 − 8 = 49), or divide 574 by 7. In either case, you will see that 7 divides the number. Therefore, 7 divides 5824. Use this divisibility test to determine if 7 is a factor of each of the following numbers.

(a) 6076   (b) 3872   (c) 527,940

(d) 31,987   (e) 591,647

13. A test for divisibility by 11 is given here for 62,678.

Beginning with the first digit and alternating to every other digit, find the sum.	6 + 6 + 8 = 20
Beginning with the second digit and alternating to every other digit, find the sum.	2 + 7 = 9
Find the difference of the two sums.	20 − 9 = 11

If this difference is divisible by 11, the original number is divisible by 11. Therefore, 62,678 is divisible by 11. Use this divisibility test to determine if 11 is a factor of each of the following numbers.

(a) 71,862   (b) 573,611   (c) 10,835

(d) 35,354   (e) 108,614

14. Determine a divisibility test for 15. Explain the test, then use it to determine if 15 is a factor of each of the following numbers.

(a) 13,455   (b) 63,840   (c) 72,245

(d) 76,560   (e) 81,580

15. Identify the indicated term of each sequence. Explain the pattern in each.

(a) $2^4, 3^9, 4^{16}, 5^{25}$ (one hundredth term)

(b) 2, 6, 24, 120, 720   (tenth term)

(c) $2^3, 5^7, 11^{13}, 17^{19}$ (seventh term)

(d) 362,880,   40,320,   5040,   720,   120   (ninth term)

(e)

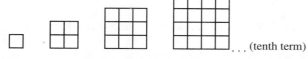

. . . (tenth term)

16. Suppose a piece of paper is folded into three equal sections as illustrated below. The resulting folded page is then folded again into three equal sections. This process is repeated five more times. The paper is now opened and examined. It has been divided into a number of small congruent rectangular regions. How many such regions are formed on *each side* of the page by these folds?

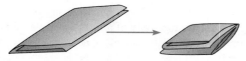

. . .

17. For the following sets, list $(A \cap B)$ and $(A \cup B)$.

(a) $A = \{$multiples of 5 between 0 and 55$\}$
     $B = \{$multiples of 10 between 0 and 100$\}$

(b) $A = \{2, 3, 4, 6, 8, 9, 10, 12, 14, 15, 16\}$
     $B = \{$multiples of 6 between 0 and 20$\}$

(c) $A = \{$even multiples of 3 between 0 and 20$\}$
     $B = \{$multiples of 2 between 0 and 19$\}$

(d) $A = \{$multiples of 12 between 0 and 65$\}$
     $B = \{$multiples of 4 between 0 and 65$\}$

(e) $A = \{2^1, 2^2, 2^3, \ldots, 2^{10}\}$
     $B = \{4^1, 4^2, 4^3, \ldots, 4^{10}\}$

(f) $A = \{$multiples of 6 that are divisible by 4 and are less than 60$\}$
     $B = \{$multiples of 4 that are divisible by 6 and are less than 60$\}$

(g) $A = \{$factors of 72 that are divisible by 4$\}$
     $B = \{$whole numbers that divide 36$\}$

18. A certain warehouse contains 720 cartons of books. Can these cartons be placed in stacks four cartons high so that each stack contains an equal number of cartons? Can they be placed in stacks five cartons high? six cartons high? seven cartons high? What is the greatest number of cartons that can be stacked so that each stack contains the same number of cartons and no stack is over 25 cartons high?

19. Determine whether each of the following results in a number that is divisible by 2. Justify your reasoning.

(a) The sum of 15 even numbers and 3 odd numbers

(b) The sum of eight even numbers and eight odd numbers

(c) The sum of 101 even numbers and 100 odd numbers

(d) The product of 17 odd numbers and 5 even numbers

(e) The product of 99 odd numbers

20. The number 77 is divisible by 7 and can be expressed as $100 - 23$. Neither 100 nor 23 is divisible by 7, and yet their difference is divisible by 7. Does this represent a counterexample for the divisibility rule of differences? Explain your answer.

21. Determine the set of all possible three-digit numbers of the form __ 4 __ such that the number is divisible by 6.

22. Determine the set of all possible three-digit numbers of the form __ 6 __ such that the number is divisible by 45. Explain your answer.

23. How can it be shown that no arrangement of the 10 digits 0 through 9 inclusive (used only once) forming a 10-digit number will result in a prime number?

24. Show that the sum of any five consecutive whole numbers will always be divisible by 5.

25. A three-digit number is divisible by both 3 and 8. Its digits are all even numbers, and the sum of its digits is 12. Find one such number.

26. A four-digit number is divisible by 2, 5, and 7. The sum of its digits is 21. Each of the digits is divisible by 3. Find one such number.

27. A certain hotel has 180 rooms. The price for a room alone is $120 per night. Use of the health club adds $25 per night to the cost. Use of the tennis courts adds an additional $25 per night. On January 6, the hotel was fully occupied.

Sixty-three people paid for rooms only. There were 98 people who wished to play tennis, and 94 people who wanted to use the health club. How much money did these 180 rooms generate on January 6?

28. A certain travel agency offers the following vacation package:

$699 per person for airfare and four-star hotel

Add $120 per person for meal option

Add $85 per person for tour option

Add $175 per person for special flight to a neighboring island

The travel agency booked a group of 61 people who took advantage of this package. Thirty people took the meal option. Twenty-one people went on the tour. Nine people visited the neighboring island. Six people chose the flight to the island and the tour. Three people chose the meals and the tour. Only one person chose all three options. Ten people chose none of the add-on options. What was the total amount of money collected by the travel agent?

In Other Words

29. Suppose that a number X has a prime factorization of $2^a \cdot 3^b \cdot 5^c$. Explain why X has a total of

$$(a + 1) \cdot (b + 1) \cdot (c + 1)$$

factors.

30. Suppose that a certain three-digit number is not divisible by 12. Is it possible for the number to be divisible by a factor of 12? Is it possible for the number to be divisible by a multiple of 12? Explain your answer.

31. Using the divisibility test for 6 as a model, define an alternate divisibility test for 10 that employs the factors of 10.

32. Explain the divisibility test for 3 on any four-digit number $ABCD$.

33. If the product of two whole numbers A and B is divisible by a whole number C, does this imply that each of the two numbers must be divisible by C? Explain your answer.

Cooperative Activity

34. Groups of three

Individual Accountability: Determine the multiples of 11 that are nearest the base ten place values; that is, what multiples of 11 are closest to 10, 100, 1000, 10,000, 100,000, and 1,000,000? Once you have determined these numbers, rewrite 3,584,614 in an "expanded" form that employs the multiples of 11 you found (see the test for divisibility by 3 outlined on page 147 for a similar expansion).

Group Goal: Use your calculator to verify that 3,584,614 is divisible by 11. As a group, examine the expansion you have written. Use the distributive property to simplify the expansion. The divisibility test for 11 is based on sums and differences of the digits in the number to be tested. Look for a pattern. Justify the rule given to you in Problem 13 of this section.

4.4 **M**aking Connections: Relations and Relationships

You have examined the set of whole numbers from a variety of vantage points. The problem-solving strategies that were introduced assisted you in exploring aspects of the whole number system. Now having completed the study of all of the whole number operations, you are ready to extend your knowledge to make connections within the set of whole numbers and between the whole number system and other mathematical systems.

Relations

Recall the Cartesian product, or cross-product, model that was used to describe whole number multiplication in Section 4.1. Given two sets A and B, the Cartesian product, $A \times B$, is defined as a set containing all of the possible pairs formed by joining, in order, one element of A with one element of B. For example, let set $A = \{2, 4, 6, 8\}$ and set $B = \{1, 3\}$. The Cartesian product $A \times B = \{(2, 1), (2, 3), (4, 1), (4, 3), (6, 1), (6, 3), (8, 1), (8, 3)\}$. Examine the subset C of $A \times B$, which contains $\{(2, 1), (4, 1), (6, 1), (8, 1), (6, 3)\}$. The ordered pairs in this set all have something in common. The first element in each is related in the same way to the second element in each. The relationship illustrated by the pairs in set C is "is a multiple of."

In (2, 1), 2 is a multiple of 1.

In (4, 1), 4 is a multiple of 1.

In (6, 1), 6 is a multiple of 1.

In (8, 1), 8 is a multiple of 1.

In (6, 3), 6 is a multiple of 3.

relation Any subset of a Cartesian product is called a **relation**. The subset C above represents the relation "is a multiple of." Other subsets might define other relations. Some other possible relations could be "is greater than," "is less than," "is half of," and "is a factor of."

Relations do not necessarily have to be numerical. Consider the following set of family members: F = {Linda (mother), Robert (father), Julie (child), Pete (child), Rich (child), Ruth (Robert's mother)}. The Cartesian product of $F \times F$ would contain all of the possible pairs that could be formed with the elements of set F. The elements of $F \times F$ are

(Linda, Linda) (Linda, Robert) (Linda, Julie) (Linda, Pete) (Linda, Rich) (Linda, Ruth)

(Robert, Linda) (Robert, Robert) (Robert, Julie) (Robert, Pete) (Robert, Rich) (Robert, Ruth)

(Julie, Linda) (Julie, Robert) (Julie, Julie) (Julie, Pete) (Julie, Rich) (Julie, Ruth)

(Pete, Linda) (Pete, Robert) (Pete, Julie) (Pete, Pete) (Pete, Rich) (Pete, Ruth)

(Rich, Linda) (Rich, Robert) (Rich, Julie) (Rich, Pete) (Rich, Rich) (Rich, Ruth)

(Ruth, Linda) (Ruth, Robert) (Ruth, Julie) (Ruth, Pete) (Ruth, Rich) (Ruth, Ruth)

The subset of $F \times F$ formed by the relation on F "is the son of" would contain the following elements: (Robert, Ruth), (Pete, Linda), (Pete, Robert), (Rich, Linda), and (Rich, Robert), since Robert is the son of Ruth, Pete is the son of Linda, Pete is the son of Robert, Rich is the son of Linda, and Rich is the son of Robert. This relation can also be illustrated using the arrow diagram shown in Figure 4.7.

Figure 4.7

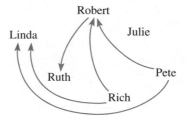

In the first example, the relation "is a multiple of" was a relation between two different sets. In the second example, the relation "is the son of" was a relation on a single set. When a relation is on a single set, three important properties may or may not be true concerning that relation. To explain these properties, we will use "is related to" to denote a generic relationship.

reflexive **1. Reflexive Property.**   A relation on a set Y is **reflexive** if it can be shown that for every element $y \in Y$, y "is related to" y; that is, the ordered pair (y, y) is an element of the relation. If every element of set Y can be shown to be related to itself, then the relation is said to be reflexive.

For example, let set $Y = \{5, 10, 15, 20\}$ and the relation be "is a multiple of." Since 5 is a multiple of 5, 10 is a multiple of 10, 15 is a multiple of 15, and 20 is a multiple of 20, the ordered pairs (5, 5), (10, 10), (15, 15), and (20, 20) will be four of the elements in the subset of the Cartesian product $Y \times Y$ defined by the relation "is a multiple of." The reflexive property can be illustrated as in the arrow diagram in Figure 4.8.

Figure 4.8

Suppose that the relation had been defined by "is an odd divisor of." Although it is true that 5 is an odd number divisor of 5 and 15 is an odd number divisor of 15, both 10 and 20 are not odd number divisors of themselves. Therefore, this relation would not be reflexive.

symmetric   **2. Symmetric Property.**   A relation on a set Y is said to be **symmetric** if it can be shown that for every $a, b \in Y$, whenever a "is related to" b, then b "is related to" a; that is, if the ordered pair (a, b) is an element of the relation, so also is (b, a).

For example, let $D = \{10, 20, 30\}$ and the relation be "has a prime factor in common with." Since all of the elements of set D are divisible by 5, the ordered pairs (10, 20), (10, 30), (20, 30), (20, 10), (30, 10), (30, 20), (10, 10), (20, 20), (30, 30) each represent the relation in which the first number in the pair has the prime factor of 5 in common with the second number in the pair. Notice that for each pair (a, b), the relation "has a prime factor in common with" also holds for (b, a). Therefore, the relation is symmetric on the set D. In addition, this relation is also reflexive, since every element has a prime factor in common with itself.

Suppose that set $T = \{10, 20, 30, 7\}$ and the relation is also "has a prime factor in common with." Is the relation on set T symmetric? The answer lies in the understanding of the wording of the symmetric property. For a relation to be symmetric on a set containing a and b as two of its elements, whenever a is related to b, b must be related to a. We have already determined that the relation on D, which is a subset of T, is symmetric. In T, the element 7 does not have a prime factor in common with any other element in the set, nor is any other element in the set a multiple of 7. Therefore, no ordered pairs with 7 as a first element can be formed that illustrate the relation, other than (7, 7). The relation holds for the remaining elements in the set and therefore is symmetric. This relation on set T is illustrated by the arrow diagram in Figure 4.9.

Figure 4.9

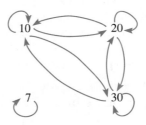

In a diagram of a symmetric relation on a set, if there is an arrow pictured from a to b, then there must be an arrow pictured from b to a.

Suppose that the relation on set T had been "is less than." The ordered pairs (10, 20), (10, 30), (20, 30), (7, 10), (7, 20), (7, 30) illustrate this relation. An arrow diagram illustrating this relation would be drawn as in Figure 4.10.

Figure 4.10

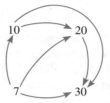

Notice that the relation does not hold when the elements in the ordered pairs are reversed. For example, although it is true that 7 is less than 10, it is not true that 10 is less than 7. Therefore, the relation "is less than" is not symmetric on the set T.

transitive **3. Transitive Property.** A relation on a set A is said to be **transitive** if it can be shown that for any $a, b, c \in A$, whenever a is related to b, and b is related to c, then a is related to c; that is, if the ordered pairs (a, b) and (b, c) are elements of the relation, then the ordered pair (a, c) must also be an element of the relation. For example, let $A = \{8, 12, 16, 24, 28, 32, 48\}$ and the relation be "is a divisor of." Notice that 8 is a divisor of 16, 16 is a divisor of 32, and 8 is a divisor of 32. This is also true for the elements 12, 24, and 48 (12 is a divisor of 24, 24 is a divisor of 48, and 12 is a divisor of 48), and for 8, 16, and 48. These are the only three cases in the set where a is related to b and b is related to c. Since in each of these cases a is also related to c, the relation on set A is said to be transitive. This relation can be illustrated by the diagram in Figure 4.11.

Figure 4.11

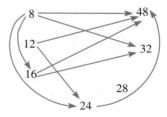

Suppose the relation on set A had been "is eight less than." It is true that 8 is eight less than 16, and 16 is eight less than 24. In order for the relation to be transitive, it *must* be true that 8 is eight less than 24. Obviously, this is not the case. Therefore, the relation "is eight less than" on set A is not transitive.

Investigation 15

Consider the following set: $C = \{19, 37, 46, 91, 109, 145, 2071\}$. Let the relation in question be "has the same sum of its digits as." Test whether the relation on set C is reflexive, symmetric, and transitive.

Each element of the set has the same sum of its digits as itself. Therefore, the relation is reflexive. For each $a, b \in C$, it follows that the relation is symmetric since whenever a has the same sum of its digits as b, b has the same sum of its digits as a. Finally, for each $a, b, c \in C$, whenever a has the same sum of its digits as b, and b has the same sum of its digits as c, then a has the same sum of its digits as c. Therefore, the relation is transitive.

equivalence relation

When a relation is reflexive, symmetric, and transitive it is said to be an **equivalence relation**. Another example of an equivalence relation is given here. Examine set X: $\{1001_{\text{two}}, 100_{\text{three}}, 21_{\text{four}}, 14_{\text{five}}, 13_{\text{six}}\}$; the relation is "is equivalent to." Each element of the set has a base ten equivalent of 9. It should be clear that the relation is reflexive (any number is equivalent to itself). The relation is symmetric (if a is equivalent to b, then b is equivalent to a). Finally, the relation is transitive (if a is equivalent to b, and b is equivalent to c, then a is equivalent to c). The relation "is equivalent to" is an equivalence relation on set X.

Consider the following set: $P = \{48, 82, 35, 26, 80, 37, 55, 39, 19\}$. Let the relation on set P be the same as the relation in Investigation 15. It is left to you to verify that the relation "has the same sum of its digits as" on set P is an equivalence relation. Examine the arrow diagram in Figure 4.12, which illustrates the equivalence relation on P.

Figure 4.12

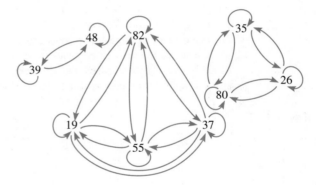

Notice that the arrows appear to separate the set into three groups. Examine these subsets:

$$\{26, 35, 80\} \qquad \{39, 48\} \qquad \{55, 82, 19, 37\}$$

partitioning

The symmetric and transitive properties do not connect these groups. These three subsets completely exhaust the elements of set C by partitioning set C into three nonempty, disjoint subsets. This **partitioning** of a set into a group of nonempty, disjoint subsets is a special characteristic of an equivalence relation. Notice that

$$C = \{26, 35, 80\} \cup \{39, 48\} \cup \{55, 82, 19, 37\}$$

Investigation 16

Let set *G* be composed of the following geometric shapes:

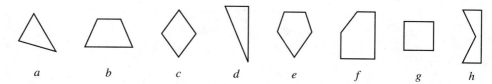

a	*b*	*c*	*d*	*e*	*f*	*g*	*h*

Verify that the relation "has the same number of sides as" is an equivalence relation on set *G*. Describe the nonempty, disjoint subsets of *G* that are formed by the equivalence relation.

Since any shape has the same number of sides as itself, it is obvious that the relation is reflexive. If a given shape has the same number of sides as a second shape, it follows that the second shape has the same number of sides as the first shape. For example, notice that (*a*, *d*) is an element of the relation, and (*d*, *a*) is also an element of the relation. Therefore, the relation "has the same number of sides as" on set *G* is symmetric. Finally, if a given shape has the same number of sides as a second shape, and that second shape has the same number of sides as a third shape, then the given shape has the same number of sides as the third shape. For example, shape *b* has the same number of sides as shape *c*, and shape *c* has the same number of sides as shape *g*. Since shape *b* has the same number of sides as shape *g*, the relation is transitive.

This equivalence relation can be pictured in the following way:

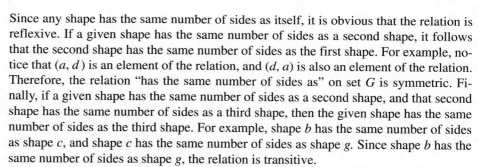

The relation "has the same number of sides as" partitions set *G* into three nonempty, disjoint subsets, which may be described as subsets containing three-sided figures, four-sided figures, and five-sided figures.

Functions

Examine the following numerical and nonnumerical relations illustrated by arrow diagrams.

(1) "prefers the sport of"

(2) "is the first-period class of"

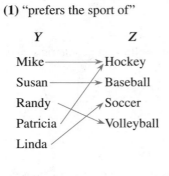

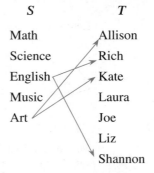

(3) "is the square of"

(4) "is two units on a number line away from"

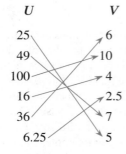

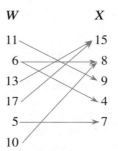

In part (1), the subset of the Cartesian product of sets Y and Z, which defines the relation "prefers the sport of," is {(Mike, Hockey), (Susan, Baseball), (Randy, Volleyball), (Patricia, Hockey), (Linda, Soccer)}. In this relation, each element of set Y is related to a single element of set Z. Although it is true that both Patricia and Mike prefer the same sport, as shown by two arrows coming from set Y to the element "Hockey" of set Z, it is not true that any one person prefers more than one sport. Therefore, there is only one arrow coming from each member of set Y.

Which of the remaining examples are analogous to part (1)? In part (2), English is the first-period class of both Rich and Shannon. Therefore, two of the ordered pairs in the subset of the Cartesian product of sets S and T, which define the relation "is the first-period class of," have the same first element, namely, (English, Rich) and (English, Shannon). This is also true of the ordered pairs (Art, Allison) and (Art, Kate). The nature of the relationship illustrated in part (1), that of a single arrow stemming from an element of the first set, is not analogous to that of part (2), since two arrows emanate from a single element of set S. Notice that this is also the case in part (4). The relation "is the square of" on sets U and V in part (3) is the only relation analogous to "prefers the sport of." In the subsets of the Cartesian products that define the relations in both part (1) and part (3), each element of the first set is paired with one and only one element of the second set. A relation of this type is called a function.

Definition: **function** A **function** is a relation from set A to set B in which each element of the first set is paired with *one and only one* element of the second set.

Functions are usually symbolized by letters in the following manner. If $a \in A$, then the function f acting on a is represented by $f(a)$ and read "f of a." The set of all ordered pairs that define a particular function, f, can be symbolized by $[a, f(a)]$.

Investigation 17

Examine the following calendar month. Based on this calendar, state two examples of relations on specific sets that are functions and two examples of relations on specific sets that are not functions.

April

Sunday	Monday	Tuesday	Wednesday	Thursday	Friday	Saturday
1	2	3	4	5	6	7
8	9	10	11	12	13	14
15	16	17	18	19	20	21
22	23	24	25	26	27	28
29	30					

Answers will vary. Some possibilities follow.

1. Relations That Are Functions.

    (a) Let A = {Sunday, Monday, Tuesday, Wednesday, Thursday, Friday, Saturday}
    Let B = {April 1, April 2, April 3, April 4, April 5, April 6, April 7}
    Let the relation R = "is the day of the week corresponding to."
    The subset of the Cartesian product $A \times B$, which defines the relation R, is

        {(Sunday, April 1), (Monday, April 2), (Tuesday, April 3),

        (Wednesday, April 4), (Thursday, April 5), (Friday, April 6),

        (Saturday, April 7)}

    The relation R is a function since each element of set A is paired with one and only one element of set B.

    (b) Let C = {April 16, April 30, April 2, April 7, April 28}
    Let D = {Monday, Saturday}
    Let the relation S = "falls on the day of the week"
    The subset of the Cartesian product $C \times D$, which defines the relation S, is

        {(April 16, Monday), (April 30, Monday), (April 2, Monday),

        (April 7, Saturday), (April 28, Saturday)}

The relation S is a function, since each element of set C is paired with one and only one element of set D.

2. Relations That Are Not Functions.

(a) Let E = {Wednesday, Friday, Sunday}
Let F = {April 4, April 29, April 6, April 22}
Let the relation T = "is the day of the week corresponding to."
The subset of the Cartesian product $E \times F$, which defines the relation T, is

{(Wednesday, April 4), (Friday, April 6), (Sunday, April 29), (Sunday, April 22)}

The relation T is not a function, since the element of set E, "Sunday," is paired with two elements of set F.

(b) Let G = {April 10, April 19, April 5, April 22}
Let H = {April 12, April 17, April 26, April 29}
Let the relation W = "is the date that is one week away from the date."
The subset of the Cartesian product $G \times H$, which defines the relation W, is

{(April 10, April 17), (April 19, April 26), (April 19, April 12),

(April 5, April 12), (April 22, April 29)}

The relation W is not a function, since the element of set G, "April 19," is paired with two elements of set H.

In addition to representing a function as a subset of the Cartesian product of two sets, a function can also be viewed as a rule. This rule can be illustrated using a table or a function machine. The function "is the triple of" is shown in Figure 4.13 in tabular form and using a function machine.

Figure 4.13

Function Table

X	Y
3	1
15	5
24	8
6	2

Function Machine

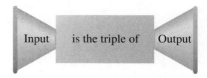

Input   is the triple of   Output

domain   In the function table, the set X is called the domain of the function. The **domain** of the function consists of values upon which the rule is applied. In the ordered pair model of a function, the X value is the first element of the ordered pair and is one of the elements of the domain of the function. Notice in the function machine model that the domain acts as the input of the machine.

range   The set Y is called the range of the function. In the set model, the **range** is all of the second elements, or the Y values of the ordered pairs. In the function machine model, the output of the function is known as the range of the function. In all function models, each value in the domain has one and only one value in the range. Examine Figure 4.14, which shows a nonfunction table and a nonfunction machine representing the relation "is a factor of."

Figure 4.14

Nonfunction Table

X	Y
2	4
2	8
2	6
3	6
5	25

Nonfunction Machine

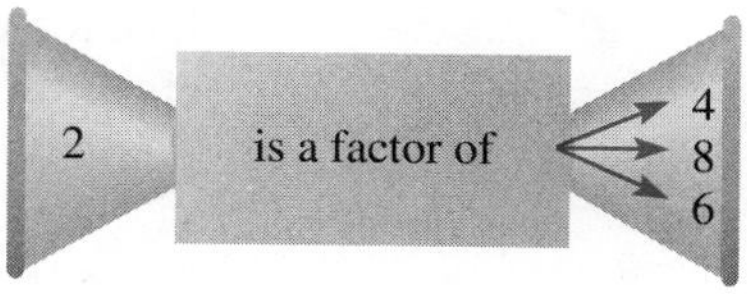

Notice that there are three different Y values associated with the X value 2. This is also evident in the function machine illustration. When a 2 is input, 4, 6, and 8 are all outputs. Clearly, "is a factor of" is not a function, since it violates the rule that each X value be paired with one and only one Y value.

Composition of Functions

Suppose that D represents the function in which the output is the double of each input, and S represents the function in which the output is the square of each input. Figure 4.15 pictures each of these two functions.

Figure 4.15

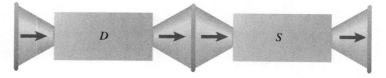

Suppose that the two functions are joined in such a way that the output of the first function immediately becomes the input of the second function, as shown in Figure 4.16.

Figure 4.16

When the input of the first function is paired with the associated output of the second **composition of two** function, a new function, called the **composition of two functions**, is formed. Notice **functions** that the range of the first function becomes the domain of the second function, as illustrated in the following table:

Function D (doubles each input)		Function S (squares each input)	
Domain	Range	Domain	Range
2	4	4	16
3	6	6	36
4	8	8	64
5	10	10	100

The ordered pairs (2, 16), (3, 36), (4, 64), and (5, 100) define the composition of the functions D and S when the domain of the first function D is $\{2, 3, 4, 5\}$. The above function composition can be symbolized in two different ways, where a is an element of the domain of function D. When the function composition is

$$S(D(a)) \qquad \text{read as "}S \text{ of } D \text{ of } a\text{"}$$

we work with the function on the inside of the parentheses first. Once the output of the inner function is determined, it becomes the input of the outer function. For example, $S(D(4)) = S(8) = 64$. This process can also be symbolized as follows:

$$(S \circ D)\,(a)$$

The output is exactly the same as $S(D(a))$. Here the function D is the first function to act on a.

Investigation 18

Let the function S be such that the output (Y value) is the square of the input (X value). Let the function T be such that the output is the triple of the input.

1. Describe $T \circ S$.

2. Describe $S \circ T$.

3. Find $T(S(2))$.

4. Find $S(T(2))$.

5. What conclusion might be drawn from the solutions to (3) and (4)?

1. In the composition symbolized by $T \circ S$, a number is first squared, then this result is tripled.

2. In the composition symbolized by $S \circ T$, a number is first tripled, then this result is squared.

3. $T(S(2)) = (T \circ S)(2) = T(4) = 12$

4. $S(T(2)) = (S \circ T)(2) = S(6) = 36$

5. $(T \circ S) \neq (S \circ T)$ since $12 \neq 36$. A conclusion that could be drawn from this single case is that it will not always be true that you can change the order of the composition without changing the result.

Investigation 19

Describe how the solution to $((10)^3)^2$ can be found using the composition of two functions.

In this situation, the number 10 will be viewed as the input. The base, 10, is first cubed. Define a function C that outputs the cube of the input. Once 10 has been cubed, the result must then be squared. Define a function S that outputs the square of the input.

$$((10)^3)^2 = (S \circ C)(10) = S(C(10)) = S(1000) = 1,000,000$$

Notice that $(S \circ C)$ is equivalent to a function that raises the input value to the sixth power. It is left to you to determine whether in the case of the functions described above, $(S \circ C) = (C \circ S)$.

Clock Arithmetic

Up to this point in the text, you have examined the whole numbers as they relate to one another. A variety of properties, rules, definitions, patterns, and relationships have been introduced, established, and explored. The set of whole numbers, together with the operations and rules that govern them, form a **mathematical system**. A mathematical system is symbolized by an ordered pair of the form $(S, *)$, where S represents a certain set of elements and $*$ represents an operation that is defined on that set of elements..

mathematical system

Traditionally, the set of whole numbers is symbolized by $\mathcal{W}$. The operations of addition, subtraction, multiplication, and division each form a system on the set of whole numbers and can be symbolized by $(\mathcal{W}, +)$, $(\mathcal{W}, -)$, $(\mathcal{W}, \times)$, and $(\mathcal{W}, \div)$. We know that statements such as $8 + 5 = 13$, $14 - 3 = 11$, $22 \times 3 = 66$, and $100 \div 20 = 5$ are all true within the defined system.

Now we will turn to another set of numbers and a new mathematical system that results from it. Examine the set $\{1, 2, 3, 4, 5, 6, 7, 8, 9, 10, 11, 12\}$. To better understand operations on this set, we will look at the analogous situation of a clock. The set can be described as the hours marked on an analog clock. Operations on this particular set (and sets similar to it) are known as **clock arithmetic**. For the purposes of notation, we will call this set Clock 12.

clock arithmetic

The first operation we will explore is clock addition. Here we will use the symbol $\oplus$ to represent the operation of addition on the set Clock 12. The statement $A \oplus B$ can be interpreted as B hours after the hour of A, or the time it will be B hours from A. Examine the results of clock addition in Figure 4.17.

Figure 4.17

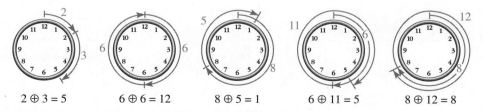

| $2 \oplus 3 = 5$ | $6 \oplus 6 = 12$ | $8 \oplus 5 = 1$ | $6 \oplus 11 = 5$ | $8 \oplus 12 = 8$ |

The first number is the starting "time" on the clock. The second number indicates an addition by moving that number of units in a clockwise direction. The sum is the resulting "time."

It is often helpful to construct a table that can assist in solving operation problems in this system. The table lists all of the elements of the set along the top and the left side, and the particular operation in the top left-hand corner (in this case, clock addition).

⊕	1	2	3	4	5	6	7	8	9	10	11	12
1	2	3	4	5	6	7	8	9	10	11	12	1
2	3	4	5	6	7	8	9	10	11	12	1	2
3	4	5	6	7	8	9	10	11	12	1	2	3
4	5	6	7	8	9	10	11	12	1	2	3	4
5	6	7	8	9	10	11	12	1	2	3	4	5
6	7	8	9	10	11	12	1	2	3	4	5	6
7	8	9	10	11	12	1	2	3	4	5	6	7
8	9	10	11	12	1	2	3	4	5	6	7	8
9	10	11	12	1	2	3	4	5	6	7	8	9
10	11	12	1	2	3	4	5	6	7	8	9	10
11	12	1	2	3	4	5	6	7	8	9	10	11
12	1	2	3	4	5	6	7	8	9	10	11	12

To use the table to find the sum of 6 and 7, locate the first number, 6, in the left-hand column. Then locate the second number, 7, in the top row. The intersection of row 6 and column 7 is the number 1. Therefore, $6 \oplus 7 = 1$.

Examine the table. The identity element in (Clock 12, $\oplus$) is 12, since $12 + x = x$ and $x + 12 = x$. To draw a parallel between the set of whole numbers and the clock set, the identity element 12 can be replaced by 0. This does not change the structure of the table, only the symbol used to identify the identity element.

Investigation 20

What value of x in (Clock 12, $\oplus$) will make the equation $x \oplus 5 = 4$ true?

The equation can be interpreted as "Five hours from hour X it will be four o'clock." Use the table above to solve this problem. Go down the 5 column until you reach the number 4. Go across to identify the row label in the left-most column. The solution is $x = 11$. Therefore, $11 \oplus 5 = 4$.

When working in a system with whole numbers, we saw that addition and subtraction were inverse relations. These two operations are also inverse relations on the set Clock 12.

In Investigation 20 we found that $11 \oplus 5 = 4$. We will use the symbol $\ominus$ to represent subtraction on the set Clock 12. In general, $A \ominus B = C$ if and only if $B \oplus C = A$. Clock subtraction can be done by rewriting the subtraction problem as an equivalent addition problem and solving as in Investigation 20, or, in the case of $A \ominus B$, beginning on the clock at A and going B units in the counterclockwise direction. Using the clock analogy, if it is now 4:00 o'clock, five hours ago it was 11:00 o'clock.

Clock multiplication, $\otimes$, relies on the knowledge that whole number multiplication can be viewed as repeated addition. Recall in the system (W, x), $5 \times 4 = 4 + 4 + 4 + 4 + 4$. We can apply this same relationship to (Clock 12, $\otimes$). To find the product $7 \otimes 5$, we write $5 \oplus 5 \oplus 5 \oplus 5 \oplus 5 \oplus 5 \oplus 5$. Figure 18 shows the solution using the clock analogy.

Figure 4.18

$7 \otimes 5 = 11$

On the set of whole numbers, multiplication and division are inverse operations, since $a \div b = c$ is equivalent to $a = b \cdot c$. In clock arithmetic, we can symbolize clock division by $\oslash$. The expression $2 \oslash 3 = x$ can be written in its equivalent form as $3 \otimes x = 2$. This can be solved if a multiplication table is available. Solving such division problems will be left for you to do in the assessments that follow this section.

With this introduction to clock arithmetic as background, we now define a set Clock N, such that the elements of the set are $0, 1, 2, \ldots, (N-1)$. For example, the elements of the set Clock 5 are $\{0, 1, 2, 3, 4\}$. The clock that could be used to explore a Clock 5 system would look like this:

Use this clock in Investigation 21.

Investigation 21

Is $4 \oplus 0$ defined in the Clock 5 system?

We are trying to discover if x has a value in the statement $4 \oplus 0 = x$. It should be clear that $4 \oplus 0 = x$ can be written in the equivalent form $0 \otimes x = 4$. A Clock 5 multiplication table can be generated by viewing multiplication as repeated addition. The entries of such a table are given here. (The process we used to generate this table will be left to you in the assessments following this section.)

$\otimes$	0	1	2	3	4
0	0	0	0	0	0
1	0	1	2	3	4
2	0	2	4	1	3
3	0	3	1	4	2
4	0	4	3	2	1

Notice that 0 times any element of the set Clock 5 is equal to 0. There is no element, x, in Clock 5 such that 0 times x is equal to 4. Therefore, division by zero has no solution in the Clock 5 system. As in whole numbers, division by zero in any Clock N system is undefined.

Modular Arithmetic

modular arithmetic

modulus

Clock arithmetic is an example of a type of mathematics that is known as **modular arithmetic**. In modular arithmetic, we work with operations on a set of numbers from 0 to $m - 1$ where m is known as the **modulus** of the system. The set Clock 12 could be viewed as the set whose modulus is 12 and that contains the whole numbers from 0 to 11. Any operations on this set would be called modulo 12, or mod 12, operations.

We will continue with the time analogy, but now let's examine the set containing the days of the week. We can make a numerical assignment to each day as follows: $0 \rightarrow$ Sunday, $1 \rightarrow$ Monday, $2 \rightarrow$ Tuesday, $3 \rightarrow$ Wednesday, $4 \rightarrow$ Thursday, $5 \rightarrow$ Friday, and $6 \rightarrow$ Saturday. If you know that the second day of July falls on a Friday, how can you determine the day of the week on which July 31 will fall? Obviously, a calendar would be the easiest tool to use to determine this information. But in lieu of a calendar, you could use a clock diagram that represents modulo 7, as shown in Figure 4.19.

Figure 4.19

Begin at 5 on the clock (because $5 \rightarrow$ Friday). In 29 days (the difference between 31 and 2), the "hand" would make four complete revolutions, plus one. This remainder of 1 is interpreted as the 31st falling one day after a Friday. July 31 would therefore be a Saturday.

Problems such as these can also be solved by generating a mod 7 addition table as shown below. This table is created in the same way that the Clock 12 addition table was created.

+	0	1	2	3	4	5	6
0	0	1	2	3	4	5	6
1	1	2	3	4	5	6	0
2	2	3	4	5	6	0	1
3	3	4	5	6	0	1	2
4	4	5	6	0	1	2	3
5	5	6	0	1	2	3	4
6	6	0	1	2	3	4	5

To use this table to add $3 + 6$ in modulo 7, find the first addend in the left-hand column and the second addend in the top row. The intersection of this row and column reveals the sum. Therefore, $(3 + 6)$ modulo 7 is equal to 2. This could also have been determined by the remainder when 9 is divided by the modulus 7. Notice that all of the entries in the modulo 7 addition table can be found by determining the remainder of that whole number sum when it is divided by 7. Certain sums will have the same remainder. For example, a sum of 11, 25, or 32 would each be equivalent to 4 modulo 7. This is a very important equivalence in modular arithmetic, known as **congruence modulo *m***.

Rule: In general, x is congruent to y modulo m, symbolized by $x \equiv y \pmod{m}$, if x and y have the same remainder when divided by modulus m.

It can be said, for example, that 11 is congruent to 25 modulo 7 since they both have a remainder of 4 when divided by 7.

Another interesting characteristic of congruence modulo m results in a closer examination of the congruent numbers. Consider set $C = \{4, 11, 25, 32, 39, 46, 53\}$. Each of the elements in C has a remainder of 4 when divided by 7. These elements are therefore congruent to each other in modulo m. Take any pair of these numbers and subtract the smaller from the larger. What do you notice? In any case, 7 will always divide the difference. An alternate definition of congruence results from this discovery:

Rule: If x, y, and m are whole numbers with $m \geq 2$ and $x \geq y$, $x \equiv y$ mod m if and only if $m \mid (x - y)$.

This definition will be revisited when the set of negative numbers is introduced in Chapter 5.

Investigation 22

Let $\mathcal{W}$ be the set of whole numbers and R be the relation defined as "is congruent to (mod 7)." Does this relation define an equivalence relation?

We must test if the relation is reflexive, symmetric, and transitive.

1. **Reflexive:** Any number x is congruent to itself mod 7 since $7 \mid (x - x)$, or $7 \mid 0$. The relation is reflexive.

2. **Symmetric:** If $x \equiv y \pmod{7}$, then $y \equiv x \pmod{7}$. The relation is symmetric.

3. **Transitive:** If $x \equiv y \pmod{7}$, and $y \equiv z \pmod{7}$, then $x \equiv z \pmod{7}$. The relation is transitive.

The relation R, "is congruent to (mod 7)" is an equivalence relation on the set of whole numbers. Further properties of this equivalence relation will be examined in the assessments that follow this section.

Assessments for Section 4.4

1. Here is an alphabetical listing of the tenants in a certain apartment building. Each apartment is identified by a three-digit number. The ones place names the individual apartment, and the hundreds place names the floor on which it is found.

J. Alvarez	203
R. Chou	301
B. Cohen	104
L. Gerver	303
G. Harron	201
M. Mollot	103
T. Richmond	202
M. Sabo	102
C. Sullivan	101
J. Toscano	302
A. Trolio	304
J. Wilhoft	204

Each floor is laid out as follows:

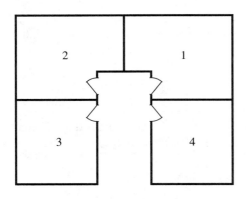

(a) List all ordered pairs of the form (tenant, tenant) in the subset defined by the relation "shares the third floor with."

(b) List all ordered pairs of the form (number, number) in the subset defined by the relation "is the apartment directly above."

(c) List all ordered pairs of the form (number, number) in the subset defined by the relation "is on the same floor as and is adjacent to."

(d) List all ordered pairs of the form (number, number) in the subset defined by the relation "is on the same floor as but is not adjacent to."

(e) For each of the relation in parts (a)–(d), determine if the reflexive, symmetric, and transitive properties hold.

2. In each case, list the ordered pairs that are depicted by the arrow diagram. Describe the relation in each.

(a) 54 ➔ 18 ➔ 6 ➔ 2

(b)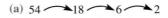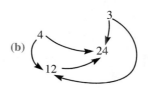

(c)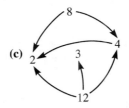

(d)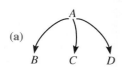

3. Find possible numbers, determined by the arrow diagram, for the letters in each case. Describe the illustrated relation using the numbers you have chosen.

(a)

(b)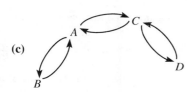

(c)

4. Let $X = \{3, 4, 6, 7, 9, 11, 16, 20, 21, 22\}$. Determine the subsets of X consisting of ordered pairs defined by each of the following relations.

   (a) "is a prime factor of"

   (b) "divides"

   (c) "is a multiple of"

   (d) "is four greater than"

5. Which of the following relations are symmetric?

   (a) "is the brother of"

   (b) "lives in the same neighborhood as"

   (c) "is the same age as"

   (d) "is the father of"

   (e) "sits at the same lunchroom table as"

   (f) "is taller than"

   (g) "is the twin of"

   (h) "is paid the same hourly wage as"

   (i) "speaks the same language as"

   (j) "is visible to"

6. List five of the relations in Problem 5 that are transitive. Explain your choices.

7. Let $A = \{16, 100, 121, 225\}$ and $B = \{3, 7, 11, 15\}$.

   (a) Find all of the elements in $A \times B$.

(b) Determine the subset of $A \times B$ defined by the relation "is the square of."

(c) Is this a symmetric relation?

(d) Describe a relation that would hold for every ordered pair listed in part (a).

8. The following arrow diagram represents the phone calls made among the coworkers in a certain office who are suspects in an embezzlement investigation. An arrow defines the relation "telephoned." One detective theorizes that the real embezzler is antisocial and tends to have little contact with others. Based on this theory, who should the prime suspects be?

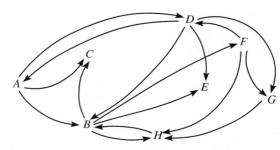

9. The following arrow diagram represents transmissions sent on a computer network. User E is suspected of spreading a computer virus. An arrow defines the relation "transmits data via a modem to." Trace a possible spread of the virus. Justify your conclusions.

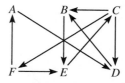

10. List all of the factors of 36. List the ordered pairs defined by the relation "is a multiple of." Determine whether or not this is an equivalence relation.

11. Which of the following relations are functions?

   (a) "is the father of"

   (b) "is the sister of"

   (c) "is twice"

   (d) "is the letter of the alphabet directly after"

   (e) "is the telephone number of"

   (f) "is two units away on the number line from"

   (g) "cubed is"

   (h) "is the first name in the phone book on the page whose last name is"

(i) "has the same number of vertices as"

(j) "rounds up to the nearest whole dollar amount of"

12. Using the calendar in Investigation 17 (see page 163), state an additional example of a relation on a specific set that is a function and an additional example of a relation on a specific set that is not a function.

13. In each of the following sets you are given the domain and the range of a function as ordered pairs. Identify the function that defines these ordered pairs.

(a) $\{(8, 2), (20, 5)\ (4, 1), (60, 15)\}$

(b) $\{(5, 2), (7, 3), (9, 4), (11, 5), (13, 6)\}$

(c) $\{(48, 5), (68, 7), (18, 2), (998, 100), (1498, 150)\}$

(d) $\{(0, 0), (1, 1), (2, 8), (3, 27)\}$

(e) $\{(36, 40), (37, 40), (123, 120), (71, 70)\}$

14. Fill in the missing domain, function, or range.

	Domain	Function	Range
(a)	20	?	12
	15	?	7
	111	?	103
(b)	?	divided by 2, minus 3 is	5
	?		0
	?		30
(c)	13	plus 2, divided by 3 is	?
	16		?
	31		?
(d)	Lincoln	?	Abraham
	Kennedy	?	John
	Ford	?	Gerald
(e)	fattest	?	fat
	best	?	good
	worst	?	bad

15. Which of the following arrow diagrams represent functions on the given sets?

(a)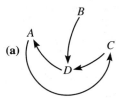

(b)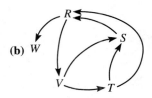

(c)

(d)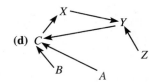

16. Let $f(x) = 3 + 3x$. Let the domain of the function be the set $\{2, 4, 6, 8\}$.

(a) Determine the ordered pairs that define this function on the given domain.

(b) Illustrate the function on the domain by means of an arrow diagram.

17. Let $f(x) = 36 - x^2$. Let the domain of the function be the set $\{0, 1, 2, 3, 4, 5, 6\}$. Determine the ordered pairs that define the function on the given domain.

18. Suppose that the function $g(x)$ is defined on a given set where $g(x) = x^3 - x^2$.

(a) What is the value of the function when $x = 0$, $x = 3$, and $x = 5$?

(b) For what value of x does the function equal 448?

19. Let the function F be such that the output is five times the input. Let the function G be such that the output is five less than the input.

(a) Describe $G \circ F$.

(b) Describe $F \circ G$.

(c) Describe $F(G(x))$.

(d) Describe $G(F(x))$.

(e) Find $G(F(10))$.

(f) Find $F(G(10))$.

(g) Find $(G \circ F)(7)$.

(h) Find $(F \circ G)(9)$.

20. Describe how the solution to each of the following could be found by using the composition of two functions. Define the functions in the composition.

(a) $((4)^5)^2$

(b) 9^3

(c) 4×5

21. Let $F(x) = 6x - 5$. Let $G(x) = 5x - 6$. Find the value of each of the following compositions.

(a) $F(G(5))$ (b) $(G \circ F)(5)$ (c) $G(F(2))$

(d) $(G \circ F)(2)$ (e) $(F \circ G)(10)$

22. (a) Let $F(x) = 2x$, and let $(F \circ G)(3) = 36$. What is a possible function for $G(x)$?

(b) Let $F(x) = 3x + 2$, and let $G(F(3)) = 6$. What is a possible function for $G(x)$?

(c) Let $G(x) = x^2 + 1$, and let $(F \circ G)(4) = 170$. What is a possible function for $F(x)$?

23. Evaluate each of the following terms.

(a) $(3 + 6) \pmod{12}$ (b) $(8 + 9) \pmod{12}$

(c) $(4 + 4) \pmod 5$ (d) $(6 + 4) \pmod 7$

24. Determine the value of each of the following operations on the Clock 12 set, $\{1, 2, 3, 4, 5, 6, 7, 8, 9, 10, 11, 12\}$.

(a) $8 \oplus 9$ (b) $9 \ominus 11$ (c) $2 \otimes 10$ (d) $4 \oplus 8$

25. Determine the value of B in each of the following.

(a) $4 + 7 = B \pmod 5$ (b) $B + 5 = 3 \pmod 4$

(c) $4 - B = 5 \pmod 8$

26. List four whole numbers that are congruent to 8 in modulo 11.

27. (a) Construct an addition table for modulo 6.

(b) Is mod 6 closed under addition? Explain your answer.

(c) What is the identity element in mod 6?

(d) Does every element have an additive inverse? (Recall that a number plus its additive inverse has a sum of zero.)

(e) Is addition mod 6 commutative? Explain your answer.

(f) Is addition mod 6 associative? Explain your answer.

28. You have seen that the relation "is congruent to (mod 7)" is an equivalence relation on the set of whole numbers. Describe how the set of whole numbers is partitioned by this equivalence relation.

In Other Words

29. What is a relation?

30. What is a function?

31. Explain the relationship between modular arithmetic and clock arithmetic.

32. What are the domain and range of a function?

33. What does it mean for two numbers, a and b, to be congruent mod c?

Cooperative Activity

34. Groups of four

Individual Accountability: The concepts involved in modular arithmetic can be used to develop and send codes. If we assign each letter of the alphabet a number from 1 to 26 and let 0 represent a space, we can use mod 27 to encode messages.

The first part of this activity is to create an addition table for mod 27. This will be divided into four parts, with each group member completing one quarter of the table. The responsibilities are listed in the following chart.

Member	Addition Table Rows
A	0–6
B	7–13
C	14–20
D	21–26

Group Goal: Combine your efforts from above into one table. Make sure that the entire table is correct. Together, use the table to decode the following message by first determining the missing value in each equation. Then, use $1 \to$ A, $2 \to$ B, . . . , $26 \to$ Z to decode the message (fill in the blank lines).

$$13 + 20 = \text{\_\_\_\_} \pmod{27}$$
$$26 + 20 = \text{\_\_\_\_} \pmod{27}$$
$$155 = \text{\_\_\_\_} \pmod{27}$$
$$4 + 17 = \text{\_\_\_\_} \pmod{27}$$
$$9 \times 11 = \text{\_\_\_\_} \pmod{27}$$
$$23 + 9 = \text{\_\_\_\_} \pmod{27}$$
$$54 = \text{\_\_\_\_} \pmod{27}$$
$$37 \times 2 = \text{\_\_\_\_} \pmod{27}$$
$$29 - 24 = \text{\_\_\_\_} \pmod{27}$$
$$109 = \text{\_\_\_\_} \pmod{27}$$

$2 \times 15 = $ _____ (mod 27)

$31 \times 2 = $ _____ (mod 27)

$2^5 = $ _____ (mod 27)

$30 + 42 = $ _____ (mod 27)

Vocabulary for Chapter 4

array

associative property of whole number
    multiplication

base

Cartesian product model of multiplication

clock arithmetic

Clock N

closure property of whole number
    multiplication

commutative property of whole number
    multiplication

composite numbers

composition of two functions

congruence modulo m

cross-product model

distributive property of whole number
    multiplication over addition

dividend

divisor

domain

drawing a diagram

Egyptian method of whole number
    division

equivalence relation

exponent

factors

function

identity property of whole number
    multiplication

lattice method of whole number
    multiplication

making a chart

mathematical system

modular arithmetic

modulus

multiplicand

multiplicative identity element

multiplier

number line model of whole number
    division

number line model of whole number
    multiplication

partial products method of whole number
    multiplication

partitioning

power

prime factorization

prime numbers

product

quotient

range

reflexive

relation

Russian peasant method of whole number
    multiplication

set model of whole number division

set model of whole number multiplication

standard algorithm method of whole
    number division

subtractive method of whole number
    division

symmetric

transitive

tree diagram

using a variable

variable

working backwards

zero property of whole number
    multiplication

Review for Chapter 4

1. The product of two adjacent page numbers in a text book is 71,556.

    (a) Estimate what these two numbers might be.

    (b) What information does the last digit give that helps to narrow down the search?

    (c) *Clue 1:* One of the numbers contains all even digits. How does this clue help narrow the search space?

    (d) *Clue 2:* The sum of the digits of one number is 15. How does this clue help narrow down the search space?

    (e) Find the two numbers. Compare your result with your estimate from part (a).

2. Illustrate the product by the indicated model.

    (a) 7×8 (set model)

    (b) 4×4 (number line model)

    (c) 1×9 (array model)

    (d) 2×5 (Cartesian product model)

3. Illustrate each problem using the indicated model.

    (a) $35 \div 7$ (set model)

    (b) $21 \div 3$ (number line model)

4. You are given the set $\{A, B, C, D, E\}$. You are told that the set is closed under multiplication, and that E is the multiplicative identity element. An element of the set may not appear more than once in any row or column of the multiplication table. Fill in the multiplication table with appropriate values.

×	A	B	C	D	E
A	—	—	—	—	—
B	—	—	—	—	—
C	—	—	—	—	—
D	—	—	—	—	—
E	—	—	—	—	—

5. Supply a real-life context to illustrate each of the following properties.

    (a) $(B + C) \div D = (B \div D) + (C \div D)$

    (b) $A \cdot (B - C) = (A \cdot B) - (A \cdot C)$

6. Rewrite each of the following expressions in two different ways in a simpler form using the distributive property.

    (a) 89×5

    (b) 173×42

    (c) $3150 \div 15$

    (d) $7825 \div 25$

7. Let $R = \{19, 105, 11\}$ and let $S = \{15, 121, 133\}$. Form the Cartesian product $R \cdot S$. Identify the ordered pairs (r, s) in which r is a factor of s, r is a multiple of s, or r divides s.

8. Find the missing digits A, B, C, D, and E in the following factor tree diagram.

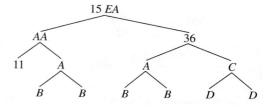

9. Write a problem that would use the following calculator keystroke sequences.

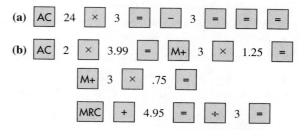

10. Write a problem in which an estimate is an appropriate solution for each of the following terms. Use any of the estimation procedures to approximate the solution.

    (a) 365×27

    (b) $2550 \div 50$

    (c) $(2200 \div 8) \times 52$

11. Find the solution for each example below using the indicated algorithm.

    (a) 853×47 (lattice multiplication algorithm)

    (b) 29×75 (Russian peasant algorithm)

    (c) $1620 \div 45$ (Egyptian division algorithm)

    (d) $1584 \div 33$ (subtractive algorithm)

12. Determine the values for A, B, and C in the accompanying lattice multiplication.

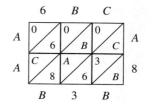

13. Express 2520 as a product of primes. How many factors does this number have?

14. A certain number has $5^2 \times 7^1 \cdot 11^2$ as its prime × factorization. List all of the factors of this number.

15. Let $A = 2^3$, $B = 2^5$, and $C = 2^{10}$. Simplify each of the following using the rules of exponents outlined in this chapter.

    (a) $A \cdot B \cdot C$ (b) $C \div (B \cdot A)$ (c) B^A

    (d) $\dfrac{B + C}{A}$ (e) $A \cdot (C - B)$

16. Find three whole numbers, none of which contain any zeros, whose product is 27,000.

17. Find two whole numbers, neither of which contain any zeros, whose product is 2 million.

18. When a coin collection is arranged in piles of 8, there are no coins remaining. When it is arranged in piles of 9, there are no coins remaining. When it is stacked in piles of 11, there are 7 coins remaining. What is the fewest number of coins that can be contained in this collection?

19. What is the value of $(666,666,667)^2$? (*Hint*: Solve a simpler problem and look for a pattern.)

20. Determine a divisibility rule for 105. Explain your answer.

21. What is the exact product of 7,777,777,777 and 5?

22. Find the missing digits (A and B) in each of the following equations.

    (a) $A8A \div 1A = 39$

    (b) $(BB)^4 = B34B56$

    (c) $A^B \cdot B^A = 7A$

23. In a certain video game, points are awarded for capturing the following aliens:

$$\text{eenie} = 2 \text{ points}$$
$$\text{meanie} = 3 \text{ points}$$
$$\text{minie} = 4 \text{ points}$$
$$\text{mo} = 10 \text{ points}$$

Al scored a total of 41 points, capturing more mo's than any other aliens. How many arrangements of captured aliens would result in this score? List these arrangements.

24. On a piece of graph paper, write the numbers from 1 to 100 as illustrated in the following grid.

1	2	3	4	5	6	7	8	9	10
11	12	13	14	15	16	17	18	19	20
21	22	23	24	25	26	27	28	29	30
31	32	33	34	35	36	37	38	39	40
41	42	43	44	45	46	47	48	49	50
51	52	53	54	55	56	57	58	59	60
61	62	63	64	65	66	67	68	69	70
71	72	73	74	75	76	77	78	79	80
81	82	83	84	85	86	87	88	89	90
91	92	93	94	95	96	97	98	99	100

This grid is known as the sieve of Eratosthenes.

(a) Circle the number 2, and cross off all subsequent multiples of 2.

(b) Circle the number 3, and cross off all subsequent multiples of 3.

(c) Repeat this process with the numbers 5, 7, and 11.

(d) Draw a conclusion about the numbers that have been crossed off the grid and the numbers that remain.

25. Find the number of dots that form the eleventh figure in this sequence.

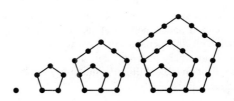

26. Determine the remainders in each of the following terms. Explain your reasoning.

    (a) $7^{100} \div 6$ (b) $5^{47} \div 3$ (c) $11^{25} \div 7$

27. Seventeen is a prime number, as is 71, the number you get when you reverse the digits in 17. Find three other prime numbers whose reverse is also prime.

28. Mathematician Christian Goldbach (1690–1764) made two hypotheses about whole numbers that have yet to be proven or disproven. These hypotheses have come to be known as *Goldbach's conjectures*. His first conjecture states that every even number greater than 2 can be written as the sum of two prime numbers. Determine two primes whose sum is given in each of the following numbers.

    (a) 36   (b) 42   (c) 78   (d) 46   (e) 198

29. Goldbach's second conjecture states that each odd number greater than 5 can be written as the sum of three prime

numbers. Determine the three primes whose sum is given in each of the following numbers.

(a) 23   (b) 59   (c) 49   (d) 107   (e) 293

30. Find a three-digit number with the following characteristics.

The square of the number is a five-digit number whose ones digit is a 6.

The cube of the number is a seven-digit number whose ones digit is a 4.

The sum of the digits of the number is 6.

The smallest digit is in the tens place.

31. The sum of the digits of a four-digit even number is 20. Two of its digits are even and two are odd. The number is divisible by the square of a prime whose ones digit is a 1. Find such a number.

32. What is the relation depicted by the following arrow diagram?

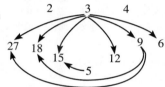

33. Examine the face of the analog clock shown below. Let C be the set of whole numbers on the face of the clock.

(a) Let A represent the relation "is the number opposite." List the subset of the Cartesian product $C \times C$ defined by relation A. Is this an equivalence relation? Explain your answer.

(b) Let D represent the relation "divides." List the subset of the Cartesian product $C \times C$ defined by the relation D. Is this an equivalence relation? Explain your answer.

(c) Let S represent the relation "has the same number of digits as." List the subset of the Cartesian product $C \times C$ defined by the relation S. Is this an equivalence relation? Explain your answer.

34. Let P be the set containing elements of the form 3^N, where N is a whole number ($P = \{3^0, 3^1, 3^2, 3^3, \ldots\}$).

(a) Is this set closed under multiplication?

(b) Describe the subset of the Cartesian product $P \times P$ defined by the relation "is a multiple of."

(c) Is the relation "is a multiple of" on set P a reflexive relation? Explain your answer.

(d) Describe the subset of the Cartesian product $P \times P$ defined by the relation "is a factor of."

(e) Is the relation "is a factor of" on set P a reflexive relation?

35. Let Y be the set containing the elements $\{1, 2, 3, 4, 7, 10\}$. Let R represent the relation "is two less than three times." Construct an arrow diagram to illustrate the relation R on set Y.

36. Let A be the set of factors of 12. Let B be the set of factors of 18.

(a) Let G be the subset of the Cartesian product $A \times B$ defined by the relation "shares a common factor with." List the ordered pairs in G.

(b) Let H be the subset of the Cartesian product $B \times A$ defined by the relation "shares a common factor with." List the ordered pairs in H.

(c) List the elements of $(G \cap H)$.

37. Let set $A = \{2, 4, 6, 8, 10, 12, 14\}$. Let set $B = \{1, 3, 5, 7, 9, 11, 13, 15, 17\}$.

(a) Let W be the relation "is three less than" from set A to set B. Does the relation W define a function? Explain your answer.

(b) Let M be the relation "is one unit on a number line away from" from set A to set B. Does the relation M define a function? Explain your answer.

38. (a) Determine the function $G(x)$ whose domain and range are given here:

Domain	Range
3	10
4	13
5	16
6	19

(b) Use the function G found in part (a) to determine the values of $G(x)$ when $x = 0$, 10, and 100.

39. Let F be the function that doubles an input value. Let G be the function that divides the input by 2. Describe each of the following compositions.

(a) $F \circ F$ (b) $G \circ G$ (c) $G \circ F$ (d) $F \circ G$

40. Let $F(x) = 8x - 4$ and let $G(x) = 4x - 8$. Find the values of each of the following.

    (a) $F(4)$ (b) $G(4)$ (c) $(G \circ F)(4)$

    (d) $(F \circ G)(4)$ (e) $F(G(5))$ (f) $G(F(5))$

41. When $x = 2$, the result of a composition $(G \circ F)(2)$ is 6^2. What might the functions F and G be that would yield this result?

42. (a) Write an addition table for mod 4.

    (b) Write a multiplication table for mod 4.

    (c) What is the additive inverse for each element in the set $\{0, 1, 2, 3\}$?

    (d) What is the multiplicative identity for each element in the set $\{0, 1, 2, 3\}$?

    (e) Is multiplication mod 4 commutative? Explain your answer.

    (f) Does $3(2 + 3) = 3 \times 2 + 3 \times 3$ in mod 4?

43. Write an addition table for mod 5. Is the relation "is the additive inverse of" reflexive and symmetric? Explain your answer.

44. The year 1992 was a leap year. Leap years occur every four years. What is the first leap year after the year 3500?

In Other Words

45. A number is written as a product of primes, but not in exponential form. Explain how grouping the prime factors together in groups of two, three, four, and so on can generate all of the factors of the original number.

46. Discuss three contexts in which tests for divisibility would be useful.

47. Can the product of two primes itself be prime? Explain your answer.

48. Why is the standard division algorithm viewed as a more efficient and compact version of the scaffold method?

49. Why does this text make a point of describing several models for each of the basic whole number operations?

Cooperative Activity

50. Groups of four

Individual Accountability: A proper factor of a number is any whole number divisor other than the number itself. A counting number is said to be *perfect* if it is equal to the sum of its proper factors. It is known that an even number is perfect if and only if it has the form $2^{n-1}(2^n - 1)$. A counting number is said to be *deficient* if it is greater than the sum of its proper factors. A counting number is said to be *abundant* if it is less than the sum of its proper factors. Find three perfect, three deficient, and three abundant numbers.

Group Goal: Share your individual results. Now examine these pairs: 220 and 284; 1184 and 1210. Each pair of counting numbers is said to be *amicable*, or *friendly*. Find the relationship that exists between each of the elements of the pairs. Write a definition of *amicable*.

5

Integer Relationships: Algorithms and Algebra

Examine the photograph at the right.

Describe what you see.

How might you estimate the length of the road?

How might you estimate the height of the mesas?

How might you determine the lowest point in the photograph?

What would a mathematical description of the photograph contain?

Introduction

To this point, most of our discussion has focused on the set of whole numbers. However, the real world presents situations that are not easily represented by the set of whole numbers. For example, we need ways to represent such things as:

- losses
- gains
- elevations above and below sea level
- deposits
- withdrawals
- credits
- debits
- temperatures

When subtraction of whole numbers was introduced in Chapter 3, we limited our discussion to situations in which the difference was a number greater than or equal to zero. By imposing such a limitation, we were able to confine the subtractive process to cases in which the minuend was greater than the subtrahend. This might have given you the false notion that in real-world contexts, subtraction is closed under the set of whole numbers. However, even the world of elementary school students involves situations in which the result of a subtraction is a number less than zero. For example, a drop in temperature on a cold January day might result in a change in the temperature reading from 2° C to –3° C.

The material covered in this chapter will broaden your concept of our number system, going beyond the set of whole numbers and into the realm of numbers that are less than zero. Section 5.1 takes the first step in extending the number line you are familiar with by introducing integer addition and subtraction. Section 5.2 discusses the models and properties of integer multiplication and division. And finally, Section 5.3 prepares you to begin to use your knowledge of whole numbers and integers and apply it to algebra. The introduction here will familiarize you with mathematical expressions used in algebra and begin to show you how using it to solve equations will increase your problem-solving capabilities and help you learn to deal with a world that contains unknowns.

5.1 Extending the Number Line: Integer Addition and Subtraction

Examine Figure 5.1, which depicts a number line of whole numbers. The whole number 2 is found by moving two units to the right of zero. Likewise, the whole number 153 would be found by moving one hundred fifty-three units to the right of zero. But what about movement to the left of zero?

Figure 5.1

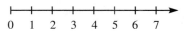

Notice on the number line in Figure 5.2 that a distance of three units "away from zero" defines the location of two different points on the number line. Because the number line is a distance model, we must introduce a new set of numbers that will indicate distance to the left of zero. The symbol "–" is placed in front of the numeral to indicate a location to the left of zero. The union of the set {–1, –2, –3, –4, . . . } with the set of whole numbers is called the set of **integers**, as shown in Figure 5.2

integers

Figure 5.2

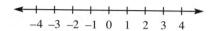

The set of integers can be partitioned into three disjoint subsets:

{–1, –2, –3, –4, . . . }	**Negative integers**
{0}	**Zero**
{1, 2, 3, 4, 5, . . . }	**Positive integers**

Sometimes a positive integer is written with the "+" symbol before the numeral to clearly distinguish it from its negative counterpart.

A balance beam is a manipulative material commonly found in elementary school classrooms. It can be used to illustrate the relationship between, for example, +4 and –4. The horizontal beam is a tangible representation of a number line. The pegs on the beam model the set of integers. Weights are hung on the pegs to the right of the center post (zero) to represent positive numbers and to the left of the center post to represent negative numbers (see Figure 5.3).

Figure 5.3

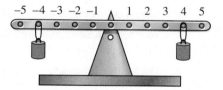

When weights are hung on both +4 and –4, the beam is balanced. This indicates that both numbers are an equal distance from zero. This distance from zero is called the **absolute value** of a number. The absolute value of +4, symbolized by | 4 |, is equal to 4, since +4 is a distance of four units from zero on the number line. The absolute value of –4, symbolized by | –4 |, is also equal to 4, since –4 is also a distance of four units from zero on the number line. The integers +4 and –4 are considered **opposites**. The negative symbol is often read as "the opposite of." For example, –5 would be read as "the opposite of 5." The relationship between 5 and –5 can be viewed as analogous to the relationship between p and ~p. Just as in logic, we encounter ~(~p), and define it to be logically equivalent to p; so also might we encounter –(–5), read it as "the opposite of the opposite of 5," and define it as 5.

absolute value

opposites

Many calculators have a +/– key that allows you to change the sign of the display to its opposite. For example, the following keystroke sequence will convert a positive 36 to a negative 36, and then back to a positive 36:

Be aware that calculators are programmed differently to operate with signed numbers. On some calculators, pressing the subtraction key results in a change of sign. Usually, these are the calculators that do not have a change-of-sign key. Read through the instruction booklet of your calculator or experiment with your calculator to familiarize yourself with its integer capabilities.

Integer Addition

A theme that has permeated this text is that in order for students to understand and remember rules, those rules must be preceded by tangible activities that illustrate the concept. If these activities are well suited to the purpose, students can often formulate the rules by themselves.

This reliance on tangible models will become obvious to you as we move through each of the four basic operations on integers. We will begin with integer addition. Integer addition can be illustrated in two ways: through the set model and the number line model.

The Set Model of Integer Addition

Before we discuss the set model, we must lay some groundwork for combining a number and its opposite. For example, what are the outcomes of each of the following situations?

- You gain one pound, and then you lose one pound.
- I give you $5, then I take away $5 from you.
- A stock price drops eight points, then it gains eight points.
- A river drops one foot below its normal level, and then rises by one foot.
- You deposit $150 into your checking account, then immediately write a check for that amount.
- The temperature drops 10 degrees, and then rises 10 degrees.

Each of these statements is a combination of two situations. Look at the second example. Initially, you were given $5. This can be represented by +5. Then you "lost" $5. Typically, losing $5 would be construed as subtracting 5. However, for our purposes here, we will view it as adding −5. The −5 represents a debit, or a removal of a certain monetary amount. The sentence can be symbolized by $+5 + (-5)$. In fact, each of the situations can be symbolized by either $+x + (-x)$ or $-x + (+x)$. The outcomes are all the same. The net effect of the combination of the two situations is that the value has not changed. When you gain a pound then lose a pound $[+1 + (-1)]$, when the temperature drops 10 degrees then rises 10 degrees $[-10 + (+10)]$, and when you deposit $150 then withdraw $150 $[+150 + (-150)]$, the net effect is zero. Therefore, for any number x,

$$+x + (-x) = -x + (+x) = 0$$

Recall the set model of whole number addition. A number was represented by a set of that many objects. In integer addition, however, we will be concerned with the *value* of a set rather than the number of objects in it. Examine Figure 5.4. Figure 5.4a shows a set with a value of +5. Figure 5.4b shows a set with a value of –5. Figure 5.4c depicts the mathematical sentence +5 + (–5) as a combination of the two sets. Although the resulting set contains 10 chips, it does not have a value of 10. Its value is determined by first pairing one positive chip with one negative chip. We have already seen that this pair has a value of zero. The set has five such pairs. Therefore, the value is zero, as shown in figure 5.4d, leading us to the mathematical statement +5 + (–5) = 0.

Figure 5.4

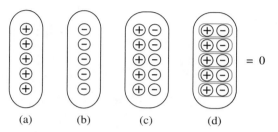

(a)   (b)   (c)   (d)

To help you understand this concept of combining positive and negative integers, try some experiments of your own. Obtain a quantity of two different objects, such as coins, poker chips, or slips of paper that can represent the positive and negative chips shown in Figure 5.4. After you have demonstrated for yourself that combining an equal number of positive items with an equal number of negative items will always equal zero, try some experiments in which the number of positive and negative items are not equal. What hapens then? Investigation 1 explores a situation in which the outcome of the combination of positive and negative integers is not zero.

Investigation 1

Use the set model of integer addition to solve the following problem: A stock price rose 7 points at the start of trading. By the end of the day, it had fallen 11 points. What was the outcome of the day's trading?

An increase of 7 points can be represented by a set containing 7 positive chips. A loss of 11 points can be represented by a set containing 11 negative chips. When these chips are combined and the negative/positive pairs are formed, the value of the remaining chips indicates the outcome of the day's trading:

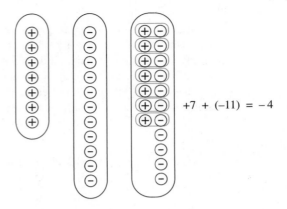

$$+7 + (-11) = -4$$

The outcome of the day's trading for this particular stock is a loss of 4 points, which can be represented by –4.

The Number Line Model of Integer Addition

An alternative model of integer addition is the number line model. In this model, positive values are represented by a directed distance to the right, and negative values are represented by a directed distance to the left. Figure 5.5 depicts how Investigation 1 would be viewed using the number line model. In Figure 5.5a a gain of 7 points is shown. In Figure 5.5b a subsequent loss of 11 points is pictured. In Figure 5.5c the final outcome, a loss of 4 points, is indicated. The number of units moved left or right on the number line is determined by the absolute value of the integer. The direction, left or right, is determined by the sign preceding the numeral. The solution would have been the same if the stock had dropped 11 points initially and then rallied for a gain of 7 points.

Figure 5.5

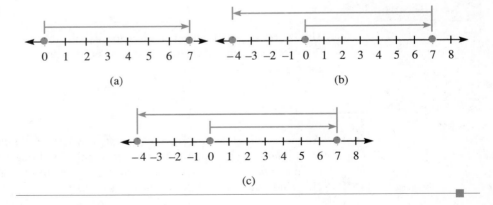

Use the number line model of integer additon to illustrate the following problem: Before midnight, the temperature dropped 6°. By 1:00 A.M. the temperature had dropped an additional 3°. What was the total temperature change as of 1:00 A.M.?

The number line below illustrates the effect of the two temperature changes:

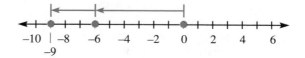

The number line shows that the total change in temperature was a drop of 9°. Symbolically, this is stated as

$$-6 + (-3) = -9$$

Notice that the set model begins with tangible manipulatives, whereas the number line model dispenses with the tangible and moves to the symbolic.

Rules and Properties of Integer Addition
The eight rules and properties of integer addition are stated here.

1. Combination of Opposites.   Any number combined with its opposite is equal to zero.

$$+x + (-x) = -x + (+x) = 0$$

2. Additon of Integers with Like Signs.   To add integers with like signs, add the absolute values of the addends. The sum will have the same sign as the addends.

$$+x + (+y) = +(|+x| + |+y|) = +(x + y)$$
$$-x + (-y) = -(|-x| + |-y|) = -(x + y)$$

3. Addition of Integers with Unlike Signs.   To add integers with unlike signs, take the absolute value of each addend and then subtract the lesser absolute value from the greater absolute value. This will result in the absolute value of the solution. The sign of the solution is dictated by the sign of the number with the greater absolute value. In the case where $|x| > |y|$,

$$+x + (-y) = +(|+x| - |-y|) = +(x-y)$$
$$-x + (+y) = -(|-x| - |+y|) = -(x-y)$$

closure property of integer addition **4. Closure Property of Integer Addition.**   The sum of any two integers is itself an integer; that is, the set of integers is closed under the operation of addition.

commutative property of integer addition **5. Commutative Property of Integer Addition.**   The order of the addends may be changed without changing the sum.

associative property of integer addition

6. Associative Property of Integer Addition. When combining more than two addends, the way in which the addends are grouped does not affect the sum.

identity property of integer addition

additive identity

7. Identity Property of Integer Addition. There exists a unique integer zero that when added to any integer addend does not change the value of the addend. Zero is called the **additive identity** element.

additive inverse property of integer addition

additive inverse

8. Additive Inverse Property of Integer Addition. Any integer added to its opposite results in a value of zero; that is, for each integer x there exists a unique integer $(-x)$, the opposite of x, such that $x + (-x) = 0$. The integer $(-x)$ is called the **additive inverse** of x.

You can see now why we introduced the set model and number line model before presenting the rules and properties of integer addition. Rules and properties are too abstract for young students to absorb without first seeing how they apply to real situations. And as we mentioned earlier, when students are presented with models of how operations work, models that have meaning in their world, they can often discover many of the rules that govern these operations on their own. Hence our progression throughout the book from the tangible to the symbolic—it is the best way for elementary school students to learn the critical skills of analyzing, making connections, and learning to apply those connections to both classroom and real-life problem-solving situations.

Investigation 3

An elevator is situated at the 50th floor of a 90-story building. The following movements of the elevator are recorded: rises 10 floors; rises 8 floors; rises 17 floors; drops 33 floors; drops 9 floors; rises 18 floors. What is the present location of the elevator?

Because of the large numbers and the many movements involved, modeling this problem with either the set model or the number line model would be awkward. Instead, we will represent the problem symbolically and follow the rules and properties of integer addition.

$$50 + [+10 + (+8) + (+17) + (-33) + (-9) + (+18)]$$

$50 + [+10 + (+8) + (+17) + (+18) + (-33) + (-9)]$ by the commutative property

$50 + [+10 + (+8) + (+17) + (+18)] + [-33 + (-9)]$ by the associative property

$50 + [+53 + (-42)]$ by integer addition of like signs

$50 + [|+53| - |-42|]$ by integer addition of unlike signs

$50 + (+11)$ by integer addition of unlike signs

$+61$ by integer addition of like signs

The elevator is now located on the 61st floor.

The calculator keystroke sequence for this problem might read as follows:

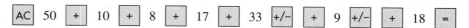

The display should be 61.

Integer Subtraction

The Set Model of Integer Subtraction.   In this model, subtraction can be interpreted as *removing* "chips" from a single set and examining what remains. Examine Figure 5.6. The $-4 - (-2)$ is viewed as "from a set containing four negative chips, remove two negative chips." The result is a set containing two negative chips. Therefore, $-4 - (-2) = -2$.

Figure 5.6

Now, $-5 - (+4)$ would be viewed as "from a set containing five negative chips, remove four positive chips." Because there are no positive chips in the set to remove, it is necessary to alter the number of chips in the set without altering the value of the set. Recall that a negative/positive pair has a value of zero. The additive identity property assures you that adding zero does not change the original value. Therefore, it is possible to include as many negative/positive pairs as necessary to result in four positive chips. Figure 5.7 depicts this process.

Figure 5.7

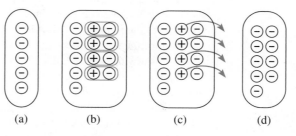

(a)   (b)   (c)   (d)

In Figure 5.7b four negative/positive pairs are incorporated into the set without changing the value of the set. In Figure 5.7c four positive chips are removed, as indicated by the original subtraction example. Figure 5.7d depicts what remains after the subtraction process, which is nine negative chips. Therefore, $-5 - (+4) = -9$.

Investigation 4

Use the set model of integer subtraction to illustrate the following situation: After writing a $5 check, the balance in your checking account is $7. You wrote the $5 check for a catalog purchase. When you find out that the item is out of stock, you tear up the check. What is the balance in your account now?

Although this problem is simple, it offers a real-world illustration of subtracting a negative amount. The checking account balance is represented as +7. The check itself is represented as –5. The voiding of the check is represented by removing the withdrawal from your account, or –(–5). This situation can be represented symbolically by +7 – (–5). It can be viewed using the set model as follows:

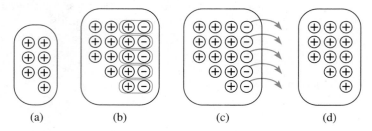

(a)   (b)   (c)   (d)

This illustration depicts a set representing the balance of $7. Part (b) shows the inclusion of five negative/positive pairs, each with a value of zero. In part (c), five negative chips are removed to represent the removal of the debit of $5, or the voiding of the $5 check. Part (d) represents the new balance in the checking account, which is $12.

The Number Line Model of Integer Subtraction.   Recall that in whole number subtraction of the form $x - y$, x is the minuend, y is the subtrahend, and the result of this operation is the difference. These labels are also used for integer subtraction. In the number line model, the difference between x and y is interpreted as the directed distance from the subtrahend to the minuend. This will become clearer in the following example.

To determine the solution of $-4 - (+3)$ using a number line, begin at zero and draw an arrow to show the directed distance represented by the minuend, –4. Then beginning at zero, draw an arrow to show the directed distance represented by the subtrahend, +3. Draw a third and final arrow from the subtrahend to the minuend. The length of the arrow indicates the absolute value of the difference. The direction in which the arrow is pointed indicates if the distance is positive or negative. As shown in Figure 5.8, the directed distance from +3 to –4 is represented by an arrow seven units long pointing in the negative direction; that is, the minuend, –4, is seven units to the left of the subtrahend, +3. Symbolically, $-4 - (+3) = -7$.

Figure 5.8

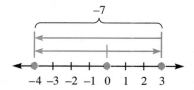

Investigation 5

Use the number line model of integer subtraction to illustrate Investigation 4.

The symbolic notation of the problem is +7 – (–5). The number line model follows:

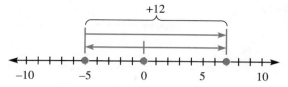

The directed distance from –5 to +7 is represented by an arrow that is 12 units long and points to the right. Thus, the difference has a value of +12.

Investigation 6

Use the number line model of integer subtraction to illustrate the following problem: Your credit card statement indicates that you owe $100. However, since you received the statement, you have returned a $20 item that had been charged to your account. If you wish to pay your balance in full, how much should you write the check for?

The $100 owed can be represented by –100. The $20 purchase charged to the account can be represented by –20. By returning the item, you have removed the $20 charge, which can be symbolized by –100 – (–20). This can be shown on the following number line:

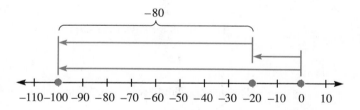

The difference is –80, which indicates that you still owe $80. A check written for $80 will cover your outstanding balance in full.

The Add-the-Opposite View of Integer Subtraction.   In Investigations 4 and 5, you may have noticed that the symbolic removal of the $5 check from the checking account statement, –(–5), had the same effect as adding a +5. In other words, the balance was increased by $5 after the order was canceled. In Investigation 6, by returning the $20 item, the debit of $20 was removed. This is symbolized by –(–20). Again, this is equivalent to adding a +20. It appears that subtracting a negative subtrahend is equivalent to adding the positive of that subtrahend. Is this the case when the subtrahend is positive to begin with? Examine the number line and set model illustrations of −8 − (+2) in Figure 5.9. The solution in both cases is −10.

Figure 5.9

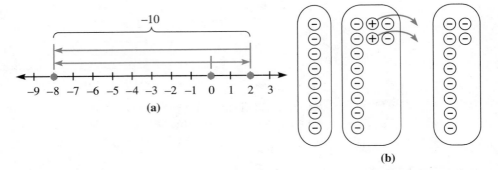

(a)

(b)

Now examine the number line and set model illustrations of the problem −8 + (−2) shown in Figure 5.10. The solution is also −10. Subtracting integers can be viewed as "adding the opposite" of the subtrahend.

Figure 5.10

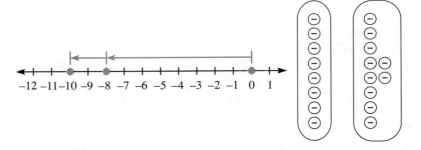

The calculator keystroke sequence for −8 − (+2) can be

The display should read −10. Notice that the keystroke sequence

which employs the add-the-opposite view, also yields a −10 in the display.

Investigation 7

Use the add-the-opposite view of integer subtraction to solve the following problem: At the beginning of the week, you deposited a $150 check in your checking account. After writing checks all week, the balance dropped to $90. On Saturday a statement from your bank indicated that the $150 check was returned for insufficient funds. What effect does this have on your checking account balance?

This is a simple subtraction problem that illustrates the relationship between integer subtraction and integer addition.

$$+90 - (+150) = +90 + (-150) = -60$$

Your account is overdrawn by $60.

Assessments for Section 5.1

1. Use the set model for integer addition or subtraction to illustrate each of the following sums.
   (a) $-3 + (-4)$
   (b) $11 + (-5)$
   (c) $-2 + (+2)$
   (d) $5 + (-6)$
   (e) $-2 + (4) + (-7)$

2. Use the set model for integer addition or subtraction to illustrate each of the following differences.
   (a) $-3 - (-5)$
   (b) $6 - (-2)$
   (c) $-5 - 4$
   (d) $-7 - 3$
   (e) $4 - (-4)$

3. Use the set model to illustrate the solution to the following problem.

$$(-3 + 6) - (-8)$$

4. Write the problem statement illustrated by each of the following illustrations.

   (a)

   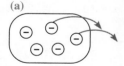

   (b)

   (c)

   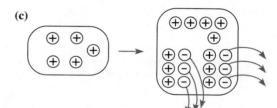

   (d)

5. Use the number line model to illustrate and determine the solution to each of the following sums.
   (a) $-5 + (-3)$
   (b) $9 + (-6)$
   (c) $-4 + (+5)$
   (d) $-15 + 13$
   (e) $-6 + 8 + (-3)$

6. Use the number line model to illustrate and determine the solution to each of the following differences.
   (a) $-11 - (-7)$
   (b) $9 - (-3)$
   (c) $-13 - 7$
   (d) $-12 - 5$
   (e) $10 - (-10)$

7. Use a number line model to illustrate and determine the solution to the expression.

$$[-3 + (+2)] - (-6)$$

8. Write a problem statement for each illustration below.

(a)

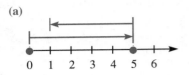

(b)

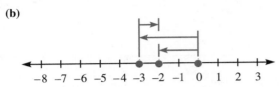

(c)

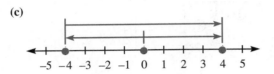

(d)

9. Rewrite each statement using the add-the-opposite view of integer subtraction, and then find the difference.

(a) $-35 - (+56)$

(b) $93 - (-27)$

(c) $117 - 98$

(d) $-75 - (-15)$

(e) $103 - (-103)$

10. Each of the following statements has been rewritten using the add-the-opposite view of integer subtraction. In each case, indicate the original subtraction problem.

(a) $-90 + (-45)$

(b) $45 + (-34)$

(c) $73 + 42$

(d) $-35 + 35$

(e) $-1342 + (-275)$

11. Write two different calculator keystroke sequences that could be used to solve each of the following problems.

(a) $-9 - (-4)$

(b) $37 - 56$

(c) $-275 - (-391)$

12. Determine the signs for each of the numbers below that will yield the given result.

(a) $[\square\, 3 + (\square\, 8)] + (\square\, 2) = -9$

(b) $\square\, 7 + [\square\, 2 + (\square\, 2)] = -7$

(c) $\square\, 231 - (\square\, 32) = -199$

(d) $\square\, 312 - (\square\, 72) = -384$

(e) $[\square\, 42 + (\square\, 36)] - (\square\, 18) = +24$

(f) $[\square\, 16 - (\square\, 20)] - (\square\, 11) = -25$

13. Simplify the following statements. Use the laws of integers outlined in this section as justification.

(a) $-23 + [+35 + (-48)] + (-29 + 83)$

(b) $[-43 + (-82) + 83 + (-29)] - (-28 + 72 + 28)$

14. Following are three illustrations of the nines' complement method of subtraction. First, identify the steps that occur and attempt to use the nines' complement method to perform the subtraction on part (d). Second, offer an explanation of *why* this method works. Your knowledge of integer addition and subtraction should help. (This alternative algorithm was first introduced in the Cooperative Activity of the Review for Chapter 3.)

(a)
$$
\begin{array}{r}
261 \\
-\ 85 \\
\hline
\end{array}
\rightarrow
\begin{array}{r}
261 \\
+914 \\
\hline
1175 \\
\curvearrowleft 1 \\
\hline
176
\end{array}
$$

(b)
$$
\begin{array}{r}
313 \\
-165 \\
\hline
\end{array}
\rightarrow
\begin{array}{r}
313 \\
+834 \\
\hline
1147 \\
\curvearrowleft 1 \\
\hline
148
\end{array}
$$

(c)
$$
\begin{array}{r}
705 \\
-278 \\
\hline
\end{array}
\rightarrow
\begin{array}{r}
705 \\
+721 \\
\hline
1426 \\
\curvearrowleft 1 \\
\hline
427
\end{array}
$$

(d)
$$
\begin{array}{r}
516 \\
-288 \\
\hline
\end{array}
$$

15. The elevation of a level plot of land is 16 feet below sea level. A 34-foot television antenna is erected on this site. How far above sea level is the top of the antenna? Express this problem symbolically, then solve it.

16. A construction crew wishes to put concrete pilings in the ground so they can construct a beach house that will sit atop the pilings. The pilings are 30 feet long. Each is to be driven 15 feet into the ground so that it reaches a point where the elevation is 18 feet below sea level. What will be the actual elevation above sea level of the house?

17. Determine the indicated term(s) in each of the following sequences.

(a) $-100, -73, -46$ (fifth term)

(b) $-17, -38, -59$ (eighth term)

(c) $-3, -2, -4, -1, -5, 0, -6, +1, -7$ (next three terms)

(d) $-40, -39, -37, -34, -30$ (seventh and eighth terms)

(e) First term, second term, −42, −53, −64, sixth term, seventh term

18. Using the numbers −4, −3, −2, −1, 0, 1, 2, 3, 4, construct a magic square whose sum is 0.

19. List five ways that you can balance a weight of 4 on the balance beam shown, using four different weights.

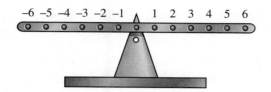

20. Describe two ways in which three weights can balance the given weight on the balance beam pictured in Problem 19.
(a) −5 **(b)** −1 **(c)** 4 **(d)** 6 **(e)** −3

21. The hourly temperature in a laboratory setting was recorded as follows:

8:00 A.M.	− 5° C
9:00 A.M.	− 1° C
10:00 A.M.	− 15° C
11:00 A.M.	− 7° C
12:00 noon	− 5° C

What is the total number of units that the mercury in the thermometer rose and fell beginning at 8:00 A.M. and ending at noon?

22. Let set T be the set of integers with the element 0 excluded. Let R be the relation "is the absolute value of." Is R reflexive, symmetric, and/or transitive? Explain your answer.

23. Let set T be the same as in Problem 22. Let R be the relation "is the opposite." Is R reflexive, symmetric, and/or transitive? Explain your answer.

24. Without using a calculator, determine the value of the following sequence. Verify your result on a calculator.

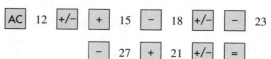

In Other Words

25. Explain absolute value.

26. Explain why subtracting a negative number is equivalent to adding the positive of that number.

27. How can the missing addends model of whole number subtraction be extended to the set of integers?

28. When illustrating integer subtraction with the set model, what must be done to model $A − B$, if $B > A$?

29. Explain the concept of directed distance on a number line.

Cooperative Activity

30. Groups of two

Individual Accountability: Each group member is given a set of equivalences. Use the first two complete statements in each column to determine an interpretation of a negative number in a particular modulus. Use the interpretation to find the missing values.

Member A	*Member B*
− 5 (mod 2) = 1	− 8 (mod 2) = 0
− 7 (mod 3) = 2	− 15 (mod 3) = 0
− 4 (mod 5) = ?	− 2 (mod 9) = ?
− ? (mod 4) = 3	− ? (mod 4) = 0
− ? (mod 9) = 2	− ? (mod 8) = 7
− 5 (mod ?) = 2	− 3 (mod ?) = 3
− 4 (mod ?) = 3	− 6 (mod ?) = 6

Group Goal: Share your results with your partner. Your interpretations of a negative number in a particular modulus should be justifiable. Together, determine the value of each.
(a) $[−5 + 2 − (−3) + 7 − 9 + (−14)]$ mod 8
(b) $[3 − 8 − (−2) − 16 + 1 − 6]$ mod 9

5.2 Models and Properties of Integer Multiplication and Division

Perhaps when you were introduced to multiplication and division of signed numbers as a young student, the goal of the activity was for you to memorize a set of rules. One of the drawbacks to learning mathematics in this way is that students see mathematics as abstract concepts that just "are"—not as a logical system of rules that applies because it makes sense in the context of tangible situations. Many students who simply memorize rules would be hard pressed to explain why, for example, a negative times a negative is a positive. For a prospective elementary school teacher, it is not enough simply to know that a negative times a negative is a positive. Rather, you must know and be able to explain *why* it is agreed that this is so. The purpose of this section is to provide the necessary background and to introduce a variety of models that will give meaning to the rules governing integer multiplication and division.

Integer Multiplication

Integer multiplication can be best illustrated using the set model, and like integer addition, it has various rules and properties that govern its use.

The Set Model of Integer Multiplication

Recall the set model that was introduced in Chapter 4 for working with whole number multiplication. In this model, whole number multiplication was based on recognizing a pattern of repeated addition. For example, when x and y are whole numbers,

$$x \cdot y = \underbrace{y + y + y + \cdots + y}_{x \text{ sets}}$$

You can see that $x \cdot y$ was interpreted as x groups of y. We will now construct an analogy between whole number multiplication and integer multiplication.

In integer multiplication, four possibilities exist: positive times positive, positive times negative, negative times positive, and negative times negative. We will use an extended version of the set model of integer addition to illustrate each of these four possibilities. We will introduce the concepts of putting groups of elements into a set and removing groups of elements from a set.

1. Positive Times Positive [$x \cdot y$ where $x > 0$ and $y > 0$]. We begin with a set that contains no elements; that is, has a value of zero. The product $x \cdot y$ where $x > 0$ and $y > 0$ is interpreted as "put x groups of y into the zero value set." These elements will be represented by positive and negative chips, and the set will be represented by a jar. At the start of integer multiplication, it is understood that an empty jar represents the zero value set. For example, $+3 \cdot (+2)$ means "Begin with an empty jar. Put three groups of two positive chips into the jar." You can see from the figure below that the product of $+3$ and $+2$ is $+6$.

2. Positive Times Negative [$x \cdot y$ where $x > 0$ and $y < 0$]. The product $x \cdot y$ where x is a positive integer and y is a negative integer is viewed as "Begin with an empty jar. Put x groups of y into the jar. The resulting product is represented by the chips in the jar." For example, +3 times –2 means that three groups of two negative chips will be put into the empty jar, as shown in the figure below. You can see that the product of +3 and –2 is – 6.

3. Negative Times Positive   [x · y where x < 0 and y > 0].
Recall the terminology used when whole number multiplication was introduced in Chapter 4. When you were given any whole number *x* of countable equal sets each containing *y* elements, *x* was known as the multiplier and *y* was known as the multiplicand. These labels are also used in integer multiplication. When viewing integer multiplication with the set model, a negative multiplier indicates a *removal* of a certain number of groups of negative or positive chips from the jar. For example, –3 times +2 means "Begin with an empty jar. Remove three groups, each containing two positive chips." But how can anything be removed from an empty jar? Recall that the empty jar represents a zero value set. You have already seen that negative/positive pairs have a value of zero. Any number of these negative/positive pairs can be put into the jar without changing its zero value. You can see in the figure below that all of the jars pictured have a value of zero.

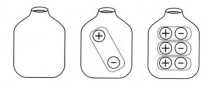

We begin with the empty (zero value) jar. We wish to remove three sets of two positive chips. There are no positive chips in the jar. However, we can put three sets of two positive chips in the jar, provided that each positive chip is paired with a negative chip, in order not to change the zero value of the jar. Now it is possible to remove three groups of two positive chips from the zero value jar. This leaves us with three groups of two negative chips, or six negative chips, leading us to see that the product of +3 and –2 is –6. This product is shown in the figure below.

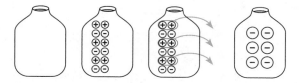

4. Negative Times Negative   [x · y where x < 0 and y < 0].
The product *x · y* where both *x* and *y* are negative integers is interpreted in a similar fashion as in the case of negative times positive. Again, the multiplier is negative, indicating a removal of a certain number of groups of chips. For example –3 · (–2) means "Begin with an empty jar. Remove

three equivalent groups each containing two negative chips." Since the jar is empty, no chips can be removed at this point. In order to remove three groups of two chips, these chips must be present in the jar. To maintain the zero value of the set, three equivalent groups of two negative chips paired with three equivalent groups of two positive chips are put in the jar, as shown in the figure below. Notice that the value of the set does not change, since each negative is paired with a positive to produce a zero value. Now the subtraction process can begin. By removing the three equivalent groups of two negative chips, you are left with six positive chips. Symbolically, this can be stated as $-3 \cdot (-2) = +6$.

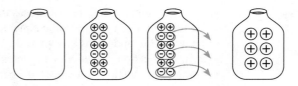

Investigation 8

You purchase three round-trip bridge tokens that cost $2 each. How could this situation and its outcome be viewed using positive and negative integers?

At the outset, this problem appears to be a straightforward multiplication of two whole numbers. The result is obviously $6. But this simple problem can also illustrate the product of a positive and a negative integer. The amount you owe for each token is expressed as -2, and the three tokens are represented as $+3$. The solution is symbolized by $(+3) \cdot (-2) = (-6)$, indicating that you owe $6 in all. The set model explanation of this process appears in the positive times negative case above and is pictured in the first figure on page 197.

Return to the results of all four possibilities in integer multiplication. They are summarized here.

1. $+3 \cdot (+2) = +6$

2. $+3 \cdot (-2) = -6$

3. $-3 \cdot (+2) = -6$

4. $-3 \cdot (-2) = +6$

Notice that in each case the absolute value of the multiplier, multiplicand, and product remains constant. This was not the case in addition and subtraction of integers. For example, $+3 + (+2) = +5$, whereas $+3 + (-2) = +1$. (See the assessments at the end of this section.) The pattern shown above would suggest that in multiplication of integers, the product of the absolute values of the factors is equal to the absolute value of the product of the factors. This is symbolically stated as

$$|x| \cdot |y| = |x \cdot y|$$

Once the product has been established, the sign of the product can be determined. The results of 1–4 above indicate that when the multiplier and the multiplicand share the same sign, the product is always positive. When the multiplier and the multiplicand have different signs, the product is always negative.

Properties of Integer Multiplication

Integer multiplication has eight rules and properties that govern its use.

1. Multiplication by Zero.   The product of any integer x and 0 is equal to zero.

$$x \cdot 0 = 0 \cdot x = 0$$

2. Multiplication of Integers with Like Signs.   The product of a multiplier x, and multiplicand, y, whose signs are alike is equal to $+|x \cdot y|$.

3. Multiplication of Integers with Unlike Signs.   The product of a multiplier x, and multiplicand y, whose signs are different is equal to $-|x \cdot y|$.

closure property of integer multiplication

4. Closure Property of Integer Multiplication.   The product of any two integers is itself an integer; that is, the set of integers is closed under the operation of multiplication.

commutative property of integer multiplication

5. Commutative Property of Integer Multiplication.   The order of the factors may be changed without changing the product; that is, if x and y are the integers, $x \cdot y = y \cdot x$.

associative property of integer multiplication

6. Associative Property of Integer Multiplication.   When multiplying more than two integer factors, the way in which the factors are grouped does not affect the product; that is, if x, y, and z are any integers, $x \cdot (y \cdot z) = (x \cdot y) \cdot z$.

identity property of integer multiplication

7. Identity Property of Integer Multiplication.   There exists a unique integer 1 that when multiplied by any integer results in a product that is the integer itself; that is, for any integer x, $1 \cdot x = x \cdot 1 = x$.

distributive property of integer multiplication

8. Distributive Property of Integer Multiplication over Integer Addition.   If x, y, and z are any integers, then

$$x \cdot (y + z) = x \cdot y + x \cdot z \qquad \text{and} \qquad (y + z) \cdot x = y \cdot x + z \cdot x$$

A final property is worth mentioning here, since it calls upon prior knowledge of integers. Recall that the symbol "–" can be interpreted as "the opposite of." Therefore, $-x$ can be read as "the opposite of x." Examine the pattern in the list that follows.

$$-1 \cdot (-3) = +3 = \text{the opposite of } -3 = -(-3)$$
$$-1 \cdot (-2) = +2 = \text{the opposite of } -2 = -(-2)$$
$$-1 \cdot (-1) = +1 = \text{the opposite of } -1 = -(-1)$$
$$-1 \cdot (+1) = -1 = \text{the opposite of } +1 = -(+1)$$
$$-1 \cdot (+2) = -2 = \text{the opposite of } +2 = -(+2)$$

Notice that multiplication by –1 has the same effect as changing the number to its opposite. In general, if x is any integer,

$$x \cdot (-1) = -1 \cdot x = -x$$

This multiplication by −1 can be used to help understand the outcome of the product of two negatives. We have already determined that −3 · (−2) = +6. The following example leads to the same result.

$$-3 \cdot (-2) =$$
$$[-1 \cdot (+3)] \cdot (-2) = \quad \text{since } -3 = -1 \cdot (+3)$$
$$-1 \cdot [+3 \cdot (-2)] = \quad \text{by the associative property}$$
$$-1 \cdot (-6) = \quad \text{integer multiplication}$$
$$-(-6) = \quad \text{"the opposite of } -6\text{"}$$
$$+6$$

Integer Division

The set model can be used to represent division of integers. Although it is more complicated than the set model of other operations, it is worth including. It serves as a foundation for understanding the rules and properties of integer division. The same terminology used in whole number division (see Chapter 4) is used in integer division. If x and y are any integers, and $y \neq 0$, then $x \div y = c$. The integer y is called the divisor and the integer x is called the dividend. The quotient, c, may or may not be an integer, depending on the values of x and y.

The set model is applicable to integer division only in the cases where the quotient, c, is itself an integer. For c to be an integer, we need to expand the definition of "divides." In Chapter 4, when we stated that y divides x, or $y \mid x$, y was assumed to be a whole number divisor other than 0. Within the context of integer division, y will be assumed to be an integer other than 0. Thus it will be shown that if y divides x, then $-y$ divides x. As with integer multiplication, four cases are possible.

1. Positive Divided by Positive [$x \div y$ where $x > 0$ and $y > 0$]. This situation can best be examined using a numerical example. Let $x = +6$ and $y = +3$. Using the set model, the statement $6 \div 3$ is read as "Begin with a set containing no elements. Three equivalent groups are put into the set so that the set has a value of +6. Determine the value of each equivalent group." The solution is shown below.

(a) Begin with a set whose value is zero.

(b) Since the set must ultimately contain six positive chips, put six positive chips in the set.

(c) These chips were to be entered as three equivalent groups. Partition the six chips into three equivalent groups.

As shown in Figure 5.16(c), each equivalent group contains two positive chips. Therefore, the value of each group is +2. This can now be written symbolically as $+6 \div (+3) = +2$.

2. Negative Divided by Positive $[x \div y$ where $x < 0$ and $y > 0]$. Let $x = -6$ and $y = +3$. Find the quotient of $-6 \div (+3)$. The figure below depicts the set model procedure.

(a) Begin with a set whose value is zero.

(b) Since the set must now contain six chips, put six negative chips in the set.

(c) These chips were to be entered as three equivalent groups. Partition the six chips into three equivalent groups.

As shown in (c), each equivalent group contains two negative chips. Therefore, the value of each group is –2. This can now be written symbolically as $-6 \div (+3) = -2$.

3. Positive Divided by Negative $[x \div y$ where $x > 0$ and $y < 0]$. In cases 1 and 2, a positive divisor was interpreted as *putting equivalent groups into a set*. In cases 3 and 4, the divisor will be negative and therefore interpreted as *removing equivalent groups from a set*. For example, $+6 \div (-3)$ is viewed as shown in the following figure.

(a) Begin with a zero value set.

(b) $(+6) \div (-3)$ is interpreted as removing three equivalent groups from a set so that the set then contains six positives. Since the set contains no removable elements, you must enter the needed number of positives, along with six negatives. This maintains the zero value of the set.

(c) Now remove three equivalent groups so that only six positives remain. Do this by removing three equivalent groups, each of which contains two negatives.

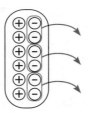

Since each of the equivalent groups contains two negatives, the quotient $+6 \div (-3)$ is -2.

4. Negative Divided by Negative $[x \div y$ where $x < 0$ and $y < 0]$. Once again, a negative divisor will be viewed as removing equivalent groups. Examine the problem $-6 \div (-3)$, as shown in the figure below.

(a) Begin with a zero value set.

(b) $(-6) \div (-3)$ is interpreted as removing three equivalent groups from a set so that the set is left with six negative chips. Since the set contains no removable elements, you must enter the needed number of negatives, along with six positives. This maintains the zero value of the set.

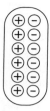

(c) Now remove three equivalent groups so that six negatives remain.

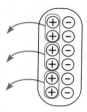

Since each of the equivalent groups contains two positives, the quotient $(-6) \div (-3) = (+2)$.

The following table summarizes the results of each of the four cases so that a pattern can be established.

x	$\div$	y	$=$	c
+6	÷	(+3)	=	+2
−6	÷	(+3)	=	−2
+6	÷	(−3)	=	−2
−6	÷	(−3)	=	+2

Notice that in each case, $|x| \div |y| = |c|$. This tells us that the *number* of elements in the equivalent sets, whether added or removed, can always be determined by simple division. In order to understand the sign of the quotient, we must recall the formal definition of division of whole numbers, which was introduced in Chapter 4. It states that if $x \div y = c$, and $y \neq 0$, then $y \cdot c = x$. This definition of whole number division also applies to integer division, as evidenced in the extension of the summary table above.

x	$\div$	y	$=$	c	$\rightarrow$	y	$\cdot$	c	$=$	x
+6	÷	(+3)	=	+2	→	+3	·	(+2)	=	+6
−6	÷	(+3)	=	−2	→	+3	·	(−2)	=	−6
+6	÷	(−3)	=	−2	→	−3	·	(−2)	=	+6
−6	÷	(−3)	=	+2	→	−3	·	(+2)	=	−6

The rules that were established about the sign of the product of integers (see 1–3 on page 199) also hold for the sign of the quotient of integers. The quotient of two integers of like signs is a positive integer. The quotient of two integers of unlike signs is a negative integer. You can see that these "rules" evolved from the set model. Obviously, real-world division problems would become overly cumbersome if always viewed through this model. But by restructuring a division problem into an associated multiplication problem, students can not only develop a better idea of the relationship between division and multiplication but can also better understand the origin of the rules governing the sign of the quotient.

Investigation 9

Use the set model to interpret the following problem: Each ton of a certain cargo lowers a ship a distance of 2 cm deeper into the water. If, at the end of loading, the ship is 10 cm lower in the water than it had been, how many tons of cargo were loaded? Once the quotient is found, verify that the solution is correct by restructuring the division problem into an associated multiplication problem.

Since the level of the ship is being lowered a total of 10 cm, 2 cm at a time, each of these two numbers is expressed as a negative integer. The problem can be stated symbolically as $-10 \div (-2)$. The set model follows:

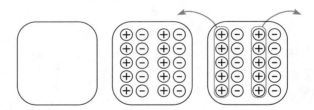

Since each equivalent group contains five positives, the quotient $-10 \div (-2)$ is $+5$. This problem could have been written as

$$-2 \cdot \, ? = -10$$

The missing factor can only be $+5$. Therefore, five tons of cargo were loaded onto the ship.

Investigation 10

Write the calculator keystroke sequence that can be used to determine the solution of $[-36 \cdot (+5)] \div (-6)$.

The following calculator keystroke sequence can be used:

$$\boxed{\text{AC}}\ 36\ \boxed{+/-}\ \boxed{\times}\ 5\ \boxed{=}\ \boxed{\div}\ 6\ \boxed{+/-}\ \boxed{=}$$

The display should read 30.

Assessments for Section 5.2

1. Use the set model of integer multiplication to illustrate each of the following statements.
   (a) $-4 \cdot (+7)$
   (b) $+3 \cdot (-6)$
   (c) $-9 \cdot (-2)$
   (d) $-5 \cdot (+5)$
   (e) $+4 \cdot (+6)$

2. Find the product in each of the following statements.
   (a) $-12 \cdot (-23)$
   (b) $-36 \cdot (+14)$
   (c) $-24 \cdot (-2)$
   (d) $+51 \cdot (-11)$
   (e) $-3 \cdot (-21) \cdot (+12)$

3. Evaluate each of the following terms.
   (a) $(-3)^2$
   (b) $(-5)^3$
   (c) $(-4)^4 \cdot (-4)^2$
   (d) $(-1)^8$
   (e) $(-1)^9$

4. Use the results from Problem 3 to help answer the following problems.
   (a) Determine the sign of the result when each of the following expressions is evaluated.
   $$(-1)^{38} \qquad (-16)^{25} \qquad (-12)^{100} \qquad (-41)^{11}$$
   (b) Explain how you were able to answer part (a) without actually performing the multiplication.

5. Classify each term as either a positive even integer, a positive odd integer, a negative even integer, or a negative odd integer.
   (a) $(-2)^{55}$ (b) $(-19)^8$ (c) $(-893)^{100}$
   (d) $(-302)^{301}$ (e) $(-93)^{19}$ (f) $(-14)^{14}$

6. Determine the missing signs that would yield the indicated result.
   $$\Box\, 3 \cdot (\Box\, 5) \cdot (\Box\, 8) \cdot (\Box\, 2) = -240$$
   Is your answer unique? Explain why or why not.

7. Determine the missing signs that would yield the indicated result.
   $$[\Box\, 5 \cdot (\Box\, 8) \div (\Box\, 4)] + [\Box\, 6 \cdot (\Box\, 3)] = +28$$
   Is your answer unique? Explain why or why not.

8. Use the set model to illustrate each division problem.
   (a) $-16 \div (-8)$
   (b) $+9 \div (-9)$
   (c) $+12 \div (-6)$
   (d) $-14 \div (+7)$
   (e) $-12 \div (+6)$

9. Determine the quotient for each of the following expressions.
   (a) $-121 \div (-11)$
   (b) $-900 \div (+25)$
   (c) $+368 \div (-16)$
   (d) $+4368 \div (-208)$
   (e) $-1,000,000 \div (+10,000)$

10. Use four 4s to write an expression equal to zero. One possibility is shown here:
    $$+44 + (-44) = 0$$

11. Estimate the following products and quotients.
    (a) $-23 \cdot (-59)$
    (b) $+78 \cdot (-11)$
    (c) $-459 \div (+3)$
    (d) $+702 \div (-18)$
    (e) $+17,595 \div (+391)$

12. Estimate each of the following expressions.
    (a) $-72 \cdot (-15) \div (-24)$
    (b) $1500 \div (-327)$
    (c) $-23,900 \div (-1000) \cdot (-300)$
    (d) $-111 \cdot (-3500) \div (-1000)$
    (e) $(-5)^5$

13. Write a word problem in which the following expressions would be used in the solution process.
    (a) $+7 \cdot (-5)$ (b) $+40 \div (-10)$

14. Which of the following expressions are equivalent to –15?
    (a) $-[-5 \cdot (-3)]$
    (b) $[+5 \cdot (-3)] \cdot (-1)$
    (c) $[-(-5)] \cdot (-3)$
    (d) $[-5 \cdot (+3)] \div [-(+3) \div (-3)]$
    (e) $[(-5)^3 \div (-5)^2] \cdot (-3)$

15. Represent the outcome of the following situation as an integer: On February 5 you purchased 50 shares of stock at $11 per share. On February 25 you sold the 50 shares for $9 per share. What is the outcome of this transaction?

16. Represent the outcome of the following situation as an integer: On October 8 you purchased 95 shares of stock at $32 per share. Each day you held the stock, you lost $2 per share. On October 15 you sold the 95 shares. What is the outcome of this transaction?

17. Find the next term in each sequence. Identify the pattern.
    (a) $3, 5, 0, 2, -3, -1, -6, -4, —$
    (b) $4, -12, 36, -108, 324, —$
    (c) $256, -128, 64, -32, 16, —$
    (d) $15, -29, 59, -117, 235, —$
    (e) $11, 52, 257, 1282, 6407, —$

18. Recall the formula $a_n = a_1 + (n-1)d$ that was used to generate the nth term of an arithmetic sequence (a_1 = first term, d = common difference, n = number of terms). Find the nth term in each.
    (a) $n = 5, d = -2, a_1 = 0$
    (b) $n = 10, d = -4, a_1 = 8$
    (c) $n = 2, d = -5, a_1 = -8$
    (d) $n = 100, d = -11, a_1 = -11$
    (e) $n = 32, d = -7, a_1 = -9$

19. In an arithmetic sequence, the common difference is –17, $a_7 = -52$. Find a_3 and a_{10}.

20. In a geometric sequence, the nth term is given as $a_1 \cdot r^{n-1}$, where a_1 is the first term and r is the common quotient of each term with its preceding term. Find the indicated term in each.
    (a) $a_6 = \underline{\quad}, a_1 = -4, r = -2$
    (b) $a_4 = \underline{\quad}, a_1 = 6, r = -5$
    (c) $a_5 = \underline{\quad}, a_1 = -7, r = 2$
    (d) $a_{10} = \underline{\quad}, a_1 = -3, r = -3$
    (e) $a_8 = \underline{\quad}, a_1 = -1, r = -1$

21. The sum of the first n terms of a geometric sequence was given as

$$s_n = \frac{a_1(1 - r^n)}{1 - r} \qquad (r \neq 1)$$

where a_1 is the first term, n is the number of terms, and r is the common quotient of a term with its preceding term. Determine the sum of each of the following geometric sequences.
    (a) $a_1 = -2, r = -1, n = 5$
    (b) $a_1 = -5, r = -6, n = 3$
    (c) $-7, 49, -343, 2401, \ldots \quad n = 6$
    (d) $24, -72, 216, -648, \ldots \quad n = 9$
    (e) $-5, 20, -80, 320, \ldots \quad n = 10$

22. Determine the following quotient:

$$(-2 + 3 - 4 + 5 - 6 + \cdots + 97 - 98) \div$$
$$(+2 - 3 + 4 - 5 + 6 - \cdots - 97 + 98)$$

23. Examine the following list. How could it be used to generate a rule for a negative times a negative?

$$-4 \cdot 4 = -16$$
$$-4 \cdot 3 = -12$$
$$-4 \cdot 2 = -8$$
$$-4 \cdot 1 = -4$$
$$-4 \cdot 0 = 0$$

(*Hint:* Look for and extend patterns.)

24. Determine the value of each of the following expressions.
    (a) $|(-5) \cdot (-6)|$
    (b) $|-5| \cdot |-6|$
    (c) $-|(-5) \cdot (-6)|$
    (d) $-|(-3)^2 - (-3)^3|$
    (e) $|4 - 10| - |(-4) - 10|$

25. (a) Does $|a \cdot b| = |a| \cdot |b|$? Explain your answer.
    (b) Does $|a - b| = |a| - |b|$? Explain your answer.
    (c) Does $|a + b| = |a| + |b|$? Explain your answer.

In Other Words

26. What is the set model interpretation of a positive and a negative multiplier?

27. In the expression x^a, if x is a negative integer, what determines the sign of the value of the expression?

28. Is it possible for every term in a geometric sequence to be negative? Explain your answer.

29. Explain why the absolute value of a quotient is equal to the quotient of the absolute values of the dividend and the divisor.

30. Is the process of integer division described in this section closer to the repeated subtraction model of whole number division or the partition model of whole number division?

Cooperative Activity

31. Groups of three

In Chapter 4, you examined the concept of a function. In this activity, you will explore functions that involve negative numbers.

Individual Accountability:

Member A: Determine the output for each of the following functions on the domain given.

	Domain	Function
(a)	$\{-5, -4, -3, -2, -1\}$	"cube +1"
(b)	$\{-15, -18, -21\}$	"three less than the double"
(c)	$\{-4, -2, 0, 2, 4\}$	"negative seven times the square"

Member B: Given a function and a particular output of the function, determine the input value associated with that output.

	Function	Output
(a)	"twice the square minus two"	96
(b)	"times negative three, plus one"	−17
(c)	"the cube times negative four plus two"	110

Member C: Given a particular set of input values and their associated output values, expressed as ordered pairs, determine the function.

(a) $\{(2, -9), (3, -14), (4, -19), (5, -24)\}$

(b) $\{(-4, 0), (-6, 1), (-8, 2), (-10, 3)\}$

(c) $\{(-2, -9), (-1, -6), (0, -3), (1, 0), (2, 3)\}$

Group Goal: Share and explain your individual work with the members of your group. As a group, determine the functions F and G, whose composition, $(F \circ G)$, would generate the following input/output table. Are your choices for F and G unique? Explain your answer.

Input	Output
−3	$(F \circ G)(-3) = -12$
−2	$(F \circ G)(-2) = -2$
−1	$(F \circ G)(-1) = 4$
0	$(F \circ G)(0) = 6$
1	$(F \circ G)(1) = 4$
2	$(F \circ G)(2) = -2$
3	$(F \circ G)(3) = -12$

5.3   Introduction to Algebra: Equations and Inequalities

Now that you have done an extensive amount of work with whole numbers and integers, you are ready to apply your knowledge in a branch of mathematics known as **algebra**.

> The origin of our word *algebra* from the title of al-Khowârizmî's treatise on the subject, *Hisab al-jabr w'al-muga-balah,* is very interesting. This title has been literally translated as "science of the reunion and the opposition" or, more freely, as "science of transposition and cancellation." The text, which is extant, became known in Europe through Latin translations, and made the word *al-jabr,* or *algebra,* synonymous with the science of equations. (From Howard Eves, *An Introduction to the History of Mathematics,* 6th ed., Philadelphia, PA: Saunders College Publishing, 1990, p. 236.)

Knowledge of algebra will increase your problem-solving abilities and allow you to deal systematically with a world that contains unknowns.

Mathematical Expressions

Some have claimed that mathematics is a language much like any other language. It is used to communicate, it has a vocabulary of numbers and symbols, and it has a syntax of various operations that can be performed on those numbers and symbols. Spoken language is often used to make statements about the world. Mathematics can also be used to do this. For example, the literal expression "three less than eight" can be translated into the mathematical expression "8 − 3." Notice that this is not a complete sentence, either in English or in mathematics. It is simply a phrase, or in mathematical terms, an expression. A **numerical expression** combines number symbols and mathematical operations. Numerical expressions can also be translated into verbal phrases and can usually be written in a simplified equivalent form. Examine each of the following examples.

numerical expression

Verbal Phrase	*Mathematical Expression*	*Simplified Equivalent*
Eight increased by seven	$8 + 7$	15
The product of eleven and four	$11 \cdot 4$	44
Five squared	5^2	25
The difference of ten and three, added to five	$5 + (10 - 3)$	12
Twenty decreased by the quotient of eight and two	$20 - (8 \div 2)$	16

order of operations

Certain rules govern the simplification of numerical expressions. These rules are called the **order of operations**. The verbal phrase "twenty decreased by the quotient of eight and two" clearly translates to $20 - (8 \div 2)$, and simplifies to 16. Suppose, however, that you were given only the numerical expression $20 - 8 \div 2$. Examine the two procedures shown here.

$$20 - 8 \div 2 \qquad 20 - 8 \div 2$$
$$12 \div 2 \qquad 20 - 4$$
$$6 \qquad 16$$

Both answers appear to be correct. Imagine the confusion if they were both correct, if a numerical expression did not have a unique equivalent. It is for this reason that mathematicians have agreed on a unified order of operations in the simplification process. This priority order of operations is listed here.

1. Parentheses take precedence. All operations within parentheses are completed first. If another numerical expression is contained within the parentheses, it follows the order of operations as well.

2. Numerical expressions involving exponents are simplified next.

3. Multiplication and division are performed in sequence from left to right.

4. Addition and subtraction are performed in sequence from left to right.

Following the order of operations, the correct simplification of $20 - 8 \div 2$ is 16.

Investigation 11

Translate the following verbal phrase into symbols and then simplify it: Ten times the quotient of sixteen and eight, decreased by the square of the difference between nine and six, plus negative twenty-eight.

The numerical translation is as follows:

$$10 \cdot (16 \div 8) - (9 - 6)^2 + (-28)$$

$$10 \cdot 2 - (3)^2 + (-28)$$

$$10 \cdot 2 - 9 + (-28)$$

$$20 - 9 + (-28)$$

$$11 + (-28)$$

$$-17$$

The verbal phrase is equivalent to -17.

Recall your work with elementary logic in Chapter 1. An open sentence was defined as one to which a truth value could not be ascribed until further information was given. "It is serious," "She will not be attending," and "The number is increased by ten" are examples of open sentences. In these cases, the replacements for "It," "She," and "The number" determine the truth value of the open sentence. They can be replaced by a variety of possibilities. Some possibilities will make the sentence true, whereas others will not. In this context, the words "It," "She," and "The number" are called variables. In algebra, a variable is a letter that is used to represent a number.

The distinction between expressions and sentences is important. For example, "a number increased by four" is an expression. It could be symbolized by "$x + 4$" where x is a variable that represents some unidentified number. Expressions of this type are known as **algebraic expressions**. The following examples are algebraic expressions:

algebraic expressions

The product of a number and 3	$x \cdot 3$ or $3x$
Twice the sum of a number and 5	$2 \cdot (x + 5)$ or $2(x + 15)$
The cube of a number decreased by 8	$x^3 - 8$

domain

In each of these three algebraic expressions, the variable can be replaced by any number. The set of replacement values for a variable is called the **domain**. In the second example, suppose that the domain was $\{1, 2, 3\}$. The variable will take on the values in the domain. When $x = 1$, $2(x + 5) = 2(1 + 5) = 2 \cdot 6 = 12$. When $x = 2$, $2(x + 5) = 2(2 + 5) = 2 \cdot 7 = 14$. Finally, when $x = 3$, $2(x + 5) = 2(3 + 5) = 2 \cdot 8 = 16$. Because algebraic expressions, like numerical expressions, are only phrases, it is impossible to assign a truth value to them.

solution set

Algebraic open sentences contain expressions that are linked by some relational operator ($=, \neq, <, >, \leq, \geq$). When given a domain, the truth of the open sentence can be determined. The subset of the domain containing the values that make the open sentence true is called the **solution set**. For example, suppose you are given the open sentence $2x + 6 = 14$ and the domain $\{3, 4, 5, 6, 7\}$. The solution set contains the element or elements that make the open sentence true. By substitution, it is easy to see that only when $x = 4$ does $2x + 6 = 14$. Therefore, the solution set contains a single element and is expressed as $\{4\}$. Open sentences that contain an equal sign are called **equations**. It is possible that none of the values in the domain satisfy the equation. In this case, the solution set is the empty set, $\{\,\}$, or $\varnothing$.

equations

Now suppose that the open sentence had been $2x + 6 > 14$, on the same domain. By substitution, the values 5, 6, and 7 all make the open sentence true. Therefore, the solution set is $\{5, 6, 7\}$. Open sentences that contain the symbols for "less than," "greater than," "less than or equal to," and "greater than or equal to" are called **inequalities**.

inequalities

Solving Equations

For this introduction of algebra, we will restrict the domain to the set of integers. In subsequent chapters we will broaden the domain to include fractions, decimals, and more. An equation, when simplified, can take any of five discernible forms. The set model is used to illustrate the algebraic solution process.

Form 1

General Form: $x + a = b$ or $a + x = b$

Example: $x + 5 = 7$.

Set Model: Set X contains an amount of chips with an unknown value, x. Set A contains five positive chips, and set B contains seven positive chips. (See the following figure.)

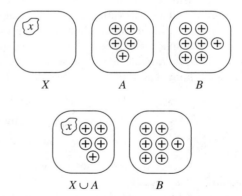

Since the set $(X \cup A)$ must be equivalent to the set B, the value of $(X \cup A)$ must be equal to the value of B. The value of the unknown number of chips needs to be determined. We can remove five positive chips from each of the two sets and still maintain the equivalence. This is analogous to a balance scale. If one side of a balanced scale is reduced by a certain amount, the other side must be reduced by the same amount in order to maintain the balance. The removal of five positive chips from both sets is shown in the following figure.

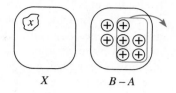

It is now clear that the unknown value x must be positive two. This process can be symbolically expressed as

$$x + 5 = 7$$
$$x + 5 - 5 = 7 - 5$$
$$x = 2$$

The solution set for the equation $x + 5 = 7$ is $\{2\}$.

Form 2

General Form: $x - a = b$. or $x + (-a) = b$

Example: $x - 7 = -3$

Set Model: To use the set model introduced in Form 1, we must rewrite this subtraction statement as an equivalent addition statement. Recall that subtraction can be viewed as adding the opposite. Therefore, subtracting 7 can be viewed as adding –7, as illustrated in the following figure.

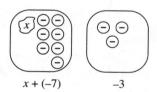

Removing –7 from both sets yields the solution of 4, as shown in the following figure.

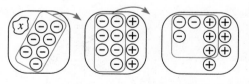

$$x + (-7) - (-7) = -3 - (-7) = (-3) + (+7) = +4$$

In order to understand the symbolic representation of this process, we must once again employ the add-the-opposite view. Subtracting –7 from both sets is equivalent to adding +7 to both sets. The algebraic solution follows.

$$x - 7 = -3$$
$$x - 7 + 7 = -3 + 7$$
$$x = 4$$

Notice that in both of the two equation forms, $x + a = b$ and $x - a = b$, the solution was achieved by "undoing" the stated operations. Addition can be "undone" by employing its inverse operation, subtraction. Likewise, subtraction can be "undone" by employing its inverse operation, addition. The use of inverse operations as a means of altering the form of an equation without altering the equality follows from two very important properties of equality.

addition property of equality

1. Addition property of equality. For all a, b, and c,

$$\text{if } a = b, \text{ then } a + c = b + c$$

This can be translated as "if the same number is added to both sides of an equation, the equivalence of both sides remains."

subtraction property of equality

2. Subtraction property of equality. For all a, b, and c,

$$\text{if } a = b, \text{ then } a - c = b - c$$

This can be translated as "if the same number is subtracted from both sides of an equation, the equivalence of both sides remains."

Investigation 12

At 6:00 A.M. the temperature was $-11°$ C. This was a rise of 15 degrees from the temperature at 2:00 A.M. What was the 2:00 A.M. temperature? Algebraically interpret and solve this problem.

Understand the Problem: What is given? The 6:00 A.M. temperature was $11°$ C. From 2:00 A.M. to 6:00 A.M., the temperature rose 15 degrees.
What is unknown? The 2:00 A.M. temperature.

Devise a Plan: Use a variable. Let x represent the unknown temperature. Represent the situation algebraically.

Carry Out the Plan:

$$x + 15 = -11$$
$$x + 15 - 15 = -11 - 15$$
$$x = -11 + (-15)$$
$$x = -26$$

Look Back: If the temperature at 2:00 A.M. was $-26°$ C, as indicated by the algebraic solution, then $-26 + 15$ should equal the 6:00 A.M. temperature:

$$-26 + 15 = -11$$

In this step, the solution is verified. It was $-26°$ C at 2:00 A.M.

Form 3

General Form: $a \cdot x = b$

Example: $3 \cdot x = -15$

Set Model: Recall that multiplication of the form $3 \cdot x$ can be read as "Begin with a zero value set. Put three groups of x into the set." The equation indicates that these three groups of x must be equivalent to -15. This is shown in the figure below.

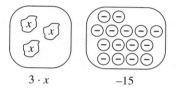

$$3 \cdot x \qquad\qquad -15$$

It is necessary to make the set on the right take the same form as the set on the left. This can be accomplished by partitioning the set on the right into three equivalent groups, as shown in the following figure.

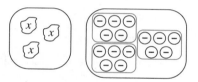

To find the value of one of the groups of x, we will examine its counterpart in the set on the right. You can see that $x = -5$. Symbolically, this can be written as

$$3x = -15$$
$$3x \div 3 = -15 \div 3$$
$$x = -5$$

Form 4

General Form: $x/a = b$ or $x \div a = b$

Example: $x \div 8 = -2$

Set Model: The division $x \div 8$ is interpreted as "Eight equivalent groups are put into a zero value set resulting in a set with a value of x." The quotient, -2, is the value of each equivalent group. Therefore, if we have eight equivalent groups, each with a value of -2, it is clear that the total value, x, can be determined by finding the product of 8 and -2. Symbolically, this can be written as

$$x \div 8 = -2$$
$$(x \div 8) \cdot 8 = -2 \cdot 8$$
$$x = -16$$

Notice that in both of the last two equation forms, $a \cdot x = b$ and $x \div a = b$, a solution was achieved by "undoing" the stated operations. Multiplication can be "undone" by employing its inverse operation, division. Likewise, division can be "undone" by employing its inverse operation, multiplication. The use of these inverse operations as a means of altering the form of an equation without altering the equality follows from the following two properties of equality.

multiplication property of equality

1. Multiplication Property of Equality. For all a, b, and c

$$\text{if } a = b, \text{ then } a \cdot c = b \cdot c$$

This can be translated as "if both sides of an equation are multiplied by the same number, the equality remains."

division property of equality

2. Division Property of Equality. For all a, b, and c where $c \neq 0$, if

$$a = b, \text{ then } a \div c = b \div c.$$

This can be translated as "if both sides of an equation are divided by the same nonzero number, the equality remains."

Form 5

General Form: $a \cdot x + b = c$ or $a \cdot x - b = c$

Example: $4x + 2 = 10$

Set Model: The set with a value of $4x + 2$ was formed by combining two sets—one whose value is $4x$ and the other whose value is 2 (see the figure below).

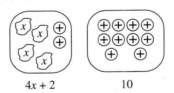

$$4x + 2 \qquad\qquad 10$$

To determine the value of x, it is necessary to remove two positives from the set $4x + 2$. This will leave a set containing four groups of x on the left. Recall that the subtraction property of equality states that in order to maintain the equivalence, it is necessary to subtract the same amount from both sides of the equation. Therefore, 2 positives will be removed from the set containing 10 positives. Symbolically, this results in the equation $4x = 8$, which is in the form of $a \cdot x = b$, or Form 3. The following figure depicts the set model solution of this equation. Each group must contain two positives.

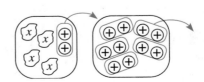

This equation can be solved symbolically as shown here.

$$4x + 2 = 10$$

$4x + 2 - 2 = 10 - 2$ "Undo" any addition or subtraction first by using the associated inverse operation.

$4x = 8$ Simplify.

$4x \div 4 = 8 \div 4$ "Undo" any multiplication or division next by using the associated inverse operation.

$x = 2$ Simplify.

You should always verify that your solution is correct. Do this by replacing the variable in the original equation with the solution.

$$4x + 2 = 10$$
$$4 \cdot 2 + 2 = 10$$
$$8 + 2 = 10$$
$$10 = 10$$

Investigation 13

A girl scout troop sold 1200 boxes of cookies. The cookie boxes were packed in cartons. Each carton contained the same number of cookie boxes. The troop leader took delivery of 70 cartons plus 10 individual boxes. How many boxes of cookies were packed in each carton?

Understand the Problem: What is given? One thousand two hundred boxes were shipped. The shipment contained 70 cartons plus 10 boxes of cookies. Each carton contains the same number of boxes.

What is unknown? The number of cookie boxes packed in each carton.

Devise a Plan: Use a variable. Let n represent the number of boxes in each carton. Let $70n$ represent the total number of boxes packed in the cartons. Let $70n + 10$ represent the total number of cookie boxes shipped. Solve for n by equating the algebraic representation of the total number of cookie boxes shipped, $70n + 10$, with the actual number of cookie boxes shipped, 1200.

Carry Out the Plan:

$$70n + 10 = 1200$$
$$70n + 10 - 10 = 1200 - 10$$
$$70n = 1190$$
$$70n \div 70 = 1190 \div 70$$
$$n = 17$$

There are 17 boxes of cookies packed in each carton

Look Back:

$$70 \cdot 17 + 10 = 1200$$
$$1190 + 10 = 1200$$
$$1200 = 1200$$

Notice that in Investigation 13, as in all of the equations solved above, there was one correct answer. This is not always the case. In an inequality, an upper or lower bound for a solution set is determined. Examine Investigation 14.

Investigation 14

Alison Guiney is paid biweekly. She has a savings account into which she deposits a fixed amount of money from each paycheck. At the beginning of the year, her account balance was $1230. How much should she deposit from each biweekly paycheck so that her balance at the end of the year is at least $2400?

Understand the Problem: What is given? Alison is paid biweekly This means that she receives 26 paychecks per year. Her balance at the beginning of the year was $1230. Her balance at the end of the year must be at least (greater than or equal to) $2400.
What is unknown? The minimum amount of each biweekly deduction that will yield a balance of $2400 at the end of the year.

Devise a Plan: Use a variable. Let a represent the amount of each biweekly deduction. Let $26a$ represent the total deduction for the year. Let $26a + 1230$ represent the balance at the end of the year. The balance at the end of the year must be greater than or equal to $2400.

Carry Out the Plan:

$$26a + 1230 \geq 2400$$
$$26a + 1230 - 1230 \geq 2400 - 1230$$
$$26a \geq 1170$$
$$26a \div 26 \geq 1170 \div 26$$
$$a \geq 45$$

Each deduction must be greater than or equal to $45.

Look Back:

$$26a + 1230 \geq 2400$$
$$26 \cdot 45 + 1230 \geq 2400$$
$$1170 + 1230 \geq 2400$$
$$2400 \geq 2400$$

Is the solution of \$45 unique? Since $a \geq 45$, any amount greater than or equal to \$45 will yield a year-end balance greater than or equal to \$2400.

Solving inequalities of this type is analogous to solving equations. The inverse operations are used with addition and subtraction preceding multiplication and division. Two cases deserve special attention.

Case 1. Examine the two sets in the figure below.

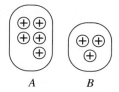

Set *A* contains five positives and set *B* contains three positives. Clearly, the value of set *A* is greater than the value of set *B* $(5 \geq 3)$. Multiplying both 5 and 3 by the same positive integer maintains the inequality in its present form. For example,

$$4 \cdot 5 \geq 4 \cdot 3$$
$$20 \geq 12$$

The value of a set containing four groups of five positives is greater than or equal to the value of a set containing four groups of three positives.

Suppose that both sides were multiplied, instead, by a negative four.

$-4 \cdot 5$ means remove four groups of five positives from a zero value set.

This leaves you with 20 negatives in the set.

$-4 \cdot 3$ means remove four groups of three positives from a zero value set.

This leaves you with 12 negatives in the set.

The value of set *A*, -20, is no longer greater than or equal to the value of set *B*, -12. It appears that the direction of the inequality has been reversed. This is known as the **multiplication property of inequalities**. In general, if *a*, *b*, and *c*, are integers, then the following relationships are true:

multiplication property of inequalities

If $a > b$ and $c > 0$, $ac > bc$.

If $a > b$ and $c < 0$, $ac < bc$.

If $a < b$ and $c > 0$, $ac < bc$.

If $a < b$ and $c < 0$, $ac > bc$.

These relationships also hold for the $\leq$ and $\geq$ inequalities.

Case 2. Examine the two sets in the figure below.

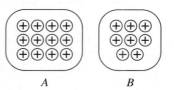

A   B

Set *A* contains 12 positives and set *B* contains 8 positives. Clearly, the value of set *A* is greater than the value of set *B* ($12 \geq 8$). Dividing both 12 and 8 by the same positive integer maintains the inequality in its present form. For example,

$$12 \div 4 \geq 8 \div 4$$

$$3 \geq 2$$

The value of a set containing four groups of three positives is greater than or equal to the value of a set containing four groups of two positives.

Suppose that both sides were divided, instead, by a negative four.

$$12 \div (-4) = -3$$

$$8 \div (-4) = -2$$

division property of inequalities   The value −3 is no longer greater than or equal to the value −2. It appears that the direction of the inequality has been reversed. This is known as the **division property of inequalities**. In general, if *a, b,* and *c* are integers, then the following relationships are true:

$$\text{If } a > b \text{ and } c > 0, (a \div c) > (b \div c).$$

$$\text{If } a > b \text{ and } c < 0, (a \div c) < (b \div c).$$

$$\text{If } a < b \text{ and } c > 0, (a \div c) < (b \div c).$$

$$\text{If } a < b \text{ and } c < 0, (a \div c) > (b \div c).$$

These relationships also hold for the $\leq$ and $\geq$ inequalities.

Investigation 15

To test the efficiency of a new type of refrigerator, it must be shown to achieve an internal temperature of $0°$ C within a limited amount of time after being turned on. If the beginning temperature is $24°$ C, assuming a constant hourly decrease in temperature of 8 degrees, what is the minimum number of hours necessary to reach the desired temperature?

Understand the Problem: What is given? The internal temperature is $24°$ C. The temperature must reach $0°$ C. The temperature decreases at a constant rate of 8 degrees per hour (-8).

What is unknown? The minimum number of hours needed to reach a temperature of $0\,°C$.

Devise a Plan: Use a variable. Let h represent the number of hours. Let $-8h$ represent the drop in temperature over h hours. Let $24 + (-8h)$ represent the temperature at the end of h hours. The temperature at the end of h hours, $24 + (-8h)$, must be at most $0°$ C, that is $24 + (-8h) \le 0$.

Carry Out the Plan:

$$24 + (-8h) \le 0$$
$$24 - 24 + (-8h) \le 0 - 24$$
$$-8h \le -24$$
$$-8h \div (-8) \ge -24 \div (-8) \quad \text{change direction of inequality when multiplying or dividing by a negative}$$
$$h \ge 3$$

It will take at least 3 hours to reach the desired temperature.

Look Back:

$$24 + (-8h) \le 0$$
$$24 + (-8) \cdot 3 \le 0$$
$$24 + (-24) \le 0$$
$$0 \le 0$$

Assessments for Section 5.3

1. Translate each of the following expressions into symbols.
   (a) Three times a number increased by seven
   (b) The quotient of forty-five and nine, decreased by five
   (c) The difference between a number and seven, multiplied by the square of six
   (d) The product of the sum of a number and three, and the difference between the same number and one
   (e) Thirty-two less twice the sum of a number and five

2. Evaluate each of the following expressions.
   (a) $3 \div 5 \cdot 8 - 20 \div 4$
   (b) $8 \cdot (12 + 24) \div (1 + 2)^2$
   (c) $(2 - 3)^3 + (2 - 4)^2 + (2 - 4)$
   (d) $162 \div [2 \cdot (-45 \div 5)] + 16 - [3 \cdot (-2)]$
   (e) The square of twelve less than nine, divided by three

3. Evaluate each of the following expressions when $a = -1$, $b = 3$, and $c = -5$.
   (a) $a \cdot b - c + 2b$
   (b) $(abc)^2 \div (-b \cdot c)$
   (c) $5a - 4b + 3c - (a^2 \cdot b)$

   (d) $ab - ac + 2c$
   (e) $36a \div 2b - 13c$

4. Simplify each of the following inequalities.
   (a) $5 \cdot 3 + 6 \ge 8 \div (-2)$
   (b) $(7 - 3)^2 + 5 > (17 - 3) \div 7$
   (c) $3 + 2 \cdot 3 \cdot 5 \le 6^2 - 3$
   (d) $-30 \div 2 + 11 < (-3)^2 \div 3$
   (e) $8 \div (-2)^2 > (2 \cdot 3 + 8) \div (-7)$

5. Evaluate each of the following inequalities when $a = 6$, $b = 5$, and $c = -1$ to determine if it is true.
   (a) $8a + c - 3b > -b \cdot 7c$
   (b) $12c \div a \le b^3 \div 25$
   (c) $7c \cdot 8 + bc \ge (abc)^2$
   (d) $ab \div c + 15 < 3b$
   (e) $2bc + a \le bc + 1$

6. Solve for x in each of the following equations.
   (a) $x - 7 = 15$
   (b) $3x = 90$
   (c) $x + 11 = 41$

(d) $x \div 7 = -1$

(e) $-4x = 12$

7. Solve for x in each of the following equations.

(a) $14 + x = 6$

(b) $3x - 5 = 10$

(c) $10 + 2x = -30$

(d) $-5x - 9 = -39$

(e) $35 = -7x + 14$

8. Solve each of the following inequalities.

(a) $-2x + 5 < 11$

(b) $5 - x > 9$

(c) $10x - 9 \le -109$

(d) $x \div (-5) \ge 8$

(e) $8x - 1 < -33$

9. Let the domain of x be the set $\{-3, -2, -1, 0, 1, 2, 3\}$. Find the solution set for each of the following.

(a) $-5x + 8 = -2$

(b) $3x \le -3$

(c) $-6x = 0$

(d) $-3x + 1 \ge -2$

(e) $12 - 4x > 24$

10. Six times some number, decreased by eleven is equal to thirty-one. Find the number.

11. Eight more than the product of a number and five is equal to negative seven. Find the number.

12. A certain video store has 2350 videos. Each shelf can hold the same number of videos. If 92 shelves are full and 1 shelf is partially filled with 50 videos, how many videos does one shelf hold?

13. An employer has 13 employees. He pays each employee the same weekly salary. He also pays a total of $250 per week to an insurance company to cover all employee benefits. His total weekly employee-related expenses are $5060. What is the weekly salary of each employee?

14. Let p: The number is eight more than three times x.
Let q: The number is less than 68.
If $p \wedge q$ is true, find the solution set of integers for x that satisfies the conjunction.

15. Let p: $2x + 3 > -9$
Let q: $x - 6 < 5$
Find an integer value for x that will make $p \rightarrow q$ false.

16. A car travels at an average speed of 55 miles per hour. Let t represent time and d represent the distance traveled.

(a) Write an equation that relates distance traveled to time.

(b) How many fewer miles does a car travel in 3 hours traveling at an average rate of 50 miles per hour than a car traveling for 3 hours at 55 miles per hour?

17. For what value(s) of x will $8x - 3$ equal $x^2 + 9$? Use a chart to solve this problem.

18. For what values of x is $x^2 > 2x + 15$? Use a chart to solve this problem.

19. The sum of the squares of two integers is 58. One integer is 10 less than the other integer.

(a) Write two algebraic expressions to represent this situation.

(b) Set up a chart with the following column headings.

Larger Integer	Smaller Integer	Sum of Squares of Integers

Choose values for the larger integer. Determine the smaller integer and the sum of the squares of the integers. Try to solve the problem by looking for patterns in the chart.

20. Find four consecutive integers such that the sum of the first and the fourth is 229.

21. If a restaurant seats a tour group at tables for four, there will be two people left over. If the group is seated at tables of five, there will be three people left over. Offer three possible numbers of people that could be on the tour.

22. Let p: $2x - 5 > 3$
Let q: $3x + 2 > 23$
For what values of x would $p \wedge q$ be a true statement?

23. Together, a pair of binoculars and a case cost $130. If the binoculars cost $110 more than the case, how much does the case cost?

24. A carpet cleaner rental company charges $18 to rent a carpet cleaner plus $3 per rental hour. Jack does not wish to spend any more than $30 to clean his carpet. What is the longest rental he can afford?

In Other Words

25. What does it mean to solve an equation?

26. What does it mean to solve an inequality?

27. What is a variable?

28. What role do inverse operations play in solving equations and inequalities?

29. Explain how a set model can be used to illustrate the solution to $3x + 4 = 13$.

Cooperative Activity

Groups of three

Individual Accountability: Examine how the distributive property can be used to write equivalent algebraic expressions:

$$y^2 - 5y - 4 = y(y - 5) - 4 = (y - 5)y - 4$$

The equivalent expression on the extreme right makes evaluation using a calculator much simpler. To determine the value of $y^2 - 5y - 4$ when $y = -7$, rewrite the algebraic expression as

$$(y - 5)y - 4$$

The following calculator keystroke sequence follows the order of operations and does not require any exponents.

The display should read 80.

We can use the distributive property twice to evaluate expressions that have y^3, as follows:

$$y^3 + 4y^2 - 3y + 4 = (y^2 + 4y - 3)y + 4 = [(y + 4)y - 3]y + 4$$

Use the order of operations (solve within parentheses first) to evaluate $y^3 + 4y^2 - 3y + 4$ in the equivalent preceding form shown at the extreme right when $y = 5$.

The display should read 214.

Each group member should rewrite the expressions below in their equivalent form. Then, evaluate the expression on a calculator using the indicated value of y.

(a) $y^2 - 4y - 3$ $y = 6$
(b) $y^2 - 7y + 8$ $y = -3$
(c) $y^3 + 2y^2 - y + 1$ $y = 4$
(d) $y^3 - 4y^2 + 5y - 3$ $y = -5$

Group Goal: Share your solutions with the other members of the group. Make sure the entire group understands the process involved. Work together on the following problem: Find the value of

$$y^5 - 4y^4 + 6y^3 - 5y^2 + 2y - 1 \quad \text{when } y = 3$$

using the procedure outlined above. Write the calculator keystroke sequence.

Chapter 5 Vocabulary Terms

absolute value

addition property of equality

additive identity

additive inverse property of integer
    addition

algebra

algebraic expressions

associative property of integer addition

associative property of integer
    multiplication

closure property of integer addition

closure property of integer multiplication

commutative property of integer addition

commutative property of integer
    multiplication

distributive property of integer
    multiplication

division property of equality

division property of inequalities

domain

equations

identity property of integer addition

identity property of integer multiplication

inequalities

integers

multiplication property of equality

multiplication property of inequalities

numerical expression

opposites

order of operations

solution set

subtraction property of equality

Review for Chapter 5

1. Suppose that square *ABCD* is cut out of a piece of cardboard and placed in front of you as shown here:

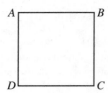

Let a negative integer indicate the number of quarter turns to the left and a positive integer indicate the number of quarter turns to the right. What line segment will be across the top as a result of each of the following situations?

   (a) $-4 + (-2) + 5$

   (b) $+6 + (-8) + (-6) + 7$

   (c) $-3 + 6 + 6 + (-10)$

2. Simplify each expression.

   (a) $+14 + (-10)$

   (b) $-8 \div (-2)$

   (c) $-35 + (-15)$

   (d) $21 \cdot (-10)$

   (e) $-12 - 21$

3. Sort each of the following illustrations into similar groups.

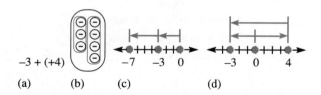

   (a)   (b)   (c)   (d)

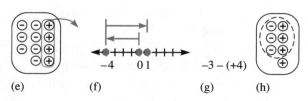

   (e)   (f)   (g)   (h)

4. Three times the product of negative seven and negative two is twice what number?

5. Negative one hundred less twice the quotient of negative twenty and five is what number?

6. Evaluate each of the following expressions:

   (a) $-5 \cdot (-2) + (-4) \div 2 - 8$

   (b) $(-1)^2 + (-2)^3 - (-3)^4$

7. Use the set model to illustrate each of the following expressions:

   (a) $-6 + 5$

   (b) $-6 - 5$

   (c) $2 \cdot (-9)$

   (d) $-14 \div 7$

8. Use the number line to illustrate each of the following expressions:

   (a) $-15 + 13$

   (b) $-15 - 13$

9. Let $x = -2$, $y = -3$, and $z = 2$. Evaluate each of the following inequalities to determine if the statement is true.

   (a) $-2x + 3y \leq 6z$

   (b) $(xy)^2 \cdot (-z) + 3x < (-x)(yz)^2 + 3z$

10. Solve each of the following equations.

   (a) $4x - 12 = -20$

   (b) $-5 + x = 12$

   (c) $x \div (-9) = 0$

   (d) $12 + 7x = -9$

11. Eight times a number, decreased by seventeen is equal to negative forty-one. Find the number.

12. Fifteen more than negative three times a number is equal to negative three. Find the number.

13. The face on a combination lock for a gym locker looks as follows:

If the combination is left 32, right 19, left 18, right 21, and assuming that you begin at zero, what is the total distance traveled from zero to the final number? How could you represent this problem using integers?

14. Solve each inequality.

    (a) $-7 + x \geq 5$

    (b) $x - 3 < -11$

    (c) $-6x - 9 \geq 3$

    (d) $15 + (-5x) < -15$

15. Does the following expression represent a negative or a positive integer? (Do not solve this problem.)

$$[(-4)^3 \cdot 2^3 \div (-8)]^3$$

16. Let p: $-3x + 5 \leq 14$

    Let q: $2x + 8 < 14$

    Determine a value for x that will yield each of the following situations.

    (a) $p \wedge q$ is true

    (b) $p \vee q$ is false

    (c) $p \leftrightarrow q$ is true

    (d) $p \rightarrow q$ is true

17. What is the relationship between $(a - b)$ and $(b - a)$ for any integer values of a and b?

18. Alex and Barbara sold 100 candy bars for a fund raiser.

    (a) If the number sold by Alex is represented by x, how would you represent the number sold by Barbara?

    (b) If the number sold by Alex is one more then twice the number sold by Barbara, find the number that each sold.

19. Set A contains all integer solutions to the equation $3x - 5 > 7$. Set B contains all integer solutions to the equation $-2x + 3 \leq 11$. Set C contains all integer solutions to the equation $5x + 3 < -7$.

    (a) Draw a Venn diagram to depict the relationship between these three sets.

    (b) Identify $A \cup B$.

    (c) Identify $B \cap C$.

    (d) Identify $A \cap C$.

    (e) Identify the set represented by $B - A$.

20. Let the vowel a be worth -5 points. Let the vowel e be worth -3 points. Let the vowel i be worth -2 points. Let the vowel o be worth -7 points. Let the vowel u be worth -1 point. The consonants have a point value equal to their numerical place in the alphabet. For example, the letter c is worth three points since it is the third letter of the alphabet. The point value for a word is the sum of the individual letter values.

    (a) What is the point value of "mathematics"?

    (b) What is the point value of "Mississippi"?

    (c) Find a word containing more than three letters that has a point value of 7.

    (d) Find a word containing more than three letters that has a negative point value.

21. Determine the equivalent of each term in the indicated modulus.

    (a) $-15 \pmod 6$

    (b) $-5 \pmod 3$

    (c) $-8 \pmod 9$

    (d) $(7 - 12) \pmod 4$

    (e) $(-2 \cdot 6) \pmod 5$

22. Examine the following statements. If the pattern were continued, what would be the next two rows and their individual values?

$$1 - 2$$
$$1 - 2 + 5$$
$$1 - 2 + 5 - 13$$
$$1 - 2 + 5 - 13 + 25$$
$$1 - 2 + 5 - 13 + 25 - 41$$

23. (a) When is $|a| < b$ a true statement?

    (b) When is $|a| > b$ a true statement?

24. The sum of 54, 86, 98, and 77, and x, all divided by 5, is greater than 70 and less than 80. If x is a whole number, what are some possible values for x?

25. Solve for x, y, and z in this magic square.

x	2	y
0	z	-4
-1	-6	1

In Other Words

26. Compare the process of solving an open sentence with the process of solving a problem.

27. Is the set of negative integers closed under addition? subtraction? multiplication? division? Explain your answers.

28. How is $-1 \cdot (-x)$ equivalent to $-(-x)$?

29. Connect the concept of directed distance (introduced in Chapter 4), with the concept of positive and negative integers and the concept of absolute value.

30. Describe a real-world situation in which you might "minus a minus."

Cooperative Activity

31. Groups of two

Individual Accountability: Identify the error in reasoning that is contained in the following "classic" situation: Three people are traveling together, and each contributes $10 toward a room rental of $30. They give this money to the bellhop. When the bellhop turns the money over to the desk clerk, he is informed that the room charge is only $25 and is asked to return the $5 to the travelers. In the elevator, the bellhop decides to keep $2 and distribute $1 to each of the three travelers. Since the travelers together contributed $27 toward the rental and the bellhop kept $2, this sums to $29. Where is the missing dollar?

Group Goal: Discuss with your partner how you worked through this problem. How did you locate the flaws in reasoning? Together, examine this "classic" proof. Determine its flaw in reasoning.

It is given that $x = y$ and both y and x are greater than zero.

(1) $x \cdot y = y^2$ — Multiply both sides of $x = y$ by y.

(2) $xy - x^2 = y^2 - x^2$ — Subtract x^2 from both sides of (1).

(3) $x(y - x) = (y + x)(y - x)$ — Factor (reverse the distributive property).

(4) $x = y + x$ — Divide both sides by $(y - x)$.

(5) $x = x + x$ — Replace y with x since you are given that $x = y$.

(6) $x = 2x$ — Add the variables.

(7) $1 = 2$ — Divide both sides by x.

How can $1 = 2$? Where is the flaw in reasoning?

6

Rational Numbers: Models, Operations, and Applications of Fractions

Examine the photograph at the right.

Describe what you see.

What relationship exists in each row?

How are the rows similar? How are they different?

Predict what the next row would look like.

What would a mathematical description of the photograph contain?

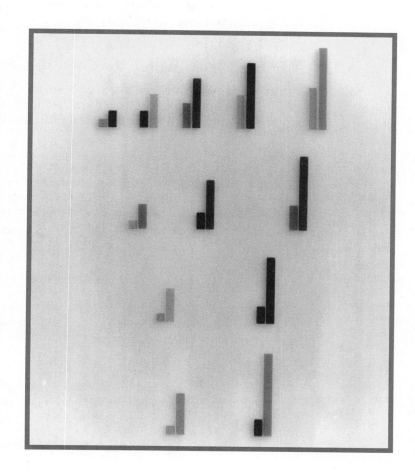

Introduction

In Chapter 5 we expanded the definition of number to include the set of integers. We showed situations in the real world that required numbers other than the set of counting numbers. Situations in the real world also involve quantities that are not whole quantities, but are *parts* of a whole. Parts of a whole can be represented in various ways—fractions, decimals, and percentages are three examples. Because the concept of fractional parts receives the most attention in elementary schools, we will spend this chapter discussing fractions.

Section 6.1 begins by relating fractions to the number theories and models we have covered in preceding chapters. A new set of numbers, rational numbers, is introduced. Locating fractions on a number line and several ways of ordering rational numbers are also covered. Section 6.2 examines models, properties, and various algorithms of rational number addition and subtraction. Section 6.3 discusses models, properties, and algorithms for rational number multiplication and division. Even though the first three sections provide real-world examples of fractions in action, Section 6.4 moves into an area of applications that is especially relevant for young children—the area of measurements. Once the basics of linear measurement are covered, we enter the more complex world of comparisons, relationships, and conversions (represented by ratios, proportions, rates, and dimensional analysis).

6.1 Number Theory Within the Context of Fractions

fraction A **fraction** is a number that can be written in the form $\frac{x}{y}$, where x and y are any number and y is not equal to zero. You may not be accustomed to this form of fraction. Although elementary school mathematics rarely considers fractions of the types

$$\frac{1.5}{8} \qquad \frac{3}{2\frac{1}{4}} \qquad \frac{\sqrt{3}}{2} \qquad \frac{\pi}{2}$$

you need to be aware of their existence in order to get a fuller picture of the set of fractions. For the purposes of this chapter, we will examine fractions of the type $\frac{x}{y}$, where x and y are both integers, and y does not equal zero. This specialized set of fractions is **rational numbers** known as the set of **rational numbers**. The set is represented by the symbol Q and is formally written as

$$Q = \left\{ \frac{x}{y} \;\middle|\; x \text{ and } y \text{ are integers, } y \neq 0 \right\}$$

This is read as "Q is the set of all $\frac{x}{y}$ such that x and y are integers and y does not equal zero." Every integer belongs to the set of rational numbers since every integer x can be written in the form $\frac{x}{1}$. In this chapter and Chapter 7, you will see how

$$\frac{1.5}{8} \qquad \text{and} \qquad \frac{2}{2\frac{1}{4}}$$

can be rewritten in an equivalent form of integer over integer and are therefore rational numbers. But, $\frac{\sqrt{3}}{2}$ cannot be expressed in such a form. The question of just which numbers are rational will be addressed in Chapter 7. There, rational numbers will be examined in terms of their decimal equivalents.

The models of fractions used at the elementary school level are, for the most part, defined on a subset of rational numbers of the form $\frac{x}{y}$, where x and y are both positive integers and $y \neq 0$. We use this form to emphasize our belief that elementary school students need tangible models when first introduced to mathematical concepts.

The first illustration of a fraction as representing equal parts of a whole can be shown using two different models, as in Figure 6.1.

Figure 6.1

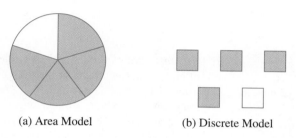

(a) Area Model   (b) Discrete Model

area model

discrete model

numerator, denominator

In Figure 6.1 we see two ways of showing four out of five. In the **area model**, a shape is partitioned into five congruent parts, four of which are shaded to show the concept "four out of five equal parts." The **discrete model**, on the other hand, compares four individual items to a whole that is composed of five individual items, again illustrating the concept "four out of five." Symbolically, this is shown as $\frac{4}{5}$. In any fraction of the form $\frac{x}{y}$, x is called the **numerator**, and y is called the **denominator**. The denominator can never be equal to zero. This stipulation can best be understood when a fraction is viewed as a quotient. For example, in the discrete model, $\frac{6}{2}$ can be interpreted as six objects partitioned into two equal groups. Each group would then contain three items. In like manner, $\frac{3}{4}$ can be interpreted as three objects partitioned into four equal groups. Figure 6.2 depicts three sandwiches shared among four children. Each child receives three-fourths of a sandwich. Since $\frac{x}{y}$ can be interpreted as x divided by y, the constraint on the divisor in whole number division must apply to the denominator. In other words, the denominator cannot equal zero.

Figure 6.2

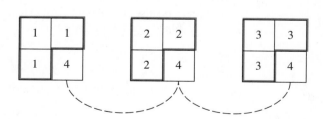

Investigation 1

What number is represented by the following area model?

  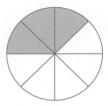

mixed number

In this illustration, three congruent circles are presented. Two whole circles and three out of eight congruent parts of the third circle are shaded. Therefore, this model can be represented by the mixed number $2\frac{3}{8}$. A **mixed number** is a number formed by the combination of a whole number and a fraction. The mixed number $2\frac{3}{8}$ can also be viewed in another way. Each of the two whole circles, like the third circle, can be divided into eight congruent parts. Each congruent part is represented by the fraction $\frac{1}{8}$. Now, superimpose the required shading as illustrated below.

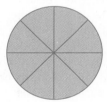 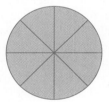 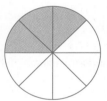

improper fraction

Notice that a total of 19 parts have been shaded. These shaded regions are represented by the fraction $\frac{19}{8}$. The mixed number $2\frac{3}{8}$ is equivalent to the fraction $\frac{19}{8}$. When written in the form $\frac{19}{8}$, this fraction is called an improper fraction. An **improper fraction** is any fraction in which the numerator is greater than or equal to the denominator. It is not always necessary to divide circles into congruent parts in order to attain an equivalent representation of a mixed number. The connection between $2\frac{3}{8}$ and $\frac{19}{8}$ can be made by recognizing that the whole number 2 represents two sets of $\frac{8}{8}$, for a total of $\frac{16}{8}$. The additional $\frac{3}{8}$ results in a total of $\frac{19}{8}$. In general, the following algorithm can be employed.

Any mixed number of the form

$$a\frac{b}{c}$$

can be written as the equivalent improper fraction

$$\frac{(ca) + b}{c}$$

The mixed number

$$2\frac{3}{8} = \frac{(2 \cdot 8) + 3}{8} = \frac{19}{8}$$

Any improper fraction can be written as a mixed number by dividing the numerator by the denominator and writing the remainder in fractional form. The improper fraction

$$\frac{19}{8} = 19 \div 8 = 2\frac{3}{8}$$

■

Locating a Fraction on a Number Line

Students often find it useful to visualize the location of a given fraction on a number line. In Figure 6.2, you examined the fraction $\frac{3}{4}$. This fraction resulted in a quotient that was less than 1 but greater than 0. This quantity can be located on a number line. Imagine that the distance representing one unit on a number line is broken into four equal portions. Starting at zero, a movement to the right spanning three of those four equal portions locates the fraction $\frac{3}{4}$ as shown in Figure 6.3a. The fraction $-\frac{3}{4}$ is found by starting at zero and moving to the left through the three of four equal portions into which the distance from 0 to −1 has been divided (Figure 6.3a).

If we wish to locate the fraction $\frac{6}{8}$ on a number line, we follow the same procedure of partitioning the distance between 0 and 1 into eight equal portions and then moving through six of those eight equal portions. The location of this fraction is shown in Figure 6.3b. Likewise, if we wish to locate the fraction $-\frac{6}{8}$, we start at zero and move left through six of the eight equal portions, as shown in Figure 6.3b. Notice the commonalities between 6.3a and 6.3b. Two sets of fractions are located at points that are the same distance from zero. To the right of zero, $\frac{3}{4}$ and $\frac{6}{8}$ name the same point on the number line. To the left of zero, $-\frac{3}{4}$ and $-\frac{6}{8}$ name the same point on the number line.

Figure 6.3

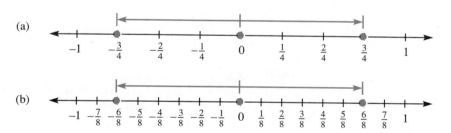

Fractions can have many different names. Fractions that are located at the same point on the number line are called **equivalent fractions**. The fractions $\frac{3}{4}$, $\frac{6}{8}$, and $\frac{12}{16}$ all name the same point on the number line and are therefore called equivalent fractions ($\frac{3}{4} = \frac{6}{8} = \frac{12}{16}$). The fractions $-\frac{3}{4}$, $-\frac{6}{8}$, and $-\frac{12}{16}$ all name the same point on the number line and are therefore also called equivalent fractions ($-\frac{3}{4} = -\frac{6}{8} = -\frac{12}{16}$).

Although the number line model visually represents fractions and their equivalences, testing whether or not fractions are equivalent by partitioning distances on a number line can be tedious and time-consuming. Equivalent fractions share other important characterists that, when recognized, can simplify work with such fractions.

Examine the fraction $\frac{12}{16}$, which we claim to be equivalent to $\frac{3}{4}$. Recall your work in Section 4.3 with factors and factor trees as they relate to prime numbers. Factors and

equivalent fractions

factor trees can also be used with equivalent fractions. Figure 6.4 depicts the prime factorization of the numerator, 12, and the denominator, 16.

Figure 6.4

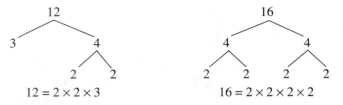

$$12 = 2 \times 2 \times 3 \qquad 16 = 2 \times 2 \times 2 \times 2$$

Comparing the prime factorization of each number gives us some insight into the relationship between the two numbers. Notice that both 12 and 16 have prime factors in common. They both share a prime factor of 2, and they both share a factor of 2×2, or 4. The factors 2 and 4 are the only factors shared by 12 and 16. Since these factors are

common factors   common to both 12 and 16, they are called **common factors**. In every set of common factors, there is always one that is the greatest (even in a set containing only one common factor, that number is both the greatest and the least common factor). The greatest

greatest common factor   number in a set of common factors is called the **greatest common factor**, sometimes

(GCF)   known as the **GCF**. Determining the greatest common factor of a numerator and denominator is one of the ways to verify fractional equivalences.

Examine the prime factorization of 12 and 16, each of which contains two 2s. The greatest common factor is formed by the product of the prime factors that 12 and 16 share:

$$12 = 2 \times 2 \times 3$$
$$16 = 2 \times 2 \times 2 \times 2$$
$$GCF = 2 \times 2 = 4$$

With this information, $\frac{12}{16}$ can be simplified and written as an equivalent fraction.

To understand the simplification process, you must recognize that every fraction is a representation of a division problem. Notice the relationship among the following division examples.

Case A	*Case B*	*Case C*
$4000 \div 1000 = 4$	$1250 \div 125 = 10$	$6 \div 3 = 2$
$400 \div 100 = 4$	$250 \div 25 = 10$	$12 \div 6 = 2$
$40 \div 10 = 4$	$50 \div 5 = 10$	$24 \div 12 = 2$
$4 \div 1 = 4$	$10 \div 1 = 10$	$48 \div 24 = 2$

In each step of case A, the divisor and the dividend were both divided by 10. In each step of case B, the divisor and the dividend were both divided by 5. In case C, the divisor and the dividend were both multiplied by 2. In all cases, notice that the quotients remained unchanged. This suggests the generalization that for any x, y, z, and a, where both y and a are nonzero, if $x \div y = z$, then $ax \div ay = z$, and $(x \div a) \div (y \div a) = z$. Pursuing this line of thought allows us to arrive at the following properties:

1. For any x, y, and a, where y and a are nonzero,

$$\frac{x}{y} = \frac{x \div a}{y \div a}$$

2. For any x, y, and a, where y and a are nonzero,

$$\frac{x}{y} = \frac{ax}{ay}$$

These two properties are extremely important to the fraction simplification process. They will be revisited when decimal division is discussed in Chapter 7. Applying property 1 to the fraction $\frac{12}{16}$ shows that:

$$\frac{12 \div 4}{16 \div 4} = \frac{3}{4}$$

relatively prime

The fraction $\frac{3}{4}$ is therefore shown to be equivalent to the fraction $\frac{12}{16}$. It is said to be *simplified, in simplest form,* or *written in lowest terms.* A fraction is said to be in lowest terms if the numerator and denominator share only a common factor of 1. When a fraction is in lowest terms, the numerator and denominator are **relatively prime**; that is, they are related as if they were both prime numbers, sharing a factor of 1. A fraction $\frac{a}{b}$ can be expressed in simplest form by dividing both a and b by the GCF of a and b.

In the past the simplification process has been known as "reducing a fraction." Recently, many math educators have taken exception to the term "reduce" when applied to fractions, since it implies that the value of the fraction decreases. As you can see, the definition of a fraction in simplest form is that it has a value that is equivalent to the original fraction. Some mathematicians insist that "reduce" is an appropriate term since the numerator and denominator are made smaller, even though the value of the fraction remains unchanged. Most elementary math textbooks use the term "simplify" to resolve any ambiguity.

Investigation 2

The financial page of a newspaper reports the daily net change in the closing price of a share of stock as $+\frac{1}{4}$. This indicates that the value of a share of the stock increased by one-fourth of a dollar. Since stock prices are traded in amounts of a half of a dollar, a fourth of a dollar, an eighth of a dollar, and a sixteenth of a dollar, how else could this increase have been represented?

Since the numerator and denominator of the fraction $\frac{1}{4}$ are relatively prime, the fraction is already in simplest form. It is therefore possible to *build* equivalent fractions as shown here:

$$\frac{1}{4} = \frac{1 \times 2}{4 \times 2} = \frac{2}{8}$$

$$\frac{1}{4} = \frac{1 \times 4}{4 \times 4} = \frac{4}{16}$$

The fraction $\frac{1}{4}$ is equivalent to both $\frac{2}{8}$ and $\frac{4}{16}$, and the increase in stock prices could have been represented with either of these equivalences.

Investigation 3

An advertisement reads "Four out of five dentists choose Chudent for their patients who chew gum." This claim was made by polling 635 dentists concerning their chewing gum preference. Five hundred eight of these dentists responded favorably to Chudent. Is the claim correct?

Understand the Problem: What is given? You are told that a claim of four out of every five dentists surveyed prefer Chudent. There were 635 dentists in this survey and 508 of those surveyed preferred Chudent.

What is unknown? You must determine whether this claim is justified based on the given information.

Devise a Plan: One of the ways to verify the claim is to simplify the fraction $\frac{508}{635}$ and compare the resulting fraction to $\frac{4}{5}$.

Carry Out the Plan: Find the GCF of 508 and 635 by examining their prime factorizations to determine the set of common factors.

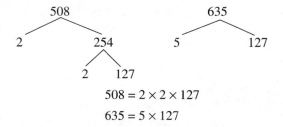

$$508 = 2 \times 2 \times 127$$
$$635 = 5 \times 127$$

The GCF of 508 and 635 is 127.

$$\frac{508}{635} = \frac{508 \div 127}{635 \div 127} = \frac{4}{5}$$

Therefore, the claim that four out of five dentists polled chose Chudent is correct.

Look Back: The claim could also have been tested by applying some of the rules of algebra outlined in Section 5.3. To test whether or not $\frac{4}{5} = \frac{508}{635}$, you could use the multiplication property of equations to "undo" the division by five on the left and the division by 635 on the right, as shown in the following five steps:

Step 1 $\dfrac{{}^1\cancel{5}\times 4}{\cancel{5}_1}=\dfrac{508\times 5}{635}$ Multiply both sides by 5 and simplify.

Step 2 $4=\dfrac{508\times 5}{635}$

Step 3 $635\times 4=\dfrac{508\times 5\times{}^1\cancel{635}}{\cancel{635}_1}$ Multiply both sides by 635 and simplify.

Step 4 $635\times 4=508\times 5$

Step 5 $2540=2540$

The claim is justified.

Suppose that 511 of the 635 dentists responded favorably. Would the claim then be justified? Since $\frac{511}{635}>\frac{508}{635}$, it follows that $\frac{511}{635}>\frac{4}{5}$. More than four out of five dentists surveyed prefer Chudent, but it is easier to report this fact when using whole number values. It is likely that the company would still report this as four out of five.

Notice in Step 4 of Investigation 3 that we have shown that the denominator of the fraction on the right times the numerator of the fraction on the left (cross product) equals the denominator of the fraction on the left times the numerator of the fraction on the right (cross product). This can be generalized into the following rule for fractional equality.

Fraction Equality Rule (Cross-Product Rule)
For any a, b, c, d, where b and d are nonzero, if

$$\frac{a}{b}=\frac{c}{d}$$

then $ad=cb$.

Ordering Rational Numbers

It is simple to order fractions that share the same denominator. For example, it is clear that $\frac{3}{8}<\frac{5}{8}$, as shown in Figure 6.5.

Figure 6.5

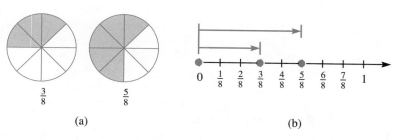

$\dfrac{3}{8}$ $\dfrac{5}{8}$

(a) (b)

The task of ordering fractions with unlike denominators is more difficult. It is not easy to determine at a glance which of the following two fractions is greater: $\frac{13}{15}$ or $\frac{5}{6}$. What you must do is rewrite them as equivalent fractions with the same denominator. Examine the set of equivalent fractions for $\frac{13}{15}$ or $\frac{5}{6}$:

$$\frac{13}{15} = \frac{26}{30} = \frac{39}{45} = \frac{52}{60} = \frac{65}{75} = \frac{78}{90}\cdots$$

$$\frac{5}{6} = \frac{10}{12} = \frac{15}{18} = \frac{20}{24} = \frac{25}{30} = \frac{30}{36} = \frac{35}{42} = \frac{40}{48} = \frac{45}{54} = \frac{50}{60} = \frac{55}{66} = \frac{60}{72} = \frac{65}{78} = \frac{70}{84} = \frac{75}{90}\cdots$$

Several pairs of fractions share the same denominator. For example,

$$\frac{26}{30} \quad \text{and} \quad \frac{25}{30} \qquad \frac{52}{60} \quad \text{and} \quad \frac{50}{60} \qquad \frac{78}{90} \quad \text{and} \quad \frac{75}{90}$$

common multiples

Notice that 30, 60, and 90 are multiples of both 15 and 6. These are called **common multiples**. The set of common multiples is infinite. We have listed only three common multiples here. For comparison purposes, it is easier to work with the fraction that has the smallest of the common multiples as its denominator. The smallest element in the set of common multiples is called the **least common multiple**, or **LCM**. When the least common multiple is used as a denominator, it is called the **least common denominator**.

least common multiple (LCM)

least common denominator

Using the common multiples as denominators, it is easy to see in all cases that $\frac{13}{15} > \frac{5}{6}$, as shown here:

$$\frac{26}{30} > \frac{25}{30} \qquad \frac{52}{60} > \frac{50}{60} \qquad \frac{78}{90} > \frac{75}{90}$$

The process outlined above appears laborious, but it is important to the understanding of the concept of equivalent fractions. Least common multiples can also be determined in several other ways. Three of those way are presented here. The first approach involves manipulatives, the second uses the calculator, and the third calls upon the number theory of prime factorization.

A Manipulative Approach to Finding Least Common Multiples Using Rods

Cuisenaire® rods are manipulatives that are commonly used in elementary school mathematics classrooms. These rods were developed in Belgium by George Cuisenaire during the 1950s to illustrate various concepts in fractions. They have since found many other applications. They consist of a set of 10 colored rods ranging in length from 1 to 10 centimeters, all 1 centimeter in width (see Figure 6.6).

These rods can be used to illustrate the multiples of a given number. For example, lining up several light-green rods, each of which measures 3 centimeters in length, creates a "train." The breaks that occur between each "car" on the train can be thought of as representing the multiples of 3. One rod measures 3 centimeters; two rods, end to end, measure 6 centimeters; three rods measure 9 centimeters; four rods measure 12 centimeters; five rods measure 15 centimeters, and so on. Another "train" can be arranged underneath the light-green train, using the purple rod, which is 4 centimeters long. The individual "cars" of this train represent the numbers 4, 8, 12, 16, and 20, or multiples of 4. If a fourth grader is asked to identify breaks that occur in both "trains" simultaneously, the child will be identifying common multiples of 3 and 4, in this case, 12 and 24. If the first common break is located, the child will be identifying the least common multiple of 3 and 4, or 12 (see Figure 6.7).

Figure 6.6

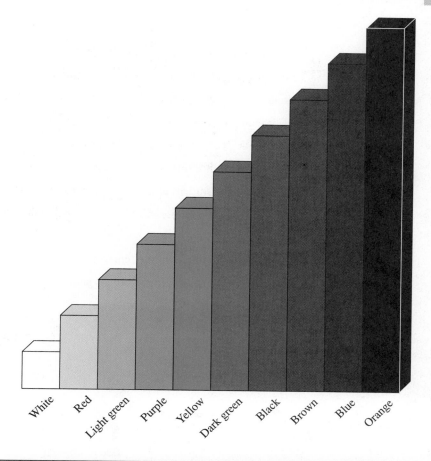

White   Red   Light green   Purple   Yellow   Dark green   Black   Brown   Blue   Orange

Figure 6.7

Light green	Light green	Light green	Light green
Purple	Purple	Purple

A Calculator Approach to Finding Least Common Multiples

Using rods to identify least common multiples is less useful when the numbers are fairly large. This limitation can be overcome by using a calculator to identify a least common multiple in much the same way as the rods are used. With a calculator, numbers of any magnitude can be used. To simulate with calculators the same procedure outlined above, you will need two calculators. (Your could perform this procedure by yourself using two calculators, but for our discussion we will assume two students are working on the problem, each using one calculator.) Let's assume that a least common denominator needs to be found for denominators of 9 and 15. Let's also assume that the calculator has the constant arithmetic feature outlined in Section 2.2.

To begin, each student clears the display. One student enters 9 $\boxed{+}$ $\boxed{=}$. The other student enters 15 $\boxed{+}$ $\boxed{=}$. At this point, the first student's display reads $\boxed{9}$, and the second student's display reads $\boxed{15}$. The student with the lower number in the display will press $\boxed{=}$, which results in a display of $\boxed{18}$. The second student then presses his or her $\boxed{=}$, which results in a display of $\boxed{30}$ on the second calculator. The first student then presses $\boxed{=}$, which again results in a display of $\boxed{27}$. Since this number is less than the display of $\boxed{30}$ on the other calculator, the first student presses $\boxed{=}$ again. The display will now read $\boxed{36}$. The second student now presses his or her $\boxed{=}$, which results in a display of $\boxed{45}$. When the first student presses $\boxed{=}$ again, that calculator will also display $\boxed{45}$. Since this is the first number common to the displays of both calculators, it is the least common multiple. This procedure is shown here:

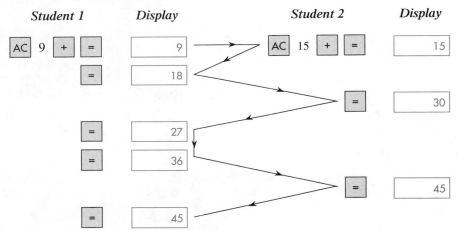

If the calculator has the constant key, $\boxed{K}$, this procedure can be repeated in much the same way. If neither of the constant features are available, the first student merely presses $\boxed{+}$ 9 $\boxed{=}$, and the second student presses $\boxed{+}$ 15 $\boxed{=}$ when their display is the lesser of the two.

The Number Theory Approach to Finding Least Common Multiples

Because this approach is more abstract than the previous two approaches, it is more appropriate for older students, or for students who have already had a concrete introduction to least common multiples. To begin determining the least common denominator of two fractions whose denominators are 15 and 6, determine the prime factorization of each denominator.

$$15 = 3 \times 5$$
$$6 = 2 \times 3$$

For a number to be a multiple of both 15 and 6, it must have both 15 and 6 as factors. If a number has 15 as a factor, then it must have 3 and 5 as factors. Therefore, the chosen multiple must have at least 3 and 5 as factors. If a number has 6 as a factor, it must have at least 2 and 3 as factors. Since the number in question already has factors of 3 and 5, it is necessary to include only the factor 2. Therefore, the smallest number that has 2, 3, and 5 as factors is the product of 2, 3, and 5, or 30. The LCM of 15 and 6 is 30. Knowing that the least common denominator is 30, it is necessary to build equivalent fractions that have 30 as their denominators. Once this is done, the fractions can be compared.

Investigation 4

Determine the greater fraction: $\frac{68}{135}$ or $\frac{37}{72}$.

Before applying any rules or algorithms, try to get a sense of the location of these fractions on a number line. In some cases, this sort of estimate may make the algorithmic process unnecessary. Both of these fractions, however, appear to be close to the fraction $\frac{1}{2}$. We must therefore find a common denominator and build both fractions into equivalent fractions with the new denominator. As mentioned earlier, the least common multiple will serve as the least common denominator. The process is outlined here:

$$135 = 3 \times 3 \times 3 \times 5 = 3^3 \times 5$$
$$72 = 2 \times 2 \times 2 \times 3 \times 3 = 2^3 \times 3^2$$

For comparison purposes, we will match the prime factorizations by introducing the missing primes and raising them to the zero power. Since a prime factor to the zero power is equal to 1, the product in each case will not be changed.

$$135 = 2^0 \times 3^3 \times 5^1$$
$$72 = 2^3 \times 3^2 \times 5^0$$

The LCM must contain all of the prime factors listed in the factorizations above, that is, 2, 3, and 5. Now, comparing each prime factorization, the LCM must be factorable by both 2^3 and 2^0. The smallest number that has both 8 and 1 as factors is 8. The LCM must therefore be factorable by 8. The LCM must be factorable by 3^3 and 3^2. The smallest number that has both 27 and 9 as factors is 27. The LCM must be factorable by 27. The LCM must be factorable by both 5^1 and 5^0. The smallest number that has both 5 and 1 as factors is 5. The LCM must be factorable by 5. The LCM must have factors 2^3, 3^3, and 5^1. The smallest number with these factors is $2^3 \times 3^3 \times 5^1$, or 1080. Notice that in each case, the prime factor raised to the greater of the two powers was chosen as a determining factor of the LCM.

In general, two numbers x and y whose prime factorization is

$$x = 2^a \times 3^b \times 5^c \times 7^d \ldots$$
$$y = 2^s \times 3^t \times 5^u \times 7^v \ldots$$

have the least common multiple $2^l \times 3^m \times 5^n \times 7^p$ where l is the greater of a and s; m is the greater of b and t; n is the greater of c and u; p is the greater of d and v; and so on.

Now that the LCM of 135 and 72 has been determined, the next step is to build equivalent fractions with a denominator of 1080.

$$\frac{68}{135} = \frac{68 \times 8}{135 \times 8} = \frac{544}{1080}$$

$$\frac{37}{72} = \frac{37 \times 15}{72 \times 15} = \frac{555}{1080}$$

Since $\frac{555}{1080} > \frac{544}{1080}$, it follows that $\frac{37}{72}$ is greater than $\frac{68}{135}$. As you can see, building equivalent fractions with like denominators establishes a commonality between the two fractions, which, in turn, makes the comparison process easier.

Assessments for Section 6.1

1. Build three equivalent fractions for each of the following fractions.

   (a) $\frac{1}{2}$ (b) $\frac{2}{3}$ (c) $\frac{7}{10}$ (d) $\frac{6}{7}$ (e) $\frac{8}{11}$

2. Build three equivalent fractions for each of the following fractions.

   (a) $\frac{4}{3}$ (b) $\frac{5}{2}$ (c) $\frac{7}{2}$ (d) $\frac{11}{4}$ (e) $\frac{19}{5}$

3. Illustrate each of the following fractions with both an area and a discrete model.

   (a) $\frac{1}{3}$ (b) $\frac{3}{5}$ (c) $\frac{4}{4}$ (d) $\frac{7}{8}$ (e) $\frac{1}{16}$

4. Illustrate each of the following mixed numbers with an area model.

   (a) $5\frac{1}{2}$ (b) $3\frac{2}{3}$ (c) $4\frac{3}{4}$ (d) $2\frac{5}{8}$ (e) $1\frac{1}{3}$

5. Simplify each of the following fractions.

   (a) $\frac{10}{15}$ (b) $\frac{18}{32}$ (c) $\frac{135}{220}$ (d) $\frac{153}{204}$ (e) $\frac{104}{182}$

6. Fill the blank space with a number that will make the fraction pairs equivalent.

   (a) $\frac{5}{8}, \frac{15}{\square}$ (b) $\frac{4}{9}, \frac{\square}{27}$ (c) $\frac{12}{15}, \frac{28}{\square}$

   (d) $\frac{16}{18}, \frac{\square}{72}$ (e) $\frac{7}{49}, \frac{12}{\square}$

7. Test whether each of the following pairs of fractions are equivalent.

   (a) $\frac{63}{77}, \frac{117}{143}$ (b) $\frac{144}{168}, \frac{54}{64}$ (c) $\frac{75}{120}, \frac{15}{24}$

   (d) $\frac{180}{280}, \frac{45}{70}$ (e) $\frac{128}{144}, \frac{152}{170}$

8. Determine the least common multiple of each pair.

   (a) 90, 60   (b) 24, 36   (c) 125, 350

9. The least common multiple of three, three-digit numbers is 540. Find three such numbers.

10. A teacher has one sixth-grade math class before lunch and another sixth-grade math class after lunch. She decided to administer the same examination to each of the classes and compare the results. In the first class, 24 students took the test. In the second class, 30 students took the test. The results are presented in the table below as fractions.

Grade	A	B	C	D	F
Class 1	$\frac{12}{24}$	$\frac{8}{24}$	$\frac{3}{24}$	$\frac{0}{24}$	$\frac{1}{24}$
Class 2	$\frac{15}{30}$	$\frac{10}{30}$	$\frac{4}{30}$	$\frac{1}{30}$	$\frac{0}{30}$

Compare the results for letter grades of A and F.

11. Jack practiced making basketball shots each day after school. On Monday he made 10 out of the 18 baskets he shot. On Tuesday he made 16 out of the 24 baskets he shot. On Wednesday he missed only 4 of the 16 baskets he shot. Did he improve as the week progressed? Justify your reasoning.

12. A farmer died, leaving a square plot of land, 1 mile on each side. According to his will, $\frac{1}{4}$ of the land was to go to his eldest child, and the remaining $\frac{3}{4}$ was to be split evenly among his other four children, in four congruent sections. Sketch at least three possible solutions for the way in which this might be done.

13. A tangram is an ancient Chinese puzzle in which a square is partitioned into seven pieces. These seven pieces can be used to form a variety of geometric shapes. (You will do more work with tangrams in Chapter 10.) Examine the tangram pictured below. Assuming that the "value" of the entire tangram square equals 1, write the fractional value for each of the seven tangram pieces. (*Hint:* Trace the tangram and cut out the individual pieces.)

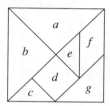

14. Martina drives along the same route to her job every day. She passes a fast-food restaurant after driving $\frac{4}{6}$ of the total trip. She passes an elementary school after driving $\frac{3}{5}$ of the total trip. She passes a service station after driving $\frac{11}{15}$ of the total trip. She passes a park after driving $\frac{5}{10}$ of the total trip. In what order does she pass these sites?

15. When Alberto jogs one way along the riverbank, he passes a coffee shop after $\frac{5}{8}$ of his run, a boathouse after $\frac{7}{12}$ of his run, an exercise course after $\frac{5}{9}$ of his run, and a newsstand after $\frac{2}{3}$ of his run.

    (a) In what order does he pass these sites?

    (b) If he also passes Pier 4 after $\frac{3}{5}$ of his run, what is the next site he will pass?

16. A fraction whose numerator is 1 is called a *unit* fraction. Arrange the following unit fractions in ascending order: $\frac{1}{6}, \frac{1}{8}, \frac{1}{2}, \frac{1}{4}$, and $\frac{1}{3}$. What do you notice about this arrangement? Generalize a statement that could be applied to any set of unit fractions.

17. A book contains 256 pages.

(a) What fractional part of the book would you have read if you are up to page 32?

(b) Build equivalent fractions to determine what page you are on when you have read $\frac{3}{4}$ of the book.

18. A concert began at 8:05 P.M. and is scheduled to end at 10:30 P.M. What fractional part of the concert is completed at 9:45 P.M.?

19. A baseball game began at 2:15 P.M. The seventh-inning stretch ended at 4:40 P.M. The game ended at 5:30 P.M. What fractional part of the game was yet to be played when the seventh-inning stretch ended?

20. Draw a circle. Divide this circle into four congruent parts. Divide each congruent part into four smaller congruent parts.

    (a) What fractional part of the circle does one of these smaller parts represent?

    (b) Assume that this process is repeated three more times. What fractional part of the circle would one of the smallest congruent parts represent?

    (c) Assume that this process is done n times in all. Write a fractional expression in terms of n that represents the smallest part.

21. An advertisement for a cola states that seven out of eight people tested prefer Pepola Cola. If 2808 people took the taste test, and 2457 preferred Pepola, is the claim correct?

22. A shipment of computer chips is considered "acceptable" if, at most, 3 out of 10,000 chips are defective. If a total shipment contained 5,800,000 chips, what is the maximum number of allowable defects?

23. Four out of every 23 students in a certain school district were absent on the day before a holiday. If 572 students were absent on that date, how many students are enrolled in the school district?

24. At the first souvenir store Lauren visited, she spent $5 more than half of her money. In the second souvenir store, Lauren again spent $5 more than half of her remaining money. She then had $12 left. How much money did she begin with? (*Hint:* Work backwards.)

In Other Words

25. Explain the concept of equivalent fractions. What does it mean when two or more fractions are said to be equivalent?

26. Some educators believe that "reduce" is an appropriate term for writing an equivalent fraction in lowest terms, whereas others do not. Make a case for each side of the issue.

27. What does it mean when one fraction is said to be greater than another.

28. Explain the difference between an area model and a discrete model of fractions.

29. We have said that when the numerator and denominator of a given fraction are relatively prime, the fraction is in lowest terms. Explain this concept. Why does "relatively prime" necessitate the simplest form of a fraction?

Cooperative Activity

30. Groups of two

Individual Accountability: Each person is to answer the following set of questions using the illustrations below. Be prepared to justify your responses to your partner.

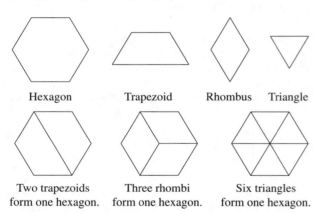

(a) If one hexagon has a value of one whole, what fractional part of the whole is the trapezoid? the rhombus? the triangle?

(b) If one hexagon has a value of one whole, show how the value of "two" can be represented in five different ways. For example, the combination of two trapezoids, two rhombi, and two triangles equal "two."

(c) Assume that you have five rhombi. If one hexagon has a value of one whole, represent the five rhombi in the form of a mixed number and an improper fraction.

(d) Assume that you have nine triangles. If one hexagon has a value of one whole, represent the nine triangles in the form of a mixed number and an improper fraction.

(e) If one hexagon has a value of $\frac{1}{2}$, what fractional part of the whole is the trapezoid? the rhombus? the triangle?

(f) If one hexagon has a value of $\frac{1}{2}$, show how the value of "three" can be represented in five different ways. For example, the combination of four hexagons, two trapezoids, and six triangles equals "three."

(g) Assume that you have six rhombi. If one hexagon has a value of one-half, represent the six rhombi in the form of a mixed number and an improper fraction.

(h) Assume that you have nine triangles. If one hexagon has a value of one-half, represent the nine triangles in the form of a fraction.

Group Goal: Compare your individual results with your partner. Together, complete the following problems using the illustrations below.

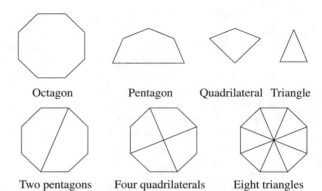

(a) If one octagon has a value of one whole, what fractional part of one whole is the pentagon? the quadrilateral? the triangle?

(b) If one octagon has a value of one whole, show how the value of "four" can be represented in five different ways.

(c) Assume that you have 35 pentagons. If one octagon has a value of one whole, represent the 35 pentagons in the form of a mixed number and an improper fraction.

(d) Assume that you have nine quadrilaterals. If one octagon has a value of one whole, represent the nine quadrilaterals in the form of a mixed number and an improper fraction.

(e) Assume that you have 17 triangles. If one octagon has a value of one whole, represent the 17 triangles in the form of a mixed number and an improper fraction.

(f) If one pentagon has the value of one whole, what fractional part of the whole is the quadrilateral? the triangle?

(g) Assume that you have 11 quadrilaterals. If one pentagon has a value of one whole, represent the 11 quadrilaterals as a mixed number and an improper fraction.

(h) Assume that you have 23 triangles. If one pentagon has a value of one whole, represent the 23 triangles as a mixed number and an improper fraction.

6.2 Models, Properties, and Algorithms of Rational Number Addition and Subtraction

As the operations of addition and subtraction on whole numbers and integers have certain models, properties, and algorithms that govern their use, so do these same operations on the set of rational numbers. In this section we present several models for working with fractions, discuss how to estimate the sums and differences of fractions, and list the properties that pertain to the addition and subtraction of rational numbers.

In Section 6.1 we introduced both an area model and a discrete illustration of a fraction. As you will remember the area model shows the fractional amount as the shaded area of a shape. We will cover area in detail in Chapter 11. But for now it is enough to recognize that the area of a two-dimensional closed shape is defined as the amount of space within that shape.

Models of Addition and Subtraction of Fractions

Three models illustrate the addition and subtraction of fractions: the area model, a manipulative model, and the number line model. Each model has specific uses within the operations of addition and subtraction of rational numbers, and some are better suited in certain situations and for particular age groups.

The Area Model of Addition and Subtraction of Fractions

You are familiar with the fact that $\frac{1}{2} + \frac{1}{2}$ is equal to one whole. Is this always the case? Examine Figure 6.8.

Figure 6.8   (a)   (b)

As you can see, Figure 6.8a shows two halves. However, they are not both halves of the same figure. The two original figures are neither the same size nor the same shape. Combining these halves in any meaningful fashion would be awkward. For the purposes of this chapter and of teaching fractions at the elementary school level, addition and subtraction are modeled only with congruent shapes, as seen in Figure 6.8b.

A Manipulative Model for Addition and Subtraction of Fractions

In Section 6.1 we introduced Cuisenaire rods as a means of illustrating the concept of the least common multiple. Here we will use Cuisenaire rods to illustrate the addition and subtraction of fractions. Fractional work with the rods usually begins by arranging a series of "one-color trains" under a train composed of an orange rod and a red rod, whose total length is 12 centimeters. The "orange-red" rod, rather than simply the orange rod, is used to represent one whole because 12 has many more factors than 10 and thus can be broken down into halves, thirds, fourths, sixths, and twelfths.

This orange-red rod will now be used to represent one whole, and all of the trains arranged under it will also have a length of 12 centimeters (see Figure 6.9). Each fraction will be defined in terms of its relation to this orange-red rod, which represents one whole.

Figure 6.9

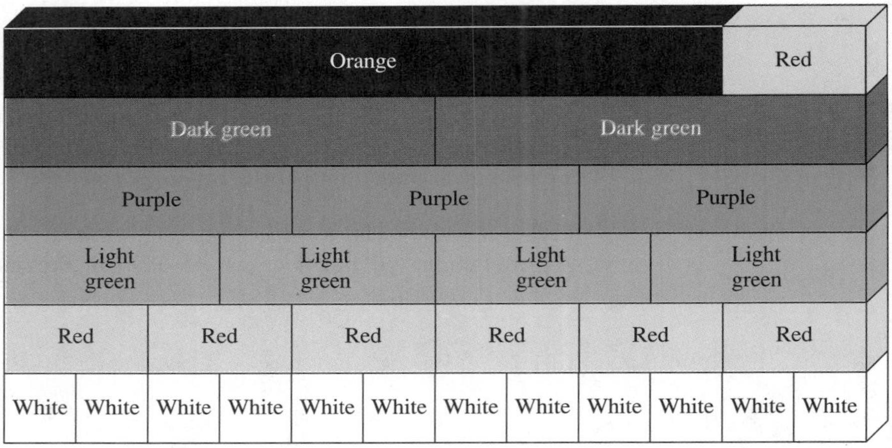

You can see that since two dark-green rods make one whole, each one can be called $\frac{1}{2}$. Since three purple rods make one whole, each purple rod can be called $\frac{1}{3}$. In similar fashion, one light-green rod can be called $\frac{1}{4}$, one red rod can be called $\frac{1}{6}$, and one white rod can be called $\frac{1}{12}$.

If we wanted to use the rods to illustrate $\frac{1}{2} + \frac{1}{3}$, we could do this by arranging a train of one dark-green rod and one purple rod under the rods that are already there (see Figure 6.10). This train is as long as 10 white rods, indicating that the sum of $\frac{1}{2}$ and $\frac{1}{3}$ is $\frac{10}{12}$. We can also see from the rods that $\frac{10}{12}$ is equivalent to $\frac{5}{6}$, since the train of dark green plus purple is also as long as five red rods.

Subtracting fractions with unlike denominators can be easily illustrated and understood using the rods. To illustrate $\frac{2}{3} - \frac{1}{4}$, arrange a train of two purples. Under this train, place one light-green rod (see Figure 6.11). The difference between the length of the two purple rods and the length of the one light-green rod represents the solution to $\frac{2}{3} - \frac{1}{4}$. You can see from Figure 6.11 that the difference is equivalent to the length of five white rods, or $\frac{5}{12}$.

Figure 6.10

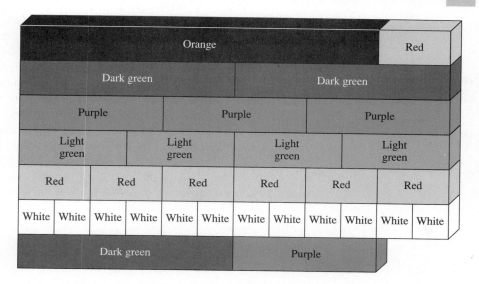

Figure 6.11

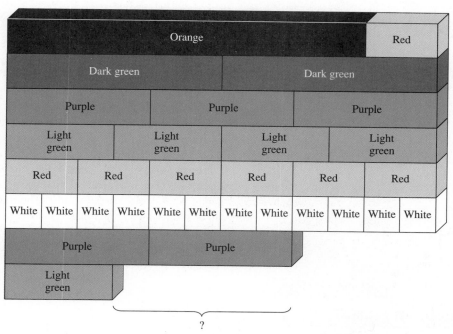

This brief discussion of addition and subtraction of fractions using rods should provide you with insight into the power of a visual, tangible manipulative. It was possible to "see" the solution to each of these examples without building equivalent fractions and performing the algorithms. As we have stressed all along, these types of tangible activities make the more abstract concepts that underlie them easier for students to grasp.

The Number Line Model for Addition and Subtraction of Fractions

The number line model is an abstract model that can help older students visualize the addition and subtraction processes of rational numbers. We will again look at the sum of $\frac{1}{3}$ and $\frac{1}{2}$. Recall how the number line model was used to illustrate the addition of whole numbers. The first addend is located on the number line as shown in Figure 6.12a. It is now necessary to move to the right (since the second addend is positive) a distance of one-half unit. This is difficult to do since the original number line is represented in thirds. We must therefore rewrite the number line in terms of fractional parts that allow for equivalences of both addends. In this case, the least common denominator of 2 and 3 will serve as the fractional unit for the number line, as shown in Figure 6.12b. Now it is possible to both locate $\frac{1}{3}$ ($\frac{2}{6}$) as well as move a distance of $\frac{1}{2}$ ($\frac{3}{6}$) to the right. The sum of these two distances is found at the point $\frac{5}{6}$ on the number line.

Figure 6.12

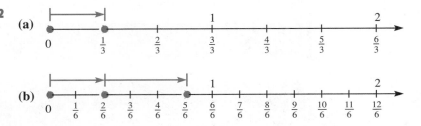

Estimating Sums and Differences of Fractions

Before discussing the addition and subtraction algorithms for fractions, we need to address the role that estimation plays in these operations. Recall the work you did with operations on whole numbers. We recommended that students develop the habit of estimating the sum, difference, product, or quotient before actually performing the algorithm. This habit is also beneficial when operating on fractions.

Since we can easily visualize 0, $\frac{1}{2}$, and 1 on a number line, we will use these three numbers as estimators. For example, before finding the actual sum of $\frac{5}{6}$ and $\frac{1}{3}$, examine each of the addends as they relate to 0, $\frac{1}{2}$, and 1. The fractional equivalent of $\frac{1}{2}$ in sixths is $\frac{3}{6}$. A whole can be represented as $\frac{6}{6}$. Since $\frac{5}{6}$ is closer to one whole than to $\frac{1}{2}$, use the estimate of 1. The fractional equivalent of $\frac{1}{3}$ in sixths is $\frac{2}{6}$, which is close to $\frac{3}{6}$, or $\frac{1}{2}$. Therefore, an estimate of the sum of $\frac{5}{6}$ and $\frac{1}{3}$ is $1\frac{1}{2}$. The actual sum is somewhat less than the estimate since each addend was rounded up.

Investigation 5

A pizza is cut into eight congruent slices. Two of the slices are topped with pepperoni, three of the slices are topped with peppers, and the remaining three slices have no extra topping. What fractional part of the pizza contains extra topping?

Employing the strategy of **drawing a diagram** may be helpful here.

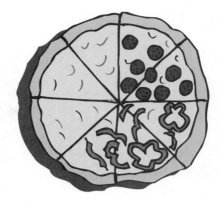

The two slices topped with pepperoni can be symbolized as $\frac{2}{8}$, since two of the eight congruent slices are topped with pepperoni. The slices topped with peppers can be symbolized as $\frac{3}{8}$. The problem now becomes one of determining the sum of $\frac{2}{8} + \frac{3}{8}$. Looking at the pizza, we see that five of the eight slices have extra toppings. Therefore, the solution must be that $\frac{2}{8} + \frac{3}{8} = \frac{5}{8}$. Look at the pattern here. When the denominators are the same, the sum of two fractions can be found by determining the sum of the numerators and leaving the denominators unchanged. Therefore,

$$\frac{2}{8} + \frac{3}{8} = \frac{2+3}{8} = \frac{5}{8}$$

The original problem in Investigation 5 can be looked at in a different way. Three of the slices have no extra topping and can be symbolized as $\frac{3}{8}$. This fractional part can be subtracted from the entire pizza, generating the solution of the fractional parts that do have extra toppings. Since eight slices comprise the entire pie, $\frac{8}{8}$ is the symbolic representation of the whole. The problem now becomes one of determining the difference between $\frac{8}{8}$ and $\frac{3}{8}$. Again referring to the illustration in Investigation 5, you can see that $\frac{5}{8}$ of the whole pie is covered with extra toppings. Therefore,

$$\frac{8}{8} - \frac{3}{8} = \frac{5}{8}$$

Notice the pattern here. When the denominators are the same, the difference between two fractions can be found by subtracting the numerators and leaving the denominators unchanged.

$$\frac{8}{8} - \frac{3}{8} = \frac{8-3}{8} = \frac{5}{8}$$

From this application, the following two generalizations can be drawn about the set of rational numbers.

addition property of rational numbers with like denominators

1. Addition Property of Rational Numbers with Like Denominators.   If a, b, and c are integers with $c \neq 0$, then

$$\frac{a}{c} + \frac{b}{c} = \frac{a+b}{c}$$

subtraction property of rational numbers with like denominators

2. Subtraction Property of Rational Numbers with Like Denominators. If a, b, and c are integers with $c \neq 0$, then

$$\frac{a}{c} - \frac{b}{c} = \frac{a-b}{c}$$

Although it is possible to have a negative solution in either of these cases, within the context of the area model a negative fraction has no meaning.

Investigation 6

At the close of trading on Tuesday, March 11, one share of Egon Industries had a net change of $+\frac{1}{4}$. At the close of trading on Wednesday, March 12, one share of Egon Industries had a closing price of $21\frac{1}{2}$. This represented a net change of $+\frac{3}{8}$ over the previous day's closing price of one share. (a) What was the total net change over these two trading days? (b) What was the closing price at the end of trading on Monday, March 10?

Understand the Problem: What is given? You are given information about changes in the closing price of a stock over a period of two days, along with the actual closing price of one share on the second day.

What is unknown? In (a) you are asked to find the total change from the opening price of the first day to the closing price of the second day. In (b) you are asked to determine the closing price on the day prior to the first day in question.

Devise a Plan: The problem asks for the sum of Tuesday's and Wednesday's net changes. Draw a diagram, using an area model to depict the situation.

Carry Out the Plan:

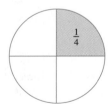 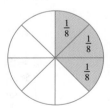

Notice that the sum is not found by counting the number of parts since these parts are not congruent. We must therefore relate each of these areas in terms of congruent parts. We can do this by determining the least common denominator of 4 and 8. When both of the fractions are rewritten as equivalent fractions with a common denominator, we can then use the addition property of rational numbers with like denominators. The least common denominator of 4 and 8 is 8. This is the smallest multiple of both 4 and 8.

Building equivalent fractions results in

$$\frac{1}{4} = \frac{2}{8}$$

$$\frac{3}{8} = \frac{3}{8}$$

The sum is $+\frac{5}{8}$ since both of the daily changes represent an increase in value of one share of stock.

To determine the closing price of one share on Monday, March 10, we must use the problem-solving strategy of working backwards. Using the closing price on Wednesday, subtract from it the total net change over the previous 2-day period. This will result in the closing price on Monday.

$$21\frac{1}{2}$$

$$-\ \ \frac{5}{8}$$

Again, we must determine the least common denominator of 2 and 8, which is 8. The problem can be rewritten as shown below. Recall the procedure followed in whole number subtraction when the digit in a particular column of the subtrahend was greater than the corresponding digit in the minuend. Regrouping was necessary. Following the strategy of **looking for a related problem**, we try to find a similar problem whose structure and/or solution might be related to the problem at hand. Just as regrouping is sometimes necessary when subtracting whole numbers, it is also sometimes necessary when subtracting fractions. Here we will need to regroup one whole into $\frac{8}{8}$ and add it to the $\frac{4}{8}$ in the minuend. Notice that the whole number 21 is thus reduced to 20. The value of the minuend has not been changed, since $21\frac{1}{2}$ is equivalent to $20\frac{12}{8}$.

$$21\frac{1}{2} = 21\frac{4}{8} = 20\frac{12}{8}$$

$$-\ \ \frac{5}{8} = \ \ \frac{5}{8} = \ \ \ \frac{5}{8}$$

$$20\frac{7}{8}$$

The closing price on Monday, March 10, of one share of Egon Industries was $20 $\frac{7}{8}$.

Look Back: Examine this problem situation on a number line as follows:

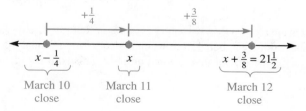

When adding or subtracting fractions with unlike denominators, the following two generalizations can be made:

addition property of rational numbers with unlike denominators

1. Addition Property of Rational Numbers with Unlike Denominators. If a, b, c, and d are integers with c, d, $\neq 0$, then

$$\frac{a}{c} + \frac{b}{d} = \frac{ad + bc}{cd}$$

subtraction property of rational numbers with unlike denominators

2. Subtraction Property of Rational Numbers with Unlike Denominators. If a, b, c, and d are integers with c, d, $\neq 0$, then

$$\frac{a}{c} - \frac{b}{d} = \frac{ad - bc}{cd}$$

Properties of Rational Number Addition and Subtraction

Recall how knowledge of the properties of whole number addition and subtraction and integer addition and subtraction helped simplify the computation processes. In the same way, becoming familiar with rational number addition and subtraction will help you understand and solve problems that involve these operations.

closure property of rational number addition

1. The Closure Property of Rational Number Addition. The sum of two rational numbers is a unique rational number. The set of rational numbers is said to be closed under addition. But is the set of rational numbers closed under subtraction? Recall the "add the opposite" model of integer subtraction, which stated that $a - b = a + (-b)$. Extend this model to rational numbers by letting a and b both be rational numbers. Since subtraction of rational numbers can be rewritten as an addition of the opposite, we can also say that the set of rational numbers is closed under subtraction.

commutative property of rational number addition

2. The Commutative Property of Rational Number Addition. The order of the addends may be changed without changing the sum. Let $\frac{a}{b}$ and $\frac{c}{d}$ be any two rational numbers. Then, by the commutative property we are assured that

$$\frac{a}{b} + \frac{c}{d} = \frac{c}{d} + \frac{a}{b}$$

associative property of rational number addition

3. The Associative Property of Rational Number Addition. When combining more than two fractional addends, the way in which the addends are grouped does not affect the sum. Let $\frac{a}{b}$, $\frac{c}{d}$, and $\frac{e}{f}$ be any three rational numbers. Then, by the associative property we are assured that

$$\left(\frac{a}{b} + \frac{c}{d}\right) + \frac{e}{f} = \frac{a}{b} + \left(\frac{c}{d} + \frac{e}{f}\right)$$

identity property of rational number addition

4. The Identity Property of Rational Number Addition. There exists a unique rational number, $\frac{0}{n}$, that when added to any rational number of the form $\frac{a}{n}$ does not change the value of that rational number. This additive identity property assures us that

$$\frac{a}{n} + \frac{0}{n} = \frac{0}{n} + \frac{a}{n} = \frac{a}{n}$$

additive inverse property of rational numbers

5. The Additive Inverse Property of Rational Numbers. For any rational number $\frac{a}{b}$ there exists a unique rational number that is the opposite of $\frac{a}{b}$, namely, $-\left(\frac{a}{b}\right)$ such that

$$\frac{a}{b} + \left(-\frac{a}{b}\right) = 0 = \left(-\frac{a}{b}\right) + \left(\frac{a}{b}\right)$$

This number is called the additive inverse of $\frac{a}{b}$.

Investigation 7

Find the sum of $\frac{1}{2}, \frac{1}{6}, \frac{1}{12}, \frac{1}{20}$, and $\frac{1}{30}$.

Understand the Problem: You are given five fractions with unlike denominators. You are asked to find the sum.

Devise a Plan: Although you could determine the least common denominator, rewrite each of these as equivalent fractions, find the sum, and then simplify, this is not the only way to solve this problem. We will use the strategy of looking for a pattern. Since the pattern in this problem is quite disguised, we will help you along by rewriting the set of fractions in an "unusual," equivalent form.

Carry Out the Plan: Examine the denominators. Notice that 2 is the product of 1 and 2. Six is the product of 2 and 3. Twelve is the product of 3 and 4. Twenty is the product of 4 and 5. Thirty is the product of 5 and 6. Therefore, the sum can be rewritten as

$$\left(\frac{1}{1 \times 2}\right) + \left(\frac{1}{2 \times 3}\right) + \left(\frac{1}{3 \times 4}\right) + \left(\frac{1}{4 \times 5}\right) + \left(\frac{1}{5 \times 6}\right)$$

It can be shown algebraically that any fraction of the form

$$\frac{1}{(n)(n + 1)}$$

where n is a nonzero integer, can be rewritten as the equivalent difference

$$\frac{1}{n} - \frac{1}{n + 1}$$

Therefore, $\frac{1}{2}$ can be written as $1 - \frac{1}{2}$, $\frac{1}{6}$ can be written as $\frac{1}{2} - \frac{1}{3}$, $\frac{1}{12}$ can be written as $\frac{1}{3} - \frac{1}{4}$, and so on. Thus, the sum can once again be rewritten as

$$\left(1 - \frac{1}{2}\right) + \left(\frac{1}{2} - \frac{1}{3}\right) + \left(\frac{1}{3} - \frac{1}{4}\right) + \left(\frac{1}{4} - \frac{1}{5}\right) + \left(\frac{1}{5} - \frac{1}{6}\right)$$

Do you notice that this sum contains several adjacent terms that are the additive inverses of each other? Using the associative property, the statement can be regrouped as follows:

$$1 + \left(-\frac{1}{2} + \frac{1}{2}\right) + \left(-\frac{1}{3} + \frac{1}{3}\right) + \left(-\frac{1}{4} + \frac{1}{4}\right) + \left(-\frac{1}{5} + \frac{1}{5}\right) - \frac{1}{6}$$

Recall from our work with integers that the sum of two opposite terms is zero. Therefore, the sum of $-\frac{1}{2}$ and $\frac{1}{2}$ is zero, the sum of $-\frac{1}{3}$ and $\frac{1}{3}$ is zero, and so on. The solution we seek is found by simplifying $1 - \frac{1}{6}$, or $\frac{5}{6}$.

Look Back: This result can be verified by expressing each fraction as an equivalent fraction whose denominator is the LCM of 2, 6, 12, 20, and 30. This LCM is 60.

$$\frac{30}{60} + \frac{10}{60} + \frac{5}{60} + \frac{3}{60} + \frac{2}{60} = \frac{50}{60} = \frac{5}{6}$$

Assessments for Section 6.2

1. Estimate each of the following sums and differences.

   (a) $\frac{3}{7} + \frac{4}{10}$ (b) $\frac{1}{3} + \frac{6}{9}$ (c) $\frac{5}{6} - \frac{1}{5}$

   (d) $\frac{9}{11} - \frac{3}{4}$ (e) $4\frac{4}{5} - 2\frac{1}{2}$ (f) $6\frac{7}{8} + 3\frac{2}{7}$

2. Estimate the missing value in each of the following equations.

   (a) $\frac{3}{7} + ? = 1\frac{1}{2}$ (b) $\frac{4}{5} - ? = \frac{1}{2}$ (c) $\frac{2}{3} + ? = 3\frac{1}{4}$

   (d) $5\frac{5}{8} - ? = 3\frac{1}{3}$

3. Find the following sums. Express your answer in simplest form.

   (a) $\frac{9}{10} + \frac{3}{4}$ (b) $\frac{5}{8} + \frac{2}{3}$ (c) $\frac{1}{5} + \frac{1}{9}$

   (d) $3\frac{4}{7} + \frac{6}{21}$ (e) $7\frac{5}{6} + 2\frac{2}{5}$ (f) $\frac{3}{4} + \frac{4}{5} + \frac{5}{6}$

   (g) $\frac{7}{16} + \frac{1}{3} + \frac{3}{8}$ (h) $\frac{3}{10} + 6\frac{5}{10} + 4\frac{7}{20}$

4. Find a fractional value(s) greater than 0 and less then 1 for the missing term(s) that would make each of the following statements true (each question mark need not be replaced with the same value).

   (a) $\frac{2}{3} + ? < 1$ (b) $1\frac{1}{4} + ? < 2$ (c) $\frac{1}{4} < ? < \frac{1}{3}$

   (d) $\frac{2}{5} < ? < \frac{9}{20}$ (e) $1 < ? + ? < 1\frac{1}{2}$

   (f) $3\frac{1}{2} - (? + ?) = 3$ (g) $? + ? + ? = \frac{5}{8}$

   (h) $? < ? + ? < ? + ? + ?$

5. Find values that will make each of the following statements true.

   (a) $\frac{?}{8} + \frac{?}{4} = 1$ (b) $\frac{?}{6} + \frac{?}{8} = 1$ (c) $\frac{4}{?} + \frac{3}{?} = 1$

   (d) $\frac{1}{?} + \frac{7}{?} = 1$ (e) $\frac{?}{3} + \frac{3}{?} = 1$

6. Use an area model to illustrate the sum of $\frac{7}{8}$ and $\frac{2}{4}$.

7. Use an area model to illustrate the sum of $\frac{1}{4}$ and $\frac{1}{3}$.

8. Examine the following sets of trains. Use symbols to represent the indicated sums. Assume that the orange-red rod represents one whole as illustrated on page 242.

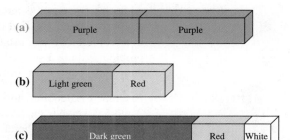

9. Examine the following sets of trains. Use symbols to illustrate the indicated differences. Assume that the orange-red rod represents one whole.

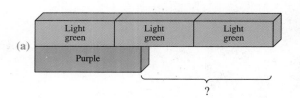

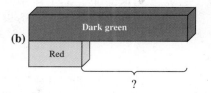

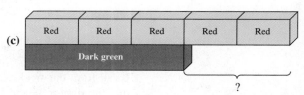

10. Illustrate and solve each of the following examples using a number line.

    (a) $\frac{5}{6} + \frac{1}{3}$ (b) $\frac{5}{8} - \frac{1}{2}$

11. Illustrate and solve each of the following equations using a number line.

    (a) $\frac{3}{4} - ? = \frac{1}{3}$ (b) $\frac{1}{8} + ? = 1\frac{1}{2}$

12. Find the difference in each of the following examples.

    (a) $\frac{7}{8} - \frac{5}{6}$ (b) $\frac{15}{16} - \frac{1}{4}$ (c) $6\frac{1}{2} - 2\frac{1}{8}$

    (d) $7\frac{2}{3} - 6\frac{1}{9}$ (e) $9\frac{1}{8} - 6\frac{5}{6}$

13. A unit fraction is a fraction in which the numerator is 1. A unit fraction can be expressed as the sum of two equal unit fractions. For example, $\frac{1}{3} = \frac{1}{6} + \frac{1}{6}$, and $\frac{1}{10} = \frac{1}{20} + \frac{1}{20}$. Express each of the following unit fractions as the sum of two identical unit fractions.

    (a) $\frac{1}{7}$ (b) $\frac{1}{15}$ (c) $\frac{1}{2}$ (d) $\frac{1}{9}$ (e) $\frac{1}{19}$

14. A unit fraction can also be rewritten as the sum of two different unit fractions. Examine each of the following equations. Determine the pattern that exists. Use this pattern to express each of the unit fractions below as a sum of two different unit fractions.

    $\frac{1}{4} = \frac{1}{5} + \frac{1}{20}$ $\frac{1}{6} = \frac{1}{7} + \frac{1}{42}$ $\frac{1}{2} = \frac{1}{3} + \frac{1}{6}$ $\frac{1}{5} = \frac{1}{6} + \frac{1}{30}$

    (a) $\frac{1}{3}$ (b) $\frac{1}{7}$ (c) $\frac{1}{10}$ (d) $\frac{1}{100}$ (e) $\frac{1}{11}$

15. For the most part, the ancient Egyptians used unit fractions in their work. This required that other fractions be rewritten in terms of unit fraction equivalents. Examine the following equations:

    $\frac{2}{3} = \frac{1}{2} + \frac{1}{6}$ $\frac{2}{9} = \frac{1}{5} + \frac{1}{45}$ $\frac{2}{15} = \frac{1}{8} + \frac{1}{120}$ $\frac{2}{13} = \frac{1}{7} + \frac{1}{91}$

    Identify the pattern. Use the recognized pattern to rewrite the following fractions as the sum of two unit fractions.

    (a) $\frac{2}{5}$ (b) $\frac{2}{7}$ (c) $\frac{2}{11}$ (d) $\frac{2}{17}$ (e) $\frac{2}{25}$

16. Four partners own a business. Dr. Trolio owns $\frac{1}{8}$ of the business, Mr. Eddio owns $\frac{2}{5}$ of the business, Ms. Video owns $\frac{9}{20}$ of the business, and Mrs. Rodeo owns the rest. What part of the business does Mrs. Rodeo own?

17. (a) One share of Beeper Company closed on Friday at $34\frac{1}{2}$. It had a net change of $+\frac{1}{4}$ at the close on Monday and a net change of $-\frac{7}{8}$ at the close on Tuesday. What was the closing price on Tuesday?

    (b) One share of Kate, Inc., closed on Monday at $23\frac{3}{4}$. It closed on Tuesday at $22\frac{1}{2}$. What was the net change?

    (c) One share of Ally Industries closed on Thursday at $19\frac{5}{8}$. This represented a net change of $-\frac{1}{4}$ over the previous day's closing price. What was the previous day's closing price?

    (d) One share of Lizatiz Corporation closed on Wednesday at $65\frac{1}{4}$. It had a net change of $-\frac{3}{8}$ on Thursday and closed on Friday at $63\frac{3}{8}$ per share. What was the net change on Friday over Thursday's closing price?

18. Annalee has only two measuring cups. One measures only $\frac{1}{4}$ cup, and the other measures only $\frac{1}{3}$ cup. Using only these two cups, how can she measure each of the following quantities?

    (a) $1\frac{1}{6}$ cup   (b) $\frac{5}{12}$ cup   (c) $\frac{5}{6}$ cup

19. In each case, use the indicated digits only once to make the greatest answer possible.

    (a) $(1, 2, 3, 4)$ $\frac{?}{?} + \frac{?}{?}$

    (b) $(1, 3, 5, 7)$ $\frac{?}{?} - \frac{?}{?}$

    (c) $(1, 2, 3, 4, 5, 6)$ $\frac{?}{?} + \frac{?}{?} - \frac{?}{?}$

20. Find the indicated term in each of the following sequences. Describe the pattern you find.

    (a) $\frac{1}{2}, \frac{3}{4}, \frac{5}{6}, \frac{7}{8}$ (one hundredth term)

    (b) $\frac{1}{3}, \frac{2}{9}, \frac{3}{27}, \frac{4}{81}$ (tenth term)

    (c) $\frac{1}{2}, \frac{1}{6}, \frac{1}{24}, \frac{1}{120}$ (fifth term)

    (d) $\frac{1}{2}, \frac{1}{5}, \frac{1}{10}, \frac{1}{17}$ (twelfth term)

    (e) $\frac{1}{2}, \frac{1}{6}, \frac{1}{12}, \frac{1}{20}$ (one thousandth term)

21. You are given the upper and lower bound of an interval. Find a fraction that falls within the interval.

    (a) $\frac{1}{2}, \frac{3}{4}$ (b) $\frac{5}{6}, \frac{7}{8}$ (c) $\frac{2}{3}, \frac{3}{4}$

    (d) $\frac{3}{8}, \frac{5}{9}$ (e) $\frac{4}{7}, \frac{5}{7}$

22. Insert five fractions between $\frac{1}{5}$ and $\frac{1}{2}$ so that the seven fractions form an arithmetic sequence.

23. Insert five fractions between $1\frac{1}{2}$ and 3 so that the seven fractions form an arithmetic sequence.

24. Find the sum of the following five fractions using the technique outlined in Investigation 7.

$$\frac{2}{3} \quad \frac{2}{15} \quad \frac{2}{35} \quad \frac{2}{63} \quad \frac{2}{99}$$

In Other Words

25. Write a realistic word problem for an elementary school student to illustrate the sum of $\frac{1}{2}$ and $\frac{2}{3}$.

26. Write a realistic word problem for an elementary school student to illustrate the difference between $\frac{5}{6}$ and $\frac{1}{4}$.

27. In your own words, explain the identity property of fraction addition.

28. Explain the need for finding a common denominator in fraction addition and subtraction.

29. List five real-world contexts in which addition and subtraction of fractions can be found.

Cooperative Activity

30. Groups of two

Individual Accountability: Use the following illustrations and information to answer the questions below.

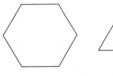

Hexagon   Trapezoid   Rhombus Triangle

Two trapezoids   Three rhombi   Six triangles
form one hexagon form one hexagon form one hexagon

(a) If one hexagon has a value of one whole, what fractional part of the whole is the trapezoid? the rhombus? the triangle?

(b) Assume that you have three hexagons, four rhombi, and eight triangles. If one hexagon has a value of one whole, how can these 15 shapes together be represented as a mixed number and an improper fraction?

(c) Assume that you have 5 trapezoids and 13 triangles. If one

hexagon has a value of one whole, how can these 18 shapes be represented as a mixed number and an improper fraction?

(d) Assume that you have two hexagons, three trapezoids, five rhombi, and two triangles. If one hexagon has a value of one whole, how can these 12 shapes be represented as a mixed number and an improper fraction?

(e) If one hexagon has a value of $\frac{1}{2}$, what fractional part of the whole is the trapezoid? the rhombus? the triangle?

(f) Assume that you have 3 hexagons, 4 rhombi, and 10 triangles. If one hexagon has a value of $\frac{1}{2}$, how can these 17 shapes be represented as a mixed number and an improper fraction?

(g) Assume that you have 5 trapezoids and 12 triangles. If one hexagon has a value of $\frac{1}{2}$, how can these 17 shapes be represented as a mixed number and an improper fraction?

Group Goal: Share your individual work with your partner. Together, use the following illustrations and information to answer the questions below.

Octagon   Pentagon   Quadrilateral   Triangle

Two pentagons   Four quadrilaterals   Eight triangles
form one octagon form one octagon   form one octagon

(a) If one octagon has a value of one whole, what fractional part of one whole is the pentagon? the quadrilateral? the triangle?

(b) Assume that you have five pentagons, five quadrilaterals, and five triangles. If one octagon has a value of one whole, how can these 15 shapes be represented as a mixed number and an improper fraction?

(c) Assume that you have three pentagons, two quadrilaterals, and nine triangles. If one octagon has a value of one whole, how can these 14 shapes be represented as a mixed number and an improper fraction?

(d) Assume that one octagon represents one whole. If you have a triangle but wish to form an octagon, what fractional part of the octagon are you missing?

(e) Assume that one octagon represents one whole. If you have a quadrilateral and a pentagon but wish to form an octagon, what fractional part of the octagon are you missing?

(f) Assume that one octagon represents one whole. If you have a pentagon, a quadrilateral, and a triangle but wish to form two octagons, what shapes are you missing? How can these missing shapes be represented as a mixed number and an improper fraction?

(g) Assume that one octagon represents one whole. If you have five triangles and three quadrilaterals but wish to form $3\frac{1}{4}$ octagons, what shapes are you missing? How can these missing shapes be represented as a mixed number and an improper fraction?

6.3   Models, Properties, and Algorithms of Rational Number Multiplication and Division

In this section, we present several models for the operations of multiplication and division of rational numbers. We examine the properties and algorithms for those operations, and investigate a variety of appropriate problems.

Rational Number Multiplication

Recall the work we did in Chapter 4 with whole number multiplication. To help you review, examine Figure 6.13. Here you are given a diagram of the ways in which whole number multiplication can be modeled. These models were applicable to any whole number multiplication.

Figure 6.13

	Cone	Dish	Sundae
Vanilla	Vanilla Cone	Vanilla Dish	Vanilla Sundae
Chocolate	Chocolate Cone	Chocolate Dish	Chocolate Sundae

$3 \div 3$

2×3 array

2×3 repeated addition

2×3 Cartesian product

This is not the case with rational number multiplication, however, where the multipliers and the multiplicands can take a variety of forms. The most appropriate model to illustrate rational number multiplication is dictated by the nature of the multiplier and the multiplicand.

Forms of Rational Number Multipliers

Three general forms of rational number multipliers are possible: whole number multipliers, fraction multipliers, and mixed number multipliers.

Form 1. Whole Number Multiplier

(a) Whole number times a fraction

$$5 \times \frac{1}{3}$$

(b) Whole number times a mixed number

$$5 \times 2\frac{1}{3}$$

In both of these cases, multiplication can be viewed as five groups of a particular quantity. In case (a) the example is read as five groups of one-third. In case (b) it is read as five groups of two and one-third. In both cases, it is most appropriate to illustrate these examples using the repeated addition model of multiplication.

(a) $5 \times \frac{1}{3} \rightarrow$ five groups of one-third $\rightarrow \frac{1}{3} + \frac{1}{3} + \frac{1}{3} + \frac{1}{3} + \frac{1}{3} = \frac{5}{3} = 1\frac{2}{3}$

(b) $5 \times 2\frac{1}{3} \rightarrow$ five groups of two and one-third $\rightarrow 2\frac{1}{3} + 2\frac{1}{3} + 2\frac{1}{3} + 2\frac{1}{3} + 2\frac{1}{3} = 10\frac{5}{3} = 11\frac{2}{3}$

Form 2. Fraction Multiplier
(a) Fraction times a whole number

$$\frac{2}{3} \times 4$$

(b) Fraction times a fraction

$$\frac{2}{3} \times \frac{1}{2}$$

(c) Fraction times a mixed number

$$\frac{2}{3} \times 2\frac{1}{2}$$

Each of these three cases can be viewed as two-thirds of a particular quantity. Case (a) can be illustrated using a number line model. Cases (b) and (c) can be illustrated using an array model.

(a) $\frac{2}{3} \times 4$ In this example, you are asked to find two-thirds of four. Begin with a number line illustrating a length of four units, as shown in Figure 6.14.

Figure 6.14

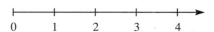

Recall the distributive property of whole number multiplication over addition. Recognizing that this property also holds for fraction multiplication over addition allows $\frac{2}{3} \times 4$ to be rewritten as

$$\frac{2}{3} \times (1 + 1 + 1 + 1)$$

By the distributive property, this is equal to

$$\left(\frac{2}{3} \times 1\right) + \left(\frac{2}{3} \times 1\right) + \left(\frac{2}{3} \times 1\right) + \left(\frac{2}{3} \times 1\right)$$

This expression can be viewed as in Figure 6.15.

Figure 6.15

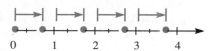

The sum of the four products,

$$\left(\frac{2}{3} \times 1\right) + \left(\frac{2}{3} \times 1\right) + \left(\frac{2}{3} \times 1\right) + \left(\frac{2}{3} \times 1\right)$$

is $\frac{8}{3}$, or $2\frac{2}{3}$, as shown in Figure 6.16.

Figure 6.16

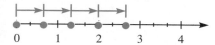

This solution can be verified by employing the commutative property of multiplication. The statement $\frac{2}{3} \times 4$ must be equal to $4 \times \frac{2}{3}$. The latter is a form 1 example and can be viewed using repeated addition:

$$4 \times \frac{2}{3} = \frac{2}{3} + \frac{2}{3} + \frac{2}{3} + \frac{2}{3} = \frac{8}{3} = 2\frac{2}{3}$$

(b) $\frac{2}{3} \times \frac{1}{2}$ This example can be read as two-thirds of one-half. Begin by vertically shading $\frac{1}{2}$ of a rectangle as shown in Figure 6.17a. Next, horizontally shade $\frac{2}{3}$ of the rectangle (Figure 6.17b). The double-shaded area represents two-thirds of one-half. Notice that this double-shaded region covers two of six equal parts. Since six equal parts make up one whole, this can be represented by $\frac{2}{6}$, or $\frac{1}{3}$.

Figure 6.17

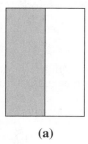   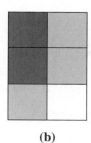

(a)   (b)

(c) $\frac{2}{3} \times 2\frac{1}{2}$ This example can be read as two-thirds of two and one-half. Begin by showing $2\frac{1}{2}$ vertically (Figure 6.18a). Next, show $\frac{2}{3}$ horizontally (Figure 6.18b). The double-shaded area represents two-thirds of two and one-half. Notice that the double-shaded area covers 10 equal parts. Since six equal parts make up one whole, these 10 parts can be represented as $\frac{10}{6}$, or $1\frac{2}{3}$.

Figure 6.18

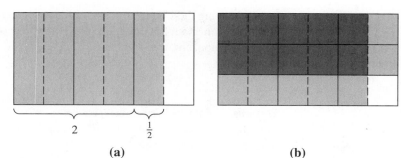

(a)   (b)

Form 3. Mixed Number Multiplier

(a) Mixed number times a whole number

$$1\frac{1}{2} \times 4$$

(b) Mixed number times a fraction

$$1\frac{1}{2} \times \frac{3}{4}$$

(c) Mixed number times a mixed number

$$1\frac{1}{2} \times 3\frac{3}{4}$$

Each of these three cases can be interpreted as one and one-half groups of a particular quantity. Although cases (a) and (b) could be modeled with array and number line models, the mechanics of the models are cumbersome. Instead, by once again recognizing that multiplication is commutative, each of these two cases can be written in either form 1 or form 2 of the multiplication examples. Understanding the laws of mathematics gives us the power to simplify situations that might otherwise appear complex. In case (c) it will be easiest to change the form of the example using the distributive property. For a mixed number multiplier and multiplicand, it is necessary to recognize that $1\frac{1}{2} = (1 + \frac{1}{2})$ and $3\frac{3}{4} = (3 + \frac{3}{4})$. Therefore,

$$1\frac{1}{2} \times 3\frac{3}{4} = \left(1 + \frac{1}{2}\right) \times \left(3 + \frac{3}{4}\right)$$

Distributing each of the numbers in the first parentheses over each of the numbers in the second parentheses generates the following statement and indicated view:

$$\underbrace{(1 \times 3)}_{\text{Whole number multiplication}} + \underbrace{\left(1 \times \frac{3}{4}\right)}_{\text{Form 1}} + \underbrace{\left(\frac{1}{2} \times 3\right) + \left(\frac{1}{2} \times \frac{3}{4}\right)}_{\text{Form 2}} =$$

$$3 \quad + \quad \frac{3}{4} \quad + \quad \frac{3}{2} \quad + \quad \frac{3}{8} \quad =$$

$$\frac{24}{8} \quad + \quad \frac{6}{8} \quad + \quad \frac{12}{8} \quad + \quad \frac{3}{8} \quad = \frac{45}{8} = 5\frac{5}{8}$$

Reviewing these three forms of rational number multipliers leads to the following generalization about fraction multiplication: If a, b, c, and d are whole numbers where b and d are nonzero, then

$$\frac{a}{b} \cdot \frac{c}{d} = \frac{a \cdot c}{b \cdot d}$$

Properties of Rational Number Multiplication

Now that we have generalized a method of rational number multiplication, we need to state the properties that hold.

closure property of rational number multiplication

1. The Closure Property of Rational Number Multiplication.   The product of two rational numbers is a unique rational number. The set of rational numbers is said to be closed under multiplication.

commutative property of rational number multiplication

2. The Commutative Property of Rational Number Multiplication.   The order of the multiplier and the multiplicand can be changed without changing the product. Let $\frac{a}{b}$ and $\frac{c}{d}$ be any two rational numbers. Then, by the commutative property we are assured that

$$\frac{a}{b} \cdot \frac{c}{d} = \frac{c}{d} \cdot \frac{a}{b}$$

The product on the left side of the equal sign is $\frac{ac}{bd}$. The product on the right side of the equal sign is $\frac{ca}{db}$. Since a, b, c, and d are whole numbers, we are assured by the commutative property of whole number multiplication that $ac = ca$ and $bd = db$. Therefore, $\frac{ac}{bd} = \frac{ca}{db}$.

associative property of rational number multiplication

3. The Associative Property of Rational Number Multiplication.   When multiplying more than two rational numbers, the way in which the rational numbers are grouped does not affect the product. Let $\frac{a}{b}, \frac{c}{d}$, and $\frac{e}{f}$ be any three rational numbers. Then, by the associative property we are assured that

$$\left(\frac{a}{b} \cdot \frac{c}{d}\right) \cdot \frac{e}{f} = \frac{a}{b} \cdot \left(\frac{c}{d} \cdot \frac{e}{f}\right)$$

distributive property of multiplication over addition of rational numbers

4. The Distributive Property of Multiplication over Addition of Rational Numbers.   Let $\frac{a}{b}, \frac{c}{d}$, and $\frac{e}{f}$ be any three rational numbers. Then,

$$\frac{a}{b} \cdot \left(\frac{c}{d} + \frac{e}{f}\right) = \left(\frac{a}{b} \cdot \frac{c}{d}\right) + \left(\frac{a}{b} \cdot \frac{e}{f}\right) \quad \text{and} \quad \left(\frac{c}{d} + \frac{e}{f}\right) \cdot \frac{a}{b} = \left(\frac{c}{d} \cdot \frac{a}{b}\right) + \left(\frac{e}{f} \cdot \frac{a}{b}\right)$$

zero multiplication property of rational numbers

5. The Zero Multiplication Property of Rational Numbers.   Let $\frac{a}{b}$ be any rational number. Then,

$$\frac{a}{b} \cdot 0 = 0 = 0 \cdot \frac{a}{b}$$

multiplicative identity property of rational number multiplication

6. The Multiplicative Identity Property of Rational Number Multiplication.   For any rational number $\frac{a}{b}$, there is a unique rational number $\frac{1}{1}$ (or 1) such that

$$\frac{a}{b} \cdot \frac{1}{1} = \frac{a}{b} \cdot 1 = 1 \cdot \frac{a}{b} = \frac{a}{b}$$

Finally, we will examine a property that is unique to the set of rational numbers. Begin with a representation of one whole—for example, $\frac{x}{x}$ where x is a nonzero whole number that can be expressed as the product of two whole numbers a and b. Then it follows that

$$1 = \frac{x}{x} = \frac{a \cdot b}{a \cdot b}$$

Since a and b are whole numbers, $a \cdot b = b \cdot a$ by the commutative property of whole number multiplication. We use this fact to write the following expression:

$$1 = \frac{x}{x} = \frac{a \cdot b}{a \cdot b} = \frac{a \cdot b}{b \cdot a}$$

Using the definition of rational number multiplication, we see that

$$1 = \frac{x}{x} = \frac{a \cdot b}{a \cdot b} = \frac{a \cdot b}{b \cdot a} = \frac{a}{b} \cdot \frac{b}{a}$$

Therefore,

$$1 = \frac{a}{b} \cdot \frac{b}{a}$$

This establishes the existence of a special fraction $\frac{b}{a}$ that, when multiplied by the fraction $\frac{a}{b}$, has 1 as its product. This leads us to the following property:

multiplicative inverse property of rational number multiplication

7. The Multiplicative Inverse Property of Rational Number Multiplication. For each nonzero rational number $\frac{a}{b}$, there exists a unique rational number $\frac{b}{a}$ such that

$$1 = \frac{a}{b} \cdot \frac{b}{a}$$

multiplicative inverse (reciprocal)

The fraction $\frac{b}{a}$ is known as the **multiplicative inverse**, or **reciprocal**, of the fraction $\frac{a}{b}$.

Investigation 8

Sky West Airlines flight 1022 flies from Salt Lake City, Utah, to Seattle, Washington. There are 240 passengers on this flight. One-eighth of the passengers are in first class. The rest of the passengers are in coach class. Two-thirds of the coach passengers are traveling together on a tour. One-fourth of the tour passengers are male. How many male passengers are on the tour?

The modeling process used to illustrate fraction and mixed number multiplication should have helped you develop a visual image of the fraction multiplication process. When attempting to solve a problem, it often helps to use the problem-solving technique of drawing a diagram. The diagram serves as a model or a picture of the situation and allows you to examine the component parts of the problem from different vantage points.

Let a rectangle represent the 240 passengers on flight 1022 (see top left). In order to show the fraction of the passengers that fly in both classes, we must partition the rectangle into two parts: one part representing the first class passengers $\left(\frac{1}{8}\right)$ and one part representing the coach class passengers $\left(\frac{7}{8}\right)$. Next, the coach section must be further partitioned to show those coach passengers who are traveling on the tour (see top right).

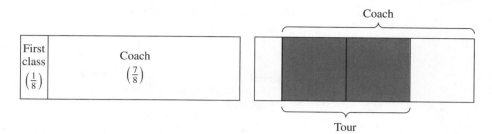

Finally, the tour passengers must be further partitioned to show those passengers who are male:

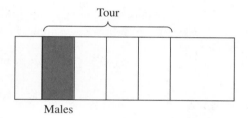

Now that a diagram of the problem situation has been drawn, we can estimate the number of tour passengers who are male. Examine the region in question. Since it is a relatively small portion of the entire rectangle, a reasonable estimate should be a relatively small portion of the 240 passengers. You might estimate the number of male tour passengers to be less than 50. The mathematical operations necessary to solve this problem follow the logic of the sequence in which the diagram was drawn.

First, the rectangle was partitioned into first-class and coach groupings. Since $\frac{1}{8}$ of the passengers are in first class, the remaining $\frac{7}{8}$ must be in coach. This number can be determined by finding $\frac{7}{8}$ of 240.

$$\frac{7}{8} \times 240 = \frac{1680}{8} = 210$$

There are 210 coach passengers.

Second, we need to partition the number of coach passengers into two groups: those who are part of the tour and those who are not. The number of passengers on the tour can be determined by finding $\frac{2}{3}$ of 210.

$$\frac{2}{3} \times 210 = \frac{420}{3} = 140$$

There are 140 coach passengers on the tour.

Finally, the number of male coach passengers who are on the tour is determined by finding $\frac{1}{4}$ of 140.

$$\frac{1}{4} \times 140 = \frac{140}{4} = 35$$

There are 35 male coach passengers on the tour.

This final step solves the original problem. But let's take a closer look at the operations performed.

$$\left(\frac{7}{8} \times 240\right) \times \frac{2}{3} \times \frac{1}{4}$$

By applying both the commutative and associative properties of multiplication, this statement becomes

$$240 \times \frac{7}{8} \times \frac{2}{3} \times \frac{1}{4} = 240 \times \left(\frac{7}{8} \times \frac{2}{3} \times \frac{1}{4}\right) = 240 \times \frac{14}{96} = 240 \times \frac{7}{48} = \frac{1680}{48} = 35$$

This indicates that the number of male coach passengers on the tour, 35, is $\frac{7}{48}$ of 240.

A procedure that greatly simplifies the multiplication process can be employed. Examine the following example: Find the product of $\frac{3}{8}$ and $\frac{4}{9}$.

$$\frac{3}{8} \times \frac{4}{9} = \frac{3 \cdot 4}{8 \cdot 9} \quad \text{by the definition of fraction multiplication}$$

$$\frac{3 \cdot 4}{8 \cdot 9} = \frac{3 \cdot 4}{9 \cdot 8} \quad \text{by the commutative property of whole number multiplication}$$

$$\frac{3 \cdot 4}{9 \cdot 8} = \frac{3}{9} \times \frac{4}{8} \quad \text{by the definition of fraction multiplication}$$

$$\frac{3}{9} \times \frac{4}{8} = \frac{1}{3} \times \frac{1}{2} = \frac{1}{6} \quad \text{by simplifying fractions}$$

A more compressed view of this process can be seen in the following simplification:

$$\frac{3}{8} \times \frac{4}{9} = \frac{\overset{1}{\cancel{3}}}{\underset{2}{\cancel{8}}} \times \frac{\overset{1}{\cancel{4}}}{\underset{3}{\cancel{9}}} = \frac{1}{6}$$

Investigation 9

In a particular textbook, $\frac{15}{16}$ of the pages contain illustrations. If $\frac{4}{5}$ of these illustrations are diagrams, what fractional part of the total page count of the textbook contains diagrams? If the book has 360 pages, how many pages contain diagrams?

Draw a picture to visualize this problem. Let one complete circle represent the total page count for the textbook. Partition the circle into 16 congruent sections, as shown at the top of page 261. Fifteen of the 16 congruent sections represent the number of pages that contain illustrations. Four-fifths of these 15 sections represent the illustrations that are diagrams. Since there are 3 sections in $\frac{1}{5}$, there are 12 sections in $\frac{4}{5}$. Therefore, $\frac{12}{16}$, or $\frac{3}{4}$, of the total page count contains diagrams.

If the book has 360 pages, $\frac{3}{4}$ of 360 is

$$\frac{3}{\underset{1}{\cancel{4}}} \times \frac{\overset{90}{\cancel{360}}}{1} = 240$$

Therefore, 240 pages contain diagrams.

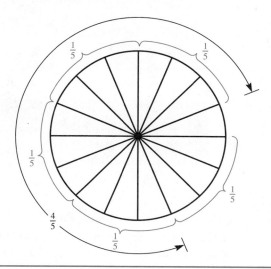

Rational Number Division

The language used to interpret rational number division is important to a full understanding of the process. We will make an analogy to the language that is used to interpret whole number division. For example, $12 \div 4 = 3$ can be interpreted as the answer to the question, "How many fours are in twelve?" In a similar fashion, $\frac{2}{3} \div \frac{1}{6} = 4$ can be interpreted as the answer to the question, "How many one-sixths are there in two-thirds?"

Fraction division can be concretely illustrated using Cuisenaire rods. Begin with the orange-red rod. Recall that the orange-red rod is often used to represent one whole in work with fractions since it represents a length of 12 centimeters. As we mentioned earlier, 12 is a "rich" number to use in fractional work because it has several factors. Under the orange-red rod, build as many one-color trains as possible (Figure 6.19).

You can see from this illustration that the fractional name given to dark green is $\frac{1}{2}$, the fractional name given to purple is $\frac{1}{3}$, the fractional name given to light green is $\frac{1}{4}$, the fractional name given to red is $\frac{1}{6}$, and the fractional name given to white is $\frac{1}{12}$. If we are asking the mathematical question, "How many one-sixths are there in two-thirds?" in color language we are asking, "How many red rods are there in two purple rods?" You can see from Figure 6.19 that four red rods are as long as two purple rods. In other words, there are four one-sixths in two-thirds.

Figure 6.19

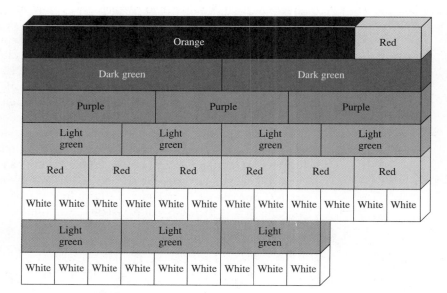

Investigation 10

A block of cheese weighs $\frac{3}{4}$ of a pound. The cook wants to slice it for sandwiches, with each sandwich containing $\frac{1}{12}$ of a pound of cheese. How many sandwiches can be made from this block of cheese?

The mathematical question being asked here is, "How many $\frac{1}{12}$s are there in $\frac{3}{4}$?" Referring to the illustration below, this question can be interpreted as, "How many white rods are as long as three light-green rods?"

Nine white rods are as long as three light-green rods, indicating that the answer to $\frac{3}{4} \div \frac{1}{12} = 9$. Nine sandwiches can be made from the given block of cheese.

Investigation 11

A child was observed dividing fractions in the same way that she had learned to multiply fractions. Examine her procedure in these two examples.

$$\frac{4}{6} \div \frac{1}{3} = \frac{4 \div 1}{6 \div 3} = \frac{4}{2} \qquad \frac{4}{12} \div \frac{2}{3} = \frac{4 \div 2}{12 \div 3} = \frac{2}{4}$$

Is this an acceptable algorithm? Will it always work?

To determine if it is an acceptable algorithm, we must first determine if it yields the correct answer in this case and in all cases. In the first example, we ask how many $\frac{1}{3}$s are in $\frac{4}{6}$. Refer to the illustration in Investigation 10 to see how many purple rods are as long as four red rods. You will see that two purple rods are as long as four red rods. The solution $\frac{4}{2}$ is therefore correct. In the second example, we need to determine how much of two purple rods are as long as four white rods. Again referring to the illustration in Investigation 10, you can see that $\frac{1}{2}$ of two purple rods are as long as four white rods. The solution $\frac{2}{4}$ is also correct.

However, you may have noticed that these two examples are special cases since both numerators and denominators divide without remainder. Will the algorithm work when this is not the case? Consider $\frac{5}{7} \div \frac{6}{11}$.

$$\frac{5}{7} \div \frac{6}{11} = \frac{5 \div 6}{7 \div 11} = \frac{\frac{5}{6}}{\frac{7}{11}}$$

complex fraction   At this point, the algorithm has generated a complex fraction. A **complex fraction** is a fraction in which the numerator and/or denominator are themselves fractions. A method for simplifying a complex fraction uses the multiplicative inverse property to result in an equivalent complex fraction with a denominator of 1. By multiplying the denominator of this fraction by $\frac{11}{7}$, the reciprocal of $\frac{7}{11}$, the denominator will equal 1. In order to maintain the equivalence, the numerator must also be multiplied by $\frac{11}{7}$, as shown here:

$$\frac{\frac{5}{6} \times \frac{11}{7}}{\frac{7}{11} \times \frac{11}{7}} = \frac{\frac{5}{6} \times \frac{11}{7}}{1} = \frac{5}{6} \times \frac{11}{7}$$

Using the definition of fraction multiplication,

$$\frac{5}{6} \times \frac{11}{7} = \frac{5 \times 11}{6 \times 7}$$

Since multiplication is commutative,

$$\frac{5 \times 11}{6 \times 7} = \frac{5 \times 11}{7 \times 6} = \frac{5}{7} \times \frac{11}{6}$$

Therefore, it appears that

$$\frac{5}{7} \div \frac{6}{11} = \frac{5}{7} \times \frac{11}{6}$$

The solution is $\frac{55}{42}$ or $1\frac{13}{42}$.

Notice that the division problem becomes an equivalent multiplication problem in which the reciprocal of the divisor is the multiplicand. This is traditionally known as the "invert and multiply" procedure. Therefore, the algorithm used by the child is correct and in fact has been used to generate the traditional procedure of "invert and multiply."

A second alternative division algorithm necessitates finding a common denominator and then performing the appropriate operation on both the numerator and the denominator. To find the quotient of $\frac{5}{7} \div \frac{6}{11}$, first express each of the fractions as equivalent fractions with a common denominator:

$$\frac{5}{7} \div \frac{6}{11} = \frac{55}{77} \div \frac{42}{77} = \frac{55 \div 42}{77 \div 77} = \frac{\frac{55}{42}}{1} = \frac{55}{42} = 1\frac{13}{42}$$

By expressing the divisor and the dividend as fractions with a common denominator, the denominator of the resulting complex fraction will always be equal to 1. The solution is the numerator itself.

The following generalizations can be made about fraction division. If a/b and c/d are any two fractions with $\frac{c}{d} \neq 0$, then

1. $\dfrac{a}{b} \div \dfrac{c}{d} = \dfrac{a}{b} \cdot \dfrac{d}{c} = \dfrac{ad}{bc}$ Here, invert the divisor, then multiply.

2. $\dfrac{a}{b} \div \dfrac{c}{d} = \dfrac{ad}{bd} \div \dfrac{cb}{db} = \dfrac{ad \div cb}{bd \div db} = \dfrac{\frac{ad}{cb}}{1} = \dfrac{ad}{cb}$

Here, rewrite both the dividend and the divisor as equivalent fractions with common denominators, then divide across and simplify the resulting complex fraction.

Investigation 12

A seedling was planted in a school science laboratory on September 2. At that time, the seedling measured $2\frac{1}{4}$ inches in height. Height measurements were taken and entered into a log. When the last entry was made, the height of the plant was $11\frac{1}{8}$ inches. This particular plant has an average growth of about $\frac{3}{4}$ inch per month in a laboratory setting. Knowing this information, approximately when was the last entry made?

Understand the Problem: What is given? You are told the original and final heights of the seedling and its average monthly growth.

What is unknown? You must determine the date of the entry recording $11\frac{1}{8}$ inches.

Devise a Plan: The first piece of information you must determine is the amount that the seedling grew from September to the day of the last log entry. You can do this by subtracting the initial height from the last recorded height.

Carry Out the Plan:

$$11\frac{1}{8} = 11\frac{1}{8} = 10\frac{9}{8}$$
$$-2\frac{1}{4} = 2\frac{2}{8} = 2\frac{1}{8}$$
$$\overline{\qquad\qquad 8\frac{7}{8}}$$

The seedling grew a total of $8\frac{7}{8}$ inches.

If the seedling grew approximately $\frac{3}{4}$ inch each month, the question can be restated as $8\frac{7}{8} \div \frac{3}{4}$, which represents the number of $\frac{3}{4}$ inches in $8\frac{7}{8}$ inches. This can be determined as follows:

$$8\frac{7}{8} \div \frac{3}{4} = \frac{71}{8} \times \frac{4}{3} = \frac{71}{6} = 11\frac{5}{6}$$

Therefore, the plant had been growing for close to 12 months. A reasonable estimate of when the last entry was made in the log is late in August.

Look Back: This problem could also have been solved in another way. Often, a solution can be found by first organizing the data in a structured fashion. This problem-solving strategy is called **constructing a table**. Constructing a table, or a chart, allows you to readily view the data, looking for patterns and/or inconsistencies that might lead to a solution. The table below models a monthly height log.

Height (in inches)	$2\frac{1}{4}$	3	$3\frac{3}{4}$	$4\frac{1}{2}$
Date Recorded	September 2	October 2	November 2	December 2
Height (in inches)	$5\frac{1}{4}$	6	$6\frac{3}{4}$	$7\frac{1}{2}$	$8\frac{1}{4}$
Date Recorded	January 2	February 2	March 2	April 2	May 2
Height (in inches)	9	$9\frac{3}{4}$	$10\frac{1}{2}$	$11\frac{1}{4}$
Date Recorded	June 2	July 2	August 2	September 2

Notice that since the last recorded height in the log was $11\frac{1}{8}$ inches (which is less than the $11\frac{1}{4}$ inches indicated in the table), this final height must have been recorded at the end of August.

Assessments for Section 6.3

1. Estimate the product in each of the following examples.

   (a) $170 \times \frac{2}{3}$ (b) $5\frac{1}{2} \times \frac{1}{2}$ (c) $80 \times \frac{1}{7}$

   (d) $\frac{15}{16} \times 100$

2. Estimate the quotient in each of the following examples.

   (a) $7 \div \frac{1}{2}$ (b) $2\frac{2}{5} \div \frac{1}{3}$ (c) $100 \div 2\frac{1}{2}$

   (d) $\frac{7}{8} \div \frac{1}{10}$

3. Find the product in each of the following examples.

   (a) $\frac{2}{5} \times \frac{16}{16}$ (b) $\frac{7}{9} \times \frac{3}{4}$ (c) $\frac{4}{5} \times \frac{3}{8}$

   (d) $3\frac{1}{4} \times \frac{8}{9}$ (e) $\frac{7}{8} \times 2\frac{2}{3}$ (f) $4\frac{2}{5} \times \frac{5}{11}$

   (g) $\frac{1}{8} \times 2\frac{2}{5}$ (h) $1\frac{1}{3} \times \frac{3}{4}$ (i) $6\frac{2}{4} \times 1\frac{1}{13}$

   (j) $\left(3\frac{1}{5}\right)^2$ (k) $\left(\frac{2}{3}\right)^3$

4. Find the quotient in each of the following examples.

   (a) $\frac{7}{16} \div \frac{1}{7}$ (b) $\frac{3}{5} \div \frac{8}{11}$ (c) $\frac{5}{9} \div \frac{2}{9}$

   (d) $8\frac{8}{14} \div 3\frac{4}{7}$ (e) $6\frac{1}{3} \div \frac{6}{7}$ (f) $18 \div \frac{2}{3}$

   (g) $\frac{2}{3} \div 18$ (h) $5\frac{1}{4} \div 21$ (i) $\left(\frac{1}{2}\right)^2 \div \left(\frac{1}{4}\right)^2$

   (j) $\left(\frac{1}{2} \times \frac{2}{5}\right) \div \frac{13}{15}$

5. Find the difference between the quotient of $\frac{3}{4}$ and $\frac{1}{2}$, and the product of $\frac{3}{4}$ and $\frac{1}{2}$.

6. Find the sum of the product of $1\frac{2}{3}$ and 15, and the quotient of $1\frac{2}{3}$ and 15.

7. Find the quotient of the sum of $\frac{4}{5}$ and $\frac{1}{2}$, and the product of $\frac{4}{5}$ and $\frac{1}{2}$.

8. Find the product of the difference between $4\frac{2}{3}$ and $1\frac{1}{5}$, and the sum of $4\frac{2}{3}$ and $1\frac{1}{5}$.

9. Explain how each of the following multiplication examples can be viewed using any model outlined in this section.

   (a) $4 \times \frac{2}{5}$ (b) $7 \times 1\frac{1}{2}$ (c) $\frac{5}{6} \times \frac{1}{3}$

   (d) $\frac{1}{4} \times \frac{2}{7}$ (e) $\frac{3}{5} \times \frac{2}{3}$ (f) $\frac{5}{8} \times 4$

10. What multiplication problem is illustrated in each of the following models?

    (a)   (b)

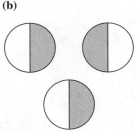

11. A coat was originally priced at \$180. It was reduced by $\frac{1}{3}$ of the original price. What was the reduction? What was the sale price?

12. A certain store pays \$50 wholesale for each radio it purchases. The store owners mark up the price of the radio by $\frac{1}{5}$ of their cost. What is the markup? What does one radio retail for?

13. A shipment contained 250 light bulbs. Each light bulb was tested. Five were found to be defective. The quality-control department recalls a shipment if over $\frac{1}{125}$ of its contents are defective. Will this shipment be recalled? Explain your answer.

14. A college library was conducting an inventory of its holdings in order to bar code each book. Of the 325,000 books on file, 6500 were missing from the shelves. The library reorders books when more than $\frac{1}{100}$ of the books are missing. Will the library reorder books?

15. Eight thousand applications were received by a certain college. After reviewing the applications, the following information was ascertained: $\frac{9}{10}$ of the applicants were state residents; $\frac{2}{5}$ of the state residents were female. How many state applications came from males?

16. A high school has 650 students enrolled. The following statistics refer to the student population: $\frac{7}{25}$ are seniors; $\frac{1}{5}$ are freshmen; $\frac{3}{10}$ are juniors. How many students are freshmen? How many students are sophomores? How many students are juniors? How may students are seniors?

17. The cabins on a cruise ship are distributed on six decks as outlined here:

> The promenade deck has $\frac{1}{8}$ of the cabins.
>
> The sun deck has $\frac{1}{6}$ of the cabins.
>
> The pool deck has $\frac{5}{24}$ of the cabins.
>
> The A deck has $\frac{6}{24}$ of the cabins.

Both B and C decks have the same number of cabins. What fractional part of the total number of cabins are on the C deck?

18. There are 40 students in a mathematics class. One-fourth of the students are math majors, one-eighth are economics majors, and two-fifths are science majors. The remainder of the class are education majors. One-third of the education majors are seniors. How many education majors are seniors? What fractional part of the total class are seniors who are education majors?

19. There are 180 seats in the rear cabin of a plane. One-fifth of those seats are occupied by passengers who purchased Super Summer tickets. Two-ninths of the seats are occupied by passengers who purchased nonrefundable bargain tickets. Five-twelfths are occupied by passengers who purchased economy coach tickets. The remaining seats are empty. How many empty seats are there in the rear cabin of this plane?

20. The 2nd, 9th, 16th, 23rd, and 30th days of a particular 30-day month fall on a Tuesday.

  (a) What fractional part of the month falls on Tuesdays?

  (b) What fractional part of the Tuesdays in that month are even-numbered dates?

  (c) In the context of this problem, what could $\frac{1}{6} \times \frac{3}{5}$ represent?

21. (a) In a 31-day month, what fractional part of the dates are prime numbers?

  (b) Of the prime number dates, what fractional part have the digit 1 in the ones place?

  (c) In the context of this problem, what could $\frac{11}{31} \times \frac{2}{11}$ represent?

22. A highway exit ramp is $1\frac{1}{2}$ miles long. A marker is to be placed at each $\frac{1}{10}$-mile interval along the side of the road starting at the first tenth of a mile. How many markers are needed?

23. A calculator in its case is $\frac{7}{8}$ inch thick. How many calculators can be stacked one on top of another in a carton that is $18\frac{3}{4}$ inches tall?

24. In a warehouse, five congruent boxes stacked one on top of the other reach a height of $22\frac{1}{2}$ feet. If the measurement from floor to ceiling in the warehouse is 57 feet, how many more of these boxes can be stacked on the pile?

25. At the close of trading on Monday, one share of a certain stock was listed at $\$23\frac{5}{8}$. Each day during the week, the stock rose by the same amount. At the close of trading on Friday, one share of the stock listed at $\$28\frac{1}{8}$. What was the daily increase?

26. At the close of trading on Friday, one share of a certain stock was listed at $\$51\frac{3}{8}$. Each day during the week, the stock had decreased by the same amount. At the close of trading on Monday of that week, the stock was listed at $\$57\frac{7}{8}$. What was the daily decrease?

27. A bolt of fabric contains $23\frac{1}{2}$ yards. How many $2\frac{3}{4}$-yard pieces can be cut from the bolt? What is the length of the remaining piece (called a remnant)?

In Other Words

28. Write a realistic problem for an elementary school child to illustrate fraction multiplication using $\frac{1}{2}$ and $2\frac{1}{4}$.

29. Write a realistic problem for an elementary school child to illustrate fraction division using $7\frac{1}{2}$ and 15.

30. Explain the commutative property of fraction multiplication.

31. What is a reciprocal, and why is the product of a fraction and its reciprocal equal to 1?

32. Define a complex fraction in your own words.

Cooperative Activity

33. Groups of three

Individual Accountability: Each group member is to individually answer the following questions.

(a) Each term in a sequence is $\frac{3}{4}$ of the term that precedes it. If the first term in the sequence is $1\frac{1}{8}$, what are the next four terms? If you were to continue this process 100 times, what might be true about each of the terms found?

(b) Each term in a sequence is $\frac{2}{3}$ of the term that precedes it. If the first term in the sequence is $\frac{5}{9}$, what are the next four terms?

(c) Each term in a sequence is $1\frac{1}{2}$ times the number that precedes it. If the eighth term in the sequence is 16, find the seventh and sixth terms.

Group Goal: Share your methods and solutions to the individual problems with the group. Together, answer each of the following questions.

(a) Each term in a sequence is $2\frac{3}{4}$ times the number that precedes it. If the tenth term is $20\frac{1}{2}$, find the thirteenth term.

(b) Each term in a sequence is $1\frac{3}{8}$ times the number that precedes it. If the fifth term is 10, find the third term and the seventh term.

Create three problems like the ones given in both the individual and group parts of this activity. Generate the solution to each and briefly describe how the solution might be determined.

6.4 Fractions in Context: Linear Measurement, Ratios, Proportions, Rates, and Dimensional Analysis

In this chapter we have used fractions in a variety of applications. An application that has significance for elementary school students is measurement. Children are very interested in such questions as "How tall am I?" "How fast can I run?" "How big is it?" "How far away are we?" Once students understand the basics of linear measurement, they begin to ask more sophisticated questions: "How tall am I compared to my sister?" "Mom says I can watch a $\frac{1}{2}$ hour of TV for every 2 hours of homework I do. How much time do I have to spend on homework if I want to watch 2 hours of TV?" "How much money can I make babysitting if I work 6 hours a week for 3 weeks and get paid $3.00 an hour?" and "If I'm riding my bike at 15 miles an hour how far do I travel in 10 seconds? All of these questions involve applications we will be learning about in this section: linear measurement, ratios, proportions, rates, and dimensional analysis. Fractions will be used to help answer these questions.

Linear Measurement

One of the earliest ways children begin to measure is to directly compare two things. Children stand back-to-back to see who is taller; they run races to see who is faster; they have staring contests to see who will blink first.

Children also engage in indirect comparisons. A child might hold up her arm to the height of a box and try to walk over to a shelf without moving her arm to determine if the box will fit on the shelf. When describing the size of a toy, a child might say to his friend that it is "this" big, while holding his hands a certain distance apart.

Children quickly become dissatisfied with these measurement processes, since they are neither efficient nor accurate. At this point, the measurement process begins to formalize into the following three steps:

1. **Attribute Identification.** What is to be measured?

2. **Unit Quantification.** What is the unit of measurement?

3. **Comparison.** How many units of measurement are equivalent to the amount of the attribute to be measured?

At first, children often employ nonstandard units of measurement. For example, a child might know that dinner will be served after two more cartoon shows; that the ride to grandma's house will be over when two cassette tapes have been played; that it takes 17 steps to get from the play area to the block area; or that it takes two boxes of animal crackers to fill up the cookie jar.

Young children often engage in nonstandard measurement activities in school. The teacher might trace a child's foot on a stack of folded newspapers. When the teacher cuts along the outline of the foot, the child is given several congruent footprints. These footprints can be used as a nonstandard unit of measurement to determine the distance from the classroom to the lunchroom, from the classroom to the library, and so on. Eventually, children question why it takes 28 of the teacher's footprints to get to the library, but 35 of Kate's footprints. A question like this can be an oppportunity to introduce the need for standard units of measurement.

The English Standard System of Measurement

Two systems of measurement are currently used in the United States: the English standard system and the metric system. Because this chapter concerns fractions, we will use the English standard system here. The metric system will be addressed in Chapter 7 when we introduce decimals, since it is a decimal system of measurement.

Linear measurement focuses on the attribute of length. Units of linear measurement are used to answer questions such as "How far?" "How long?" "How wide?" and "How deep?" The English standard system of measurement was arbitrary and nonstandard in its origins. Many of the units of measurement currently in use were originally defined in unique ways. For example, hands, arms, feet, and kernels of barley were used as units of measurement. The common units of linear measurement in the English standard system were eventually standardized and are summarized below.

Unit	Equivalence	
Inch	12 inches	= 1 foot
	36 inches	= 1 yard
Foot	3 feet	= 1 yard
	5280 feet	= 1 mile
Yard	1760 yards	= 1 mile
Mile		

The inch is the smallest unit of linear measurement commonly used in the English standard system. The inch can be subdivided into a number of fractional parts. Measurement tools with a wide range of precision are available. An elementary school student's ruler could measure length to the nearest sixteenth of an inch, whereas some artists' scales (rulers) are capable of measuring to the nearest fiftieth of an inch. The amount of accuracy needed defines the type of measurement device used.

Investigation 13

A $1 bill is given to an early elementary school student, a middle school student, and a college art student. Each is asked to measure its length with varying degrees of accuracy: the young child measures to the nearest inch; the middle school student measures to the nearest sixteenth of an inch; and the art student measures to the nearest thirty-second of an inch. What length would each student give as an answer?

The young child places a ruler, perhaps marked only in inches, along the top of the dollar bill, as shown here. The length of the bill to the nearest inch measures six inches.

The middle school student places a standard ruler (marked to the nearest sixteenth of an inch) along the top of the bill, as shown below. Each division of an inch is one-sixteenth. The bill measures six full inches and approximately $\frac{3}{16}$ of an inch ($6\frac{3}{16}$ inches).

The art student uses a ruler with a scale in which the inch is divided into 32 parts. The length of the bill is approximately $6\frac{5}{32}$, as shown here.

In actuality, the U.S. Bureau of Printing and Engraving reports that the length of a bill is approximately $6\frac{14}{100}$ inches. Examine the fractional parts of the middle school student's measurement ($\frac{3}{16}$), the art student's measurement ($\frac{5}{32}$), and the official length ($\frac{14}{100}$). To determine how close these measurements are to each other, you must find a common denominator. Recall the method that uses the prime factorization of each number:

$$16 = 2 \times 2 \times 2 \times 2 \quad = 2^4 \times 5^0$$
$$32 = 2 \times 2 \times 2 \times 2 \times 2 = 2^5 \times 5^0$$
$$100 = 2 \times 2 \times 5 \times 5 \quad = 2^2 \times 5^2$$

The least common multiple of 16, 32, and 100 is $2^5 \times 5^2$, or 800. Rewriting each of the fractions in terms of the least common denominator, 800, yields

$$\frac{3}{16} = \frac{150}{800} \qquad \frac{5}{32} = \frac{125}{800} \qquad \frac{14}{100} = \frac{112}{800}$$

Notice that the measurement taken by the art student was closer to the official measurement.

Ratios

ratio   Comparisons are the basis of measurement. A comparison of one numerical quantity to another is called a **ratio**. In more sophisticated terms, a ratio is an ordered pair of numbers that can be expressed as $a:b$, or as the fraction $\frac{a}{b}$, and is read as "the ratio of a to b." As with any fraction, b must be nonzero. Although is is possible to have a ratio of $a:0$ within a realistic context (the ratio of grams of protein to grams of fat in nonfat yogurt), these instances are unusual. In this text we will consider ratios only of the type $a:b$ where b is nonzero.

It is natural to think of a fraction as a ratio. Examine Figure 6.20.

Figure 6.20

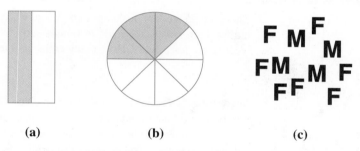

(a)   (b)   (c)

In Figure 6.20a the fraction $\frac{1}{2}$ can be interpreted as "one part for every two parts," or "one to two." In Figure 6.20b you see a circle divided into eight congruent regions. The shaded regions depict $\frac{3}{8}$ of the entire circle. Notice that this illustration could be viewed as the ratio $3:8$ and read as "three shaded regions for every eight regions." In Figure 6.20c the letters M and F represent males and females in a group of 11 people. Notice that the ratio of females to males could be written as $7:4$, or $\frac{7}{4}$, and read as "seven females for every four males." Many other ratios can be expressed using the information in Figure 6.20c. The ratio $\frac{7}{11}$ represents the number of females to the total number of people in the group. The ratio $4:11$ represents the number of males to the total number of people in the group. The ratio $\frac{11}{4}$ represents the total number of people in the group to the number of males.

Notice the difference in the ratios that were derived from Figure 6.20c. Some ratios represented comparisons that were made between two parts of the entire group. Other ratios represented comparisons that were made between a part of the group and the entire group itself, or between the entire group and a part of the group.

Examine the following group of letters:

F F F F F F F F F F F F F F F F F F F F

M M M M M M M M M M M M

The letters represent a group composed of 21 females and 12 males. The ratio of females to males can be expressed as $21:12$ or as $7:4$. In the first case, the ratio reflects the composition of the entire group. By knowing that the ratio of females to males is $21:12$, in addition to knowing that the group has 21 females and 12 males, you are able to state that the group has a total population of 33 people. But the ratio could have been reported in its equivalent form, $7:4$; that is, for every seven females there are four males. Adding seven and four does not yield the total number of people in the group. This is a very important concept when working with ratios. A ratio yields a comparison indicating how one quantity relates to another quantity. Unless it is clearly stated, you cannot assume that the sum of the two numbers in a ratio will yield the total amount or number under consideration.

Investigation 14

There are 35 student desks in room 304 at Columbia Middle School. The teacher reports that on February 8, the male to female ratio of students present was $3:2$ and that there were five empty desks. How many males and females were present on February 8?

Understand the Problem: What is given? You are told that there are 35 student desks in the room and that all but 5 are occupied on February 8. You are also told that the ratio of males to females in the class on that date is 3 to 2.
What is unknown? You are asked to determine the number of males and the number of females that were present on February 8.

Devise a Plan: The ratio $3:2$ tells you the relationship between one quantity and the other. To better understand this idea, examine the ratio $\frac{3}{2}$ as presented in fraction form. Notice that 3 and 2 are relatively prime, and therefore the fraction $\frac{3}{2}$ is said to be in simplest terms. What other fractions are equivalent to $\frac{3}{2}$ and have meaning within the context of this problem? Any fraction of the type

$$\frac{3 \cdot a}{2 \cdot a}$$

where a is a nonzero integer would be equivalent to $\frac{3}{2}$. Making a table will help solve this problem.

Carry Out the Plan: It is important to recognize that both positive a and negative a will yield the same result. Therefore, it is sufficient to use only positive values of a.

a	$\dfrac{3 \cdot a}{2 \cdot a}$	Ratio	Problem Context
1	$\dfrac{3 \cdot 1}{2 \cdot 1}$	$\dfrac{3}{2}$	3 males, 2 females, 5 students
2	$\dfrac{3 \cdot 2}{2 \cdot 2}$	$\dfrac{6}{4}$	6 males, 4 females, 10 students
3	$\dfrac{3 \cdot 3}{2 \cdot 3}$	$\dfrac{9}{6}$	9 males, 6 females, 15 students
4	$\dfrac{3 \cdot 4}{2 \cdot 4}$	$\dfrac{12}{8}$	12 males, 8 females, 20 students
5	$\dfrac{3 \cdot 5}{2 \cdot 5}$	$\dfrac{15}{10}$	15 males, 10 females, 25 students
6	$\dfrac{3 \cdot 6}{2 \cdot 6}$	$\dfrac{18}{12}$	18 males, 12 females, 30 students
7	$\dfrac{3 \cdot 7}{2 \cdot 7}$	$\dfrac{21}{14}$	21 males, 14 females, 35 students

Look Back: Since five desks were empty, 30 students were present on February 8. The number of males and females that results in a total of 30 students and a male-to-female ratio of 3:2 is 18 males and 12 females.

The problem in Investigation 14 can also be solved in another way. To do so, recall the fraction equality rule (cross-product rule) presented in Section 6.1. If two fractions $\frac{a}{b}$ and $\frac{c}{d}$ are equal, then $ad = bc$. This rule also applies to two equal ratios, as stated here.

Ratio Equality Rule   For any ratio $a:b$ and $c:d$, if

$$\frac{a}{b} = \frac{c}{d}$$

then $ad = bc$.

The ratio equality rule leads us to a very important concept. The statement

$$\frac{a}{b} = \frac{c}{d}$$

proportion   where two ratios are equal, is called a **proportion**. A statement of this type is a proportion if and only if the ratio equality rule holds. For example, $\frac{5}{7} = \frac{15}{21}$ is a proportion since $5 \cdot 21 = 7 \cdot 15$. Knowing that these two ratios form a proportion allows us to infer that the relationship that holds in one ratio is equivalent to the relationship that holds in the other. For example, a mini-size pack of candy coated chocolate pieces contains 7 green candies out of a total of 28 candies. The pound bag contains 125 green candies out of a total of 500 candies. The ratio of the number of green candies to the total number of candies in the mini-size pack is $7 : 28$. The ratio of the number of green candies to the total number of candies in the pound bag is $125 : 500$. Let's apply the ratio equality rule to this situation to determine if the ratio of green candies to the total number of candies is the same in both bags.

$$\frac{7}{28} \overset{?}{=} \frac{125}{500}$$

$$7 \cdot 500 \overset{?}{=} 125 \cdot 28$$

$$3500 = 3500$$

The two ratios form a proportion since the cross products are equal. Therefore, we can conclude that for these two bags, the relationship between the number of green candies and the total number of candies is the same in each instance. You might also have arrived at this conclusion by noticing that both ratios, $\frac{7}{28}$ and $\frac{125}{500}$, simplify to $\frac{1}{4}$.

With this knowledge, we return to Investigation 14. Rather than employing the problem-solving technique of making a table, we will use the strategy of **using a variable**. (Recall that a variable is a symbol that is used to represent a number.) We know that 30 students were present on February 8. The class consists of two groups: males and females. Let X represent the number of males present. Therefore, the statement *X + the number of females present = 30* is a true statement. Although we might be tempted to introduce another variable to represent the number of females present, it is important to first try to represent this missing amount in terms of X. If we can do this, the problem is reduced to one that involves only a single variable.

How can the number of females be represented in terms of what is already known and the variable X? Let's solve a simpler problem and see if that makes this situation easier to comprehend. Suppose that there were 15 males. The number of females would be expressed as $30 - 15$, or 15. If there were 8 males, the number of females would be $30 - 8$, or 22. There are X males. Therefore, the number of females can be written as $30 - X$.

Using this information, you can now set up the ratio of males to females in terms of the variable X in the following manner:

$$\frac{X}{30 - X}$$

This ratio must be equivalent to the ratio $\frac{3}{2}$. Set up a proportion as follows:

$$\frac{X}{30 - X} = \frac{3}{2}$$

Applying the ratio equality rule, we have

$$2 \cdot X = 3 \cdot (30 - X)$$

$$2X = 90 - 3X \qquad \text{by the distributive property}$$

This equation has the variable X on both sides of the equal sign. We have already seen that an equation can be manipulated by adding the same amount to each side of the equal sign without altering the truth of the equation. Adding $3X$ to both sides of the equation yields the following equations:

$$2X + 3X = 90 - 3X + 3X$$

$$5X = 90$$

Solving for X, we see that $X = \frac{90}{5}$, or 18. At this point, we have completed the computation necessary to solve for the variable. Now we must put this information back into the context of the problem and determine if we have answered the question. Since there are 18 males, there must be $30 - 18$, or 12, females. To check your solution, it is important to verify that these results conform to the requirements of the problem. This step is necessary in all problem solving. The ratio of males to females must be $\frac{3}{2}$, and the total number of students must be 30. Setting up the proportion $\frac{3}{2} = \frac{18}{12}$ yields $3 \cdot 12 = 2 \cdot 18$, which is a true statement, since $36 = 36$. Since the sum of 18 and 12 is 30, this solution conforms to the requirements stipulated in the problem statement. There were 18 males and 12 females present on February 8.

Investigation 15

The Elm Street Elementary School is going on a field trip to the Science Museum. The museum requires the chaperone-to-student ratio for students under 10 years of age to be $1:10$, and for students 10 years of age and older to be $2:40$. There are 240 students planning to go on the trip. If 160 students are under the age of 10, and 20 chaperones are going, will the museum's requirements be satisfied?

Understand the Problem: The information in this problem is easier to understand if it is organized as follows:

	Under 10	10 and Over	Total
Number of students	160	?	240
Number of chaperones	?	?	20
Chaperone-to-student ratio	1:10	2:40	

Devise a Plan: You can now determine the number of students who are 10 and over ($240 - 160$). There are 80 students in this category. The strategy of using a variable suggests that C represents the number of chaperones who will be assigned to the Under 10 group. We can therefore represent the remaining chaperones as $20 - C$. The chart now appears as follows:

	Under 10	*10 and Over*	*Total*
Number of students	160	80	240
Number of chaperones	C	$20 - C$	20
Chaperone-to-student ratio	$1:10$	$2:40$	

Carry Out the Plan: Two conditions must be met. For every 10 children under the age of 10, one chaperone is needed. For every 40 children 10 years of age and older, two chaperones are needed. This information can be represented and solved with the following two proportions:

$$\frac{1}{10} = \frac{C}{160} \qquad \frac{2}{40} = \frac{20 - C}{80}$$

$$10 \cdot C = 160$$

$$C = 16$$

Since C represents the number of chaperones for the younger children, the museum therefore requires that there be 16 chaperones for this age group. Since there are only 20 chaperones on the trip, this leaves 4 chaperones for the older children ($20 - C = 4$). The second proportion must hold in order that the museum's requirements be satisfied.

$$\frac{2}{40} = \frac{4}{80}$$

Look Back: Since $40 \cdot 4 = 2 \cdot 80$, there are a sufficient number of chaperones on the trip.

In Investigations 14 and 15, the ratios that were used represented comparisons of numbers expressed in the same units of measure. Sometimes ratios compare amounts **rates** that are not expressed in the same units of measurement. These ratios are called **rates**. Some examples of ratios that are rates are given here:

3 bottles for $4	$3:4$
55 miles per hour	$55:1$
12 inches in 1 foot	$12:1$
$750 in three weeks	$750:3$

Since rates are ratios, proportions can also be used to test for equivalences of rates. Examine Investigations 16 and 17.

Investigation 16

On a map, 1 inch represents 200 miles. Using a ruler, you determine the distance between Des Moines, Iowa, and Duluth, Minnesota, to be $1\frac{3}{4}$ inches. What is the actual distance between these two cities?

A map is a scaled-down version of an actual area. A map scale tells us the ratio between distances measured on the map and actual distances. On this map, the ratio can be expressed as $1:200$; that is, every 1 inch on the map represents 200 miles. This ratio can be expressed as the fraction $\frac{1}{200}$. Let X represent the actual distance between Des Moines and Duluth. The ratio of the map distance between these two cities to the actual distance between these two cities must be $1:200$. This ratio can be expressed as the complex fraction

$$\frac{\text{Map distance}}{\text{Actual distance}} = \frac{1\frac{3}{4}}{X}$$

Since the numerator of this ratio is greater than the numerator of the ratio $\frac{1}{200}$, it is reasonable to estimate that the actual distance between Des Moines and Duluth will be greater than 200 miles and will actually be close to 400 miles (since $1\frac{3}{4}$ is close to 2).

Set up a proportion and solve for the unknown distance.

$$\frac{1}{200} = \frac{1\frac{3}{4}}{X}$$

$$X = 200 \cdot 1\frac{3}{4}$$

$$X = 200 \cdot \frac{7}{4}$$

$$X = 350$$

The distance between Des Moines and Duluth is (approximately) 350 miles. Notice that the solution is close to the estimate of 400 miles.

Investigation 17

A rectangular garage is 22 feet long by 20 feet wide. A scale drawing of this garage measures $5\frac{1}{2}$ inches long by $5\frac{1}{4}$ inches wide. Is this an accurate representation of the actual garage? If so, what is the ratio between the measurements on the drawing and the actual measurements of the garage?

Understand the Problem: What is given? You are told the actual and scale dimensions of a garage.

What is unknown? It is unclear if the scale drawing is a proportional model of the garage. If so, you need to determine the ratio between the measurements of the scale drawing and the actual garage measurements.

Devise a Plan: If the measurements in the scale drawing are accurate, a proportion should hold between the ratios of lengths and widths of both the drawing and the actual garage.

Carry Out the Plan: The proportion can be symbolized and tested as follows:

$$\frac{\text{Scale measurements}}{\text{Actual measurements}} = \frac{5\frac{1}{2}}{22} \overset{?}{=} \frac{5\frac{1}{4}}{20}$$

$$5\frac{1}{2} \cdot 20 \overset{?}{=} 5\frac{1}{4} \cdot 22$$

$$\frac{11}{2} \cdot 20 \overset{?}{=} \frac{21}{4} \cdot 22$$

$$110 \neq 115\frac{1}{2}$$

Look Back: Since the ratios are not in proportion, the scale drawing is not accurate. One or both of the scale measurements could be incorrect. Since scale drawings are often constructed using a quarter-inch scale, that is, $\frac{1}{4}$ inch represents one unit of actual measurement (feet, yards, miles, etc.), it might be useful to test the ratios of the dimensions to see if either conform to the quarter-inch scale.

$$\frac{5\frac{1}{2}}{22} \overset{?}{=} \frac{\frac{1}{4}}{1}$$

$$5\frac{1}{2} \overset{?}{=} 22 \cdot \frac{1}{4}$$

$$\frac{11}{2} = \frac{22}{4}$$

Since the ratio between the scale length and the actual length conforms to the quarter-inch scale, the error might lie in the scale measurement of the width. Let X be the scale measurement of the width. The following proportion can be used to find the value of X:

$$\frac{X}{20} = \frac{\frac{1}{4}}{1}$$

$$X = 20 \cdot \frac{1}{4}$$

$$X = 5$$

It appears that the scale measurement of width may have been incorrect. If the scale measurement of width had been 5 inches, the ratios of lengths and widths would be in proportion.

Verify the accuracy of the scale measurements.

$$\frac{5\frac{1}{2}}{22} \overset{?}{=} \frac{5}{20}$$

$$22 \cdot 5 \overset{?}{=} 5\frac{1}{2} \cdot 20$$

$$110 = 110$$

Dimensional Analysis

dimensional analysis

Measurement and ratios play an important role when trying to convert from one unit of measurement to another. Although this conversion can be accomplished in a variety of ways, a method often used in scientific study is dimensional analysis. **Dimensional analysis** is a method in which ratios equivalent to 1 are used to make unit conversions. A ratio that is equivalent to 1 can be shown in the following ways:

1. The ratio $\frac{a}{a} = 1$ when the units of measurement are the same in both the numerator and denominator of the fraction. For example, the ratio of the *number* of desks in room 304 to the *number* of desks in room 305 might be $\frac{35}{35}$, which is equivalent to 1. The ratio of the *length in inches* of a pencil to the *length in inches* of a pen might be $\frac{6}{6}$, which is equivalent to 1.

2. The ratio $\frac{a}{b} = 1$ when the units of measurement are not the same, but $\frac{a}{b}$ is a unit ratio that represents the conversion equivalence between the two units. For example, the ratio of 60 *minutes* to 1 *hour* can be expressed as $\frac{60 \text{ min}}{1 \text{ hr}}$, which is equivalent to 1 since both numerator and denominator represent the same amount of time. The ratio of 5280 *feet* to 1 *mile* can be expressed as $\frac{5280 \text{ ft}}{1 \text{ mi}}$, which is equivalent to 1 since both numerator and denominator represent the same distance.

In dimensional analysis, we use the latter of these two forms of ratios that are equivalent to 1. For example, the following procedure can be used to express 32 miles in feet:

$$32 \text{ mi} = 32 \text{ mi} \times \frac{5280 \text{ ft}}{1 \text{ mi}}$$

$$32 \text{ mi} = 32 \times 5280 \text{ ft} = 168,960 \text{ ft}$$

Investigation 18

Suppose you are driving on a dry, level surface at a speed of 55 miles per hour ($55 \frac{\text{mi}}{\text{hr}}$). If it takes you approximately 1 second to move your foot from the gas pedal to the brake pedal, how far will your car have traveled in that time?

Understand the Problem: You are given a speed in miles per hour and an approximate reaction time. You are asked to determine the distance that a car travels during the reaction time.

Devise a Plan: It is clear that the car will travel a small fractional part of a mile in 1 second. To get a better understanding of this distance, it is more reasonable to express this distance in feet rather than miles. Therefore the answer to this problem will be a number of feet traveled in 1 second, or feet per second ($\frac{\text{ft}}{\text{sec}}$).

Carry Out the Plan: Some equivalences are necessary in order to use dimensional analysis here:

$$60 \text{ min} = 1 \text{ hr}$$
$$60 \text{ sec} = 1 \text{ min}$$
$$5280 \text{ ft} = 1 \text{ mi}$$

$$\frac{55 \text{ mi}}{\text{hr}} = \frac{55 \text{ mi}}{1 \text{ hr}} \times \frac{1 \text{ hr}}{60 \text{ min}} = \frac{55 \text{ mi}}{60 \text{ min}} \qquad \text{55 mi for each 60 min}$$

$$= \frac{55 \text{ mi}}{60 \text{ min}} \times \frac{1 \text{ min}}{60 \text{ sec}} = \frac{55 \text{ mi}}{3600 \text{ sec}} \qquad \text{55 mi for each 3600 sec}$$

$$= \frac{55 \text{ mi}}{3600 \text{ sec}} \times \frac{5280 \text{ ft}}{1 \text{ mi}} = \frac{290{,}400 \text{ ft}}{3600 \text{ sec}} \qquad \text{290,400 ft for each 3600 sec}$$

$$= \frac{80\frac{2}{3} \text{ ft}}{\text{sec}} \qquad 80\frac{2}{3} \text{ ft for each sec}$$

Look Back: In 1 second, the car will travel $80\frac{2}{3}$ feet. If a car is approximately 12 feet long, the car will travel a distance of approximately six car lengths in 1 second. This information clearly illustrates the need for careful attention when operating a motor vehicle. Keep in mind that the car travels $80\frac{2}{3}$ feet in the 1 second that it takes the driver to shift from the gas pedal to the brake. It also takes time and distance for the car to slow down to a complete stop!

Assessments for Section 6.4

1. Name three measurable attributes in each of the following situations.
   (a) In a classroom
   (b) At a post office
   (c) In a recording studio
   (d) At a track meet
   (e) In a pool

2. Name two different nonstandard units of measurement that a young child might use to "measure" each of the following.
   (a) Body height
   (b) Length of a baseball bat
   (c) Distance from a couch to the TV set
   (d) Distance around the child's head
   (e) The width of a table

3. Use a 12-inch ruler to measure the length of each of the following line segments to the nearest inch, half-inch, quarter inch, and eighth inch.
   (a) ————————————————
   (b) ————————————

4. Measure each of the following line segments to the nearest sixteenth inch.
   (a) ————————————————————
   (b) ——————————
   (c) ————————————————

5. Measure the length of each of the following line segments as accurately as possible

   A————B
   C————————D
   E————————————————F
   G————————————H
   I ————————————————J

   Determine the lengths stated below.
   (a) $AB + CD$
   (b) $GH + IJ$
   (c) $EF - AB$
   (d) The distance around the outside of a square whose side is the same measure as CD

(e) The distance around the outside of a triangle, two of whose sides are each the same measure as *IJ*, and whose third side is the same measure as *AB*

(f) Three times the length of *AB* added to twice the length of *EF*

(g) The distance around the outside of a six-sided figure, each of whose sides is the same measure as *IJ*

6. A wire of a given length is used to form a particular figure. Find the length of each side of the figure. (In each figure all sides are equal in length.)

   (a) Wire length: 10 in   [square]

   (b) Wire length: $8\frac{3}{4}$ in   [five-sided figure; pentagon]

   (c) Wire length: $5\frac{1}{4}$ in   [six-sided figure; hexagon]

   (d) Wire length: $8\frac{1}{4}$ in   [three-sided figure; equilateral triangle]

   (e) Wire length: $19\frac{1}{2}$ in   [twelve-sided figure; dodecagon]

7. Write three different ratios for each of the following situations.

   (a) A class contains 12 boys and 13 girls.

   (b) A kennel houses eight kittens and four puppies.

   (c) A fruit basket contains seven apples, six bananas, and five oranges.

8. Obtain a tape measure. Measure the lengths of (a) the distance around your head; (b) your arm from shoulder to fingertips; (c) your foot; (d) your leg from knee to ankle. Develop each of the following ratios: $a:b$, $b:c$, $c:d$, $d:a$, and $d:b$.

9. A map scale indicates that $\frac{1}{2}$ inch = 50 miles. What actual distance corresponds to the following map distances?

   (a) 2 in

   (b) $3\frac{1}{2}$ in

   (c) $7\frac{1}{4}$ in

   What map distance would be used to represent the following actual distances?

   (d) 475 mi

   (e) 550 mi

10. A map scale indicates that 1 inch = 60 miles. What actual distance corresponds to the following distances?

    (a) $4\frac{1}{4}$ in

    (b) $5\frac{3}{4}$ in

    (c) $3\frac{1}{2}$ in

    What map distance would be used to represent the following actual distances?

    (d) 390 mi

    (e) 420 mi

11. A portion of the map of Phoenix, Arizona is shown on page 282. On this map $\frac{5}{8}$ inch represents 3 miles. Find the distances between each of the following locations on the map.

    (a) Along Peoria Avenue from the intersection of Route 60 to Interstate 17

    (b) Along Bell Road from the intersection of Route 60 to Interstate 17

    (c) Along Scottsdale Road from the intersection of Route 60 to Shea Boulevard

    (d) Along Glendale Avenue from the intersection of 83rd Avenue to Interstate 17

    (e) Along Interstate 10 from the intersection of 115th Avenue to 7th Avenue

12. A portion of the map of Providence, Rhode Island is shown on page 283. On the map, 1 inch represents $\frac{1}{4}$ mile. Find the distances between each of the following locations on the map.

    (a) Along Brook Street from the intersection of Waterman Street to Wickenden Street

    (b) Along George Street from the intersection of Benefit Street to Hope Street

    (c) Along Westminster Mall from the intersection of Green Street to Route 44

    (d) Along Friendship Street from the intersection of Lockwood Street to Route 44

    (e) Along Pine Street from the intersection of Summer Street to Claverick Street

13. Solve each of the following proportions for *X*.

    (a) $\dfrac{32}{48} = \dfrac{X}{12}$ (b) $\dfrac{75}{225} = \dfrac{X}{45}$ (c) $\dfrac{18}{27} = \dfrac{26}{X}$

    (d) $\dfrac{X}{44} = \dfrac{42}{56}$ (e) $\dfrac{X}{720} = \dfrac{8}{90}$ (f) $\dfrac{21}{24} = \dfrac{14}{X}$

    (g) $\dfrac{150}{X} = \dfrac{3}{8}$ (h) $\dfrac{5}{40} = \dfrac{2}{X}$ (i) $\dfrac{89}{5} = \dfrac{X}{15}$

    (j) $\dfrac{X}{31} = \dfrac{45}{9}$

14. Julie was practicing her basketball shots. On Monday she made 16 baskets out of the 24 shots she tried. On Tuesday, she made 30 baskets out of the 45 shots she tried.

    (a) Julie claimed that she didn't improve nor did she get any worse. How can she mathematically justify this claim?

    (b) Assume that Julie was to continue making baskets at the same rate that she did on Tuesday. If she tries 54 times on Wednesday, how many baskets might you expect her to make?

Exercise 11 Map

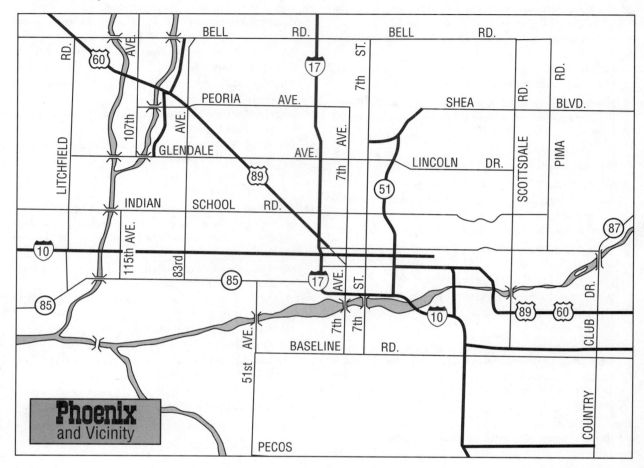

15. Two authors worked together on a book. Of the 12 chapters written, Mike wrote 5 and Ellen wrote 7. All chapters required the same amount of time and effort. After the first year of sales, the publishing company sent them a check for $14,472. How should Mike and Ellen fairly divide the money?

16. Marianne, Celine, and Winnie want to open a pizzeria. Celine contributes twice as much as Winnie, and Winnie contributes three times as much as Marianne.

   (a) What is the contribution ratio of Celine's share to Marianne's share?

   (b) If the initial investment is $80,500, how much money did each person contribute?

   (c) If at the end of the first year the pizzeria shows a profit of $23,000, how should this profit be fairly shared among the three women?

17. The lengths of two line segments are in the ratio of $3:5$. The smaller of the two line segments is $3\frac{3}{4}$ inch. What is the sum of the actual lengths of the two line segments?

18. A carton of 1000 light bulbs averages about 36 defective bulbs. At this rate, how many defective bulbs would you expect in a shipment of $2\frac{3}{4}$ cartons?

19. For every 5-degree change measured on a Celsius thermometer, there would be a corresponding 9-degree change on a Fahrenheit thermometer. If a Celsius thermometer showed an 8-degree increase, what would be the corresponding increase on a Fahrenheit thermometer?

20. An employee earns 5 vacation days for every 2 months she works.

   (a) At the end of 18 months, how many full vacation days has she accumulated?

Exercise 12 Map

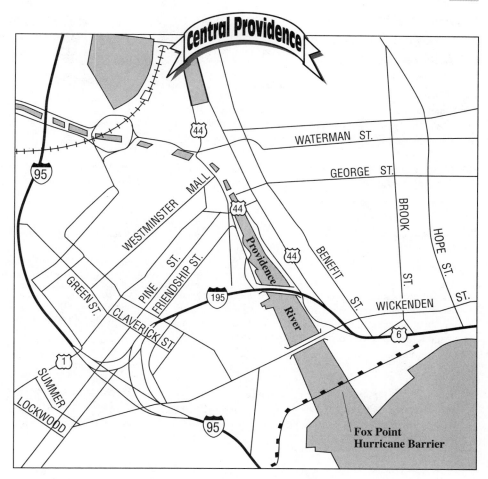

(b) At the end of 2 years, how many full vacation days has she accumulated?

(c) If the employee wishes to spend the summer in Europe (the equivalent of 40 working days), how long will she need to work in order to have enough vacation time?

21. A car is traveling at $45 \frac{mi}{hr}$. How many feet per second is the car covering?

22. A bicyclist is cycling at a constant rate of $12 \frac{mi}{hr}$. How many yards per minute does the cyclist cover?

23. A certain aircraft covers a ground distance of $\frac{3}{20}$ mile in 1 second. At this rate, how fast in miles per hour is it traveling?

24. Jessica works 7 hours per day, 5 days a week. If she makes a weekly salary of $525, how much does she earn per minute?

25. One complete revolution of a bicycle pedal advances a particular bicycle about 90 inches. How many feet will the bicycle travel in 100 turns of the pedal?

In Other Words

26. When increasing or decreasing a recipe, the ingredients must be in the correct proportion. Why is this important?

27. Explain what is meant by a one-to-one ratio. Give a real-world example in which comparing two quantities might yield such a ratio.

28. When the telephone company lists its phone rates, are these rates ratios?

29. What does it mean when something is said to be "drawn to scale"?

30. Explain the process used in dimensional analysis. What is it modeled after?

Cooperative Activity

31. Groups of two

Individual Accountability: Each group member is to complete the assigned portion below:

Member A

(a) Scale: $\frac{1}{4}$ inch represents 3 miles. Draw a line segment that would represent 18 miles. Draw a line segment that would represent 28 miles. Draw a line segment that would represent $1\frac{1}{2}$ miles.

(b) Scale: $\frac{3}{4}$ inch represents 10 miles. What distances would be represented by the following three line segments?

```
├──────────────────────────┤
A                          B

├────────────────────────────────┤
C                                D

├──────────────────────────────────────┤
E                                      F
```

(c) The following line segment represents the distance between two cities (1 inch represents 150 miles). Suppose that a car travels at an average rate of 50 miles per hour. How long would it take to drive from one city to the other city?

```
├──────────────────────────────────┤
```

Member B

(a) Scale: $\frac{1}{4}$ inch represents 5 miles. Draw a line segment that would represent 20 miles. Draw a line segment that would represent 24 miles. Draw a line segment that would represent $2\frac{1}{2}$ miles.

(b) Scale: $\frac{3}{4}$ inch represents 20 miles. What distances would be represented by the following three line segments?

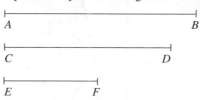

```
├────────────────────────────────────┤
A                                    B

├──────────────────────────────┤
C                              D

├────────────────┤
E                F
```

(c) The following line segment represents the distance between two cities (1 inch represents 80 miles). Suppose that a car travels at an average rate of 55 miles per hour. How long would it take to drive from one city to the other city?

```
├────────────────────────────────────────┤
```

Group Goal: Share your methodology with your partner. In order to verify the correctness of the solutions, Member A should now do Member B's assignment, and vice versa. Once this is completed, both members should work together on the following activity.

Let $\frac{1}{4}$ inch represent 1 foot. Sketch a scale drawing of a room with the following attributes:

One 17-ft solid wall

Two 3-ft-wide windows

One 5-ft-wide window

One $3\frac{1}{2}$-ft-wide entranceway

One $2\frac{1}{2}$-ft $\times$ $2\frac{1}{2}$-ft closet

Vocabulary for Chapter 6

additive inverse property of rational
    numbers

addition property of rational numbers
    with like denominators

addition property of rational numbers
    with unlike denominators

area model

associative property of rational number
    addition

associative property of rational number
    multiplication

closure property of rational number
    addition

closure property of rational number
    multiplication

common factors

common multiples

commutative property of rational number
    addition

commutative property of rational number
    multiplication

complex fraction

denominator

dimensional analysis

discrete model

distributive property of multiplication over addition of rational numbers

drawing a diagram

equivalent fractions

fraction

greatest common factor (GCF)

identity property of rational number addition

improper fraction

least common denominator

least common multiple (LCM)

mixed number

multiplicative inverse property of rational number multiplication

multiplicative inverse (reciprocal)

multiplicative property of rational numbers

numerator

proportion

rates

ratio

rational numbers

relative prime

subtractive property of rational numbers with like denominators

subtractive property of rational numbers with unlike denominators

zero multiplication property of rational numbers

Review for Chapter 6

1. Simplify each of the following fractions.

(a) $\dfrac{14}{49}$ (b) $\dfrac{48}{72}$ (c) $\dfrac{25}{20}$ (d) $\dfrac{45}{60}$

(e) $\dfrac{26}{39}$ (f) $\dfrac{24}{32}$ (g) $\dfrac{35}{36}$ (h) $\dfrac{33}{44}$

(i) $\dfrac{28}{91}$ (j) $\dfrac{30}{18}$

2. Build three equivalent fractions for each of the following fractions.

(a) $\dfrac{2}{3}$ (b) $\dfrac{7}{9}$ (c) $\dfrac{10}{11}$ (d) $\dfrac{9}{8}$ (e) 1

3. Write each of the following fractions as an equivalent fraction with the indicated denominator.

(a) $\dfrac{1}{3}$ denominator: 15

(b) $\dfrac{6}{7}$ denominator: 42

(c) $\dfrac{4}{5}$ denominator: 100

(d) 5 denominator: 6

(e) 13 denominator: 13

4. Write each of the following statements using symbols.

(a) One-half of one-half

(b) The sum of two-thirds and five-eighths

(c) Twice the sum of five-sixths and three-fourths, divided by one-half

(d) Three less than one-third of twelve

(e) The quotient of the sum of seven-eighths and one-fourth, and the difference between four-fifths and one-half

5. Arrange each set of fractions in ascending order.

(a) $\dfrac{2}{5}, \dfrac{1}{4}, \dfrac{3}{8}, \dfrac{3}{10}$

(b) $\dfrac{2}{3}, \dfrac{8}{9}, \dfrac{1}{2}, \dfrac{5}{6}, \dfrac{7}{18}$

6. Arrange each set of fractions in descending order.

(a) $\dfrac{4}{5}, \dfrac{5}{7}, \dfrac{7}{10}, \dfrac{1}{2}, \dfrac{17}{35}$

(b) $\dfrac{7}{9}, \dfrac{9}{7}, \dfrac{2}{3}, \dfrac{3}{2}, \dfrac{1}{1}$

7. Illustrate and explain each of the following expressions using any appropriate model.

(a) $\dfrac{4}{9} \times \dfrac{3}{8}$ (b) $\dfrac{2}{5} + 1\dfrac{1}{2}$ (c) $\dfrac{7}{8} - \dfrac{1}{2}$

(d) $2\dfrac{3}{4} \div \dfrac{1}{8}$ (e) $\dfrac{9}{10} \div \dfrac{3}{8}$

8. Perform the indicated operation in each expression.

(a) $\dfrac{2}{7} + \dfrac{1}{2}$ (b) $4\dfrac{2}{3} + \dfrac{1}{9}$ (c) $11 + 2\dfrac{3}{4}$

(d) $6\dfrac{1}{5} + 3\dfrac{2}{3}$ (e) $\dfrac{1}{4} + 15 + 3\dfrac{5}{12}$ (f) $\dfrac{5}{8} - \dfrac{1}{10}$

(g) $8\frac{2}{3} - 6$ **(h)** $8 - 6\frac{2}{3}$ **(i)** $12\frac{3}{4} - 3\frac{5}{6}$

(j) $14\frac{1}{3} - 12\frac{7}{8}$ **(k)** $\frac{2}{5} \times \frac{15}{16}$ **(l)** $1\frac{1}{2} \times 16$

(m) $2\frac{1}{3} \times 3\frac{1}{4}$ **(n)** $\frac{25}{20} \times 7\frac{1}{5}$ **(o)** $1\frac{1}{4} \times 1\frac{1}{3} \times 1\frac{1}{2}$

(p) $6 \div \frac{2}{3}$ **(q)** $\frac{2}{3} \div 6$ **(r)** $5\frac{1}{4} \div \frac{3}{8}$

(s) $3\frac{3}{4} \div 2\frac{1}{2}$ **(t)** $\left(\frac{3}{4} \div \frac{1}{8}\right) \div 1\frac{1}{2}$

9. Find the missing term in each expression.

(a) $\frac{1}{6} + \frac{?}{3} = \frac{1}{2}$ **(b)** $\frac{?}{12} - \frac{1}{4} = \frac{1}{3}$ **(c)** $\frac{2}{5} + \frac{1}{?} = \frac{1}{2}$

(d) $1 \div \frac{2}{?} = 1\frac{1}{2}$ **(e)** $\frac{4}{?} \div 1\frac{1}{4} = \frac{16}{25}$ **(f)** $1\frac{3}{5} \times \frac{?}{8} = \frac{3}{5}$

10. A roll contained $14\frac{5}{8}$ yards of fabric. A shopper purchased $\frac{1}{3}$ of the roll. Half of the remaining fabric was sold to another shopper. What is the length of the piece that is left on the roll?

11. Eighteen and one-half feet of phone wire is needed to run an extension. One-fourth of this wire runs along a baseboard. Two-thirds of the remaining wire goes around a doorway. The remaining portion of the wire is left free-standing and leads into the telephone. What is the length of the freestanding portion of the wire?

12. A computer printer has three type styles. The full print style prints 12 characters per inch. The italics print style prints 12 characters in $1\frac{1}{2}$ inches. The bold print style prints 12 characters in $1\frac{3}{4}$ inches. What is the length of a sentence containing the following print types?

> Full print: 20 characters
>
> Italics: 18 characters
>
> Bold: 6 characters

13. A moving company uses three boxes of varying sizes: a wardrobe box that is $4\frac{3}{4}$ feet high; a utility box that is $3\frac{5}{6}$ feet high; and a linens box that is $2\frac{1}{3}$ feet high. The height of the interior portion of their van is 15 feet. Boxes can only be stacked upright in the van. Offer four different combinations of stacked boxes that will fit in the van with as little wasted space as possible. State the number of each type of box used, the total height, and the amount of space remaining.

14. Dry wallboard is manufactured in half-inch thickness and three-eighths-inch thickness. A warehouse operator wishes to store 100 sheets of each type of wallboard by stacking them one on top of the other in two separate piles. Strips of wood that are seven-eighths-inch thick are used as separators between each set of 25 sheets of wallboard. How tall will each stack measure? Assume that the first sheet of wallboard rests on the ground.

15. On the map of Harrisburg, Pennsylvania, shown on page 287, $1\frac{1}{2}$ inches represent 3 miles. Determine the distance between the following locations on the map.

    (a) Along Cameron Street from the intersection of Herr Street to Sycamore Street

    (b) Along the Harrisburg Expressway from the intersection of Route 15 to Interstate 83

    (c) Along Interstate 83 from the intersection of Interstate 81 to Interstate 76

    (d) Find two locations that are approximately 5 miles apart.

    (e) Find two locations that are approximately 8 miles apart.

16. A train is traveling at 60 miles per hour. How many feet per second is this rate?

17. One cyclist is traveling at 63,360 feet per hour. A second cyclist is traveling at 294 yards per minute. Which is the faster speed? Explain your method for obtaining the answer.

18. There are 12 numbers (1–12) on an analog clock. What time is it in nearest whole numbers when the ratio of the minute-hand number to the hour-hand number is 1 : 3? Find four such times.

19. The ratio of boys to girls in a particular classroom is 3 : 4. If 16 girls are in the class, how many boys are there?

20. A college lecture hall has 400 seats. During a presentation, the ratio of empty seats to occupied seats is 3 to 5. How many seats are occupied?

21. The ratio of a father's whole number age to his younger daughter's whole number age is 10 to 1. The ratio of the same father's whole number age to his older daughter's whole number age is 10 to 3. Is it possible that the ages of the children are 3 and 6? Explain.

22. Eighty-five people are on a mailing list to receive advertisements from a small clothing store. The ratio of people on the list who live in town to those on the list who are out-of-towners is 13 : 4. How many of the advertisements are mailed to out-of-towners?

Exercise 15 Map

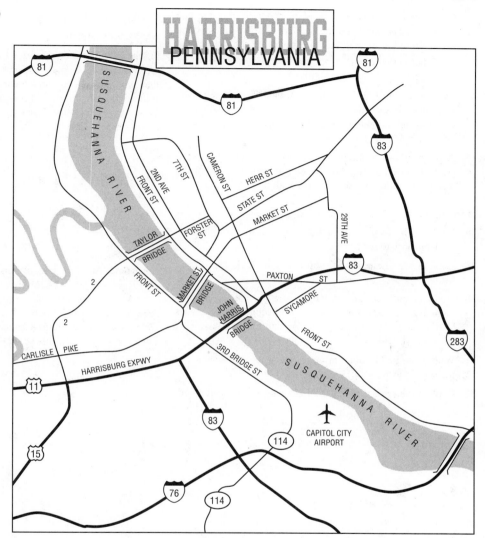

23. Determine the pattern in each sequence. Find the indicated term.

    (a) $\dfrac{1}{2 \times 3}, \dfrac{1}{3 \times 4}, \dfrac{1}{4 \times 5}, \dfrac{1}{5 \times 6}$ [sixth term]

    (b) $2, \dfrac{2}{5}, \dfrac{2}{25}, \dfrac{2}{125}, \dfrac{2}{625}$ [next term]

    (c) $\dfrac{7}{100^2}, \dfrac{7}{100^4}, \dfrac{7}{100^6}, \dfrac{7}{100^8}$ [tenth term]

24. Examine the following sum:

    $$\left(1 + \frac{1}{2}\right) + \left(1 + \frac{1}{3}\right) + \left(1 + \frac{1}{4}\right) + \left(1 + \frac{1}{5}\right)$$

    (a) What is the actual sum of the above four terms?

    (b) Explain the pattern for identifying the terms.

    (c) If another term were to be added to this sum, what would the next term be?

    (d) How many terms of the above type are needed to get as close to a sum of 10 without exceeding it?

25. A ball is dropped from a height of 8 feet. Each time it hits the ground it rebounds a distance of $\frac{3}{4}$ of the height it fell.

    (a) How high does the ball rebound after it hits the ground for the fifth time?

(b) What is the ratio of the rebound height after the ball hits the ground for the second time to the rebound height after the ball hits the ground for the third time?

(c) What is the total distance this ball has traveled before it rebounds for the fourth time?

26. A roll contains 80 feet of electrical wire. How many $14\frac{1}{2}$-foot pieces can be cut from the roll? What is the length of the remaining piece? What fractional part of the original roll is the remnant?

27. A punch bowl contains $4\frac{3}{4}$ gallons of punch. If a given recipe makes $\frac{2}{3}$ gallon, how many times must the recipe be made in order to exactly fill the punch bowl?

In Other Words

28. Explain why the repeated addition model of multiplication is inappropriate for $\frac{7}{8} \times \frac{1}{2}$.

29. Explain why the repeated subtraction model is appropriate for $\frac{7}{8} \div \frac{1}{2}$.

30. One student reported the length of a particular line segment as $5\frac{1}{4}$ inches. Another reported a length of $5\frac{8}{32}$ inches of the same segment. Are both measurements equivalent? Why, or why not?

31. What is a rate? Explain how the set of rates is a subset of the set of ratios.

32. Explain the error made in the following subtraction example.

$$
\begin{array}{r}
6\frac{1}{2} \;\rightarrow\; 6\frac{7}{8} \rightarrow\; 5\frac{14}{8} \\
-\,2\frac{7}{8} \;\rightarrow\; 2\frac{7}{8} \rightarrow\; 2\frac{7}{8} \\
\hline
3\frac{7}{8}
\end{array}
$$

Cooperative Activity

33. Groups of two

Individual Accountability: In each of the following equations, you are to estimate whole number replacements for the variables that would make the statement true. Test your estimates by finding the value of the expression. Adjust the estimates if necessary and recalculate. Each group member is to complete the entire set.

(a) $\frac{3}{4} \cdot A + \frac{1}{2} \cdot B = 7\frac{3}{4}$

(b) $2\frac{1}{2} \cdot C + 3\frac{1}{8} \cdot D = 35\frac{5}{8}$

(c) $10\frac{3}{4} \cdot E - 3\frac{1}{2} \cdot F = 118\frac{1}{2}$

(d) $6\frac{5}{8} \cdot G - 9\frac{1}{2} \cdot H = 34$

Group Goal: Share your results and methodology with your partner. Together, solve the following problem.

A gift wrapper makes two types of bows. A small bow requires $3\frac{1}{4}$ feet of ribbon and a large bow requires $5\frac{1}{2}$ feet of ribbon. A spool contains 128 feet of ribbon. How many bows of each type can be made so that no ribbon is left over?

7

Decimals, **P**ercents, and **R**eal **N**umbers

Examine the photograph at the right.

Describe what you see.

What mathematical questions can you ask?

What mathematical questions can be answered?

What mathematical questions cannot be answered?

What would a mathematical description of this photograph contain?

3.181

3.179

Introduction

Because our number system is a base ten system, it is natural to express quantities smaller than one whole in terms of tenths. In Chapter 6 we saw that comparisons among rational numbers are more obvious when parts of a whole are expressed using the same denominator. Rewriting rational numbers as equivalent decimals performs this function, allows us to extend the definition of rational numbers, and also facilitates computation in many contexts. These computations can readily be performed and interpreted using a calculator, since most calculator displays are decimal displays.

This chapter provides an in-depth look at all facets of decimal numbers and percents and completes our introduction to the various sets of numbers within our number system. In our society the use of decimal numbers and percents is pervasive. Whether you realize it or not, you probably encounter situations involving decimal numbers and percents almost every day. Such activities as varied as using money, investing in the stock market, filling your car with gas, hearing a weather report, figuring out interest rates on a new house you plan to buy, or measuring different distances, heights, lengths, and thicknesses all involve decimal numbers and percents. Section 7.1 starts off the discussion of decimals by showing them used in a variety of everyday situations. The section continues by discussing the subjects of place value, ordering and comparing decimals, and estimating the decimal values of fractions. Section 7.2 discusses the four basic operations—addition, subtraction, multiplication, and division—on decimals and also introduces various estimation strategies. Section 7.3 covers percents, yet another way in which fractions can be written. Many situations in which percents are commonly used are presented. Section 7.4 examines decimals in the context of linear metric measurement, using both the metric system and scientific notation. Finally, in Section 7.5 the "missing pieces" of the number line—the sets of rational numbers, irrational numbers, and real numbers—are filled in so that by the time you are finished studying this chapter, your understanding of our numbers and number systems should be complete.

7.1 Decimals: Modeling, Ordering, Comparing, and Estimating

Decimal numbers offer an alternate way of representing fractions in our base ten system. Recall our discussion of whole number place value in Chapter 2. The value of each digit in a number is a function of both the digit itself and the place it occupies. This is also true for decimals. We will begin our discussion of decimals by examining them in the context of their most widely used form, money. Since you are very familiar with money, this is a natural point of entry. The symbols 13.82 take on a special meaning when viewed as a monetary amount. Let's examine that meaning more closely by viewing the total amount as the sum of its individual parts.

$$\$\ 1\ 3\ .\ 8\ 2$$

1 ten-dollar bill ⎯⎯⎯⎯⎯⎯⎯⎯⎯⎯⎯⎯⎯⎯⎯⎯⎯

3 one-dollar bills ⎯⎯⎯⎯⎯⎯⎯⎯⎯⎯⎯⎯⎯⎯

8 dimes ⎯⎯⎯⎯⎯⎯⎯⎯⎯⎯⎯⎯⎯⎯⎯⎯⎯

2 pennies ⎯⎯⎯⎯⎯⎯⎯⎯⎯⎯⎯⎯⎯⎯⎯⎯

Although this amount could have been expressed using other currency denominations (such as 2 five-dollar bills, 12 quarters, 16 nickels, and 2 pennies), these denominations were chosen because they illustrate how our monetary system is also a base ten system.

A dime can be viewed in two different ways: It is equivalent to 10 pennies, and it is equivalent to $\frac{1}{10}$ of a dollar. Eight dimes are therefore equivalent to $8 \times \frac{1}{10}$ of a dollar, or $\frac{8}{10}$ of a dollar.

A penny can also be viewed in terms of its relationship to a dollar. A penny is equivalent to $\frac{1}{100}$ of a dollar. Two pennies are therefore equivalent to $2 \times \frac{1}{100}$ of a dollar, or $\frac{2}{100}$ of a dollar.

The amount $13.82 can now be expressed in expanded form as

$$(1 \times 10) + (3 \times 1) + \left(8 \times \frac{1}{10}\right) + \left(2 \times \frac{1}{100}\right) =$$

$$10 \ + \ 3 \ + \ \frac{8}{10} \ + \ \frac{2}{100} \ =$$

$$13 \ + \ \frac{80}{100} \ + \ \frac{2}{100} \ =$$

$$13 \ + \ \frac{82}{100} \qquad\qquad = 13\frac{82}{100}$$

Compare the decimal and fractional equivalents of thirteen dollars and eighty-two cents.

$$13.82$$

$$13\frac{82}{100}$$

It is easy to see how the whole number (dollar) amounts relate. Notice that 82 cents can be written in two equivalent forms: as .82 and as $\frac{82}{100}$. When removed from the monetary context, .82 and $\frac{82}{100}$ are both read as "eighty-two hundredths." This relationship between a fraction and a decimal can be extended to encompass the entire set of decimals. Examine the number 1234.5678:

1	**2**	**3**	**4**	**.**	**5**	**6**	**7**	**8**
1000	100	10	1	.	$\frac{1}{10}$	$\frac{1}{100}$	$\frac{1}{1000}$	$\frac{1}{10,000}$
Thousands	Hundreds	Tens	Ones		Tenths	Hundredths	Thousandths	Ten-Thousandths

This number can be written in expanded form as

$$(1 \times 1000) + (2 \times 100) + (3 \times 10) + (4 \times 1) + \left(5 \times \frac{1}{10}\right) + \left(6 \times \frac{1}{100}\right) + \left(7 \times \frac{1}{1000}\right) + \left(8 \times \frac{1}{10,000}\right)$$

$$1000 + 200 + 30 + 4 + \frac{5}{10} + \frac{6}{100} + \frac{7}{1000} + \frac{8}{10,000}$$

$$1234 \qquad + \frac{5000}{10,000} + \frac{600}{10,000} + \frac{70}{10,000} + \frac{8}{10,000}$$

$$1234 + \frac{5678}{10,000}$$

$$1234 \frac{5678}{10,000}$$

Therefore, $1234.5678 = 1234\frac{5678}{10,000}$. Both the decimal and fractional representations are read as "one thousand two hundred thirty-four and five thousand six hundred seventy-eight ten-thousandths."

Investigation 1

Examine the following gasoline pump digital display.

Read the total number of gallons for the purchase shown. Express that amount as an equivalent fraction.

The display 9.568 represents 9 full gallons and a fractional part of a gallon. The decimal .568 is read as "five hundred sixty-eight thousandths" and is interpreted as $\frac{568}{1000}$ of a gallon. Therefore, 9.568 is equivalent to the mixed number $9\frac{568}{1000}$.

Investigation 2

The business section of the newspaper reports that the price of one share of a particular stock is up $2\frac{5}{8}$ points. What is the monetary equivalent of this increase?

Stock prices are quoted in dollar amounts. An increase of $2\frac{5}{8}$ "points" is actually an increase in the price per share of $2\frac{5}{8}$ dollars. To express $\frac{5}{8}$ as an equivalent decimal, it must be written as an equivalent fraction whose denominator is either 10, 100, 1000, 10,000 and so on. The smallest of these numbers that is divisible by 8 without a remainder is 1000. Therefore,

$$\frac{5}{8} = \frac{5 \cdot 125}{8 \cdot 125} = \frac{625}{1000}$$

The increase of $2\frac{5}{8}$ dollars is equivalent to $2\frac{625}{1000}$ dollars, or 2.625 dollars. The rules of rounding whole numbers apply to decimal numbers as well. Consequently, 2.625 dollars rounded to the nearest hundredth is $2.63. One share of stock rose approximately $2.63. The rounding we have done here is for ease of computation and interpretation. In actual stock transactions, rounding does not take place at this point. Monetary amounts for stock prices are quoted to three decimal places. Computations are carried out with this degree of accuracy. Out of necessity, rounding takes place only after the final monetary computation is made, since we do not have a coin that is less than $\frac{1}{100}$ of a dollar.

The fraction $\frac{5}{8}$ chosen above was purposefully selected as an illustration for two reasons. First, stock prices are actually quoted in halves, quarters, and eighths (and occasionally sixteenths). Second, this fraction yields a decimal equivalent with a countable number of decimal places in its simplest form. Such a decimal is called a

terminating decimal   **terminating decimal**. To determine whether or not a rational number has a terminating decimal representation, examine the decimal places in terms of their prime factorizations shown here:

$$10 = 2 \times 5 \qquad\qquad = 10^1 = 2^1 \times 5^1$$
$$100 = 2 \times 2 \times 5 \times 5 \qquad\qquad = 10^2 = 2^2 \times 5^2$$
$$1000 = 2 \times 2 \times 2 \times 5 \times 5 \times 5 \qquad\qquad = 10^3 = 2^3 \times 5^3$$
$$10,000 = 2 \times 2 \times 2 \times 2 \times 5 \times 5 \times 5 \times 5 = 10^4 = 2^4 \times 5^4$$

Do you recognize a pattern? In general, when n is any whole number, $10^n = 2^n \times 5^n$. Therefore, a proper fraction in lowest terms has a terminating decimal equivalent if and only if its denominator is itself a factor of $2^n \times 5^n$, that is, if it can be written as $2^a \times 5^b$ where a and b are whole numbers. Only denominators that are factors of this type can be multiplied by a nonzero whole number to achieve a new denominator of the form 10^n.

Some calculators have the capability of converting a fraction into a decimal by pressing a key such as

$$\boxed{F \circlearrowright D}$$

On these calculators, fractions are entered in a special way and are displayed as fractions. For example, the fraction $\frac{5}{8}$ would be entered and displayed as shown here:

Keystroke Sequence   *Display*

$\boxed{\text{AC}}$ 5 $\boxed{/}$ 8 $\boxed{5/8}$

$\boxed{\text{AC}}$ 5 $\boxed{/}$ 8 $\boxed{F \circlearrowright D}$ $\boxed{0.625}$

nonterminating decimal

The $\boxed{/}$ key on this type of calculator is the fraction bar key. Notice that $\frac{5}{8}$ can be written as a terminating decimal since $8 = 2^3 \times 5^0$. Examine the calculator display. Only three decimal places are used. Sometimes it is not obvious from the display whether or not the decimal terminates. For example, the fraction $\frac{7}{9}$ has a **nonterminating decimal** equivalent, which means that an exact decimal equivalent for the fraction $\frac{7}{9}$ cannot be found no matter how many decimal places are computed. Some calculators would display 0.7777777; others would display 0.7777778. Both displays are misleading. In actuality, the digit 7 repeats infinitely. This is verifiable since the denominator 9 cannot be written in the form $2^a \times 5^b$.

Now examine the decimal equivalent of the fraction $\frac{9}{1024}$. The calculator displays 0.008789. Three interpretations are possible:

1. The fraction has a terminating decimal equivalent and the display is the actual six-place equivalent.

2. The fraction has a nonterminating decimal equivalent and the display shows either a rounded version, or just the first six decimal places of the equivalent.

3. The fraction has a terminating decimal equivalent, but the display is too small to depict the actual equivalent.

Examine the denominator, 1024. It can be written as 2^{10}. Since 2^{10} is of the form $2^a \times 5^b$ where $a = 10$ and $b = 0$, the fraction has a terminating decimal equivalent. Whether or not the display is the actual equivalent cannot be established at this time. (The decimal equivalent of $\frac{9}{1024}$ terminates at the tenth decimal place.) For now, you should be aware that when a fraction is converted to its decimal equivalent on a calculator and the entire display is filled with digits, the display is not necessarily the exact decimal equivalent of the fraction. Computations with this decimal equivalent may yield answers that are close to, but not exactly, the desired result. The degree of specificity needed to answer a particular question will dictate the number of decimal places necessary in the decimal equivalent.

A Place Value Model of Decimals

When whole number place value was discussed in Chapter 2, we introduced a manipulative material called powers-of-ten blocks. These blocks can also be used to illustrate decimal place value, simply by changing the value of the unit block. If the large cube, previously used to represent 1000, is now used to represent one whole, all of the other blocks will represent parts of the whole. The numerical equivalents can be shown as in Figure 7.1.

Figure 7.1

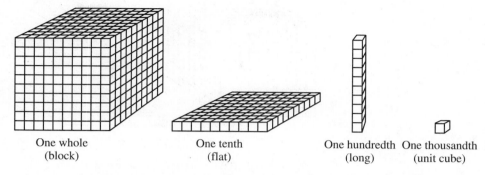

One whole (block)   One tenth (flat)   One hundredth (long)   One thousandth (unit cube)

One flat can be used to represent one-tenth, since 10 flats are equivalent to 1 block. Additionally, 1 flat is composed of 100 unit cubes. These 100 unit cubes, when compared to the 1000 unit cubes that make up the block, yield a ratio of $\frac{100}{1000}$, or $\frac{1}{10}$.

One long can be used to represent one one-hundredth, since 100 longs are equivalent to 1 block. Additionally, 1 long is composed of 10 unit cubes. These 10 unit cubes, when compared to the 1000 unit cubes that make up the block, yield a ratio of $\frac{10}{1000}$, or $\frac{1}{100}$.

One unit cube can be used to represent one one-thousandth, since 1000 unit cubes are equivalent to 1 block. One unit cube, when compared to the 1000 unit cubes that make up the block, yields a ratio of $\frac{1}{1000}$.

Investigation 3

Use the powers-of-ten blocks to represent one and four hundred sixty-eight thousandths.

Express the number using symbols.

$$1.468$$

To represent one whole, one large block is needed. To represent four one-tenths, four flats are needed $\left(4 \times \frac{1}{10}\right)$. To represent six one-hundredths, six longs are needed $\left(6 \times \frac{1}{100}\right)$. To represent eight one-thousandths, eight unit cubes are needed $\left(8 \times \frac{1}{1000}\right)$. The number 1.468 is expressed in powers-of-ten blocks as follows.

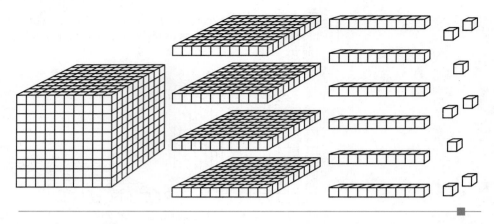

Ordering and Comparing Decimals

We must be able to compare the relative size of decimals. This skill becomes necessary when comparing lengths or prices. Investigation 4 shows two ways of accomplishing this task.

Investigation 4

The strings on stringed instruments are labeled by the measure of their diameter. The differences in these small measurements are reflected in the differences in the sounds that the string can make. Usually, the strings are put on the instruments in ascending or descending order. Examine the following four measurements of the thicknesses of strings: .1 inch, .075 inch, .062 inch, .08 inch. Assuming that the strings will be put on a guitar in ascending order, what will the order of the strings be according to the measures of their diameters?

To compare the sizes of these strings, we must establish some commonality among them. One way to do this is by expressing each of the decimals as equivalent fractions:

$$.1 = \frac{1}{10} \qquad .075 = \frac{75}{1000} \qquad .062 = \frac{62}{1000} \qquad .08 = \frac{8}{100}$$

Now that the decimals have been expressed as fractions, we can compare them by writing them using a common denominator. The least common multiple of 10, 100, and 1000 is 1000. Therefore, the following equivalences can be written:

$$.1 = \frac{1}{10} = \frac{100}{1000} \qquad .075 = \frac{75}{1000} \qquad .062 = \frac{62}{1000} \qquad .08 = \frac{8}{100} = \frac{80}{1000}$$

It is easy to see that

$$\frac{62}{1000} < \frac{75}{1000} < \frac{80}{1000} < \frac{100}{1000}$$

Consequently, $.062 < .075 < .08 < .1$. The strings should be put on the guitar in the following order: .062 inch, .075 inch, .08 inch, .1 inch. This method of comparison relies on knowledge of the fraction equivalents of decimals, which leads to the following extension of the method.

Align the decimals to be compared:

$$.1$$
$$.075$$
$$.062$$
$$.08$$

Once again, look for commonalities to compare. The largest number of decimal places present in these four numbers is three. Therefore, writing each of these decimals as thousandths will make the comparison process easy. But how can .1 be written as a three-place decimal? From the work above, you saw that $\frac{1}{10} = \frac{100}{1000}$. It therefore follows that $.1 = .100$. Also, $\frac{8}{100} = \frac{80}{1000}$. Consequently, $.08 = .080$. Trailing zeros do not change the value of the decimal. With this fact in mind, you should enter as many trailing zeros as necessary so that all of the decimals have the same number of decimal places. This can be done as follows:

$$.100$$
$$.075$$
$$.062$$
$$.080$$

Now you can see that $.062 < .075 < .080 < .1$, which yields the same ascending order of the original decimals as found using the first technique. The decimals appear in ascending order as follows:

$$.062$$
$$.075$$
$$.080$$
$$.100$$

Estimating Decimal Values of Fractions

The fraction $\frac{5}{10}$ is equivalent to the fraction $\frac{1}{2}$. Therefore, the decimal .5 is also equivalent to the fraction $\frac{1}{2}$. Every fraction that is equivalent to $\frac{1}{2}$ has a decimal representation of .5. We will use this knowledge as a starting point for estimating decimal equivalents of fractions.

Suppose that an estimate of the decimal equivalent of $\frac{5}{8}$ is needed. It is easy to mentally determine that $\frac{4}{8}$ is equal to $\frac{1}{2}$. Therefore, $\frac{4}{8} = .5$. Since $\frac{5}{8} > \frac{4}{8}$, it follows that $\frac{5}{8} > .5$. Examining a number line, $\frac{5}{8}$ is relatively close to $\frac{4}{8}$. Therefore, the decimal equivalent of $\frac{5}{8}$ should be relatively close to .5. A reasonable estimate of the decimal equivalent of $\frac{5}{8}$ might be .6. The following calculator keystroke sequence yields the exact decimal equivalent of $\frac{5}{8}$.

AC 5 / 8 FCD   0.625

Investigation 5

Suppose that the division key on a certain calculator does not work, nor does the calculator have a fraction bar key. You want to perform calculations with the fraction $\frac{3}{7}$ in a context where a ballpark figure is sufficient. What approximate decimal equivalent might be appropriately entered for the fraction $\frac{3}{7}$?

The complex fraction $\dfrac{3\frac{1}{2}}{7}$ is equivalent to $\frac{1}{2}$, or .5. Since $\frac{3}{7}$ is slightly less than $\dfrac{3\frac{1}{2}}{7}$, a reasonable approximation of $\frac{3}{7}$ might be .45. (The actual equivalent of $\frac{3}{7}$ is .428571....)

Sometimes it is useful to round decimals before performing operations with them. Perhaps the simplest form of rounding takes place when a decimal is rounded to the nearest integer. We often do this when reporting monetary amounts, tuning into radio stations, or determining approximate sales tax. The rounding techniques we introduced in Chapter 3 can also be applied to decimals. If we wish to round a decimal to the nearest integer, look at the digit to the right of the ones place. If this number is 5 or greater, the ones digit is increased by one, and decimal places are dropped. If the digit to the right of the ones place is less than 5, the ones digit remains unchanged, and the decimal places are dropped.

Examine the various results of rounding 72.7291:

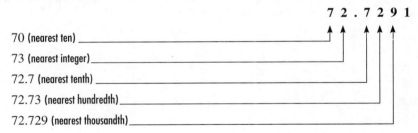

70 (nearest ten)
73 (nearest integer)
72.7 (nearest tenth)
72.73 (nearest hundredth)
72.729 (nearest thousandth)

Assessments for Section 7.1

1. Are the following statements true or false? Explain your reasoning.

(a) $\frac{2}{3} > .5$ (b) $\frac{5}{11} > .5$ (c) $\frac{8}{17} < .5$

(d) $\frac{3}{5} < .5$ (e) $\frac{5}{9} < .5$

(d) $\frac{2}{3}$ — .6   (e) $\frac{5\frac{1}{2}}{11}$ — .5   (f) $\frac{3}{8}$ — .35

(g) $\frac{3}{4}$ — .7   (h) $\frac{1.5}{3}$ — .5   (i) $\frac{7}{8}$ — .857

2. Fill in the blank space with a >, <, or = symbol.

(a) $\frac{3}{7}$ — .5   (b) $\frac{2}{5}$ — .45   (c) $\frac{1}{8}$ — .125

(j) $\frac{3}{4}$ — $\frac{6}{8}$

3. Write each of the following numbers in decimal notation.

   (a) Thirty-eight hundredths

   (b) Five thousandths

   (c) One hundred twenty-three ten-thousandths

   (d) Six and twenty-two hundredths

   (e) Fifteen and twelve ten-thousandths

   (f) Five and five hundred five thousandths

4. Write each of the following numbers in words.

   (a) .23   (b) .012   (c) 5.008

   (d) 23.1   (e) .308

5. A fuel gauge can be digital (usage reported in decimals) or fractional (usage reported as a fractional part of the entire tank). Assume that one full tank is one whole, and that the digital type reports the fuel remaining as the decimal equivalent of the fractional part of one whole. (Later you will see that this decimal represents the percent of fuel remaining.) Trace five copies of the fuel gauge illustrated here. Indicate where the fractional representation of the gauge might be located for each of the following digital representations.

   (a) .71   (b) .125   (c) .8   (d) .455   (e) .375

6. Write each of the following numbers in decimal notation. (Be careful; some intermediary steps are necessary.)

   (a) Thirty-five tenths

   (b) Five hundred fifteen hundredths

   (c) Three and one hundred five tenths

   (d) Eight hundred seven hundredths

   (e) Thirty-two thousand thousandths

   (f) Two thousand sixteen hundredths

   (g) Eighty-three and thirty-eight tenths

7. Write the decimal representation for the quantities illustrated here, if one large block has a value of one whole.

   (a)

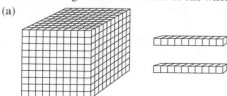

(b)

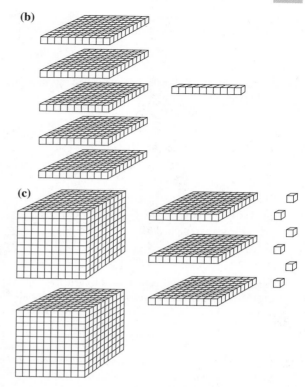

(c)

8. Arrange the following decimals in ascending order.

   (a) .015, .6, .912, .178, .34

   (b) 2.35, 2.035, 2.305, 2.0355

   (c) .01, .0101, .1101, .1001

   (d) .234, .1, .21, .301, .03

   (e) .09, .00090, .9909, .99099

9. Arrange the following decimals in descending order.

   (a) .72, .76, .03, .5, .532

   (b) 5.314, 5.34, 5.034, 5.3, 5

   (c) .269, .296, .29, .206, .09

   (d) 3.7, 7.3, 3, 7, .37, .73, .3377, .7733

   (e) 1.06, 1.6, .06, .60, .66, .161

10. State two decimals that can replace the question mark to make each statement true.

   (a) .5 < ? < .6

   (b) .25 < ? < .295

   (c) .75 < ? < .755

   (d) .07 < ? < .09

   (e) −.9 < ? < −.85

   (f) −1.2 < ? < −1.15

11. Express each of the following stock price changes in monetary amounts rounded to the nearest cent.

(a) $+1\frac{5}{8}$ (b) $-2\frac{1}{2}$ (c) $+\frac{7}{8}$ (d) $+3\frac{1}{8}$ (e) $-2\frac{3}{4}$

12. Round each of the following numbers to the specified decimal place.

(a) 3.876 (tenth)
(b) 1.0099 (tenth)
(c) 2.354 (hundredth)
(d) 34.965 (integer)
(e) .04534 (thousandth)
(f) .789 (integer)
(g) 3.061 (tenth)
(h) .1234567 (hundredth)
(i) .67 (tenth)
(j) 5.012 (hundredth)

13. Determine the decimal equivalent of each fraction. State whether each decimal equivalent has terminating or nonterminating decimal representations. Explain your reasoning.

(a) $\frac{7}{200}$ (b) $\frac{17}{80}$ (c) $\frac{5}{12}$ (d) $\frac{234}{1250}$ (e) $\frac{12}{30}$

14. The five finalists in a swimming competition were clocked with the following times. Arrange the swimmers in order from first place to fifth place.

Jessica	37.39 seconds
Allison	38.03 seconds
Sara	36.58 seconds
Liz	37.37 seconds
Kate	37.73 seconds

15. The rate of change of the depth of a body of water because of tides is expressed as the ratio

$$\frac{\text{Change in time}}{\text{Change in depth}}$$

At 9:00 A.M. the water is 8 meters deep. At 1:00 P.M. the water is 13 meters deep. Express this rate of change in hours per meter as a decimal.

16. The rate of change in the height of a tree is expressed as the ratio

$$\frac{\text{Change in height}}{\text{Change in time}}$$

In 1979 a sapling was 2 inches tall. In 1993 it had grown to a height of 3 feet, 8 inches. Express this rate of change in feet per year as a decimal.

17. Express each of the following sums as a decimal.

(a) $\frac{1}{10} + \frac{2}{5}$ (b) $\frac{3}{4} + \frac{1}{8}$ (c) $\frac{2}{5} + \frac{1}{100}$

(d) $4\frac{1}{2} + 5\frac{3}{4}$ (e) $2\frac{3}{10} + \frac{1}{5}$

18. Express each of the following sums as a decimal.

(a) $\frac{1}{10} + \frac{2}{100} + \frac{3}{100}$

(b) $\frac{1}{10} + \frac{4}{1000}$

(c) $\frac{3}{100} + \frac{4}{10} + \frac{9}{1000}$

(d) $\frac{7}{100} + \frac{9}{1000} + 9$

(e) $\frac{2}{100,000} + \frac{1}{10}$

19. What year was it when sixty-four hundredths of the 20th century had already passed? Explain your reasoning.

20. On an assembly line, a certain product is considered acceptable if its weight falls between .05 pound and .125 pound. Any product that does not meet this requirement is defective and immediately removed from the line. Which of the following products would be considered defective?

(a) .105 pound (b) .005 pound (c) .152 pound
(d) .1 pound (e) .0125 pound

21. Line segment $\overline{VZ}$ is divided into 5 equal parts and labeled as shown here:

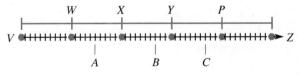

Each of the 5 equal parts is further divided into 10 equal parts. Consider $\overline{VW}$ to have a length of one unit. What is the decimal representation of each of the following points on the segment? (Assume V represents zero on the number line.)

(a) A (b) B (c) C

In Other Words

22. Explain the difference between a terminating and a nonterminating decimal.

23. Many supermarkets are abandoning the traditional pan scales that report weights as fractions ($\frac{1}{2}$ pound, $\frac{3}{4}$ pound, etc.) and replacing them with digital scales that report weights to the nearest thousandth of a pound. Why do you think this change is occurring?

24. Many teachers discourage students from reporting whole numbers using the conjunction *and*, as in one hundred and thirty-two (132). From what you have learned in this section, why might this deletion of *and* be a good idea?

25. In Investigation 2 we noted that stock prices are not rounded to the nearest penny until the final computations are made. Explain why this rounding is delayed. Does it seem easier to work with money reported in dollars and cents rather than decimal parts of a dollar?

Cooperative Activity

26. Groups of four

Individual Accountability: This activity involves collecting stock market data over five days. You will also need this information for the Cooperative Activity at the end of Section 7.2.

Each group member is to choose any three corporations. Look in the business section of the newspaper for five consecutive trading days. Chart the closing price for one share of each corporation's stock. Write each closing price as an equivalent fraction and a decimal.

Group Goal: Combine the stocks chosen from all four group members. Devise a plan in which the 20 stocks can be ordered from the "best performing" to the "worst performing" over the five-day period. Explain your method.

7.2 Operations with Decimals

You probably make estimates that involve decimal numbers almost every day, such as when you determine the approximate cost of a sale item, figure out the tax and tip on a restaurant bill, mentally compute batting averages, or try to decide whether to get a 24- or 36-month auto loan. Getting into the habit of estimating the answer before performing any algorithms on decimals is a good idea, partly because mental estimation is a beneficial skill and partly because it will guard against errors. The latter is true whether the algorithm is done by hand or with a calculator. This section will outline the formal algorithms for the four basic operations on decimals and also introduce you to estimation strategies.

Decimal Addition and Subtraction

Recall your work with fraction addition and subtraction. Fractions had to have common denominators before you could add and subtract them. This is also the case with decimals. For example, to find the sum of $\frac{9}{10}$, $\frac{67}{100}$, and $\frac{136}{1000}$, you would first have to rewrite the fractions with a common denominator of 1000. The problem would then appear as

$$\frac{900}{1000} + \frac{670}{1000} + \frac{136}{1000} = \frac{1706}{1000} = 1\frac{706}{1000}$$

If these fractions were written as decimals, the problem would have been to find the sum of .9, .67, and .136. Before these decimals can be added, they must be rewritten in common form, or carried out to the same decimal place. Annexing trailing zeros to the right of a decimal does not change the value of the decimal. Therefore, the problem can be rewritten as

$$.900 + .670 + .136 = 1.706$$

Do you see the similarity between the procedure followed with fractions and the procedure followed with decimals? To generalize, when adding or subtracting decimal fractions, first rewrite the terms so that they are carried out to the same number of decimal places, and then align the numbers according to place value.

Investigation 6

The precipitation amounts for the month of July were recorded as .2 centimeter, .03 centimeter, 1.05 centimeters, .671 centimeter, 2 centimeters, and 1.9 centimeters. What was the total precipitation recorded for the month of July?

First, estimate the sum by rounding each addend to the nearest integer.

.2   rounds to 0
.03   rounds to 0
1.050   rounds to 1
.671   rounds to 1
2   rounds to 2
1.9   rounds to 2

An estimate obtained by adding $1 + 1 + 2 + 2$ is 6 centimeters of rainfall.

To obtain a precise sum, rewrite the addends vertically, annexing zeros so that they are all carried out to the same number of decimal places.

$$
\begin{array}{r}
.200 \\
.030 \\
1.050 \\
.671 \\
2.000 \\
+\ 1.900 \\
\hline
5.851 \text{ cm}
\end{array}
$$

The total rainfall for the month of July was 5.851 centimeters. This comes close to the estimate of 6 centimeters. Notice that although it was necessary to align the decimal points, the sum would not have changed if the trailing zeros had not been included.

Investigation 7

The total weight of a package of lunch meat (packaging plus meat) is 1.5 kilograms. If the packaging weighs .005 kilogram, what is the actual weight of the meat?

An estimate of the difference between 1.5 and .005 should be very close to 1.5, since .005 is such a small amount. Remember that the procedure requires rewriting the minuend and the subtrahend in vertical form and carrying them out the same number of decimal places.

$$
\begin{array}{ccc}
1.5 & & 1.500 \\
-\ \underline{.005} & \rightarrow & -\ \underline{.005} \\
& & 1.495
\end{array}
$$

The actual weight of the lunch meat is 1.495 kilograms, which compares favorably to the estimate.

Investigation 8

A carton contains three items of the following weights: 3.25 kilograms, 1.5 kilograms, .875 kilogram. The total weight of the carton is 6.23 kilograms. What is the weight of the packaging?

You are asked to determine the difference between the weight of the carton and the sum total of the weight of the three items. A good estimate of the weight of the three items is 6 kilograms (3 + 2 + 1). Therefore, the weight of the packaging should be less than 1 kilogram.

First, determine the total weight of the three items as follows:

$$
\begin{array}{l}
3.250 \\
1.500 \\
+\ \underline{.875} \\
5.625
\end{array}
$$ The three items weigh 5.625 kilograms.

Now subtract this total weight from the weight of the carton:

$$
\begin{array}{l}
6.230 \\
-\ \underline{5.625} \\
.605
\end{array}
$$ The total weight of the packaging is .605 kilogram, which agrees with the estimate of less than 1 kilogram.

This problem could also have been solved using either of the following two calculator keystroke sequences.

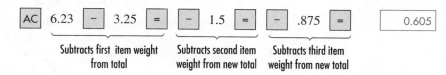

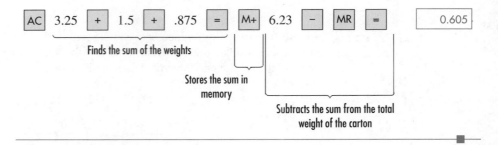

Finds the sum of the weights

Stores the sum in memory

Subtracts the sum from the total weight of the carton

Decimal Multiplication and Division

Students often know the procedures for multiplying and dividing decimals, but are at a loss when asked to explain the reasoning behind those procedures. If students are taught only to "count the number of decimal places" in multiplication or to "move the decimal point in the divisor and the dividend the same number of places," the algorithms have no meaning. The placement of the decimal in the product and the quotient need not be a mystery. Examine Investigations 9, 10, and 11.

Investigation 9

Ribbon sells at $.75 a meter. What is the cost of 2.25 meters of ribbon?

Many times, verbal problems containing fractions and/or decimals seem to unsettle students. When faced with a problem involving 2.25 meters of ribbon at $.75 per meter, the strategies of solving a related problem and solving a simpler problem can be used in tandem. A related, simpler problem might contain only whole dollar amounts and an integer length.

For example, if ribbon sells at $1 a meter, what would be the cost of 2 meters of ribbon? The total price of the purchase is found by multiplying the price per meter by the number of meters purchased. The result will be a dollar amount. This is easily verified by examining the resulting units when the problem is analyzed using dimensional analysis.

The ribbon sells at .75 $\frac{\text{dollars}}{\text{meter}}$. The amount needed is 2.25 meters.

$$.75\ \frac{\text{dollars}}{\text{meter}} \times 2.25\ \text{meters} = ?\ \text{dollars}$$

Before performing the multiplication, an estimate should be obtained. Two methods are possible:

1. Rounding to the Nearest Whole Number. The decimal .75 rounds to 1, and the decimal 2.25 rounds to 2. Therefore, the product should be close to 1×2, or $2.

2. Obtaining Upper and Lower Bounds. Rewrite the multiplication in two different forms. In the first form, obtain a lower bound by rounding each number down to the nearest whole number. This is accomplished by just removing the decimal portion. For the second form, obtain an upper bound by rounding each number *up* to the nearest whole number. These forms are shown here.

$$
\begin{array}{ccccc}
2 & \leftarrow & 2.25 & \rightarrow & 3 \\
\times\,0 & \leftarrow & \times\ .75 & \rightarrow & \times\,1 \\
\hline
0 & & ? & & 3
\end{array}
$$

We now have an upper and lower bound between which the solution will be found. Now multiply the two original numbers as if they were whole numbers, as shown here:

$$
\begin{array}{r}
225 \\
\times\ \ 75 \\
\hline
16875
\end{array}
$$

Where can the decimal point be placed so that the product falls between the upper and lower bounds?

$$
\begin{array}{ll}
16875. & \rightarrow \text{No, this is greater than the upper bound of 3.} \\
1687.5 & \rightarrow \text{No, this is greater than the upper bound of 3.} \\
168.75 & \rightarrow \text{No, this is greater than the upper bound of 3.} \\
16.875 & \rightarrow \text{No, this is greater than the upper bound of 3.} \\
1.6875 & \rightarrow \text{Yes, this falls in the acceptable range.} \\
.16875 & \rightarrow \text{Yes, this falls in the acceptable range.}
\end{array}
$$

There are two possible answers here. The answer of .16875, which would be interpreted as $.17, obviously does not make sense as an answer in the context of this problem. The solution must be 1.6875, which rounds to $1.69. Therefore, the cost of the ribbon is $1.69.

Of course, this procedure isn't followed every time you do a multiplication problem. But it helps set the stage for understanding why the decimal point is positioned in a certain place in the product. An additional explanation follows.

Express each of the decimals as fractions, then multiply:

$$
\frac{75}{100} \times 2\frac{25}{100} = \frac{75}{100} \times \frac{275}{100} = \frac{16.875}{10,000} = 1\frac{6875}{10,000} = 1.6875
$$

Once again, we obtain an answer of 1.6875, or $1.69. Notice that in the fractional representation of the answer the denominator is 10,000 ($100 \times 100 = 10,000$). In decimal notation, this would require four decimal places. Therefore, an *n*-place decimal times an *m*-place decimal will yield an $(n + m)$-place decimal product. When multiplying decimals, a simple way of determining the number of decimal places in the product is to count the number of decimal places in both of the factors.

Division operations on decimals can take several forms: a decimal divided by a whole number, a whole number divided by a decimal, and a decimal divided by a decimal. These various operations are not treated as special cases since they can all be viewed as extensions of the process used for whole number division.

Recall from Chapter 6 that a fraction is a form of a quotient. The fraction $\frac{1}{2}$ results from dividing 1 by 2. The fraction $\frac{7}{8}$ results from dividing 7 by 8. In general, the fraction $\frac{x}{y}$ results from the operation $x \div y$ (when $y \neq 0$).

To help estimate the decimal equivalent of a fraction, estimate the relative value of that fraction. For example, if $0 < (\frac{x}{y}) < 1$, then the decimal equivalent of $\frac{x}{y}$ is also restricted to that range. The procedure for converting a fraction to its decimal equivalent relies on the degree of specificity you wish to attain in the answer. Examine the process used to determine the decimal equivalents of $\frac{1}{2}, \frac{7}{8}, \frac{5}{80}$, and $\frac{23}{24}$.

$$
\begin{array}{llll}
.50 & .875 & .0625 & .958333\overline{3} \\
2)\overline{1.00} & 8)\overline{7.000} & 80)\overline{5.0000} & 24)\overline{23.000000} \\
\underline{-1\,0} & \underline{-6\,4} & \underline{-4\,80} & \underline{-21\,6} \\
00 & 60 & 200 & 1\,40 \\
& \underline{-56} & \underline{-160} & \underline{-1\,20} \\
& 40 & 400 & 200 \\
& \underline{-40} & \underline{-400} & \underline{-192} \\
& 0 & 0 & 80 \\
& & & \underline{-72} \\
& & & 80 \\
& & & \underline{-72} \\
& & & 80
\end{array}
$$

Notice that the first three decimal equivalents are terminating decimals. Although each could have been terminated at any decimal place by rounding, decimal equivalents are commonly carried out to at least three decimal places. In the case of $\frac{23}{24}$, notice that only after three decimal places does a recurring pattern become apparent. This decimal equivalent is a nonterminating, repeating decimal.

Although it is acceptable to state that $\frac{23}{24} \approx .958$, it is more accurate to write $\frac{23}{24} = .958\overline{3}$. A bar over the repeating portion indicates that the decimal is a nonterminating, repeating decimal. Some examples of repeating decimals are given here:

$$
\begin{array}{llll}
\dfrac{1}{3} \approx .333 & \dfrac{5}{9} \approx .555 & \dfrac{37}{99} \approx .374 & \dfrac{123}{999} \approx .123 \\[2mm]
= .\overline{3} & = .\overline{5} & = .\overline{37} & = .\overline{123}
\end{array}
$$

The calculator keystroke sequence used to find the decimal equivalent of any rational number $\frac{x}{y}$ is

$$\boxed{AC} \quad x \quad \boxed{\div} \quad y \quad \boxed{=}$$

Remember that calculators have no way of indicating whether or not a decimal equivalent repeats. Although it is easy to see in the calculator display that $\frac{5}{9}$ repeats, it is not that easy to see that $\frac{2}{7}$ is a repeating decimal. Its equivalent, .285714, repeats after six decimal places. Keep this in mind when using decimal equivalents of rational numbers. Any simplified fraction $\frac{x}{y}$ whose denominator cannot be written in the form $2^a \times 5^b$ where a and b are whole numbers will be nonterminating and repeating.

Is it possible to determine the fractional equivalent of a nonterminating, repeating decimal? A closer look at the decimal itself will reveal the answer to this question. You have already seen that $.\overline{123} = \frac{123}{999}$. This decimal can be expressed as a sum in the following way:

$$.\overline{123} = .123 + .000123 + .000000123 + .000000000123 + \cdots$$

We will employ the technique of **using a variable** here to help simplify this sum. Let $S = .\overline{123}$. Then

$$S = .123 + .000123 + .000000123 + .000000000123 + \cdots$$

This decimal repeats after three decimal places. By multiplying each side of the equation by 1000, the equality will be maintained and a whole number portion will appear on the right-hand side.

$$1000 \times S = 1000(.123 + .000123 + .000000123 + .000000000123 + \cdots)$$
$$1000 \times S = 123 + \underbrace{.123 + .000123 + .000000123 + .000000000123 + \cdots}_{S}$$
$$1000 \times S = 123 + S$$
$$1000 \times S - S = 123 + S - S$$
$$999 \times S = 123$$
$$S = \frac{123}{999}$$

Since we already know that S is equal to the original nonterminating, repeating decimal, we have now determined its fractional equivalent to be $\frac{123}{999}$.

The decimal does not have to be expressed in the expanded notation as above. The procedure could have been simplified as follows:

$$S = .123\overline{123}$$
$$1000S = 123.\overline{123}$$
$$1000S = 123 + .\overline{123}$$
$$1000S = 123 + S$$
$$999S = 123$$
$$S = \frac{123}{999}$$

This technique can be utilized to determine the fractional equivalent of any nonterminating, repeating decimal.

1. Set up the appropriate equation and multiply by a power of 10 dictated by the size of the repeating portion of the decimal (e.g., if three digits repeat, multiply by 10^3.)

2. Represent the right side of the equation as the sum of a whole number and a repeating decimal.

3. Substitute the variable for the repeating decimal portion of the sum.

4. Subtract the variable from both sides of the equation.

5. Divide both sides of the equation by the coefficient of the variable. The result is the fractional equivalent of the repeating decimal.

Investigation 10

A class treasury contains $57.75. Each student in the class contributed $1.75. How many students are in the class?

To estimate the contribution per student, round each number to its largest place value and then divide. The estimate will result from $60 \div 2$, or 30. Approximately 30 students are in this class.

To obtain a precise answer, you must find $57.75 \div 1.75$. This division is easier to perform when the divisor is a whole number. Since any division $x \div y$ can be represented as $\frac{x}{y}$, $57.75 \div 1.75$ can be rewritten as

$$\frac{57.75}{1.75}$$

Since any number multiplied by 1 is itself, we will multiply the fraction

$$\frac{57.75}{1.75}$$

by an equivalent form of 1 in order to obtain a fraction in which the denominator is a whole number. This can be accomplished by multiplying by $\frac{100}{100}$.

$$\frac{57.75}{1.75} \times \frac{100}{100} = \frac{5775}{175}$$

The multiplicative identity property assures us that

$$\frac{57.75}{1.75} = \frac{5775}{175}$$

Therefore,

$$57.75 \div 1.75 = 5775 \div 175 = 33$$

There are 33 students in the class.

This method of dividing decimals employs the problem-solving strategy of solving an equivalent problem. To perform this division in standard form, multiply both the dividend and the divisor by an appropriate power of 10 to result in a whole number divisor, and then divide as with whole numbers.

Investigation 10 was deliberately chosen to result in a whole number quotient. When dividing decimals, the results are not always whole numbers. For example, examine Investigation 11.

Investigation 11

The price for 1.2 kilograms of bananas is $.42. What is the cost per kilogram of the bananas?

In order to determine the price per kilogram, the total cost must be divided by the total weight. Remember to multiply the divisor and the dividend by an appropriate power of 10 to result in a whole number divisor. Rather than writing out this procedure as in Investigation 10, a simple way of indicating that this multiplication has taken place is to move the decimal point to the right in both the divisor and the dividend. (Recall that multiplying by 10^n, where n is a whole number, moves the decimal point to the right n places.) The decimal is then placed in the quotient directly above the decimal in the dividend.

$$1.2\,\overline{)\,.4\,2}$$

$$
\begin{array}{r}
.35 \\
12\,\overline{)\,4.20} \\
3\,6 \\
\hline
60 \\
60 \\
\hline
0
\end{array}
$$

The bananas cost $.35 per kilogram.

Assessments for Section 7.2

1. Find each of the following sums.
   (a) $4.8 + 3.25 + 1.008$
   (b) $16.2 + 3.75 + 3 + .08$
   (c) $1.5 + \dfrac{3}{4}$
   (d) $4 + .125 + \dfrac{1}{8}$
   (e) $42.012 + 78 + .654 + 3.056$

2. Find each of the following differences.
   (a) $23.975 - 14.8$
   (b) $32.19 - 7.875$
   (c) $5.98 - 5$
   (d) $7 - 3.275$
   (e) $16 - .001$
   (f) $6.625 - \dfrac{1}{20}$
   (g) $\dfrac{7}{8} - .1$

3. Find each of the following products.
   (a) 34×1.25
   (b) $.01 \times .001$
   (c) $(.05)^2$
   (d) $6.5 \times 1.2 \times 3.4$
   (e) $1.25 \times .75 \times .01$

4. Find each of the following quotients.
   (a) $57.5 \div 46$
   (b) $223.2 \div 18$
   (c) $78 \div 19.5$
   (d) $38 \div 4$
   (e) $.247 \div .19$
   (f) $2.0625 \div 5.5$

5. Set $W = \left\{ \dfrac{3}{5}, \dfrac{4}{11}, \dfrac{13}{25}, \dfrac{17}{20}, \dfrac{15}{18}, \dfrac{61}{64} \right\}$. Let set A equal the subset of W containing only those fractions that have terminating decimal equivalents. Let set B equal the subset of W containing only those fractions that have nonterminating decimal equivalents. Find the elements of sets A and B. Explain why $A \cap B = \varnothing$.

6. Express each of the following fractions as decimal equivalents rounded to three decimal places.

    (a) $\frac{5}{7}$ (b) $\frac{1}{9}$ (c) $\frac{13}{15}$ (d) $\frac{45}{100}$ (e) $\frac{3}{13}$

7. Determine the missing value in each of the following.

    (a) $3.25 + ? = 14.1$

    (b) $? + .0125 = .125$

    (c) $13 - ? = 9.75$

    (d) $? - 1.25 = 8$

    (e) $9.75 \times ? = 2.925$

    (f) $? \times .34 = .1972$

    (g) $7.65 \div ? = 9$

    (h) $? \div 1.5 = 3.75$

8. Express each of the following fractions as nonterminating, repeating decimals.

    (a) $\frac{2}{9}$ (b) $\frac{2}{7}$ (c) $\frac{19}{33}$ (d) $\frac{10}{11}$ (e) $\frac{5}{999}$

9. Express each of the following repeating decimals as fractional equivalents.

    (a) $.\overline{15}$ (b) $.\overline{02}$ (c) $.\overline{375}$

    (d) $.\overline{8}$ (e) $.\overline{1001}$

10. Marta purchased five sheets of sandpaper at the hardware store. The purchase consisted of two sheets of one grade of sandpaper, two of a second grade, and one of a third grade. The three grades of sandpaper were priced at $.85, $.65, and $1.09 per sheet, but not necessarily in that order. Her total bill before tax was $4.53. How many sheets of each grade did she purchase?

11. Tom's bill before tax at the drugstore was $8.41. He bought as many items as the price in cents of one item. How many items did he buy?

12. Determine two decimal factors whose product falls within the given range.

    (a) $5 < ? \times ? < 8$

    (b) $5 < ? \times ? < 7$

    (c) $5 < ? \times ? < 6$

    (d) $5 < ? \times ? < 5.5$

    (e) $5 < ? \times ? < 5.1$

    (f) $3.5 < ? \times ? < 5$

    (g) $100 < ? \times ? < 110$

    (h) $0 < ? \times ? < 1$

    (i) $-5 < ? \times ? < -3$

    (j) $-1.5 < ? \times ? < 0$

13. If three-quarters of a pound of chocolate costs $5.85, how much does one pound cost?

14. In a three-game series, a particular baseball player came up to bat 13 times. He successfully hit in four of the at bats. What is his batting average (to three decimal places) for the three-game series?

15. The distance on a map from point A to point B along the interstate is 1.5 cm. Points C, D, and E lie, in that order, along the same interstate, but do not lie between points A and B. The distance from B to C is one and one-half times the distance from A to B. The distance from C to D is three times the distance from B to C. The distance from D to E is 1.7 cm less than twice the distance from A to D.

    (a) Find the map distance in centimeters from A to E.

    (b) On this map, 1 cm represents 38.5 km. What is the actual distance from A to E?

16. A drilling company spent three days drilling through rock. On Monday the drill reached a depth of 6.375 meters. On Tuesday, because of poor weather conditions on the surface, the operators were able to drill only a distance equal to one-third of Monday's depth. On Wednesday the drill went to a depth that was equivalent to 1.5 times the total of Monday's and Tuesday's depth. Juan was operating the drill on Monday, Russ was operating the drill on Tuesday, and Dolores was operating the drill on Wednesday. Who was operating the drill when the point was reached that was half of the final depth reached on Wednesday?

17. Bob uses a mixture of unleaded gasoline and super octane gasoline each time he fills up his tank. The unleaded sells for $1.21 per gallon, and the super octane sells for $1.47 per gallon. He filled the tank with 5.025 gallons of unleaded and 4.371 gallons of super.

    (a) What was the total number of gallons added to the tank?

    (b) What was the cost of the gasoline?

18. Place decimal points anywhere in each of the numbers in parentheses to achieve a solution that is in the desired range.

    (a) $0 < (48 + 372 + 17 + 8) < 10$

    (b) $300 < (37 \times 873) < 350$

    (c) $100 < (19773 - 2863) < 200$

    (d) $0 < (21024 \div 24) < 1$

    (e) $-50 < (18 \times (36 + 15 - 6)) < 0$

19. The total monthly rainfall for Galveston, Texas, during a particular year was reported as follows: January, 7.62 cm; February, 5.84 cm; March, 5.33 cm; April, 6.6 cm; May, 8.4 cm; June, 8.9 cm; July, 9.65 cm; August, 11.18 cm; September, 14.73 cm; October, 6.6 cm; November, 8.13 cm; December, 9.14 cm.

(a) What is the total rainfall for the year?

(b) Suppose that the following year the total rainfall increases by 3.6 cm. In addition, suppose that four of the months report no change in total monthly rainfall from the previous year, four of the months report an increase in total monthly rainfall from the previous year, and four of the months report a decrease in total monthly rainfall from the previous year. Based on this information, how might you determine the monthly rainfall amounts?

20. One cup of sherbet contains 2.4 grams of saturated fat.

(a) If a single serving consists of three-quarters of a cup of sherbet, how many grams of saturated fat are in this serving?

(b) One cup of sherbet contains 270 calories. What is the ratio of saturated fat to calories?

(c) How many calories are in a single serving of sherbet?

(d) If one cup of ice cream contains 8.9 grams of saturated fat, how many times greater is the fat content of one cup of ice cream than one cup of sherbet? (Round your answer to the nearest thousandth.)

(e) If a single serving of ice cream consists of two-thirds of a cup, how many grams of saturated fat are in a single serving? (Round your answer to the nearest hundredth.)

In Other Words

21. Explain the relationship between any fraction and its decimal equivalent.

22. The decimal equivalent of a fraction $\frac{a}{b}$ terminates at the fifth decimal place. What significance does this have when $\frac{a}{b}$ is interpreted as a quotient?

23. How is it possible for a decimal that repeats indefinitely to have a fractional equivalent?

24. The decimal equivalent of $\frac{2}{3}$ is a repeating decimal. Which will result in a more accurate product: a whole number times $\frac{2}{3}$, or a whole number times the decimal equivalent of $\frac{2}{3}$? Explain your answer.

25. From time to time, an argument has been made to dispose of the penny in our currency system. Offer an opinion on this issue. Is your argument based on mathematics, economics, practicalities, or some other viewpoint?

Cooperative Activity

26. Groups of four (preferably different groups than in the Cooperative Activity in Section 7.1)

Individual Accountability: For the next five consecutive trading days, collect closing-price stock data on the corporation that performed the best out of the four that you chose in Cooperative Activity in Section 7.1. Suppose that you had purchased 250 shares of the stock on the first of the five days at the closing price of that day. Suppose that you sold those shares at the closing price of the fifth day. Determine your profit or loss.

Group Goal: Compare the four different corporate stocks. Together, choose a single corporation that the group feels has the best performance of the four and determine each of the following amounts.

(a) The closing price of a single share of stock on the fifth day (round to the nearest penny)

(b) The cost of purchasing 750 shares at the price in part (a)

(c) The total cost of the purchase

(d) The closing price of a single share of this stock at the end of trading on the upcoming Friday

(e) The selling price of 750 shares of the stock at the price per share found in part (d)

(f) The amount received from the sale of the stock

(g) The total amount of money made or lost on the entire transaction for this corporate stock.

7.3   Percents

You have seen a variety of ways in which fractional equivalences can be represented and interpreted: as quotients, as decimals, and as ratios and rates. Yet another view of fractions is as percents, whose use (and misuse) is extremely widespread when reporting information. The word *percent* literally means "out of one hundred," or "per hundred." If you had 100 blocks before you, 18 painted red and the remainder white, you could report that 18 out of 100 are red, or 18% of the blocks are red. Likewise, if 18 of the 100 blocks are red, this leaves 82 out of the 100 to be white, or 82% white.

Applications of Percents

The origin of the percent symbol (%) is unknown. Some say that the symbol is a re-arranged version of the digits in the number 100. Others report that the symbol represents a fraction. In either case, the symbol % is usually used in place of the word *percent* when reporting information. Three forms are commonly used to represent parts per 100: the percent symbol form, the fraction form, and the decimal form. All three forms are equivalent. Examine the table below, which illustrates the equivalents of 5%, 10%, 15%, 30%, 100%, and 130%.

Percent Symbol Form	Fraction Form	Decimal Form
5%	$\frac{5}{100}$	.05
10%	$\frac{10}{100}$	.10
15%	$\frac{15}{100}$	.15
30%	$\frac{30}{100}$	.30
100%	$\frac{100}{100}$	1.00
130%	$\frac{130}{100}$	1.30

Investigation 12

In a package of candy-coated chocolate pieces, 20 out of the 50 pieces are dark brown. Express this as a ratio of dark-brown pieces to the total number of pieces in the package. Rewrite this ratio as both a decimal and a percent. Explain what the percent means in this context.

The ratio of dark-brown pieces to the total number of pieces in the package is 20:50. This ratio can be written as $\frac{20}{50}$. This fraction can be written as the equivalent decimal .4, or .40. The latter form of the decimal is read as "forty hundredths." This can also be written as $\frac{40}{100}$, which leads us to 40%.

A particular ratio exists in this package. Had this ratio remained constant and the package size increased to 100 pieces, 40 of the 100 pieces would have been dark brown.

Investigation 13

Suppose the package of candy in Investigation 12 contained 48 pieces of candy and 6 were green. What percent of the package was green? What percent of the package was not green?

Once again, set up the ratio of green pieces to total pieces. This is represented as $\frac{6}{48}$. This fraction has a decimal equivalent of .125. The decimal .125 is equivalent to $\frac{125}{1000}$. But percents have fractional equivalents that are out of 100. Therefore, to rewrite this fraction with a denominator of 100, divide both the numerator and the denominator by 10 as shown here:

$$\frac{125 \div 10}{1000 \div 10} = \frac{12.5}{100}$$

The fraction can be interpreted as 12.5 out of 100, or 12.5% ($12\frac{1}{2}$%). If 12.5% of the package is green, 87.5% of the package is not green, since 12.5% + 87.5% = 100%, or the total package.

A percent of a whole is a part of that whole. When percents are greater than 100, the part is bigger than the whole itself. Applications that involve percents usually ask one of three questions:

1. What is the part?

2. What is the whole?

3. What is the percent?

An example of each of these questions is given in Investigations 14, 15, and 16.

Investigation 14

The sales tax rate in Ulster County is $7\frac{1}{2}$%. What is the sales tax on a $20 purchase?

You are asked to find a part of $20 that will be added on as tax. The operation used here is easy to identify if we examine a similar problem. The question could have been worded as follows: Ulster County residents must pay a tax of 7.5 cents for every 100 cents in the purchase price. What is the sales tax on a $20 purchase? Or, in another equivalent form, the question could have been written as: Ulster County residents must pay as tax $\frac{7.5}{100}$ of all purchases. What is the sales tax on a $20 purchase?

Each problem statement is equivalent. Notice how the problem statement has been converted from the unfamiliar to the familiar. To solve the problem as it was first stated, solve the simpler equivalent problems of $\frac{7.5}{100} \times 20$, as shown here:

$$.075 \times 20 = 1.50$$

The sales tax is $1.50. The statement "7.5% of 20" is equivalent to ".075 × 20." To find a percent of a whole, you can solve an equivalent problem by expressing the percent as a decimal and then multiplying.

The following calculator keystroke sequences could have been used to solve this problem. Be aware that the percent key operates differently on many calculators. Some calculators require that the equal key be pressed after the percent key, whereas others do not. Experiment with your calculator to obtain the correct result of $1.50 for this problem.

| AC | .075 | × | 20 | = | | 1.50 |

| AC | 20 | × | 7.5 | % | | 1.50 |

Investigation 15

In a certain elementary school, a third-grade teacher is responsible for 20% of the third graders. If she teaches 21 students, what is the total number of third graders at this school?

Understand the Problem: What is given? You are told that 20% of a certain total is equal to 21 students.
What is unknown? You are asked to find the total number of third graders. Although this problem is asking for a different category of unknown, it has the same form as Investigation 14. A good estimate of the total number of third graders is slightly more than 100, since 20% of a class of 100 is 20 students.

Devise a Plan: Use a variable to solve this problem.

Carry Out the Plan: Let T represent the total number of third-grade students. The problem statement can be expressed symbolically as follows:

$$20\% \text{ of } T = 21$$
$$20\% \times T = 21$$
$$.20 \times T = 21$$
$$T = \frac{21}{.20} = 105$$

There are 105 third graders in this school. This number comes close to the estimate.

Look Back: The following calculator keystroke sequences could be used to determine the solution.

| AC | 21 | ÷ | .20 | = | | 105 |

| AC | 21 | ÷ | 20 | % | | 105 |

Investigation 16

In a basketball game, Dave successfully made 12 baskets out of 15 attempts. What percent of his attempts were successful?

Understand the Problem: What is given? You are told that a certain percent of 15 is equal to 12.
What is unknown? You are asked to find the percent of success.

Devise a Plan: To obtain an estimate, recognize that since $\frac{7.5}{15}$ is equivalent to $\frac{1}{2}$, or 50%, Dave's percent of success will be greater than 50%. Now use a variable to solve this problem.

Carry Out the Plan: Let $P\%$ represent the percent of success. The problem statement can be expressed symbolically as

$$P\% \times 15 = 12$$

$$P\% = \frac{12}{15} = .80$$

$$\frac{P}{100} = .80$$

$$P = .80 \times 100 = 80$$

Dave was successful on 80% of his attempts.

Look Back: The following calculator keystroke sequences could be used to solve this problem.

| AC | 12 | ÷ | 15 | = | × | 100 | = | | 80 |

| AC | 12 | ÷ | 15 | % | | 80 |

Percents Used in Consumer Mathematics

Percents play a significant role in consumer mathematics. Sales tax, discount rates, markups, interest rates, and profit margins all involve percents. Investigations 17 and 18 set operations with percents in some of these contexts.

Investigation 17

Alexis purchased a new car for \$14,500. The sales tax rate in her county is $8\frac{1}{4}\%$. She will make a down payment of \$5500. How much should she borrow from the bank in order to cover the remaining cost of the car, including tax?

To estimate the size of the "tax bite," round $8\frac{1}{4}\%$ to 10%. Ten percent of $14,500 is $1450. Alexis might estimate that the tax on her new car will come to $1200. The problem statement can be expressed symbolically as

$$14{,}500 + (14{,}500 \times 8\tfrac{1}{4}\%) - 5500 = \text{Amount of the loan}$$

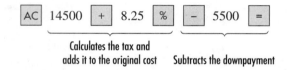

$$14{,}500 + (14{,}500 \times .0825) - 5500 =$$
$$14{,}500 + \quad 1196.25 \quad - 5500 = 10{,}196.25$$

Alexis must borrow $10,196.25.

Some calculators have the capability of calculating a percent increase in one step. On these calculators, the following keystroke sequence would yield an answer of 10,196.25.

$$\boxed{\text{AC}}\ \ 14500\ \ \boxed{+}\ \ 8.25\ \ \boxed{\%}\ \ \boxed{-}\ \ 5500\ \ \boxed{=}$$

$\underbrace{\qquad\qquad\qquad\qquad}$ $\underbrace{\qquad\qquad\qquad}$
Calculates the tax and   Subtracts the downpayment
adds it to the original cost

Investigation 18

A particular compact disc (CD) player, originally priced at $299, is on sale for 15% off the original price. What is the sale price?

To estimate the discount, realize that 10% of $300 is $30, and half of this again (an additional 5%) is $15. Therefore, the discount should be approximately $45. The problem can be expressed symbolically as

$$299 - (299 \times .15) =$$
$$299 - \quad 44.85 \quad = 254.15$$

The CD player is on sale for $254.15. Notice that the estimate of the discount, $45, was very accurate.

Some calculators have the capability of calculating a percent decrease in one step. On these calculators, the following keystroke sequence would yield the correct answer of 254.15.

Simple and Compound Interest

This application warrants special attention. Banks advertise their interest rates, but do not always specify the way in which the interest is computed. Interest is computed on the amount of money in the account, called the principal. The frequency with which the interest is computed and added to the principal determines if the interest is compounded annually, semiannually, quarterly, monthly, or daily. (There is such a thing as continuous compounding of interest, but that topic is beyond the scope of this book.)

Determining the interest on principal requires the same algorithm as determining the percent of a number. The percent used is equivalent to the interest rate paid by the bank. Examine the simple interest problem in Investigation 19, in which the interest is compounded once a year (annually).

Investigation 19

If $15,000 is invested at an interest rate of 6% compounded annually, what will be the balance in the account at the end of 2 years, assuming that no deposits or withdrawals are made during that 2-year period?

The interest earned on this money will be determined in the same way as the sales tax was determined on Alexis's car in Investigation 17.

$$15,000 + (15,000 \times .06) = 15,900$$

$$\underbrace{15,000}_{\text{Principal}} + \underbrace{(15,000 \times .06)}_{\substack{\text{Interest at the} \\ \text{end of 1 year}}} = \underbrace{15,900}_{\substack{\text{New Principal at the} \\ \text{end of 1 year}}}$$

$$\underbrace{15,900}_{\substack{\text{Principal at} \\ \text{the beginning} \\ \text{of the second} \\ \text{year}}} + \underbrace{(15,900 \times .06)}_{\substack{\text{Interest at the} \\ \text{end of the second} \\ \text{year}}} = \underbrace{16,854}_{\substack{\text{Balance in the} \\ \text{account at the} \\ \text{end of two years}}}$$

The balance in the account at the end of two years would be $16,854.

Investigation 20

How would the amount of interest change if the bank had compounded the interest quarterly rather than annually in Investigation 19?

When interest is compounded quarterly, it is computed and added to the principal four times a year. Since only one quarter of the year constitutes the interest period, the principal can earn only one quarter of the annual interest. It is for this reason that the interest at the end of any period is determined by dividing the annual interest by 4. The following table illustrates the growth of principal over the two-year period. Interest amounts have been rounded to the nearest penny.

Interest Period	Principal	Interest		New Principal
1	$15,000.00	$\dfrac{15,000 \times .06}{4}$	= 225	$15,225.00
2	$15,225.00	$\dfrac{15,225 \times .06}{4}$	= 228.38	$15,453.38
3	$15,453.38	$\dfrac{15,453.38 \times .06}{4}$	= 231.80	$15,685.18
4	$15,685.18	$\dfrac{15,685.18 \times .06}{4}$	= 235.28	$15,920.46
5	$15,920.46	$\dfrac{15,920.46 \times .06}{4}$	= 238.81	$16,159.27
6	$16,159.27	$\dfrac{16,159.27 \times .06}{4}$	= 242.39	$16,401.66
7	$16,401.66	$\dfrac{16,401.66 \times .06}{4}$	= 246.02	$16,647.68
8	$16,647.68	$\dfrac{16,647.68 \times .06}{4}$	= 249.72	$16,897.40

The balance at the end of two years in an account that is compounded quarterly at 6% is $16,897.40. Notice that had this same account been compounded annually, the balance would have been $16,854, a difference of $43.40. Therefore, it is to the consumer's advantage to invest money at a bank where the interest is compounded frequently.

Assessments for Section 7.3

1. Use Investigation 14 as a model. Write an equivalent problem statement for each of the following problems and then solve them.

   (a) There are 28 students registered in the class. Twenty-five percent of them were absent on March 16. How many students were absent?

   (b) Nineteen percent of Rosa's weekly salary goes to taxes. How much tax does she pay on a gross weekly salary of $700?

   (c) Only 1% of the 1000 light bulbs in a shipment were defective. How many light bulbs were defective?

2. Solve each of the following problems.

   (a) Find 18% of 58.
   (b) Find $9\frac{3}{4}$% of 80.
   (c) Find 12.5% of 150.
   (d) Find 120% of 80.
   (e) 30% of what number is 54?
   (f) $6\frac{1}{2}$% of what number is 13?
   (g) 7.5% of what number is 135?
   (h) 110% of what number is 55?
   (i) What percent of 25 is 20?
   (j) Express $\dfrac{2\frac{1}{2}}{25}$ as an equivalent percent.
   (k) Express $\dfrac{14}{16}$ as an equivalent percent.

3. A large bag of candy-coated chocolate pieces contains 8 red pieces, 16 green pieces, 12 yellow pieces, 24 dark-brown pieces, and 20 light-brown pieces. Each color is what percent of the bag?

4. A coat originally sold for $240. It is presently on sale at 30% off the original price.

(a) What is the discount?

(b) What is the sale price?

5. Crazy Freddie marks down all appliances by 5% off the retail price. What is the markdown and the markdown price for a washing machine that retails at $350?

6. The Asher Family is driving to Florida. They set out on Monday and drove a total of 500 miles that day. On Tuesday they drove 60% of Monday's distance. On Wednesday they drove 40% of Tuesday's distance. On Thursday they drove 120% of Tuesday's distance. What was the total mileage driven over the four-day period?

7. A certain company packages cookies in boxes that are sold by weight. The computerized assembly line removes any boxes that are more than 1% overweight or more than 1% underweight. What is the range of acceptable weights of a 2-kilogram package of cookies?

8. The manufacturer lists the price of a dining room set at $1200. The store owner marks up the price by 15%. After three months, when the set does not sell, the store owner reduces the price by 10%. The Gibsons purchase the set at the sale price. They must pay 9% sales tax for their purchase. What is the total cost of the dining room set, with tax?

9. Last year, 800 freshman enrolled at a certain university. This year, 976 freshmen enrolled. What percent increase over last year's enrollment is this year's enrollment?

10. Forty-five percent of the people surveyed chose Brand A soft drink in a taste test. There were 144 people who chose Brand A. How many people were surveyed?

11. One ounce of a fortified breakfast cereal contains 3 grams of protein. The nutrition label on the box states that this represents 4% of the U.S. Recommended Daily Allowance of protein. How many grams of protein constitute the recommended daily allowance?

12. Three-quarters of an ounce of a powdered chocolate malt beverage mix contains 8% of the U.S. Recommended Daily Allowance (U.S. RDA) of phosphorus. How many ounces of the beverage mix would constitute 100% of the U.S. RDA of phosphorus?

13. Marina deposited $2000 in a certificate account that compounded interest annually at $5\frac{1}{2}\%$. Assuming that she did not alter the balance during the year, what was the new balance at the end of the year after the interest was posted to the account?

14. What is the minimum amount of money that Liz must deposit in a savings account that compounds interest annually at 6% in order to receive $300 in interest at the end of the year?

15. What annual percentage rate would yield $200 in interest on a principal of $2500 at the end of one year?

16. Gabby deposited $8000 in a savings account that compounds interest quarterly at 7%. What will her balance be at the end of the second quarter?

17. Adrianna deposited $8000 in a savings account that compounds interest monthly at 7%. What will her balance be at the end of the second month?

18. Marty won $50,000 in a state lottery. The government took 36% of his winnings in taxes. He deposited 65% of the remaining money in a savings certificate that compounds interest annually at $8\frac{1}{4}\%$. He had to pay an income tax of 15% on the interest that he made on this account at the end of one year. How much income tax did he pay on the interest.

19. There are 5000 seats in a theater. Twenty percent of the seats are on the stage level. Fifty percent of the seats are one level above the stage. The remainder of the seats are on the second level above the stage. At last night's concert, 90% of the second-level seats were sold. How many second-level seats were not sold for this concert?

20. Allison, Elizabeth, and Katie opened up a yogurt store. Allison owns 35% of the business, Elizabeth owns 32% of the business, and Katie owns the remainder of the business. The initial expenditure to open the yogurt store was $80,000. At the end of the year, the store had made $120,000. Twenty percent of the difference between the end-of-year revenue and the initial expense was considered profit. What is each of the owner's share of the profit?

In Other Words

21. If an item is discounted the same percent as the sales tax rate, what effect does it have on the amount paid by the customer? Explain your logic.

22. What might "an allowable percent of error" mean?

23. Many people leave a waiter or a waitress a 15% tip. In certain states, a good approximation of what to leave as a tip is found by doubling the sales tax. What might the sales tax rate be in those states?

24. When someone states that your changes are "50-50," what might this mean?

25. Do the following two statements always yield the same result? Explain your answer.

$$X\% \text{ of } Y \qquad Y\% \text{ of } X$$

Cooperative Activity

26. Groups of three (Before beginning this activity, review Investigation 20 on page 317.)

Individual Accountability: Each group member is to solve the following problem: Suppose you deposit $20,000 at 6% interest compounded monthly on January 1. If you do not make any deposits or withdrawals, what is the balance at the end of each month for the entire year?

Group Goal: Compare the results from the individual problem. Together, determine why the following calculator keystroke sequences can each be used to solve the problem.

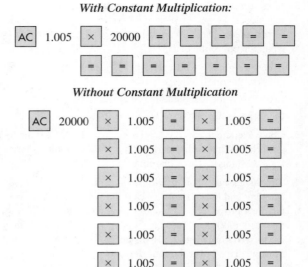

With Constant Multiplication:

Without Constant Multiplication

■
7.4 Decimals in Context: Linear Metric Measurement

In Chapter 6 we examined fractions in the context of the English standard system of linear measurement. The metric system of measurement is very different from the English standard system, both in origin and in structure. The English standard system evolved over time, and the origins of its units were arbitrary. The metric system, on the other hand, was developed in its entirety at about the time of the French Revolution. The French Academy of Sciences determined the distance from the North Pole to the equator along the meridian that passes through Paris. One ten-millionth $\left(\frac{1}{10,000,000}\right)$ of this distance was chosen to represent 1 **meter**. The meter is the basis for metric measurement. The metric system is an important decimal system of measurement and is used extensively around the world.

meter

Linear Measurement Using the Metric System

Visualizing one ten-millionth of the distance from the North Pole to the equator is virtually impossible. It is more reasonable to remember that a meter is approximately the distance from the floor to a door knob on an average door, or the length of a baseball bat. For ease of conversion from one unit to another within the metric system, each unit of measurement is related to every other unit of measurement by a power of 10. The name of each metric unit of measurement is formed by a prefix and a root unit. The prefixes are the same whether you are measuring length, weight (mass), or capacity. The root unit for measuring length is the meter; the root unit for measuring mass is the **gram**; and the root unit for measuring capacity is the **liter**. The uses of the gram and the liter as root units of measurement are addressed in Chapter 11.

gram, liter

The relationships among the metric units of linear measure are illustrated in the following table. (Notice that the prefixes used throughout the metric system are set in boldface type.)

Unit	Symbol	Relationship to Root Unit	
kilometer	km	1000	meters
hectometer	hm	100	meters
dekameter	dam	10	meters
meter	m		Root unit
decimeter	dm	.1	meter
centimeter	cm	.01	meter
millimeter	mm	.001	meter

kilo-
hecto-
deka-

deci-
centi-
milli-

Decimeters, centimeters, and millimeters are units of measurement smaller than 1 meter. These units can be clearly identified on a meter stick. Since 1 decimeter is equivalent to .1 meter, 10 decimeters equal 1 meter. The actual length of 1 decimeter is pictured in Figure 7.2.

Figure 7.2

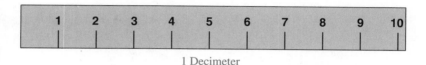

1 Decimeter

Since 1 centimeter is equivalent to .01 meter, 100 centimeters equal 1 meter. The actual length of 1 centimeter is pictured in Figure 7.3. Finally, since 1 millimeter is equivalent to .001 meter, 1000 millimeters equal 1 meter. The actual length of 1 millimeter is also shown in Figure 7.3.

Figure 7.3

cm   mm

The convenience of the metric system is obvious. You already know that 10 decimeters equal 1 meter. Examine 1 decimeter. How many centimeters are equivalent to 1 decimeter? The answer is 10. Ten centimeters equal 1 decimeter. Now examine 1 millimeter. How many millimeters are equivalent to 1 centimeter? Again, the answer is 10. Ten millimeters equal 1 centimeter. These units are related to one another as multiples or quotients of 10. The same relationship holds with units that are greater than 1 meter: 10 meters equal 1 dekameter; 10 dekameters equal 1 hectometer; and 10 hectometers equal 1 kilometer. Because multiplying and dividing by a power of 10 results in a shift of the decimal point to the right and left, respectively, it is simple to convert from one unit to another within the metric system. Examine Investigation 21.

Investigation 21

Three windows are side by side in a living room. The width of each window is indicated in the following illustration.

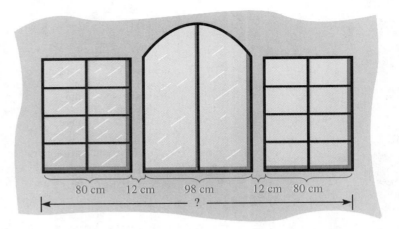

What is the total width in meters represented by the question mark in this illustration?

   The total width in centimeters can be found by finding the sum of the individual widths.

$$80 + 12 + 98 + 12 + 80 = 282 \text{ cm}$$

The total width is 282 centimeters. Now examine the following chart, which illustrates the relationships among the metric units. (Notice that this includes the same information as the table on page 321 but is set up horizontally rather than vertically to better illustrate the movement of the decimal point.)

1000 m	100 m	10 m	1 m	.1 m	.10 m	.001 m
kilo	hecto	deka	root	deci	centi	milli

Set up the symbolic notation for the problem statement in such a way that when reading from left to right the unknown unit of measure is to the right.

$$282 \text{ cm} = \underline{\hspace{1cm}} \text{ m}$$

Since 1 centimeter is equal to .01 meter, to convert from centimeters to meters, it is necessary to multiply by .01. This multiplication moves the decimal point two places to the left. Therefore, 282 centimeters are equivalent to 2.82 meters. Notice that the root unit, 1 meter, is two places to the left of the unit centimeter. The relative positions of each unit on the chart determine the movement of the decimal when converting from one unit to another.

Investigation 22

A company manufactures machinery parts on an assembly line. The work order calls for a part that is 2.5 centimeters wide. The computer has been programmed to reject any defective parts that are greater than 2% above or below the acceptable width. (a) What are the boundaries of acceptable widths? (b) What is the length of this range in millimeters?

Understand the Problem: You are told that a computerized assembly line is programmed to reject any part greater than 2% above or below an acceptable width of 2.5 centimeters. You are asked to determine the boundaries of acceptability and express them in centimeters and millimeters.

Devise a Plan:
subgoals

This question has several parts. The solution involves setting **subgoals,** which are intermediate goals that are necessary to achieve in order to attain the major goal, the solution of the problem.

Carry Out the Plan:

Subgoal #1. Determine 2% of 2.5.

Subgoal #2. Determine the upper bound of the acceptable range.

Subgoal #3. Determine the lower bound of the acceptable range.

Subgoal #4. Determine the difference between the upper bound and the lower bound; convert this difference to millimeters.

Once you have decided what your subgoals should be, carry out the computations they entail:

1. Two percent of 2.5 can be determined using the following equation:

$$.02 \times 2.5 = .05$$

The computer will reject any part whose width is .05 centimeter above 2.5 centimeters or .05 centimeter below 2.5 centimeters.

2. The upper bound is determined by adding .05 to 2.5. This sum is 2.55 centimeters.

3. The lower bound is determined by subtracting .05 from 2.5. This difference is 2.45 centimeters.

4. The difference between the lower bound and the upper bound is 2.55 – 2.45, or .1 centimeter. Use the chart in Investigation 21 to convert this measurement from centimeters to millimeters:

$$.1 \text{ cm} = \underline{\hspace{1cm}} \text{ mm}$$

Since there are 10 millimeters in 1 centimeter, it is necessary to multiply .1 by 10. In so doing, the decimal point moves to the right one place. This can also be seen by the relative positions in the chart of the centimeter and the millimeter. The millimeter is one position to the right of the centimeter. Therefore, the difference between the lower bound and the upper bound is 1 millimeter, or approximately the thickness of one dime.

Look Back: Does this answer make sense? Test a variety of width sizes that might be acceptable and unacceptable. Once you have sorted these into the two categories, check to see if the acceptable ones indeed fall within the 2% range.

To help you become more familiar with the metric system, study the following table, which offers examples of common uses of metric units of length. Notice that the hectometer, dekameter, and decimeter are missing from this table. These units of measure are rarely used when reporting real-world data.

Situation	English Standard System	Metric Measurement
Travel distances	Miles	Kilometers (1km ≈ .6 mi)
Room dimensions	Yards or feet	Meters (1m ≈ 1.1 yd); (1 m ≈ 3.3 ft)
People's height	Feet or inches	Centimeters (1 cm ≈ .4 in)
Socket wrenches	Inches	Millimeters (1 mm ≈ .04 in)

The following examples of metric measurements should give you a better sense of how linear measurements within the metric system compare to the English standard system measurements you are probably more used to.

- The distance from Los Angeles, California, to New York, New York, is approximately 4000 kilometers.

- The distance from Dallas, Texas, to Chicago, Illinois, is approximately 1400 kilometers.

- An average-size classroom measures approximately 8 meters by 8 meters.

- An average-size door measures approximately 1 meter by 2.5 meters.

- An average woman's height is approximately 170 centimeters.

- An average infant's length is approximately 50 centimeters.

- The length of a pen is approximately 15 centimeters.

- The seat of a chair is approximately 55 centimeters from the floor.

- The thickness of a textbook might be approximately 35 millimeters.

Linear Measurement Using Scientific Notation

For convenience, positive numbers that are very large or very small are often reported in a form that uses powers of 10. Rather than writing long strings of digits to express such numbers, the numbers are written in the form of a product. This product consists of a factor greater than or equal to 1 and less than 10, and a factor of the form 10 raised to an integer power. The form $A \times 10^b$, where A and b are limited as mentioned here, is **scientific notation** called **scientific notation**. Scientific notation usually reports an approximate value rather than an actual value. For example, the approximate maximum distance from the planet Pluto to earth is 7,430,400,000 kilometers. This distance can be converted to scientific notation in the following manner.

significant digits Determine the degree of accuracy you need to report, or the number of original digits that must be maintained. This process is known as identifying the **significant digits**. If you need the scientific notation to have three significant digits, then 7, 4, and 3 will be called significant and will be used in the first factor. The second factor will supply the appropriate power of 10 to correctly interpret the first factor. Therefore, this number in scientific notation is 7.43×10^9. Compare the original number to the product of 7.43 and 10^9 to see the accuracy that has been lost.

Actual distance = 7,430,400,000

$$7.43 \times 10^9 = 7,430,000,000$$

Numbers between 0 and 1 can also be reported in scientific notation. To do so, it is necessary to understand the concept of a negative exponent. Examine the following lists. Look for a pattern.

Place Value	*Exponential Form*
10,000	10^4
1000	10^3
100	10^2
10	10^1
1	10^0
$\dfrac{1}{10}$	10^{-1}
$\dfrac{1}{100}$	10^{-2}
$\dfrac{1}{1000}$	10^{-3}

Notice that a negative exponent is used to denote division by powers of 10, but a positive exponent is used to denote multiplication by powers of 10. In general,

$$10^{-N} = \frac{1}{10^N}$$

For example, the mass of an object on Pluto is .0025 of its mass on earth. This number can be represented in scientific notation using two significant digits. Zero is never used as a leading significant digit. Therefore, .0025 can be written as 2.5×10^{-3}. This can be interpreted either as

$$2.5 \times \frac{1}{1000} \qquad \text{or} \qquad 2.5 \div 1000$$

In contexts other than scientific notation, the negative exponent is not restricted to a base of 10. In general, for any nonzero number X,

$$X^{-N} = \frac{1}{X^N}$$

The justification for this notation has its basis in the algebra of exponents and can be clearly seen in the example that follows, where $N = 1$. Assume a and b are integers with $b = a + 1$. Then,

$$\frac{X^a}{X^b} = \frac{X^a}{X^{a+1}} = \frac{X \times X \times X \times \cdots \times X}{X \times X \times X \times \cdots \times X \times X} = \frac{1}{X}$$

since there is one more factor of X in the denominator. Therefore,

$$\frac{X^a}{X^{a+1}} = X^{a-(a+1)} = X^{-1} = \frac{1}{X}$$

The rules for exponents that were outlined in Chapter 4 for positive exponents hold for any nonzero integer exponents. Let X and Y be any nonzero numbers. Let a and b be nonzero integers. Then,

$$X^a \times X^b = X^{a+b}$$

$$(X^a)^b = X^{ab}$$

$$\frac{X^a}{X^b} = X^{a-b}$$

$$(XY)^a = X^a \times Y^a$$

$$\left(\frac{X}{Y}\right)^a = \frac{X^a}{Y^a}$$

$$\left(\frac{X}{Y}\right)^{-a} = \frac{X^{-a}}{Y^{-a}} = \frac{\frac{1}{X^a}}{\frac{1}{Y^a}} = \frac{Y^a}{X^a}$$

These properties can be used when performing operations on numbers expressed in scientific notation. Examine Investigations 23 and 24.

Investigation 23

The maximum distance from the earth to the sun is 9.46×10^7 miles. The maximum distance from the planet Neptune to the sun is 2.82×10^9 miles. Assume that the two planets are aligned at these distances. How far would earth be from Neptune?

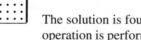

The solution is found by subtracting the smaller distance from the larger distance. This operation is performed only on the decimal portion of the scientific notation. In order to add or subtract, both numbers must be multiplied by the same power of 10. Therefore, 2.82×10^9 can be rewritten as

$$2.82 \times 10^2 \times 10^7 = 2.82 \times 100 \times 10^7 = 282 \times 10^7$$

The subtraction can now be performed as follows:

$$(282 \times 10^7) - (9.46 \times 10^7) = (282 - 9.46) \times 10^7$$
$$= 272.54 \times 10^7 \text{ miles}$$

To report this number in scientific notation, use three significant digits and adjust the exponent accordingly. Therefore, Neptune is approximately 2.73×10^9 miles from earth when the planets are aligned as stated above.

Investigation 24

The approximate diameter of an atomic nucleus is 3.2×10^{-13} centimeters. If light travels at approximately 3.0×10^{10} centimeters per second, how long will it take for light to traverse this distance?

Understand the Problem: You are given a distance and a rate. You are asked to determine the time it takes for light to travel this distance at the given rate.

Devise a Plan: Use variables and the relationship among distance, rate, and time.

Carry Out the Plan: You already know that distance can be determined by the product of the rate and the time traveled $(D = R \times T)$. Therefore, the unknown time is equal to the quotient of the distance and the rate $\left(T = \frac{D}{R}\right)$. It is necessary to divide the diameter of the nucleus by the speed of light and to use dimensional analysis to determine the unit of measure for the outcome.

$$\frac{(3.2 \times 10^{-13}) \text{ cm}}{(3.0 \times 10^{10}) \frac{\text{cm}}{\text{sec}}}$$

First, divide the decimal factors:

$$\frac{3.2}{3.0} = 1.067$$

Second, use the rules of exponents to continue the division operation. Notice that for both multiplication and division of numbers written in scientific notation it is not necessary to express the numbers with the same powers of 10.

$$\frac{10^{-13}}{10^{10}} = 10^{(-13 - 10)} = 10^{-23}$$

Using dimensional analysis, determine the units of the answer as follows:

$$\frac{\text{cm}}{\frac{\text{cm}}{\text{sec}}} = \text{cm} \times \frac{\text{sec}}{\text{cm}} = \text{sec}$$

(The numbers have been omitted to make it easier for you to see the process.) Light takes 1.067×10^{-23} seconds to travel across the atomic nucleus.

Look Back: Although it may be difficult to get a feel as to whether or not your answer is correct, you can check your work by using the solution. Since $D = RT$, the product of the rate and the time determined should be equal to the distance. We leave it to you to verify this solution.

Some calculators automatically convert very large and very small numbers to scientific notation. Examine the following keystroke sequences and their respective displays.

| AC | 98765432 | × | 1000 | = | 9.8765 E 10 |

| AC | .0001258 | × | .000009 | = | 1.322 E –9 |

In the first case, the display $\boxed{9.875\,\text{E}10}$ is interpreted as 9.875×10^{10}. In the second case, $\boxed{1.1322\,\text{E}-9}$ is interpreted as 1.1322×10^{-9}.

Certain calulators have a key labeled $\boxed{\text{EE}}$. This allows you to enter numbers in scientific notation. Examine the following keystroke sequence, which finds the product of 450,000,000 and 32,000. You must first convert the factors into scientific notation, since the display may not be large enough to accommodate the numbers in standard notation.

$$450,000,000 = 4.5 \times 10^8 \qquad 32,000 = 3.2 \times 10^4$$

| AC | 4.5 | EE | 8 | × | 3.2 | EE | 4 | = | 1.44 E 13 |

The display is interpreted as 1.44×10^{13}, which is equivalent to 14,400,000,000,000. This number is read as fourteen trillion, four hundred billion.

Assessments for Section 7.4

1. Choose the most reasonable answer for each of the following measurements.
   (a) Height of a door: 2.5 cm   2.5 m   25 m   .25 km   .025 km
   (b) Length of a credit card: 7 cm   .7 cm   .7 m   7 mm   .07 cm
   (c) Height of a tree: 8 mm   8 cm   8 m   .8 km   .008 m
   (d) Diameter of a quarter: .23 cm   .023 mm   2.3 mm   2.3 cm   .0023 mm
   (e) Distance from Los Angeles, California, to Houston, Texas: 210 km   2.1 km   210,000 km   2100 km   210,000 m
   (f) Height of the Empire State Building: 5000 m   50 km   5 km   500 m   .5 km

2. Fill in the blank with the correct measurement.
   (a) 10 km = _____ m
   (b) 10 m = _____ km
   (c) 3.5 cm = _____ mm
   (d) 8 mm = _____ cm
   (e) .04 m = _____ mm
   (f) 5.5 km = _____ mm
   (g) 10,000 mm = _____ km
   (h) (5×10^3) cm = _____ m

   (i) (2.6×10^{-7}) km = _____ m
   (j) (1.47×10^{-5}) m = _____ mm

3. Give an approximate metric measurement for each of the following.
   (a) Length of a toothbrush
   (b) Distance around your wrist
   (c) Width of a door
   (d) Height of a 10-story building
   (e) Length of a couch
   (f) Thickness of an index card
   (g) Distance from Washington, D.C., to Boston, Massachusetts
   (h) Length of a tennis racket
   (i) Height of a soda can
   (j) Thickness of this textbook

4. On a map, 1 cm represents 45 km. What is the actual distance in kilometers between two cities that are 5.5 cm apart on the map? What is this actual distance in meters?

5. Last year the length of a race was 25 km. This year the planning committee increased the length by 15%.
   (a) What is the new distance that is to be run?
   (b) How many meters longer is this year's race than last year's race?

6. The distance from the floor to the ceiling in the den of a home is 2.8 m. A carpenter is building shelves across one of the walls. Each shelf is 3 cm thick. The distance between each shelf must be at least 34 cm. The first shelf must start 50 cm off the ground. How many such shelves are possible?

7. A desk measures 1.2 m across. An upright piano measures 1.36 m across. Two bookshelves are each 61 cm across. All of this furniture is arranged along a wall that is 4 m long. Can a file cabinet that measures 40 cm across also fit along this wall?

8. Choose the better price in each pair.

  (a) 1.25 m of ribbon for $3.25
    $1\frac{1}{4}$ yds of ribbon for $3.25

  (b) 3.5 m of wood molding for $7
    .35 m of wood molding for $.75

  (c) 2.5 m of telephone cord for $35
    200 cm of telephone cord for $26

9. A certain brand of ballpoint pen refills are 15 cm long. The manufacturer rejects any refills that are greater than 2% above or below this length. What is the acceptable range of refill lengths in both centimeters and millimeters?

10. The plans for a rectangular addition to a house show dimensions of 4.5 m by 5 m. If the builder decreases the shorter side by 10% and the longer side by 6%, what are the new dimensions of the room?

11. A new model of car is 420 cm long.

  (a) How many such cars can fit end to end in a showroom that is 25 m long?

  (b) Suppose the dealer wants to leave at least 1 m between each car and between the cars and the showroom walls. How many cars can be aligned according to these specifications?

12. The odometer on a car read 23,745 km at the beginning of a trip. At the end of the trip, the odometer reads 24,008 km. If the car averaged 80 km/hr on this trip, approximately how long did the trip take?

13. A ski resort reports a snow base of 140 cm. During the night, 15 cm of new snow accumulated. What is the percent of increase to the nearest tenth?

14. Use the ruler below to answer the following questions. Report your answers in centimeters and millimeters.

  (a) What is the distance from A to B?

  (b) What is the distance from A to C?

  (c) How much longer is the distance from C to E than the distance from D to F?

  (d) Which two letters identify the endpoints of a distance that is 10% greater than the distance from B to C?

  (e) Which two letters identify the endpoints of a distance that is 25% less than the distance from A to D?

15. The length and width of a rectangle are in a 3 to 2 ratio. What is the width of the rectangle if the length is 1.5 m?

16. Express each of the following numbers in scientific notation using three significant digits.

  (a) 42,628,087

  (b) 1,096,945,856,000

  (c) 1,000,000

  (d) .0000045678

  (e) .123456

17. The mass of a hydrogen atom is

$$0.00000000000000000000000000167 \text{ kg}$$

Express this number in scientific notation.

18. Write each of the following numbers in scientific notation using three significant digits, and then perform the indicated operation. Express the answer in scientific notation using three significant digits.

  (a) The sum of 536,874,823,987 and 673,000,003

  (b) The difference between 894,732,925 and 87,098

  (c) The quotient of 101,876,463 and 74,097

  (d) The product of .000234 and .376534

  (e) The sum of .0000034, .00098543, and .12367

  (f) The square of .000000085

19. Light travels at approximately 3.0×10^{10} cm/sec. If it takes 1.3 sec for light from the moon to reach the earth, approximately how far away is the moon from the earth in kilometers? Express your answer in scientific notation.

20. Light travels at approximately 3.0×10^{10} cm/sec. If it takes 8 years for light to travel from a particular star to the earth, approximately how far away is the star? Express your answer in scientific notation.

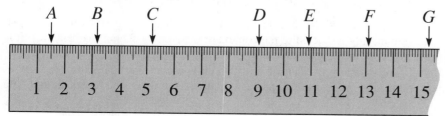

In Other Words

21. Describe three important differences between the metric system and the English standard system of measurement.

22. Explain the use of commutative and associative properties when multiplying two numbers in scientific notation.

23. In the discussion of negative exponents of the form X^{-n}, X was limited to nonzero values. Why was this done?

24. Explain how the following equivalence is established:

$$\frac{\frac{1}{X^a}}{\frac{1}{Y^a}} = \frac{Y^a}{X^a}$$

25. Describe a real-world situation appropriate for this text that would necessitate the use of millimeters as a unit of measurement.

Cooperative Activity

26. **Groups of three**

Individual Accountability: Each member is assigned one activity to perform. The solutions to the unassigned activities should be estimated.

Tape together strips of paper (or use adding machine tape) in the indicated length. First estimate the length of the final folded piece. Then test your estimate by folding the paper as instructed.

Member A: Length = 1.5 m   Fold in half, then in thirds, then in half again.

Member B: Length = 1.75 m   Fold in thirds, then in fourths, then in half.

Member C: Length = 1.6 m   Fold in fourths, then in thirds, then in thirds again.

Group Goal: Compare your estimates with the actual measurements. Discuss how the estimates were ascertained. You will need more strips of paper or adding machine tape for this portion of the activity.

Estimate each other's height in meters. Estimate the average height of the group. Using only the paper (and tape), but no measuring devices, determine the average height of the group. Describe your method.

7.5   The Bigger Picture: Rational Numbers, Irrational Numbers, and Real Numbers

Throughout this text, we have used the number line to model a variety of sets of numbers and operations. However, the restrictions we placed on those sets of numbers consequently made the number line incomplete. In this section, the missing pieces will be filled in so that you are able to get the complete picture of our numbers and number systems.

Rational Numbers

natural numbers   You have already been introduced to the set of counting numbers, or **natural numbers**, the set of whole numbers, the set of integers, and the set of rational numbers. These sets are given formal symbols as shown here:

The set of counting numbers $N = \{1, 2, 3, 4, 5, \ldots\}$

The set of whole numbers $W = \{0, 1, 2, 3, 4, \ldots\}$

The set of integers $I = \{\ldots -3, -2, -1, 0, 1, 2, 3, \ldots\}$

The set of rational numbers $Q = \{\frac{a}{b} \mid a \text{ and } b \text{ are integers, } b \neq 0\}$

In the preceding chapters, the models and operations that were performed on rational numbers were usually restricted to the context of elementary school mathematics. It is important, however, to know how these numbers relate to each other in a broader context.

Recall the beginning of Chapter 6, in which you were introduced to a variety of fractions. Some of these fractions represented rational numbers, and others did not. The reasons for this distinction was not discussed in depth there because you needed to fully understand both fractions and decimals before such a discussion could make sense. By now, you should have such an understanding.

You now know that every rational number can be expressed in the form of a fraction. Here are some examples:

$$3 = \frac{3}{1} \qquad 5\frac{1}{3} = \frac{16}{3} \qquad 12.8 = 12\frac{8}{10} = \frac{128}{10}$$

$$-.05 = \frac{-5}{100} \qquad -6\frac{2}{3} = \frac{-20}{3} \qquad -5.99 = -5\frac{99}{100} = \frac{-599}{100}$$

You also know that to express any rational number that is in the form of a fraction as an equivalent decimal, the numerator is divided by the denominator. Some possible outcomes are

$$\frac{1}{3} = 1 \div 3 = .3333333\ldots = .\overline{3}$$

$$\frac{1}{8} = 1 \div 8 = .1250000\ldots = .125\overline{0} = .125$$

$$6\frac{1}{6} = \frac{37}{6} = 37 \div 6 = 6.16666\ldots = 6.1\overline{6}$$

$$\frac{1}{2} = 1 \div 2 = .500000\ldots = .5\overline{0} = .5$$

$$2\frac{62}{999} = \frac{2060}{999} = 2060 \div 999 = 2.062062\ldots = .2.\overline{062}$$

repeating decimals   All of the above decimals belong to the set of **repeating decimals**, since some single digit or sequence of digits repeats indefinitely in the decimal places. The set of repeating decimals is made up of two subsets: those repeating decimals that are terminating and those that are nonterminating. In a terminating decimal, the division process is completed at some point. Keep in mind that the digit 0, although not necessary at the end of .125000000 . . . (or .1250) and .50000000 . . . (or .50), can be used to express a terminating decimal as a repeating decimal. In the subset containing nonterminating decimals, the division process continues infinitely, generating a sequence of digits that repeats in the quotient. Every rational number can be expressed as a repeating decimal, and every repeating decimal can be expressed as a rational number. Because both of these statements must be true, they can be combined to form the biconditional statement that follows:

Rule: A number belongs to the set of rational numbers if and only if it can be expressed as a repeating decimal.

The properties of rational numbers that were discussed in Chapter 6 related to operations on fractions. We will now look at properties that define the relationships among rational numbers.

Order Properties of Rational Numbers
Rational numbers have four order properties:

trichotomy property

1. **The Trichotomy Property.** Let $\frac{a}{b}$ and $\frac{c}{d}$ be rational numbers. Then only one of the following three situations is true:

$$\frac{a}{b} > \frac{c}{d} \qquad ad > bc, \text{ and } \frac{a}{b} \text{ is to the right of } \frac{c}{d} \text{ on the number line}$$

$$\frac{a}{b} = \frac{c}{d} \qquad ad = bc, \text{ and } \frac{a}{b} \text{ and } \frac{c}{d} \text{ name the same position on the number line}$$

$$\frac{a}{b} < \frac{c}{d} \qquad ad < bc, \text{ and } \frac{a}{b} \text{ is to the left of } \frac{c}{d} \text{ on the number line}$$

transitive property of rational number inequalities

2. **The Transitive Property of Rational Number Inequalities.** Let $\frac{a}{b}, \frac{c}{d},$ and $\frac{e}{f}$ be rational numbers.

$$\text{If } \frac{a}{b} > \frac{c}{d} \text{ and } \frac{c}{d} > \frac{e}{f}, \text{ then } \frac{a}{b} > \frac{e}{f}$$

$$\text{If } \frac{a}{b} < \frac{c}{d} \text{ and } \frac{c}{d} < \frac{e}{f}, \text{ then } \frac{a}{b} < \frac{e}{f}$$

addition properties of rational number inequalities

3. **The Addition Properties of Rational Number Inequalities.** Let $\frac{a}{b}, \frac{c}{d},$ and $\frac{e}{f}$ be rational numbers.

$$\text{If } \frac{a}{b} > \frac{c}{d}, \text{ then } \frac{a}{b} + \frac{e}{f} > \frac{c}{d} + \frac{e}{f}$$

$$\text{If } \frac{a}{b} < \frac{c}{d}, \text{ then } \frac{a}{b} + \frac{e}{f} < \frac{c}{d} + \frac{e}{f}$$

multiplication properties of rational number inequalities

4. **The Multiplication Properties of Rational Number Inequalities.** Let $\frac{a}{b}, \frac{c}{d},$ and $\frac{e}{f}$ be rational numbers.

$$\text{If } \frac{a}{b} > \frac{c}{d} \text{ and } \frac{e}{f} > 0, \text{ then } \frac{ae}{bf} > \frac{ce}{df}$$

$$\text{If } \frac{a}{b} < \frac{c}{d} \text{ and } \frac{e}{f} > 0, \text{ then } \frac{ae}{bf} < \frac{ce}{df}$$

$$\text{If } \frac{a}{b} > \frac{c}{d} \text{ and } \frac{e}{f} < 0, \text{ then } \frac{ae}{bf} < \frac{ce}{df}$$

$$\text{If } \frac{a}{b} < \frac{c}{d} \text{ and } \frac{e}{f} < 0, \text{ then } \frac{ae}{bf} > \frac{ce}{df}$$

density property of rational numbers

dense set

The Density Property of Rational Numbers
The set of rational numbers is said to be a **dense set**, since between any two rational numbers $\frac{a}{b}$ and $\frac{c}{d}$, there exists another rational number $\frac{e}{f}$. This density property can be seen in the context of Investigation 25.

Investigation 25

A fuel gauge on an oil tank shows measurements in sixteenths. The level shows a reading somewhere between $\frac{7}{16}$ and $\frac{1}{2}$. (a) Assume that the level appears to be at the halfway mark between these two readings. What rational number can be assigned to the fuel level? (b) Assume that it is difficult to determine a specific reading by eyeing the level between $\frac{7}{16}$ and $\frac{1}{2}$. What might some other possible readings be?

(a) Determine the distance between the two endpoints, then add half of that distance to the lesser of the two endpoints, as shown here:

$$\frac{1}{2} - \frac{7}{16} = \frac{8}{16} - \frac{7}{16} = \frac{1}{16}$$

This is the distance on the gauge between the two markings.

$$\frac{1}{16} \times \frac{1}{2} = \frac{1}{32}$$

This is half the distance between the two markings. This amount will be added to $\frac{7}{16}$.

$$\frac{7}{16} + \frac{1}{32} = \frac{14}{32} + \frac{1}{32} = \frac{15}{32}$$

The reading $\frac{15}{32}$ is halfway between $\frac{7}{16}$ and $\frac{1}{2}$.

This method can be generalized to any readings A and B as follows:

$$B + \left[(A - B) \times \frac{1}{2} \right] =$$

$$B + \frac{1}{2}A - \frac{1}{2}B = \qquad \text{by the distributive property of rational numbers}$$

$$\left(B + \frac{1}{2}A \right) - \frac{1}{2}B = \qquad \text{by the associative property of rational numbers}$$

$$\left(\frac{1}{2}A + B \right) - \frac{1}{2}B = \qquad \text{by the commutative property of rational numbers}$$

$$\frac{1}{2}A + \left(B - \frac{1}{2}B \right) = \qquad \text{by the associative property of rational numbers}$$

$$\frac{1}{2}A + \frac{1}{2}B = \frac{1}{2}(A + B)$$

arithmetic mean, average

The properties of rational numbers assure us that the method used to solve the problem is equivalent to finding half of the sum of the two readings. This particular rational number, which lies halfway between A and B, is called the **arithmetic mean**, or **average**, of A and B (averages will be discussed in greater detail in Chapter 9). Therefore, the arithmetic mean of any two rational numbers lies halfway between the two numbers. The arithmetic mean can be used to verify the fact that rational numbers are dense.

(b) From part (a) we have determined that $\frac{7}{16} < \frac{15}{32} < \frac{1}{2}$. Two more rational numbers that lie between the gauge readings can be found by applying the density property and determining the average of $\frac{7}{16}$ and $\frac{15}{32}$, and the average of $\frac{15}{32}$ and $\frac{1}{2}$. These averages are $\frac{29}{64}$ and $\frac{31}{64}$, respectively.

Irrational Numbers

Examine the following nonterminating decimals:

$$.20220222022220222220\ldots \qquad \pi = 3.14159265358979\ldots$$

irrational numbers

No discernible sequence of digits repeats in either of these two decimals. In the first example, although a pattern does exist, no particular set of digits repeats. In the second example, no matter how many places of π are calculated, a pattern never repeats. Decimals of this type are called **irrational numbers**. An irrational number has a nonterminating, nonrepeating decimal representation. The first 14 decimal places of π are given in the second example above. The exact value of π cannot be written using a countable number of decimal places. However, computation with π appears in many places. For our purposes, and the purposes of elementary school classrooms, $\pi \approx \frac{22}{7}$, or $\pi \approx 3.14$. Some calculators have a $\boxed{\pi}$ key. Pressing this key displays the value of π correct to the maximum number of places in the display.

The rest of this chapter will make better sense if we briefly review the concept of square numbers. Examine Figure 7.4.

Figure 7.4

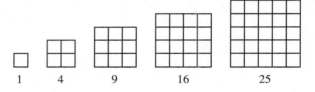

| 1 | 4 | 9 | 16 | 25 |

square numbers (perfect squares)

What would be the next term in this sequence? The sides of the square are increased by one unit in each term. Therefore, a square whose dimensions are 6 units by 6 units, containing 36 unit squares, would be the next term in the sequence. In general, a square of dimensions s by s, where s is a whole number, is composed of s^2 unit squares. This sequence generates the set of **square numbers**, or **perfect squares**. Every whole number perfect square (s^2) defines the number of square units contained within a square whose side is equal to s. Geometrically, s^2 is also the area of the square whose side is equal to s, since area is the number of unit squares that cover a closed shape.

Investigation 26 ▪

A set of children's blocks contains 256 wooden cubes. Is it possible to arrange these cubes in a configuration that forms an s by s square?

For these blocks to be arranged in an s by s square, 256 must be a perfect square. You might anticipate that the number of blocks forming the sides of the square will fall between 10 blocks and 20 blocks since $10^2 = 100$, and $20^2 = 400$. Further refining your estimate may lead you to realize that $15^2 = 225$. Therefore, the number of blocks per side must be between 15 and 20—but much closer to 15. If your next estimate is 16, you have solved the problem, since $16^2 = 256$. The blocks can be arranged in a square of dimensions 16 by 16.

square root

radical

radicand

This solution can also be obtained using a calculator. The length of a side of a square can be determined when given only the area of that square by finding the **square root** of the area. Many calculators have a square root key, $\boxed{\sqrt{\ }}$, which displays a value, s, when $\boxed{\sqrt{\ }}$ s^2 is entered. The symbol, $\sqrt{\ }$, is called the **radical**, and the number under the radical is called the **radicand**. The following keystroke sequence could be used to find the correct solution:

$$\boxed{\text{AC}} \quad 256 \quad \boxed{\sqrt{\ }}$$

The display should read 16.

It is important to recognize that $\sqrt{x}$, where x is any positive number, has two values. Examine $\sqrt{256}$. The product of 16 and 16 is equal to 256, and the product of -16 and -16 is equal to 256. Therefore, the square root of any positive number will yield two answers. Because this problem involves length, and length is represented by a positive number, only the positive square root is an acceptable solution. This positive square root is called the **principal square root**. In general, the principal square root of any whole number x is the positive value y such that $y^2 = x$. Calculators display only the principal square root of a number.

principal square root

Square roots can be rational numbers or irrational numbers. For example, $\sqrt{49}$ is equal to the rational numbers 7 and -7, and $\sqrt{.16}$ is equal to the rational numbers .4 and $-.4$. There are radicands, such as 5, 7, and 11, whose square roots result in nonterminating, nonrepeating decimal representations. The square roots of these radicands are irrational numbers.

Investigation 27

Prove that $\sqrt{2}$ is an irrational number.

Understand the Problem: You are given the number $\sqrt{2}$. You are asked to prove that it is irrational, that is, that it cannot be expressed as a rational number $\frac{x}{y}$ where x and y are integers and $y \neq 0$.

Devise a Plan: Use the problem-solving strategy of contradiction to prove that $\sqrt{2}$ is irrational.

Carry Out the Plan: First, assume that $\sqrt{2}$ is rational. Therefore, $\sqrt{2}$ can be expressed in the form $\frac{x}{y}$ where x and y are integers and $y \neq 0$.

$$\sqrt{2} = \frac{x}{y}$$

$$(\sqrt{2})^2 = \left(\frac{x}{y}\right)^2 \qquad \text{Square both sides of the equation.}$$

$$2 = \frac{x^2}{y^2}$$

$$2y^2 = x^2 \qquad \text{Multiply both sides by } y^2.$$

This equation states that $2y^2$ represents the same number as x^2. Since every whole number has a unique prime factorization, the product of primes of each of these representations must be the same. An even number of primes will appear on the right-hand side, but an odd number of primes will appear on the left-hand side (the factor 2 will supply the extra prime number). Here is our contradiction. These two representations cannot be equal; therefore, $\sqrt{2}$ cannot be expressed in the form of a rational number. If $\sqrt{2}$ is not rational, it must be irrational.

Look Back: Review the technique of contradiction. Every step must logically follow from the previous step. Work backwards from the conclusion to verify the accuracy of your work.

We began this section by talking about incomplete number lines. The rational number line is one such number line. It is filled with "holes" in places that represent irrationals such as $\sqrt{2}$, $\sqrt{5}$, $\sqrt{7}$, and so on. The location of these holes can be determined by employing a well-known geometric theorem known as the Pythagorean theorem. The origin and geometric development of this theorem will be presented in Chapter 11. For now, it is enough to establish its existence and use it to locate irrational numbers on the number line. The Pythagorean theorem states that in a right triangle (a triangle that contains a 90° angle called a right angle), the square of the side opposite the right angle (the hypotenuse) is equal to the sum of the squares of the other two sides (see Figure 7.5).

Figure 7.5

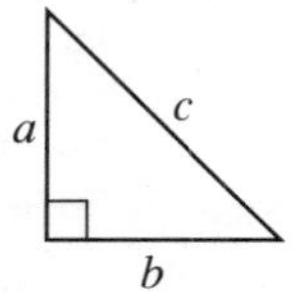

In general, $a^2 + b^2 = c^2$, where c is the hypotenuse of a right triangle and a and b are the other two sides. We will use the Pythagorean theorem in Investigation 28.

Investigation 28

Locate $\sqrt{2}$ on the number line.

Intuitively, $\sqrt{2}$ is somewhere between $\sqrt{1}$ and $\sqrt{4}$. Therefore, $1 < \sqrt{2} < 2$. We will draw a number line that focuses on the range from 0 to 2 (see below left). On this number line, a right triangle is constructed whose sides are one unit and whose hypotenuse is determined using the Pythagorean theorem.

$$1^2 + 1^2 = c^2$$
$$2 = c^2$$
$$\sqrt{2} = c$$

The length of the hypotenuse is equal to $\sqrt{2}$. The hypotenuse is fixed at 0 and rotated clockwise until it "hits" the horizontal number line. Its length is then marked off as A. The point A represents the irrational number $\sqrt{2}$ as the distance from 0 to A (see below right).

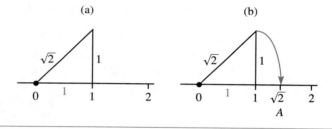

Other irrational numbers (and some rational ones) can be generated from the right triangle whose dimensions are 1 by 1 by $\sqrt{2}$, as shown in Figure 7.6.

Figure 7.6

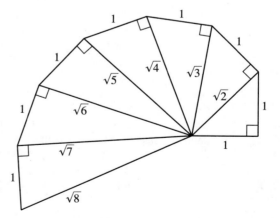

The hypotenuse of the first triangle becomes a side of the second triangle. The Pythagorean theorem is then used to generate the length of the hypotenuse of the second triangle, or $\sqrt{3}$. This process continues. Notice that repeated use of the Pythagorean theorem generates $\sqrt{n}$, where n is a whole number greater than or equal to 2.

Investigation 29

To raise money for a local charity, Marina participated in a walkathon in which people pledged to pay as many cents per kilometer as kilometers walked. If each of her sponsors paid $3.80, how many kilometers did Marina walk?

Understand the Problem: You are told that each sponsor paid $3.80, which represents as many cents per kilometer as kilometers walked. You are asked to determine the number of kilometers that Marina walked.

Devise a Plan: Use the technique of solving a simpler problem.

Carry Out the Plan: If each of Marina's sponsors had paid 25 cents, this would indicate that she had walked 5 kilometers at 5 cents per kilometer ($\sqrt{25} = 5$). If each of Marina's sponsors had paid $1.21, this would indicate that she had walked 11 kilometers at 11 cents per kilometer ($\sqrt{121} = 11$). To solve this problem, we must determine the square root of 380.

A technique for approximating the square root without a calculator involves recognizing upper bounds and lower bounds. Examine the following progression:

Lower Bound	Upper Bound	Comparison
$15^2 = 225$	$20^2 = 400$	$\sqrt{225} < \sqrt{380} < \sqrt{400}$
$18^2 = 324$	$20^2 = 400$	$\sqrt{324} < \sqrt{380} < \sqrt{400}$
$19^2 = 361$	$20^2 = 400$	$\sqrt{361} < \sqrt{380} < \sqrt{400}$

We have exhausted the whole number possibilities. It is clear from this progression that Marina walked between 19 and 20 kilometers. Choose two decimal values between 19 and 20, say 19.3 and 19.5.

$$19.3^2 = 372.49 \qquad 19.5^2 = 380.25$$

As you can see, 19.5 kilometers is a good approximation of the distance Marina walked. If a greater degree of accuracy is needed, this procedure could be continued by extending the number of decimal places in the lower bound and upper bound in order to better close in on the number 380. Assuming that Marina walked 19.5 kilometers, her sponsors had to pay 19.5 cents per kilometer. The total paid, $3.80, is a monetary amount rounded to the nearest penny for 380.25 (19.5^2).

Look Back: Use a calculator to verify the accuracy of your solution.

Real Numbers

We are now ready for one more step back (not backwards) to look at the bigger picture. The union of the set of rational numbers and the set of irrational numbers is called the **real numbers** set of **real numbers** *(R)*. Real numbers can take a variety of forms: whole numbers, integers, fractions, and decimals. The fractions can be of the type $\frac{\sqrt{5}}{2}$, $\frac{2}{\sqrt{7}}$, or any $\frac{x}{y}$ where $y \neq 0$. The decimals can be repeating, nonrepeating, terminating, or nonterminating. The four basic operations are defined on the real numbers as they were defined on the rational numbers (see Chapter 6). The closure properties, commutative properties, and associative properties hold for both addition and multiplication. Zero is the unique additive identity element for the real numbers, and 1 is the unique multiplicative identity. For every real number x, $-x$ is its unique additive inverse; and for every nonzero real number y, $\frac{1}{y}$ is its unique multiplicative inverse. The distributive property of multiplication over addition holds for the real numbers, and the real numbers are a dense set. The real number line is a complete number line with no gaps.

Investigation 30

The braking distance of a car is related to the speed of the car. A car was traveling on a wet, concrete road when the driver applied the brakes and left a 50-foot skid mark. A good approximation of the speed the driver was going can be determined by finding the square root of the product of 12 and the length of the skid. Approximately how fast was the driver going?

Understand the Problem: What is given? You are told that the skid mark is 50 feet long and that multiplying this number by 12 and taking the square root of the product will approximate the speed of the car.
What is unknown? You are looking for the speed of the car.

Devise a Plan: The problem-solving strategy of using a variable can be employed here. Let S represent that speed.

Carry Out the Plan: Set up an equation and solve for S:

$$S = \sqrt{12 \times 50}$$
$$= \sqrt{600}$$

Since 600 is not a perfect square, the speed, S, is an irrational number. Its decimal equivalent can only be approximated. Use the method called "divide and average" to approximate the square root as outlined here.

1. Estimate the square root of 600. Since $20^2 = 400$ and $30^2 = 900$, an estimate should fall somewhere in between these two. Try 25. Divide the radicand, 600, by 25.

$$\boxed{AC} \quad 600 \quad \boxed{\div} \quad 25 \quad \boxed{=}$$

The display should read 24. You have now determined that the square root of 600 falls between 24 and 25.

2. Take the average of these two boundaries and repeat step 1 using the average as the divisor.

The display should read 24.489796. The square root of 600 lies between 24.489796 and 24.5. Average these two boundaries and once again divide.

$$\boxed{\text{AC}}\ \ 24.489796\ \ \boxed{+}\ \ 24.5\ \ \boxed{=}\ \ \boxed{\div}\ \ 2\ \ \boxed{=}$$

The display should read 24.494898. This process can be continued as many times as you wish. To check the degree of accuracy of 24.494898 as the square root of 600, square it. The square of 24.494898 is 600.00003. This is a reasonable and acceptable approximation. Therefore, the car was traveling at about 24.5 miles per hour.

Of course if your calculator has a square root key, this problem could have been solved with the following keystroke sequence:

$$\boxed{\text{AC}}\ \ 600\ \ \boxed{\sqrt{\ }}$$

The display should read 24.494897. This is only a .000001 difference from our estimate using the "divide-and-average" method, which may not be fast, but certainly is accurate.

Assessments for Section 7.5

1. Express each of the following numbers as rational numbers in the form a/b where a and b are both integers and $b \neq 0$.

   (a) $2\frac{2}{5}$ (b) 5.09   (c) .875   (d) $-3\frac{1}{4}$

   (e) -7.45 (f) $.\overline{3}$ (g) $-3.\overline{12}$

2. Determine two rational numbers that lie between the two given numbers.

   (a) 1.2, 1.22   (b) $\frac{2}{3}, \frac{7}{10}$ (c) $-\frac{11}{12}, -\frac{5}{6}$

   (d) $.05, \frac{3}{50}$ (e) $\frac{1}{10}, .\overline{1}$ (f) $.3\overline{1}, .\overline{3}$

3. The gauge on the dashboard of a car looks as follows:

   (a) What rational boundaries might this reading fall between?

   (b) Use your answer in part (a) to narrow the boundaries.

   (c) What is the difference between the lower boundary and the upper boundary?

   (d) Suppose that the gas tank holds 16 gallons when full. If the tank contained 10.8 gallons of gas at the time of the reading, express the gauge reading as a rational number.

4. The decimal representation of π is 3.14159265328979, correct to 14 places. The rational number $\frac{22}{7}$ is often used as a good approximation of π.

   (a) For how many decimal places do the decimal equivalents of $\frac{22}{7}$ and π match?

   (b) Some people have used the rational number $\frac{355}{113}$ as an approximation of π. How well does the decimal equivalent of this rational number compare with π?

5. In the mid-1600s, an English mathematician named John Wallis proved that the following infinite product was equal to $\pi/2$:

   $$\frac{2}{1} \times \frac{2}{3} \times \frac{4}{3} \times \frac{4}{5} \times \frac{6}{5} \times \frac{6}{7} \times \frac{8}{7} \times \frac{8}{9} \times \cdots$$

   (a) Describe the pattern that generates the terms of this infinite product.

   (b) What are the next three terms of the infinite product?

   (c) A decimal approximation of π correct to 14 decimal places is 3.14159265328979. What would be the decimal approximation of $\pi/2$ correct to 14 decimal places?

   (d) Complete the following chart:

Number of Terms	Product of Rational Numbers	Decimal Equivalent
1	$\frac{2}{1}$	?
2	$\frac{2}{1} \times \frac{2}{3}$	?
3	$\frac{2}{1} \times \frac{2}{3} \times \frac{4}{3}$	?
4	$\frac{2}{1} \times \frac{2}{3} \times \frac{4}{3} \times \frac{4}{5}$	?
5	$\frac{2}{1} \times \frac{2}{3} \times \frac{4}{3} \times \frac{4}{5} \times \frac{6}{5}$	?
6	$\frac{2}{1} \times \frac{2}{3} \times \frac{4}{3} \times \frac{4}{5} \times \frac{6}{5} \times \frac{6}{7}$	?
7	$\frac{2}{1} \times \frac{2}{3} \times \frac{4}{3} \times \frac{4}{5} \times \frac{6}{5} \times \frac{6}{7} \times \frac{8}{7}$	?
8	$\frac{2}{1} \times \frac{2}{3} \times \frac{4}{3} \times \frac{4}{5} \times \frac{6}{5} \times \frac{6}{7} \times \frac{8}{7} \times \frac{8}{9}$	?
9	$\frac{2}{1} \times \frac{2}{3} \times \frac{4}{3} \times \frac{4}{5} \times \frac{6}{5} \times \frac{6}{7} \times \frac{8}{7} \times \frac{8}{9} \times \frac{10}{9}$	?

(e) How close was the approximation of $\pi/2$ using nine terms to the approximation that you determined in part (c)?

6. In 1674 a German mathematician named von Leibniz proposed the following for π:

$$\pi = 4 \times \left(1 - \frac{1}{3} + \frac{1}{5} - \frac{1}{7} + \frac{1}{9} - \frac{1}{11} + \frac{1}{13} - \cdots\right)$$

(a) Describe the pattern that generates the terms of this infinite series.

(b) What are the next three terms of the infinite series?

(c) Compete the following chart.

Number of Terms	Series of Rational Numbers	Decimal Equivalent
1	$4 \times [1]$	?
2	$4 \times [1 - \frac{1}{3}]$	?
3	$4 \times [1 - \frac{1}{3} + \frac{1}{5}]$	?
4	$4 \times [1 - \frac{1}{3} + \frac{1}{5} - \frac{1}{7}]$	?
5	$4 \times [1 - \frac{1}{3} + \frac{1}{5} - \frac{1}{7} + \frac{1}{9}]$	?
6	$4 \times [1 - \frac{1}{3} + \frac{1}{5} - \frac{1}{7} + \frac{1}{9} - \frac{1}{11}]$	?
7	$4 \times [1 - \frac{1}{3} + \frac{1}{5} - \frac{1}{7} + \frac{1}{9} - \frac{1}{11} + \frac{1}{13}]$	?
8	$4 \times [1 - \frac{1}{3} + \frac{1}{5} - \frac{1}{7} + \frac{1}{9} - \frac{1}{11} + \frac{1}{13} - \frac{1}{15}]$	?
9	$4 \times [1 - \frac{1}{3} + \frac{1}{5} - \frac{1}{7} + \frac{1}{9} - \frac{1}{11} + \frac{1}{13} - \frac{1}{15} + \frac{1}{17}]$	?

(d) How close is this approximation of π after nine terms when compared to the approximation of π given in problem 4?

7. Use the divide-and-average method to approximate the square roots of each of the following numbers to two decimal places.

(a) 15   (b) 29   (c) 98   (d) 150.5   (e) 2000

8. Let N = the set of natural numbers, W = the set of whole numbers, I = the set of integers, Q = the set of rational numbers, $\overline{Q}$ = the set of irrational numbers and R = the set of real numbers.

(a) Name two sets whose intersection is the empty set.

(b) Find $n(W - N)$.

(c) Name two subsets of I.

(d) Which of the above sets are subsets of R?

(e) Find $Q \cup \overline{Q}$.

(f) Identify the elements in $I - W$.

9. Let X be the set containing elements greater than -3 and less than or equal to 3. Describe or list the elements in set X that satisfy the following conditions.

(a) X contains only whole numbers.

(b) X contains only integers.

(c) X contains only real numbers.

10. Arrange each of the following groups of numbers in ascending order.

(a) $1\frac{2}{3}, 1.41, \sqrt{3}, \frac{7}{5}, \frac{\sqrt{5}}{2}$

(b) $-\frac{3}{4}, -\sqrt{2}, -.5\overline{6}, -.03, -\frac{\sqrt{3}}{2}$

11. Arrange the following groups of numbers in descending order.

(a) $-\sqrt{5}, 1\frac{2}{5}, -1.04, \sqrt{5}, .\overline{1}$

(b) $-\sqrt{1.2}, -1.2, -\frac{1}{2}, .1\overline{2}, (2 \times \sqrt{2})$

12. Identify each as "always yields a rational number," "always yields an irrational number."

(a) The square of a rational number

(b) The square root of an irrational number

(c) The product of two rational numbers

(d) The sum of a rational number and an irrational number

(e) A rational number subtracted from an irrational number

13. (a) State an example in which an irrational number divided by an irrational number would equal a rational number.

(b) State an example in which an irrational number times an irrational number would equal a rational number.

14. **(a)** Identify two rational numbers between 1 and 2.

(b) Identify two irrational numbers between −3 and −2.

15. Use the Pythagorean theorem to determine the missing side in each of the following right triangles. State whether the missing side is a rational number or an irrational number.

16. Trace the following number line. Use it and your knowledge of the Pythagorean theorem to locate $\sqrt{3}$.

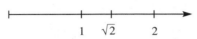

17. The maximum visibility distance (in kilometers) that can be seen from atop a tall structure is approximately 112 times the square root of the height of the building given in kilometers. What is the maximum visibility distance for each of the following to the nearest tenth of a kilometer?

(a) World Trade Center in New York City ≈ .41 km

(b) Eiffel Tower in Pairs ≈ .3 km

In Other Words

18. Give your interpretation of why $\sqrt{2}$ is called the "square root of two."

19. You have been introduced to natural numbers, whole numbers, integers, rational numbers, irrational numbers, and real numbers. Explain how these sets relate to one another; that is, which sets are subsets of other sets?

20. We have said that a rational number is a number that can be expressed in the form $\frac{x}{y}$ where x and y are integers and $y \neq 0$. Since $\sqrt{2}$ can be expressed as $\frac{\sqrt{2}}{1}$, why isn't it considered to be a rational number?

21. Explain why the rational numbers are dense but the set of integers is not.

22. The set of irrational numbers is not closed under addition. Explain why this is so.

Cooperative Activity

23. Groups of three

Individual Accountability: Each member is to complete the assigned portion of this activity. You are given three numbers.

First estimate the square root of each number. Then use a calculator to determine the square root correct to five decimal places. Finally, use the divide-and-average method repeatedly until your solution is correct to five decimal places.

Member A: 43, 127, 2672

Member B: 84, 161, 1912

Member C: 58, 192, 3950

Group Goal: Discuss your findings and your methodology. Together, you will now examine an alternate method of determining the square root of a number. It is outlined here for $\sqrt{73}$.

Using the square root key on the calculator, the square root of 73 is 8.54401 (rounded to five decimal places). We will repeatedly use the expression

$$\left(\frac{73}{s} + s\right) \div 2$$

for different values of s. This can be determined using the calculator keystroke sequences:

$$\boxed{AC}\ \ 73\ \ \boxed{\div}\ \ s\ \ \boxed{=}\ \ \boxed{+}\ \ s\ \ \boxed{=}\ \ \boxed{\div}\ \ 2\ \ \boxed{=}$$

(a) Let $s = 1$. Calculate

$$\left(\frac{73}{s} + s\right) \div 2 = \left(\frac{73}{1} + 1\right) \div 2 = 37$$

(b) Let $s = 37$. Calculate

$$\left(\frac{73}{37} + 37\right) \div 2 = 19.48649 \text{ (rounded to five decimal places)}$$

(c) Let $s = 19.48649$. Calculate

$$\left(\frac{73}{19.48649} + 19.48649\right) \div 2 = 11.61634$$

(d) Let $s = 11.61634$. Calculate

$$\left(\frac{73}{11.61634} + 11.61634\right) \div 2 = 8.95030$$

(e) Let $s = 8.95030$. Calculate

$$\left(\frac{73}{8.95030} + 8.95030\right) \div 2 = 8.55323$$

If this process is continued, the result will approach the square root of 73.

Together, use this process to determine an approximation of the square root of 43, 84, and 58. Compare the approximations with your individual work. How is this process similar to the divide-and-average method?

Chapter 7 Vocabulary Terms

addition properties of rational number
    inequalities

arithmetic mean (average)

centi-

deci-

deka-

dense set

density property of rational numbers

gram

hecto-

irrational numbers

kilo-

liter

meter

milli-

multiplication properties of rational
    number inequalities

natural numbers

nonterminating decimal

Pythagorean theorem

principal square root

radical

radicand

real numbers

repeating decimals

scientific notation

significant digits

square numbers (perfect squares)

square root

subgoals

terminating decimal

transitive property of rational number
    inequalities

trichotomy property

Review for Chapter 7

1. Arrange the following sets in ascending order.

  (a) $.125, \sqrt{3}, .108, .1\overline{2}, \frac{1}{9}$

  (b) $-\sqrt{9}, \sqrt{3}, -2\frac{2}{3}, -2.7\overline{6}, -\frac{2.5}{5}$

2. Arrange the following sets in descending order.

  (a) $-\sqrt{5}, -\sqrt{4}, -2.\overline{2}, -\frac{1}{100}, (1.3 \times 10^{-2})$

  (b) $(3.5 \times 10^{-3}), \frac{5}{13}, .1\overline{3}, \sqrt{2}, 1\frac{1}{8}$

3. Give an integer estimate for each of the following problems.

  (a) $45.987 + 16.25 + .91 + 12.4568$

  (b) $13.98 - 2.45 + 1.9 - 7$

  (c) $8.98 \times .75$

  (d) 65.12×3.21

  (e) $614.7 \div 25.1$

  (f) $12.854 \div .53$

4. Perform the operations indicated in each part of problem 3. Compare your estimates with the actual results.

5. Write each of the following numbers in scientific notation using three significant digits.

  (a) 236,986   (b) .002056

  (c) .0000000381   (d) 12,825,924,987

  (e) 193,972

6. Give the closest integer estimate for the principal value of each square root. Then determine the actual square roots to the nearest thousandth.

  (a) $\sqrt{17}$ (b) $\sqrt{93}$ (c) $\sqrt{50}$

  (d) $\sqrt{700}$ (e) $\sqrt{9999}$

7. Use the divide-and-average method to determine an approximation of the principal value of each square root to the nearest tenth.

  (a) $\sqrt{117}$ (b) $\sqrt{23}$ (c) $\sqrt{500}$

  (d) $\sqrt{27}$ (e) $\sqrt{99}$

8. Write each of the following rational numbers in the form $\frac{a}{b}$ where a and b are integers and $b \neq 0$.

  (a) 3.51 (b) $.\overline{8}$ (c) $\frac{2\frac{1}{2}}{7}$ (d) $4\frac{1}{5}$ (e) $(\sqrt{1.2})^2$

9. Fill in the blank with the correct metric measurement.
   (a) 2.5 km = _____ m
   (b) .065 km = _____ m
   (c) 4.5 cm = _____ mm
   (d) 6 mm = _____ cm
   (e) 734 cm = _____ m

10. Express each fraction as an equivalent percent rounded to the nearest tenth.

    (a) $\frac{2}{6}$ (b) $\frac{23}{50}$ (c) $\frac{875}{100}$ (d) $\frac{4}{5}$ (e) $\frac{2}{16}$

11. Express each of the following percents as equivalent decimals.
    (a) 35%   (b) 1%   (c) 123%
    (d) $7\frac{3}{4}\%$ (e) 37.5%

12. When a certain number is raised to the fourth power, the result is a rational number. When the original number is raised to the fifth power, the result is an irrational number. Find one such number.

13. A clothing warehouse has the following pricing policy. The item is first marked down by 5% of the manufacturer's listed price. If the item stays on the rack for over 30 days, an additional 30% is taken off. If the item stays on the rack for over 60 days, it is further reduced by 40%. In each of the following cases, you are given the first date the item appeared on the rack, the manufacturer's listed price, and the date the item was purchased. Determine the purchase price. Include 8% sales tax.
    (a) May 15, $180, May 21
    (b) May 15, $150, June 8
    (c) May 15, $50, August 3
    (d) May 15, $300, July 27

14. The Gazette News computes charges for classified ads by the number of characters in the ad. The first 90 characters cost $12.50, the next 45 characters cost $5.50, and each additional character over 135 characters costs $.03. What is the total cost of a 213-character advertisement?

15. When 15 gallons of gasoline are added to a partially filled fuel tank, the tank is 75% full. The tank holds 28 gallons. How many gallons were in the tank before the filling began?

16. A repair shop charges an hourly labor fee of $38. Rachel had the following air-conditioning parts replaced on her car: condenser, $380.00; compressor, $365.00; fan belt, $15.50. The job took the mechanic $3\frac{1}{4}$ hours. What is the total cost of Rachel's repairs, including $7\frac{1}{4}\%$ sales tax?

17. A certain photocopy machine can print copies whose dimensions are .1 larger than the original. Assume that a 5 cm by 9 cm original is placed in the machine, and then an enlarged copy is made of the original. If this process is repeated three more times (a copy made of the copy), what are the dimensions of the last copy (to the nearest hundredth centimeter)?

18. A certain photocopy machine can print a copy of an original whose dimensions have been reduced by 15%. Assume that the original is 10 cm by 15 cm, and a reduced copy is made of the original. If this process is repeated three more times (a copy made of the copy), what are the dimensions of the last copy (to the nearest hundredth centimeter)?

19. A certain type of glass is 2 cm thick and filters light by allowing only 60% of the light to go through. How much light would go through if four thicknesses of this glass were put together (to the nearest hundredth of a percent)?

20. *R* values are assigned to many building materials. This indicates the resistance of the material to loss of heat. The higher the *R* value, the better the material insulates. The *R* value is proportional to the thickness of the material. If a $\frac{3}{4}$" thickness of Styrofoam has an *R* value of 3.725, what is the *R* value of a piece of Styrofoam that is $\frac{1}{2}$" thick?

21. Compare the following two situations. Before performing any computations, predict which person chose the better savings plan. Then determine the balance for each person at the end of the three-year period. Assume that no deposits or withdrawals were made during this time.
    (a) Richard deposited $1000 in an account that compounded interest annually. The interest rates were 7.5% the first year, 8% the second year, and 8.5% the third year.
    (b) Laura deposited $1000 in an account that compounded interest annually. The interest rate remained at 8% throughout the three-year period.

22. All 800 rooms in a certain hotel are booked for the weekend of June 12. Eighty percent of the rooms were booked in advance by a conference of math teachers. Sixty-five percent of the conference-room reservations were made before February 8. The remaining conference-room reservations were made after that date. Twenty-five percent of those people who made their reservations for the conference after February 8 requested nonsmoking rooms. Twelve and one-half percent of those requests could not be

filled. How many people who made conference-room reservations after February 8 were able to get a nonsmoking room?

23. The maximum distance from the planet Saturn to the sun is 9.38×10^8 miles. The maximum distance from the planet Mercury to the sun is 4.34×10^7 miles. What would be the distance from Mercury to Saturn when these two planets are aligned?

24. A unit of distance used to measure atomic dimensions is called the angstrom. One angstrom is equal to 10^{-8} cm. Suppose that the distance between two atoms is identified as 3.15 angstroms. If the speed of light is approximately 3×10^{10} cm/sec, how long does it take light to traverse this distance? (Time = Distance/Rate.)

25. When Lee opened his textbook, the product of the page numbers on the two pages that faced him was 125,670. What were the two page numbers.

In Other Words

26. Explain how the decimal equivalent of $\frac{3}{4}$ is considered an element of the set of repeating decimals.

27. Explain why when converting a measurement in meters to centimeters you move the decimal point two places to the right.

28. Offer some arguments in favor of adopting the metric system of measurement throughout the United States.

29. Suppose that X can be written as the product of primes $(p_1)^2 \cdot (p_2)^3 \cdot (p_3)$, and Y can be written as the product of primes $(p_1) \cdot (p_2)^2 \cdot (p_3)^3$. Explain why the least common multiple of X and Y is $(p_1)^2 \cdot (p_2)^3 \cdot (p_3)^3$.

30. Is the square root of a prime number rational or irrational?

Cooperative Activity

31. Groups of three

You have seen that a decimal of the form $.abcd$ can be expressed as the sum of fractions in the following manner:

$$\frac{a}{10} + \frac{b}{10^2} + \frac{c}{10^3} + \frac{d}{10^4}$$

We now introduce you to a new type of fraction called a radix fraction. A *radix fraction* is a fraction that is expressed in another base. For example, $(.5214)_{six}$ is a radix fraction in base six. It is equivalent to

$$\frac{5}{6} + \frac{2}{6^2} + \frac{1}{6^3} + \frac{4}{6^4} = \frac{5}{6} + \frac{2}{36} + \frac{1}{216} + \frac{4}{1296}$$

$$= \frac{1162}{1296} \approx .897 \text{ (base ten)}$$

Individual Accountability: Each group member is to express the radix fractions as a sum, and then determine the base ten decimal equivalent.

Member A:	$.11001_{two}$	$.2673_{eight}$	$.888_{nine}$
Member B:	$.10011_{two}$	$.737_{eight}$	$.1734_{nine}$
Member C:	$.10101_{two}$	$.4661_{eight}$	$.284_{nine}$

Group Goal: Discuss your methods with your group members. Together, determine the sum of the base ten decimal equivalents of the base two, base eight, and base nine radix fractions. Determine a method of adding the radix fractions within the given base; that is, find the missing part of each of the following radix fractions.

$$.11001_{two} + .10011_{two} + .10101_{two} = ?_{two}$$

$$.2673_{eight} + .737_{eight} + .4661_{eight} = ?_{eight}$$

$$.888_{nine} + .1734_{nine} + .284_{nine} = ?_{nine}$$

Compare the radix fraction sums with the base ten equivalent sums.

8

Using **S**tatistics as an **I**nterpretive **T**ool

Examine the photograph at the right.

Describe what you see.

What do all the pieces of identification in this photograph have in common?

What information is represented?

What generalizations might you make?

What might a mathematical description of this photograph contain?

Introduction

"The average precipitation for the month of January was 7.3 centimeters."

"The winner of the Cy Young Award had an ERA of 2.86."

"Salaries for teachers in that school district range from $23,000 to $63,000."

"The computer predicts that there is a 35% chance of Hurricane Liz hitting the shore."

"The median selling price of homes in the village was $135,000."

"Your child's reading score is at the 87th percentile."

You have probably heard or read some or all of these comments in one form or another. The revolution in technology and the easier access to enormous amounts of information over the past several decades have made our society an increasingly quantitative one. Within the last 30 years, statistics has moved to the forefront as one of the most important tools for making sense out of a barrage of real-world data. Students can no longer afford to wait until high school or college to be introduced to statistics. An introduction to the basic principles of the statistical method needs to begin in the elementary grades. Statistics has permeated the lives of ordinary citizens. No longer is statistics just a tool used by mathematicians, engineers, scientists, economists, and other professionals. It is an investigative branch of mathematics that should be accessible to everyone. A basic knowledge of statistics can help us make and understand predictions and decisions, evaluate claims, refute or support findings, and validate hypotheses in our everyday lives as well as in professional settings.

In this chapter we will introduce various ways of organizing, displaying, analyzing, and summarizing data. In Section 8.1 we examine the various ways to organize and display data graphically. We focus on stem-and-leaf plots, histograms, bar graphs, line graphs, circle graphs, and picture graphs. In Section 8.2 we go beyond data presentation and delve into several techniques used to analyze and summarize data: frequency analysis, measures of central tendency, measures of dispersion, measures of individual performance, and box-and-whisker plots. By the time you have finished studying this chapter, you will have the rudimentary tools you will need to make sense of the deluge of data you are inundated with every day and to understand and evaluate the graphical displays you encounter in the media.

8.1 Looking for Trends: Organizing and Displaying Data

data

What are data? **Data** are pieces of information that can be either qualitative or quantitative. Qualitative data about a person might include gender, health status, eye color, hair color, and so on. Quantitative data about a person might include height, weight, age, blood pressure, visual acuity, hat size, shoe size, and the like.

statistics

Data can be organized, summarized, analyzed, and interpreted using techniques from a branch of mathematics called **statistics**. We will begin our study of statistics by examining the following set of data.

Number of College Mathematics Courses Taken by the
20 Applicants for a Summer Teaching Position

Applicant 1:	5	Applicant 11:	4
Applicant 2:	3	Applicant 12:	5
Applicant 3:	5	Applicant 13:	3
Applicant 4:	2	Applicant 14:	2
Applicant 5:	1	Applicant 15:	6
Applicant 6:	7	Applicant 16:	2
Applicant 7:	3	Applicant 17:	5
Applicant 8:	8	Applicant 18:	4
Applicant 9:	5	Applicant 19:	2
Applicant 10:	6	Applicant 20:	3

In the above list, the set of applicants and the set of data are in a one-to-one correspondence. A particular applicant can be connected to a specific number of college courses. Looking at the data, you can see that 20 pieces of data are in this set ($n = 20$).

range   The least number of college math courses taken by these applicants is 1, and the greatest number is 8. The **range** of a set of data is the difference between the greatest and least values in the set. Therefore, the range of number of college math courses for these applicants is $8 - 1$, or 7.

To make this set of data more meaningful, it would help to arrange the data in tabular form. To do so, the data must be grouped in some way. Here are some possible ways to organize these data.

Number of College Mathematics Courses Taken by the
20 Applicants for a Summer Teaching Position

Table 1

Number of Courses	Number of Applicants
1–4	11
5–8	9

Table 2

Number of Courses	Number of Applicants
1–2	5
3–4	6
5–6	7
7–8	2

Table 3

Number of Courses	Number of Applicants
1	1
2	4
3	4
4	2
5	5
6	2
7	1
8	1

frequency In each table, the values listed under "Number of Applicants" describe the **frequency**, or the number of times that a particular piece of data was observed in the set. In Table 1, the frequency of the value describing those applicants who took fewer than five math courses is 11. In Table 2, the frequency of the value describing those applicants who took three or four math courses is 6. In Table 3, the frequency of the value describing those applicants who took eight math courses is 1.

Notice that the arrangement of the "Number of Courses" column is different in each table. The difference lies in the size of the interval that was chosen to organize the data. In Table 1, two intervals are given. Table 2 lists four intervals. And Table 3 shows eight intervals. The size of the interval depends on how compactly the analyst wants to organize the data.

lower interval limits Let's examine Table 1. This frequency table has two intervals. The **lower interval limits** are 1 and 5, since these are the lowest numbers that can belong to the different in-

upper interval limits tervals. The **upper interval limits** are 4 and 8, since these are the largest numbers that

interval width can belong to the different intervals. The **interval width** is constant for each interval and is equal to the difference between any two consecutive lower interval limits. The interval width for Table 1 is 4, since 5 – 1 is equal to 4. In Table 3, eight intervals are used to organize the data. Both the lower interval limits and the upper interval limits are 1, 2, 3, 4, 5, 6, 7, and 8. The interval width is 1.

Depending on the needs of the person studying the data, one or more of these tables might be useful. Examine Investigation 1, which explains how to construct a frequency table.

Investigation 1

The following data represent the class enrollments for all of the course offerings in the School of Education at a particular college during the spring semester.

4	43	19	42	22	17	9	29	36	24
28	39	27	45	27	11	25	39	37	16
36	48	17	34	16	37	10	38	23	19
33	18	40	35	33	39	43	8	47	22
38	13	25	21	35	38	13	36	16	16

Organize the data into a frequency table.

Once the range of these data is determined, equal intervals can be established based on the needs of the analyst. The lowest enrollment is 4, and the highest is 48. Therefore, the range of these data is 48 – 4, or 44.

Assume that an analyst wants seven intervals. The width of an interval can be determined by dividing the range by the desired number of intervals. In this case, that quotient is $\frac{44}{7}$, or ≈ 6.3. Although it is possible to have intervals whose widths are not whole numbers, we will restrict the frequency tables in this text to intervals with whole number widths. Rounding *up* any quotient obtained to the next largest whole number will result in a whole number interval width that will be large enough to capture all of the data. This rounding up takes place even if the quotient is a whole number. Rounding off in the traditional sense is not done, since it may result in some data being lost.

Let's examine this problem using nine intervals. The width of an interval can be determined by rounding up the quotient of 44 and 9. Here, $4.\overline{8}$ rounds up to 5. It is not necessary for the least number in the first interval and the greatest number in the last interval to be elements in the data set. Any convenient endpoints that provide intervals of equal width to capture all of the data can be chosen.

tally   We will now use the width determined above to set up intervals. These intervals will be used to create a **tally** chart, which in turn will be used to determine the frequencies. In the table below, notice that tally marks account for each member of the set under consideration. These marks are then counted. The number of marks for a given interval represents the frequency of the data in that interval.

Enrollment	Tally	Frequency
4–8	||	2
9–13	ЖЖ	5
14–18	ЖЖ ||	7
19–23	ЖЖ |	6
24–28	ЖЖ |	6
29–33	|||	3
34–38	ЖЖ ЖЖ |	11
39–43	ЖЖ ||	7
44–48	|||	3

This is the frequency table that results from intervals of width 5. Many different tables are possible, depending on the interval width chosen.

Stem-and-Leaf Plots

stem-and-leaf plot   The class enrollment data from Investigation 1 could have been organized in other ways as well. A **stem-and-leaf plot** is a method of displaying data in a visual form that retains the numerical values of each piece of data. This method of display partitions the data into groupings according to place value. For example, in order to prepare for a stem-and-leaf plot, the data on enrollments would be partitioned into the following groups:

4, 9, 8

19, 17, 11, 16, 17, 16, 10, 19, 18, 13, 13, 16, 16

22, 29, 24, 28, 27, 27, 25, 23, 22, 25, 21

36, 39, 39, 37, 36, 34, 37, 38, 33, 35, 33, 39, 38, 35, 38, 36

43, 42, 45, 48, 40, 43, 47

The stem of each piece of data is determined by the digit in the tens place. The leaf of a piece of data is the digit in the ones place. Notice that only five stems are under consideration: 4, 3, 2, 1, and 0 (4 = 04, 9 = 09, 8 = 08). Each category has many different leaves. The stem-and-leaf plot for this set of data would look like this:

Stems	Leaves
0	4 9 8
1	9 7 1 6 7 6 0 9 8 3 3 6 6
2	2 9 4 8 7 7 5 3 2 5 1
3	6 9 9 7 6 4 7 8 3 5 3 9 8 5 8 6
4	3 2 5 8 0 3 7

Both frequency tables and stem-and-leaf plots depict the entire data set. However, the stem-and-leaf plot of a large set of data would be as unwieldy as the data itself. Other graphical displays are better suited to large sets of data.

Histograms

After a frequency table has been constructed, the data can be presented graphically in the form of a histogram. A **histogram** is a graph that uses rectangles to represent the frequency of scores on a particular interval. The number of rectangles used in the histogram is equal to the number of intervals set up in the frequency table. Each rectangle represents a single interval. The rectangles are the same width, but they vary in height according to the frequency of the interval represented.

histogram

A stem-and-leaf plot can be used to construct a histogram merely by turning the plot counterclockwise on its side, as shown in Figure 8.1a. The leaves can be "boxed" by rectangles, and the numbers removed, forming the histogram shown in Figure 8.1b.

The same data can also be illustrated in a different histogram. The histogram in Figure 8.2 depicts the class enrollment figures whose frequency table was completed in Investigation 1.

Despite the usefulness of graphs in displaying data meaningfully, they can be deceiving, and conclusions drawn from them must be viewed cautiously. For example, Figure 8.3 depicts two histograms of the same data set pictured in Figure 8.2. By changing the scale on the axes, very different representations of the data are achieved. What conclusions might you make on the basis of each of these histograms?

Some statisticians have a rule of thumb that governs the number of intervals in a histogram. Usually, if n represents the group size, the number of intervals is k, where k

Figure 8.1

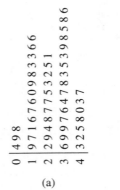
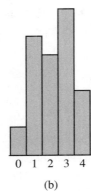

(a)   (b)

Figure 8.2

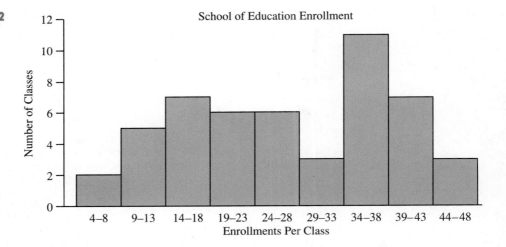

Figure 8.3

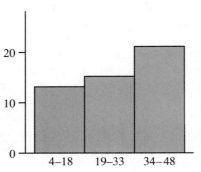
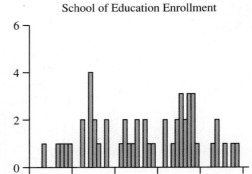

is the smallest number such that $2^k \geq n$. For example, if 25 pieces of data were in the group, 2^5 is the smallest number that is greater than 25. Therefore, five intervals would be desirable. If 70 pieces of data were in the group, 2^7 is the smallest number that is greater than 70. Seven intervals could be used for this histogram.

Bar Graphs

bar graph
A graphic representation of data that is similar to a histogram is a bar graph. Like a histogram, a **bar graph** uses rectangles of varying length to depict quantity. In a histogram the bars always touch each other, but in a bar graph, the rectangles do not touch each other. Bar graphs are used for quantitative comparisons of categories. Generally, bar graphs are not used to depict continuous changes over a period of time. As with all graphs, the numerical labels of the horizontal and vertical axes of the graph must be consistent; that is, the increments along a given axis must use a consistent scale throughout.

In Figure 8.4a a bar graph is constructed to depict the average entry age of the students in four kindergarten classes at a particular elementary school. Notice that the differences in the lengths of the rectangles are barely distinguishable. The same data are represented in Figure 8.4b But here the vertical axis does not begin at zero but with a number that allows the vertical axis to be divided into more specific intervals. Far more specific information is communicated by the second graph. If the teacher of Class 1 wanted to make the case that the children in his class were unusually "young," he might choose Figure 8.4b, since this bar graph emphasizes the differences, rather than the similarities, in average ages.

Bar graphs can also be constructed in other forms to depict larger amounts of information. *Adjacent bar graphs* and *stacked bar graphs* can be used to make comparisons within and among categories by placing bars that represent the same categories close to each other.

Figure 8.4a

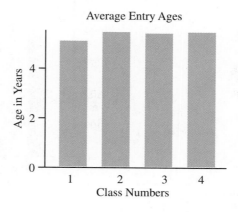

Average Entry Ages

Figure 8.4b

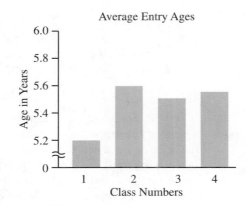

For example, electricity is sold and consumed in kilowatt-hours. The bar graphs in Figure 8.5a depict the May, June, and July kilowatt-hour usage of electricity by a single family in 1990, 1991, and 1992. The bars representing usage in 1990 are represented by dark gray; the bars representing usage in 1991 are represented by white; and the bars representing usage in 1992 are represented by light gray. In Figure 8.5a the data are depicted with adjacent bars. In Figure 8.5b notice that the bars for a given month are stacked one behind the other, with the smallest value in front and the largest in the back. This particular family consistently used more electricity during May, June, and July of 1991. No other usage trend is obvious from the remaining bars.

Bar graphs can be created to illustrate data that fluctuate above and below a particular value. This type of bar graph is known as a *hanging bar graph*. Investigation 2 uses a hanging bar graph to illustrate the net changes of a particular stock.

Figure 8.5a

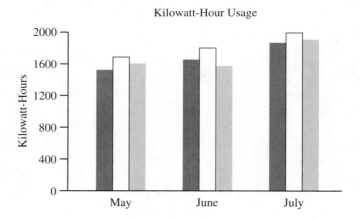

Figure 8.5b

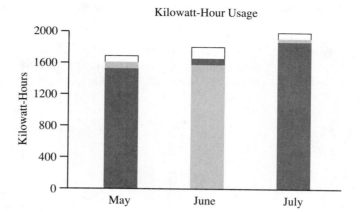

Kilowatt-Hour Usage

Investigation 2

The net changes in the price of a single share of Bruno Industries for the last seven trading days is as follows:

Day 1: $+\dfrac{1}{2}$

Day 2: $+\dfrac{1}{8}$

Day 3: Unchanged

Day 4: $-\dfrac{1}{4}$

Day 5: $-\dfrac{1}{2}$

Day 6: $+\dfrac{1}{8}$

Day 7: $-\dfrac{3}{4}$

(a) Illustrate the net changes on a bar graph.

(b) If the stock had a closing price of $48\frac{3}{4}$ dollars per share on Day 7, what was the opening price on Day 1?

Understand the Problem: You are given the daily change in the price of a share of stock over a seven-day period. You are asked to determine the opening price on Day 1, given that the closing price on Day 7 was $48\frac{3}{4}$ dollars.

Devise a Plan: For part (a) we will construct a graph. For part (b) we will use the strategy of working backwards.

Carry Out the Plan: Notice that the net-change values fall above and below zero. We will use zero as our baseline in this bar graph. Rather than building up only from the base, we will position the baseline in the middle of the graph so that bars can hang below the baseline as well as rise above it.

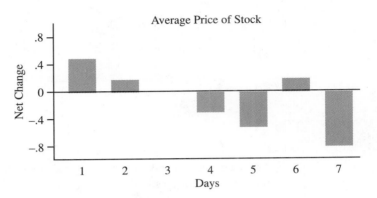

Hanging bar graphs can be used to depict situations involving gains and losses, increases and decreases, deposits and withdrawals, rises and falls, and so on. In each of these cases, a baseline (not necessarily zero) upon which the bars are built and hung is identified.

(b)   To solve this problem we will work backwards from the closing price on Day 7. A price of $48\frac{3}{4}$ represents a drop of $\frac{3}{4}$ from the closing price on Day 6. Let X be the closing price on Day 6. This situation can therefore be expressed as

$$X - \frac{3}{4} = 48\frac{3}{4}$$
$$X = 49\frac{1}{2}$$

The closing price on Day 6 was $49\frac{1}{2}$ dollars.

   Now, $49\frac{1}{2}$ dollars represents an increase of $\frac{1}{8}$ from Day 5. Let $Y =$ the closing price on Day 5. This situation can be expressed as

$$Y + \frac{1}{8} = 49\frac{1}{2}$$
$$Y = 49\frac{3}{8}$$

The closing price on Day 6 was $49\frac{3}{8}$ dollars.

   We can continue in this fashion, or recognize that working backwards from the final day's closing price to the first day's opening price can be achieved by subtracting the net changes from the closing price on Day 7. This can also be viewed as "undoing" the net changes and can be expressed as follows:

$$48\frac{3}{4} - \left(-\frac{3}{4} + \frac{1}{8} - \frac{1}{2} - \frac{1}{4} + \frac{1}{8} + \frac{1}{2}\right) = 48\frac{3}{4} - \left(-\frac{3}{4}\right) = 49\frac{1}{2}$$

The stock opened at $49.50 per share on the first trading day.

Look Back: Use your calculator and the decimal equivalents of the net changes to verify the solution.

Line Graphs

Data that represent a change over time are often collected. The average monthly rainfall for a particular year, the heartbeat rate over a 5-minute period, and the sales figures for a particular item over a 10-day period are three situations that would appropriately be **line graph** depicted on a **line graph**.

In Figure 8.6 two line graphs are drawn on the same set of axes. Although each graph could have been drawn separately, using a double line graph allows for comparison within and between categories. Figure 8.6 depicts the number of beach chair rentals at a certain hotel during the first week of August in 1991 and 1992. Not only does the double line graph show that beach chair rentals increase on weekends, but it also shows that more beach chairs were rented in 1991. The differences could have been because of a change in weather, a variation in the number of hotel guests from 1991 to 1992, or a price increase in beach chair rentals.

Figure 8.6

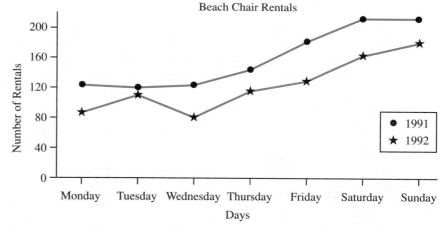

Circle Graphs

We have said that bar graphs are useful for representing categories of data, and line graphs are used primarily to chart changes over time. When we want to represent data that is part of a whole, circle graphs can be an appropriate choice. (In Chapter 11 you will learn how to use a protractor to construct a circle graph. This section examines the component parts of a circle graph.)

circle graph A **circle graph** is an area graph that shows how one category relates to another. The circle is partitioned into pie-shaped regions called *sectors*. The percentage of area in each sector is directly related to the percentage of data it represents. The size of the sector is a function of the measure of the angle that is formed at the center of the circle. This angle is called the *central angle*. (More detail on circle graphs will be given in Chapter 11.) The measure, in degrees, of the central angle also reflects the percentage of data the sector represents. For example, a central angle of 90° forms 25% of the circle, since 25% of 360° equals 90°. A sector containing a 90° angle would be used to represent data that are 25% of the whole. Examine Investigation 3, which outlines the procedure for constructing and interpreting a circle graph.

Investigation 3

A person wishes to invest $60,000. The investment counselor suggests putting the money into a portfolio that will divide the investment as follows:

$15,000	Transportation stock
$9,000	Utility stock
$6,000	Money-market fund
$3,000	Bonds
$27,000	Tax-sheltered annuities

Construct a circle graph to represent this investment portfolio.

 We must first determine the percentage of the whole amount represented by each individual investment. These percentages are then used to determine the measure of the central angle that will form the representative sector in the circle graph. This information is organized in the following table.

Investment	Amount of Investment	Fraction	Percentage	Measure of Central Angle
Transportation stock	$15,000	$\frac{15,000}{60,000}$	25%	25% of 360° = 90°
Utility stock	$9,000	$\frac{9,000}{60,000}$	15%	15% of 360° = 54°
Money-market fund	$6,000	$\frac{6,000}{60,000}$	10%	10% of 360° = 36°
Bonds	$3,000	$\frac{3,000}{60,000}$	5%	5% of 360° = 18°
Tax-sheltered annuities	$27,000	$\frac{27,000}{60,000}$	45%	45% of 360° = 162°
Totals	$60,000	$\frac{60,000}{60,000}$	100%	360°

Using the angle measures in the last column, the circle graph that depicts the investment portfolio is given here:

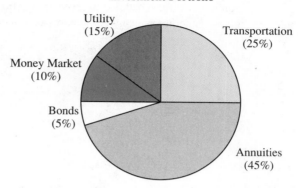

Investment Portfolio

Picture Graphs

picture graph   The final type of graph we will consider is the picture graph. In a **picture graph**, an icon is chosen and assigned a numerical value. Repetitions of the icon in the graph represent multiples of that numerical value. Fractional parts of the numerical value can also be represented by fractional parts of the icon.

Picture graphs are appropriate for showing broad differences in categories, since it is difficult to visually discriminate between one-third of an icon and three-eighths of the same icon. Figure 8.7 depicts a picture graph of departures at a particular airport.

Figure 8.7

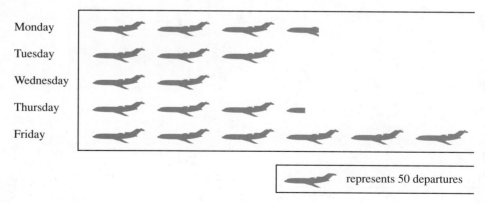

The value ascribed to the icon is a critical component of this graph. An advantage of a picture graph is that it communicates information clearly and quickly. For example, in Figure 8.7 you can easily see that 175 flights (50 + 50 + 50 + 25) departed on Monday.

Investigation 4

Examine the following series of graphs, which represent information about a daily commuter train scheduled to arrive in a major city at 8:30 A.M. On the basis of the data given, generate as many conjectures as you can about the situation presented.

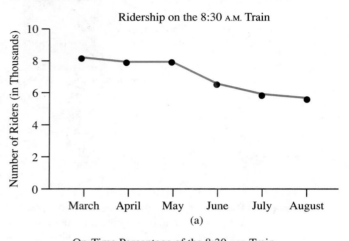

(a)

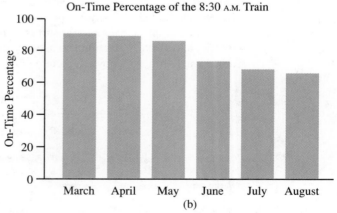

(b)

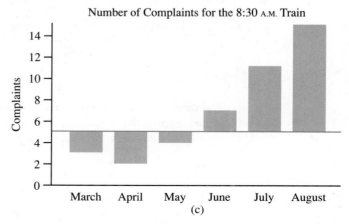

(c)

Types of Tickets Purchased

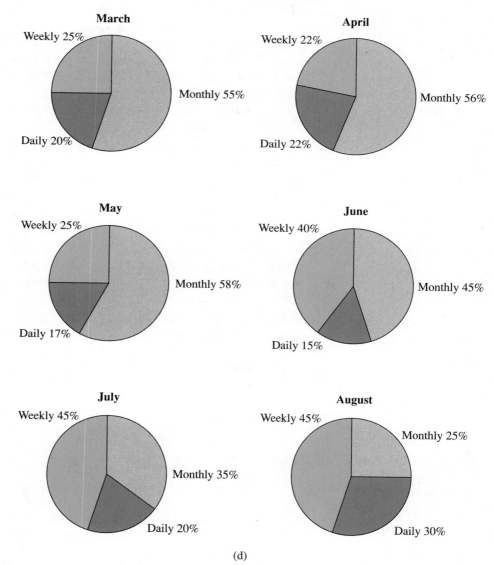

(d)

The following conjectures appear to be supported by the data. (Where appropriate, the graph supporting these conjectures is given in parentheses following each statement.)

- Ridership decreased from March to August (a).
- On-time percentage decreased from March to August (b).
- The number of complaints increased, with March, April, and May showing fewer than average complaints (indicated by the baseline 5), and June, July, and August showing a greater than average number of complaints (c).

▪ The month with the lowest on-time percentage and the fewest riders (August) generated the greatest number of complaints (b and c).

▪ Graphs (a), (b), and (c) indicate reasonable consistency in ridership, on-time percentage, and number of complaints for March, April, and May. In June, July, and August, the data change. The ridership decreases, the on-time percentage decreases, and the number of complaints increases. In addition, the number of monthly tickets purchased sharply decreases (d).

▪ It is possible that there is a connection among ridership, on-time percentage, and number of complaints.

▪ The circle graphs (d) indicate that the percentage of monthly tickets sold remained relatively stable during the months of March, April, and May. In June, July, and August, the percentage of monthly tickets sold significantly decreased, whereas the percentages of weekly and daily tickets sold increased significantly.

▪ The sharper decrease in ridership from May to August could be because of a poor on-time record during the summer months (a and b).

▪ The sharper decrease in ridership from May to August could be because many people go on vacation during the summer months (a and b). This conjecture is supported by the fact that fewer monthly and more daily and weekly tickets are sold in June, July, and August (a).

Graphical representations of data should be interpreted cautiously. As you can see, even with this limited amount of data, we can come up with several possible explanations for the decrease in ridership on the 8:30 A.M. train. When you see graphs in the media, realize that you are probably not being given all of the relevant information. Further information may support or refute the argument being made.

Assessments for Section 8.1

1. You are given the following data:

18	29	52	18	39	58	26	52	57	62
42	47	36	28	35	27	17	19	52	41
34	15	8	45	2	9	56	41	87	9
15	18	30	20	8	11	13	23	47	22

(a) What is the range of this set of data?

(b) Suppose that the data were to be partitioned into 5 intervals of equal length. What would the length of each interval be?

(c) Determine 8 intervals of equal length that capture all of the data. Identify each of the intervals.

(d) Determine 4 intervals of equal length that capture all of the data with 0 as the lower boundary of the first interval. Identify each of the intervals.

(e) Determine 6 intervals of equal length that capture all of the data with 0 as the lower boundary of the first interval. Identify each of the intervals.

(f) Construct a frequency table that partitions the data into 10 intervals of equal length that capture all of the data.

2. You are given the following set of data:

1	3	6	2	7	4	2	8	2	6	4	1	8
2	0	7	0	3	5	4	2	7	5	3	7	2
0	3	7	1	7	3	6	2	6	8	1	9	
6	0	1	6	2	7	3	8	2	9	5	6	

(a) What is the range of this set of data?

(b) Determine three intervals of equal length that capture all of the data. Identify each of the intervals.

(c) Determine two intervals of equal length that capture all of the data. Identify each of the intervals. What percentage of the data would fall into each interval?

(d) Construct a frequency table that partitions the data into five intervals of equal length that capture all of the data.

3. (a) Give an example of a set of 10 pieces of data whose range is 24.

(b) Suppose your data were accounted for in equal intervals of length 3. How many intervals would you have?

(c) Suppose your data were accounted for in equal intervals of length 4. How many intervals would you have.

(d) Suppose your data were accounted for in equal intervals of length 5. How many intervals would you have?

(e) Suppose your data were accounted for in seven equal intervals. What would the length of each interval be?

4. (a) Construct a frequency table for the following data, which present the area in square miles for each of the 50 states.

Alabama: 51,609	Montana: 147,138
Alaska: 586,412	Nebraska: 77,227
Arizona: 113,909	Nevada: 110,540
Arkansas: 53,104	New Hampshire: 9,304
California: 158,693	New Jersey: 7,836
Colorado: 104,247	New Mexico: 121,666
Connecticut: 5,009	New York: 49,576
Delaware: 2,057	North Carolina: 52,586
Florida: 58,560	North Dakota: 70,655
Georgia: 58,876	Ohio: 41,222
Hawaii: 6,450	Oklahoma: 69,919
Idaho: 83,557	Oregon: 96,981
Illinois: 56,400	Pennsylvania: 45,333
Indiana: 36,291	Rhode Island: 1,214
Iowa: 56,290	South Carolina: 31,055
Kansas: 82,264	South Dakota: 77,047
Kentucky: 40,395	Tennessee: 42,244
Louisiana: 48,523	Texas: 267,339
Maine: 33,215	Utah: 84,916
Maryland: 10,577	Vermont: 9,609
Massachusetts: 8,257	Virginia: 40,817
Michigan: 58,216	Washington: 68,192
Minnesota: 84,068	West Virginia: 24,181
Mississippi: 47,716	Wisconsin: 56,154
Missouri: 69,686	Wyoming: 97,914

(a) Use the following intervals:

0–49,999 sq mi

50,000–99,999 sq mi

100,000–149,999 sq mi

150,000–199,999 sq mi

200,000–249,999 sq mi

250,000–299,999 sq mi

300,000–349,999 sq mi

350,000–399,999 sq mi

400,000–449,999 sq mi

450,000–499,999 sq mi

500,000–549,999 sq mi

550,000–599,999 sq mi

(b) Suppose a portion of Iowa that measures 18,490 sq. mi wishes to secede from the state and form a new state. How would this change the frequency table?

(c) Use the frequency table constructed in part (a) to draw a histogram representing the area in square miles of the 50 states.

5. The customer relations department of a major airline conducted a study to determine the amount of time a customer waits on hold when calling to speak with a reservations agent. The following data (in minutes) were collected.

2.5	2.8	3.5	1.0	2.7	4.9	6.1	4.2	2.6
0.5	1.1	3.2	2.4	0.6	2.0	4.6	5.1	1.9
5.1	3.9	3.7	0.7	1.0	0.3	2.2	2.7	1.7
3.2	2.8	1.8	0.3	3.0	6.3	5.1	3.2	1.9

(a) Construct a stem-and leaf plot to organize the data.

(b) Construct a histogram that uses the intervals determined by the stem-and-leaf plot.

(c) What is the relationship between the stem-and-leaf plot in part (a) and the histogram in part (b)?

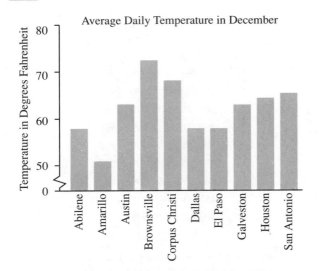

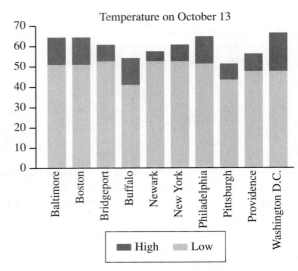

6. Examine the bar graph above, which illustrates the average daily temperature during December in 10 major cities in Texas.

(a) The bar representing the average daily temperature in Corpus Christi appears to be more than twice the height of the bar representing the average daily temperature in Dallas. Does this mean that the temperature in Corpus Christi is more than twice that of Dallas? Explain your answer.

(b) How might the bar graph be redrawn to suggest that there is little difference in average December temperatures among the 10 cities?

(c) Using the data represented in the bar graph, sketch a hanging bar graph with a baseline average temperature of 60°.

(d) Using the data represented in the bar graph, construct a stacked bar graph that includes the following average December temperatures recorded last year.

Abilene: 56°	Dallas: 61°
Amarillo: 53°	El Paso: 56°
Austin: 64°	Galveston: 65°
Brownsville: 68°	Houston: 66°
Corpus Christi: 67°	San Antonio: 66°

7. The following bar graph illustrates the high and low temperatures recorded on October 13 in 10 eastern cities.

(a) Which city appears to have the greatest difference in high and low temperatures?

(b) Which city appears to have the least difference in high and low temperatures?

(c) Which city appears to have a difference between high and low temperatures that is double that of Pittsburgh?

(d) Which city appears to have a difference between high and low temperatures that is 50% greater than that of Pittsburgh?

(e) Which city appears to have a difference between high and low temperatures that is 75% of the difference between the high and low temperatures in Pittsburgh?

8. Examine the following line graph, which illustrates the closing price of a single share of stock at the end of seven trading days.

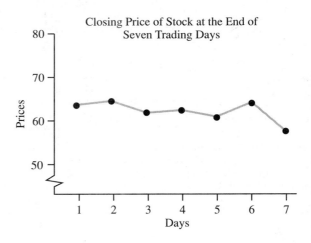

(a) Estimate an average closing price.

(b) Approximate the difference between the price on Day 1 and the price on Day 7.

(c) Assume that the price on Day 8 was 25% less than the price on Day 7. Estimate the Day 8 closing price.

(d) Instead of dropping on Day 7, if the closing price of the stock had continued rising at the same rate as between Day 5 and Day 6, at what price might the stock have closed on Day 7?

(e) Generalize the performance of this stock over the seven-day period based solely on the closing prices.

9. The following line graphs illustrate the same information concerning the number of complaints lodged against a car dealership in a given year.

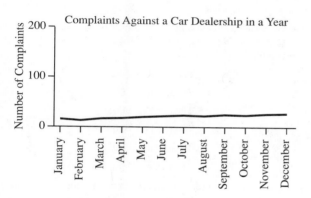

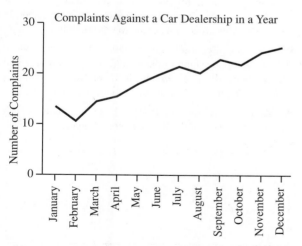

(a) Describe the general trend depicted in the first graph.

(b) Describe the general trend depicted in the second graph.

(c) Describe a context in which the first graph might be used.

(d) Describe a context in which the second graph might be used.

(e) Why do some people say that you can "lie" with statistics?

10. The following hanging bar graph illustrates the monthly difference in home sales between 1992 and 1991. Use the graph to estimate the sales figures. Sketch a double line graph that pictures both the 1991 and 1992 sales figures. The sales for 1991 are as follows: January, 32; February, 22; March, 41; April, 37; May, 42; June, 48; July, 52; August, 60; September, 78; October, 80; November, 61; December, 57.

11. The following are the monthly payments on a $70,000 loan borrowed at a 9% interest rate.

> 10 years: $886.73
>
> 15 years: $709.99
>
> 20 years: $629.81
>
> 25 years: $587.44

(a) Construct a bar graph to illustrate this information.

(b) Based on the bar graph drawn in part (a), estimate the monthly payment for a 30-year loan.

12. The following circle graph illustrates the land area of the continental states and territories in mainland Australia.

Mainland Australia

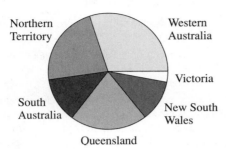

(a) Without performing any calculations, estimate the percentage of the total mainland area for each of the continental states and territories.

(b) If the toal area of mainland Australia is approximately 2,940,600 sq mi, what is the approximate area of each of the continental states and territories?

(c) Use the data to construct a bar graph. Which of the two types of graphs (circle or bar) appears more useful for land-area comparisons?

13. The areas in square miles of three Canadian provinces are as follows:

    Northwest Territory: 1,304,903 sq mi

    Quebec: 594,860 sq mi

    Ontario: 412,582 sq mi

The total land area of Canada is 3,851,809 sq mi. If a circle graph were constructed of the total land area of Canada, determine the percentage of the graph that would be used to form the sectors that represent each of these three provinces.

14. Construct a picture graph using the following data. Select and identify the value of a suitable icon.

Number of Buildings over 500 Feet Tall in Selected U.S. Cities

    Atlanta: 9

    Boston: 12

    Chicago: 43

    Houston: 26

    Los Angeles: 18

    Philadelphia: 9

15. You are given the following stem-and-leaf plot.

Stems	Leaves
8	4 1 7 4 8 9 0
9	2 6 1 9 6 1 2 5 3
10	7 2 8 0 1 7 8 2
11	3 9 1 6
12	2 0 2

(a) What is the range of this set of data?

(b) Determine eight intervals of equal width that capture all of the data.

(c) Describe a possible context for which these data might be representative.

16. Construct a picture graph that illustrates the total ticket sales for a single day in each of the six theaters of a sixplex cinema.

    Theater A: 1200

    Theater B: 600

    Theater C: 900

    Theater D: 450

    Theater E: 1000

    Theater F: 1500

17. Engage in some form of vigorous exercise for five minutes. Count your pulse for one minute immediately after stopping, and again after three minutes, six minutes, and nine minutes. Construct a line graph to represent these data.

18. Keep track of your total calorie intake for one day. Indicate if the calories belong to the meat/fish/egg group, the grain group, the dairy group, or the fruits/vegetables group. Sketch an estimated circle graph to illustrate these data.

19. Examine the following rectangle. Use your centimeter ruler to measure each of the line segments shown.

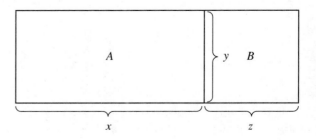

(a) The area of region A can be found by multiplying x times y. What is that area?

(b) The area of region B can be found by multiplying z times y. What is that area?

(c) Suppose that region A represented the number of hours in a day that you were awake, and region B represented the number of hours in a day that you were asleep. How many hours were you awake? How many hours were you asleep? Explain your answer.

20. Construct an adjacent bar graph depicting the following:

Major Fields of Study at a Particular College		
	Number of Students, 1992	Number of Students, 1993
Liberal arts	2150	2460
Engineering	115	190
Business	1500	1450
Education	900	950
Performing arts	335	310

In Other Words

21. Why is a bar graph inappropriate for displaying changes over a period of time?

22. When setting up a frequency table, is it possible that intervals that have no data contained within them will be generated. Explain your answer.

23. Explain how adjusting the scales used on a graph can change the way the information might be interpreted.

24. Each of the five secretaries for a corporation uses the same fax machine at work. The secretaries wish to make a point that they spend too much time waiting to fax documents. During the course of one day, they each record the amount of time spent waiting at the fax machine. What would be an appropriate graph to display their waiting times?

25. Is it possible for the interval width in a frequency table to be equal to 1? If so, give an example of a set of data that might require such a frequency table.

Cooperative Activity

26. Groups of two

Individual Accountability: Find three different types of graphs in the print media. Without making any reference to the type of graph, write a description of each of the situations portrayed. Include a listing of the actual data in your summaries.

Group Goal: Share your graphs and summaries with your partner. Discuss why the graph chosen by the author is or is not suitable to portray the situation.

Select two exemplary summaries that represent two different types of graphs. Submit these to your instructor. Your instructor will then redistribute the summaries to different groups. Each group is to examine the summaries given to them and then construct appropriate graphs to illustrate the situations. Students will then compare their versions of a graphical representation of data with the published graph.

8.2   Analyzing and Summarizing Data

In Section 8.1 we introduced several methods for organizing and displaying data. We pointed out that different representations of the same set of data suggest different interpretations. This section will help you develop skills that will enable you to go beyond the surface level of data presentation and begin learning ways to analyze and summarize data.

Frequency Analysis

You have already learned how to organize data using a frequency table. These tables were used primarily for sorting the data and subsequently translating them into some graphical form.

In frequency analysis we examine the data as they are presented in the frequency table itself. To illustrate this, we will use the frequency table in Investigation 1 (see p. 349), which represented the enrollment in all of the classes in the School of Education at a particular college. Recall that the frequency column represented the number of

cumulative frequency

times a piece of data appeared on the particular interval. We now introduce a new column, called the **cumulative frequency**. This column is formed by keeping a running total of the frequencies that are less than or equal to that particular interval. Notice that the final entry in the cumulative frequency column is the total number of pieces of data under consideration.

Enrollment	Frequency	Cumulative Frequency
4–8	2	2
9–13	5	7
14–18	7	14
19–23	6	20
24–28	6	26
29–33	3	29
34–38	11	40
39–43	7	47
44–48	3	50

The cumulative frequency in this table tells the reader the number of classes whose enrollment is less than or equal to a particular class size. For example, 26 classes have an enrollment of 28 students or less.

relative frequency

We now add a fourth and fifth column to the table. The **relative frequency** is the ratio of the frequency of a particular interval to the total number of pieces of data collected. The relative frequency represents the proportion of data that falls into a particular interval. Notice that .22, or 22%, of all of the data fall into the interval from 34–38. The **relative cumulative frequency** is the ratio of the cumulative frequency to the total number of pieces of data. It can also be computed by keeping a running total of the relative frequencies that are less than or equal to that of a particular interval. Thus, it can also be known as the cumulative relative frequency.

relative cumulative frequency

For example, the relative cumulative frequency of the data in the interval 39–43 is $\frac{47}{50}$, or .94. It is also the sum of the relative frequencies of the intervals less than or equal to 39–43 (.04 + .10 + .14 + .12 + .12 + .06 + .22 + .14 = .94). The relative cumulative frequency of .94 on this interval can be interpreted as 94% of the enrollments having 43 students or less.

Enrollment	Frequency	Cumulative Frequency	Relative Frequency	Relative Cumulative Frequency
4–8	2	2	.04	.04
9–13	5	7	.10	.14
14–18	7	14	.14	.28
19–23	6	20	.12	.40
24–28	6	26	.12	.52
29–33	3	29	.06	.58
34–38	11	40	.22	.80
39–43	7	47	.14	.94
44–48	3	50	.06	1.00

Investigation 5

A teacher gave a quiz that was worth a total of 20 points. The scores on the quiz were as follows:

15 19 13 15 17 18 19 20 17 12 18 17 15

14 13 20 14 18 15 19 17 14 20 16 13

Construct a frequency table with three intervals. Include the relative frequency, the cumulative frequency, and the relative cumulative frequency. Reach some conclusions about the students' performance on the quiz.

The width of the interval is determined by

$$\frac{\text{Range}}{\text{Number of intervals}}$$

rounded to the next highest whole number. In this case, the interval width is 3, and the range is 20 – 12, or 8.

Score	Frequency	Cumulative Frequency	Relative Frequency	Relative Cumulative Frequency
12–14	7	7	.28	.28
15–17	9	16	.36	.64
18–20	9	25	.36	1.00

Some conclusions that can be drawn based on this frequency table follow:

- Twenty-eight percent of the students scored less than 15 out of 20.
- Seventy-two percent of the students scored 15 out of 20 or better.
- An equal number of students scored on the intervals of 15–17 and 18–20.
- Sixty-four percent of the students scored 17 or less out of 20.

Measures of Central Tendency

Examine the scores on the quiz from Investigation 5. How did the students "typically" do on the quiz? What would be your best estimate of their overall performance? To answer this question, you must determine a single score that is representative of the group as a whole. This typical score is commonly represented by one of the **measures of central tendency**.

measures of central tendency

The Mean

arithmetic average
arithmetic mean

One of the most common statistics that serves this purpose is known as the **arithmetic average**, or the **arithmetic mean**. Most people are familiar with the concept of the mean. The word *average* is used in everyday language. Phrases like "the average citizen," "an average price for a meal," "an average height," and "average miles per gallon" all represent the central tendency of a group of data. When referring to numerical data, the average is determined by dividing the sum of the individual scores by the total number of scores.

In general, for a collection of n scores, $x_1, x_2, x_3, \ldots, x_n$, the average (denoted by $\bar{x}$) is found by

$$\frac{x_1 + x_2 + x_3 + \cdots + x_n}{n}$$

This formula can be simplified by using the Greek letter sigma to represent the sum:

$$\sum_{i=1}^{n} x_i = x_1 + x_2 + x_3 + \cdots + x_n$$

The symbol $\sum_{i=1}^{n} x_i$ is read as "the sum of x sub i, for $i = 1$ to n." The letter i is known as the *index* and it represents the integers from 1 through n. The formula for the mean, $\bar{x}$, can therefore be expressed as

$$\frac{\sum_{i=1}^{n} x_i}{n} \qquad \text{where } n \text{ is the number of pieces of data}$$

The average of the scores in Investigation 5 can be determined as follows:

$$\frac{\sum_{i=1}^{25} x_i}{25} = (15 + 19 + 13 + 15 + 17 + 18 + 19 + 20 + 17 + 12 + 18 + 17 +$$

$$15 + 14 + 13 + 20 + 14 + 18 + 15 + 19 + 17 + 14 + 20 + 16 + 13) \div 25$$

$$= \frac{408}{25}$$

$$= 16.32$$

The mean quiz score is 16.32.

The Median

The next measure of central tendency we will consider is the median. To determine the median, the data must be arranged in numerical order. This is called **ranked data**. The **median** is the value that partitions the ranked data in such a way that half of the data fall below it and half of the data fall above it.

ranked data
median

The median does not necessarily have to be one of the pieces of data under consideration. If the number of scores is odd, the median will be the middle score in the set. If the number of scores is even, the median is defined as the average of the two middle scores.

In the case of the quiz scores above, the data can be arranged in ascending order as follows:

12   13   13   13   14   14   14   15   15   15   15   16   17

17   17   17   18   18   18   19   19   19   20   20   20

Since there is an odd number (25) of scores, the median is the 13th score, which is 17.

Had there been 24 scores, the median would have been the average of the 12th and the 13th scores.

In some cases, the median is a better choice than the mean for locating the central tendency of a set of data. Examine Investigation 6.

Investigation 6

Eleven homes were sold in a certain village during the week of October 20. The selling prices of these homes are listed here:

| $95,990 | $101,000 | $115,000 | $98,000 | $102,999 | $107,000 |
| $545,000 | $103,000 | $111,999 | $99,500 | $104,500 | |

What is the typical selling price of the homes that were sold last week in the village?

Looking at the selling prices, it appears that a typical price was in the low hundred-thousand-dollar range. We can determine the mean of the 11 prices using a calculator as shown here:

AC 95990 + 101000 + 115000 + 98000 + 102999 + 107000

+ 545000 + 103000 + 111999 + 99500 + 104500

= ÷ 11 =

The display should read 143998.9091. The mean selling price was approximately $144,000. This value does not agree with our estimate, and only one price is higher than this amount. Yet this answer is mathematically correct.

Examine the data set carefully. Although 10 of the prices appear to hover around the low hundred-thousand-dollar mark, one price is about five times that amount. This extreme value inflates the sum, which results in a mean that does not accurately represent the typical selling price.

Now, examine the median (in boldface type).

95,990 98,000 99,500 101,000 102,999 **103,000** 104,500 107,000 111,999 115,000 545,000

The median selling price is $103,000. This agrees with our estimate that the prices of homes sold in the village last week were typically in the low hundred-thousand-dollar range. Notice that the extreme value of $545,000 does not inflate the median statistic as it inflates the mean statistic.

The Mode

mode   Finally, we examine the measure of central tendency known as the mode. The **mode** is the most frequently appearing piece of data in the set. The mode has limited usage depending on the situation. When we refer to the "average citizen," we are probably using the mode rather than the median or the mean as our measure of central tendency.

In the set of quiz scores we have been examining, the scores of 15 and 17 both appear the most and an equal number of times. This set of scores therefore has two modes **bimodal** rather than one. We call this set of data **bimodal**.

A real-world example of the use of the mode can be found in a hospital emergency room. Suppose a certain hospital wants to make sure that the correct specialists are on call. For one week, they might make a list of the reasons why people came to the emergency room. At the end of that week, the mode reason might determine the specialists who need to be on call.

Measures of Dispersion

A commuter flight has a capacity of 10 people. The following table lists the weights of 10 pieces of luggage on two of its flights from New York to Boston.

Date	Luggage Weight (in pounds)									
October 20	45	45	50	47	45	43	45	40	45	45
October 21	7	75	18	90	8	82	65	25	10	70

Let A represent the set of luggage weights on the October 20 flight. The mean, $\overline{A}$, is 45 pounds. Let B represent the set of luggage weights on the October 21 flight. The mean, $\overline{B}$, is also 45 pounds. In addition, the median for both sets of data is also 45.

Although both sets of data have the same mean and median, when we examine the individual weights we find that the two data sets are quite different. This can be seen by arranging the data on the number lines in Figure 8.8.

Figure 8.8

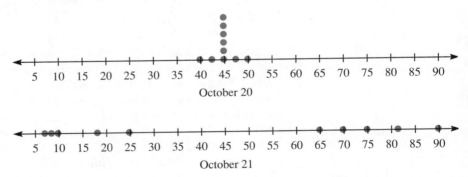

October 20

October 21

Notice that in set A, the data tend to cluster around the mean of 45. The range of this set of data is 10. In set B, the data appear to be much more spread out, or dispersed, with a range of 83.

Reporting only the mean weight for each of these two sets of data does not give us **measures of dispersion** a good indication of the elements of the sets. For this reason, **measures of dispersion**, or variability, are often reported when examining a set of data. Measures of dispersion give the analyst an indication of how varied the data are in a set. We will examine two such measures in this section: the variance and the standard deviation. These measures of dispersion can be used in conjunction with the measures of central tendency to give an overall picture of the entire set of data.

The Variance

The mean weight for each of the two data sets was 45 pounds. Let's examine the directed distance of each of the pieces of data from the mean.

October 20		October 21	
A_i	$A_i - \bar{A}$	B_i	$B_i - \bar{B}$
43	$40 - 45 = -5$	7	$7 - 45 = -38$
43	$43 - 45 = -2$	8	$8 - 45 = -37$
45	$45 - 45 = 0$	10	$10 - 45 = -35$
45	$45 - 45 = 0$	18	$18 - 45 = -27$
45	$45 - 45 = 0$	25	$25 - 45 = -20$
45	$45 - 45 = 0$	65	$65 - 45 = 20$
45	$45 - 45 = 0$	70	$70 - 45 = 25$
45	$45 - 45 = 0$	75	$75 - 45 = 30$
47	$47 - 45 = 2$	82	$82 - 45 = 37$
50	$50 - 45 = 5$	90	$90 - 45 = 45$

Both $A_i - A$ and $B_i - \bar{B}$ yield numbers that indicate the deviation of a piece of data from the mean. Let's examine the sum of the deviations from the mean for each data set. These sums can be symbolized as

$$\sum_{i=1}^{10} (A_i - \bar{A}) \qquad \text{and} \qquad \sum_{i=1}^{10} (B_i - \bar{B})$$

In each case, the sum of the deviations from the mean is equal to zero. This will always be true for the sum of the deviations from the mean. Do you see why? To get a cumulative indication of the dispersion about the mean, each deviation is squared before determining the sum. The squaring eliminates any negatives. The sum of the squares of the deviations from the mean is determined for each set as illustrated here:

October 20			October 21		
A_i	$A_i - \bar{A}$	$(A_i - \bar{A})^2$	B_i	$B_i - \bar{B}$	$(B_i - \bar{B})^2$
43	$40 - 45 = -5$	25	7	$7 - 45 = -38$	1444
43	$43 - 45 = -2$	4	8	$8 - 45 = -37$	1369
45	$45 - 45 = 0$	0	10	$10 - 45 = -35$	1225
45	$45 - 45 = 0$	0	18	$18 - 45 = -27$	729
45	$45 - 45 = 0$	0	25	$25 - 45 = -20$	400
45	$45 - 45 = 0$	0	65	$65 - 45 = 20$	400
45	$45 - 45 = 0$	0	70	$70 - 45 = 25$	625
45	$45 - 45 = 0$	0	75	$75 - 45 = 30$	900
47	$47 - 45 = 2$	4	82	$82 - 45 = 37$	1369
50	$50 - 45 = 5$	25	90	$90 - 45 = 45$	2025

$$\sum_{i=1}^{10} (A_i - \bar{A})^2 = 58 \qquad\qquad \sum_{i=1}^{10} (B_i - \bar{B})^2 = 10,486$$

Notice that the set whose data was more widely dispersed about the mean *(B)* has a much greater sum of the squares of the deviations from the mean. The greater this sum, the more variable is the set of data.

What if the mean had been 45.36527? You can see that the computations above would have been tedious and complex. For this reason, an alternate procedure is used to determine the sum of the squares of the deviations from the mean. This computational formula is stated in symbolic form as:

$$\sum_{i=1}^{n} (X_i - \bar{X})^2 = \sum_{i=1}^{n} (X_i^2) - \frac{\left(\sum\limits_{i=1}^{n} X_i\right)^2}{n}$$

The sum of the squares of the deviations from the mean is equivalent to the sum of the squares of each individual piece of data minus the quotient of the square of the sum of the data and the number of pieces of data.

We are now able to use the sum of the squares of the deviations from the mean to determine the variance. The **variance** is a statistic used for making comparisons. The larger the numerical value of the variance, the more dispersed, or variable, the values in the set are from the mean and from each other. The variance is denoted by the symbol σ^2 ("sigma squared") and is computed as follows:

variance

$$\frac{\sum\limits_{i=1}^{n} (X_i - \bar{X})^2}{n}$$

that is, it is the average of the sum of the squares of the deviations from the mean.

No set boundaries delineate "widely dispersed" from "somewhat dispersed" and "clustered about the mean." These phrases have meaning only within a particular context.

The variance can be used to compare sets of scores. Consider Investigation 7.

Investigation 7

A certain teacher teaches two classes of sixth-grade mathematics. He decides to give the same exam to both his first-period class and his second-period class. The scores on the exam in each class are as follows:

First Period: 85 83 74 70 88 95   89 72 90 83 77 91 98
               89 82 84

Second Period: 95 89 82 81 72 69 100 97 75 91 82 79 96
               81 80 95 89 97 83   71

Discuss the test results in terms of the mean and the variance.

 The mean scores in each of the classes are as follows:

First Period: 84.375

Second Period: 85.200

The averages are relatively close to one another; that of the second-period class is slightly higher.

We will determine the variance (using the computational formula and a calculator) to see how the grades in each class are dispersed about the respective means. The following procedures can be used to determine the variance.

First, we will determine the sum of the squares of the scores. This sum is then stored in the calculator's memory. Next, we will compute the value for

$$\frac{\left(\sum\limits_{i=1}^{n} X_i\right)^2}{n}$$

This value is then subtracted from the sum of the squares that has been stored in memory.

The sum of the squares can be found in a number of ways, depending on the capability of your calculator. If your calculator has a $\boxed{y^x}$ key, the first score of 85 would be squared as follows:

$$85 \quad \boxed{y^x} \quad 2 \quad \boxed{=}$$

The display should read 7225.

If your calculator has constant arithmetic capability, the square of 85 can be determined by using the following sequence:

$$85 \quad \boxed{\times} \quad \boxed{=}$$

The display should read 7225.

If your calculator has an $\boxed{x^2}$ key, this key squares the value that is in the display and can be used as follows:

$$85 \quad \boxed{x^2}$$

The display should read 7225.

If your calculator has none of the above capabilities, the square of 85 can be determined by

$$85 \quad \boxed{\times} \quad 85 \quad \boxed{=}$$

We will use this last case along with the $\boxed{M+}$ key. After each score is squared, the value is added to that in the memory. The final value in memory will be the sum of the squares.

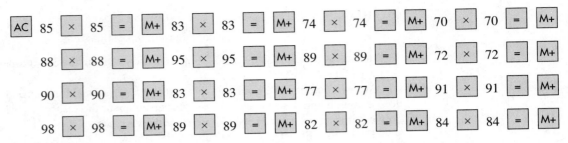

The total value in memory can be displayed by pressing the MR (memory recall) key. This display should read 114868.

Next, the quotient

$$\frac{\left(\sum_{i=1}^{n} X_i\right)^2}{n}$$

is determined as follows:

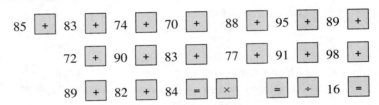

This portion finds the sum of the scores, squares it, then divides that number by 16.

The display should read 113906.25.

The sum of the squares of the deviations from the mean is the difference between the amount stored in memory and the last value that was computed. It can be calculated using *either* of the following calculator keystroke sequences:

113906.25 M– MR

This subtracts 113906.25 from the value that is stored in memory. It then displays 961.75.

113906.25 +/– M+ MR

This changes the sign of 113906.25 to a negative and then adds that amount to the value in memory. In effect, 113906.25 has been subtracted from 114868. The display then reads 961.75.

Finally, the variance of the test scores in the first class is determined by dividing 961.75 by 16. The variance is 60.109375.

The above procedure is followed for the test scores in the second-period class. That variance is found to be 86.86. The variance of the scores in the second-period class is greater than the variance of the scores in the first-period class. In other words, the scores in the first-period class fall closer to the mean than those in the second-period class. The scores of the second-period class are more variable in relation to the mean and to each other. The teacher might interpret this to mean that the performance of the students in his first-period class was more homogeneous than in his second-period class.

Statistical calculators and computer software that can perform a wide variety of statistical computations are available. If you use these tools, you will still have to know how to interpret the data and information they generate.

The Standard Deviation

standard deviation (SD) Because the variance is the result of a statistic that has been squared, it is difficult to relate it to the original data. For this reason, statisticians use a measure of dispersion called the standard deviation when reporting information about a set of data. The **standard deviation (SD)** is the positive square root of the variance and is denoted by σ. In Investigation 7 the standard deviation for the scores in the first-period class is $\sqrt{60.10937}$, ≈ 7.753. The standard deviation for the scores in the second-period class is $\sqrt{86.86}$, ≈ 9.32. To understand the meaning of the standard deviation, we plot all of the scores on two separate number lines, shown in Figure 8.9 and Figure 8.10.

Figure 8.9

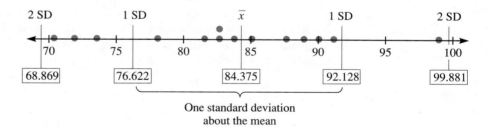

One standard deviation
about the mean

Notice that the scores of 77, 82, 83, 84, 85, 88, 89, 90, and 91 fall within one standard deviation above and below the mean. The remainder of the scores are two standard deviations above and below the mean. All of the scores on the test in the first-period class are within two standard deviations of the mean.

We repeat this procedure for the second-period class in Figure 8.10.

Figure 8.10

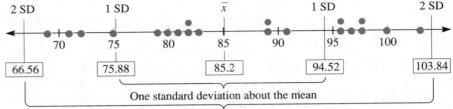

One standard deviation about the mean

Two standard deviations about the mean

All of the scores in the second-period class are also captured within two standard deviations of the mean, but here the standard deviation is greater than in the first-period class since the scores are more widely dispersed about the mean.

Measures of Individual Performance

The standard deviation and the variance gave us information about sets of scores and allowed us to interpret class performance. We now shift our attention to individual performances.

z-Scores

Suppose that Marc is a student in the first-period class, and that he scored 95% correct on the exam. Zoe, a student in the second-period class, also scored 95% correct. Are the two scores equivalent in relation to the scores in their respective classes?

In the first-period class, a score of 95 was 10.625 points above the mean. In the second-period class, a score of 95 was 9.8 points above the mean. The difference between the deviations from the mean appears slight, and comparisons made using such numbers do not reflect the relative performance of the rest of the class. Since we have already seen that comparisons can be made using the standard deviation, we will examine how many standard deviations from the mean each score is. We can do this by dividing the deviation from the mean by the respective standard deviation, as shown here:

Marc	*Zoe*
First-period mean score: 84.375	Second-period mean score: 85.2
Standard deviation: 7.753	Standard deviation 9.32
Deviation from the mean: $(95 - 84.375)$ 10.625	Deviation from the mean: $(95 - 85.2)$ 9.8
$\dfrac{\text{Deviation from mean}}{\text{Standard deviation}} = \dfrac{10.625}{7.753} \approx 1.37$	$\dfrac{\text{Deviation from mean}}{\text{Standard deviation}} = \dfrac{9.8}{9.32} \approx 1.05$

z-score　　The last statistic in each column is known as the z-score. The **z-score** is a standard score that indicates the number of standard deviations an individual piece of data is from the mean. A general formula for the z-score, z, of a particular piece of data, x, where $\bar{x}$ represents the mean and σ represents the standard deviation, is

$$z = \frac{x - \bar{x}}{\sigma}$$

Using z-scores allows for comparisons of individual scores between sets of data. Since Marc's z-score of 1.37 is greater than Zoe's z-score of 1.05, Marc's score of 95% was a better performance in the first-period class in relation to the performances of the others in that class.

Let's compute the z-scores of two grades that fell below the mean in each class. A score of 72 occurred in both of the class sections.

First Period

$$z = \frac{72 - 84.375}{7.753} \approx -1.6$$

Second Period

$$z = \frac{72 - 85.2}{9.32} \approx -1.4$$

Notice that both z-scores are negative. A negative z-score indicates that the original piece of data fell below the mean; a positive z-score indicates that the original piece of data was above the mean. A score of 72 in the first-period class is 1.6 standard deviations below the mean of that class. A score of 72 in the second-period class is 1.4 standard deviations below the mean of that class. Therefore, in relation to the performance of the class, a score of 72 in the first-period class is not as good as a score of 72 in the second-period class.

Notice that a score of 88 in the first-period class has a z-score equivalent of approximately .468. A score of 89 in the second-period class has a z-score equivalent of approximately .408. What conclusion can you draw from this?

Investigation 8

Twenty students took a science test. The class mean was 82.25 with a standard deviation of 7.5. Adriana's z-score equivalent of her test score was +1.3. What was Adriana's actual score on the exam?

Understand the Problem: You are given several descriptive statistics about a specific test. You are asked to interpret and use this information in order to determine Adriana's exam score.

Devise a Plan: To solve this problem, work backwards using the z-score formula.

Carry Out the Plan: Since

$$z = \frac{x - \overline{x}}{\sigma}$$

it follows that

$$1.3 = \frac{x - 82.25}{7.5}$$

The following calculator keystroke sequence can be used to determine the test score:

$$\boxed{\text{AC}} \quad 1.3 \quad \boxed{\times} \quad 7.5 \quad \boxed{+} \quad 82.25 \quad \boxed{=}$$

The display should read 92. Adriana's test score was 92.

Look Back: Verify that the score of 92 is equivalent to the z-score of 1.3 in this testing situation.

Normal Curves

Examine the following set of test scores:

100   85   82   95   90   93   93   87   99   88

87   91   91   90   97   92   89   90   81   83

The data can be organized into a frequency table and pictured in the histogram shown in Figure 8.11.

Figure 8.11

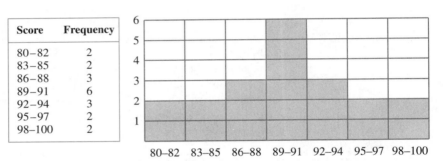

Score	Frequency
80–82	2
83–85	2
86–88	3
89–91	6
92–94	3
95–97	2
98–100	2

Because the frequency table illustrates how the scores are distributed, we call the list a frequency distribution. Notice the symmetry in the histogram, which pictures this frequency distribution. We can present this information in a different way. First, locate the midpoint of the top of each bar in the histogram (see Figure 8.12a). Then connect these midpoints with a smooth curve to produce a bell-shaped graph as shown in Figure 8.12 b.

Why does this graph have such a shape? Examine the distribution. Much of the data can be found in the middle portion of the distribution. The mean of this distribution is 90.15, the median is 90, and the mode is also 90, all of which occur toward the center of the bell-shaped curve.

In Figure 8.12 the data were selected so that a smooth, symmetrical bell-shaped curve would result. Not all data sets produce such curves. Statisticians have found that certain distributions will result in curves that are approximately bell-shaped. A few of the many such distributions are heights of American females, IQ scores, and the sums obtained when a fair set of dice are tossed many times. Obviously, not all distributions **normal curve** are that predictable. The bell-shaped curve, or **normal curve** as it is often called, is theoretical in nature. Many important actual frequency distributions closely approximate it.

Let's examine some other characteristics of the normal curve. Notice that the frequency distribution is at its highest in the center of the graph. As you move away from the center, the graph declines, indicating a decrease in the frequencies. In the theoretical

Figure 8.12

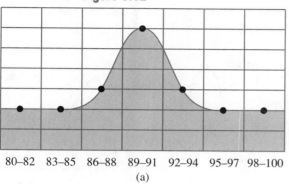

(a)

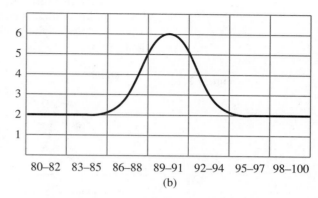

(b)

normal curve, the mean, median, and mode scores are all found at the same point. The vertical line drawn through this point will intersect the peak of the graph, partitioning it into two congruent regions. For this reason, the theoretical normal curve is said to be symmetric about the measures of central tendency (see Figure 8.13).

Figure 8.13

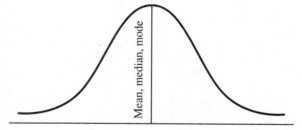

Another interesting characteristic of a normal distribution (a distribution whose graph resembles the normal curve) is that a somewhat predictable percentage of scores will be found between easily located boundary points. These boundary points are determined using the standard deviation and the mean. About 68% of the data in a normal distribution fall between one standard deviation above and below the mean. About 95% of the data in a normal distribution fall between two standard deviations above and below the mean. And about 99.7% of the data fall between three standard deviations above and below the mean (see Figure 8.14).

Figure 8.14

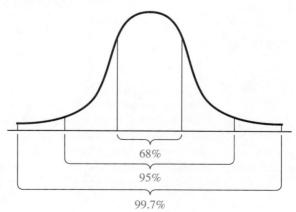

Be aware that distributions considered to be normal are in actuality only approximately so. In addition, some distributions do not approximate the normal distribution. Some examples of the graphical representations of these distributions are shown in Figure 8.15.

Figure 8.15

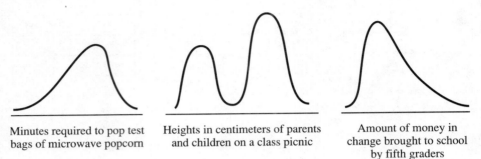

Minutes required to pop test
bags of microwave popcorn

Heights in centimeters of parents
and children on a class picnic

Amount of money in
change brought to school
by fifth graders

When discussing the mean, median, and mode, measures of central location were important. We now turn to data that may or may not be centrally located in the distribution.

Notice in Figure 8.16 that the center of the distribution, the median, is labeled as 50%. The median can be defined as the score that is better than 50% of the other scores in the distribution. Recall that one standard deviation above and below the mean in the normal distribution captured approximately 68% of the scores in the distribution. The z-scores of -1 and $+1$ are labeled 16% and 84%, respectively. In a normal distribution, 16% of the scores have a z-score equivalent that is less than -1, and 84% of the scores have a z-score equivalent that is less than $+1$.

Figure 8.16

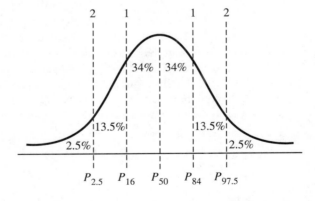

As you already know, not all distributions are normal distributions. But even in distributions that are not normal, we are able to compare scores by examining the relative location of the data in terms of percentages. A statistic commonly reported on standardized test results that allows a particular score to be interpreted in terms of the percentage of scores falling below that score is known as the **percentile equivalent**, or **percentile rank**, of a score. If a score on a certain reading exam is reported at the 85th percentile, this means that 85% of the grades scored on that particular test fell below

percentile equivalent
percentile rank

that score. This can be symbolized by P_{85}. In general, if a score has a percentile equivalent of x, it can be symbolized by P_x and interpreted as "$x\%$ of the data falls below P_x." For example, suppose there are 25 scores in a distribution, and a particular score ranks 21st when the list is arranged in increasing numerical order. There are 20 scores that fall below the 21st score in this distribution. Therefore, since $\frac{20}{25} \times 100 = 80\%$, 80 percent of the scores are less than the 21st score. The percentile rank is 80.

quartiles

first quartile (lower quartile)

second quartile

third quartile (upper quartile)

Identifying the percentile rank of a particular score in a distribution allows us to make comparisons between and among scores. It is common for a distribution to be divided into four parts such that P_{25}, P_{50}, and P_{75} are identified as **quartiles**. We give each of these values a special name and notation. The **first quartile**, Q_1, is the smallest number that is greater than 25% of the scores (P_{25}). This quartile is sometimes known as the **lower quartile**. The **second quartile**, Q_2, is the median (P_{50}). The **third quartile** is the smallest number that is greater than 75% of the scores (P_{75}). This quartile is sometimes known as the **upper quartile** (Q_3).

For computation purposes, if the number of scores in a distribution is divisible by 4, ($\frac{n}{4} = a$ where a is an integer), then Q_1 is the average of the ath and the $(a + 1)$th scores in the ranked distribution. For example, if 12 scores were in the distribution, the lower quartile would be the average of the third and fourth scores.

If $\frac{3}{4} \times n$ is an integer (75% of $n = b$ where b is an integer), the upper quartile is the value that is the average of the bth and the $(b + 1)$th scores in the distribution. For example, if 32 scores are in the distribution,

$$\frac{n}{4} = \frac{32}{4} = 8$$

The value of Q_1 will be the average of the eighth and ninth scores in the ranked distribution.

If $\frac{n}{4}$ and $\frac{3}{4}n$ are not integers, the respective quartiles are found by rounding up the quotients. For example, if 25 scores are in the distribution,

$$\frac{n}{4} = \frac{25}{4} = 6.25$$

The value of Q_1 will be the seventh score in the ranked distribution. The value of Q_3 will be the nineteenth score in the ranked distribution since $\frac{3}{4} \times 25 = 18.75$.

It is easy to see why quartiles and percentiles are measures of location. These equivalents divide a distribution in such a way that scores can be compared in relation to other scores in the distribution. Examine Investigation 9.

Investigation 9

Recall the situation from Investigation 7.

First Period: 85 83 74 70 88 95   89 72 90 83 77 91 98
89 82 84

Second Period: 95 89 82 81 72 69 100 97 75 91 82 79 96
81 80 95 89 97 83   71

We have already examined Marc's score of 95 in the first-period class and Zoe's score of 95 in the second-period class. These scores were discussed in relation to the mean in each class. Examine Rich's score of 91 in the first-period class and Allison's score of 91 in the second-period class. Interpret these scores in terms of their percentile rank equivalents. What are the first, second, and third quartiles in each of the classes? How does this information give you a better picture of each of the grades in their respective classes?

To solve this problem, we must arrange the data from each of the classes in ascending order as shown here:

First Period: 70 72 74 77 82 83 83 84 85 88 89 89 90
                91 95 98

Second Period: 69 71 72 75 79 80 81 81 82 82 83 89 89
                91 95 95 96 97 97 100

The quartiles in each distribution are determined as follows:

	First Period		*Second Period*

Q_1 $\dfrac{16}{4} = 4$ (Average of 4th and 5th scores) $\dfrac{20}{4} = 5$ (Average of 5th and 6th scores)

$Q_1 = \dfrac{77 + 82}{2} = 79.5$ $Q_1 = \dfrac{79 + 80}{2} = 79.5$

Q_2 $Q_2 = \text{Median} = \dfrac{84 + 85}{2} = 84.5$ $Q_2 = \text{Median} = \dfrac{82 + 83}{2} = 82.5$

Q_3 $\dfrac{3}{4} \times 16 = 12$ (Average of 12th and 13th scores) $\dfrac{3}{4} \times 20 = 15$ (Average of 15th and 16th scores)

$Q_3 = \dfrac{89 + 90}{2} = 89.5$ $Q_3 = \dfrac{95 + 95}{2} = 95$

Since 13 out of the 16 scores in the first-period class were below Rich's score of 91, the percentile rank of 91 in that distribution is $\frac{13}{16} \times 100 = 81.25$. In the second-period class, 13 out of the 20 scores were below Allison's score of 91. The percentile rank of this grade is $\frac{13}{20} \times 100 = 65$.

Clearly, a case can be made that Rich's score of 91 represents a better performance in relation to the scores of the other students in the first-period class than does Allison's score of 91 in relation to those in her class. Rich's score falls above the third quartile and is better than 81.25% of those who took the test in his class. Allison's score is between the second and third quartiles in her distribution and is better than only 65% of the grades in her class.

Notice how a knowledge of the relative location of the same numerical scores in each class leads to a completely different interpretation in relation to the other performances in the respective classes.

Box-and-Whisker Plots

box-and-whisker plot

lowest extreme value
highest extreme value

The mathematician J. W. Tukey developed a simple graphical method of displaying the data in a distribution. This design is known as the **box-and-whisker plot** because of its appearance. To construct a simple box-and-whisker plot, the following information is needed: Q_1, Q_2, and Q_3; the **lowest extreme value**, which is the lowest value in the distribution; and the **highest extreme value**, which is the highest value in the distribution.

We will construct a box-and-whisker plot for the set of test scores from the first-period class of Investigation 9.

$$Q_1 = 79.5 \qquad Q_2 = 84.5 \qquad Q_3 = 89.5$$

Lowest extreme value: 70

Highest extreme value: 98

A number line is first drawn that begins and ends at any convenient points whose values will capture all of the data in the distribution. In this case, we will construct a number line from 60 to 100 with equal intervals of five units. On that number line we will locate the extreme values and the values of the first, second, and third quartiles. Below the number line, the box-and-whisker plot is drawn as shown in Figure 8.17. Notice that the extreme values are the endpoints of the line segment. The box is formed by the first and third quartiles. The median partitions the box into two regions.

Figure 8.17

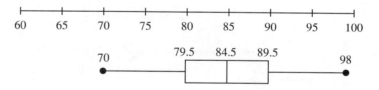

The line segment from the lower extreme value to the lower quartile and the line segment from the upper quartile to the upper extreme value form the "whiskers" of the plot. The box captures approximately 50% of the scores in the distribution, and each whisker captures approximately 25% of the scores. The "width" of the box is the difference between the upper quartile and the lower quartile. This value is known as the **interquartile range**

outliers

interquartile range. The interquartile range is a very important value since it is used to classify the set of values that are widely dispersed from the median. These values are called **outliers** and are defined as those values that are more than 1.5 interquartile ranges above the upper quartile and more than 1.5 interquartile ranges below the lower quartile. In the distribution shown in Figure 8.17, the interquartile range is 89.5 – 79.5, or 10. Since more than 15 units (1.5 interquartile ranges) yield values that are greater than the highest extreme value and less than the lowest extreme value, this particular distribution of grades has no outliers.

The box-and-whisker plot allows the user to view at a glance the nature of the dispersion of a distribution and the relative locations of particular pieces of data within it. The box-and-whisker plot for the second-period class in Investigation 9 is shown in Figure 8.18. Compare this visual representation with that of Figure 8.17. What can you conclude?

Figure 8.18

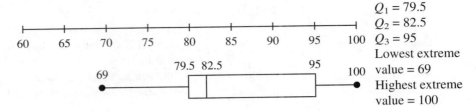

$Q_1 = 79.5$
$Q_2 = 82.5$
$Q_3 = 95$
Lowest extreme
value = 69
Highest extreme
value = 100

Investigation 10

A physical education teacher records the time it takes each of her students to run a mile. The box-and-whisker plots for her first-period class and her eighth-period class are given here:

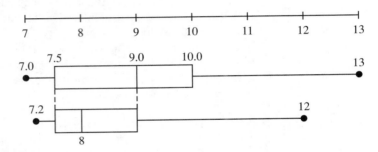

Discuss a time of 9.0 minutes in each of the two classes.

In this situation, a shorter time is "better" than a longer time. Determine the location of the value of 9.0 in each distribution. In the first-period class, 9.0 is the median. Therefore, 50% of the students had a better time than 9.0. In the eighth-period class, 9.0 is the upper quartile. Therefore, 75% of the students in this class had a better time than 9.0. A time of 9.0 in the first-period class is a better time than in the eighth-period class.

A possible interpretation of the differences between the two classes might be that some of the track team members are in the afternoon class.

Assessments for Section 8.2

1. Examine the following frequency table, which illustrates the duration in minutes of phone calls made from a certain extension on March 21.

Duration (in minutes)	Number of Calls
0–4	2
5–9	4
10–14	8
15–19	10
20–24	6
25–29	6

(a) Complete the table by determining the cumulative frequency, the relative frequency, and the relative cumulative frequency.

(b) Based on the information compiled in your table, what generalizations can you make concerning calls that lasted 20–24 minutes?

2. A teacher gave a 15-point quiz. The scores are as follows:

11 13 15 10 13 15 8 9 14 15 7 5 15
14 13 15 14 9 10 13 12 7 9 10 15

(a) Construct a frequency table with the intervals 0–1, 2–3, 4–5, 6–7, 8–9, 10–11, 12–13, 14–15. Include the frequency, cumulative frequency, relative frequency, and relative cumulative frequency.

(b) Draw three conclusions based on the information in this table.

(c) Suppose the teacher incorrectly graded a student's quiz. The score written on his paper was 9, but should have been 14. How will this affect the table? Explain rather than calculate your answer.

3. Suppose there are 200 scores in a distribution. The distribution has been partitioned into five equal intervals (A, B, C, D, and E) whose relative frequencies are listed here:

Interval	Relative frequency
A	.06
B	.25
C	.55
D	.10
E	.04

Determine the frequencies in each of the intervals.

4. Suppose there are 80 scores in a distribution. The distribution has been partitioned into five equal intervals (A, B, C, D, and E) whose relative cumulative frequencies are listed here:

Interval	Relative Cumulative Frequency
A	.05
B	.40
C	.55
D	.75
E	1.00

Determine the frequencies and relative frequencies in each interval.

5. A certain brand of battery is tested in a child's toy. The following list consists of the "life span" of the batteries reported, in hours.

8.2 9.5 7.0 4.5 10.8 8.75 9.25 11.0 9.25 8.0
8.9 9.0 10.5 9.5 10.2 9.50 7.25 7.0 9.10 9.7

(a) What is the mean lifetime of this brand of battery?

(b) What is the median lifetime of this brand of battery?

(c) What is the mode lifetime of this brand of battery?

6. The net change in the price of one share of stock over a 10-day period is given here:

$$+\frac{1}{2} \quad +1\frac{1}{2} \quad -1 \quad 0 \quad -\frac{1}{8} \quad -\frac{1}{4} \quad +\frac{1}{2} \quad -\frac{5}{8} \quad -\frac{1}{4} \quad +\frac{7}{8}$$

(a) What is the mean net change over this 10-day period?

(b) What is the median net change over this 10-day period?

(c) What is the mode net change over this 10 day period?

7. A certain student has the following test scores: 85, 75, 90, and 88. His instructor is giving one more exam. What score must the student achieve on the exam so that the average of the five tests is 87?

8. Determine a set of eight test scores whose mean, median, and mode are the same. The distribution should be such that all scores are not identical.

9. Determine a set of five test scores whose mean is 85, median is 84, and mode is 84.

10. The following stacked bar graph illustrates the absentee figures for two weeks at Marlton High School. The official enrollment at the school is 500 students. The bar representing the week of May 5 is dark grey. The bar representing the week of May 12 is light grey.

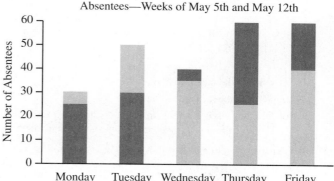

Absentees—Weeks of May 5th and May 12th

(a) What is the mean daily number of absentees during the week of May 5?

(b) What is the mean daily number of absentees during the week of May 12?

(c) What is the mean daily attendance during the week of May 5?

(d) What is the mean daily attendance during the week of May 12?

(e) What is the mean daily attendance over the 10-day period?

(f) What is the median number of absentees over the 10-day period?

(g) What conclusions can you draw?

11. Two elementary schools are located in a certain district. The class-size figures for each school are given here:

Grades:	K	1	2	3	4	5	6
School A:	15 18	23 27	34 33	29 25	23 24	30 33	28 28
School B:	14	20	35	35	28	29	32

(a) Determine the average class enrollment in each of the two schools (round to nearest tenth).

(b) Determine the variance for each of the two sets of data.

(c) Draw a conclusion based on a comparison of the variance figures.

12. The following stem-and-leaf plots depict the scores on two math exams given by a particular teacher to the same class. (The exam was scored out of 100 possible points.)

Exam 1

Stems	Leaves
5	8 7 5
6	7 9 5
7	3
8	5 1 0 3 7 1 7
9	2 9 3 6 1 9 1 0 0 2 7
10	0 0 0

Exam 2

Stems	Leaves
6	2 6 8 7
7	1 9 5
8	3 8 2 9 3 7 1 0 6 8 1
9	2 9 3 7 1 7 1 2 9 2

(a) What is the mean score on Exam 1?

(b) What is the mean score on Exam 2?

(c) Discuss a score of 92 on each of the two exams in terms of the standard deviation and z-score equivalent.

13. Construct a stem-and-leaf plot and a bar graph for the following set of test scores.

85 77 54 67 89 99 90 94 65 79 64

73 66 85 88 94 72 71 98 81 83 59

60 92 74 79 85 88 99 91 90 66 71

14. A swimming relay team recorded the following times at their 10 meets during the season. The times are reported in minutes.

4.3   4.5   4.4   3.9   4.8   5.0   4.7   4.4   3.8   4.0

Construct a box-and-whisker plot for the relay times.

15. A certain theater has 400 seats. The theater shows a particular movie six times during the course of one day. On a particular Saturday, the following sales were reported:

10:00 show:	55% occupied
12:10 show:	70% occupied
2:30 show:	65% occupied
4:50 show:	60% occupied
6:45 show:	85% occupied
9:10 show:	95% occupied

(a) What was the average number of occupied seats per show?

(b) Construct a box-and-whisker plot for the show occupancies.

16. Examine the following box-and-whisker plot.

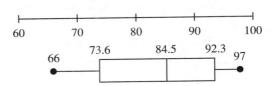

(a) What is the value of the lower quartile?

(b) What is the value of the upper quartile?

(c) What is the interquartile range?

(d) Would 95 be considered an outlier? Explain your answer.

17. The following box-and-whisker plots compare the scores on a pretest in two classes.

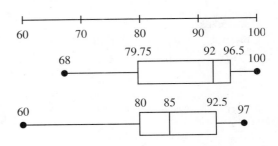

(a) Is there any way to determine the exact mean of each distribution? Explain your answer.

(b) Is there any way to determine the exact median of each distribution?

(c) Discuss a grade of 87 in each class.

(d) What is the interquartile range for each plot?

(e) Give two values that would be considered outliers in the second distribution.

18. Arthur took an examination. He knows that his z-score is .5, the mean of the scores is 87, and the standard deviation of the scores is 2.5. What was Arthur's score on the test?

19. Marta took an examination on which she scored 88. She knows that the z-score is 1.3 and the mean of the scores is 83. What was the standard deviation for this set of test scores?

20. Rich took an examination. The mean score was 90 with a variance of 64. His z-score equivalent is $-.2$. What is Rich's test grade?

21. The following scores are reported on a 50-point quiz:

45   38   23   34   45   29   40   40   42   33
15   40   29   31   37   41   25   43   41   36

If the teacher adds 5 points to every grade (keeping the total point value equal to 50), what effect does this change have on each of the following?

(a) The mean

(b) The median

(c) The mode

(d) The standard deviation

(c) The upper quartile

(d) The lower quartile

(e) The interquartile range

22. Flour is packaged in 5-lb bags. Each bag of flour is weighed as it comes off the assembly line. The following list contains 20 weights of randomly chosen bags. The weights are reported in pounds.

4.95   4.96   5   5.2   5   5.25   5   5.01   5.1   5
5.3   4.75   4.875   5   4.99 4.95   5.02   5   4.8   5

(a) Determine the mean, median, and mode weights.

(b) Determine the values of Q_1, Q_2, and Q_3.

(c) What is the percentile rank of a weight of 4.99?

(d) Determine P_{80}.

23. Fifty cereals were tested for their fat content per serving. The following circle graph illustrates the results of this study.

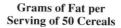

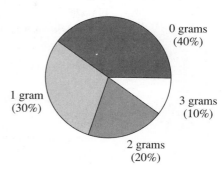

Grams of Fat per Serving of 50 Cereals

(a) Determine the mean, median, and mode fat content per serving

(b) What is the standard deviation of this distribution?

In Other Words

24. Why are the mean, median, and mode known as measures of central tendency?

25. What is the difference between measures of central tendency and measures of location?

26. What is the limitation of the variance statistic?

27. Suppose that a teacher wished to "curve" a test using the normal curve. What might that mean?

28. Explain the significance of a test score at the 80th percentile.

Cooperative Activity

29. Groups of four

Individual Accountability: Each member of the group is responsible for collecting the measure in centimeters of the lengths of the left foot of 20 people. Determine the mean, median, mode, and standard deviation of your distribution. Construct a box-and-whisker plot to illustrate the data.

Group Goal: Combine the data. Determine the mean, median, mode, and standard deviation for the total distribution of 80. Construct a box-and-whisker plot for this larger set. Compare the individual statistics with the group statistics. Draw some conclusions.

Vocabulary for Chaper 8

arithmetic average	mode
arithmetic mean	normal curve
bar graph	outliers
bimodal	percentile equivalent
box-and-whisker plot	percentile rank
circle graph	picture graph
cumulative frequency	quartiles
data	range
first quartile (lower quartile)	ranked data
frequency	relative cumulative frequency
highest extreme value	relative frequency
histogram	second quartile
interquartile range	standard deviation (SD)
interval width	stem-and-leaf plot
line graph	statistics
lower interval limits	tally
lowest extreme value	third quartile (upper quartile)
measures of central tendency	upper interval limits
measures of dispersion	variance
median	z-score

Review for Chapter 8

1. Examine the following set of data:

   45 35 25 30 22 18 10 36 45 50
   19 43 16 18 35 22 29 31 43 49
   28 37 41 22 13 19 27 22 33 42

   (a) Construct a frequency table using seven intervals with the lowest value in the first interval equal to 10.

   (b) Construct a stem-and-leaf plot with the stem equal to the tens place digit.

2. Examine the following set of data in this stem-and-leaf plot.

Stems	Leaves
0	9 8 5
1	4 2 6 1 4
2	3 1 2
3	0 7 6 1 7 5
4	2
5	0 7

   Construct a histogram using the partitions of the stem-and-leaf plot.

3. You are given the following tally chart. Construct a frequency table that includes the relative frequency, cumulative frequency, and relative cumulative frequency.

70–74	II
75–79	ЦНТ
80–84	IIII
85–89	ЦНТ ЦНТ II
90–94	ЦНТ
95–99	ЦНТ III
100–104	IIII

4. Determine the missing values in the following frequency table.

Interval	Frequency	Relative Frequency	Cumulative Frequency	Relative Cumulative Frequency
1	30	.2	(a)	(b)
2	(c)	.3	(d)	.5
3	60	.4	(e)	(f)
4	(g)	.06	(h)	(i)
5	(j)	(k)	(l)	(m)

5. Determine the relative frequency, cumulative frequency, and relative cumulative frequency from the following histogram.

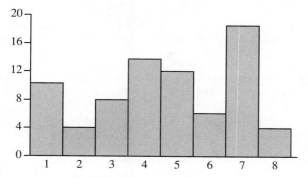

6. The bar graph below illustrates the daily number of car sales at a dealership over a 10-day period.

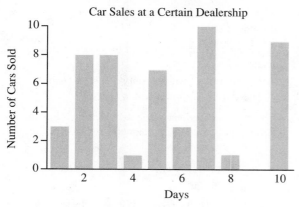

(a) What is the average number of cars sold daily?

(b) What is the median number of cars sold?

(c) What is the percent decrease in sales from Day 7 to Day 8?

(d) What percentage of the total sales were made on Day 3?

7. A certain hotel considers 25 no-shows per day to be average. The following hanging bar graph depicts the number of no-shows over an eight-day period.

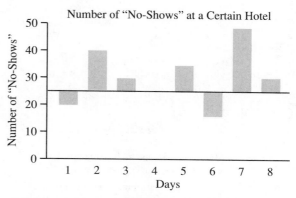

(a) Interpret the data represented by the Day 2 bar.

(b) Interpret the data represented by the Day 4 bar.

(c) How many more no-shows than average occurred on Day 7?

(d) What is the median number of no-shows over the eight-day period?

(e) Convert these data into a form that can be used to construct a regular bar graph. Construct the bar graph.

8. The variable mortgage rates that were reported on the 15th of each month for a one-year period are listed here.

January: 9.75%	July: 10.5%
February: 9.5%	August: 10.25%
March: 9.0%	September: 10%
April: 9.25%	October: 9.75%
May: 9.75%	November: 9.5%
June: 10.0%	December: 8.75%

(a) What might be an appropriate graph to illustrate these data. Explain your reasoning.

(b) What are the mean, median, and mode variable percentage rates.

9. The following stacked bar graph on page 392 illustrates the number of emergency road-service calls that an automobile club received during the first 10 days of 1992 and the first 10 days of 1993.

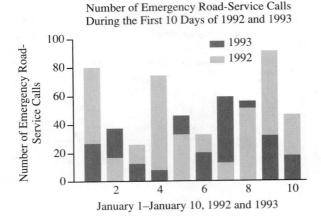

Number of Emergency Road-Service Calls
During the First 10 Days of 1992 and 1993

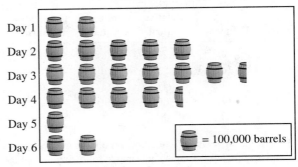

Barrels of Oil Shipped

Determine the median and mean daily shipment.

(a) Estimate (rather than compute) the average daily number of road-service calls received over this 10-day period in 1992.

(b) Estimate (rather than compute) the average daily number of road-service calls received over this 10-day period in 1993.

(c) Between which two days did the sharpest increase occur (in either year)?

10. The water reserves at a particular reservoir are reported as percentages below and above a predetermined normal level. These daily percentages are listed here for February. A positive number indicates a percentage above the normal level, and a negative number indicates a percentage below the normal level.

1.5	1.45	1.4	1.35	1.3	1	.8
.75	.7	.63	.63	.63	.62	.6
.5	.4	.3	.1	−.1	−.25	−.3
−.5	−.5	−.2	0	.5	.6	.4

(a) What is the average daily water reserve percentage for February?

(b) What is the standard deviation of the percentages reported for February?

(c) What are the values of the lower quartile, median, and upper quartile for this set of data?

11. Examine the following picture graph.

12. Examine the following circle graph, which depicts a single day's activities of a particular school teacher from 8:00 A.M. to 4:00 P.M.

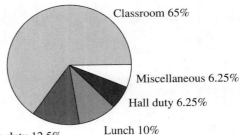

**One Day's Activities of
a Particular School Teacher**

Classroom 65%

Miscellaneous 6.25%

Hall duty 6.25%

Lunch 10%

Bus duty 12.5%

Use the circle graph to determine the duration, in hours and minutes, of each category.

(a) Classroom   (b) Bus duty   (c) Lunch
(d) Hall duty   (e) Miscellaneous

13. Construct a stacked bar graph to depict the following data concerning total course enrollments for an academic year in five subjects.

Course Number	Fall	Spring
64050	250	200
64140	120	140
64240	180	170
64250	130	100
54340	90	90

14. Examine the following line graph. Estimate the data indicated for each month. Develop a situation in which this graph might be used.

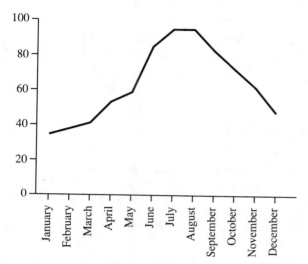

15. A certain college administers a common final examination at the end of a calculus course to all sections of the course. The results are tabulated in the following table:

Section	Number of Students	Mean	Median	Standard Deviation
01	35	75.6	88	10.2
02	30	82.5	83	2.5
03	30	83	80	5.5
04	25	85.25	85	4.75
05	30	87.5	90	6

(a) Determine the z-score equivalent of a grade of 83 in each of the sections. Rank the sections in terms of the relative performance of a grade of 83.

(b) Assume that the classes were ranked from the lowest standard deviation to the highest standard deviation. What might this ranking indicate.

16. Construct a box-and-whisker plot from the following stem-and-leaf plot. All data are less than 60.

Stems	Leaves
0	2 4 3 1
1	9 7 3 4 3 1 6
2	2 8 5 1 3 5 1
3	1 3 0 0 2 4 9 1
4	7 6 5 7 1 0 1 9
5	0 1 7 2 9 0

17. Suppose that a set of 50 scores is normally distributed with a mean of 83.5 and a standard deviation of 6.5.

(a) Determine the raw-score boundary points that are equivalent to one standard deviation above and below the mean.

(b) Determine the z-score equivalent of a score of 80.

(c) Determine the raw-score equivalent of a z-score of −1.5.

(d) Approximately how many of the scores fall within one standard deviation of the mean?

18. Use the state-area data presented in Problem 4 of Section 8.1 (see page 363) to answer the following questions.

(a) What is the median area? Is this the exact area of a state? If so, which state? If not, explain your answer.

(b) What is the lower quartile?

(c) What is the upper quartile?

(d) What is the interquartile range?

(e) Identify the states whose areas would be considered outliers. Explain your answer.

19. A distribution consists of 15 whole number scores, 3 of which are missing. The remaining 12 are given here:

75 86 62 91 89 65 88 100 95 79 76 89

You know that the range is 40, with 100 as the upper extreme. Score A is the lower extreme value. Score B is the median. Score C is the upper quartile. Find scores A, B, and C.

20. Suppose that the test scores on a math exam are normally distributed with the mean score at 84 and a standard deviation of 8. The teacher has the following grading policy:

A: More than 1.25 standard deviations above mean

B: mean < test score ≤ 1.25 standard deviations above mean

C: 1.25 standard deviations below mean < test score ≤ mean

D: 2 standard deviations below mean < test score ≤ 1.25 standard deviations below mean

F: Test score ≤ 2 standard deviations below mean

Determine test-score boundaries for each letter grade.

21. Examine the following grades given on a 50-point cooperative group project in three different classes.

Class 1: 45 40 42 47 48 43 49 50 43
        46 48 50 42 47 45 44

Class 2: 33 37 45 45 45 47 49 38 42
        46 44 42

Class 3: 50 50 47 49 46 32 40 39 50
        50 49 50 40 41 50

(a) Determine the mean grade for each class.

(b) Construct a box-and-whisker plot for each class.

(c) Discuss a score of 45 in each class.

22. Examine the following two graphs. Discuss the possible
nature of the test scores they might represent.

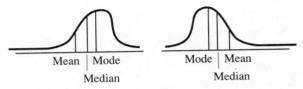

23. The mean of the squares of a set of scores can be represented as

$$\frac{\sum\limits_{i=1}^{n} x_i}{n}$$

The square of the mean of a set of scores can be represented as

$$\left(\frac{\sum\limits_{i=1}^{n} x_i}{n}\right)^2$$

Develop a set of 10 scores in order to test whether

$$\frac{\sum\limits_{i=1}^{n} x_i^2}{n} = \left(\frac{\sum\limits_{i=1}^{n} x_i}{n}\right)^2$$

In Other Words

24. How is the mean influenced by outliers in the distribution?

25. Why might the mode be considered the least dependable
(reliable) measure of central tendency?

26. What is the interpretation of a z-score of 0?

27. Summarize the appropriate uses of bar, line, picture, and
circle graphs.

28. Which measure(s) of central tendency need not be the actual data in the distribution?

Cooperative Activity

29. Groups of four

Individual Accountability: Each member is to toss a fair set of dice
50 times and record the sum of the dots that appear face up on
each die. Construct a complete frequency table based on the
data, with 11 intervals of width 1 (2, 3, 4, . . . , 12). In addition,
determine the mean, variance, and standard deviation of the
distribution.

Group Goal: Compile all of the frequencies into one table. Complete a new frequency table for this compilation. Determine the
mean, median, variance, and standard deviation. What generalizations can you make from the compiled results?

9

Probability

Examine the photograph at the right.

Describe what you see.

What information is available to you?

What predictions might you make?

What information is missing?

What might a mathematical description of this photograph contain?

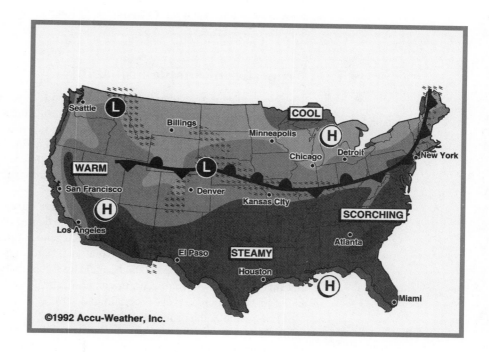

©1992 Accu-Weather, Inc.

Introduction

In Chapter 8 we examined techniques to help you organize, display, analyze, and summarize events that had already taken place. In this chapter, we will introduce a branch of mathematics, called probability, that will help you understand events that have not yet occurred.

Statistics and probability are often taught in sequence. Together, they help us make sense of certain past, present, and future events. The roles of these two branches of mathematics are expanding in our increasingly quantitative society. Decision making involves analyzing the trends found in events that have already occurred with the hope of recognizing patterns and regularities that will help us understand future events. Statistics and probability can assist us in this endeavor. They are not merely tools for mathematicians, but are subjects that informed citizens and consumers as well as professionals in most fields need to be familiar with.

In Section 9.1 we present the terminology and properties of simple probability. Section 9.2 discusses several ways of picturing probabilistic situations, such as with probability tree diagrams, and goes beyond simple probability into some types and characteristics of more complex probability situations, covering such topics as conditional probability, independent events, and expected value. Finally, Section 9.3 explores some additional counting techniques: Pascal's triangle, permutations, and combinations.

9.1 Properties of Simple Probability

The forecaster on a weather channel makes the following statement: "There is a 60% chance of rain tomorrow." Most people interpret this statement as "There is somewhat more of a chance that it will rain than it will not rain tomorrow." The actual calculation of the 60% figure is a complicated process. In general, "a 60% chance of rain" can be viewed as follows. After examining numerous situations in which atmospheric conditions were similar to current conditions, meteorologists found that it rained 60% of those times.

Quantifying situations whose outcomes are uncertain is part of probability. In
probability
probability we assign a numerical value to the degree of belief that we have in the occurrence of a particular event (or the nonoccurrence of that event). The numerical value can be expressed as a fraction, a decimal, or a percentage, all of which are equivalent. This value is always between 0 and 1 inclusive. A probability of 0 is interpreted as a belief that an event will not occur, or cannot occur. A probability of 1 is interpreted as a belief that a particular event is certain to occur.

For example, the probability that the Empire State Building is standing at this very moment is very close to 1 (seismologists have discovered a fault line under New York City, so the probability is not exactly 1). The probability that the Pacific Ocean will dry up in 5 years is very close to 0. This event is extremely unlikely to occur.

The science of probability has its own terminology and properties that you should become familiar with. We will define the basic terms used in probability in the context of the following experiment, which we encourage you to perform as you read through it.

Six strings of equal length, color, and texture are held together at the center by a stapled strip of paper as shown in Figure 9.1a. The strings are not tied, but the center is covered so that it is difficult to match one end of a string with its other end. You are to tie pairs of the strings together at the top, as shown in Figure 9.1b. Now do the same to the bottom so that you have six knots in all (three on the top and three on the bottom).

Figure 9.1

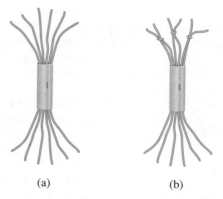

(a) (b)

Stop here! Predict the configuration of the tied strings when the paper is removed.

outcome   Each possible configuration is known as an **outcome** of this experiment. The set of
sample space   all possible outcomes is called the **sample space** of the experiment. Try to envision the sample space for this experiment.

Three outcomes are possible as shown in Figure 9.2. Each outcome in an experi-
event   ment is known as an **event**. The possible events in this experiment are three circles, two circles, or one circle.

Figure 9.2

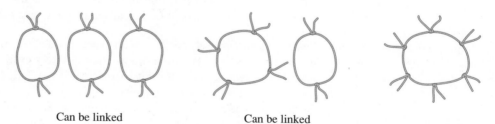

Can be linked   Can be linked

This string problem is particularly interesting because even in its simplicity it conveys some of the basic questions probability tries to answer. We encourage you think about it, since we will be referring to it again as the chapter progresses.

Theoretical and Experimental Probability

Examine the following two experiments:

Experiment A: A coin is flipped 500 times. The outcome is recorded each time.

Experiment B: A paper cup is tossed 500 times. The outcome is recorded each time.

What are the similarities and differences between these two experiments?

In each case, an object is tossed 500 times and the outcome recorded. In Experiment A, certain aspects of the object are well known. It is common knowledge that only two outcomes are possible when a coin is tossed: heads or tails. If the coin is a fair coin, that is, it is not altered to produce a certain outcome, the chance of it landing and showing heads or tails is considered to be equal by the very nature of the coin itself. Here, the sample space is well defined, and characteristics of each of the outcomes are known. As you will see, it is easy to assign a numerical probability to each of these outcomes based on the knowledge you already have. Such an assignment, without regard to the 500 outcomes of the experiment, is known as a **theoretical probability**. We often say that there is a 50-50 chance of a coin landing on heads or tails. This refers to notion that the coin is expected to land on heads 50% of the times tossed, and tails 50% of the times tossed.

theoretical probability

In Experiment B, our knowledge of the set of outcomes is not well defined. Not all paper cups are manufactured in the same way or out of the same kind of paper. We do know that the cup can land bottom up, top up, or on its side. Assigning numerical probabilities to these outcomes is more difficult. In this case, it is necessary to examine the results of the experiment by determining the relative frequencies of each outcome. On the basis of the "after-the-fact" knowledge, a probability can then be assigned. Such a probability is known as an **experimental probability**.

experimental probability

In both theoretical and experimental probability, the probability of a certain event relates directly to the relative frequency with which the event is likely to occur. Because experimental probabilities can vary markedly from experiment to experiment, we will narrow the discussion of probability in this text to theoretical probabilities only.

Probability Properties

If a particular outcome is under consideration for its occurrence, that event is known as a **favorable event** (or **favorable outcome**). Six properties, or rules, are important when studying the probabilities of favorable and nonfavorable events.

favorable event (favorable outcome)

Property 1: Equally Likely Events.   If all events in a sample space have an equal chance of occurring, these events are known as **equally likely events**. Suppose that a fair die is tossed. The sample space for this experiment is {1, 2, 3, 4, 5, 6}. There is an equally likely chance that any of these numbers will appear face up once the die comes to a rest. Because there is a 100% chance that a number in the sample space will result, the probability of a given number is the percentage that results when 100% is divided by 6. ($16.\overline{6}\%$). This probability can also be achieved by generating an equivalent ratio. In general, if E is an equally likely outcome in a sample space, then the probability of the event E occurring, symbolized by $P(E)$, can be stated as

property 1: equally likely events

$$P(E) = \frac{1}{n} \qquad \text{where } n \text{ is the number of elements in the sample space}$$

Therefore, in the case of rolling a die,

$$P(1) = P(2) = P(3) = P(4) = P(5) = P(6) = \frac{1}{6} \text{ (or } 16.\overline{6}\%)$$

Examine the two spinners pictured in Figure 9.3. Both spinners have the same sample space of outcomes, namely, $\{A, B, C, D\}$. In the spinner on the left, each sector contains 25% of the area of the circle. Therefore, there is an equal chance of the arrow landing on any of these four sectors. The probability of it landing on any one of these sectors is $\frac{1}{4}$, or 25%. In the spinner on the right, the sectors do not have equal areas. Because region A is larger than any of the other regions, it appears more likely that the spinner will land in region A. The outcomes of this experiment are not equally likely. Probabilities cannot be assigned to each of the four outcomes in the same way as they were with the equally likely outcomes of the left spinner. Assigning probabilities to events with not equally likely outcomes will be addressed in Section 9.2.

Figure 9.3

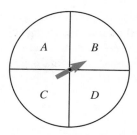   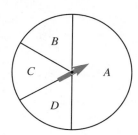

property 2: more than one favorable event in a sample space

Property 2: More Than One Favorable Event in a Sample Space.   The examples used in the explanation of equally likely events each contained single, distinct outcomes that were considered favorable. In the case of the die, all of the outcomes are equally likely. If rolling a 5 is favorable, $P(5) = \frac{1}{6}$, since there is one favorable outcome out of the six equally likely outcomes. In the case of the spinner on which all of the regions are equally likely outcomes, we might consider landing on region B to be favorable. Since there is only one favorable region B on the spinner out of the four equally likely outcomes, $P(B) = \frac{1}{4}$.

If a sample space consists of more than one equally likely event that can be considered favorable, then the probability of the events is the quotient of the frequency (f) of the favorable event and the total number (n) of elements in the sample space. If E is such an event, then $P(E) = \frac{f}{n}$. Both favorable and nonfavorable events will be addressed in Property 4.

Investigation 1 uses Property 2 in its solution.

Investigation 1

A bag contains eight marbles. Three are blue, four are green, and one is red. What is the probability of randomly selecting a red marble? a green marble? a blue marble?

Notice the phrase "randomly selecting" in the problem statement. These words are necessary so that the reader of the problem is assured of an unbiased selection process. For example, suppose the marbles were not in the bag, but rather spread out in plain view on a table. The probability that a person would select a red marble is 1, or 100% (provided that the person isn't color blind), since he or she would go right for the red marble. Random selection allows us to employ the predictive properties of theoretical probability.

Let's examine the sample space in terms of the individual marbles that can be chosen:

$$\{B, B, B, G, G, G, G, R\}$$

There is an equally likely chance of selecting any one marble. Choosing a marble is therefore an equally likely event. The selection of a particular color is not equally likely.

Suppose that selecting a red marble is considered a favorable event. Only one red marble is in the bag; therefore, the frequency (f) of red in the sample space is equal to one: $P(R) = \frac{1}{8}$. Now suppose that selecting a green marble is considered a favorable event. Four green marbles are in the bag. The frequency (f) of green in the sample space is equal to 4. Therefore,

$$P(G) = \frac{4}{8} = \frac{1}{2}$$

by Property 2. Likewise, if blue is considered a favorable event, the probability of selecting a blue marble is $\frac{3}{8}$. Since the probability ratio for green is the greatest, there is more of a chance of selecting a green marble than any other color.

---

property 3: the sum of all probabilities in a sample space

Property 3: The Sum of All Probabilities in a Sample Space.   Assume you are given a particular sample space for some experiment. When the experiment is conducted, there is a 100% chance of getting an outcome from the sample space. Because a 100% chance is equivalent to a probability of 1, the sum of the individual probabilities in the sample space must be equal to 1. This can be seen in the problem presented in Investigation 1.

$$P(\text{red}) = \frac{1}{8} \qquad P(\text{green}) = \frac{1}{2} \qquad P(\text{blue}) = \frac{3}{8}$$

Since the colors red, green, and blue partition the sample space into three disjoint sets, a marble that is selected must be an element of one of these three sets. The probability of choosing any marble at random is equal to 1. Therefore, the sum of the probabilities in the sample space will also equal 1.

$$P(\text{randomly selecting a marble from the bag}) = P(\text{red marble}) + P(\text{green marble}) \\ + P(\text{blue marble})$$

$$P(\text{randomly selecting a marble from the bag}) = \frac{1}{8} + \frac{1}{2} + \frac{3}{8} = 1$$

property 4: the probability of the complement of an event

complement

Property 4: The Probability of the Complement of an Event.   The probability that an event will occur is equal to 1 minus the probability that an event will not occur. Examine the sample space in Investigation 1. Let E be the event that a red marble is chosen. The **complement** of event E, written as $\overline{E}$, includes all outcomes in the sample space that are not in the event E. In other words, the event $\overline{E}$ is the event that the marble chosen is not red. This can be visualized in the Venn diagram in Figure 9.4.

Figure 9.4

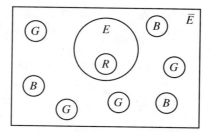

The complement of an event is the set of all outcomes that lie outside the set that symbolizes the favorable event. Property 4 can be restated as the probability of an event is equal to 1 minus the probability of its complement, and symbolized as $P(E) = 1 - P(\bar{E})$. It is also true that $P(\bar{E}) = 1 - P(E)$, which can be interpreted as the probability that an event will not occur is equal to 1 minus the probability that the event will occur. Therefore, since the probability in Investigation 1 that a red marble will be chosen is equal to $\frac{1}{8}$, the probability that the marble chosen is not red is $1 - \frac{1}{8}$, or $\frac{7}{8}$.

In general, if N is the total number of elements in a sample space, and the sample space is partitioned into two disjoint events E and $\bar{E}$, then

$$P(E) = \frac{n(E)}{N} \qquad \text{and} \qquad P(\bar{E}) = \frac{n(\bar{E})}{N}$$

Notice that $n(\bar{E}) = N - n(E)$. Therefore,

$$P(\bar{E}) = \frac{N - n(E)}{N} = \frac{N}{N} - \frac{n(E)}{N} = 1 - P(E)$$

Consider Investigation 2.

Investigation 2

The search committee to fill the position of high school principal consists of six teachers, three administrators, four parents, and two students. One of the committee members will be randomly selected as the recording secretary.

(a) What is the probability that Dr. Adams, one of the committee members, will be the secretary?

(b) What is the probability that the secretary will be a student?

(c) What is the probability that the secretary will be a parent?

(d) What is the probability that the secretary will not be a teacher?

(a) The sample space has 15 elements. Since each individual is equally likely to be selected, the probability that any one particular person is chosen is equal to $\frac{1}{15}$. Therefore,

$$P(\text{Dr. Adams}) = \frac{1}{15} \approx .067$$

(b) We will consider the choice of a student as a favorable event. Since the sample space has two favorable events, the probability that a student will be chosen is $\frac{2}{15}$, or $\approx .133$.

(c) We will consider the choice of a parent as a favorable event. Since the sample space has four favorable events, the probability that a parent will be chosen is $\frac{4}{15}$, or $\approx .267$.

(d) The event that the choice will not be a teacher is the complement of the event that the choice will be a teacher. Let T be the event that the choice is a teacher. Then, $P(\overline{T}) = 1 - P(T)$. If we consider the choice of a teacher to be a favorable event, then $P(T) = \frac{6}{15} = .4$. From Property 4, it follows that the probability that the secretary will not be a teacher is $1 - .4$, or .6. There is a 60% chance that the secretary chosen at random will not be a teacher.

Investigation 3

Examine the following spinner:

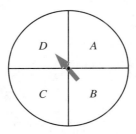

The spinner face is a circle that has been partitioned into four equal sectors. The experiment consists of spinning the spinner once, recording the sector on which the arrowhead lands, then spinning the spinner once again and recording the sector. For example, the outcome DB represents landing on D the first time and on B the second time.

(a) What are the elements of the sample space in this experiment?

(b) What is the probability of spinning BB?

(c) What is the probability of not spinning BB?

(d) What is the probability of landing on B on the first spin and C on the second spin?

(e) What is the probability that both spins will match (AA, BB, CC, DD)?

(f) What is the probability that there will not be a match?

(g) What is the probability of landing on C at least once?

(a) The elements of the sample space, S, can be listed systematically. Pair A with itself and every other sector label; B with itself and every other sector label; and so on. The elements of the sample space S are listed as follows.

$$AA \quad AB \quad AC \quad AD$$
$$BA \quad BB \quad BC \quad BD$$
$$CA \quad CB \quad CC \quad CD$$
$$DA \quad DB \quad DC \quad DD$$

(b) Notice that $n(S) = 16$. Each of the outcomes is equally likely since each of the sectors covers the same area of the circle. Therefore, $P(BB) = \frac{1}{16}$, or .0625.

(c) Let X be the event of spinning BB. Then the complement of this event, not spinning BB, can be symbolized by $\overline{X}$. Therefore, $P(\overline{X}) = 1 - P(X) = 1 - .0625 = .9375$, or $\frac{15}{16}$.

(d) Only one outcome in the sample space represents B on the first spin and C on the second spin. Therefore, $P(BC) = \frac{1}{16}$.

(e) We will consider matching spins as a favorable event. The relative frequency of matching spins in the sample space is .25. Therefore, the probability of matching spins is .25. This agrees with the notion that if a sample space consists of more than one equally likely outcome that can be considered a favorable event, the probability of the events is the quotient of the frequency (f) of the favorable event and the total number (n) of elements in the sample space. Here, the frequency of favorable events is 4. Therefore, $P(\text{match}) = \frac{f}{n} = \frac{4}{16}$, or .25.

(f) $P(\text{not match}) = 1 - P(\text{match}) = 1 - .25 = .75$. There is a 75% chance that the result of the two spins will not match.

(g) Examine the sample space. The event of landing on C at least once consists of the outcomes in which the spinner lands on C on the first spin, the spinner lands on C on the second spin, and the spinner lands on C on both spins. Let F be the set of these favorable outcomes. Then, $F = \{CA, CB, CD, AC, BC, CC, DC\}$. Since $n(F) = 7$, $P(F) = \frac{7}{16}$, or .4375.

---

property 5: the odds in favor of and against an event

Property 5: The Odds in Favor of and Against an Event. If you look at the back of a lottery ticket or in the rules for a sweepstakes, you will notice that probabilities of winning or losing are not mentioned, but odds are. The odds in favor of an event E are the ratio $P(E):P(\overline{E})$. The odds against an event E occurring are the ratio $P(\overline{E}):P(E)$. For example, when a fair die is tossed, the odds in favor of tossing a 3 are $\frac{1}{6}:\frac{5}{6}$, or $1:5$ (1 to 5). The odds against tossing a 3 are $\frac{5}{6}:\frac{1}{6}$, or $5:1$ (5 to 1).

property 6: mutually exclusive events

Property 6: Mutually Exclusive Events. Examine the following situation. A fair die is tossed. The sample space, S, is $\{1, 2, 3, 4, 5, 6\}$. Event A contains all of the outcomes that are multiples of two: $A = \{2, 4, 6\}$. Event B contains all of the outcomes that are factors of five: $B = \{1, 5\}$. Notice that $A \cap B = \varnothing$; that is, events A and B are disjoint.

mutually exclusive events

These events are known as **mutually exclusive events**. Events A and B are mutually exclusive events since they do not share any outcomes. If A occurs, then B cannot occur; and if B occurs, then A cannot occur. Written in symbolic logic form, this would be $(A \rightarrow {\sim}B) \wedge (B \rightarrow {\sim}A)$.

We will now determine the probability of randomly obtaining an outcome in A or B. Here, we consider as favorable any outcome that is a multiple of 2 or a factor of 5. Examining the sample space, we can see that this event is $\{1, 2, 4, 5, 6\}$. There are five favorable outcomes out of the six possibilities in the sample space. Therefore, $P(A \text{ or } B) = \frac{5}{6}$.

Notice that the set $\{1, 2, 4, 5, 6\}$ is the union of the disjoint sets A and B. We note that

$$P(A \cup B) = \frac{n(A \cup B)}{n(S)} = \frac{5}{6} = \frac{3+2}{6} = \frac{3}{6} + \frac{2}{6}$$

But it is clear from our work above that $P(A) = \frac{3}{6}$ and $P(B) = \frac{2}{6}$. Therefore,

$$P(A \cup B) = P(A) + P(B)$$

Does this property apply to events that are not mutually exclusive? Examine the following situation. Suppose that an experiment consists of tossing a fair die once and recording the outcome. Let event A contain the outcomes that are even numbers. Let event B contain the outcomes that are multiples of 3. What is the probability that the die will land on an even number or a multiple of 3, that is, $P(A \cup B)$. The situation can be shown in the Venn diagram in Figure 9.5.

Figure 9.5

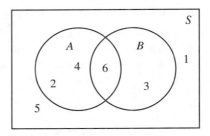

You can see that event $A = \{2, 4, 6\}$ with $P(A) = \frac{3}{6} = \frac{1}{2}$, and event $B = \{3, 6\}$ with $P(B) = \frac{2}{6} = \frac{1}{3}$. Then $(A \cup B) = \{2, 3, 4, 6\}$. It follows that

$$P(2, 3, 4, 6) = \frac{n(A \cup B)}{n(S)} = \frac{4}{6} = \frac{2}{3}$$

We previously stated that the probability of the union of two disjoint simple events is equal to the sum of the individual probabilities. Is it true in this situation?

$$P(A \cup B) \overset{?}{=} P(A) + P(B)$$

$$\frac{4}{6} \quad \neq \quad \frac{3}{6} \quad + \quad \frac{2}{6}$$

Obviously not. But we can cope with this discrepancy by recognizing that $(A \cap B) = \{6\}$ and $P(A \cap B) = \frac{1}{6}$. Therefore,

$$P(A \cup B) = P(A) + P(B) - P(A \cap B).$$

The probability of the union of two events is equal to the sum of the individual probabilities only when the two events are mutually exclusive. But if the two events are mutually exclusive, then their intersection is the empty set. Therefore, we can always use the above addition rule of probability to determine the probability of event A or B occurring whether or not A and B are mutually exclusive.

If A and B are two events with $P(A)$ and $P(B)$, then the probability of A or B, $P(A \cup B)$, can be computed as follows:

$$P(A \cup B) = P(A) + P(B) - P(A \cap B)$$

Investigation 4

A standard 52-card deck of playing cards consists of four suits.

(a) What is the probability of randomly selecting a red ace or a 5?

(b) What is the probability of randomly selecting a black card or a king?

Understand the Problem: What is given? You have a standard deck of playing cards. What is unknown? You must determine the probabilities of selecting certain cards at random.

Devise a Plan: Let S be the sample space for this experiment. There are 52 equally likely outcomes when a card is randomly chosen from the deck.

(a) Let A be the event that consists of the outcomes that are red aces {ace of hearts, ace of diamonds}, with $P(A) = \frac{2}{52} = \frac{1}{26}$. Let B be the event that consists of the outcomes that are 5s, {5 of hearts, 5 of diamonds, 5 of spades, 5 of clubs}, with $P(B) = \frac{4}{52} = \frac{1}{13}$.

(b) Let C be the event that consists of the outcomes that are black cards. Since $n(C) = 26$, $P(C) = \frac{26}{52}$, or $\frac{1}{2}$. Let D be the event that consists of the outcomes that are kings. Since $n(D) = 4$, $P(D) = \frac{4}{52}$, or $\frac{1}{13}$. Notice that C and D are not mutually exclusive events since $(C \cap D) = $ {king of spades, king of clubs}.

Carry Out the Plan: **(a)** Events A and B are mutually exclusive events since $(A \cap B) = \emptyset$. Consequently, $P(A \cap B) = 0$. We can use the addition rule of probability as follows:

$$P(A \cup B) = P(A) + P(B) - P(A \cap B)$$

$$= \frac{2}{52} + \frac{4}{52} - 0 \qquad = \frac{6}{52} = \frac{3}{26}$$

The probability of randomly selecting a red ace or a 5 is $\frac{6}{52}$, or approximately .115. There is approximately an $11\frac{1}{2}\%$ chance that a red ace or a 5 will be randomly selected.

(b) We use the addition rule to determine the desired probability:

$$P(C \cup D) = P(C) + P(D) - P(C \cap D)$$

$$= \frac{1}{2} + \frac{1}{13} - \frac{2}{52} = \frac{7}{13} \approx .538.$$

There is approximately a 54% chance that a black card or a king will be randomly selected.

Look Back: Examine the results for reasonableness. What does it mean when we say that there is a 54% chance that a black card or a king will be randomly selected?

Assessments for Section 9.1

1. List the elements of a sample space in each of the following experiments.
   (a) A coin is tossed.
   (b) A die is rolled.
   (c) A thumbtack is tossed.
   (d) A tin can is tossed.
   (e) A cone-shaped party hat is tossed.

2. Examine the following spinner. Each sector has the same area.

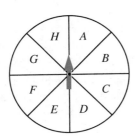

   (a) What is the probability of the spinner landing on A?
   (b) What is the probability of the spinner not landing on A?
   (c) What is the probability of the spinner landing on a vowel?
   (d) What are the odds in favor of the spinner landing on a consonant?
   (e) What are the odds against the spinner landing on a letter in the word BEACH?

3. A fair octahedral die is pictured here. Each of its eight congruent faces contains one number from 1 to 8.

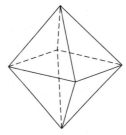

   (a) What is the probability that the die will land on 3?
   (b) What is the probability that the die will land on an even number?
   (c) What is the probability that the die will land on a factor of 8?
   (d) What is the probability that the die will land on 9?
   (e) What is the probability that the die will land on a multiple of 4 or a multiple of 3?
   (f) What is the probability that the die will land on a factor of 6 or a factor of 4?
   (g) What are the odds in favor of landing on an odd number?
   (h) What are the odds against landing on a prime number?
   (i) Let event A consist of the outcomes that are prime numbers. Let event B consist of the outcomes that are even numbers. Let event C consist of the outcomes that are factors of 6. Determine $P(A \cup B \cup C)$.

4. Marbles of equal size are placed in an empty bag. There are five white marbles, four green marbles, two blue marbles, and three orange marbles.

(a) What is the probability of getting a marble when reaching in and taking something out of the bag?

(b) What is the probability of randomly selecting an orange marble?

(c) What is the probability of not randomly selecting a white marble?

(d) What is the probability of randomly selecting a blue or a green marble?

(e) What are the odds in favor of selecting a white marble?

(f) What are the odds against selecting a blue marble?

(g) What percent chance do you have of not selecting a green marble?

5. An experiment consists of tossing a fair die, then flipping a fair coin. An outcome of this experiment would be symbolized by 3H, which indicates that a 3 was tossed on the die and the coin landed on heads.

(a) List all of the elements in the sample space.

(b) What is the probability that the outcome will be 4T?

(c) What is the probability that the outcome will be 2H or 5T?

(d) What is the probability that the outcome will include tails?

(e) What is the probability that the outcome will not include a prime number?

6. Each letter from A through E is written on separate sheets of paper and put into a bag. The distribution of letters in the bag is illustrated in the following bar graph.

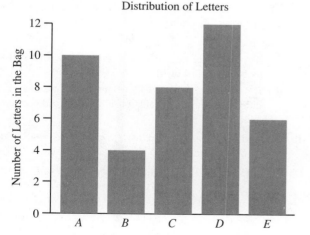

Distribution of Letters

Assume a sheet is selected at random and then returned to the bag.

(a) What is the probability of selecting an A?

(b) What is the probability of selecting an A or an E?

(c) What is the probability of not selecting a B?

(d) What is the probability of not selecting a C or a D?

7. A spinner face is partitioned into six unequal sectors: A, B, C, D, E, F. The spinner is spun 50 times. The following frequencies are recorded:

A	B	C	D	E	F
5	13	18	11	2	1

(a) What experimental probabilities would be assigned to each sector based on the results of these 50 spins?

(b) Why might region C have the greatest probability?

8. A loaded die is tossed 50 times. The following relative frequencies are recorded:

1	2	3	4	5	6
.12	.4	.28	.06	.08	.06

What experimental probabilities, expressed as fractions out of 50, would be assigned to each outcome?

9. Ten floppy disks are randomly arranged in a box. Three of the disks contain only word processing programs. Two of the disks are only data disks. Four of the disks contain only graphics software. One disk is an unformatted disk. An experiment consists of selecting a disk from the box without looking at the label.

(a) What is the probability that the unformatted disk will not be chosen?

(b) What are the odds against the unformatted disk not being chosen?

(c) What is the probability of selecting a word processing or graphics program?

(d) What are the odds against selecting a word processing or graphics program?

(e) What is the probability of selecting neither a data disk nor the unformatted disk?

10. Sketch a spinner in which the sample space, S, is {A, B, C, D} and each of the outcomes is equally likely in each of the following cases.

(a) $n(S) = 4$ and $P(A) = .25$

(b) $n(S) = 8$ and $P(B) = .25$

(c) $n(S) = 16$ and $P(\overline{C}) = .75$

11. Sketch a spinner that yields the following probabilities:

$$P(A) = \frac{1}{3} \qquad P(B) = \frac{1}{6} \qquad P(C) = \frac{1}{2}$$

12. An experiment consists of randomly selecting a card from a standard deck of cards. Let event A consist of the red-card outcomes. Let event B consist of the picture-card outcomes (J, Q, K). Let event C consist of the number-card outcomes (2–10). Let event D consist of the outcomes that are black cards. Let event E consist of the outcomes that are aces. Let event F consist of the outcomes that are queens and 3s. Let event $G = \{4$ of hearts, 3 of spades, queen of diamonds, ace of clubs$\}$. Determine the indicated probabilities.

   (a) $P(A)$ (b) $P(B)$ (c) $P(C)$

   (d) $P(D)$ (e) $P(E)$ (f) $P(F)$

   (g) $P(G)$ (h) $P(A \cup D)$

13. A green die and a blue die are both tossed at the same time.

   (a) The sample space consists of the ordered pair (g, b) where g is the number landed on the green die and b is the number landed on the blue die. Assume that these outcomes are equally likely. What are all of the elements in this sample space?

   (b) What is the probability that the green die will land on 3?

   (c) What is the probability that the first number in the ordered pair is 3?

   (d) What is the probability that the sum of the numbers rolled on the green and blue dice, $g + b$, is equal to 2?

   (e) What is the probability that the sum of the numbers rolled on the dice is equal to 7?

   (f) What is the probability that the green die will show a 4 or the blue die will show a 4?

   (g) What is the probability that the sum of the numbers rolled will be 5 or the outcome will be $(1, 6)$?

14. Determine whether or not each pair of events is mutually exclusive. State your reasoning.

   (a) Rolling a 2 on a die.
       Rolling a 3 on a die.

   (b) Rolling an even number on a die.
       Rolling a prime number on a die.

   (c) Picking a black card from a deck of cards.
       Picking a red card from a deck of cards.

   (d) Picking an ace from a deck of cards.
       Picking a red card from a deck of cards.

   (e) Selecting a registered Democrat's name from a telephone book.
       Selecting the name of a person whose age is over 55.

15. A math class consists of 30 students. Two-thirds of the students are female. Twenty percent of the female students are education majors. If all of the names of the students are written on separate sheets of paper and put into a bag, what are the odds in favor of selecting a female education student?

16. There are 150 seats on a certain airplane. Ten percent of the seats are in first class. Twenty percent of the seats are in business class. The remainder of the seats are in economy class. On a certain flight, one-third of the first-class seats were empty, 40% of the business-class seats were empty, and one-fifth of the economy seats were empty. As a promotion, the airline company put all of the boarding passes of the people on board this flight into a box. They will pick one name and award a free round-trip ticket to anywhere in the United States.

   (a) You are seated in economy class. What is the probability that your boarding pass will be selected?

   (b) What is the probability that a first-class passenger's boarding pass will be selected?

   (c) What is the probability of selecting a boarding pass of a first-class or a business-class passenger?

   (d) What is the probability of not selecting an economy-class passenger's boarding pass?

   (e) What are the odds against selecting a first-class passenger's boarding pass?

   (f) What are the odds in favor of not selecting a first-class passenger's boarding pass?

17. Assume that $P(A) = .35$ and $P(B) = .25$

   (a) If A and B are mutually exclusive events, what is the probability of $(A$ or $B)$?

   (b) If A and B are not mutually exclusive events, what additional piece of information is needed to determine $P(A \cup B)$?

18. If C and D are mutually exclusive events, $P(C) = .45$, and $P(C \cup D) = .7$, find $P(D)$.

19. Find $P(S \cap T)$ if $P(S) = .15$, $P(T) = .5$, and $P(S \cup T) = .3$.

20. Determine the odds in favor of rolling one die and getting an odd number or a number greater than 2.

21. Determine the odds against rolling one die and getting a prime number or an odd number.

22. Examine the following frequency table, which represents the spin of a spinner whose face has four regions, *A, B, C,* and *D*.

Region	Number of Spins
A	49
B	10
C	20
D	21

Sketch a spinner that might yield such outcomes.

In Other Words

23. What is a sample space?

24. What are mutually exclusive events?

25. Suppose an event is likely, but not certain to occur. What numerical probability might it have? Explain your answer.

26. What is the difference between experimental and theoretical probability?

27. The probability of an event not occurring is close to 0. What does this imply about the probability of the event occurring?

Cooperative Activity

28. Groups of four

Individual Accountability: In the beginning of this section, you were introduced to a string experiment. You will be investigating this problem in groups here: more work will be done with it in Section 9.2. Each member is to make 10 string sets like those in Figure 9.1a. When the group convenes, you should have 40 sets of strings. When you actually meet, you will tie the strings together as shown in Figure 9.1b; but for now, write down your best guess at the expected frequency of the three different outcomes shown in Figure 9.2.

Group Goal: Compare your expected frequencies. Determine a group average for each outcome. Put all of the strings into a pile. Each member is to randomly select 10 sets of strings and then tie those sets as shown in Figure 9.1b. Once all the string sets have been tied, open the sets and construct a tally chart for the outcomes. Compare the frequency of each outcome with your expected frequency.

Assign the outcome of one circle a 1, two circles a 2, and three circles a 3. Find the average of these values. What does this average indicate? Assign experimental probabilities for each outcome. Join together as a class and compare and discuss your results.

9.2 Picturing Probabilistic Situations

In Assessment 5 at the end of Section 9.1, you were asked to identify the sample space of an experiment in which a die is tossed and then a coin is flipped. If you did not complete that problem, stop here and do so now.

Reflect for a moment on how you structured your work so that you were sure to identify all possible elements in the sample space. In this section, we will examine a pictorial way of representing the sample space. In a multistep experiment such as this one, it is often desirable to attempt to visualize the components of the experiment by **tree diagram** drawing a diagram. A useful diagram in this situation is called a tree diagram. A **tree diagram** serves as a means of exploring a probabilistic situation. Figure 9.6 depicts the tree diagram for the die/coin experiment.

Figure 9.6

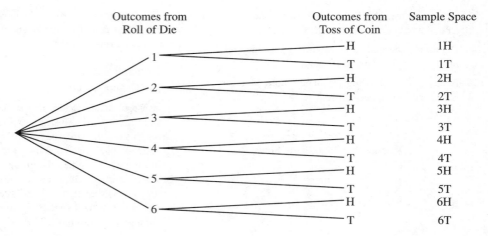

The tree diagram accounts for every possible outcome in this experiment. An individual outcome can be traced by following one of the "branches" from left to right. For example, the experiment begins by tossing a die. There are six possible outcomes, each of which is listed in the first column. The next part of the experiment is to toss a coin. For each outcome on the die, two outcomes of the coin toss are possible. If a 6 is rolled, the second part of the experiment has two possible outcomes. If a tail is then tossed, we follow the path to the T and list the outcome of the experiment as 6T. As you can see, tree diagrams allow you to investigate experiments before you run them.

If we assume that each of the 12 outcomes is equally likely, we can assign probabilities to the outcomes since we are assured that the sample space is complete. Examine Investigation 5.

Investigation 5

In Section 9.1 a string experiment was used to introduce basic probability terminology. The Cooperative Activity at the end of the Assessments section also investigated this experiment.

On numerous occasions throughout this text, we have suggested that you use the problem-solving technique of solving a simpler problem. In this investigation, you will do just that as we work our way toward a better understanding of the probabilistic situation of the six tied strings. For instance, we can simplify the problem by reducing the number of strings. Suppose you have four strings of equal color, length, and texture, held together by a stapled slip of paper, as shown here:

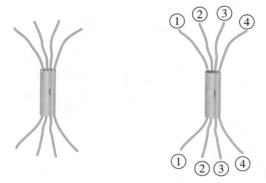

Let the outcomes of this experiment be the results of tying the strings. List the sample space for the string problem when four strings are used. Determine the probability of each outcome in the sample space.

Label the top and bottom of the strings as shown in the right of the illustration. We will use the notation (1, 2) to represent String 1 tied to String 2.

In this two-step experiment, the tops of the strings are tied, then the bottoms are tied. Therefore, the outcome of this experiment is the result of two pairs tied at the top and two pairs tied at the bottom. For example, String 1 can be tied to String 2 and symbolized as (1, 2). String 3 can be tied to String 4 and symbolized as (3, 4). Examine the tree diagram on page 412.

The sample space has nine elements that result in two different figures: four strings forming two circles (either linked or separate) and four strings forming one circle. The frequency of the two-circle outcome is 3. The frequency of the one-circle outcome is 6. Therefore,

$$P(\text{two circles}) = \frac{3}{9} = \frac{1}{3} = .\overline{3} \quad P(\text{one circle}) = \frac{6}{9} = \frac{2}{3} = .\overline{6}$$

There is a $66\frac{2}{3}\%$ chance, or approximately a 67% chance, that the experiment will result in a single circle.

In Assessment 21 at the end of this section, you will be asked to investigate the probability of a single circle resulting when six strings are tied. Do you expect the probability to be greater or less than with four strings? Why?

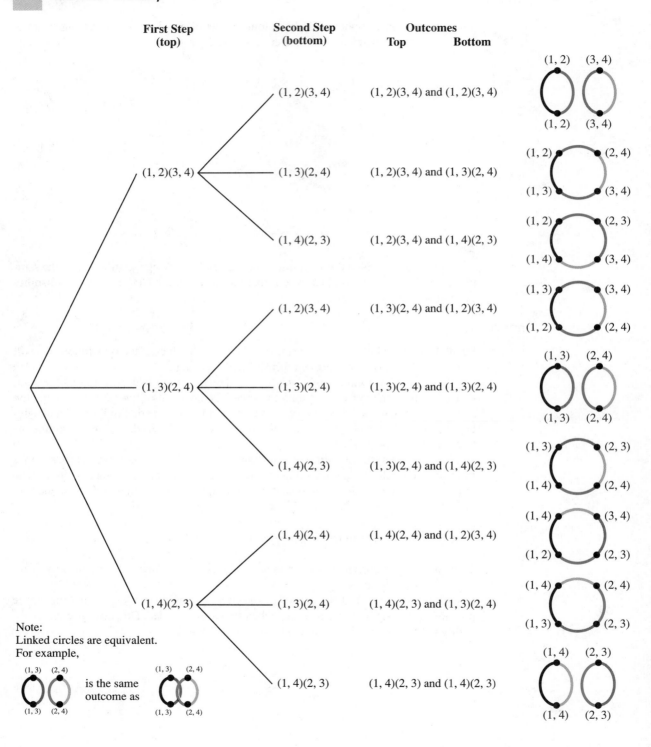

Fundamental Counting Principle of Probability

Examine the two tree diagrams that have been presented in this section. The number of outcomes in the sample space of each experiment could have been determined without actually generating the tree diagrams. In the case of the die and coin toss (Figure 9.6), the tree diagram pictured 12 possible outcomes. Notice that there were six branches in the first step, with two branches leading from each. This resulted in a sample space of 12 outcomes (6×2). In Investigation 5, there were three branches in the first step, with three branches leading from each. This resulted in a sample space of nine outcomes (3×3). The relationship between the number of branches and the number of outcomes in the sample space is formalized in a property known as the **fundamental counting** **principle** and is generalized as follows:

fundamental counting
principle

Principle: If the first step of a two-step experiment has m outcomes and the second step has n outcomes, there are $m \cdot n$ outcomes in the two-step experiment.

The counting principle can be extended to experiments with any number of steps. For example, suppose that an experiment consisted of selecting one card from a standard deck of playing cards, then tossing a fair die, and finally tossing a fair coin. How many outcomes would comprise the sample space? Obviously, the tree diagram for such an experiment would be unwieldy. However, the fundamental counting principle allows us to determine that there will be $52 \times 6 \times 2$, or 624, possible outcomes. Assuming that each outcome is equally likely, the probability of the outcome (5 of diamonds, 3, and heads) is $\frac{1}{624}$.

Investigation 6

A teacher gives a 10-question true/false exam. Suppose that a student does not study and just tosses a coin to determine the answers (heads = true, tails = false). What is the probability that the student will get all of the answers correct?

Let's assume that the correct answers to this exam are TFFTTFTFFT, in that order. If we treat each question as one step of a multistep experiment, then each step has two outcomes. By the fundamental counting principle, there are $2 \times 2 \times 2 \times 2 \times 2 \times 2 \times 2 \times 2 \times 2 \times 2$, or 2^{10} (1024), different configurations of 10 true/false answers possible on this exam. Since only the one set listed above is the correct response set, the probability that the student will correctly get this correct set of 10 is $\frac{1}{1024}$, or $\approx .00098$. There is less than a .1% chance that this student will get all of the answers correct.

Probability Tree Diagrams

The numerical probability of a particular outcome can also be determined in an alternate way using the tree diagram. Let's look at a more manageable true/false exam that has only five questions. We already know that the fundamental counting principle assures us that there are $2 \times 2 \times 2 \times 2 \times 2$, or 32, different sets of answers on this exam. We will now elaborate on the tree diagram by including the probability of an event along the branch that leads to the event. The probability tree diagram in Figure 9.7 depicts how each outcome can be represented.

Figure 9.7

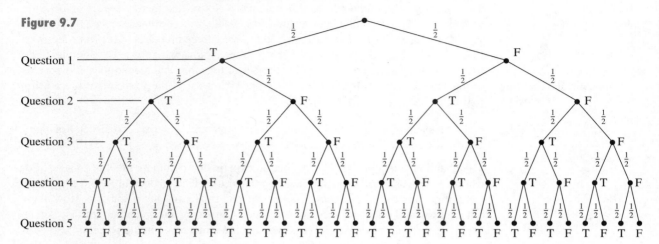

Question 1

Question 2

Question 3

Question 4

Question 5

probability tree diagram

multiplication principle of probability

The probability of each individual outcome is $\frac{1}{32}$. Notice that $\frac{1}{32} = \frac{1}{2} \times \frac{1}{2} \times \frac{1}{2} \times \frac{1}{2} \times \frac{1}{2}$. Each of these halves can be viewed as an individual probability along a given branch. For example, in Figure 9.7, trace the path that leads to the outcome TTTTT. The respective probabilities have been included on each branch of the path in this **probability tree diagram**. It is not a coincidence that the product of the individual probabilities is equal to the probability of the final outcome. This leads us to a very important property. The **multiplication principle of probability** states that the probability of a particular outcome in a multistep experiment is equal to the product of the probabilities of the individual events that comprise it.

We can view the outcome of five trues as (T and T and T and T and T). Therefore, by the multiplication principle,

$$P \text{ (T and T and T and T and T)} = P(T) \times P(T) \times P(T) \times P(T) \times P(T)$$

$$= \frac{1}{2} \times \frac{1}{2} \times \frac{1}{2} \times \frac{1}{2} \times \frac{1}{2}$$

$$= \frac{1}{32}$$

Investigation 7

Suppose a bag contains 10 marbles: two green, three white, and five blue. An experiment consists of randomly selecting a marble from the bag, recording the outcome, returning the marble to the bag, and repeating the process.

(a) What is the probability that you will select a green on the first pick and a blue on the second pick?

(b) What is the probability that both selections will match in color?

The marbles are indistinguishable other than by color. Three different color choices are possible. The first step of the experiment has three outcomes and the second step has three outcomes. The fundamental counting principle assures us that this experiment has nine possible outcomes.

Construct a probability tree diagram to illustrate this experiment. Include the individual probabilities for each step of the experiment, as shown here.

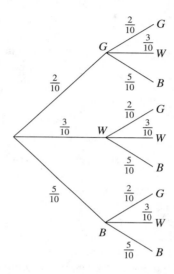

(a) The probability of a green on the first pick and a blue on the second, $P(GB)$, is equal to the product of the probabilities along the path leading to this outcome.

$$P(GB) = P(G) \times P(B)$$

$$= \frac{2}{10} \times \frac{5}{10} = \frac{10}{100} = .1$$

You can see that the probability of this outcome is not $\frac{1}{9}$. This is because each of the outcomes is not equally likely.

(b) Each probability is given here:

Outcome	GG	GW	GB	WG	WW	WB	BG	BW	BB
Probability	$\frac{4}{100}$	$\frac{6}{100}$	$\frac{10}{100}$	$\frac{6}{100}$	$\frac{9}{100}$	$\frac{15}{100}$	$\frac{10}{100}$	$\frac{15}{100}$	$\frac{25}{100}$

Notice that the sum of the probabilities is equal to 1. If we consider matching colors as a favorable event, this event has three elements: *GG*, *WW*, and *BB*. Since $P(GG) = \frac{4}{100}$, $P(WW) = \frac{9}{100}$, and $P(BB) = \frac{25}{100}$, $P(GG \text{ or } WW \text{ or } BB) = P(GG) + P(WW) + P(BB) = \frac{38}{100}$. There is a 38% chance that the colors will match in this particular experiment.

Conditional Probability

We will now investigate a different type of probability situation. We have already examined the probability of getting all answers correct on a five-question true/false exam by randomly assigning T or F according to the outcomes of a coin toss. Suppose the experiment were narrowed to consider the sample space when the first three questions were marked true. The original experiment had a sample space with 32 elements. This new restriction reduces that sample space by placing a condition on the experiment. Only four outcomes are possible when the first three questions are marked as true: {TTTTT, TTTTF, TTTFT, TTTFF}.

Let A be the event that exactly four trues appear on the final answer sheet, and let B be the event that the first three questions are marked as true. Then,

$$A=\{TTTTF, TTTFT, TTFTT, TFTTT, FTTTT\}$$

and

$$B=\{TTTTT, TTTTF, TTTFT, TTTFF\}$$

If we impose the condition that the first three responses must be marked as true, that is, event B must occur, then there are two ways that A could then occur: {TTTTF, TTTFT}.

What is the relationship between the outcomes {TTTTF, TTTFT} and events A and B? Notice that {TTTTF, TTTFT}, the outcomes of A given that B has occurred, is the intersection of events A and B. The probability of A given B is $\frac{2}{4}$, or $\frac{1}{2}$. This is because there are four elements in set B, two of which are elements of set A. Therefore, the probability of A occurring given that B has occurred is $\frac{1}{2}$. We use the notation $A \mid B$ to represent "A given B." Therefore, $P(A \mid B) = \frac{1}{2}$.

The related Venn diagram, which is shown in Figure 9.8, can also offer some insight into this situation. The intersection of A and B consists of the answers that contain exactly four trues with the first three answers true. Notice that $n(A \cap B) = 2$. We are trying to determine the probability that there are exactly four trues in the response set, given that the first three responses are true, or $P(A \mid B)$. The Venn diagram indicates that out of the four response sets with the first three as true, two have exactly four trues in each set. Therefore, $P(A \mid B)=\frac{2}{4}$, or $\frac{1}{2}$, which agrees with our calculations.

Figure 9.8

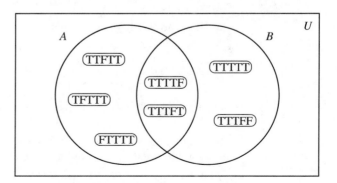

This result could also have been derived by setting up the ratio

$$\frac{P(A \cap B)}{P(B)}$$

Notice that

$$P(A \mid B) = \frac{P(A \cap B)}{P(B)} = \frac{\frac{2}{32}}{\frac{4}{32}} = \frac{1}{2}$$

conditional probability

When a restriction, or a condition, is placed on the outcome of an experiment, the resulting probability is known as **conditional probability**. In general, if A and B are two events in sample space S, and $P(B) \neq 0$, the conditional probability that event A will occur given that event B occurs is symbolized by

$$P(A \mid B) = \frac{P(A \cap B)}{P(B)}$$

Investigation 8

Suppose a bag contains five green marbles, three red marbles, and four orange marbles. An experiment consists of randomly selecting a marble, recording the color, then selecting another marble without replacing the first marble in the bag. What is the probability that the second marble will be red given that the first marble is green?

Understand the Problem: What is given? You are told the number of each of three colors of marbles in a bag and the nature of the experiment.
What is unknown? You must determine the probability that the second pick is red given that the first pick is green.

Devise a Plan: Solve this conditional probability problem by drawing a probability tree diagram.

Carry Out The Plan:

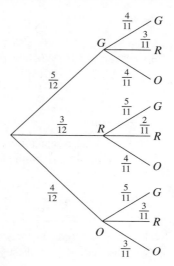

The probabilities assigned to each of the branches of the first step are simple relative frequencies of the colored marbles in a bag of 12 marbles. Since this experiment is conducted without replacement, only 11 marbles are in the bag when the second marble is to be selected. Notice that the probabilities assigned on the branches of the second step are conditional probabilities. These probabilities are dependent upon the results of the first pick. For example, the probability of a green marble being selected on the first pick is $\frac{5}{12}$. If the green marble is in fact picked, it is not replaced in the bag. There is one less green marble, and a total of 11 marbles in the bag. The probability of selecting a green marble on the second pick given that a green marble was selected on the first pick is $\frac{4}{11}$. In a similar fashion, the other probabilities are affected by the color of the first marble chosen.

Let B be the event that a green marble is chosen on the first pick. Let A be the event that a red marble is chosen on the second pick. The probability tree diagram can be used to determine $P(A \mid B)$ by following the branch that leads to a green marble on the first pick and then to a red marble on the second pick. Therefore, $P(A \mid B) = \frac{3}{11}$.

Look Back: It is interesting to see that the multiplication rule we used to determine the probabilities of multistep experiments can be used to derive the formula for determining conditional probabilities. Examine a single branch (taken from the tree diagram on page 417), that illustrates a green on the first pick and a red on the second pick, as illustrated here:

$P(G$ on first pick$) \times P(R$ on second pick given G on first pick$)$

$$= P(\text{green on first pick and red on second pick})$$

$$= P(\text{green on first pick} \cap \text{red on second pick})$$

$$= \frac{5}{12} \times \frac{3}{11} = \frac{5}{44}$$

Since $P(B) \times P(A \mid B) = P(A \cap B)$, we can divide both sides of the equation by $P(B)$, provided that $P(B) \neq 0$. The resulting formula is the rule for conditional probability:

$$P(A \mid B) = \frac{P(A \cap B)}{P(B)} = \frac{\frac{5}{44}}{\frac{5}{12}} = \frac{3}{11}$$

Sometimes a probability tree diagram cannot be drawn because some needed information is missing. Examine Investigation 9.

Investigation 9

There are 600 students enrolled in the teacher education program at a particular college. Two hundred fifty of these students are in their first semester of the program. One hundred fifty of the first-semester students are seeking secondary school teacher certification. If a student in the program is randomly selected to be on a committee, what is the probability that the student will be one seeking secondary school certification given that the student is in his or her first semester?

Understand the Problem: What is given? You are given a specific breakdown of the enrollment in a teacher education program.

What is unknown? You need to determine the probability that if a student selected is in his or her first semester, then that student is seeking secondary certification.

Devise a Plan: Make a diagram to illustrate the situation.

Carry Out the Plan: This situation can be pictured as follows:

	First-Semester Students	Others
Secondary	150	
		350
Others	100	

There are 250 first-semester students out of 600 students enrolled in the teacher education program. Therefore,

$$P(\text{first-semester student}) = \frac{250}{600}$$

There are 150 first-semester students seeking secondary certification in the program. Therefore,

$$P(\text{first-semester and secondary}) = \frac{150}{600}$$

We wish to determine P(a student seeking secondary certification given that the student is a first-semester student). Let A be the event that the student is seeking secondary certification, and B be the event that the student is a first-semester student. The situation can be symbolized as follows:

$$P(A \mid B) = \frac{P(A \cap B)}{P(B)} = \frac{\frac{150}{600}}{\frac{250}{600}} = \frac{150}{250} = \frac{3}{5}$$

The probability that the student selected for the committee will be a student seeking secondary certification given that the student is a first-semester student is .6.

Look Back: We leave it to you to construct a partial probability tree diagram as means of verifying the accuracy of this probablistic situation.

Independent Events

In the conditional probability situations we investigated, the probability of one event was directly affected by the probability of another event. For example, in Investigation 8, the probability of selecting a red marble on the second pick was determined by the outcome of the first pick. How could this experiment be altered so that the probabilities of the second step of the experiment are independent of the outcomes of the first step?

In Investigation 8, once a marble was chosen, it was not replaced in the bag. If, instead, the experiment was conducted with the marble being replaced each time it was chosen, the probabilities of the second step would be the same as the probabilities of the first step. The probability tree diagram for this situation is given in Figure 9.9. The

independent events events illustrated in this tree diagram are **independent events**, since the probability of the outcomes are not influenced by any other outcomes.

Figure 9.9

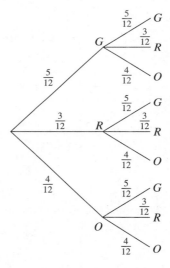

Suppose a coin is tossed twice. The outcomes of each toss are independent events since the probabilities of the outcomes of the second toss are not influenced by the outcome of the first toss.

Many people are hesitant to play numbers in a state lottery that were winning numbers the week before. Somehow the belief is that the probability of the same set of numbers being chosen again the next week is low. In fact, weekly lottery drawings are independent events. The numbers chosen are not "conscious" of the fact that they were already chosen the week before. The numbers that have been chosen in the past should not influence the numbers you choose in the future.

In general, if A and B are independent events, $P(A \mid B) = P(B)$. For example, the probability that a particular set of lottery numbers will be chosen on May 12, given that those same numbers were chosen on May 5, is equal to the probability of those numbers being chosen on May 5.

Expected Value

Examine the "wheel of chance" shown in Figure 9.10. Suppose the owner of this wheel charges a player $2 to spin the wheel. The player has the option of betting on ☆, ◯, △, ▢. The payoff for this game is $5 if the wheel lands on ☆, $4 if the wheel lands on △, $2 if the wheel lands on ◯, and $1 if the wheel lands on ▢. Is this game profitable for the owner?

Figure 9.10

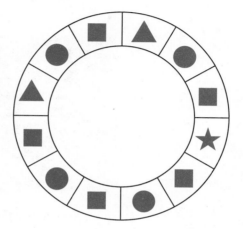

Obviously, the owner's profit/loss status is going to change from spin to spin. Will the owner make a profit, however, over the long run? Although we cannot be certain of the actual profit or loss, we can get a good indication of the average payout per spin in the following way. Multiply the probability of the spinner landing on each particular region by the amount that will be paid to the winner who has bet on that region. The sum **expected value** of these values is known as the **expected value**, E, or the expectation of an experiment. The expected payoff value for this experiment is computed as follows:

$$E = 5\left(\frac{1}{12}\right) + 4\left(\frac{1}{6}\right) + 2\left(\frac{1}{3}\right) + 1\left(\frac{5}{12}\right) = \frac{26}{12} \approx \$2.17$$

$$\underbrace{\hspace{1cm}}_{\text{for ☆}}\ \underbrace{\hspace{1cm}}_{\text{for △}}\ \underbrace{\hspace{1cm}}_{\text{for ◯}}\ \underbrace{\hspace{1cm}}_{\text{for ▢}}$$

The owner can therefore expect to pay out an average of about $2.17 per spin. Since the owner collects $2 from the bettor, his or her average loss is about $.17 per spin. This wheel will probably not generate a profit over the long run.

We can generalize the expected value formula as follows: If the sample space of an experiment consists of real numbers $n_1, n_2, n_3, \ldots, n_m$, each of which has a respective probability of $p_1, p_2, p_3, \ldots, p_m$, then the expected value E of the experiment is

$$E = n_1 \times p_1 + n_2 \times p_2 + n_3 \times p_3 + \cdots + n_m \times p_m$$

The example of the wheel of chance determined the expected value from the owner's point of view. Investigation 10 will examine the expected value from the player's point of view.

A slot machine consists of three identical wheels as shown at the left of the illustration below. The outer surface of the wheel is partitioned into 15 equal regions. Each region is either blank, marked with a single bar, or marked with a double bar (see right portion of the illustration). There are three single bars and one double bar. The remainder of the regions are blank.

 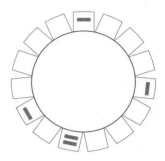

It costs one silver dollar to pull the arm of the slot machine. The payout is as follows:

> Three double bars: $30
>
> Three single bars: $3
>
> Two single bars and a double bar: $5
>
> Two double bars and a single bar: $10

(a) What is the owner's expected payout for each pull of the slot machine arm?

(b) If a person plays this slot machine 25 times, what might he or she expect to win?

Understand the Problem: You are given information about a slot machine and the payouts for that machine. You are asked specific questions about expected payouts and expected winnings.

Devise a Plan: Use the strategies of drawing a picture and making a table.

Carry Out the Plan: A "modified" probability tree diagram is shown on page 423. Notice that each wheel has three possible outcomes: double, single, and blank. Since payouts are made only when all three wheels show double and/or single bars, the branches that would lead to and from a blank outcome are not continued. The probability of any combinations with blanks can easily be determined by finding the complement of payout probabilities, although it will not be necessary since the payout value of these outcomes is zero.

Let D represent the outcome of a double bar, S represent the outcome of a single bar, and B represent the outcome of a blank.

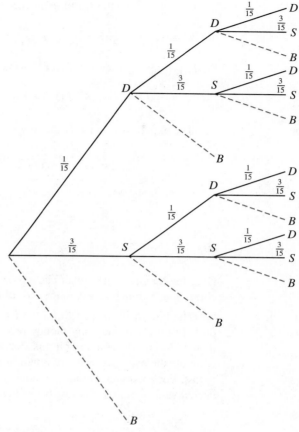

Outcome	Probability	Payout
DDD	$\frac{1}{15} \times \frac{1}{15} \times \frac{1}{15} = \frac{1}{3375}$	$30
SSS	$\frac{3}{15} \times \frac{3}{15} \times \frac{3}{15} = \frac{27}{3375}$	$3
DDS	$\frac{1}{15} \times \frac{1}{15} \times \frac{3}{15}$	
DSD	$\frac{1}{15} \times \frac{3}{15} \times \frac{1}{15} \quad = \frac{3}{3375}$	$10
SDD	$\frac{3}{15} \times \frac{1}{15} \times \frac{1}{15}$	
DSS	$\frac{1}{15} \times \frac{3}{15} \times \frac{3}{15}$	
SDS	$\frac{3}{15} \times \frac{1}{15} \times \frac{3}{15} \quad = \frac{9}{3375}$	$5
SSD	$\frac{3}{15} \times \frac{3}{15} \times \frac{1}{15}$	

(a) Let event W be the winning outcomes. Then,

$$P(W) = \frac{1}{3375} + \frac{27}{3375} + \frac{3}{3375} + \frac{3}{3375} + \frac{3}{3375} + \frac{9}{3375} + \frac{9}{3375} + \frac{9}{3375} = \frac{64}{3375} \approx .019$$

Therefore, $\overline{W}$ represents the set of losing outcomes (any wheel showing a blank).

$$P(\overline{W}) = 1 - P(W) = \frac{3311}{3375} \approx .981$$

The expected value over the long run of this slot machine is computed as follows:

$$E = 30 \times \frac{1}{3375} + 3 \times \frac{27}{3375} + 10 \times \frac{3}{3375} + 10 \times \frac{3}{3375} + 10 \times \frac{3}{3375} +$$

$$\approx \quad .009 \quad + \quad .024 \quad + \quad\quad\quad .027 \quad\quad\quad +$$

$$5 \times \frac{9}{3375} + 5 \times \frac{9}{3375} + 5 \times \frac{9}{3375} + 0 \times \frac{3311}{3375}$$

$$.04 \quad\quad\quad\quad\quad\quad = \$.10$$

Over the long run, the owner can expect to pay out about $.10 per pull of the slot machine. This is much less than the cost of a single play, so the owner will make money.

(b) The lure of winning $30 for a $1 bet is sure to attract people. But notice that the probability of winning any money prize is .019. This means that there is slightly less than a 2% chance of a win on this slot machine, and about a 98% chance of a loss. To compute the expected value of a win, we will let -1 represent the situation in which $1 is lost. Each winning amount is reduced by $1 to account for the cost of play. The expected value formula can now be written as:

$$E = 29 \times \frac{1}{3375} + 2 \times \frac{27}{3375} + 9 \times \frac{3}{3375} + 9 \times \frac{3}{3375} + 9 \times \frac{3}{3375} +$$

$$\approx \quad .009 \quad + \quad .016 \quad + \quad\quad\quad .024 \quad\quad\quad +$$

$$4 \times \frac{9}{3375} + 4 \times \frac{9}{3375} + 4 \times \frac{9}{3375} + (-1) \times \frac{3311}{3375}$$

$$.032 \quad\quad\quad\quad + \quad (-.981) \quad = -.90$$

On the average, you can expect to lose about $.90 per pull. If you play 25 times, you can expect to lose about $22.50.

Look Back: Notice the relationship between the expected payout ($.10) and the expected winnings (−$.90). The owner expects to pay out $.10 for every dollar of play over the long run. Since the player expects to be paid $.10 per play over the long run, he or she will lose $.90 for each play ($ −.90).

In Problem 23 of the following Assessments section, you will be asked to adjust this game in a variety of ways.

Assessments for Section 9.2

1. An experiment consists of randomly selecting a state, then randomly selecting a state capital. The equally likely outcomes are of the form (state, capital).

   (a) What is the probability that (Maine, Augusta) is selected?

   (b) What is the probability that (California, Tallahassee) is selected?

   (c) What is the probability that the state selected will be paired with its correct capital?

2. An experiment consists of rolling three dice. What is the probability that the sum of the numbers rolled is even? What is the probability that the sum of the numbers rolled is odd? Explain your answer.

3. Tickets for a concert are distributed by lottery. The rows AA, BB, CC, DD, EE, FF, and A–Z are each written on a sheet of paper and placed in a box. The seat numbers 1–80 are each written on a sheet of paper and placed in a bag. Individual seats are assigned by randomly selecting a row letter and a seat number. The double-letter seats are the first six rows of the theater. Seats 1–20 are on the left side of the theater. Seats 21–60 are in the center. Seats 61–80 are on the right side of the theater. Seats numbered 1, 2, 79, and 80 are considered obstructed-view seats. Assume that you are the first person to be given a seat assignment.

   (a) What is the probability that you will be in the double-letter rows?

   (b) What is the probability that you will not be assigned an obstructed-view seat?

   (c) What is the probability that you will be assigned a center seat?

   (d) What is the probability that you will be assigned an obstructed-view seat given that you are in the double-letter rows?

   (e) What is the probability that you will be assigned a center seat given that you are not in the double-letter rows?

4. Five green, two blue, and one white chip are placed in a bag. An experiment consists of randomly selecting a chip from the bag, recording the color, then replacing it in the bag and repeating the process.

   (a) Construct a probability tree diagram to illustrate this situation.

   (b) List the elements in the sample space of this experiment.

   (c) What outcome has the smallest probability?

   (d) What outcome has the greatest probability?

   (e) What is the probability of selecting matching-color chips?

   (f) What is the probability of an outcome that contains no white chips?

5. Spinner A and spinner B are illustrated here.

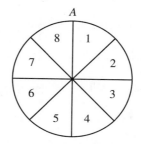 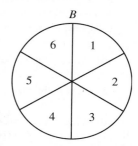

   In spinner A, the face of the spinner has been partitioned into eight congruent regions. In spinner B, the face of the spinner has been partitioned into six congruent regions. An experiment consists of spinning A first, then spinning B. Outcomes of this experiment are of the form (A, B).

   (a) Construct a probability tree diagram to illustrate this situation.

   (b) How many elements are in the sample space of this experiment?

   (c) What is the probability that the number appearing on A will also appear on B?

   (d) What is the probability that the number appearing on A is greater than the number appearing on B?

   (e) What is the probability that the number appearing on A is less than the number appearing on B?

6. Each question on a 10-question multiple-choice quiz has five choices. What is the probability that a person will get all 10 questions correct by randomly guessing the choices for all 10 questions?

7. A set of index cards is divided into five sets. Four of the sets have pictures on them, and one set is blank, as follows: 30% have stars, 25% have circles, 20% have squares, 15% have triangles, and the remainder blank. In a collection of chips, 40% are red, 30% are blue, and 30% are white. An experiment consists of randomly selecting a card, then randomly selecting a chip.

   (a) Construct a probability tree diagram for the outcomes of this experiment.

   (b) What is the probability of selecting a circle with a white chip?

(c) What is the probability of selecting a blue chip?

(d) What is the probability of not selecting a square with a white chip?

(e) What is the probability of selecting a red chip given that you have selected a star?

8. An experiment consists of randomly drawing colored markers from a box consisting of four green markers and six yellow markers. The markers are picked four times without replacement.

(a) Construct a probability tree diagram to illustrate this experiment.

(b) What is the probability that you will get four green markers?

(c) What is the probability that you will not get four yellow markers?

(d) What is the probability that you will get exactly two markers of each color?

(e) What is the probability that you will get a yellow marker on the second pick given that you selected a green marker on the first pick?

(f) Are these picks independent events? Explain your answer.

9. Blue and pink marbles are placed in a bag. An experiment consists of selecting a marble, recording the color, replacing the marble in the bag, then repeating the process. How many marbles might initially be in the bag if the probability of getting two blue marbles is .16, and the probability of getting one of each color is .48?

10. Red, white, and blue marbles are placed in a bag. An experiment consists of selecting a marble without replacement, and then selecting a second marble. How many marbles might initially be in the bag if the probability of a red on the second pick given that a red was chosen on the first pick is zero, the probability of two blue marbles is $\frac{1}{5}$, and the probability of two white marbles is $\frac{1}{15}$?

11. Thirty-two seniors are on the cheerleading squad. Twelve of the seniors are male, and three of the males were on the team last year. Eighteen squad members were on the team last year. What is the probability that a randomly selected cheerleader was on the team last year, given that the cheerleader is male?

12. The probability that Margaret will take out a home-equity loan is .75. The probability that Margaret will take out a home-equity loan and buy a new car is .40. What is the probability that Margaret will buy a new car given that she takes out a home-equity loan?

13. A political science club is considering inviting a certain controversial speaker on campus. Before doing so, they surveyed 1035 students to find out their opinions. The results are shown here:

	For	Against
Freshmen	125	100
Sophomores	150	90
Juniors	210	65
Seniors	250	45

Suppose that the name of a person surveyed was randomly selected.

(a) What is the probability that the person is a junior?

(b) What is the probability that the person is a junior given that he or she is in favor of inviting the speaker?

(c) What is the probability that the person is in favor of inviting the speaker given that he or she is a junior?

14. Three cards are drawn from a standard deck.

(a) What is the probability that all three cards will be aces if each card drawn is replaced before the next card is picked?

(b) What is the probability that all three cards will be aces if each card drawn is not replaced before the next card is picked?

15. Two well known runners are in a marathon. The probability that François will complete the marathon is .98. The probability that David will complete the marathon is .72. What is the probability that they both complete the marathon?

16. Examine the following Venn diagram. Write a problem that would use the number of elements shown in sets A, B, and $(A \cap B)$ in order to determine the probability of $A \mid B$.

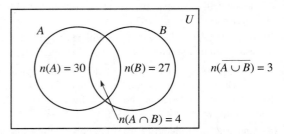

17. Eight 1-dollar bills, four 5-dollar bills, three 10-dollar bills, two 20-dollar bills, and one 50-dollar bill are put into a bag. For $5 a turn, a player chooses one bill at random and

keeps whatever bill is chosen. As each bill is chosen from the bag, a bill of the same denomination is put back in the bag.

(a) What is the expected value of this game?

(b) On the average, what should a player's winnings/losses be?

18. Assume that the situation is the same as in Problem 17. A player must pay $5 to pick from the bag. This fee must be put into the bag before the selection is made.

(a) What is the expected value of the game if the player puts one 5-dollar bill into the bag?

(b) What is the expected value of the game if the player puts five 1-dollar bills into the bag?

(c) What is the expected value of the game if the player puts a 10-dollar bill into the bag and takes out a 5-dollar bill as change?

19. A game consists of tossing a quarter, a nickel, a dime, and a penny. If all four coins show heads or all four coins show tails, you win $10. If exactly three coins show heads or exactly three coins show tails, you win $5. You lose with any other combination of heads and tails. If it costs $5 to play this game once, what are your expected winnings/losses if you play this game 100 times?

20. A game consists of rolling a painted cube. Three faces of the cube are blue, two faces of the cube are white, and one face is green. If a person wins $2 for blue, $3 for white, and $6 for green, what price should the owner charge so that this game could be considered a fair game? What is your definition of a fair game in this context?

21. Recall the string experiment whose tree diagram was shown in Investigation 5.

(a) Assign probabilities to the branches of the tree diagram.

(b) Suppose that it costs $4 for a set of these strings. The owner will pay you $5 if you tie them to form a complete circle and $2 if you tie them to form separate circles. Will the owner make or lose money over the long run?

22. Recall the string experiment involving four tied strings (see Investigation 5). In this problem, assume that you have six strings rather than four.

(a) Determine the probability of getting a complete circle.

(b) Suppose that is costs $4 for this set of strings. The owner will pay you $5 if you tie them to form a com-

plete circle. Will the owner make or lose money over the long run?

23. In Investigation 10 you were given a problem concerning the outcomes from the pull of the arm of a slot machine. Assume that the number of bars and blanks on the wheel remains fixed.

(a) If you raise the price of play to $2, what happens to the expected value?

(b) If you lower the price of play to $.50, what happens to the expected value?

(c) What are the odds in favor of three double bars?

(d) What are the odds in favor of three single bars?

(e) What are the odds in favor of two double bars and a single bar?

(f) What are the odds in favor of two single bars and a double bar?

24. An experiment consists of randomly selecting a number from 0–9 inclusive, spinning a spinner that is partitioned into four congruent regions labeled $+$, $-$, $\times$, and $\div$, respectively, and finally once again selecting a number from 0–9 inclusive. The sample space, S, of this experiment consists of arithmetic expressions of the type "first number   operation   second number" (e.g., $3 + 8$).

(a) What is $n(S)$?

(b) What is the probability of the experiment resulting in an expression that is undefined?

(c) What is the probability of the experiment resulting in an expression whose value is less than 1?

(d) What is the probability of the experiment resulting in an expression whose value is 0?

In Other Words

25. What is the difference between mutually exclusive events and independent events?

26. Suppose that the probability of the occurrence of a certain event is .70. If the experiment is run 500 times, how many times might you expect this event to occur? Why?

27. The multiplication rule for independent events can apply to more than two independent events. Create a situation in which it might be necessary to determine $P(A) \times P(B) \times P(C)$ if A, B, and C are independent events. Explain your reasoning.

28. Explain the meaning of this notation $P(A \mid \bar{B})$. Describe a context in which it might be clearly illustrated.

29. Explain how a knowledge of probability can help a person become a more informed citizen.

Cooperative Activity

30. Groups of four: In this activity, you will try to determine if the last four digits in the phone numbers of a certain area are randomly assigned.

Individual Accountability: Meet with your group before beginning the individual part of this activity. Make sure that all group members have access to the same phone book (white pages of the same area).

Prepare a tally sheet with the digits 0–9. Prepare a second sheet of paper numbered from 1–50. Begin with any page in the phone book. Randomly select any phone number on that page. Count down from the top of the page to determine the number of phone numbers that are above the one you selected. Write the last four digits of the phone number selected next to the number 1 on the second sheet of paper. Go to the next page of the phone book. Count down the same number of phone num-

bers. Write the last four digits of the phone number selected. Repeat this process until 50 phone numbers have been used. Once the 50 sets of numbers are found, tally the frequencies of the digits used. Use the completed tally chart to assign experimental probabilities to each of the digits.

Review the list of "phone numbers." Answer the following questions:

(a) What is the probability that the first digit is 0?

(b) What is the probability that the second digit is 0?

(c) What is the probability that the second digit is 0 given that the first digit is 0?

Group Goal: Compile your frequencies into one tally chart. Determine the experimental probabilities of the digits from the compiled chart. Compare the group tally with the individual tally. Discuss the individual results of the three questions (a), (b), and (c). Determine if the last four digits are randomly assigned. Justify your determination.

9.3 Counting Techniques: Pascal's Triangle, Permutations, and Combinations

The probability of an event has been viewed as the ratio of the number of ways a favorable outcome can occur to the total number of possible outcomes. The frequency of successes (favorable outcomes) can be determined in a number of ways. In Section 9.2, probability tree diagrams were used to represent the experiment, identify the sample space, and assign probabilities to the various outcomes.

Unfortunately, tree diagrams have their limitations. As discussed previously, in some cases tree diagrams are inefficient for determining relative frequencies of successes. For example, suppose an experiment consists of tossing a fair die and then randomly selecting a card from a standard deck of playing cards. Using the fundamental counting principle, we determine that there are 6 × 52, or 312, outcomes in the sample space. Obviously, a tree diagram would be inappropriate here. But notice that we were able to determine the number of elements in the sample space without actually creating the tree diagram.

The fundamental counting principle is one of many counting techniques that are used to identify the number of different outcomes, both favorable and unfavorable, in a sample space. In this section, we will investigate three additional counting techniques.

Examine the following illustration. How many different paths are possible that spell the word CAP?

Four different paths successfully spell the word CAP. The number at the end of each path in the following illustration indicates the number of paths that end there. Notice that more than one path can end at one letter:

How many different paths in the following illustration spell the word CAPE?

Eight different paths can successfully spell the word CAPE. These paths are shown here:

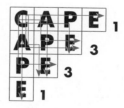

Finally, the following illustration depicts the number of possible paths that spell the word CAPER. Notice that 16 successful paths are possible:

Can you establish a pattern that permits you to predict the number of paths possible to spell the word CAPERS? This pattern can be established by examining the number of paths possible for each word. For the three-letter word CAP, 4 paths were possible. For the four-letter word CAPE, 8 paths were possible. For the five-letter word CAPER, 16 paths were possible. You have likely predicted that 32 paths will be possible for the six-letter word CAPERS. But how many paths would be possible for the word MATHE-MATICS? Examine the following table.

Number of Letters	Number of Possible Paths
3	$4 = 2^2$
4	$8 = 2^3$
5	$16 = 2^4$
6	$32 = 2^5$

In general, it appears that an n-letter word can be traced in $2^{(n-1)}$ ways. Since MATHE-MATICS contains 11 letters, it can be traced in 2^{10}, or 1024, different ways.

Pascal's Triangle

Pascal's triangle

The pattern just described was established in the seventeenth century by the famous French mathematician Blaise Pascal (1623–1662) and has been formalized into what is now known as **Pascal's triangle**. Examine the triangle below. Attempt to connect the entries in the triangle with the above spelling investigation.

$$
\begin{array}{c}
1 \\
1 \quad 1 \\
1 \quad 2 \quad 1 \\
1 \quad 3 \quad 3 \quad 1 \\
1 \quad 4 \quad 6 \quad 4 \quad 1 \\
1 \quad 5 \quad 10 \quad 10 \quad 5 \quad 1
\end{array}
\qquad
\begin{array}{l}
\rightarrow \quad 1 = 2^0 \\
\rightarrow \quad 2 = 2^1 \\
\rightarrow \quad 4 = 2^2 \\
\rightarrow \quad 8 = 2^3 \\
\rightarrow \quad 16 = 2^4 \\
\rightarrow \quad 32 = 2^5
\end{array}
$$

Notice that the sums of the rows in the triangle are 1, 2, 4, 8, 16, and 32, respectively. Another interesting pattern can be found in Pascal's triangle. Notice that each row begins and ends with a 1. All other numbers can be determined by adding the entries that appear immediately above them to the right and the left. For example, notice that the 10 in the last row is the sum of the 4 and 6 in the row above. The next row would contain the entries 1 6 15 20 15 6 1. What numbers would be in the next row?

Pascal's triangle can be used to determine the probabilities that are assigned to experiments containing two outcomes. We will examine the case of a true/false test where the choices are randomly made. On a two-question true/false test, the sample space contains {TT, TF, FT, FF}, or four entries. Notice that there is one way to have two trues, two ways to have one true, and one way to have no trues. On a three-question true/false test, the sample space is {TTT, TTF, TFT, FTT, FFT, FTF, TFF, FFF}. Here, there is one way to have three trues, three ways to have two trues, three ways to have one true, and one way to have no trues. The number of possible ways to have "trues" can be determined by Pascal's triangle. You can see that 1 2 1 is the third row in the triangle, and 1 3 3 1 is the fourth row. Extending this, on a five-question true/false test where the entries are randomly made, 32 different combinations are possible. Since the sixth row of Pascal's triangle contains the entries 1 5 10 10 5 1, it is possible to describe the sample space as containing 1 way to have five trues, 5 ways to have four trues, 10 ways to have three trues, and so on.

Investigation 11

Suppose a fair coin is tossed 10 times. Determine (a) the number of different arrangements of groups of 10 heads/tails; (b) the number of ways to get exactly 7 heads; (c) the probability of getting exactly 7 heads; and (d) the probability of getting at least 4 heads.

Understand the Problem: You are told that a single fair coin is tossed 10 times. You are asked to find a variety of outcomes and probabilities.

Devise a Plan: Since this experiment has two possible outcomes at each stage (heads/tails), we can use Pascal's triangle to answer each of the questions. (Refer to p. 430.)

Carry Out the Plan:

(a) On the five-question true/false test there were 32, or 2^5, possible true/false arrangements. This situation is similar to tossing a fair coin five times and examining the set of outcomes. From this and other findings, we can conclude that if a coin is tossed 10 times, there are 2^{10}, or 1024, possible sets of outcomes.

(b) In Pascal's triangle, the sum of the entries in the 11th row is equal to 1024. The actual entries are

$$1 \quad 10 \quad 45 \quad 120 \quad 210 \quad 252 \quad 210 \quad 120 \quad 45 \quad 10 \quad 1$$

Reading from left to right, these numbers can be interpreted as 1 way of getting exactly 10 heads, 10 ways of getting exactly 9 heads, 45 ways of getting exactly 8 heads, and 120 ways of getting exactly 7 heads, and so on.

(c) If event A consists of getting exactly 7 heads, then the probability of event A is equal to the relative frequency of the favorable outcomes, or $\frac{f}{n}$. Since there are 120 ways of getting exactly 7 heads, and 1024 different arrangements of heads/tails in the sample space,

$$P(\text{exactly 7 heads}) = \frac{120}{1024} = \frac{15}{128}$$

or approximately 12%.

(d) The event "at least 4 heads" consists of the outcomes that include exactly 4 heads, exactly 5 heads, exactly 6 heads, exactly 7 heads, exactly 8 heads, exactly 9 heads, and exactly 10 heads. The probability of getting at least 4 heads is the sum of the probabilities of each of the preceding outcomes. Therefore,

$$P(\text{at least 4 heads}) = \frac{210}{1024} + \frac{252}{1024} + \frac{210}{1024} + \frac{120}{1024} + \frac{45}{1024} + \frac{10}{1024} + \frac{1}{1024} = \frac{848}{1024}$$

$$\approx .828$$

Look Back: Could the solutions have been found in any other way? For example, the probability in (d) could also have been determined by subtracting the probability of its complement (exactly 3, 2, 1, or 0 heads) from 1.

Permutations

Suppose a committee consists of five members. A chairperson and a recording secretary must be selected from the group. How many different sets of assignments to these positions are possible?

We will model the situation using the letters A, B, C, D, and E to represent the committee members. We wish to generate every possible pair such that the first member of the pair would serve as the chairperson and the second member would serve as the secretary. The following list contains all possible pairs:

$$AB \quad AC \quad AD \quad AE$$
$$BA \quad BC \quad BD \quad BE$$
$$CA \quad CB \quad CD \quad CE$$
$$DA \quad DB \quad DC \quad DE$$
$$EA \quad EB \quad EC \quad ED$$

Notice that the pair AB is distinct from the pair BA. In the first case, Andy could be the chairperson and Barbara could be the secretary. In the second case, Barbara could be the chairperson and Andy could be the secretary. The order of the pair is an important factor. From a group of 5 people, 20 ordered pairs are possible.

permutation In mathematics, an arrangement of distinct "objects" in a particular order is known as a **permutation**. In the 20 permutations of chairpersons and secretaries, the "objects" are people. We use the word *objects* in a generic sense to mean any elements of a particular group.

Listing all of the possible permutations of groups of two out of the committee of five was easy, since the numbers were manageable. If the committee contained 15 members, and if a chairperson, associate chairperson, secretary, and treasurer needed to be selected, then the list of all possible "quartets" would have been much longer and more difficult to generate.

factorial The number of permutations can be determined without actually listing and counting them. It requires a new notation, known as the **factorial**. The symbol $n!$ is read as "n factorial" and symbolizes a special type of multiplication that can best be explained by some examples.

$$5! = 5 \times 4 \times 3 \times 2 \times 1 = 120$$
$$4! = 4 \times 3 \times 2 \times 1 = 24$$
$$3! = 3 \times 2 \times 1 = 6$$
$$2! = 2 \times 1 = 2$$

Notice that the factorial notation results in a product whose factors are the counting numbers less than or equal to the stated number. There is one exception to this rule, namely, that 0! is defined as being equal to 1. (You will see the reason for this shortly.) Some calculators have a key labeled $\boxed{n!}$ that displays the desired product.

Now, let's focus our attention on the committee permutations. The original problem asked us to determine the number of possible permutations of two objects out of five possible objects. We introduce the notation $_5P_2$ to represent this situation. There are five ways to choose the first person. Once that person is chosen, there are four ways to choose the second person. Notice that $5 \times 4 = 20$. Therefore, $_5P_2 = 20$. In general, $_nP_r$ represents the number of possible permutations of n objects taken r at a time. We have already determined that $_5P_2 = 20$ by listing and counting the outcomes. This could also have been achieved by noting that

$$20 = \frac{5!}{(5-2)!} = \frac{5!}{3!} = \frac{5 \times 4 \times 3 \times 2 \times 1}{3 \times 2 \times 1} = 20$$

In general, the number of possible permutations of n objects taken r at a time is

$$_nP_r = \frac{n!}{(n-r)!}$$

You can now see why it was important for 0! to be defined as 1. Suppose that the committee of five needed a president, vice president, secretary, treasurer, and representative. How many different permutations of the five members out of the five possible members are there? Here, we need to determine $_5P_5$, which is $\frac{5!}{(5-5)!}$. Notice that the denominator is 0!. Had 0! been defined as 0, the permutation formula would have been undefined at values where $n = r$. Rather,

$$_5P_5 = \frac{5 \times 4 \times 3 \times 2 \times 1}{1} = 120$$

There are 120 possible permutations of the five-member group to fill the five different positions.

Investigation 12

A 12-member cheerleading squad has a routine in which 10 of the members form a pyramid, with rows of four, three, two, and then one cheerleader at the top.

(a) How many different permutations of pyramids are possible for this team?

(b) Suppose that one of the permutations is to be randomly selected to be photographed and appear on the cover of a weekly sports magazine. What is the probability that any one given permutation will be selected, assuming that all outcomes are equally likely?

(c) What is the probability that the photograph will contain the pyramid in which Mike, the captain of the cheerleaders, is at the top?

(a) We wish to determine the number of ordered arrangements of 12 cheerleaders taken 10 at a time.

$$_{12}P_{10} = \frac{12!}{(12-10)!} = \frac{12!}{2!} = \frac{12 \times 11 \times 10 \times 9 \times 8 \times 7 \times 6 \times 5 \times 4 \times 3 \times 2 \times 1}{2 \times 1}$$

$$= 239{,}500{,}800$$

There are 239,500,800 different pyramids possible.

(b) Since each pyramid is distinct, the probability of any given pyramid would be $\frac{1}{239{,}500{,}800}$.

(c) We wish to determine the number of different pyramids possible that would have Mike at the peak. Removing Mike from the pool of possible participants leaves 11 cheerleaders with 9 openings in the pyramid. We therefore wish to determine the number of permutations of 11 cheerleaders taken 9 at a time, or $_{11}P_9$.

$$\frac{11!}{(11-9)!} = \frac{11!}{2!} = \frac{11 \times 10 \times 9 \times 8 \times 7 \times 6 \times 5 \times 4 \times 3 \times 2 \times 1}{2 \times 1}$$

$$= 19{,}958{,}400$$

There are 19,958,400 different pyramids possible with Mike at the top. Therefore, the probability that the randomly selected photograph would have Mike at the top is $\frac{19{,}958{,}400}{239{,}500{,}800}$, or $\frac{1}{12}$. This is the same probability as that of Mike being chosen out of the group of 12 cheerleaders for a single position.

■

Some calculators have an $\boxed{_nP_r}$ key. The calculator keystroke sequence that would determine the number of permutations of 11 objects taken 9 at a time is

$$\boxed{AC} \quad 11 \quad \boxed{_nP_r} \quad 9 \quad \boxed{=}$$

Combinations

Recall the committee of five that was used to introduce the concept of permutations. The order of the pairs chosen was important in the context given, since the first member would serve as chairperson and the second member as secretary. Suppose, instead, that a two-member team was to be selected that would serve as a small subcommittee. How many such two-member subcommittees are possible?

Let's review the list of 20 permutations. Here, we see that a subcommittee consisting of *Andy* and *Barbara* is exactly the same as the subcommittee consisting of *Barbara* and *Andy*. Therefore, *AB* and *BA* represent the same pair of people, and we can go through the list and cross off any duplicate pairs:

AB	*AC*	*AD*	*AE*
~~*BA*~~	*BC*	*BD*	*BE*
~~*CA*~~	~~*CB*~~	*CD*	*CE*
~~*DA*~~	~~*DB*~~	~~*DC*~~	*DE*
~~*EA*~~	~~*EB*~~	~~*EC*~~	~~*ED*~~

combination Only 10 distinct pairs now remain. The order is irrelevant in this context. In mathematics, an arrangement of distinct objects in which order is not important is called a **combination**. The number of combinations of n objects taken r at a time is symbolized by $_nC_r$.

There are fewer combinations possible of five objects taken two at a time than there are permutations. In this situation, the number of permutations, $_5P_2$, is twice the number of combinations, $_5C_2$. We can express this relationship in the following equations:

$$_5C_2 \times 2 = {_5P_2} \qquad \text{or} \qquad _5C_2 = \frac{_5P_2}{2}$$

Notice that $2 = 2!$. Dividing both sides of the equation by $2!$ yields an equivalence for $_5C_2$ in terms of $_5P_2$.

$$_5C_2 = \frac{_5P_2}{2!}$$

In general,

$$_nC_r = \frac{_nP_r}{r!}$$

This can be simplified and yields the following formula for the number of combinations of n objects taken r at a time:

$$\frac{n!}{r!(n-r)!}$$

Investigation 13

How many different five-card hands can be dealt from a standard deck of 52 playing cards?

The order in which the hand is dealt or arranged is irrelevant. Therefore, we are looking for the number of combinations of 52 cards taken 5 at a time.

$$_{52}C_5 = \frac{52!}{(5!(52-5)!)} = \frac{52!}{5!47!}$$

It would be time-consuming and practically impossible (even on some calculators) to get a value for 52!. On one calculator that can perform this calculation, the value is displayed as $\boxed{8.065817517\ \text{E}\ 67}$, which is obviously a very large approximation. But notice that 52! can be expressed as $52 \times 51 \times 50 \times 49 \times 48 \times 47!$. We will use this fact to simplify the expression as follows:

$$\frac{52!}{5!47!} = \frac{52 \times 51 \times 50 \times 49 \times 48 \times 47!}{5!47!} = \frac{52 \times 51 \times 50 \times 49 \times 48}{5 \times 4 \times 3 \times 2 \times 1} = 2{,}598{,}960$$

There are 2,598,960 different five-card hands possible.

This result could have been determined using a calculator that has the $\boxed{_nC_r}$ key as follows:

$$\boxed{\text{AC}} \quad 52 \quad \boxed{_nC_r} \quad 5 \quad \boxed{=}$$

The following list shows the number of combinations of five objects taken 5, 4, 3, 2, 1, and 0 at a time. Look for regularities. Where have you seen this pattern before?

$$_5C_5 = \frac{5!}{5!(5-5)!} = 1$$

$$_5C_4 = \frac{5!}{4!(5-4)!} = 5$$

$$_5C_3 = \frac{5!}{3!(5-3)!} = 10$$

$$_5C_2 = \frac{5!}{2!(5-2)!} = 10$$

$$_5C_1 = \frac{5!}{1!(5-1)!} = 5$$

$$_5C_0 = \frac{5!}{0!(5-0)!} = 1$$

The outcomes 1 5 10 10 5 1 appear in the sixth row of Pascal's triangle. Pascal's triangle can be used to determine the number of combinations of n objects taken r at a time by examining the entries in the $(n + 1)$th row. For example, if you wish to determine the number of combinations of six objects taken four at a time, examine the entries in the seventh row: 1 6 15 20 15 6 1. Start at the left and move across, counting down from 6 until you get to 4. Therefore, $_6C_4 = 15$. This can be verified using the formula

$$_6C_4 = \frac{6!}{4!(6-4)!} = \frac{6!}{4!2!} = 15$$

Prior to the discussion of combinations, we had viewed the third entry in the sixth row as the number of ways to have exactly four trues (or heads) out of six possibilities. In addition, you can see that Pascal's triangle can be used to determine the number of ways that four indistinguishable objects can be arranged in six locations.

Assessments for Section 9.3

1. Trace the number of paths possible that would spell each of the following words:

(a)

(b)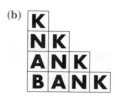

(c)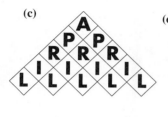

(d)

2. Use Pascal's triangle to answer the questions below.

$$
\begin{array}{ccccccccccccc}
 & & & & & & 1 & & & & & & \\
 & & & & & 1 & & 1 & & & & & \\
 & & & & 1 & & 2 & & 1 & & & & \\
 & & & 1 & & 3 & & 3 & & 1 & & & \\
 & & 1 & & 4 & & 6 & & 4 & & 1 & & \\
 & 1 & & 5 & & 10 & & 10 & & 5 & & 1 & \\
1 & & 6 & & 15 & & 20 & & 15 & & 6 & & 1
\end{array}
$$

(a) What are the entries in the 8th row?

(b) What are the entries in the 10th row?

(c) What is the sum of the entries in the 15th row?

(d) What is the sum of the entries in the 20th row?

(e) Examine the portion of Pascal's triangle shown above. You can view the triangle as being composed of seven diagonals that are slanted to the right. Determine the sum of the numbers in each of these diagonals. Look for a regularity. What generalization can you make?

3. Use Pascal's triangle to answer the following questions.

(a) On a nine-question true/false exam, how many different arrangements of answers will have exactly seven trues?

(b) On an eight-question true/false exam, how many different arrangements of answers will have exactly six falses?

(c) On a seven-question true/false exam, how many different arrangements of answers will have at least two trues?

(d) On a seven-question true/false exam, how many different arrangements will have at most two trues?

(e) On a seven-question true/false exam, what is the probability that a randomly selected arrangement of trues and falses will all be correct?

4. Use Pascal's triangle to answer the following questions.

(a) Suppose a coin is flipped 7 times. How many different arrangements of head/tails are possible?

(b) Suppose a coin is flipped 6 times. What is the probability that you will get exactly five tails?

(c) Suppose a coin is flipped 6 times. What is the probability that you will get at most four tails?

(d) Suppose a coin is flipped 8 times. What is the probability that you will get exactly one tail or exactly one head?

(e) Suppose a coin is flipped 10 times. What is the probability that you will get an even number of heads?

5. A couple is planning to have another child. Assume that the events "male" and "female" are equally likely.

(a) If the couple has three boys, what is the probability that their fourth child will be a girl?

(b) If the couple has five children, what is the probability that they have exactly three girls?

(c) If the couple has four children, what is the probability that they have at least two boys?

(d) If the couple has four children, what is the probability that they have at most two boys?

(e) If the couple has six children, what is the probability that they are all girls or all boys?

6. Determine the value of X in each of the following equations.

(a) $_4P_3 = X$

(b) $_4C_3 = X$

(c) $X! = 720$

(d) $\dfrac{(X+2)!}{X!} = 110$

(e) $\dfrac{(X+2)!}{(X-1)!} = 720$

(f) $_XP_4 = 840$

(g) $_XC_7 = 6435$

7. (a) How many different ways can the letters M, A, T, and H be arranged?

(b) If one arrangement is selected at random, what is the probability that it will be the word MATH?

8. Eighteen people volunteered to test a new drug. Five of these volunteers will be administered a placebo, and the remainder will get the actual drug. How many different placebo groups are possible?

9. A high school student must take math, English, physical education, science, global studies, and a language. Her schedule must include a lunch and a study hall. The entire school has lunch fifth period. The school day is divided into eight periods. How many different schedules are possible that would contain these six classes and a study hall?

10. Suppose you are dealt five cards from a standard 52-card deck. What is the probability that the five cards will be the 2, 3, 4, 5, and 6 of diamonds?

11. Fifty-two seventh-grade girls will be going on an overnight field trip. The principal will randomly assign four girls to each hotel room.

   (a) How many different groups of four are possible?

   (b) What is the probability that a particular group of four girls will room together?

   (c) Beth wants to room with Kate. What is the probability that the two girls will room together?

   (d) Allison, Erin, and Sara want to room together. What is the probability that the three girls will be assigned the same room?

   (e) Stacey and Tracy do not want to be in the same room with each other. What is the probability that they will not be rooming together?

12. Social Security numbers are in the form # # #-# #-# # # #. If each position can be filled with any digit, how many Social Security numbers are possible?

13. How many seven-digit phone numbers are possible in a particular area code if the first digit of the phone number cannot be zero and if each of the other positions can be filled with any digit from zero through nine.

14. The license plates in a certain state consist of three letters followed by three digits.

   (a) How many different license plates of this type are possible?

   (b) If a license plate is selected at random, what is the probability that RJS 123 will be selected?

   (c) If a license plate is selected at random, what is the probability that the first three letters will be RJS, in that order?

   (d) If a license plate is selected at random, what is the probability that the first three letters will contain an R, a J, and an S?

   (e) If a license plate is selected at random, what is the probability that the first three letters will all be vowels?

15. One marble of each of the following colors is placed into a hat: blue, red, green, orange, and purple. The five marbles are drawn from the hat one at a time without replacement.

   (a) How many different color sequences drawn are possible?

   (b) How many different color sequences drawn are possible with orange as the first color?

   (c) How many different color sequences drawn are possible with orange as the first color and green as the last color?

   (d) What is the probability that the color sequence drawn will be the same as the alphabetical listing of the colors?

16. A certain state has several different types of lottery drawings.

   (a) In CASH 40, you must select six numbers from 1–40. If your six numbers, in any order, match the six numbers that are drawn without replacement, you win the grand prize. What is the probability that a single set of six numbers will be the grand-prize numbers?

   (b) In LOTTO 54, you must select six numbers from 1–54. If your six numbers, in any order, match the six numbers that are drawn without replacement, you win the grand prize. What is the probability that a single set of six numbers will win the grand prize?

   (c) In PICK 4, you must select a number from 0000 to 9999. The number you select must match the number drawn. What is the probability that a particular four-digit number will be the winning number?

17. Fourteen people have been selected to be the jury on a particular case. Two of these people will be randomly chosen as alternates. Nancy Lewis and Liz Kane are 2 of the 14 people.

   (a) What is the probability that Nancy and Liz will be the alternates?

   (b) What are the odds against Nancy and Liz being the alternates?

   (c) Suppose that 3 people are randomly selected out of the 14. The first chosen is the chairperson of the jury. The second chosen is the first alternate. The third chosen is the second alternate. How many different groups of three are possible for these assignments?

18. A college committee consists of seven full-time students and five transfer students. A five-member subcommittee is to be randomly selected.

   (a) How many different five-member subcommittees are possible?

   (b) Suppose that three and only three of the subcommittee members must be full-time students. How many different subcommittees are possible?

19. In a small condominium complex, six of the units are owned and four are rented. A four-member tenants' advisory group is to be randomly selected. One representative from each of the units has volunteered to serve on the board.

  (a) How many different four-member advisory boards are possible?

  (b) Suppose that the advisory board must consist of two owners and two renters. How many different advisory boards are possible?

  (c) Ms. Olmos is an owner and Mrs. Philips is a renter. If the advisory board must consist of two owners and two renters, what is the probability that Ms. Olmos and Mrs. Philips will be on the board together?

  (d) Suppose that the board must consist of three owners and one renter. How many different advisory boards are possible?

In Other Words

20. Why is "combination lock" a misnomer?

21. Explain how Pascal's triangle can be used to determine the number of three-member teams that are possible out of a group of 10 people.

22. Under what circumstance(s) of n objects taken r at a time is only one combination possible? Explain your answer.

23. Under what circumstance(s) of n objects taken r at a time are n permutations possible? Explain your answer.

24. Under what circumstance(s) of n objects taken r at a time are the number of combinations equal to the number of permutations? Explain your answer.

Cooperative Activity

25. Groups of two (Further explorations of Pascal's triangle)

Individual Accountability: Construct Pascal's triangle with 12 rows. Investigate each of the following problems.

  (a) Begin at any 1. Follow down along the diagonal that begins at that 1. Find the sum of the first four numbers along that diagonal (including the 1). Record your sum. Repeat this procedure at a different starting point. Record your sum. Repeat this procedure at a different starting point using more than four consecutive addends along the diagonal. Record your sum.

  (b) Select any entry in the interior of Pascal's triangle. Locate the two diagonals that meet at that entry. Find the sum of the entries that fall within, but not on, those two diagonals. Repeat this procedure three more times. Record your results.

Group Goal: Compare the results of each member's investigations. What generalizations can you make on the basis of your findings?

Vocabulary for Chapter 9

combination

complement

conditional probability

equally likely events

event

expected value

experimental probability

factorial

favorable event (favorable outcome)

fundamental counting principle

independent events

multiplication principle of probability

mutually exclusive events

outcome

Pascal's triangle

permutation

probability

probability tree diagram

property five: the odds in favor of and against an event

property four: the probability of the complement of an event

property one: equally likely events

property six: mutually exclusive events

property three: the sum of all probabilities in a sample space

property two: more than one favorable event in a sample space

sample space

theoretical probability

tree diagram

Review for Chapter 9

1. Identify the sample space in each of the following experiments.
   (a) Two dice are tossed. An outcome is the product of the numbers that appear on each die.
   (b) Three dice are tossed. An outcome is the sum of the numbers that appear on each die.
   (c) A closed box of cereal is tossed. An outcome is the "side" that lands face up.

2. An experiment consists of spinning a spinner whose face is partitioned into five regions. The results of 500 spins are given in the following table:

Sectors	A	B	C	D	E
Frequency	180	50	22	150	98

   (a) What is the experimental probability of the spinner landing on each region?
   (b) Sketch a spinner face that might yield the same results.

3. The following bar graph depicts the outcomes of spinning a spinner whose face is partitioned into six regions.

   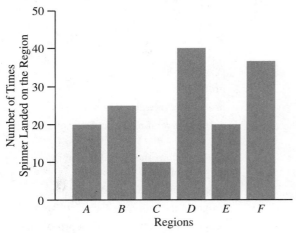

   (a) What is the experimental probability of the spinner landing on each region?
   (b) Sketch a spinner face that might yield the same result.

4. A spinner is partitioned into a number of congruent sectors. The sectors are colored red, white, green, or blue. The probability of landing on red is $\frac{3}{8}$. The probability of landing on green is $\frac{1}{3}$. The probability of landing on white is $\frac{1}{6}$. The probability of landing on blue is $\frac{1}{8}$.
   (a) What is the minimum number of these sectors that would yield these probabilities?
   (b) If the spinner were partitioned into the number of sectors determined in part (a), how many sectors of each color would there be?

5. Three sides of a cube are painted orange. Two sides of the cube are painted purple. One side of the cube is painted black. Determine each of the following probabilities or odds.
   (a) $P(\text{orange})$
   (b) $P(\text{not black})$
   (c) $P(\text{orange or purple})$
   (d) The odds against purple
   (e) The odds in favor of black

6. Suppose you have two of the cubes described in Problem 5. Both cubes are tossed.
   (a) What is the probability that you will get two orange sides facing up?
   (b) What is the probability that you will not get two black sides facing up?
   (c) What is the probability that you will get two matching faces?
   (d) What are the odds in favor of a black and a purple facing up?

7. A card is selected from a standard deck of 52 cards. Determine each of the following probabilities.
   (a) $P(\text{king})$
   (b) $P(\text{heart})$
   (c) $P(\text{red card})$
   (d) $P(\text{jack or queen or king})$
   (e) $P(\text{9 of spades})$

8. Two fair dice are tossed and the sum of the dots appearing face up are counted. Determine the following probabilities.

(a) $P(\text{sum} = 7)$

(b) $P(\text{sum} < 7)$

(c) $P(\text{sum} > 7)$

(d) $P(\text{sum} = \text{a prime number})$

(e) $P(\text{sum} = 1)$

9. The property taxes in a certain town for single-family dwellings are tabulated as follows:

Taxes (in dollars)	Number of homes
0–999	157
1000–1999	425
2000–2999	751
3000–3999	610
4000–4999	320
≥ 5000	98

If a single-family home is selected at random, find the probability that the tax on that dwelling is

(a) $2000–$2999 inclusive.

(b) greater than or equal to $4000.

(c) less than $2000.

(d) at most $2999.

(e) at least $1000.

10. Jack owns 7 sports jackets, 6 pairs of pants, 12 shirts, and 20 ties. How many different outfits of jacket, pants, shirt, and tie are possible?

11. A grandmother has five grandchildren. She is having a grandmother's ring made with the birthstones of her grandchildren. One birthstone is a ruby, one is a diamond, one is an emerald, one is an aquamarine, and one is an opal. The stones are to be placed in a line across the band of the ring. How many different arrangements of stones are possible?

12. An experiment consists of rolling a fair die and then picking a card from a set of cards containing the ace of spades, the ace of hearts, the ace of diamonds, and the ace of clubs.

(a) Construct a probability tree diagram.

(b) List all pairs in the sample space.

(c) What is the probability of rolling a 2 and selecting the ace of spades?

(d) What is the probability of rolling an even number and selecting the ace of hearts?

(e) What is the probability of rolling a prime number and selecting a black ace?

(f) What is the probability of not rolling a 4 and not selecting the ace of diamonds?

13. A bag consists of five green marbles, two blue marbles, one gold marble, and three black marbles. An experiment consists of randomly selecting a marble from the bag, recording the color, returning the marble to the bag, and repeating the process one more time. Determine the following probabilities.

(a) Getting a green marble on the first pick and a gold marble on the second pick

(b) Getting a gold marble on the first pick and a green marble on the second pick

(c) Getting two green marbles

(d) Not getting two gold marbles

(e) Getting matching-color marbles

(f) Getting a blue marble on the second pick given that you got a green marble on the first pick

(g) Getting a black marble on the second pick given that you got a gold marble on the first pick

(h) Getting a green and a blue marble in any order

14. Determine the probabilities listed in Problem 13, parts (a)–(h), if the experiment in Problem 13 is performed without replacing the marbles.

15. Examine the following probability tree diagram. Determine the missing probabilities.

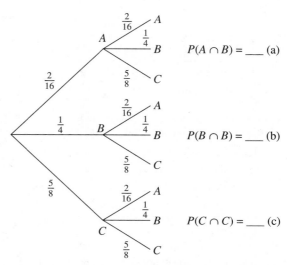

$P(A \cap B) = \underline{\quad}$ (a)

$P(B \cap B) = \underline{\quad}$ (b)

$P(C \cap C) = \underline{\quad}$ (c)

16. Examine the following probability tree diagram, which reflects the probabilities of randomly selecting two marbles from a bag containing brown, yellow, and pink marbles.

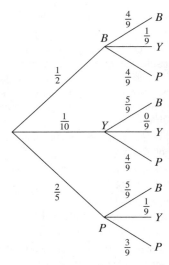

(a) Is this experiment run with or without replacement? Explain your answer.

(b) What is the minimum number of marbles in the bag that would correspond to this probability tree diagram? Explain your answer.

17. A shipment of computers arrived at a warehouse. All computers have two drives: a hard drive and a floppy drive. The packing order lists the following information about the shipment.

Hard Drive	Floppy Disk Drive	
	$3\frac{1}{2}$" Drive	$5\frac{1}{4}$" Drive
20 megabytes	20	50
40 megabytes	55	25

All computers are packaged in identical boxes with no indication of the drive specifications contained within.

Let A be the event "the computer has a $3\frac{1}{2}$" drive."

Let B be the event "the computer has a $5\frac{1}{4}$" drive."

Let C be the event "the computer has a 20-megabyte hard drive."

Let D be the event "the computer has a 40-megabyte hard drive."

Suppose a computer is selected at random.

(a) What is the probability that the computer has a 20-megabyte hard drive?

(b) Suppose you have identified the boxes that contain $5\frac{1}{4}$"drives. What is the probability that a computer selected from those boxes will have a 40-megabyte hard drive?

(c) $P(D \mid A)$

(d) $P(A \mid D)$

(e) $P(C \mid B)$

(f) $P(B \cap D)$

18. A deck of "cards" is composed of an arrow ($\rightarrow$) on a blue background, a dot ($\bullet$) on a blue background, a triangle ($\triangle$) on a blue background, an arrow ($\rightarrow$) on a white background, a dot ($\bullet$) on a white background, and a triangle ($\triangle$) on a white background. The number of each type of card is given here:

	$\rightarrow$	$\bullet$	$\triangle$
Blue	8	10	5
White	3	9	7

A card is selected at random. Determine each of the following probabilities.

(a) Selecting a blue $\bullet$

(b) Selecting a white card

(c) Selecting a card with a $\triangle$ or a $\bullet$

(d) Not selecting a card with an $\rightarrow$

(e) Selecting a card with a $\bullet$ given that it is white

(f) Selecting a blue card given that it has an $\rightarrow$ on it

19. (a) Given $P(A) = .4$, $P(B) = .55$, and $P(A \cap B) = .05$, find $P(A \mid B)$, $P(B \mid A)$, and $P(A \cup B)$.

(b) Given $P(C \mid D) = .38$ and $P(D) = .6$, find $P(C \cap D)$.

(c) Given $P(X \cap Y) = .2$, and $P(X \mid Y) = .5$, find $P(Y)$.

20. A coin is tossed. If it lands on heads you select a marble from a bag that contains three white marbles and two green marbles. If the coin lands on heads, you select a marble from a bag that contains four white marbles and three green marbles. Let event T represent the coin lands on tails, event H represent the coin lands on heads, event W represent a white marble is selected, and event G represent a green marble is selected. Determine each of the following probabilities.

(a) $P(G \mid T)$

(b) $P(W \mid H)$

(c) $P(H \mid G)$

21. Suppose a bag contains N marbles. Each marble is either red, white, or blue. The red, white, and blue marbles are in the ratio of $1 : 2 : 3$.

(a) What is the probability of a red marble being randomly selected?

(b) What is the probability of a blue marble being randomly selected?

(c) Determine two values of N (N_1 and N_2) that would represent different situations where the marbles are in the indicated ratios. Does $P(\text{blue})$ for N_1 equal $P(\text{blue})$ for N_2? Explain your answer.

22. Determine each of the following values.
    (a) $8!$ **(b)** $\frac{7!}{3!}$ **(c)** $\frac{100!}{98!}$ **(d)** $_5C_4$
    (e) $_8C_5$ **(f)** $_{10}P_7$ **(g)** $_{100}P_{100}$

23. A zip code consists of five digits, each of which can be 0–9.
    (a) How many different zip codes are possible?
    (b) Four more digits have been added to each zip code. How many more different zip codes does this addition produce?

24. Eight oil paintings are to be displayed along a corridor wall in an art museum. In how many different linear arrangements can these paintings be displayed?

25. There are 48 members in the school chorus. Five chorus members will be randomly selected to represent the school at the All-County Choral Presentation.
    (a) How many different five-member groups are possible?
    (b) What is the probability that Gina, a member of the chorus, will be selected in the first pick?
    (c) What is the probability that the group consisting of Gina, Marc, Dave, Phyllis, and Akiko will be selected?
    (d) What is the probability that a group containing Gina and Marc will be selected?

26. A shelf contains three math books, four English books, and two global studies books.
    (a) In how many different ways can the books be arranged on the shelf?
    (b) In how many different ways can the books be arranged on the shelf if the math books must all be together at the left side of the shelf?
    (c) In how many different ways can the books be arranged on the shelf if the math books must be together, the English books must be together, and the global studies books must be together?

27. A game consists of spinning a spinner twice. There are four regions (A, B, C, and D) on the spinner. Each outcome is equally likely. It costs $4 to spin the spinner twice. If the outcomes match, you win $6. If the outcome is A on the first spin and B on the second spin, you win $10. If the outcome is CD or DC, in either order, you win $4. What is the expected value of this game?

28. A game consists of tossing two coins and one fair die all at the same time.

(a) Construct a probability tree diagram for the outcomes of this game.

(b) It costs $2 to play the game. You win $1 if you get two heads with a 3 on the die or two tails with a 3 on the die. You win $2 if you get two heads with an even number on the die. You win $3 if you get two tails with a factor of 5 on the die. You win $4 if you get one head and one tail in any order, and a 6 on the die. What is the expected value of this game?

29. A true/false test consists of six questions. If the answers are randomly chosen, determine each of the following probabilities.
    (a) Getting all correct
    (b) Getting all incorrect
    (c) Getting exactly one wrong
    (d) Getting at most one wrong
    (e) Getting two or three wrong

30. A lab technician is testing the reaction when two chemicals are mixed together. She has 18 different chemicals to test.
    (a) How many tests must she make?
    (b) If before combining the two chemicals, one chemical must first be mixed in a solution of 60% alcohol and the other chemical first mixed in a solution of 60% hydrochloric acid, how many tests must now be made?

In Other Words

31. Explain how an experimental probability is viewed as a relative frequency.

32. Under what condition(s) is the probability of an event equal to the probability of the complement of that event?

33. Describe two events that are mutually exclusive but not independent.

34. A row of Pascal's triangle is 1 8 28 56 70 56 28 8 1. Describe a context in which this row would be helpful in determining a number of combinations of n objects taken r at a time.

35. Explain the relationship between the fundamental counting principle and permutations.

Cooperative Activity

36. **Groups of four** (Buffon's needle problem)
To do this problem, you will need some materials. Each group member must have one blank $8\frac{1}{2}" \times 11"$ sheet of paper and a toothpick. The toothpick must be cut so that it is exactly $\frac{1}{2}$ inch long.

Individual Accountability: Draw lines on the paper 1 inch apart that are parallel to the $8\frac{1}{2}$" side. Hold the toothpick above the paper. Drop the toothpick onto the surface of the paper 50 times. Each time, record whether the toothpick touches a line or does not touch a line. Determine the relative frequencies of the events "on the line" and "not on the line." Let X equal the relative frequency of the toothpick touching the line. Determine $\frac{1}{X}$.

Group Goal: Compare your results. Discuss the similarities and/or differences. Compile the results into a single table that represents 200 drops of the toothpick. Determine the relative frequency of the toothpick falling across a line (X). Determine $\frac{1}{X}$. Discuss this numerical value. What do you think Count Buffon (1707–1788) discovered through this activity?

10

Spatial **V**isualization

Examine the photograph at the right.

Describe what you see.

What similarities do you observe in the windows?

What similarities do you observe in the domes?

What patterns are repeated?

What might a mathematical description of this photograph contain?

Introduction

This chapter begins a series of chapters devoted to the study of geometry; not the geometry of rigor and proof, but rather the geometry of exploration, investigation, and problem solving.

Geometry is a branch of mathematics with a long, rich, and diverse history. There is evidence that ancient Egyptians used their knowledge of geometry to measure property boundaries after the annual flooding of the Nile River. Geometry was used by the Greeks to construct aesthetically pleasing buildings. Geometry has helped us to recognize regularities in nature from the hexagonal shape of the honeycomb to the predictable pattern found in the chambers of the Nautilus shell.

This chapter and those that follow will help you to develop a full understanding of that branch of mathematics which grew out of an attempt to measure the earth; hence, its name from the Latin, *geo-metry*. The study of geometry currently permeates all levels of the curriculum. The National Council of Teachers of Mathematics (NCTM) in their *Curriculum and Evaluation for School Mathematics* (1989) makes the following comments concerning the role of geometry at the primary, middle-school, and secondary-school levels.

> **Grades K–4:** Geometry is an important component of the K–4 mathematics curriculum because geometric knowledge, relationships, and insights are useful in everyday situations and are connected to other mathematical topics and school subjects. Geometry helps us represent and describe in an orderly manner the world in which we live. . . . Children should have many opportunities to explore geometry in two and three dimensions, to develop their sense of space and relationships in space, and to solve problems that involve geometry and its application to other topics in mathematics or to other fields. (pp. 49–50)

> **Grades 5–8:** Students discover relationships and develop spatial sense by constructing, drawing, measuring, visualizing, comparing, transforming, and classifying geometric figures. Discussing ideas, conjecturing, and testing hypotheses precede the development of more formal summary statements. In the process, definitions become meaningful, relationships among figures are understood, and students are prepared to use these ideas to develop informal arguments. (p. 112)

> **Grades 9–12:** High school geometry should build on the strong conceptual foundation students develop in the new K–8 programs (p. 157). The interplay between geometry and algebra strengthens a student's ability to formulate and analyze problems from situations both within and outside mathematics. . . . The study of geometry should provide students with the ability to recognize and apply effectively the geometric concepts and methods most appropriate to a given problem situation. (pp. 161–162)

The geometry the NCTM speaks of is an active field of study. Definitions, rules, and proofs all make sense through exploration and analysis, which is what we will be doing in this chapter and throughout the rest of the book. This chapter will introduce you to some basic geometric terminology so that the language of geometric communication will be easier to understand. A more formalized (but not less exploratory) treatment will be found in the chapters that follow. The development of spatial sense in both two and three dimensions affords us many interesting problems. Like the other topics we have covered in this book, geometry is most useful when it helps us solve problems.

Section 10.1 covers the concepts you will need to know in order to observe, describe, and classify two-dimensional objects. Topics such as points, line segments, and lines; collinearity; planes; closed and open shapes; and levels of geometric development are examined. Section 10.2 explores three-dimensional figures and their properties, including polyhedra such as prisms and pyramids; curved solids such as cylinders, cones, and spheres; and cross sections. As you complete this chapter, you will understand the basic language of geometry and be familiar with some of its most frequently occurring shapes and solids. This knowledge will be necessary as we proceed to Chapter 11 and begin using geometry as a tool for measurement.

10.1   Observing, Describing, and Classifying in Two Dimensions

point

The three concepts most elementary and secondary school geometry is based on are point, line, and plane. A **point** is a single location in space. It has no size and therefore cannot be measured. A period at the end of a sentence and a dot on a piece of paper are visual representations of a point. Although both the period and the dot show a particular location, they are merely analogous to a point, which is a mental construct—an idea—and therefore has no physical representation.

Points, Line Segments, and Lines

line segment

line

Examine the two points M and N in the left portion of the illustration below. It is reasonable to assume that there are an infinite number of points between M and N. The set of points that connect M and N along the shortest path between them is called **line segment** MN (see middle portion) and is symbolized as $\overline{MN}$. If this line segment is extended indefinitely through both M and N, it is called **line** MN (see right portion) and is symbolized as $\overleftrightarrow{MN}$. Line segments and lines are assumed to be straight.

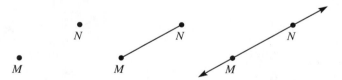

Collinearity

collinear

A special characteristic of pairs of points is that there is a unique (one and only one) line through any two points. Consequently, because a line segment is a part of a line, there is also a unique line segment between any two points. All points that lie on the same line are said to be **collinear**. Every line and line segment contain an infinite number of collinear points.

Planes

Building on the concepts of point and line is the concept of a plane. Consider the following analogy. A sheet of graph paper contains horizontal and vertical line segments.

Each intersection of the line segments can be thought of as a point. Try to visualize the line segments being extended indefinitely off the edges of the graph paper, as in Figure 10.1.

Figure 10.1

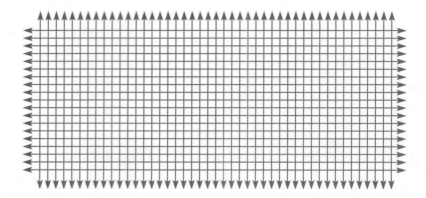

Now imagine connecting every pair of points on the graph paper with infinitely extending lines. Eventually, these lines would completely cover the surface of the graph paper. This infinitely extending flat surface is called a **plane**. The line that passes through any two points that lie in a plane must itself lie entirely in that plane. Points, lines, and line segments that lie in the same plane are said to be **coplanar**. An analogy of points and line segments that are coplanar would be figures drawn on a chalkboard. Anything drawn on the chalkboard lies in the plane of the chalkboard. Although the chalkboard is not an infinitely extending flat surface, it is a good concrete illustration of this abstract concept. Taken together, points, lines, and planes can form a variety of figures, as illustrated in Figure 10.2.

plane

coplanar

Figure 10.2

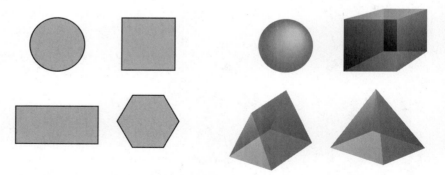

Figure 10.2 depicts two types of objects. The group on the left contains objects that are commonly referred to as shapes. **Shapes** lie entirely in a single plane and therefore have no thickness. Thus, they are considered **two-dimensional**. In contrast, **solids** protrude from a plane. They have thickness and are considered **three-dimensional**. The solid pictured in Figure 10.3 is formed by intersecting planes.

shapes

two-dimensional, *solids*

three-dimensional

Figure 10.3

When young children attempt to make sense of the world, they begin by observing. Teachers can capitalize on this natural curiosity by encouraging students to look around them, both inside and outside the classroom. The appearance and form of an object, specifically its color, size, shape, texture, and smell, contain characteristics that children can immediately identify. Once children have had experience observing and describing, they can begin to group or classify objects according to specific criteria.

Closed and Open Shapes

Eight two-dimensional figures are shown in Figure 10.4. Some are recognizable shapes, whereas others are not. These figures can be classified in a variety of ways. A classification based on the nature of the figures could result in A, D, G, and H being separated from B, C, E, and F. The figures in the first group contain straight-line segments, and the figures in the second group contain curves.

Figure 10.4

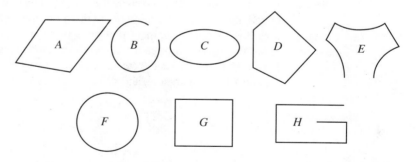

simple closed shape (simple closed curve)

simple open shape (simple open curve)

The figures can also be categorized according to whether or not they partition the plane into "inside" and "outside" regions. A **simple closed shape** (also known as a **simple closed curve**) is a shape that encloses a single portion of a plane, separating the plane into two regions—a region inside the shape and a region outside the shape. Therefore, figures A, C, D, F, and G are simple closed shapes. A **simple open shape** (also known as a **simple open curve**) does not enclose a portion of a plane, nor separate it into an inside region and an outside region. Shapes B, E, and H are open shapes. An analogy to a simple closed shape is a rubber band lying on a table. An analogy to a simple open shape is a broken rubber band lying on the table.

We will now examine the set of simple closed shapes and the variety of subsets it contains.

Circles

A particular type of simple closed shape can be formed by the set of all points that are

equidistant the same distance from a given point, A. This set of points is said to be **equidistant** from A. To help you visualize this, you will need a blank sheet of notebook paper, a small piece of string, a pencil, and a thumbtack. Tie one end of the string around the pencil. Tack the other end of the string to approximately the center of the notebook paper. Stretch the string until it is taut. Put the pencil to the paper and begin to rotate the pencil around the thumbtack, as illustrated in Figure 10.5.

Figure 10.5

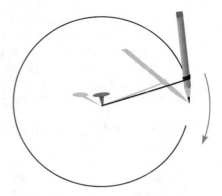

The shape drawn is a circle. All of the points that form the circle are the same distance

circle from the thumbtack. A **circle** is the set of points that are equidistant from a fixed point, called the center. Any line segment that joins the center to a point on the circle is called

radius, chord a **radius**. Any line segment that joins two points on the circle is called a **chord**. The

diameter chord that passes through the center of the circle is called the **diameter** of the circle. In Figure 10.6, point O is the center, $\overline{OC}$, $\overline{OA}$, $\overline{OE}$, $\overline{OF}$, and $\overline{OB}$ are radii (plural of radius), $\overline{CA}$ and $\overline{EF}$ are diameters, and $\overline{CG}$ and $\overline{EA}$ are other chords.

Figure 10.6

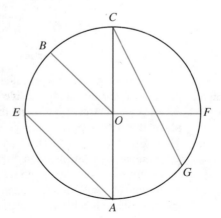

Polygons

Another subset of the set of simple closed shapes are those shapes with straight sides. Many of these closed shapes are frequently found in our surroundings, if you look closely enough. Look around and see how many you can spot. They may be described and classified in the following manner.

	Name	Description	Illustration
triangle	Triangle	Closed figures, each with 3 straight sides	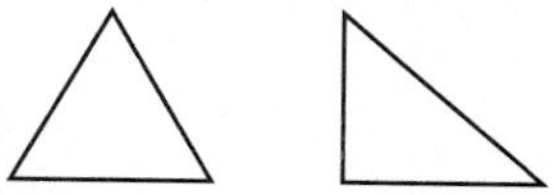
quadrilateral	Quadrilateral	Closed figures, each with 4 straight sides	
pentagon	Pentagon	Closed figures, each with 5 straight sides	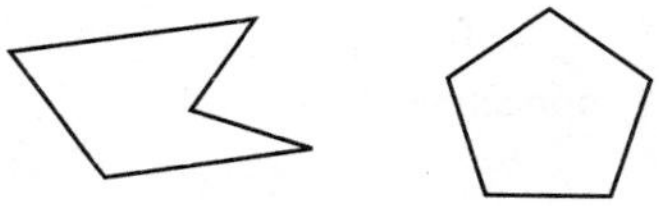
hexagon	Hexagon	Closed figures, each with 6 straight sides	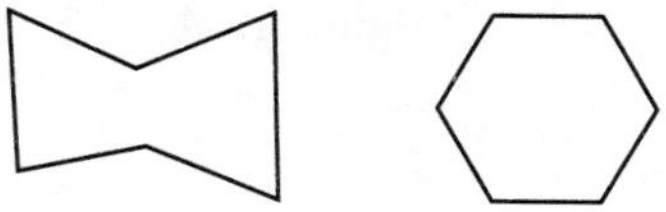
octagon	Octagon	Closed figures, each with 8 straight sides	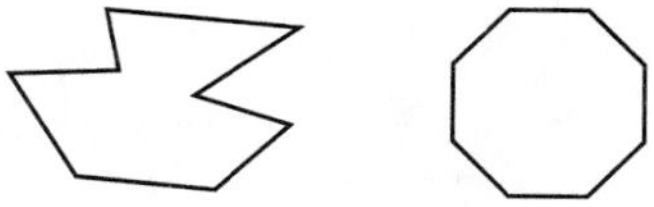
decagon	Decagon	Closed figures, each with 10 straight sides	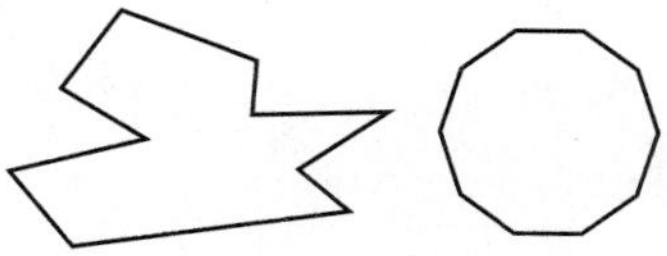

polygons

regular polygons

All of the above sets of closed figures are themselves subsets of a larger set of closed figures. This set contains all simple closed curves made up of line segments that are connected at the endpoints. This set is called the set of **polygons**. Triangles, quadrilaterals, pentagons, hexagons, octagons, decagons and others all belong to the set of polygons. Polygons, with all sides congruent and all angles congruent are said to be **regular polygons**. For example, an equilateral triangle (three sides of equal length) and a square (four sides of equal length) are both regular polygons, whereas a scalene triangle (with no sides equal) is not a regular polygon.

Convex Polygons

A further classification of simple closed shapes is possible. Compare the two hexagons in Figure 10.7.

Figure 10.7

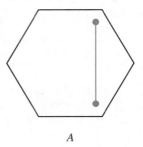 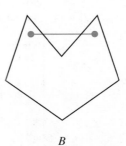

A   B

They are both simple closed polygons containing six straight sides. In hexagon *A*, a line segment connecting any two points in the shape will lie entirely within the interior.

convex Polygons that have this characteristic are called **convex**. In hexagon *B*, two points in the interior of the figure can be chosen so that a portion of the line segment connecting

nonconvex (concave) them lies outside the shape. Figures of this type are called **nonconvex**, or **concave**. Figure 10.8 depicts a variety of convex and nonconvex polygons.

Figure 10.8

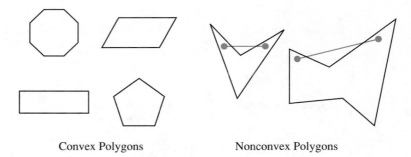

Convex Polygons   Nonconvex Polygons

Investigation 1

Ten people are attending a party. If everyone shakes hands with everyone else, how many handshakes will occur?

Understand the Problem: If 10 people exchange handshakes, how many handshakes are exchanged?

Devise a Plan: To better understand this situation, we will solve a simpler problem first. Suppose that there are four people at the party, and the same handshaking routine occurs. The strategy of drawing a diagram will be useful here.

Carry Out the Plan: Use four points to represent the partygoers, as shown below. Let the line segments that join two points represent "a handshake." There are six line segments in this picture. Therefore, six handshakes took place. Four of the line segments form the polygon, and **diagonal**   two of the line segments are known as diagonals of the polygon. A **diagonal** of a polygon is a line segment that joins nonadjacent vertices.

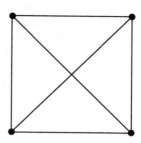

We could solve the original problem by drawing line segments for a 10-sided figure, but counting these segments would be difficult. Instead, let's take a closer look at each "handshake" as it occurs. We will do this for a party of five, as shown below.

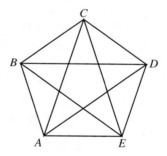

There are four line segments from *A* (person *A* shakes hands with four people). There are three new line segments from *B* (although person *B* also shakes hands with four people, the handshake with *A* has already been accounted for). There are two new line segments from *C* (although person *C* shakes hands with four people, the handshakes *C-A* and *C-B* have already been accounted for). There is one new line segment from *D* (handshakes *D-A*, *D-B*, and *D-C* have already been accounted for). Since all of the diagonals and sides of the pentagon have been drawn, our situation is complete. Ten handshakes are possible (4 + 3 + 2 + 1 + 0).

Is this a pattern? Test it for the party of four. Clearly, 6 = 3 + 2 + 1 + 0.

Solving a simpler problem and looking for a pattern help us now extend our findings to the original problem. Without actually drawing the representation, we can see that there will be 9 + 8 + 7 + 6 + 5 + 4 + 3 + 2 + 1 + 0, or 45 handshakes.

Look Back: How many handshakes would occur if 15 people were at the party?

The Van Hiele Levels of Geometric Development

Observation, description, and classification of a variety of shapes are conducted by examining the form, or appearance, of the shapes. You can focus on the number of sides, whether or not those sides are straight, whether the shapes are closed or open, whether they are convex or nonconvex. Names are given to certain groups of shapes that share a common form. This type of analysis, based on the appearance, or form, of a shape is characteristic of the way young children first begin to learn about geometry. The necessity of such a beginning was first recognized by two Dutch mathematics educators in the late 1950s. Dina and Pierre van Hiele researched children's geometric knowledge as part of their work on their doctoral dissertations. They formulated a theory that stated that children must pass through several levels of geometric development. It is critical for teachers to be aware of these levels so that their instruction matches the level of geometric maturity of each child. In this section, you will learn about the five van Hiele levels.

Level 0: Visualization. This is the most basic of the van Hiele levels. Descriptions and classifications of geometric shapes are made solely on the basis of the appearance of those shapes. Children view figures as a whole rather than the sum of characteristic parts. They recognize and name a shape because of its form. A shape would be called a square because it looks like other shapes that have been correctly called squares. Instruction at this level must enhance the student's ability to recognize form through a variety of techniques. Children who are functioning at this level of development enjoy building with blocks, assembling puzzles, arranging colored shapes to form a design, and constructing tracks on which trains or cars can ride.

Level 1: Analysis. At this level, students begin to recognize the properties of shapes. This allows them to refine their classifications. Examine the set of quadrilaterals in Figure 10.9.

Figure 10.9

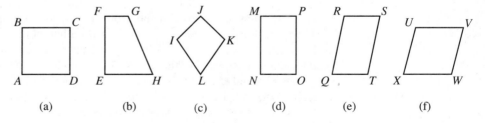

(a)   (b)   (c)   (d)   (e)   (f)

Although it is true that shapes (a) through (f) all have four sides, students functioning at this level of analysis can identify certain distinguishing characteristics that separate these figures.

A student might recognize the similarities between shapes (a) and (d), whose corners are all "square" corners. This leads us to the concept of angle. An **angle** is the union of two line segments that share a common endpoint. This endpoint is called a **vertex**. In Figure 10.9a, line segments $\overline{AD}$ and $\overline{DC}$ meet at point D, forming an angle at D. This angle can be named in three ways: $\angle D$, $\angle ADC$, and $\angle CDA$. In the first case, the vertex is used as the name for the angle. Since the square in Figure 10.9a contains four vertices, we can name the angles formed at these vertices as ∠A, ∠B, ∠C, and ∠D. The second and third cases use the endpoints of the line segments as labels, with the vertex in the middle. Therefore, the four angles in Figure 10.9a can also be labeled ∠DAB (or ∠BAD), ∠ABC (or ∠CBA), ∠BCD (or ∠DCB), and ∠CDA (or ∠ADC).

right angle

A student functioning on the van Hiele level 1 might notice that all of the angles in Figure 10.9a and Figure 10.9d look the same. They are formed by the intersection of vertical and horizontal line segments and are called right angles. A **right angle** is an angle whose measure is 90°. It is symbolized by the use of an identifying square at the vertex, as shown in Figure 10.10.

Figure 10.10

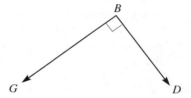

Angle GBD is a right angle. Notice that this right angle is not formed by the intersection of horizontal and vertical line segments. For example, the sides of a sturdy picture frame meet at right angles even if the frame is askew on the wall. Therefore, right angles need not be formed only by horizontal and vertical line segments. In Chapter 11 you will learn more about ways of identifying a right angle.

perpendicular

Any two segments that intersect to form a right angle are said to be **perpendicular**. The symbol used to indicate that two line segments are perpendicular is ⊥. It may be stated that sides $\overline{GB}$ and $\overline{BD}$ are perpendicular to one another by using the symbols $\overline{GB} \perp \overline{BD}$.

Now, let's examine the shapes from Figure 10.9 superimposed on graph paper, which are shown in Figure 10.11. By showing these shapes on graph paper, further attributes become apparent.

Figure 10.11

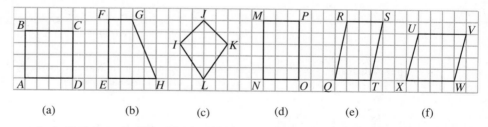

(a)   (b)   (c)   (d)   (e)   (f)

parallel

A similarity can be found in the relationship between opposite sides in both Figure 10.11a and Figure 10.11d. In both figures, the opposite sides lie along the graph paper lines and appear to be equidistant from one another. If these opposite line segments were extended indefinitely, they would never meet. Lines or line segments with this quality are said to be **parallel**. The symbol used to indicate that two lines or line segments are parallel is ∥. In Figure 10.11d it may be stated that $\overline{MN}$ and $\overline{PO}$, and $\overline{MP}$ and $\overline{NO}$, are pairs of parallel sides by using the symbols $\overline{MN} \parallel \overline{PO}$ and $\overline{MP} \parallel \overline{NO}$. But it is not enough to assume that lines and line segments are parallel or perpendicular based solely on appearances. As the text progresses, you will see that certain requirements are necessary in order to label lines and line segments as parallel or perpendicular.

Recognizing the characteristic of parallel sides allows us to further analyze the shapes given. Parts (a), (d), (e), and (f) of Figure 10.11 each have two pairs of parallel sides. Figure 10.11b has one pair of parallel sides. There are no parallel sides in Figure 10.11c.

Continuing to focus on the sides leads us to recognize certain other regularities. Parts (a) and (f) of Figure 10.11 each have four equal sides. Parts (d) and (e), although not having all sides equal, do have opposite sides equal. Part (c) has two pairs of equal sides. However, the equal sides are not opposite each other; they are next to each other. **adjacent** Sides that are next to each other are called **adjacent** sides. In other words, the adjacent sides $\overline{IJ}$ and $\overline{JK}$ are equal in length, and the adjacent sides $\overline{KL}$ and $\overline{LI}$ are equal in length. Figure 10.11b has no equal sides.

Children who are functioning at van Hiele level 1 should be given the opportunity to manipulate, fold, and cut out shapes. It would be useful for them to recognize similarities and differences in shapes by engaging in classification tasks.

deduction **Level 2: Informal Deduction.** **Deduction** is the process by which certain facts are found to necessarily follow from the acceptance of other facts. Deductive reasoning can be formal or informal. Formal deduction, which is appropriate at van Hiele level 3, incorporates the rules of logic and geometric proof. This level of geometric reasoning is not generally reached by elementary school students. Informal deduction, however, can be taught to and understood by elementary school students. During the observation and description processes, students come to accept certain things as true. These truths necessitate the acceptance of other truths. Informal deduction allows conclusions to be drawn based on the acceptance of facts, without the rigor of mathematical proof.

At this level, students can begin to understand definitions of shapes and classes of shapes. A shape can be defined by the properties of its sides and/or angles. Referring back to the quadrilaterals in Figure 10.11, students at this level should be able to offer formal definitions of each individual shape, and the class of shapes to which it belongs. A hierarchy of shapes within each class can now be recognized.

Name	Description	Illustration
parallelogram Parallelogram	A quadrilateral with two pairs of opposite sides parallel	
rhombus Rhombus	A parallelogram with four sides of equal length	
rectangle Rectangle	A parallelogram with four right angles	

Name	Description	Illustration
Square	A rectangle with four sides of equal length	
Trapezoid	A quadrilateral with only one pair of parallel sides	
Kite	A quadrilateral with two pairs of adjacent sides each of equal length, and no parallel sides	

square

trapezoid

kite

Triangles can also be named and defined by students at van Hiele level 2. Classifications of triangles can be made on the basis of the lengths of their sides, as shown in Figure 10.12.

Figure 10.12

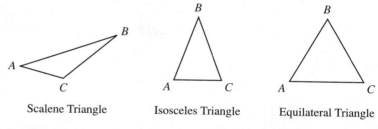

Scalene Triangle   Isosceles Triangle   Equilateral Triangle

scalene triangles
isosceles triangles
equilateral triangles

Triangles with no sides of equal length are called **scalene triangles**. Triangles with two sides of equal length are called **isosceles triangles**. Finally, triangles in which all three sides are equal in length are called **equilateral triangles**. Some authors extend the definition of isosceles triangles to include equilateral triangles. Those authors would state that an isosceles triangle contains at least two equal sides, and that an equilateral triangle is an isosceles triangle with three equal sides. This interpretation of the definitions of isosceles and equilateral triangles is as correct as our interpretation. We have chosen the definition stated above because it is more appropriate in an elementary school context, where children focus on broad distinctions.

Students who are at this level should be provided with opportunities to explore implications of certain facts. For example, knowing that a closed shape has three straight sides implies that it is a triangle, but does not imply that it is any specific type of triangle. Students could also be encouraged to investigate the necessary steps needed for changing one shape into another. The focus of this level is the examination of the properties of figures and the ramifications of these properties.

Level 3: Formal Deduction. At this level, students are able to fully understand the deductive reasoning process. They can construct their own proofs and create alternate proofs for theorems. This van Hiele level is commonly seen in the instruction of high school and college geometry. This level, as well as level 4, is included here in order to give you a complete picture of the van Hiele model.

Level 4: Rigor. Students who are functioning at level 4 are proficient in mathematics reasoning and logic. They are able to work in a variety of abstract geometric systems. Level 4 instruction and curriculum are found in intensive math courses at and above the college level.

Investigation 2

A shape is gradually revealed in four steps. Identify all of the possible figures that the shape could be at each of the stages shown.

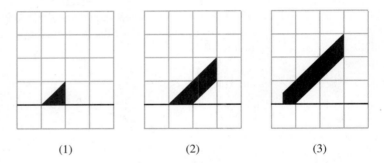

(1)   (2)   (3)

(1) The portion of this shape that is shown reveals more about what the figure cannot be than what it can be. Because the shape contains an angle that is not a right angle, both a square and a rectangle must be ruled out.

(2) Step 2 reveals a third side of the figure that appears to be parallel to the opposite side. Because these parallel sides can never meet, the entire figure must have at least four sides. All triangles are therefore ruled out. In addition, the figure cannot be a rhombus, because all visible sides are not of equal length.

(3) A fourth side, which appears to be parallel to its opposite side, is now visible. The possibility of a kite is eliminated, because no adjacent sides appear to be equal. A trapezoid is ruled out, because there appears to be two pairs of parallel sides. This indicates that the figure is most likely a parallelogram. However, it is possible that a fifth side is still hidden from view.

We now examine the fourth illustration. The revealed figure is a parallelogram.

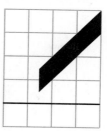

Investigation 3

tangram   A **tangram** is an ancient Chinese geometric puzzle composed of seven shapes. A tangram can be made from a sheet of unlined paper, using only a pair of scissors. In this investigation, you will be shown the steps necessary to make a tangram. At each step, identify the shapes that are being created and offer a justification for each. A summary of responses to the questions raised follows step 9.

(1) Fold a sheet of unlined paper so that two adjacent sides meet, as shown below.

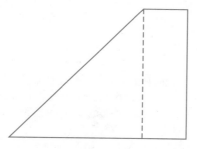

(2) Cut along the dotted line, as shown below. Identify the shape that results when the paper is unfolded. Justify your answer.

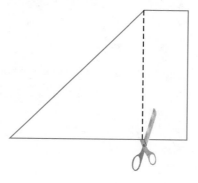

(3) Cut along the diagonal crease. Identify the two figures that result. Justify your answer.

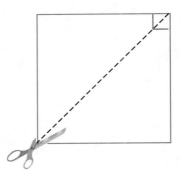

(4) Fold one of the two pieces in half, as shown below. Cut along this fold. Label one of the halves *A* and one *B*. Identify these two shapes, and justify your answer.

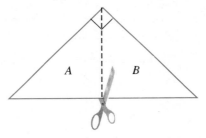

(5) Put pieces *A* and *B* aside. Take the other piece and fold two of the vertices up to meet the third vertex, as shown below. Unfold, and then fold the top vertex down to meet its opposite side, also as shown below.

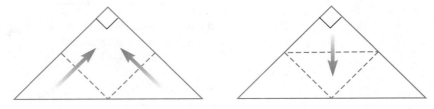

(6) Unfold and cut along the horizontal dotted line. Label this shape *C*, and identify it.

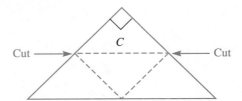

(7) Flatten the paper out. Identify its shape. Fold the shape in half, along its line of symmetry, as shown here. Cut along this fold, and identify each half. Justify your identification.

(8) Put one half aside. Fold the other half along the dotted line as shown below. Cut along this dotted line. Label the pieces *D* and *E*, as pictured. Identify both shapes.

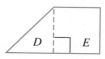

(9) Take the remaining piece and fold on the dotted line, as shown here. Label these pieces *F* and *G*. Cut along the dotted line. Identify the shapes.

If all the separate pieces you have just cut out have been done correctly, your assembled tangram should look like this:

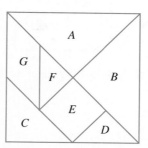

Summary of Responses

(2) The figure is a square because it has four sides of equal length and four right angles.

(3) The two shapes that result are congruent isosceles right triangles because they have two sides of equal length and one right angle. If they are placed over each other, they are shown to be congruent.

(4) Shapes *A* and *B* are congruent isosceles right triangles, for the same reasons as listed in step 3.

(6) Shape *C* is also an isosceles right triangle because it has two sides of equal length and one right angle.

(7) The shape that results is a trapezoid because it is a quadrilateral with one pair of parallel sides. When this trapezoid is cut in half along the line of symmetry, two congruent right trapezoids result.

(8) Shape *D* is an isosceles right triangle. It can be shown that the two sides that form the right angle are equal in length, because they are both as long as the sides of shape *E*. Because all sides of shape *E* are of equal length and because it contains four right angles, it is a square.

(9) Shape *F* is also an isosceles right triangle because it is congruent to shape *D*. Shape *G* is a parallelogram because its opposite sides are parallel.

Investigation 4

The following shapes are "shipshapes":

These shapes are not "shipshapes":

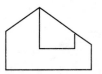

Is the following shape a "shipshape"? Justify your answer. Define a "shipshape."

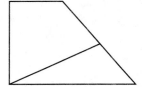

Understand the Problem: You are given four shapes that share a commonality. That commonality is not present in the second set. You must determine if a particular shape has that commonality.

Devise a Plan: Examine the figures. Make a list of the characteristics that the shapes appear to share.

Carry Out The Plan: First, identify all of the characteristics that are shared by the "shipshapes."

> Straight-sided figures (polygons)
>
> Closed figures
>
> Shapes within shapes
>
> Horizontal base

Do you see any other properties that could be added to this list?

Now, examine those shapes that are not shipshapes. If any of the figures have a characteristic mentioned above, it cannot be the defining characteristic of the ship-shape. Because all of the figures that are not shipshapes are straight sided, are closed, contain a shape within a shape, and have a horizontal base, none of these can be the defining characteristics of a shipshape.

Return to the first set. The pentagon has a triangle enclosed within it. The hexagon has a rectangle within it. The square has a rectangle. But what of the triangle? It can be viewed as containing a triangle at the top, or a trapezoid at the bottom. What is special about these interior figures? They all have a side that is congruent to one of the sides of the exterior figure, as shown here.

  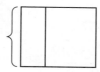

Do the figures in the second group have this quality? No! It appears therefore that a shipshape is a figure that contains a polygon within another polygon such that both share one complete side. With this as a definition, look for any contradictions in the test shape. The shape is a trapezoid with a triangle inside it. Both the trapezoid and the tri-angle share a single side. Therefore, the shape is a shipshape.

Look Back: Were there other defining characteristics of a shipshape? Draw another figure that would be considered a shipshape.

Assessments for Section 10.1

1. Use the diagram below to answer the following questions.

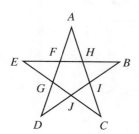

(a) Name three noncollinear points.

(b) Name three collinear points.

(c) Name two line segments.

(d) Name two line segments that share a single point. Iden-tify the point.

(e) Name three line segments that share a single point. Iden-tify the point.

(f) Name four line segments that share a single point. Iden-tify the point.

(g) Identify eight different triangles.

(h) Identify four different quadrilaterals.

(i) Identify one convex pentagon.

(j) Identify two different nonconvex pentagons.

2. Identify each of the following shapes as closed or open. Explain your answers.

(a)   **(b)**   **(c)**   **(d)**

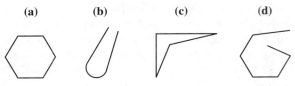

3. Identify each of the following shapes as convex or nonconvex. Explain your answers.

(a)   **(b)**   **(d)**

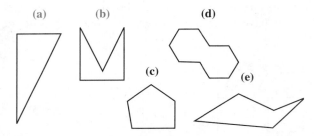

(c)

       (e)

4. Draw a convex and a nonconvex example of each of the following polygons.

(a) Decagon   **(b)** Hexagon

(c) Octagon   **(d)** Quadrilateral

5. Use the diagram below to answer the following questions.

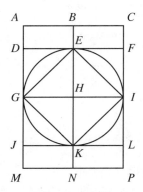

(a) Name two chords that are diameters.

(b) Name two chords that are not diameters.

(c) Name two radii.

(d) Name a triangle that has one of its points at the center of the circle.

(e) Name a triangle that has a diameter as one of its sides.

(f) Name a quadrilateral that has a diameter as one of its sides.

(g) Name a triangle that has a radius as one of its sides.

(h) Name a nonconvex figure that has a radius as one of its sides.

(i) Name a nonconvex figure that has a diameter as one of its sides.

(j) Name two figures that are composed entirely of line segments that are neither diameters nor radii.

6. Indicate whether the following statements are true or false. Justify your answers.

(a) A square is a parallelogram.

(b) A rhombus is a rectangle.

(c) A square is a rhombus.

(d) A kite is a parallelogram.

(e) An isosceles triangle is equilateral.

7. How many angles are pictured below? Name them.

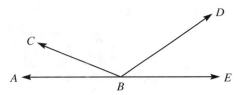

8. Indicate if the following definitions of a kite are illustrative of van Hiele level 0, 1, or 2. Explain your reasoning.

(a) A kite is a shape with four sides: two long sides next to each other, and two short sides next to each other.

(b) A kite is a quadrilateral with two pairs of adjacent sides each of equal length and no parallel sides.

(c) A kite looks like a kite you would fly.

9. Write a definition of a right trapezoid appropriate for each of the van Hiele levels 0, 1, and 2.

10. Imagine that a mirror is placed on line segment AB in each of the following figures. Identify the new shape formed by the joining of the figure and its reflection.

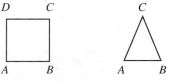

(a) Square $ABCD$ **(b)** Isosceles $\triangle ABC$

                               $AC = BC$

(c) Scalene △ABC (d) Trapezoid ABCD
$\overline{AB} \parallel \overline{DC}$

11. Draw a figure such that if a mirror is placed along one of its sides, the figure and its reflection will form the following shapes. Identify the characteristics of the figure drawn.

(a) Hexagon (b) Pentagon (c) Square

(d) Circle (e) Rectangle

12. Identify all of the possible figures that a shape could be at each of the stages shown.

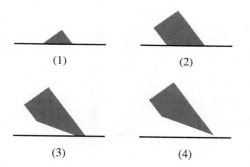

13. Given hexagon ABCDEF with all sides equal, draw segments $\overline{AC}$, $\overline{AD}$, and $\overline{AE}$.

(a) Name four triangles.

(b) Name two pairs of congruent triangles.

(c) Name two pentagons.

(d) Name one kite (justify that this figure fits the definition of a kite).

14. Use all seven tangram pieces to form each of the following shapes.

(a) Square

(b) Rectangle

(c) Isosceles right triangle

(d) Parallelogram

(e) Trapezoid

15. These are "misshapes":

These are not "misshapes":

Is this a "misshape"? Justify your answer. Define "misshape."

16. These are "getinshapes."

These are not "getinshapes."

Is this a "getinshape"? Explain your answer.

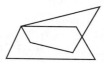

17. Examine the following sequence. The numbers below each illustration indicate the number of squares that can be identified.

1 5 14

(a) Draw a 4 × 4 square. How many squares can be identified in this shape?

(b) Examine the numerical sequence 1, 5, 14, and the answer from part (a). Look for a pattern. Use the pattern to predict the number of squares that can be identified in a 10 × 10 square.

18. How many equilateral triangles are pictured in the following figure?

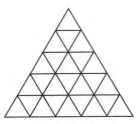

19. Examine the following figure and determine each of the following relationships.

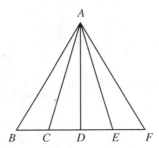

(a) $\overline{BC} \cup \overline{CD}$ (b) $\overline{BE} \cap \overline{CF}$
(c) $\overline{BA} \cap \overline{FA}$ (d) $\overline{BE} \cup \overline{CF}$
(e) $(\overline{AB} \cap \overline{BF}) \cup (\overline{AC} \cap \overline{BF}) \cup (\overline{AD} \cap \overline{BF}) \cup$
    $(\overline{AE} \cap \overline{BF}) \cup (\overline{AF} \cap \overline{BF})$

20. Can a simple closed shape be drawn that passes through the points A, B, C, D, E, and F if four of those points are collinear? If so, draw such a shape.

21. Place four points on a page so that no three are collinear. Draw possible shapes that can be constructed using line segments with these four points as vertices. Identify each shape.

22. You are given the following four shapes with the measures of $\overline{AB}$ in each shape being equal. Suppose that the following pairs of shapes are joined at segment $\overline{AB}$. (No shape should overlap the interior of another shape.) Identify the new shape that is formed. Include whether or not the shape is convex. Justify your reasoning.

Shape 1   Shape 2   Shape 3   Shape 4

(a) Shape 1 and shape 2
(b) Shape 1 and shape 3
(c) Shape 2 and shape 3
(d) Shape 2 and shape 4
(e) Shape 3 and shape 4

In Other Words

23. Which capital letters of the alphabet represent simple closed shapes? Justify your reasoning.

24. Define the terms convex and nonconvex in your own words.

25. Discuss the ways in which an understanding of the laws of logic can enhance an understanding of geometry.

26. When is it possible for the intersection of two lines to contain an infinite number of points? Explain your answer.

27. Suppose that three lines, L_1, L_2, and L_3, lie in the same plane such that both L_1 and L_2 are perpendicular to L_3. What must be true about L_1 and L_2? Explain your answer.

Cooperative Activity

28. Groups of two

Individual Accountability:

This is a domino: This is not a domino:

These are triominoes: These are not triominoes:

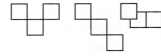

These are tetrominoes: These are not tetrominoes:

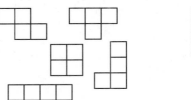
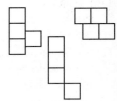

Draw the set of 12 pentominoes.

Group Goal: Compare the pentominoes you drew with those your partner drew. Make sure you have 12 distinct pentominoes. Arrange the 12 pentominoes into a rectangle.

10.2 Exploring Three-Dimensional Figures

In Section 10.1 we introduced the concept of a plane figure. Since such a figure was shown to lie totally within a single plane, it was said to be two-dimensional. In contrast, a three-dimensional figure can be formed by the intersections of several planes. A three-dimensional figure can have flat surfaces or curved surfaces. It may be convex or nonconvex. Convex three-dimensional figures are analogous to convex polygons, because the line segment connecting any two points in the interior of the figure must remain totally within the figure (see Figure 10.13a). A nonconvex three-dimensional figure is pictured in Figure 10.13b.

Figure 10.13

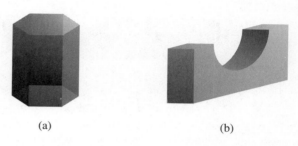

(a)   (b)

Polyhedra

polyhedron   A figure formed by polygonal surfaces is called a **polyhedron**. It is the three-dimensional analog of a polygon. Parts (a), (c), and (d) of Figure 10.14 are examples of polyhedra. Parts (a) and (c) are convex polyhedra, and part (d) is a nonconvex polyhedron. Figure 10.14b, although a three-dimensional figure, is not a polyhedron because one of its surfaces is curved.

Figure 10.14

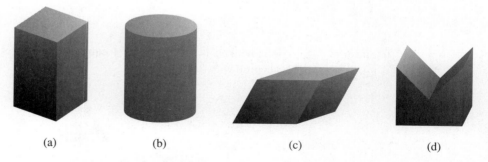

(a)   (b)   (c)   (d)

Examine how a polyhedron is formed. In Figure 10.15a the figure is formed by the intersections of six planes. A distinguishing characteristic of this figure is that adjacent planes are perpendicular and opposite planes are parallel. The planes meet in such a way that the surfaces are three pairs of congruent rectangles. The two-dimensional

faces   polygons that make up the surfaces are called **faces**. The line segments along which
edges   faces meet are called **edges**. Points at which edges meet are called **vertices**. (*Vertices* is the plural of *vertex*, which was defined on page 454.)

In Figure 10.15b the figure is formed by the intersections of five planes. The planes meet in such a way that the faces of the figure formed are two congruent triangles and three congruent rectangles. The two congruent triangles lie in parallel planes. The planes of the rectangles are perpendicular to those of the triangles.

In Figure 10.15c the figure is formed by the intersections of seven planes. The planes meet in such a way that the faces formed are two congruent pentagons and five rectangles. The pentagons lie in parallel planes, and the planes of the rectangles are perpendicular to those of the pentagons. Had the sides of the congruent pentagons been of equal length, the rectangles would have been congruent.

Figure 10.15

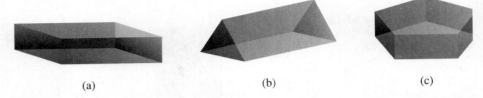

(a)   (b)   (c)

There are five special polyhedra, some of which were studied by the Egyptians, and all of which were studied by the Greeks. These five polyhedra are all composed of congruent polygonal faces and are known as **regular polyhedra**. The regular polyhedra were examined in depth by Plato and his followers and are consequently known as the five "Platonic solids."

regular polyhedra

cube

1. A **cube** (hexahedron) is composed of 6 congruent squares. The Greeks identified the cube with the *earth*.

tetrahedron

2. A **tetrahedron** is composed of 4 equilateral triangles. The Greeks identified the tetrahedron with *fire*.

octahedron

3. An **octahedron** is composed of 8 equilateral triangles. The Greeks identified the octahedron with *air*.

icosahedron   **4.** An **icosahedron** is composed of 20 equilateral triangles. The Greeks identified the icosahedron with *water*.

dodecahedron   **5.** A **dodecahedron** is composed of 12 regular pentagons. The Greeks identified the dodecahedron with the *universe*.

Only five regular polyhedra have been found to exist. These solids have intrigued mathematicians through the ages.

Investigation 5

This is a classic problem. A spider is at the vertex of a cube. Some food is at the opposite vertex, as shown here.

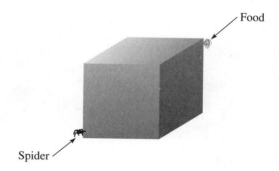

Food

Spider

The spider can travel only along the walls of the cube. What is the shortest path to the food?

Understand the Problem: The location of the spider and the food is known. You must determine the most direct route from the spider to the food.

Devise a Plan: You know that the shortest distance between two points is the line segment that joins them. Unfortunately, such a line segment would travel through space and thus contradict the given information that the spider must travel only along the walls of the cube. We must therefore change our point of view.

Carry Out the Plan: Rather than looking at this as a three-dimensional problem, "open up" the cube and attempt to solve the problem as a two-dimensional one. Examine the following diagram.

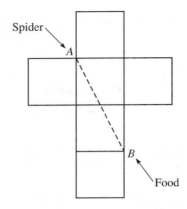

The spider is at point *A*, and the food is at point *B*. Now draw the segment that connects these two points. This segment represents the path that the spider should take along the walls of the cube.

Look Back: It is left to you to sketch a three-dimensional cube with the spider's path traced on the surface of the cube.

━━━ ■

Prisms

Examine Figure 10.16.

Figure 10.16

(a) Rectangular Prism (b) Triangular Prism (c) Pentagonal Prism

Parts (a), (b), and (c), of Figure 10.16 are examples of a set of three-dimensional figures that have similar features. Included in this set are those figures that contain at least two congruent faces lying in parallel planes. Two such opposite and congruent **bases** faces are known as **bases**. The faces that are formed by joining the corresponding **lateral faces** points on the edges of the bases are called **lateral faces**. A figure that is composed of two congruent polygonal bases in separate parallel planes, connected by lateral faces **prism** that are parallelograms, is called a **prism**. If the lateral faces are all rectangles, the **right prism** three-dimensional figure is called a **right prism**. The figures pictured in Figure 10.16 are all right prisms because the lateral faces in each are rectangles. Part (a) is called **right rectangular prism** a **right rectangular prism** because the bases are rectangles. Part (b) is called a

right triangular prism
right pentagonal prism

right triangular prism because the bases are triangles. Part (c) is called a **right pentagonal prism** because the bases are pentagons. In most elementary school textbooks, these prisms are simply referred to as rectangular, triangular, and pentagonal prisms.

Pyramids

In addition to prisms, another subset of the set of polyhedra can be seen in Figure 10.17. Compare and contrast these figures with those in Figure 10.16.

Figure 10.17

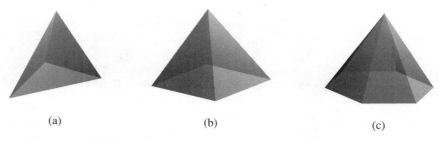

(a)   (b)   (c)

apex
pyramids

These polyhedra are formed by a single base and a point that is not in the plane of the base. This point is called the **apex**. Line segments join the apex to the vertices of the base, forming triangular faces. These polyhedra are called **pyramids**. Notice that a pyramid has no parallel faces.

A pyramid is named according to the polygon that forms its base. Figure 10.17a is a triangular pyramid. A square pyramid is depicted in Figure 10.17b, and a hexagonal pyramid is shown in Figure 10.17c.

Investigation 6

Examine each of the following polyhedra. Look for a relationship among the number of faces, edges, or vertices.

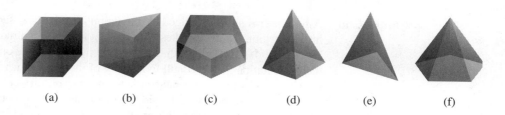

(a)   (b)   (c)   (d)   (e)   (f)

Understand the Problem: You are given six polyhedra. You must determine a common relationship among the faces, vertices, and edges.

Devise a Plan: Use the problem-solving strategy of making a table, and fill it in by counting the numbers of faces, edges, and vertices.

Carry Out the Plan:

Name	Faces	Edges	Vertices
(a) Rectangular prism	6	12	8
(b) Triangular prism	5	9	6
(c) Pentagonal prism	7	15	10
(d) Square pyramid	5	8	5
(e) Triangular pyramid	4	6	4
(f) Pentagonal pyramid	6	10	6

The relationship among the faces (F), edges (E), and vertices (V) of a polyhedron was made famous by the Swiss mathematician and physicist Leonhard Euler (1707–1783). Euler recognized that for every polyhedron the sum of the number of vertices and the number of faces is equal to the number of edges plus two. This relationship is now known as **Euler's theorem** and can be expressed using the following symbolic notation:

Euler's theorem

$$V + F = E + 2$$

We will verify this theorem for each of the polyhedra above.

A rectangular prism has eight vertices (**8** + 6 = 12 + 2).

A triangular prism has nine edges (6 + 5 = **9** + 2).

A pentagonal prism has seven faces (10 + **7** = 15 + 2).

A square pyramid has five vertices (**5** + 5 = 8 + 2).

A triangular pyramid has six edges (4 + 4 = **6** + 2).

A pentagonal pyramid has six faces (6 + **6** = 10 + 2).

Look Back: Sketch a polyhedron with 7 faces, 12 edges, and 7 vertices. What is the name of this polyhedron?

Three-Dimensional Figures with Curved Surfaces

polyhedral solid A **polyhedral solid** is formed by the union of polygonal surfaces and all points in the interior region formed by these surfaces. When children play with wooden polyhedral blocks (solids), they notice that prisms and pyramids have only flat faces. Regardless of their orientation, it is difficult to roll any of these solids across a table. This is not true for all solids. Some solids have at least one curved surface. Therefore, they do not belong to the set of polyhedral solids and their surfaces do not form polyhedra. The most common of these curved solids are the cylinder, cone, and sphere.

Recall that a prism was defined as a figure composed of two parallel congruent bases connected by lateral faces that are parallelograms. Examine Figure 10.18, in which the bases of the prisms are regular polygons. (In these illustrations, the lateral faces are perpendicular to the bases. This does not always need to be true.)

Figure 10.18

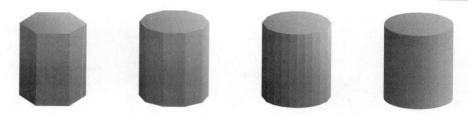

Notice that the number of lateral faces increases as you move from left to right. What might a prism look like that has 100 lateral faces? 1000 lateral faces? 100,000 lateral faces? The lateral faces would begin to resemble a curved surface. The parallel bases would begin to resemble circles. A figure composed of two parallel congruent circular **cylinder** bases connected by a curved lateral surface is called a **cylinder**.

A relationship analogous to that of the prism and the cylinder can be found between a pyramid and another curved figure. Recall that a pyramid is a polyhedron formed by a single base and a point not in the plane of the base. Line segments join the apex to the vertices of the base, forming triangular faces. Examine Figure 10.19, in which the bases of the pyramids are regular polygons. (In these illustrations, a perpendicular line can be drawn from the apex to the center of the base, although this does not always have to be the case.)

Figure 10.19

Notice that again the number of lateral faces increases as you move from left to right. What might a pyramid look like that has 100 lateral faces? 1000 lateral faces? 100,000 lateral faces? The lateral faces would begin to resemble a curved surface. The base **cone** would begin to resemble a circle. A **cone** is formed by a single circular base and a point not in the plane of the base. Line segments join the apex with points on the base circle forming a curved lateral surface.

Hemispheres and Spheres

Recall the activity illustrated in Figure 10.5 (page 450), in which you generated a circle. String was attached to a pencil and a thumbtack. The string was stretched taut from the center and all points equidistant from the center were connected. This activity led you to the definition of a circle. Because a circle is a two-dimensional shape, the points that you connected were all in the plane of the paper. Now imagine a similar activity. This time you are to connect all points equidistant from the center that are both in the plane of the circle and above the plane of the circle. Of course, this cannot actually be done. The points equidistant from the center that lie off the plane of the circle also lie off the paper and therefore cannot be drawn. Figure 10.20 shows some of the points that would lie in the set of all points equidistant from a fixed point, both in and above the plane of the fixed point.

Figure 10.20

hemisphere

sphere

The three-dimensional figure formed is called a **hemisphere**. Now, remove the condition that the points can lie only in or above the plane of the fixed point. The set of all points in space that are equidistant from a fixed point is called a **sphere**. Figure 10.21 depicts such a figure. You can also envision a sphere as being formed by a circle rotating around a diameter.

Figure 10.21

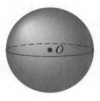

center of the sphere
radius of the sphere
diameter of the sphere

Point O is the **center of the sphere**. Any line segment from the center to a point on the sphere is called a **radius of the sphere**. Any line segment that connects two points on the sphere and passes through the center is called the **diameter of the sphere**.

Cross Sections

When a plane and a solid intersect, some interesting results occur. In Figure 10.22 a plane "cuts through" a rectangular prism parallel to the base of the prism.

Figure 10.22

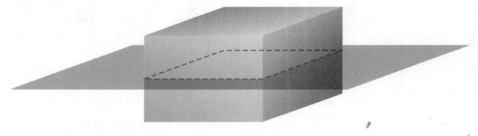

cross sections

Think of this figurative "cut" as if it were an actual straight slice, dividing the solid into two pieces. Separate the pieces and examine the new surfaces that are now exposed. Because these two surfaces must fit back together to form the solid, they are congruent. Two-dimensional surfaces formed by the intersection of a plane and a solid are called **cross sections** of the solid. In Figure 10.22 the cross section of the rectangular prism is a rectangle.

Investigation 7

Show how a plane and a rectangular prism could be made to intersect so that the cross section is

(a) a triangle,

(b) a trapezoid, and

(c) a pentagon.

Look for possible regularities in the relationship between the solid being "cut" and the cross section formed. In Figure 10.22 a plane intersected a rectangular prism to form a rectangular cross section. The number of faces of the prism that were "cut" by the plane was equal to the number of sides of the cross section. We will use this information to find each of the required cross sections. It might be helpful to use clay and actually perform the straight cuts with a knife.

(a) The required cross section is a triangle. Because a triangle has three sides, only three surfaces of the solid must be cut by the plane. This can be accomplished in a number of ways, one of which is illustrated here.

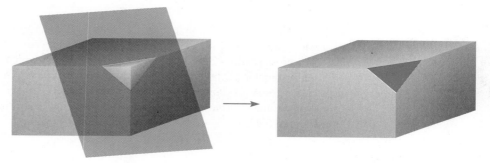

Notice that one of the vertices of the rectangular prism has been "sliced off" in order to attain the desired triangular cross section.

(b) The required cross section is a trapezoid. Recall the definition of a trapezoid. It is a quadrilateral with only one pair of parallel sides. Any slice you make that is parallel to a surface of the rectangular prism will result in a rectangular cross section. In order to obtain a trapezoid, the plane must intersect the prism in such a way that it cuts through only four faces and is not parallel to any of the surfaces of the prism. The intersection and the resulting cross section are illustrated below.

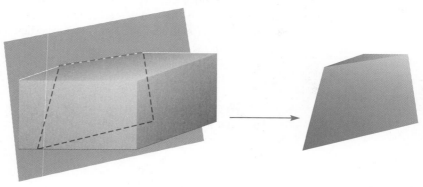

(c) The required cross section is a pentagon. A pentagon is a polygon with five sides. The plane must intersect the solid in such a way that it slices through exactly five surfaces. One of the surfaces of the rectangular prism must not be cut. The intersection and the resulting pentagonal cross section are shown here.

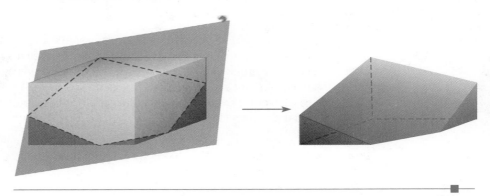

The Greek mathematician Apollonius (c. 262–c. 190 B.C.) is credited with investigating a variety of cross sections that can be achieved when a plane intersects a cone. The cross sections described here apply to cones in which the line through the apex is perpendicular to the circular base at the center of the circle. Such cross sections are called **conic sections** and are used extensively in a branch of mathematics called analytic geometry. Two conic sections, the circle and the ellipse (oval), are illustrated in Figure 10.23.

conic sections

Figure 10.23

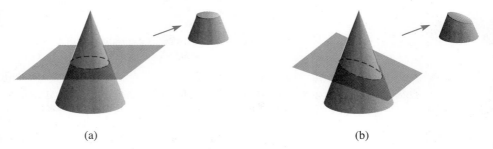

(a)   (b)

The circular cross section (Figure 10.23a) is formed when the plane intersects the cone parallel to its base. As you can see, the elliptical cross section (Figure 10.23b) is not parallel to the base of the cone and is formed when the plane cuts only through the lateral surface of the cone.

Investigation 8

A plane cuts a polyhedron in such a way that the resulting cross section is a square. Name two such solids and explain or illustrate the way in which the plane might intersect the solid.

The simplest way to envision this activity is to think of a solid that has a surface that is a square. Two such solids are a cube and a square pyramid. The plane must intersect the cube parallel to any one of the square faces. One such cut is shown here.

The resulting cross section will be a square that is congruent to all of the faces of the cube.

A square pyramid is formed by a square base and four congruent triangles. A slice parallel to the base will result in a square that is not congruent to that of the base, but smaller in size than the square base. This is illustrated below.

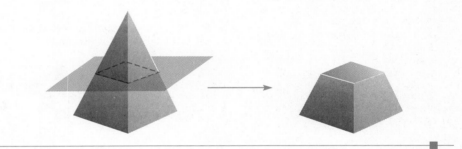

Assessments for Section 10.2

1. Identify each of the following three-dimensional figures as convex or nonconvex. State your reasoning.

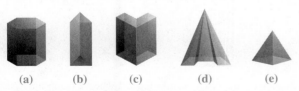

(a)   (b)   (c)   (d)   (e)

2. Identify the polyhedra in the following set of three-dimensional figures. Explain your reasoning.

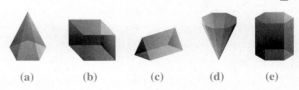

(a)   (b)   (c)   (d)   (e)

3. A prism is composed of 6 congruent, rectangular lateral faces and 2 congruent, parallel hexagonal bases. Identify the number of edges, vertices, and faces.

4. A prism is composed of 10 congruent, rectangular lateral faces and 2 congruent, parallel decagonal bases. Identify the number of edges, vertices, and faces.

5. A pyramid is composed of 6 congruent, triangular faces and 1 hexagonal base. Identify the number of edges, vertices, and faces.

6. A pyramid is composed of 10 congruent, triangular faces and 1 decagonal base. Identify the number of edges, vertices, and faces.

7. Complete the following table using Euler's theorem.

	Name	Faces	Edges	Vertices
(a)	Cube	6	12	?
(b)	Octagonal prism	?	24	16
(c)	Nonagonal prism	11	?	18
(d)	Onagonal pyramid	12	22	?
(e)	Dodecagonal pyramid	13	?	13

8. Given the following information, determine if a polyhedron exists with the given number of faces, edges, and vertices. Justify your answer.

	Faces	Edges	Vertices
(a)	9	21	14
(b)	14	27	14
(c)	15	32	15
(d)	6	10	6
(e)	11	19	11

9. Is it possible to paint the surfaces of the following solids using at most three different colors (one color on each surface) in such a way that no two adjacent surfaces are the same color? Justify your answers.

(a) Cube   (b) Pentagonal prism

(c) Hexagonal prism   (d) Pentagonal pyramid

(e) Triangular prism   (f) Square pyramid

(g) Cylinder   (h) Cone

10. The bases of a pentagonal prism and a pentagonal pyramid are congruent. The base of the pentagonal pyramid is glued to one of the bases of the pentagonal prism as illustrated below. The pentagonal prism is shown in three-dimensional format and outline style.

 or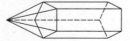

Identify the number of faces, edges, and vertices in the resulting figure. Is this a polyhedral solid? Explain your reasoning.

11. Match the pattern in (a)–(d) with the resulting folded figure in (1)–(4).

(a)
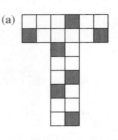

(1)

(b)
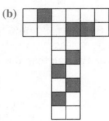

(2)

(c)
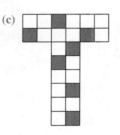

(3)

(d)
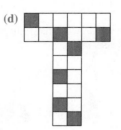

(4)
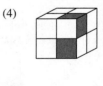

12. Identify the cross section formed when a plane intersects the given solid parallel to the base.

(a)   (b)   (c)

13. Identify the cross section formed when a plane intersects the given solid as shown in each of the following figures.

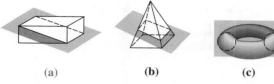

(a)   (b)   (c)

14. A plane intersects a solid in such a way that a pentagonal cross section is formed. Name three such solids in which this could occur. Explain or illustrate your results.

15. What cross sections are formed when a plane intersects a hemispherical solid in each of the following cases?

(a) The plane is parallel to the base of the hemisphere.

(b) The plane is perpendicular to the base of the hemisphere.

16. (a) A plane intersects a square pyramid through the apex, perpendicular to its base. What is the shape of the cross section formed?

(b) A plane intersects a pentagonal pyramid through the apex, perpendicular to the base. What is the shape of the cross section formed?

(c) A plane intersects a triangular pyramid through the apex, perpendicular to the base. What is the shape of the cross section formed?

(d) A plane intersects a cone through the apex, perpendicular to the base. What is the shape of the cross section formed?

(e) What can you generalize about the four cross sections in parts (a) through (d)?

17. A plane intersects a square pyramid as shown below. What is the shape of the cross section formed?

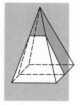

18. What cross sections are formed when a plane intersects a cylindrical solid in each of the following cases?

(a) The plane is parallel to the base of the cylinder.

(b) The plane is perpendicular to the base of the cylinder.

19. A solid is formed by joining the congruent bases of a triangular prism and a triangular pyramid. A plane perpendicu-

lar to the base of the prism passes through the apex of the pyramid.

(a) What is the shape of the cross section formed?

(b) What other combination of solids could form the same cross section?

20. A plane intersects a cube in such a way that the cross section formed is a rectangle, as shown below. How many faces, edges, and vertices does the resulting solid below have? Is this solid a polyhedron?

21. A plane intersects a pentagonal pyramid in such a way that the cross section formed is a pentagon, as shown below. How many faces, edges, and vertices do each of the two resulting solids have? Are these solids polyhedra?

22. A set is composed of the following polyhedra: rectangular prism, triangular prism, pentagonal prism, square pyramid, pentagonal pyramid, and trapezoidal pyramid. Does the relation "has the same number of faces as" define an equivalence relation on this set of polyhedra? Defend your answer. If this is an equivalence relation, describe the subsets formed by the partitioning. If it is not an equivalence relation, add or delete polyhedra from the set in order to make the relation an equivalence relation and then describe the subsets formed by the partitioning.

In Other Words

23. Explain how a plane can intersect a rectangular prism so that the cross section is a hexagon.

24. How is the edge of a polyhedron formed?

25. If a plane intersects a hemisphere perpendicular to the circular base, what is the shape of the cross section? Explain your answer.

26. Under what conditions might the triangular faces of a pyramid not be congruent to each other?

27. Describe a nonconvex prism.

Cooperative Activity

28. Groups of two

Individual Accountability: An interesting characteristic of solids is that they cast very different shadows depending on the location of the light source. For example, examine the silhouette of a tin can when placed in two different positions on an overhead projector:

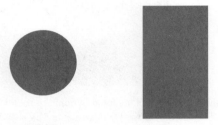

Identify several objects, commonly found around the house, that would cast the following shadows.

Object	Location of Light Source	Shadow
1	Bottom	○
	Side	▽
2	Top	◁▷
	Side	▭
3	Bottom	●
	Side	▱

Group Goal: Compare the answers you got in the individual accountability section. Settle any disagreements by actually placing the object in question on an overhead projector. Sketch possible solids that would cast the following shadows.

Solid	Location of Light Source	Shadow
1	Bottom	⬡
	Side	▲
2	Bottom	●
	Side	●
3	Bottom	●
	Front	▽
	Side	▽

Vocabulary for Chapter 10

adjacent
angle
apex
bases
chord
center of a sphere
circle
collinear
cone
conic sections
convex
coplanar
cross sections
cube
cylinder
decagon
deduction
diagonal
diameter of a sphere
dodecahedron
edges
equidistant
equilateral triangles
Euler's theorem
faces
hemisphere
hexagon
icosahedron
isosceles triangle
kite
lateral faces
line
line segment
nonconvex (concave)
octagon
octahedron

parallel
parallelogram
pentagon
perpendicular
plane
point
polygons
polyhedral solid
polyhedron
prism
pyramids
quadrilateral
radius of a sphere
rectangle
regular polygons
regular polyhedra
rhombus
right angle
right pentagonal prism
right prism
right rectangular prism
right triangular prism
scalene triangles
shapes
simple closed shape (simple closed curve)
simple open shape (simple open curve)
solids
sphere
square
tangram
tetrahedron
three-dimensional
trapezoid
triangle
two-dimensional
vertex

Review for Chapter 10

1. Use the following diagram to answer the questions below.

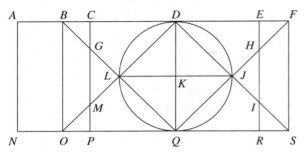

(a) Name a chord that is not a diameter.

(b) Name two radii.

(c) Name two radii that form a diameter.

(d) Name a nonconvex figure with two radii as two of its sides.

(e) Name two quadrilaterals with a diameter as one of their sides.

(f) Name a nonconvex pentagon composed of three chords and two radii.

(g) Name two convex quadrilaterals that appear to be congruent.

(h) Name two nonconvex pentagons that appear to be congruent.

2. Use the following diagram to answer the questions below.

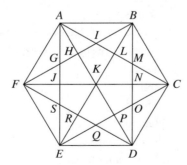

(a) Name three noncollinear points.

(b) Name three collinear points.

(c) Name four line segments.

(d) Name four line segments that share a common point. Name the point.

(e) Identify six different triangles.

(f) Identify six different quadrilaterals.

(g) Identify two different pentagons. Indicate if they are convex or nonconvex.

3. In each case, sketch a figure whose line of symmetry divides it into the following shapes.

(a) Two scalene triangles

(b) Two trapezoids

(c) Two convex pentagons

4. How many angles less than or equal to 180° are contained in this shape? Name each angle you find.

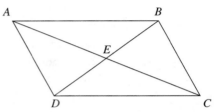

5. With a square piece of paper, make your own "tangram" consisting of six pieces. Arrange the pieces into three different figures. Trace the outline of each figure. Challenge a partner to fit the six pieces into the outlines. Then challenge a partner to arrange the six pieces back into the original square.

6. Given regular octagon *ABCDEFGH*, draw two line segments beginning and ending at vertices that divide the octagon into the following shapes.

(a) Two trapezoids and a rectangle

(b) Two pentagons and two triangles

(c) Four kites

(d) One kite and two trapezoids

(e) One triangle, one trapezoid, and one pentagon

7. In each of the following cases, sketch a convex hexagon with the given characteristics.

(a) Two sides perpendicular to the same side

(b) Two pairs of perpendicular sides, neither of which is perpendicular to the same side

(c) One pair of parallel sides

(d) Two pairs of parallel sides

(e) No parallel sides

8. What is the least number of faces, vertices, and edges that a polyhedron can have?

9. A pyramid is composed of 8 vertices, 14 edges, and 8 faces. Identify the solid.

10. The base of a rectangular pyramid and one of the faces of a rectangular prism are congruent. If these two faces are glued together, a new solid is formed. How many faces, edges, and vertices does the new solid have? Is this a polyhedral solid? Explain your answer.

11. The base of a pyramid is a nonconvex decagon. How many faces, edges, and vertices does the solid have? Is it a polyhedral solid? Explain your answer.

12. Complete the following table using Euler's theorem.

	Name	Faces	Edges	Vertices
(a)	Rectangular prism	6	?	8
(b)	Octagonal prism	9	16	?
(c)	Hexagonal prism	?	18	12
(d)	Pentagonal pyramid	?	10	6
(e)	Triangular prism	5	?	6

13. Given the following information, determine if a polyhedron exists with the given number of faces, edges, and vertices. Justify your answer. Offer a possible name for each polyhedron.

	Faces	Edges	Vertices
(a)	4	6	4
(b)	5	6	7
(c)	7	12	7
(d)	10	24	16
(e)	6	12	8

14. How might a square pyramid be sliced to form the following cross sections?

(a) Triangle   (b) Square

(c) Trapezoid   (d) Pentagon

15. A cone is sliced perpendicular to its base. Sketch the cross section. Is this the only cross section possible? Explain your answer.

16. How might the solid formed in Problem 10 be sliced to get the following cross sections?

(a) Triangle   (b) Square

(c) Trapezoid   (d) Pentagon

17. Use the following illustration to determine the set relationships that follow:

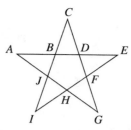

(a) $\overline{AD} \cap \overline{BE}$ (b) $\overline{BC} \cap \overline{JB}$

(c) $\overline{CF} \cap \overline{DF}$ (d) $\overline{CG} \cap \overline{EF}$

(e) $\overline{HJ} \cup \overline{JB} \cup \overline{BD} \cup \overline{DF} \cup \overline{FH}$

18. Illustrate how a convex pentagon and a square can be drawn so that they intersect at each of the following number of points. There are no restrictions on the sizes of the square and hexagon.

(a) At one point   (b) At two points

(c) At three points   (d) At four points

(e) At five points   (f) At eight points

19. Six points are evenly distributed around a circle, as shown here. The distance along the circle between any two consecutive points is the same.

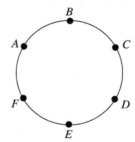

The points are labeled A, B, C, D, E, and F, respectively. Suppose that any three of these points are chosen as endpoints of a triangle. What is the probability that the triangle is an equilateral triangle?

20. Suppose that the notation $A \square B$ means "figure A superimposed over figure B." Examine the following figures.

$A \square B$ $B \square D$ $C \square A$

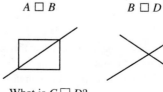

What is $C \square D$?

21. Determine if the following patterns can result in the object named when folded into a three-dimensional shape.

    (a) Triangular pyramid

    (b) Octagonal prism

    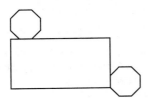

    (c) Cone

    (d) Cylinder

    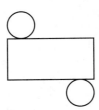

    (e) Square pyramid

    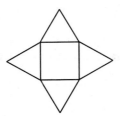

22. Imagine the face of an analog clock. If you drew the following lines, what shape would result?

    (a) Begin at 12 o'clock and connect every other number.

    (b) Begin at 12 o'clock and connect every third number.

    (c) Begin at 12 o'clock and connect every fourth number.

    (d) What instructions might you give to form a rectangle?

    (e) What instructions might you give to form a scalene triangle?

23. Examine the following addition table for this pentagonal system

    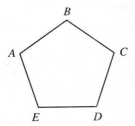

+	A	B	C	D	E
A	C	D	E	A	B
B	D	E	A	B	C
C	E	A	B	C	D
D	A	B	C	D	E
E	B	C	D	E	A

    The addition of $X + Y$ in this pentagonal system is defined as "begin at vertex X and move Y sides in a clockwise direction." The resulting vertex is the "sum."

    (a) What is the identity element in this system?

    (b) $A + B + C + D + E = ?$

    (c) $3A + 2B = ?$

24. A geoboard is a manipulative device used in elementary schools. It is a wooden or plastic square covered at regular intervals with pegs or nails, around which rubber bands are stretched. Sketch the position of a rubber band that would divide the square into two congruent polygons as described below. The laminated card that came with this text can be used to trace these solutions. An example, two isosceles right triangles, is done for you here.

    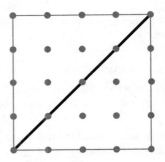

    (a) Two congruent rectangles

    (b) Two congruent nonconvex hexagons

    (c) Two congruent nonconvex decagons

In Other Words

25. Describe three differences between a right angle prism and a right angle pyramid.

26. When is a solid not a polyhedral solid?

27. Is it possible for the apex of a pyramid to be located in the same plane as all of the points in the base? Is it possible that it be located in the same plane as some of the points in the base? Is it possible that it be located in the same plane as none of the points in the base? Explain your answers.

28. What is necessarily true about a cross section that is parallel to the base of any right prism?

29. Why do you think manhole covers are circular?

Cooperative Activity

30. Groups of two

Individual Accountability: Trace and cut out eight copies of the square and equilateral triangle shown here.

 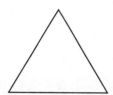

Arrange the shapes in such a way that adjacent sides touch completely. Each of the following polygons can be formed with more than one of the squares and/or triangles. Trace your pattern.

(a) Square   **(b)** Equilateral triangle

(c) Rectangle   **(d)** Pentagon in two different ways

Group Goal: Share the patterns with your partner. Are they unique? Together, determine arrangements of the squares and triangles that will yield the following shapes.

(a) seven-sided convex polygon

(b) seven-sided nonconvex polygon

(c) eight-sided convex polygon

(d) eight-sided nonconvex polygon

(e) ten-sided convex polygon

(f) ten-sided nonconvex polygon

Geometry as **M**easurement

Examine the photograph at the right.

Describe what you see.

How can you estimate the number of jelly beans in the jar?

How many grains of rice might this same jar hold?

On what did you base this estimate?

What might a mathematical description of this photograph contain?

Introduction

Chapter 10 contained a somewhat nonnumerical introduction to the study of geometry. Shapes and solids were identified and classified, and their defining characteristics were explored. In this chapter and Chapters 12 and 13, we will examine geometry in greater depth and learn how it can be used as a tool to study other branches of mathematics.

Measurement is one of the earliest experiences elementary students have with geometry. Chapters 6 and 7 introduced you to the English standard system and metric system of linear measurement. In this chapter, you will extend your knowledge of measurement into many new areas. Section 11.1 explains how to use a protractor and a compass, the basic measurement tools for angles and circles. Various kinds of angles and their characteristics and seven different geometric constructions are also presented. Section 11.2 extends the concept of measurement to include perimeters, circumferences, areas, and surface areas. Formulas for finding these measurements are developed, and examples are presented to show how these formulas apply. Section 11.3 examines characteristics of weight, volume, and temperature and describes the various units and formulas that apply to measurement in each of these areas. When you are finished with this chapter, you will have a solid foundation in the basics of geometric measurement—a foundation you will draw on as we move into the final two chapters of the book.

11.1   Tools of Geometry

Recall the terminology we used in Chapter 10. The concepts of point, line, and plane were said to be basic to geometry. Extracted from the concept of a line was the definition of a line segment. A line segment is the set of points that connect two points along the shortest path between them. The line that passes through points A and B is labeled as $\overleftrightarrow{AB}$ (see Figure 11.1a).

Because a line segment has two fixed ends, it has the attribute of length. When you name a line segment that joins points A and B, the notation $\overline{AB}$ (or $\overline{BA}$) is used. When identifying the length of the segment that joins A and B, the notation AB (or BA) is used. A line, which extends indefinitely in both directions, does not have measurable length.

Imagine a collection of points that extends indefinitely in only one direction. Such **endpoint** a portion of a line, beginning at one fixed point called an **endpoint** and extending in-**ray** definitely from that point, is called a **ray** (see Figure 11.1b). A ray also has no measurable length. The ray that begins at point A and passes through point B is labeled $\overrightarrow{AB}$. The first letter of the ray notation must name the endpoint.

Figure 11.1

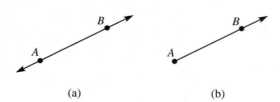

(a)   (b)

angle

vertex

Basic to any understanding of geometry is the concept of angle. An **angle** is formed by the union of two rays that extend from a common endpoint. This common endpoint is called the **vertex** of the angle. Angles can also be formed by two line segments that extend from a common endpoint, as well as at the intersection of two lines (see Figure 11.2).

Figure 11.2

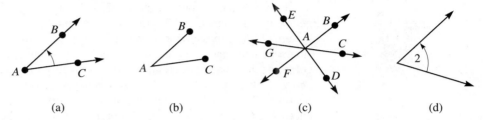

(a)   (b)   (c)   (d)

Angles can be named in a variety of ways. The angle pictured in Figure 11.2a is formed by $\overrightarrow{AB}$ and $\overrightarrow{AC}$ ($\overrightarrow{AB} \cup \overrightarrow{AC}$). The angle pictured in Figure 11.2b is formed by $\overline{AB}$ and $\overline{BC}$ ($\overline{AB} \cup \overline{BC}$). In both cases, the vertex is at point A. This angle can be symbolized as $\angle A$ and read as "angle A." It can also be named as $\angle BAC$ and as $\angle CAB$. When you name angles using three letters, the vertex is always the center letter. Certain situations necessitate the use of three letters to name an angle. In Figure 11.2c, for example, many angles have a vertex at A. Four such angles are $\angle EAB$, $\angle BAC$, $\angle CAF$, and $\angle DAE$. An angle can also be named by using a number, as shown in Figure 11.2d.

Angular measurement is not linear measurement. Therefore, a ruler cannot be used to measure an angle. Recall how the units of linear measure evolved. A particular length was subdivided into smaller congruent lengths resulting in the desired unit of measure. The object to be measured was compared with these units of measurement, and a numerical value was assigned to the object. This procedure of defining an attribute, determining a unit of measure, comparing what is to be measured with the unit of measurement, and finally quantifying the attribute is also followed when measuring an angle. Whereas the units of measure are marked on a straightedge for linear measurement, the units are marked on a curved surface for angular measure.

arc

Any two points on a circle define a portion of the circle called an **arc** (see Figure 11.3). In Figure 11.3a, the portion of the circle from A to B is called arc AB, and symbolized as $\overparen{AB}$ or $\overparen{BA}$. In Figure 11.3b, it is necessary to introduce two other points on the circle in order to delineate between the major arc $\overparen{AXB}$ and the minor arc $\overparen{AYB}$.

Figure 11.3

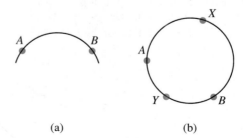

(a)   (b)

A circle can be divided into 360 congruent arcs. Line segments can be drawn from each point of division to the center of the circle. This yields 360 congruent pie-shaped **sectors** figures called **sectors** of a circle. In this particular instance, each sector represents $\frac{1}{360}$ th **degree** of the circular region. The central angle of each of these sectors measures 1 **degree**, symbolized as 1°. Sectors, however, can have a central angle whose measure is less than or equal to 360°.

protractor The tool used to measure the number of degrees in an angle is called a **protractor**. The protractor pictured in Figure 11.4 measures an angle of 20°. The base of the protractor coincides with one of the rays forming the angle. The "center" of the protractor is placed on the vertex of the angle. But how is it possible to determine that the angle measures 20° and not 160°, since the point at which $\overrightarrow{BC}$ intersects the protractor shows both numbers?

Figure 11.4

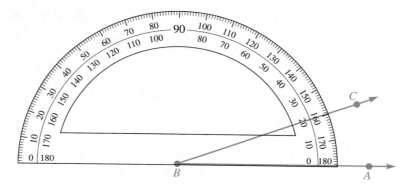

This protractor has two scales. You can easily determine which scale is the appropriate one to use by first recognizing the type of angle to be measured. There are four basic types of angles, as shown in the following table.

	Name	Definition	Illustration
acute angle	Acute angle	Measures between 0° and 90°	
right angle	Right angle	Measures 90°	
obtuse angle	Obtuse angle	Measures between 90° and 180°	
straight angle	Straight angle	Measures 180°	

Since it is clear in Figure 11.4 that $\angle ABC$ is an acute angle, it must measure 20°, not 160°. If an angle is visually categorized as belonging to the set of either acute or obtuse angles, this will dictate the angle measurement.

Investigation 1

A common way of picturing information is by means of a circle graph. The following graph illustrates sport preferences among elementary school students at a particular school.

Notice that the graph contains five sectors. What is the measure of each of the angles that form the sectors of this circle graph?

Visually classify each angle. The sector labeled "Baseball" contains an angle that appears to be obtuse. The sector labeled "Basketball" contains an angle that appears to be right. The remaining three sectors each appear to contain acute angles. The following five illustrations show a correct use of a protractor to determine the angle measurements.

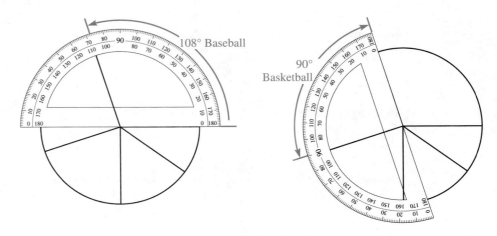

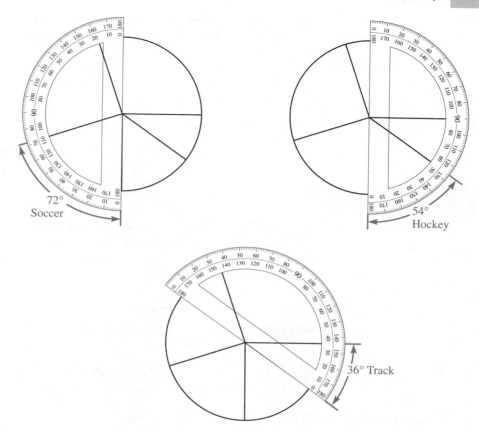

The angles that define the sectors representing each sport measure as follows:

Baseball	108°
Basketball	90°
Soccer	72°
Hockey	54°
Track	36°

Notice that the sum of the measures of these five angles is 360°. In the future, the measure of any angle ABC, will be symbolized by $m\angle ABC$, as opposed to the symbol $\angle ABC$, which simply names the angle.

Complementary and Supplementary Angles

complementary angles

complement

There are two commonly identified pairs of angles. Two angles are said to be **complementary angles** if the sum of their measures is 90°. In such a case, one angle is said to be the **complement** of the other angle. If $\angle a$ has a measure of x degrees, its complement has a measure of $(90 - x)$ degrees. A pair of complementary angles forms a right angle, as shown in Figure 11.5(a) on page 492.

supplementary angles

supplement

Two angles are said to be **supplementary angles** if the sum of their measures is 180°. In such a case, one angle is said to be the **supplement** of the other angle. If $\angle a$

has a measure of x degrees, its supplement has a measure of $(180 - x)$ degrees. A pair of supplementary angles can form a straight angle (as shown in Figure 11.5(b).

Figure 11.5

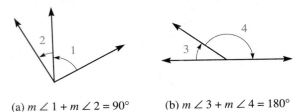

(a) $m \angle 1 + m \angle 2 = 90°$ (b) $m \angle 3 + m \angle 4 = 180°$

Investigation 2

The hinged side of a door makes a right angle with the wall beside it. In order for the door to remain open, an eye hook is attached from the wall to the door. When the door is hooked in the open position, the door makes a 15° angle with the wall. What is the angle of the opening of the door?

Understand the Problem: When a door is open it makes a 15° angle with a wall. What is the angle measure of the opening?

Devise a Plan: To better understand this problem, it would be helpful to draw a diagram. Rather than sketching a door and a wall, reduce the picture to its bare necessities.

Carry Out the Plan: Examine the following illustration:

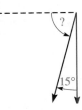

Notice that the two angles in question are complementary angles. Let A represent the number of degrees in the angle of opening of the door. Therefore,

$$15 + A = 90$$
$$A = 90 - 15 = 75$$

There are 75° in the angle of opening of the door.

Look Back: Use the diagram and your protractor to verify the accuracy of the results.

In the following diagram, $\overline{FB}$ is perpendicular to $\overline{AC}$, and $\angle ABC$ is a straight angle. Determine the measures of $\angle FBE$ and $\angle ABE$.

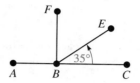

Since $\overline{FB}$ is perpendicular to $\overline{AC}$, $\angle ABF$ and $\angle FBC$ are both right angles. Clearly, from the diagram, $m\angle FBE + m\angle EBC = m\angle FBC$. Since these two angles form a right angle, they are complementary. The complement of an angle that measures 35° is an angle that measures 55°. Therefore, $m\angle FBE = 55°$.

Again, from the diagram we can see that $\angle ABE + \angle EBC = \angle ABC$. Since these two angles form a straight angle, they are supplementary. The supplement of 35° is 145°. Therefore, $m\angle ABE = 145°$.

Triangles

In Chapter 10 triangles were classified according to relationships found among the lengths of their sides. The following table extends those definitions to include angle characteristics.

Type of Triangle	Characteristics
Scalene	All sides of different length; all angles of different measure
Isosceles	At least two sides of equal length; the angles opposite the equal sides are congruent
Equilateral	All sides of equal length; all angles of equal measure
Right	Contains one right angle
Acute	Contains three acute angles
Obtuse	Contains one obtuse angle

Every triangle that can be drawn falls into one or more of these categories. It is possible for a triangle to be an isosceles right triangle, an acute scalene triangle, or an obtuse scalene triangle. It is not possible to have an equilateral right triangle or an equilateral obtuse triangle. The reason for these distinctions lies in knowing a critical characteristic about the sum of the interior angles of every triangle. To discover this relationship, follow the three steps outlined here with any type of triangle.

1. Draw a triangle on a sheet of paper. Cut it out. (The larger the triangle, the easier it will be to identify the relationship.)

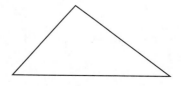

2. Draw arrows pointing to each of the vertices, as shown below.

3. Tear off each of the three vertices. Arrange the three torn angles around a common point, as shown here.

This exercise illustrates that the three vertex angles of a triangle form a straight angle. Therefore, the sum of the measures of the interior angles of any triangle is equal to 180°.

Performing the same activity with any quadrilateral would result in the four vertex angles forming one complete revolution of 360° (see Figure 11.6). Therefore, the sum of the measures of the interior angles of any quadrilateral is equal to 360°.

Figure 11.6

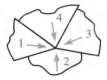

Knowing that the sum of the measures of the interior angles in any triangle is equal to 180° allows you to understand why there cannot be an equilateral right triangle or an equilateral obtuse triangle. Equilateral triangles are also equiangular, which means they contain three congruent angles. A right triangle contains a 90° angle. If all three angles were right angles, the sum of the measures of the interior angles would be 270°. This contradicts what we have just discovered about the sum of the measures of the interior angles of a triangle. A similar argument can be made to disallow the existence of an equilateral obtuse triangle.

Investigation 4

A carpenter has a piece of wood that is in the shape of a right trapezoid. She wishes to cut it into three triangles as shown here:

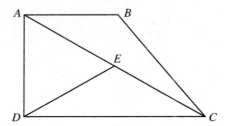

$\triangle AED$ is equilateral and $\triangle DEC$ is isosceles, with $DE = EC$. If $\overline{CD}$ is perpendicular to $\overline{AD}$, $\overline{BA}$ is perpendicular to $\overline{AD}$, and $m\angle BCD = 50°$, find the measures of the interior angles of $\triangle ABC$. What type of triangle is $\triangle ABC$?

Understand the Problem: What is known? You are given that $\triangle AED$ is equilateral, $\triangle DEC$ is isosceles, $DE = EC$, $\overline{CD} \perp \overline{AD}$, $\overline{BA} \perp \overline{AD}$, and $m\angle BCD = 50°$.
What is unknown? You must determine the measures of the interior angles of $\triangle ABC$.

Devise a Plan: What can you extract from the given information? Since $\triangle AED$ is equilateral, then $m\angle DAE = m\angle AED = m\angle EDA = 60°$. Since $\triangle DEC$ is isosceles with $DE = EC$, then $m\angle EDC = m\angle ECD$ (base angles of an isosceles triangle are congruent). Since $\overline{CD} \perp \overline{AD}$, $\angle ADC$ is a right angle. Since $\overline{BA} \perp \overline{AD}$, $\angle BAD$ is a right angle.

Carry Out the Plan: Draw a diagram and label the angles with their measures as shown here:

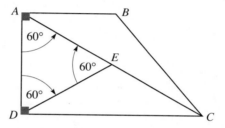

$\angle BAC$ is the complement of $\angle CAD$ and therefore measures $30°$. $\angle CDE$ is the complement of $\angle EDA$ and therefore measures $30°$. Since base angles of an isosceles triangle are equal, $\angle DCE$ also measures $30°$. Since $\angle BCD$ measures $50°$ and $\angle DCE$ measures $30°$, $m\angle BCE = 20°$. Since the sum of the measures of the interior angles of a triangle is $180°$, $m\angle ABC = 180° - (30° + 20°)$, or $130°$. Therefore, $\triangle ABC$ is a scalene triangle.

Look Back: Use your protractor to verify the measures you have determined.

Investigation 5

azimuth circle   The **azimuth circle** is used in air and sea navigation to help identify the location of a plane or a ship. It assigns $0°$ to the direction "north," $90°$ to the direction "east," $180°$ to the direction "south," and $270°$ to the direction "west." An air-traffic controller spots a private plane at point A and an airliner at point B, as shown in the following diagram. What is the measure of the angle formed by the private plane and the airliner at the location of the control tower? Find this measure in two different ways.

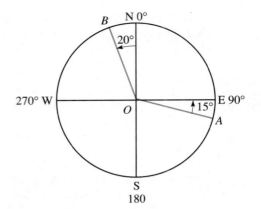

$m\angle BOA = m\angle BON + m\angle NOE + m\angle EOA$

$= 20° + 90° + 15°$

$= 125°$

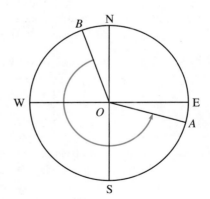

There is also another $\angle BOA$ in the circle, as shown here.

$m\angle BOA = m\angle BOW + m\angle WOS + m\angle SOA$

$= 70° + 90° + 75°$

$= 235°$

Notice that $125° + 235° = 360°$.

Exterior Angles of a Triangle

exterior angles

Every line segment that forms a triangle can be extended. The angles formed at the vertices on the exterior of a triangle by a side and an extension of a side are called **exterior angles**. Examime $\triangle RST$ given in Figure 11.7.

Figure 11.7

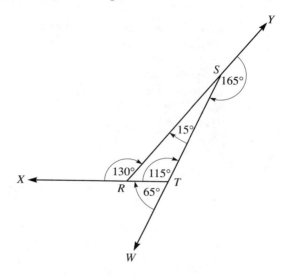

Each side has been extended in one direction, creating three exterior angles. What relationships do you observe about the measures of the angles in Figure 11.7?

Notice that the interior and exterior angles formed at a single vertex are supplementary.

$$m\angle XRS + m\angle SRT = 180°$$

$$m\angle YST + m\angle TSR = 180°$$

$$m\angle WTR + m\angle STR = 180°$$

In addition to this relationship, the measurement of each exterior angle is equal to the sum of the measures of the two opposite interior angles. For example,

Since $m\angle XRS + m\angle SRT = 180°$, it follows that $m\angle SRT = 180° - m\angle XRS$.

$$m\angle TSR + m\angle SRT + m\angle RTS = 180° \quad \text{(Why?)}$$

$$m\angle TSR + (180° - m\angle XRS) + m\angle RTS = 180° \quad \text{(Why?)}$$

$$m\angle TSR - m\angle XRS + m\angle RTS = 0 \quad \text{(Why?)}$$

$$m\angle TSR + m\angle RTS = m\angle XRS \quad \text{(Why?)}$$

This development can be shown for each of the exterior angles.
Therefore,

$$m\angle XRS = m\angle RTS + m\angle TSR$$

$$130° = 115° + 15°$$

$$m\angle YST = m\angle SRT + m\angle RTS$$
$$165° = 50° + 115°$$
$$m\angle WTR = m\angle TSR + m\angle SRT$$
$$65° = 15° + 50°$$

Knowing the measures of the exterior angles of a triangle leads to knowing the measures of the interior angles. The reverse is also true.

Angles Formed by a Transversal

transversal   In Figure 11.8, lines l and m are intersected by line n. Line n is called a **transversal**. Notice that the transversal forms eight angles at the intersection with lines l and m. These angles are labed $1-8$.

Figure 11.8

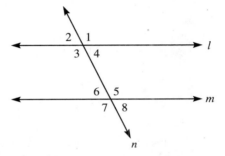

Recognizing that supplementary angles are formed along lines l, m, and n results in the following statements:

$$m\angle 1 + m\angle 2 = 180°$$
$$m\angle 1 + m\angle 4 = 180°$$
$$m\angle 2 + m\angle 3 = 180°$$
$$m\angle 4 + m\angle 3 = 180°$$
$$m\angle 5 + m\angle 6 = 180°$$
$$m\angle 5 + m\angle 8 = 180°$$
$$m\angle 6 + m\angle 7 = 180°$$
$$m\angle 8 + m\angle 7 = 180°$$

Examine the first two statements in the list. It follows that

$$m\angle 1 + m\angle 2 = m\angle 1 + m\angle 4$$

Subtracting $m\angle 1$ from both sides of the equation results in the equality $m\angle 2 = m\angle 4$. This can be repeated with the other equations to result in pairs of congruent angles **vertical angles**   called vertical angles. **Vertical angles** are nonadjacent angles that share a common vertex and are formed by two intersecting lines or line segments.

Investigation 6 will allow you to examine the special case in which the transversal intersects parallel lines.

Investigation 6

A rectangular sheet of plywood is to be cut at a 60° angle as shown in the following diagram:

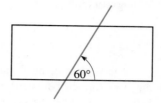

What are the measures of the interior angles formed on the surface of the plywood in each of the two trapezoidal shapes?

Understand the Problem: What is known? The wood is in the shape of a rectangle, and the cut forms a 60° angle with the base of the rectangle.

What is unknown? The measures of the interior angles formed on the surfaces of the two plywood pieces.

Devise a Plan: For ease of reference, number each angle.

Carry Out the Plan:

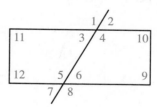

Notice that ∠5 and ∠6 are supplementary angles. Therefore, $m\angle 5 = (180° - 60°) = 120°$. Since ∠5 and ∠8 are vertical angles, they have the same angle measurement. Therefore, $m\angle 8 = 120°$. Since ∠7 and ∠8 are supplementary angles, $m\angle 7 = (180° - 120°) = 60°$. You also could have determined that $m\angle 7 = 60°$, since ∠6 and ∠7 are vertical angles. Since the original sheet of plywood was rectangular, $m\angle 9 = m\angle 10 = m\angle 11 = m\angle 12 = 90°$. Since the sum of the measures of the interior angles of a quadrilateral equals 360°, $m\angle 4 = 360° - [m\angle 6 + m\angle 9 + m\angle 10] = 360° - (60° + 90° + 90°) = 360° - 240° = 120°$.

By following the same procedure as above, it is left to you to determine why $m\angle 1 = 120°$, and $m\angle 2 = m\angle 3 = 60°$.

Examine the measures of the angles formed by the transversal. The following equalities exist:

$$m\angle 6 = m\angle 2$$
$$m\angle 5 = m\angle 1$$
$$m\angle 8 = m\angle 4$$
$$m\angle 7 = m\angle 3$$

corresponding angles

These pairs of angles are called **corresponding angles** because they share the same position relative to the parallel lines and the transversal. When parallel lines are cut by a transversal, the measures of the corresponding angles thus formed are congruent.

Examine the measures of the following angles formed by the transversal. The following equalities exist:

$$m\angle 6 = m\angle 3$$
$$m\angle 5 = m\angle 4$$

alternate interior angles

These pairs of nonadjacent angles are called **alternate interior angles** because they are formed between the two parallel lines on alternate sides of the transversal. When parallel lines are cut by a transversal, the alternate interior angles thus formed are congruent.

Look Back:

If you can imagine a clockwise rotation of one piece around the center of the cut, you will "see" that the cut edges of the board will be superimposed over each other, further indicating the congruency of $\angle 6$ and $\angle 3$, and $\angle 5$ and $\angle 4$.

Interior and Exterior Angles of Convex Polygons

Through tearing off and reassembling the vertices, we have already determined that the sum of the measures of the interior angles of a quadrilateral equals 360°. This information is also apparent if you realize that any quadrilateral can be partitioned into two triangles (see Figure 11.9).

Figure 11.9

Since the sum of the measures of the interior angles of one triangle equals 180°, the sum of the measures of the interior angles of two triangles equals 360°.

But what about the sum of the measures of the interior angles of other polygons? Figure 11.10 shows a quadrilateral, pentagon, hexagon, and octagon that have been partitioned into the fewest possible number of triangles by drawing diagonals from a single vertex.

Figure 11.10

Examine the following table, which will help you understand the data presented in Figure 11.10.

Polygon	Number of Sides	Number of Triangles Formed
Quadrilateral	4	2
Pentagon	5	3
Hexagon	6	4
Octagon	8	6

There appears to be a relationship between the number of sides of the polygon and the least number of triangles that can be formed that partition the polygon. Let N represent the number of sides in the polygon. Then $(N - 2)$ represents the number of triangles formed. Notice that the vertices of each triangle formed are at the vertices of the polygon. Since the sum of the interior angles of any triangle is $180°$, the sum of the interior angles of the triangles that partition the polygon can be represented as $180(N - 2)$. Establishing the visual pattern first leads to a more meaningful formula for the sum of the interior angles of a polygon. The sum of the interior angles of any polygon can be represented as

$$180(N - 2)$$

where N is the number of sides of the polygon.

Although it is difficult to determine the measures of each interior angle of every polygon without a protractor, it is not difficult to do so in the special case of regular polygons. Recall that a regular polygon has congruent sides. In addition, the interior angles of a regular polygon are congruent. Therefore, knowing the sum of the interior angles in a particular regular polygon will lead to the individual measure of each interior angle through division by the number of sides. In general, the measure of each interior angle of regular N-gon (a regular polygon with N sides) can be represented as

$$\frac{180(N - 2)}{N}$$

Regular polygons can also be partitioned into triangles in a different way. Every regular N-sided polygon (N-gon) has a center. Segments drawn from the center to the vertices partition the polygon into N congruent isosceles triangles (see Figure 11.11a). **central angles** Angles formed at this center are called **central angles**. Since one complete rotation about the center of the polygon measures $360°$, the measure of each central angle in a regular polygon is determined by $\frac{360}{N}$.

Figure 11.11

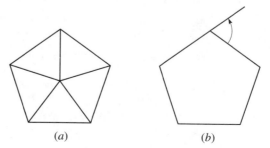

(a)　　　　　(b)

Interestingly, this is also the algebraic representation of the measure of any exterior angle of a regular polygon. Figure 11.11b depicts an exterior angle formed at the vertex of a regular pentagon. Since the interior angle, whose measure is represented by $\frac{180(N-2)}{N}$, and the exterior angle are supplementary, the sum of their measures must equal 180°. Therefore, it can be stated that

$$\text{Measure of exterior angle} = 180 - \text{Measure of interior angle}$$

$$= 180 - \frac{180(N-2)}{N}$$

$$= \frac{180N - 180N + 360}{N}$$

$$= \frac{360}{N}$$

In summary, the following generalizations can be made about the measures of the angles of a regular N-gon:

Measure of Each Interior Angle	*Measure of Each Exterior Angle*	*Measure of Each Central Angle*
$\frac{180(N-2)}{N}$	$\frac{360}{N}$	$\frac{360}{N}$

Geometric Constructions

The Greek mathematician Euclid wrote a set of 13 books called *The Elements* in approximately 300 B.C. This work forms the basis of Euclidean geometry, which is commonly taught in schools today. An important part of Euclidean geometry is the construction of plane geometric figures using only two tools: a straightedge and a compass. A **straightedge** is similar to a ruler except that it does not contain any marks used for measuring length. A **compass** is a tool that can be used to copy a line segment, draw a circle of a given radius, and draw an arc. We will now demonstrate the use of both of these tools, through seven simple constructions. More sophisticated constructions will be addressed in Chapters 12 and 13.

straightedge
compass

Many of the constructions that follow can be justified by referring to the properties of a rhombus, which are listed here:

1. A rhombus is a special type of parallelogram in which all sides are congruent.

2. The diagonals of a rhombus are perpendicular to each other.

3. The point of intersection of the diagonals in a rhombus is the point that divides each diagonal into two congruent segments (midpoint).

4. The diagonals of a rhombus divide each vertex angle into two congruent angles.

Construction 1: Copying a Line Segment

You are given line segments $\overline{AB}$ and $\overline{CD}$ (see Figure 11.12). Copy $\overline{AB}$ onto $\overline{CD}$ so that point A corresponds to point C and point B corresponds to point E, which will be located on $\overline{CD}$.

Figure 11.12

A B C D

1. Place the point of the compass at A. Open the compass leg to length AB. The figure below shows the open compass on $\overline{AB}$.

2. Without changing the expansion of the compass, move the point from A to C and mark off an arc on $\overrightarrow{CD}$. Label the point of intersection E. $\overline{CE}$ is congruent to $\overline{AB}$.

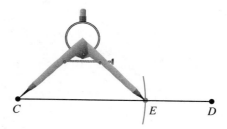

Construction 2: Bisecting a Line Segment

Given $\overline{AB}$, determine the point on $\overline{AB}$ that partitions it into two congruent line seg-

midpoint ments. This point is called the **midpoint** of $\overline{AB}$ (see Figure 11.13).

Figure 11.13

1. With the point of the compass at A, open the leg of the compass to a distance slightly more than half the length of $\overline{AB}$. Mark off arcs above and below $\overline{AB}$.

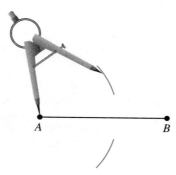

2. Without changing the expansion of the compass, put the point of the compass at B and again mark off arcs above and below $\overline{AB}$.

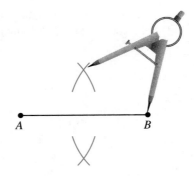

3. Label the points of intersection of the arcs C and D. With the straightedge, construct $\overline{CD}$. Line segment $\overline{CD}$ bisects line segment $\overline{AB}$ at point E, the midpoint.

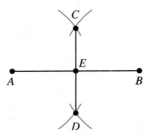

perpendicular bisector

A consequence of this construction is that the bisector $\overline{CD}$ is perpendicular to $\overline{AB}$. Therefore, it is called a **perpendicular bisector**. The justification of this construction can be found in the properties of a rhombus. By connecting points A, C, B, and D, a rhombus is formed, as shown in Figure 11.14.

Figure 11.14

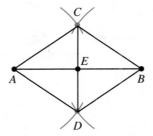

Segments $\overline{AB}$ and $\overline{CD}$ are diagonals of the rhombus. The diagonals of a rhombus are perpendicular bisectors of each other.

Construction 3: Copying an Angle
Given $\angle ABC$ and $\overline{EF}$, copy $\angle ABC$ onto $\overline{EF}$ with the vertex at E (see Figure 11.15).

Figure 11.15

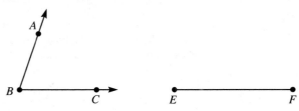

1. Place the point of the compass at vertex *B*. Open the compass and draw an arc that intersects both sides of the angle. Label the points of intersection *G* and *H*.

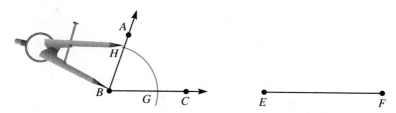

2. Without changing the extension of the compass, place the point of the compass at *E*. Draw an arc as shown below. Label the point of intersection of the arc *I*.

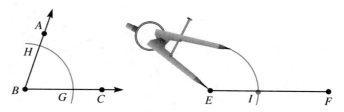

3. Return to the original angle. Place the point of the compass at *G*. Open the compass to length $\overline{GH}$. Without changing this extension of the compass, place the point at *I* and mark off an arc that will intersect the first arc drawn in this figure. Label the point of intersection *J*.

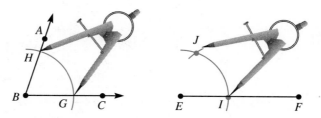

4. Construct $\overline{EJ}$. Angle *JEI* is congruent to ∠*ABC*.

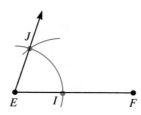

The justification of this construction lies in a knowledge of triangle congruence, a topic we will cover in Chapter 12.

Construction 4: Bisecting an Angle
Given $\angle ABC$, partition this angle into two congruent, adjacent angles, as in Figure 11.16.

Figure 11.16

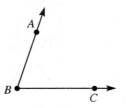

1. With the point of the compass at vertex B, mark off an arc that intersects both $\overline{AB}$ and $\overline{BC}$. Label the points of intersection D and E.

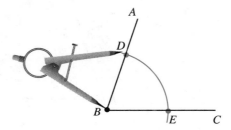

2. Without changing the extension of the compass, place the point of the compass at D and draw an arc as shown below. Repeat the same procedure with the point of the compass at E. Label the point of intersection of the two arcs F.

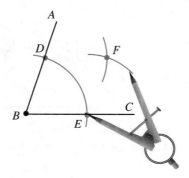

3. Construct $\overline{BF}$ using a straightedge. $\overline{BF}$ is the angle bisector of $\angle ABC$. Therefore, $\angle DBF$ is congruent to $\angle EBF$.

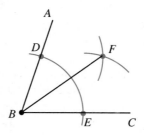

The justification for $\overline{BF}$ as an angle bisector is once again found in the properties of a rhombus. By connecting points B, E, F, and D, a rhombus is formed, as shown in Figure 11.17.

Figure 11.17

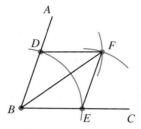

The diagonal $\overline{BF}$ of rhombus $BEFD$ divides $\angle DBE$ into two congruent parts. Therefore, $\overline{BF}$ is an angle bisector.

Construction 5: Constructing a Perpendicular from a Point Not on a Given Line to the Line
Given $\overleftrightarrow{AB}$ and point C not on $\overleftrightarrow{AB}$, construct a perpendicular line through C to $\overleftrightarrow{AB}$ (see Figure 11.18).

Figure 11.18

1. Place the point of the compass at C. Mark off an arc that will intersect $\overleftrightarrow{AB}$ in two places. Label these points of intersection D and E.

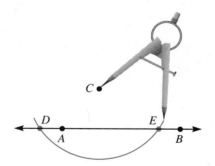

2. Place the point at D and mark off an arc under $\overleftrightarrow{AB}$, as shown on page 508. Repeat this procedure with the point of the compass at E. The two arcs should intersect. Label the point of intersection F.

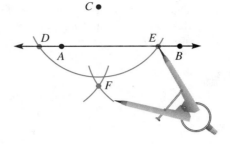

3. Construct $\overline{CF}$, which will be perpendicular to $\overleftrightarrow{AB}$ through point C.

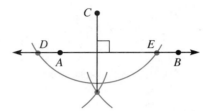

The justification of this construction will be left to you in the In Other Words portion of the assessments at the end of this section (see Problem 26).

Construction 6: Constructing a Perpendicular Through a Given Point on a Line
Given $\overleftrightarrow{AB}$ and C on $\overleftrightarrow{AB}$, construct a line segment that is perpendicular to $\overleftrightarrow{AB}$ at point C (see Figure 11.19).

Figure 11.19

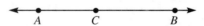

1. Place the point of the compass at C. Open the compass to any length and mark off two arcs on $\overleftrightarrow{AB}$. Label the points of intersection D and E.

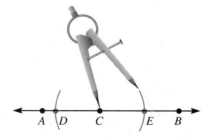

2. Place the point of the compass at D. Open the compass to a distance slightly more than $\overline{DC}$. Mark off an arc as shown here. Without changing the compass opening, repeat this procedure with the point of the compass at E. Label the point of intersection of the two arcs F.

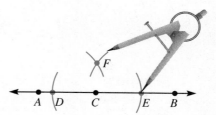

3. Construct $\overline{CF}$, which will be perpendicular to $\overline{AB}$ at C.

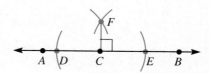

The justification is left to you (with a little help from us) in the In Other Words portion of the assessments at the end of this section (see Problem 28).

Construction 7: Constructing Parallel Lines

Given $\overleftrightarrow{AB}$ and point C off $\overleftrightarrow{AB}$, construct a line through C that is parallel to $\overleftrightarrow{AB}$ (see Figure 11.20).

Figure 11.20

1. Place the point of the compass at A. Expand the compass to point C. Mark off an arc from C through $\overrightarrow{AB}$ as shown here. Label the point of intersection D.

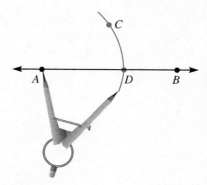

2. Without changing the extension of the compass, place the point of the compass at C and mark off an arc as shown on page 510 (Arc #1). Repeat this procedure with the point of the compass at D. Label the point of intersection of the two arcs E.

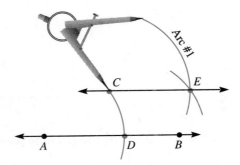

3. With a straightedge, construct $\overleftrightarrow{CE}$, which is parallel to $\overleftrightarrow{AB}$.

The justification is again left to you in the In Other Words portion of the assessments at the end of this section (see Problem 27).

Investigation 7

median   The **median** of a triangle is the line segment that is drawn from a vertex to the midpoint of the opposite side. Use any of the preceding constructions to find the median of $\triangle ABC$ from vertex B.

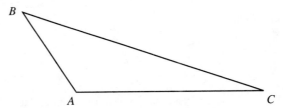

The first step is to determine the midpoint of the side opposite $\angle B$. Recall that the bisector of $\overline{AC}$ intersects $\overline{AC}$ at its midpoint. Therefore, use the construction that bisects a line segment as shown here.

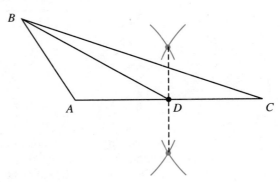

Label the midpoint D. Construct $\overline{BD}$, which is the median of $\triangle ABC$ from B.

Investigation 8

altitude The **altitude** of a triangle is the line segment drawn from a vertex perpendicular to the line containing the opposite side. In some cases, as you will see in this investigation, the side must be extended since the altitude cannot always be constructed within the triangle. Construct an altitude from point C to its opposite side.

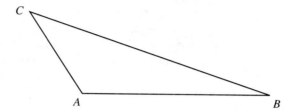

It is necessary to extend side $\overline{AB}$ as shown here.

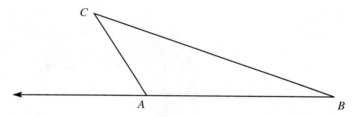

The strategy appropriate here is to look for a similar problem. Essentially, you need to view point C as a point off $\overleftrightarrow{AB}$ and to construct a perpendicular through C to $\overleftrightarrow{AB}$. (Refer to Construction 5.)

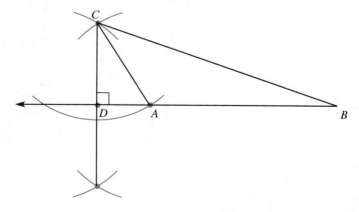

The altitude is sometimes referred to as the *height* of the triangle. In this instance, $\overline{CD}$ is the height of $\triangle ABC$, even though it is constructed outside of the triangle.

golden ratio (golden section)

Investigation 9 employs a variety of constructions. The **golden ratio**, or **golden section**, is a visually pleasing ratio of two lengths that is found in environments as varied as art, architecture, $\sqrt{5}$ anatomy, nature, and advertising. Simply, the golden ratio is

$$\frac{1 + \sqrt{5}}{2}$$

or approximately 1.618. The golden ratio is visible in the dimensions of the Parthenon in Athens, Greece, and in the famous sketch of a man by Leonardo da Vinci showing the "divine proportions" (see photo below), as well as in numerous other areas. Euclid developed an elegant construction for partitioning a line segment into two lengths that illustrates the golden ratio. A simplified version of this classic construction is offered in Investigation 9. [For further information, see John Baumgart, ed., *Historical Topics for the Mathematics Classroom* (Reston, Va: National Council of Teachers of Mathematics, 1969).]

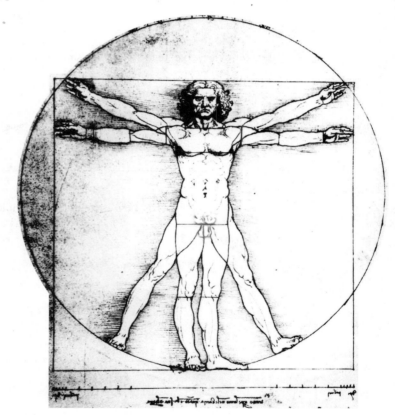

Investigation 9

Given $\overline{AB}$, locate point C on $\overline{AB}$, which partitions $\overline{AB}$ into two segments whose lengths are in the golden ratio.

1. Extend $\overline{AB}$ through A. Construct a line segment at A that is perpendicular to $\overline{AB}$. Extend this perpendicular above and below point A (see Construction 6).

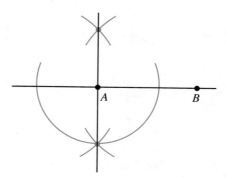

2. Use the compass to "measure" $\overline{AB}$. With the point of the compass at A, draw an arc that intersects the perpendicular at a point below A. Label this point C. Notice that $\overline{AC} = \overline{AB}$ (see Construction 1).

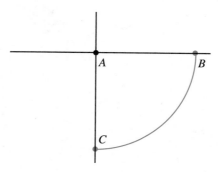

3. Bisect $\overline{AC}$ (see Construction 2). Label the midpoint D.

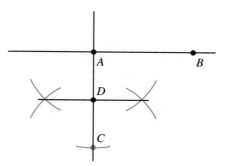

4. Use the compass to measure $\overline{DB}$. With the point of the compass at D, mark an arc on the perpendicular above point A. Label this point E (see Construction 1).

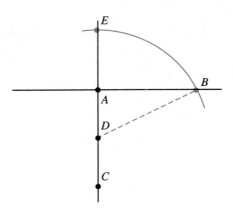

5. With the point of the compass at A, measure the distance of $\overline{AE}$ and mark off an arc on $\overline{AB}$. Label this point of intersection G.

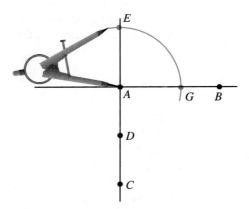

6. Use your ruler to measure the lengths of $\overline{AG}$ and $\overline{GB}$. Take measurements in both inches and centimeters. Determine the value of the ratio $\dfrac{AG}{GB}$ (in both units of measure). Your result should be close to 1.618, or the golden ratio.

The golden ratio appears in many real-world settings, both natural and manufactured. For example, measure the dimensions of an index card and a credit card. The ratio of the larger side to the smaller side approximates the golden ratio.

Assessments for Section 11.1

1. Estimate the measures of each of the following angles.

(a)   (b)   (c)

(d)   (e)

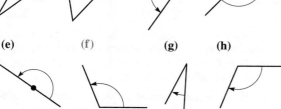

2. Classify each of the following angles as acute, right, obtuse, or straight.

(a)   (b)   (c)   (d)

(e)   (f)   (g)   (h)

3. Measure each of the following angles with your protractor.

(a)   (b)   (c)

(d)   (e)

4. Use a protractor to find the measures of each of the following angles.

(a) $\angle ABC$ (b) $\angle ABD$ (c) $\angle CBF$

(d) $\angle EBA$ (e) $\angle EBF$ (f) $\angle DBC$

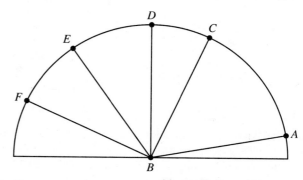

5. Two angles are complementary. Identify the measures of one such pair of angles in each of the cases stated here. Explain your answers.

(a) The measure of one angle is twice the measure of the other angle.

(b) The measure of one angle is 1 degree greater than the measure of the other angle.

(c) The measure of one angle is 10 degrees greater than three times the measure of the other angle.

6. Two angles are supplementary. Identify the measures of one such pair of angles in each of the cases stated here. Explain your answers.

(a) The measure of one angle is four times the measure of the other angle.

(b) The measure of one angle is 100 degrees more than the measure of the other angle.

(c) The measure of one angle is 3 degrees more than the measure of the other angle.

7. $\triangle ABC$ and $\triangle ADC$ are both isosceles triangles. $\overline{AD} \cong \overline{DC}$ and $\overline{AB} \cong \overline{BC}$. Examine the following illustration. List as many true statements about the figure as you can.

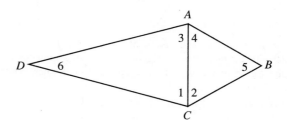

8. A square is partitioned as shown below.

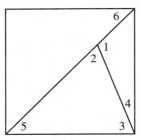

(a) What relationship holds between angles 1 and 2? Explain your reasoning.

(b) What relationship holds between angles 3 and 4? Explain your reasoning.

(c) What relationship holds between angles 5 and 6? Explain your reasoning.

9. Both a square and an equilateral triangle have congruent sides, as shown below. Determine the sum of the interior (vertex) angles of the new figure formed by combining the square(s) and the triangle(s).

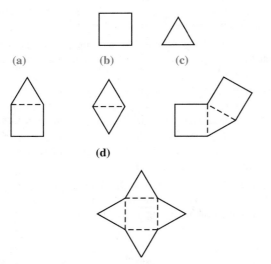

10. Given $\overline{AB} \parallel \overline{CD}$, $m\angle EDC = 50°$, and $m\angle BAE = 60°$, determine the measures of each of the following angles using the figure at the top of the next column. Explain your reasoning.

(a) $\angle AEB$ (b) $\angle DEC$ (c) $\angle BEC$ (d) $\angle AED$

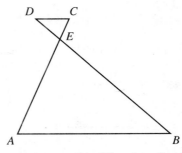

11. Given $L_1 \parallel L_2 \parallel L_3$, $m\angle 2 = 30°$, and $m\angle 9 = 105°$, find the sum of the interior vertex angles of the nonconvex hexagon *ACEHFD*. Determine all angle measures.

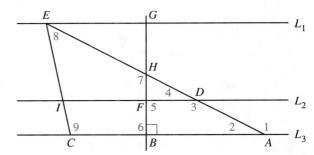

12. Draw a 7-cm line segment. Using only the geometric constructions outlined in this section, construct a square with this 7-cm line segment as one of its sides. Explain (in paragraph form) your methodology.

13. Draw a 7-cm line segment. Label the endpoints *A* and *B*. Explain how you can use only the geometric constructions outlined in this section to construct an isosceles triangle on $\overline{AB}$ with two 45° angles at points *A* and *B*.

14. On a map, 1 cm represents 88 km. Suppose the point of a compass is located at a certain town on the map, and circles are drawn with the following radii. Determine the straight-path distance from two cities that lie at the endpoints of the diameters of the circles drawn.

(a) $r = 2$ cm

(b) $r = 5$ cm

(c) $r = 2.5$ cm

(d) $r = 8.2$ cm

(e) $r = 10.7$ cm

15. Draw a line segment that is 10 cm long. Label the endpoints *A* and *B*. Use Euclid's construction to determine the point on $\overline{AB}$ that divides it into segments that are in the golden ratio.

16. Draw a line segment that is $4\frac{3}{4}$ in. long. Label the endpoints A and B. Use Euclid's construction to determine the point on $\overline{AB}$ that divides it into segments that are in the golden ratio.

17. Use your compass to draw a circle of any radius. Label the center C. Draw any diameter in the circle.

(a) Construct a diameter that is perpendicular to the diameter you have just drawn at point C.

(b) Label the points at which both diameters intersect the circle E, F, G, and H, respectively. Connect the points in order. Prove that $EFGH$ is a square.

18. Trace the following figures. Construct the three altitudes in each of the figures.

(a)   (b)

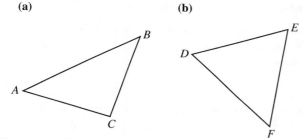

19. Given that figure $ABCD$ is a rhombus and that $m\angle CBA = 80°$, determine the measure of $\angle DBA$. Explain your answer.

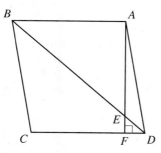

20. A regular hexagon is partitioned into two isosceles triangles and a rectangle as shown here. The measure of the exterior angle is $60°$.

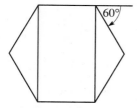

What is the sum of the interior angles of the regular hexagon? Justify your reasoning.

21. Fill in the cells in the following chart with two examples where possible.

	Acute Angle	Right Angle	Obtuse Angle	Straight Angle
Measure in degrees				
Depicted in a closed shape				
Found in a real-world setting				

22. Use your protractor and a straightedge to draw a triangle that has an exterior angle of $65°$. Write and answer two questions that a teacher might ask about this figure.

23. A car begins at a particular location and is driven due north along a straight road. After a distance, the car turns $50°$ to the right onto another straight road and continues in that direction. A short distance later, the car turns to the right once again and is now on a straight road headed due south. Determine the number of degrees that the car turned onto the southbound road. Justify your reasoning.

24. How can you use only a rectangular sheet of paper to produce an angle of approximately $22°$? Explain your reasoning.

In Other Words

25. What is an angle? How is a protractor used to measure an angle?

26. Give a justification for Construction 5, in which a perpendicular was dropped from a point to a line (see page 507).

27. Give a justification for Construction 7, in which parallel lines were drawn (see page 509).

28. Give a justification for Construction 6, in which a perpendicular was drawn through a point on a line (see page 508). (*Hint:* View the construction as if you were constructing a rhombus.)

29. Explain the difference between the two scales on a protractor. When would you use one rather than the other?

Cooperative Activity

30. Groups of four

Individual Accountability: Each member of the group is to use a straightedge to draw a nonregular convex pentagon, hexagon, and octagon. Extend each side in order as shown here:

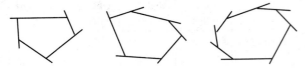

Use your protractor to determine the measures of the exterior angles formed.

Group Goal: Construct a chart for each type of polygon drawn. Use the following column headings:

Group Member	Measure of Each Exterior Angle	Sum of Exterior Angles

As a group, compare all of the charts and try to reach a generalization about the sum of the measures of the exterior angles of any convex polygon. Justify any generalizations algebraically.

11.2   Perimeter, Circumference, Area, and Surface Area

In this section, we extend the concept of measurement to include the measure of the distance around closed shapes, the amount of space within closed shapes, and the amount of space covering a three-dimensional solid.

Perimeter

Real-life situations such as enclosing a garden with a fence, trimming a blanket with binding, framing a picture, and finishing a ceiling with decorative molding require a knowledge of the distance around a closed shape. This measurement is defined as the **perimeter** of a closed shape.

perimeter

Investigation 10

Prior to the sale of a parcel of land, surveyors need to mark off and determine its precise dimensions. If the prospective buyers wish to fully enclose this land with fencing, how many meters of fencing will be needed for the parcel pictured here?

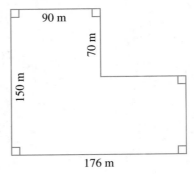

Understand the Problem: What is given? You are told certain dimensions about a plot of land.
What is unknown? You must determine the perimeter.

Devise a Plan: Use the problem-solving strategy of using variables to represent and solve this problem.

Carry Out the Plan: Let X equal the unknown vertical distance, and let Y equal the unknown horizontal distance. The perimeter P can be represented as

$$P = 150 + 176 + X + Y + 70 + 90$$

Since boundaries of this parcel meet at right angles,

$$70 + X = 150 \quad \text{and} \quad 90 + Y = 176$$

Using the commutative and associative properties, P can be represented as follows:

$$P = 150 + 176 + (X + 70) + (Y + 90)$$
$$= 150 + 176 + 150 + 176$$
$$= 652$$

The perimeter of this parcel of land is 652 meters. The problem could also have been solved by determining the individual lengths of X and Y first. Notice that

$$70 + X = 150 \qquad 90 + Y = 176$$
$$X = 80 \qquad\qquad Y = 86$$

and

$$P = 150 + 176 + 80 + 86 + 70 + 90 = 652$$

Look Back: Alternately, this problem can be solved by beginning with a rectangular parcel of land whose dimensions are 176 meters by 150 meters. We leave it to you to develop this strategy.

Determining the perimeter of a particular closed shape requires a knowledge of the characteristics of the shape itself. Recall that if a shape is labeled as regular, its sides are congruent. Therefore, if you are asked to find the perimeter of a regular pentagon each of whose sides measure 8.5 centimeters, you would merely multiply the number of sides by the length of each side ($5 \times 8.5 = 42.5$ cm).

Circumference of a Circle

circumference   The perimeter of a circle is known as its **circumference**. Because the distance around a circle obviously cannot be measured using a straight-edged ruler, it is necessary to examine some characteristics of a circle that will allow the circumference to be determined in a different way.

Early experiences with circumference involve students in measuring the distance around a circle using string, then laying off that string on a ruler. This measurement of a circle's circumference is then compared with the measurement of its diameter, resulting in a consistent ratio. Examine the following table, which might result from students measuring the diameter and circumference of various circles using string.

Circle	Diameter	Circumference	Circumference / Diameter
1	18.5 cm	60 cm	$\frac{60}{18.5} \approx 3.24$
2	12 in.	$36\frac{1}{2}$ in.	$\frac{36\frac{1}{2}}{12} \approx 3.04$
3	6 ft	19 ft	$\frac{19}{6} \approx 3.16$
4	2.2 m	7 m	$\frac{7}{2.2} \approx 3.18$

Notice that the ratio of the circumference to the diameter in each case is approximately 3. In other words, for every circle, the circumference is approximately three times the length of the diameter. You can easily illustrate this point to yourself by measuring the diameter of the rim of a coffee cup or a soda can using string. Determine how many times this string length will fit around the rim of the cup or can. You will see that it takes a little more than three diameters to fit around the rim. This will always be true, regardless of the size of the can or cup. This relationship between the diameter and the circumference, therefore, is said to be *constant*. It was formalized by Greek mathematicians as the irrational number 3.141592 . . . , which is represented by the Greek letter π.

Since the ratio of the circumference (C) to the diameter (D) is equal to π, the following relationships can be symbolized:

$$\frac{C}{D} = \pi \qquad \text{and} \qquad C = \pi D$$

Furthermore, since the diameter is equal to twice the radius (r),

$$C = \pi(2r) \qquad \text{or more commonly} \qquad C = 2\pi r$$

Investigation 11

A bicycle has two wheels whose diameters each measure 27 inches. If the cyclist travels 5 miles, how many complete revolutions of the wheel are made?

Understand the Problem: What is known? The diameter of the bicycle wheels. What is unknown? How many times the wheel revolves through a distance of 5 miles.

Devise a Plan: Use formulas and dimensional analysis to solve the problem.

Carry Out the Plan: The diameter measure can be used to determine the circumference measure of the wheel. If we find out how many of these circumference lengths are contained within 5 miles (since the distance traveled in one revolution of the wheel is equal to the circumference of the wheel), we will know how many revolutions occur in 5 miles.

$$C = \pi D$$
$$C \approx 3.14 \times 27$$
$$C \approx 84.78 \text{ in.}$$

The solution is found by dividing 5 miles by 84.78 inches. Use dimensional analysis to accomplish this task.

$$5 \text{ mi} \div 84.78 \text{ in.} =$$
$$\left(5 \text{ mi} \times \frac{5280 \text{ ft}}{1 \text{ mi}}\right) \div 84.78 \text{ in.} =$$
$$26{,}400 \text{ ft} \div 84.78 \text{ in.} =$$
$$\left(26{,}400 \text{ ft} \times \frac{12 \text{ in}}{1 \text{ ft}}\right) \div 84.78 \text{ in.} =$$
$$316{,}800 \text{ in} \div 84.78 \text{ in.} \approx 3737$$

The bicycle wheel will make approximately 3737 complete revolutions in 5 miles.

Look Back: Estimate the number of revolutions the wheel will make in 12 miles.

Area

Recall the continuous model of fractions, in which a shape was partitioned into congruent parts. One or more of these parts were shaded, resulting in a visual model of the relationship between the shaded portion(s) and the entire shape. A fraction represented a comparison between the shaded region and the shape as a whole. The measure of a **area** closed two-dimensional region is called its **area**. Therefore, the continuous model of fractions is actually an area model of fractions.

The development of area in this section will evolve through three phases: area as covering; area using upper and lower bounds; and area using formulas.

Area as Covering

Area is frequently measured using the unit square, that is, a square that measures one unit by one unit. Determining the number of unit squares required to cover a shape yields the area measurement. For example, in Figure 11.21, a rectangle that measures four units by two units can be completely covered by eight unit squares. The area of this shape is said to be eight square units, commonly symbolized as 8 units².

Figure 11.21

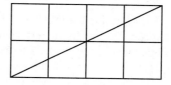

Notice that a rectangle is composed of two congruent triangles formed by the diagonal. Since the area of the entire rectangle is eight square units, it is reasonable and correct that the area of each congruent triangle is four square units.

Investigation 12

The triangular stairway landing pictured here is to be covered by carpet squares that measure 1 foot by 1 foot. What is the area of the landing in square feet, or how many carpet squares will be needed?

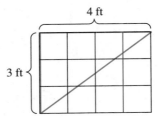

A related rectangle can be drawn using the dimensions of the legs of the right triangle. Since 12 squares will cover the related rectangle, the area of the rectangle is 12 square feet. Therefore, the area of the triangular landing must be 6 square feet, and can be covered by six carpet squares.

Area Using Upper and Lower Bounds

Finding the area by covering the shape in question with square units is not easy when the shape is irregular. Examine Figure 11.22. Here a square grid is superimposed over an irregular figure. The top and the left do not correspond to the grid lines.

Figure 11.22

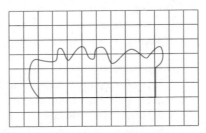

In cases like this, we can find the area by determining the upper and lower bounds. We can do this using the following three steps.

1. Determine the number of full square units that are completely contained within the shape. Do this by merely counting all the unit squares that fall completely within the boundary of the shape. There are 16 full square units enclosed in this shape (see Figure 11.23a). The area of the shape must therefore be *at least* 16 square units. We will use this number as a lower bound for the area and will symbolize this relationship as $A \geq 16$, where A is the area.

2. Determine the number of squares that are partially contained within the shape. There are 20 such squares (see Figure 11.23b). Add this number of squares to the number determined in the first step. The area of the shape must therefore be *at most* 36 square units. We will use this number as an upper bound for the area and will symbolize the relationship as $A \le 36$.

Figure 11.23

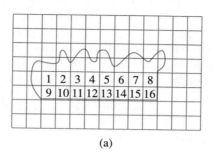

(a)

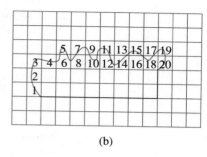

(b)

3. Let A represent the actual area of the shape. The relationship among the lower bound, actual area, and the upper bound can be symbolized as

$$16 \le A \le 36$$

One common estimate of the area is the value that falls directly between 16 and 36, or 26. Notice that using 26 square units locates the estimate at a point that is equidistant from the upper and lower boundaries. This estimate is the average, or mean, of the lower and upper boundary points.

Investigation 13

A developer owns a plot of land whose boundaries are indicated on the survey map given here. He wishes to build a boathouse on the plot.

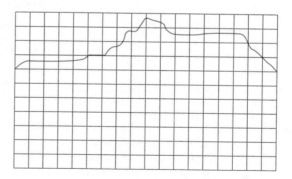

The northernmost boundary of this property is the shoreline of a lake. By superimposing a grid in which each square represents 1 square yard, determine an estimate for the area of this parcel of property.

The lower bound for the area is the number of complete squares that are fully enclosed within the interior of the figure. In the figure above, the shaded region covers 147 such squares. The lower bound is 147 square yards. The sum of the number of partially en-closed squares and the number of complete squares yields the upper bound for the area. The figure also depicts 20 partial squares. The upper bound for the area of this region is 20 + 147, or 167, square yards. An estimate for the area of this region is (147 + 167) ÷ 2, or 157, square yards.

acre   In the English standard system, common units of land measure are the acre and the square mile. An **acre** is equivalent to 4840 square yards. The estimated area of the lake-front property could be reported in acres by using the following keystroke sequence:

$$\boxed{\text{AC}} \quad 157 \quad \boxed{\div} \quad 4840 \quad \boxed{=} \qquad \boxed{.03243801}$$

Therefore, the approximate area of the lakefront property is .03 acre.

The following table will help you make connections among the various units of area measurement:

Unit	Equivalent in Square Feet
Square yard	9 square feet (ft²)
Acre	43,560 ft²

For comparison purposes, a football field measures 100 yards by $53\frac{1}{3}$ yards. This is equivalent to 300 feet by 160 feet, or 48,000 square feet. You can see that a football field is somewhat larger than an acre.

Although the acre is a common unit of measure, the unit of measurement used to form the acre is not. An acre is equivalent to 160 square rods. A rod is a unit of linear measure that is no longer used. It is equivalent to 16.5 feet (5.5 yards). The following keystroke sequence uses the rod measurement to determine the square foot equivalence of an acre.

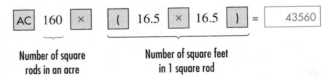

Number of square rods in an acre   Number of square feet in 1 square rod

The display of 43,560 square feet agrees with the value listed in the table.

are   Area measurement in the metric system is commonly reported in square centime-ters (cm²), square meters (m²), and square kilometers (km²). A square that is 10 meters on a side, with an area of 100 square meters, is called an **are** (pronounced "air"). An **hectare**   area containing 100 ares is called a **hectare** (ha). A hectare can also be viewed as the equivalent of 1 square hectometer (hm). The following keystroke sequence can be used to verify this equivalence:

1 are   100 ares   1 ha in m²

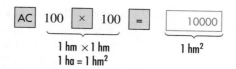

1 hm ×1 hm
1 ha = 1 hm²   1 hm²

Area Using Formulas

Determining the area of shapes through covering and using grids is limited to situations in which counting squares or parts of squares is possible. Although beginning a study of area in this concrete fashion is desirable, it is necessary to generalize from these specific situations to situations involving many varied shapes. The following treatment of area develops each subsequent formula from previous formulas. You will soon see that memorizing area formulas is unnecessary. All the formulas for finding the area of polygons can be generated from a basic understanding of area.

Area of a Rectangle.   We will begin with the area of a rectangle, as shown in Figure 11.24.

Figure 11.24

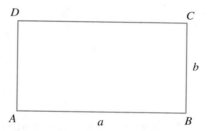

The area of rectangle *ABCD* is the number of square units that cover and are fully contained within the interior of the rectangle. By dividing the sides of the rectangle into unit lengths, it can be seen that the area is equal to the product of the length and the width. Therefore, the following generalization can be made.

Formula: **Area of a Rectangle.**   Given: rectangle *ABCD* with $AB = a$ and $BC = b$. The area of *ABCD* is equal to $a \cdot b$.

Because a square is a rectangle whose length and width are congruent, the area of a square can be symbolized as $a \cdot a$, or a^2, where a is the length of a side (see Figure 11.25).

Figure 11.25

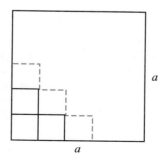

Area of a Triangle. The area of a triangle bears a special relationship to the area of a related rectangle. Recall from the covering model of area that the area of a right triangle is equivalent to half the area of its related rectangle. This relationship will be central to the development of area in each of the following four types of triangles.

right triangle **1. Right triangle.** As shown in the covering model, a rectangle can easily be extended from a right triangle. Notice in Figure 11.26 that the hypotenuse of the right triangle becomes the diagonal of the related rectangle. The dimensions of the rectangle are dictated by the lengths of the legs of the right triangle. Therefore, the area of the rectangle in Figure 11.26 is $a \cdot b$. The area of the right triangle ABC is equal to $\frac{1}{2}(a \cdot b)$. This can be expressed as one-half the product of the base of the right triangle and the height of the right triangle.

Figure 11.26

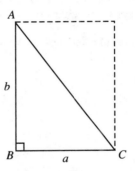

isosceles triangle **2. Isosceles triangle.** Examine Figure 11.27. Triangle ABC is an isosceles triangle with $\overline{BD} \perp \overline{AC}$. Because the sides of this triangle are not perpendicular to one another, we will use line segment $\overline{BD}$ to build two related rectangles. For ease of notation, let $\overline{BD} = h$. Both $\overline{AD}$ and $\overline{DC}$ will equal x since the altitude in an isosceles triangle is a perpendicular bisector of the base. The two new rectangles formed are $AEBD$ and $DBFC$. The area of $AEBD$ is equal to $h \cdot x$. Therefore, the area of $\triangle ABD = \frac{1}{2}(h \cdot x)$. The area of $DBFC$ is equal to $h \cdot x$. Consequently, the area of $\triangle CBD = \frac{1}{2}(h \cdot x)$. It follows that the area of the isosceles triangle ABC is the sum of the areas of $\triangle ABD$ and $\triangle CBD$.

$$\text{Area of } \triangle ABC = \text{Area of } \triangle ABD + \text{Area of } \triangle CBD$$
$$= \tfrac{1}{2}(h \cdot x) + \tfrac{1}{2}(h \cdot x)$$
$$= (h \cdot x)$$

Notice that if $\overline{AC}$ is represented as b, where $b = 2x$, it therefore follows that $x = \frac{1}{2}b$. Substituting this into the expression for the area of $\triangle ABC$ and applying the commutative property of multiplication yields $\frac{1}{2}(b \cdot h)$. The area of isosceles triangle ABC is equal to one-half of the product of the length of its altitude and the length of its base.

Figure 11.27

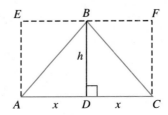

equilateral triangle   **3. Equilateral triangle.**   The area of an equilateral triangle whose side measures s follows the same development as the area of the isosceles triangle, since by definition, an equilateral triangle is an isosceles triangle. The development of the formula for the area of an equilateral triangle is left to you in the problems that follow this section.

Formula: **Area of an Equilateral Triangle.**   Given equilateral triangle ABC with side s. The area of ABC is

$$\frac{\sqrt{3}}{4}s^2$$

(See Figure 11.28.)

Figure 11.28

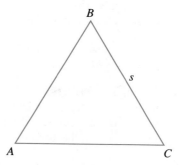

scalene triangle   **4. Scalene triangle.**   Examine $\triangle ABC$ in Figure 11.29. Extend side $\overline{AC}$ and construct the altitude $\overline{BD}$. Let $\overline{DA} = x$, $\overline{AC} = y$, and $\overline{BD} = h$, as shown in Figure 11.29a.

Figure 11.29

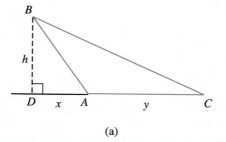

(a)

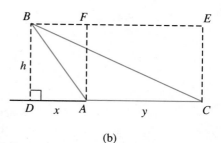

(b)

Using $\overline{BD}$ and $\overline{DC}$, build rectangle $DBEC$, as shown in Figure 11.29b. Rectangle $DBEC$ is partitioned into three regions, the sum of whose areas will yield the area of the rectangle as stated here:

$$\text{Area of } DBEC = \text{Area of } \triangle DBA + \text{Area of } \triangle ABC + \text{Area of } \triangle BEC$$

The area of rectangle $DBEC$ is equal to $h(x + y)$. The area of $\triangle BEC$ is equal to one-half the area of rectangle $DBEC$, or $\frac{1}{2}h(x + y)$. The area of $\triangle DBA$ is equal to one-half the area of rectangle $BDAF$, or $\frac{1}{2}h \cdot x$. Substituting, we get

Area of $DBEC$ = Area of $\triangle DBA$ + Area of $\triangle ABC$ + Area of $\triangle BEC$

$$h(x + y) = \tfrac{1}{2}h \cdot x + \text{Area of } \triangle ABC + \tfrac{1}{2}h(x + y)$$

$$h(x + y) - \tfrac{1}{2}h(x + y) - \tfrac{1}{2}h \cdot x = \text{Area of } \triangle ABC$$

$$\tfrac{1}{2}h(x + y) - \tfrac{1}{2}h \cdot x = \text{Area of } \triangle ABC$$

$$\tfrac{1}{2}hx + \tfrac{1}{2}hy - \tfrac{1}{2}hx = \text{Area of } \triangle ABC$$

$$\tfrac{1}{2}hy = \text{Area of } \triangle ABC$$

The area of the scalene triangle ABC is equal to one half the product of the length of its base and the length of its altitude.

Notice the similarities in each of the preceding examples. In each case, the area of the triangle was found to be one-half of the product of the length of its base and its height. Therefore, the following generalization can be made:

Formula: **Area of a Triangle.** Given: $\triangle ABC$ with $\overline{BD} \perp \overline{AC}$, $\overline{BD} = h$ and $\overline{AC} = b$. The area of $\triangle ABC = \tfrac{1}{2}bh$.

Area of a Parallelogram. The area of a parallelogram is generalized from the area formulas of a rectangle and a triangle as follows. In Figure 11.30a, you are given parallelogram $ABCD$ with height $\overline{CE} = h$, and $\overline{AD} = b$. The area of $\triangle ACD$ is equal to $\tfrac{1}{2}bh$. In Figure 11.30b, the altitude of $\triangle ABC$ is drawn to the extension of $\overline{BC}$.

Figure 11.30

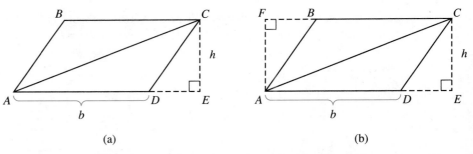

(a)   (b)

Notice that both $\overline{AF}$ and $\overline{CE}$ are transversals that are perpendicular to the same pair of parallel line segments. Therefore, $\overline{AF} = \overline{CE} = h$. By the definition of a parallelogram, opposite sides are congruent. Consequently, $\overline{BC} = \overline{AD} = b$. The area of $\triangle ABC = \tfrac{1}{2}bh$. Finally, the area of the parallelogram can be stated as

$$\text{Area of } ABCD = \text{Area of } \triangle ABC + \text{Area of } \triangle ADC$$

$$= \tfrac{1}{2}bh + \tfrac{1}{2}bh$$

$$= bh$$

The area of parallelogram $ABCD$ is equal to the product of the length of its base and its height.

Formula: **Area of a parallelogram.** Given: parallelogram $ABCD$. Area of $ABCD = bh$.

Area of a Trapezoid.   The area of a trapezoid is also generalized from the area of a triangle, since every trapezoid can be partitioned into two triangles as shown in Figure 11.31.

Figure 11.31

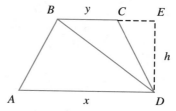

Here, trapezoid *ABCD* is partitioned into triangles *ABD* and *BCD*. Both triangles have height *h*. The area of the trapezoid can be stated as

$$\text{Area of } ABCD = \text{Area of } \triangle ABD + \text{Area of } \triangle BCD$$
$$= \tfrac{1}{2}hx + \tfrac{1}{2}hy$$
$$= \tfrac{1}{2}h(x + y)$$

The area of a trapezoid is equal to one-half the product of the height and the sum of the lengths of its two parallel sides. These parallel sides in a trapezoid are commonly called its bases.

Formula: **Area of a Trapezoid.**   Given: trapezoid *ABCD* with *h* as its height and *x* and *y* as its bases. The area of trapezoid $ABCD = \tfrac{1}{2}h(x + y)$.

Investigation 14

You are given regular hexagon *ABCDEF*, each of whose sides measure *s* units. Explain three different ways that the hexagon can be partitioned. Use shapes for which you already know the area formula in order to explain the process for finding the area of this hexagon.

1.

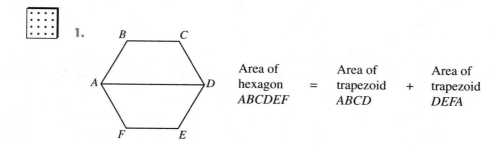

2.

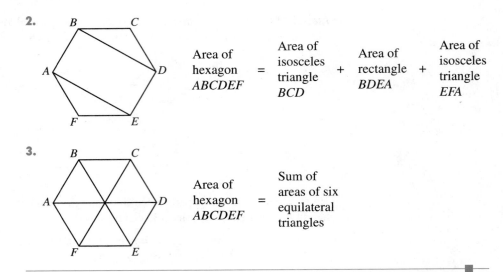

$$\begin{array}{c}\text{Area of} \\ \text{hexagon} \\ ABCDEF\end{array} = \begin{array}{c}\text{Area of} \\ \text{isosceles} \\ \text{triangle} \\ BCD\end{array} + \begin{array}{c}\text{Area of} \\ \text{rectangle} \\ BDEA\end{array} + \begin{array}{c}\text{Area of} \\ \text{isosceles} \\ \text{triangle} \\ EFA\end{array}$$

3.

$$\begin{array}{c}\text{Area of} \\ \text{hexagon} \\ ABCDEF\end{array} = \begin{array}{c}\text{Sum of} \\ \text{areas of six} \\ \text{equilateral} \\ \text{triangles}\end{array}$$

Investigation 15

Determine the area of the shaded square in the figure below. Points B, D, F, and H are the midpoints of their respective sides. Figure $ACEG$ is a square whose side measures 12 centimeters.

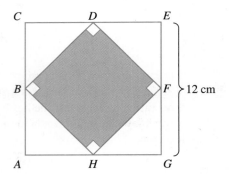

Understand the Problem: You are given a shaded region within a figure and information about the points that make up the region. You are asked to determine the area of the shaded region.

Devise a Plan: Although the area of the shaded region can be determined in many different ways, here we will change our point of view and construct a slightly different diagram.

Carry Out the Plan: Draw diagonals $\overline{BF}$ and $\overline{DH}$. These diagonals partition $ACEG$ into four congruent squares. Direct your attention to one of these squares.

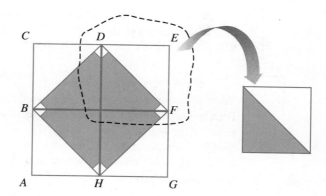

Notice that half of this square is shaded. Therefore, half the area of the square will contribute to the total area of the shaded region. This relationship is true for each of the four smaller squares formed by diagonals $\overline{AF}$ and $\overline{HD}$. Therefore, the area of the shaded region is half the area of square $ACEG$, or 72 square units.

Look Back: The area could also have been attained in the following manner. Partition the square $ACEG$ into four congruent triangles and one square. The area of one triangle is equal to $\frac{1}{2}(6 \cdot 6)$, or 18, square units. The area of four of these triangles is equal to $18 \cdot 4$, or 72, square units. The area of square $ACEG$ is equal to 12^2, or 144, square units. Therefore, the area of the shaded region can now be determined in the following manner.

Area of square $ACEG$ = Area of square $BDFH$ + Area of four congruent right triangles

144 square units = Area of square $BDFH$ + 72 square units

72 square units = Area of square $BDFH$

Notice that the area of the shaded region is half the area of the square $ACEG$.

Investigation 16

You have already been introduced to the Pythagorean theorem. This theorem expresses the special relationship among the sides of a right triangle as follows: In right triangle ABC with $m\angle C = 90°$, the sides opposite the angles are labeled a, b, and c, respectively, as illustrated here.

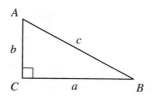

In every right triangle, the square of the length of the hypotenuse is equal to the sum of the squares of the lengths of the other two sides. Symbolically, this is written as $a^2 + b^2 = c^2$. Verify the validity of the Pythagorean theorem.

The Pythagorean theorem can be proved and visualized in a number of different ways. Perhaps the simplest way to do this is to view a^2, b^2, and c^2 as the area of squares whose sides are a, b, and c, respectively. The statement of the Pythagorean theorem would then be interpreted as the area of a square whose side is a plus the area of a square whose side is b is equal to the area of a square whose side is c. This can be seen in the following illustration.

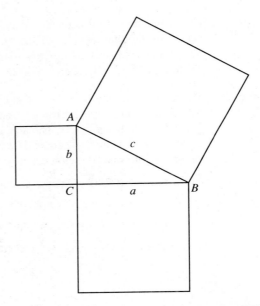

pythagorean triples Sides of squares that are related in this way are called **Pythagorean triples**, since they always form a right triangle. Some examples are 3, 4, and 5 ($5^2 = 3^2 + 4^2$); 5, 12, and 13 ($13^2 = 5^2 + 12^2$); and 9, 40, and 41 ($41^2 = 40^2 + 9^2$).

An elegant proof of the Pythagorean theorem consists of partitioning a square into four congruent right triangles and a smaller square. The lengths of the sides of the triangles are indicated in the following illustration.

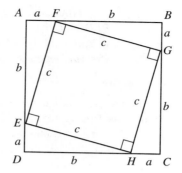

The configuration of shapes in this illustration should not be new to you. A similar drawing was used in Investigation 15 to determine the area of a shaded square that was enclosed within a larger square.

$$\text{Area of square } ABCD = 4 \cdot (\text{Area of one right triangle}) + \text{Area } EFGH$$
$$= 4(\tfrac{1}{2}ab) + c^2$$
$$= 2ab + c^2$$

Each side of square $ABCD$ measures $(a + b)$ in length. Therefore, another representation of the area of square $ABCD$ is $(a + b)^2$.

$$\text{Area of square } ABCD = (a + b)^2$$
$$= (a + b)(a + b)$$
$$= a^2 + ab + ba + b^2$$
$$= a^2 + ab + ab + b^2$$
$$= a^2 + 2ab + b^2$$

Since the area of square $ABCD$ has been symbolized in two different ways, both of these expressions must be equivalent. We can therefore set them equal to each other as follows:

$$2ab + c^2 = a^2 + 2ab + b^2$$
$$c^2 = a^2 + b^2$$

This last statement is itself the statement of the Pythagorean theorem for a triangle whose hypotenuse is c and whose legs are a and b.

■

Although the recognition of this relationship is attributed to Pythagoras (c. 585–500 B.C.), a Babylonian tablet that dates from 1900–1600 B.C. contains a list of numbers that belong to sets of Pythagorean triples. This leads us to believe that the Babylonians had some knowledge of this special relationship among numbers. For example, the numbers 2291 and 3541 are found adjacent to each other in two separate columns on the tablet. Upon close examination, experts determined that

$$(3541)^2 - (2291)^2 = (2700)^2$$

Clearly, 2291, 2700, and 3541 make up a Pythagorean triple. This ancient tablet, now known as *PLIMPTON 322*, is a part of the G. Plimpton collection at Columbia University in New York City. [For further information see Howard Eves, *An Introduction to the History of Mathematics*, 6th ed. (Philadelphia: Saunders, 1990).]

Area of a Circle

Finding the area of a circle is challenging. The process will be easier for you to understand if we first approximate the area using an upper bound and a lower bound and then develop the area formula for a circle.

Examine the following circle, whose radius is 4 centimeters (Figure 11.32a).

Figure 11.32

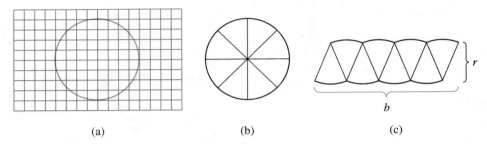

(a) (b) (c)

The lower bound for the area is 32 cm². The upper bound for the area is 60 cm². Recall that a good estimate for the area is the average of the lower bound and upper bound, that is, (32 + 60) ÷ 2, or 46 cm².

In order to develop a formula for the area of a circle, it is helpful to partition the circle into an even number of sectors. In Figure 11.32b, the circle with a radius of 4 centimeters has been partitioned into eight congruent sectors. Separate each of the sectors and arrange them as shown in Figure 11.32c. Notice that the figure formed looks somewhat like a parallelogram. If the circle were to be partitioned into a great number of sectors, the arcs that form the top and bottom of the figure would be much less pronounced. The greater the number of sectors, the straighter the top and bottom of the figure will appear, and the closer the figure will be to a parallelogram.

Let the base of the related parallelogram be represented by b. The height of the parallelogram is equal to the radius r of the circle, as shown in Figure 11.32c. The sum of the lengths of the arcs of the sectors is equal to the circumference of the circle. Therefore, the sum of the lengths of the base and the side opposite the base in the related parallelogram will approximate the circumference of the circle. This can be symbolized as

$$C = 2b$$

and leads us to the fact that $b = \frac{C}{2}$. Using the knowledge that $C = 2\pi r$, it follows that $b = \frac{2\pi r}{2}$, or πr.

The area of the related parallelogram is equal to the product of the lengths of the base and height. Consequently,

$$A = bh$$
$$A = (\pi r)r = \pi r^2$$

The area of the related parallelogram is πr^2 and is equal to the area of the circle. Therefore, the area of the circle whose radius is 4 centimeters is $\pi(4^2)$, or approximately 50.24 cm² (3.14 × 16). Notice that the lower bound/upper bound estimate of 46 cm² was reasonable when compared with the actual area.

Finding Area Using a Geoboard

A geoboard, shown in Figure 11.33, is a manipulative device often found in elementary school classrooms.

Figure 11.33

Pegs are placed to form a grid, so that students can use rubber bands to make a variety of shapes. Examine the four shapes in Figure 11.34 that have been created on a geoboard.

Figure 11.34

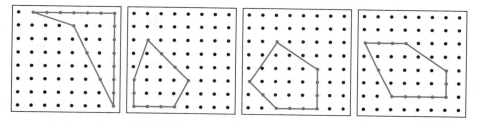

Notice that each of the pegs (henceforth called points) falls into one of three categories: a point is either in the interior of the shape, on the boundary of the shape, or in the exterior of the shape. An interesting relationship exists among the area, interior points, and boundary points.

Investigation 17

Determine the area of each figure shown in Figure 11.34 on page 536. Count the number of boundary points and interior points for each figure. Establish a relationship among the area, boundary points, and interior points.

To find the area of each irregular shape, we will use the notion that the area of a right triangle is half the area of some related rectangle. First, partition the figure into rectangular and triangular regions. By superimposing rectangles over the geoboard figure, the area of the triangular regions can be determined. This can be done most simply by copying these shapes onto the laminated card that accompanies this text.

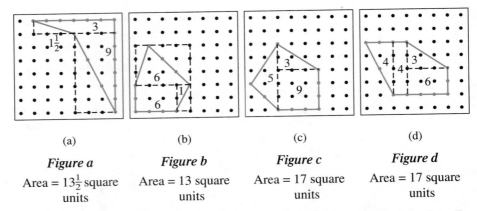

| (a) | (b) | (c) | (d) |

Figure a
Area = $13\frac{1}{2}$ square units

Figure b
Area = 13 square units

Figure c
Area = 17 square units

Figure d
Area = 17 square units

When trying to establish a pattern, a table might be helpful in organizing the data. Examine the following table, which lists the area, number of boundary points, and number of interior points for each of the figures.

Figure	Area	Boundary Points	Interior Points
a	$13\frac{1}{2}$	17	6
b	13	10	9
c	17	10	13
d	17	12	12

In 1899, Georg Pick, a German mathematician, discovered that the area of a polygon could be determined by knowing the number of boundary points and interior points when the polygon was drawn on a grid. Stop here. Examine the data. Can you see the relationship that Pick discovered?

It is significant in Figure (a) that the area is not a whole number and that the number of boundary points in this figure is odd. This might cause you to speculate that Pick's rule involves dividing the number of boundary points by 2. Let's pursue this line of reasoning to see what develops.

Figure	Area	Boundary Points	Boundary Points ÷ 2	Interior Points
a	$13\frac{1}{2}$	17	$8\frac{1}{2}$	6
b	13	10	5	9
c	17	10	5	13
d	17	12	6	12

How can you relate half the number of boundary points, the number of interior points, and the area of each figure? You may have noticed that in each case the sum of half the number of boundary points and the number of interior points is 1 greater than the area. It appears that the relationship discovered by Pick is that the area of a polygon on a grid is equal to 1 less than the sum of half the number of boundary points and the number of interior points. This can be symbolized by letting B equal the number of boundary points, I equal the number of interior points, and A equal the area, as follows:

$$A = \frac{B}{2} + I - 1$$

Verify this by constructing any polygon on a geoboard, graph paper, or the laminated card, determining the area by superimposing rectangles and checking this area using Pick's rule.

Surface Area

surface area

It is sometimes necessary to determine the area that covers a three-dimensional solid. If, for example, a cube is to be covered in gold leaf to be used as jewelry, the surface area of the cube would need to be determined. The **surface area** of a three-dimensional figure is the sum of the areas of its faces.

right prism

right regular pyramid

To determine the surface area of a prism and a pyramid, we must find the polygons that form the surfaces of these solids. For the purposes of this section, we will examine only the surface area of right prisms and right regular pyramids. A **right prism** is a prism whose lateral faces are all rectangles. A **right regular pyramid** is a pyramid whose lateral faces are all isosceles triangles. Henceforth, we will refer to these solids as prisms and pyramids. Figure 11.35 depicts some polyhedra and details the shapes of the polygons that make up the surfaces of the solids.

Figure 11.35

Rectangular Prism
Three pairs of
congruent rectangles

Triangular Prism
Three congruent rectangles;
two congruent triangles

Square Pyramid
Four congruent isosceles triangles;
one square

The following two generalizations can be made about the surface areas of right prisms and right regular pyramids.

Formula: **Surface Area of a Right Prism.**   The surface area S of a prism with height h, and whose base has n edges each of length b, and an area A is

$$S = 2A + n(bh)$$

Formula: **Surface Area of a Right Regular Pyramid.**   The surface area S of a pyramid whose base has n edges each of length b, and an area of A, and whose lateral faces are isosceles triangles with altitude a (known as the slant height) is

$$S = A + n(\tfrac{1}{2}ba)$$

The Great Pyramid of Cheops at Gizeh in Egypt was said to have been built around 2900 B.C. It is believed that its height was originally 482 feet and its base was a square whose sides each measured 768 feet. Suppose that the exposed surfaces of the pyramid were flat. What was the original exposed surface area of the Great Pyramid?

Understand the Problem: You are given information about the dimensions of a pyramid and asked to determine its surface area.

Devise a Plan: It is important to determine exactly what is being asked here. Upon rereading the question, you should see that the phrase "exposed surface area" is critical to the solution of this problem. By knowing the nature of a right square pyramid, you should realize that the square base is not exposed and therefore should not be included in the surface area calculations. Therefore, the original surface area is equal to the sum of the areas of the four isosceles triangles that are the lateral faces of the pyramid. We will now draw a sketch and use formulas to solve the problem.

Carry Out the Plan: A sketch of the pyramid is helpful here:

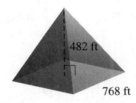

The perpendicular distance from the apex of the pyramid to the base was 482 feet, and the length of a side of the base was 768 feet. What information is missing?

To find the area of an individual isosceles triangle that makes up one of the exposed faces, it is necessary to know the altitude of that triangle. This altitude is called the **slant height** of a pyramid. The illustration below depicts a line segment $\overline{AB}$ that represents the height of the pyramid. This line segment is perpendicular to $\overline{BC}$, whose length is half that of the side of the square.

slant height

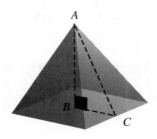

Notice that the slant height, $\overline{AC}$, is the hypotenuse of $\triangle ABC$ and can be determined by using the Pythagorean theorem as follows. Let c represent the slant height. It follows that

$$c^2 = 482^2 + 384^2$$
$$c = \sqrt{(482^2 + 384^2)}$$
$$c = \sqrt{(232{,}324 + 147{,}456)}$$
$$c = \sqrt{379{,}780}$$
$$c \approx 616.26 \text{ ft}$$

The slant height of the pyramid is about 616 feet. To find the area of one triangular face, use the formula for the area of a triangle:

$$A = \tfrac{1}{2}(768)(616) = 236{,}544 \text{ ft}^2$$

Since there were four such congruent triangles, the total exposed surface area was $4 \times 236{,}544$, or 946,176, square feet.

Look Back: To get a feel for the size of the exposed region, convert the amount into acres. There are approximately 44,000 square feet in one acre. Using 950,000 square feet as an approximation for the exposed surface area, we find that about 22 acres of stone were exposed on the Great Pyramid ($950{,}000 \div 44{,}000$).

If the four surfaces were rearranged in the fashion of the following figure, the area of the parallelogram would be approximately $600 \times (750 + 750)$, or 900,000, square feet. This verifies our solution.

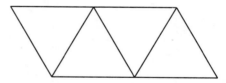

We now turn our attention to the surface areas of nonpolyhedral shapes. In Chapter 10, you were introduced to a cylinder and a cone. Here, we will restrict our work to a special type of cylinder and cone. A **right circular cylinder** is a cylinder whose bases are congruent circles. In addition, if a line segment is drawn that connects the centers of each of the circular bases, it is perpendicular to the plane of each base. A **right circular cone** is a cone in which the base is a circle. In addition, if a line segment is drawn from the apex to the center of the circular base, it is perpendicular to the plane of the base. (See Figure 11.36 on page 540.)

right circular cylinder

right circular cone

Figure 11.36

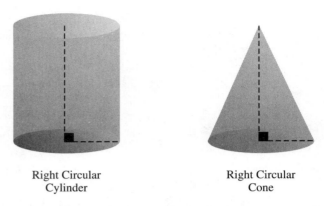

Right Circular
Cylinder

Right Circular
Cone

Figure 11.37 a depicts a right circular cylinder (henceforth called a cylinder) whose height is h and whose radius of its circular base is r. It is easy to see that the area of two circles are part of the total surface area of the cylinder.

Figure 11.37

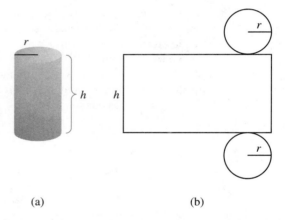

(a)   (b)

But what is the area of the face that forms the curved surface of the cylinder? A good problem-solving technique is to change your point of view. Rather than viewing the cylinder in its three-dimensional form, "open it up" and examine each of the two-dimensional surfaces that form the cylinder. Figure 11.37b depicts a cylinder that has been "opened" to reveal its component parts. Notice that the surface of a cylinder can be partitioned into three shapes: two congruent circles and a rectangle. The width of the rectangle is equal to the height of the cylinder. The length of the rectangle is equal to the circumference of the circular base, namely, $2\pi r$. Therefore, the following generalization can be made about the surface area of a cylinder.

Formula: **Surface Area of a Right Circular Cylinder.** The surface area of S of a right circular cylinder whose base has a radius r and whose height is h is

$$S = 2(\pi r^2) + 2\pi rh$$

The right circular cone can also be "opened up" as shown in Figure 11.38.

Figure 11.38

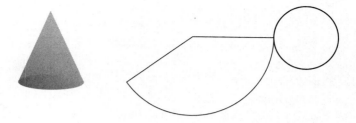

Unfortunately, the figure formed by the curved face of the cone is not one of the shapes we have worked with up to this point. Recall that when we were developing the formula for the area of the circle, we partitioned the circle into an even number of sectors and then formed a figure that resembled a parallelogram. We will use this technique again to develop the formula for the surface area of a cone.

In Figure 11.39a, the curved surface of the cone has been partitioned into an even number of sectors.

Figure 11.39

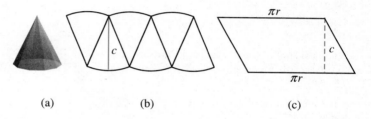

(a)   (b)   (c)

The cone is then opened, and the sectors are rearranged to form the parallelogramlike figure in Figure 11.39b. As was true with the partitioning of the circle, the more the cone is partitioned and rearranged, the more the figure formed will resemble a parallelogram. Notice that the sum of the lengths of the top and bottom edges of the parallelogram must be equal to the circumference of the circular base of the cone, that is, $2\pi r$. The length of the parallelogram is therefore equal to πr, and the height of the parallelogram is the slant height, c, of the cone. The area of the parallelogram is therefore equal to πrc. The sum of the areas of the parallelogram and the circle will yield the surface area of the cone. This leads to the following generalization.

Formula: **Surface Area of a Right Circular Cone.**   The surface area S of a right circular cone whose base has a radius of r and whose slant height of c is

$$S = \pi r^2 + \pi rc$$

Although you might now expect the surface area of a sphere to be addressed, we will wait until Section 11.3 to discuss that topic. At that point, the formula for the surface area of a sphere will be developed from the formula for the volume of a sphere.

Assessments for Section 11.2

1. Determine the perimeter of each of the following shapes.
   (a) A square whose side is 3.5 cm
   (b) An equilateral triangle whose side is $7\frac{3}{4}$ in.
   (c) A regular pentagon whose side is 5.25 cm
   (d) A right triangle with legs measuring 6 in. and 8 in.
   (e) A right triangle with a leg of 40 in. and a hypotenuse of 50 in.

2. Determine the measurement of each side of the following regular polygons.
   (a) A hexagon with a perimeter of 28.5 cm
   (b) A square with a perimeter of 113.2 cm
   (c) A pentagon with a perimeter of $4\frac{3}{8}$ in.
   (d) A triangle with a perimeter of 26 m
   (e) An octagon with a perimeter of 100 cm

3. An equilateral triangle has a perimeter of 24 ft. What is the length of its altitude?

4. A square has a side of 7.5 cm. What is the measure of the side of a square whose perimeter is twice that of this square?

5. A square has a perimeter of 400 in. What is the length of one of its diagonals?

6. A regular pentagon and a regular hexagon both have sides of 12 cm. If one side of the pentagon is coincident with one side of the hexagon, what is the perimeter of the resulting shape?

7. The area of a square is 169 cm². What is its perimeter?

8. The perimeter of a square is 68 ft. What is its area?

9. (a) If the perimeter of a square is doubled, what is the effect on the area of the square?
   (b) If the perimeter of a square is tripled, what is the effect on the area of the square?
   (c) Make a generalization about the effect on the area of a square when the perimeter is multiplied by a whole number n.

10. (a) A square has a side that measures 3 cm. Another square has a side that measures 6 cm. What is the ratio of their areas?
    (b) The sides of two squares are in the ratio of 1 to 4. What is the ratio of their areas?
    (c) The perimeter of one square is 8 m. The perimeter of a second square is 40 m. What is the ratio of their areas?

   (d) Make a generalization about the ratio of the area of two squares whose sides are in the ratio of $1 : r$.

11. In each of the following diagrams, estimate the area by determining a lower bound and an upper bound for the area.

(a) 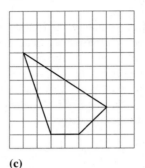   (b)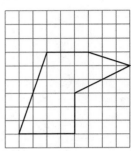

(c) 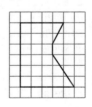   (d)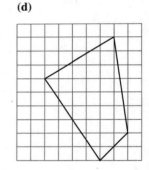

12. Find the area of each closed figure.

(a) 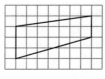   (b)

(c) 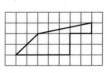   (d)   (e)

13. Use Pick's rule to determine the area of each of the following polygons.

(a) (b)

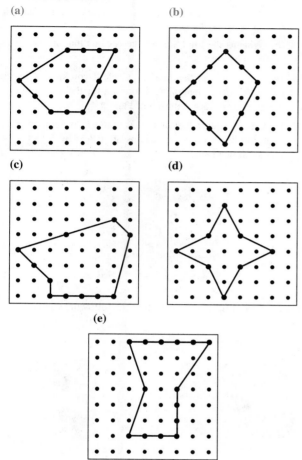

(c) (d)

(e)

14. The area of a polygon is seven square units. There are three grid points in its interior. How many grid points lie on its boundary? Sketch a possible figure.

15. The area of a polygon is six square units. There are eight grid points on its boundary. How many grid points lie in its interior? Sketch a possible figure.

16. You are given equilateral triangle *ABC*. Use the same line of reasoning that was developed for the justification of the area formulas for the isosceles, right, and scalene triangles to justify the area formula for equilateral triangle *ABC*.

17. Six equilateral triangles, each of whose sides are 10 cm, are joined to form a regular hexagon.

    (a) What is the area of the hexagon?

    (b) Generalize a formula for the area of a regular hexagon with side *s*.

18. A trapezoid is formed by joining the edges of a square and a right triangle. The perimeter of the square is 48 in. The hypotenuse of the right triangle is 13 in. What is the area of the trapezoid?

19. Illustrate and explain three ways to determine the area of a regular pentagon by partition.

20. Determine the area of the shaded region in each of the following figures.

(a) (b)

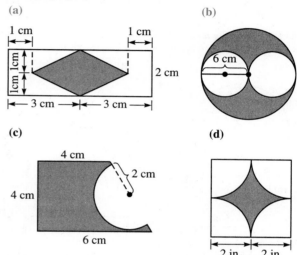

(c) (d)

21. The minute hand on a clock is 8 cm long. The second hand is 9 cm. The hour hand is 5 cm. How far does the tip of each hand travel in 1 hour?

22. The dimensions of a dirt racetrack are shown in the following diagram. The interior portion of the track is covered with grass.

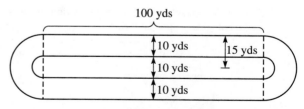

    (a) What is the distance around the dirt track along its outer edge?

    (b) What is the distance around the dirt track along its inner edge?

    (c) What is area of the dirt track itself, to the nearest integer?

23. (a) A gardener has 60 ft of fencing. She wishes to use all of the fence to enclose a rectangular plot with the largest area possible. What would be the dimensions of her rectangular garden?

(b) Suppose that the gardener in part (a) wishes to use a stone wall as a boundary for one side of her rectangular plot. What would be the dimensions of her garden that result in a maximum enclosed area if she once again wishes to use all of the fencing?

(c) Suppose she wishes to use all of the fencing to enclose a circular garden. What would be the area of this garden to the nearest integer?

24. Determine the area and the perimeter or circumference of each of the following shapes to the nearest integer.

(a) **(b)**

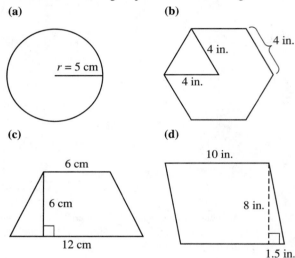

(c) **(d)**

25. What are the dimensions of a rectangular prism whose surface area measures 400 in². Is this answer unique? Explain your reasoning.

26. Four-foot-wide gravel paths intersect within a grass-covered rectangular region as shown here.

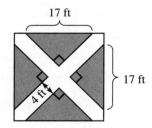

What is the total area covered by grass?

27. A sheet of paper measures $8\frac{1}{2}$ in. by 11 in. The page is covered with circles each of whose diameter measures $\frac{1}{2}$ in.

(a) What is the largest number of circles of this size that could fit on the page?

(b) What is the total area of the regions that are not covered by circles?

28. How can you find the area of a circle if you know only its circumference? Generalize a formula for the area of a circle in terms of its circumference and π.

29. How many square feet of wood are needed to construct an open-top box whose dimensions are 6 feet by 6 feet by 4 feet as shown here?

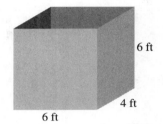

30. Find the surface area of each of the following solids.

(a) **(b)**

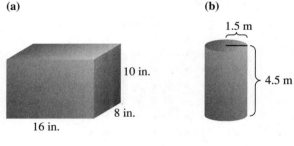

(c)

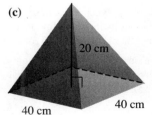

31. You are given a square pyramid whose base has an edge that is 10 cm long. A "slice" is made in the pyramid parallel to the square base. Two solids result: a smaller square pyramid and a frustum (the lower part of the pyramid that is formed by cutting off the top by a plane parallel to the base), as shown on page 545.

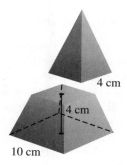

4 cm

4 cm

10 cm

The edge of the square that results from the slice is 4 cm. The perpendicular distance between the two square faces of the frustum is 4 cm. Determine the surface area of the frustum.

32. A room measures 16 ft by 18 ft, with a floor-to-ceiling distance of 9 ft. The room has three rectangular windows, each measuring 3 ft by 4 ft. The doorway is 3 ft wide and 8 ft tall. The ceiling and the exposed wall space are to be painted white. It will take two coats of paint to complete the job. If one can of paint has a listed coverage of 400 ft^2, how many cans of paint are needed for this job?

33. A cylinder and a cone are both the same height and have congruent bases. What is the ratio of their surface areas in terms of the radius and the height?

34. Paper is stored in rolls at a paper mill. Each roll is 5 m high and has a radius of 1 m. The hole at the center of the roll has a radius of .1 m, as illustrated below.

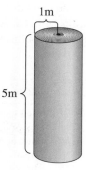

1m

5m

(a) What is the exposed area of the paper portion of the roll (including the paper at both ends)?

(b) A quantity of paper is removed from the roll, which results in a roll that has a diameter that is 75% that of the

original roll. What is the percent of decrease in the amount of exposed paper? (Express your answer to the nearest tenth of a percent.)

35. A cone has a height of .5 m and a base radius of .5 m. A slice is made through the cone that is perpendicular to the plane of the base and passes through the apex. What is the surface area of one of the resulting solids?

In Other Words

36. What does π visually represent in any circle?

37. Is is possible for two figures to have the same area but not the same shape? Support your conclusion with an example.

38. Explain the difference between area and surface area.

39. You are given the following illustration:

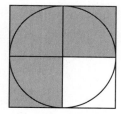

Explain how the shaded region illustrates the approximate area formula of a circle.

40. Describe two possible methods for determining the number of circles of diameter 3 in. that can be cut from a larger circle of diameter 30 in. Which method is preferable? Why?

Cooperative Activity

41. Groups of two

Individual Accountability: Each group member is to construct a circle whose radius is 4 cm and a square whose side is 7 cm. The first group member is to cut the circle into pieces that will totally cover the interior of the square. The second group member is to cut the square into pieces that will totally cover the interior of the circle.

Group Goal: It should be clear to the members of the pair that the area of a circle with radius 4 cm is approximately equal to the area of a square with a side of 7 cm. The group goal is to find the dimensions of another circle and square whose areas approximate one another.

11.3 Measuring Weight, Volume, and Temperature

Understanding the differences between weight and volume is important for future elementary school teachers. Many children have difficulty distinguishing between the two concepts. We will begin this section by examining units of weight and volume in both the metric and English standard systems of measurement. With these units well defined, we will develop the rules for assigning a numerical value to the volume of three-dimensional solids.

Weight

weight

mass

The attribute of **weight** is a measurement of the force of gravity on a particular object. Although the material that composes a particular object, its **mass**, does not change based on its location, the weight of an object does. For example, you would weigh slightly more at the bottom of Death Valley (the lowest point in the continental US) than you would at the top of Mt. McKinley. This is because the gravitational pull of the earth is greater as you get closer to the center of the earth. The attribute of mass remains unchanged.

You are familiar with the English standard unit called the pound. The pound is a basic unit of weight as well as a basic unit of mass. A pound is defined as the gravitational force at sea level on an object that has a mass of 1 pound. Since the numerical difference between weight and mass on the surface of the earth is virtually indistinguishable, the terms will be used interchangeably within the context of this book.

The English standard units of measure for weight follow:

16 ounces (oz) = 1 pound (lb)

2000 pounds = 1 ton

In the metric system, the basic root unit of measure for weight is the gram. A raisin weighs approximately 1 gram. In the metric system, the units of weight conform to the pattern that was established for the metric system units of linear measurement. The relationship among the metric units of weight measurement is illustrated in the following table.

Unit	Symbol	Relationship to Root Unit	Real-World Example
Kilogram	kg	1000 grams	Textbook
Hectogram	hg	100 grams	Box of gelatin dessert mix
Dekagram	dag	10 grams	Stick of gum
Gram	g	Root unit	Raisin
Decigram	dg	.1 gram	These small units are
Centigram	cg	.01 gram	commonly used within
Milligram	mg	.001 gram	a pharmaceutical context.

In addition, 1000 kilograms is equal to a metric ton. Although conversion between the metric system and the English standard system is not recommended, we will mention here that 1 kilogram is approximately equal to 2.2 pounds. Therefore, 1 metric ton is approximately equal to 2200 pounds.

Investigation 19

An interesting rule of physics can be used to determine a person's weight above the earth's surface. Apply this rule to determine the numerical change in weight for a 60-kilogram person traveling in an airplane approximately 10 kilometers above sea level. The rule is given here. Let W represent a weight at a given height, in this case 10 kilometers above sea level. Let r represent the radius of the earth, which is approximately 6400 kilometers. Let h represent the height above sea level of the plane. Let S represent the weight at sea level.

$$W = \left(\frac{r}{r + h}\right)^2 \cdot S$$

Substituting, we get

$$W = \left(\frac{6400}{6400 + 10}\right)^2 \cdot 60$$

Obviously, a calculator should be used here.

$$W = \frac{40,960,000}{41,088,100} \cdot 60$$

$$\approx .9968823 \cdot 60 \approx 59.81$$

A person who weighs 60 kilograms on the surface of the earth will weigh approximately 59.81 kilograms on a plane flying at an altitude of 10 kilometers. However, the mass of the person, the amount of matter composing the body, remains unchanged. What has changed is the effect of gravity on the mass. Even at this great distance from the earth, you can see the change is slight.

Volume

volume The **volume** of a three-dimensional object is a measure of the amount of space it occupies. When we speak of the volume of a container, we typically refer to the amount of matter it can contain.

It is easy to confuse the concepts of volume and weight. Children, especially, think that the larger an object, the greater its weight. Compare for example, two rectangular solids of equal dimensions: one a sponge, and the other a brick. Both the sponge and the brick occupy the same amount of space and therefore have equal volumes. But picking up these items can attest to the fact that their weights are not equal.

Recall when area was introduced. The basic unit of measure, the square unit, was used to cover a closed region and assign a numerical value to the amount of space within that closed, two-dimensional region. The basic unit of volume measure is the **cubic unit** cubic unit. A **cubic unit** is defined as the amount of space enclosed within a cube that measures 1 unit on each edge. Rather than "covering" as in area, the volume of an object is found by "filling" it with cubic units.

Examine the rectangular solid in Figure 11.40 on page 548. This solid has a length of 8 units, a width of 4 units, and a height of 3 units. In order to find the volume, we "fill" the solid with unit cubes. As you can see, there are three layers of unit cubes filling the solid. Each layer contains 32 (8 × 4) unit cubes for a total of 96 unit cubes. We report the volume of this solid as 96 cubic units, or 96 units^3.

Figure 11.40

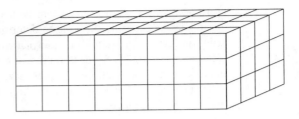

The standard units of volume in the English standard system are the cubic inch (in^3), cubic foot (ft^3), and cubic yard (yd^3). In addition, the following units of volume are commonly used when referring to liquid capacity.

$$1 \text{ fluid ounce (fl oz)} \approx 1.8 \text{ cubic inches}$$

$$1 \text{ quart (qt)} \approx 57.75 \text{ cubic inches}$$

$$1 \text{ gallon (gal)} = 231 \text{ cubic inches}$$

It follows, therefore, that there are 32 fluid ounces in a quart and 4 quarts in a gallon. For ease of use, other intermediary units of volume measure are used. They are listed here:

$$1 \text{ tablespoon (tbsp)} = \tfrac{1}{2} \text{fluid ounce}$$

$$1 \text{ cup (c)} = 8 \text{ fluid ounces}$$

$$1 \text{ pint (pt)} = 2 \text{ cups}$$

$$1 \text{ quart} = 2 \text{ pints}$$

Comparing these equivalences with the following metric equivalences will clearly illustrate how much simpler the metric system is.

In the metric system, the basic root unit of measure for volume is the liter. A liter is equivalent to a cubic decimeter, or the amount of space enclosed within a cube that measures 1 decimeter on each edge. In addition, 1 cubic decimeter of distilled water at approximately 40° F weighs 1 kilogram. The metric system clearly connects measures of volume, length, and weight.

The metric system units of volume conform to the pattern that was established for the metric system units of linear measurement and measurement of weight. The relationship among the metric units of volume measurement are illustrated in this table.

Unit	Symbol	Relationship to Root Unit	Real-World Example
Kiloliter	kL	1000 liters	Two-person hot tub
Hectoliter	hL	100 liters	Small bathtub
Dekaliter	daL	10 liters	Water-cooler container
Liter	L	Root unit	Bottle of seltzer
Deciliter	dL	.1 liter	Juice glass
Centiliter	cL	.01 liter	Serving spoon full
Milliliter	mL	.001 liter	Eyedropper full

Investigation 20

Many people leave the water running while brushing their teeth. The amount of water wasted is estimated at 2 liters per brushing. If the 500,000 residents of a city all ran the water when they brushed their teeth twice a day, how much water would be wasted in a year?

The following calculator keystroke sequence can be used to solve this problem:

$$\boxed{\text{AC}}\ \ 2\ \ \boxed{\times}\ \ 2\ \ \boxed{\times}\ \ 365\ \ \boxed{\times}\ \ 500000\ \ =\ \ \boxed{7.3\,\text{E}\,8}$$

Two liters used   Days in 1 year   Number of Residents
twice a day

The answer is displayed in scientific notation since it contains more digits than the display can handle.

$$7.3 \text{ E } 8 = 7.3 \times 10^8 = 730{,}000{,}000 \text{ L}$$

In 1 year, this city would waste 730 million liters of water. (This amount could fill approximately 8000 backyard pools!)

Volume Formulas

We have already examined the features of a variety of three-dimensional solids. The differences between polyhedra and nonpolyhedra were discussed, and Euler's formula was employed. There is however, another important characteristic of three-dimensional solids.

Prisms and Cylinders

dihedral angle

When two planes intersect, an angle is formed along the line of intersection. This angle is called a **dihedral angle**. It is the union of two planes along a common line, or edge. Figure 11.41a depicts a dihedral angle. Since a polyhedron is formed by the intersection of many planes, the resulting solid contains many dihedral angles. These angles are the union of an edge and the two faces that meet at the edge. In Figure 11.41b, all of the dihedral angles formed at the intersection of a base and a lateral face are right angles. This is not the case in Figure 11.41c.

Figure 11.41

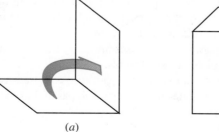 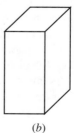 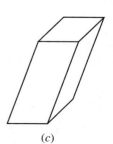

(a)   (b)   (c)

In a prism, if the dihedral angles formed at the intersection of a base and a lateral face are right angles, then the prism is a right prism (Figure 11.41b). If these dihedral **oblique prism** angles are not right angles, then the prism is known as an **oblique prism** (Figure 11.41c).

The distinction between right and oblique prisms is an important one, since the volume of any prism can be determined by examining a related right prism. For example, suppose you begin with a stack of paper to form a right rectangular prism, as pictured in Figure 11.42a. By shifting the paper slightly to the right, an oblique prism is formed (Figure 11.42b). However, the volume of both prisms must be the same, since the amount of paper is the same.

Figure 11.42

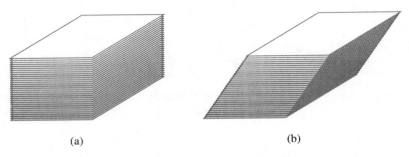

(a)   (b)

Let's look at other ways the paper could have been shifted to form new three-dimensional solids (see Figure 11.43).

Figure 11.43

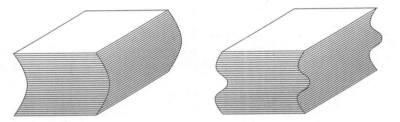

Notice that the amount of paper used to form the solids has not changed, and that the bases of each of the solids pictured are congruent (each sheet of paper is still the same size). Therefore, the volume of the solids must be the same as the volume when the paper was stacked to form a rectangular solid. In addition, suppose that each solid was to be separated by lifting off exactly the same number of sheets of paper from each stack. The area of the cross sections formed would be the same. These paper models are a simplification and a special case of an important discovery made in the early seventeenth century by Italian mathematician Bonaventura Cavalieri. Cavalieri found that two solids of the same height with bases of equal area will have the same volume if every plane parallel to the bases intersects the solids at cross sections of equal area. Figure 11.44 depicts two such solids.

It is important to note that checking only one cross section is not sufficient. Cavalieri's principle states that *every* plane parallel to the bases must intersect the solids at cross sections of equal area. It is important to know the nature of the solids being examined before drawing any conclusions based on one or two cross sections.

In Figure 11.44, A_1 and A_2 represent the areas of the bases of solids 1 and 2, respectively, and X_1 and X_2 represent the areas of the cross sections of solids 1 and 2, respectively. Notice that the bases do not necessarily have to be congruent; only the areas need to be equal.

Figure 11.44

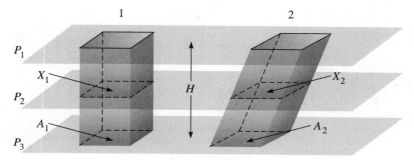

If $A_1 = A_2$ and $X_1 = X_2$ and $P_1 \parallel P_2 \parallel P_3$ then $V_1 = V_2$

The volume of a right rectangular prism can be found by determining the number of unit cubes that fill its enclosed space. Recognize in Figure 11.44 that the volume of **right rectangular prism** the **right rectangular prism** pictured is the product of its length, width, and height. The following generalization can be made:

Formula: **Volume of a Right Rectangular Prism.** The volume V of a right rectangular prism whose length is l, width is w, and height is h can be determined by finding the product $l \cdot w \cdot h$.

Notice that in the formula $l \cdot w \cdot h$, $(l \cdot w)$ is the area of the base of the prism. Therefore, it can be stated that the volume of a rectangular prism is the product of the area of its base A_b and its height. This formula can be extended to oblique prisms as well, as shown by Figure 11.44.

Remember that the height of a prism is the perpendicular distance between the two bases. When the lateral faces are rectangular, the height will be the length of one of the edges of a lateral face. In an oblique prism, the height is not one of the dimensions of its faces. The volume of any prism can therefore be symbolized as follows:

Formula: **Volume of a Prism.** The volume V, whose base has an area of A_b and whose height is h, can be determined by finding the product $A_b \cdot h$.

Investigation 21

A desk aquarium is in the shape of a right hexagonal prism, whose bases are regular hexagons. The height of the aquarium is 40 centimeters, and the length of an edge on the base is 20 centimeters. When full, how many liters of water does the aquarium contain?

Understand the Problem: What is known? You are told the dimensions of a right hexagonal prism.

What is unknown? You must determine the volume, in liters, of the filled tank.

Devise a Plan: Draw and label a sketch in order to visualize the tank in question.

Carry Out the Plan:

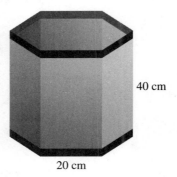

40 cm

20 cm

The volume of this right prism can be found by finding the area of the hexagonal base and multiplying it by the height. The area of the hexagon is most easily determined by first dividing it into six congruent equilateral triangles as pictured here:

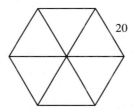

20

The altitude of a triangle can be found by using the Pythagorean theorem as shown here:

$$10^2 + a^2 = 20^2$$
$$100 + a^2 = 400$$
$$a = \sqrt{300} \approx 17.3 \text{ cm}$$

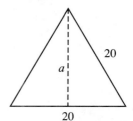

20

a

20

20

The area of an equilateral triangle is approximately $\frac{1}{2} \cdot 20 \cdot 17.3$, or 173, square centimeters. Since six such equilateral triangles make up the hexagonal base, the area of the base is approximately $6 \cdot 173$, or 1038, square centimeters. The volume of the aquarium can be represented as follows:

$$V = A_b \cdot h$$
$$= 1038 \cdot 40 = 41{,}520 \text{ cm}^3$$

You will recall that a cubic decimeter can hold 1 liter of water. Since there are 10 centimeters along each edge of a cubic decimeter, it is equivalent to 1000 cubic centimeters. Therefore, the aquarium holds 41.52 liters of water.

Look Back: Inherent in this solution is the equivalence between 1000 cubic centimeters and 1000 milliliters (1 liter). It therefore follows that 1 cubic centimeter can hold 1 milliliter of water.

If the aquarium had an octagonal base, its volume would have been found by determining the area of the octagon and multiplying by the height. If the aquarium had a dodecagonal base (12 sides), its volume would have been found by determining the area of the dodecagon and multiplying by the height. As the number of sides of the base becomes infinitely great, the base begins to resemble a circle and the solid begins to resemble a cylinder. It follows, therefore, that the volume of a cylinder can be found by finding the area of the circular base and multiplying by the height. This can be generalized as follows:

Formula: **Volume of a Right Circular Cylinder.**   The volume V of a cylinder is equal to the product of the area of its base, A_b, and its height, h:

$$V = A_b \cdot h = \pi r^2 h$$

Pyramids and Cones

Figure 11.45a depicts two types of open-top containers: a rectangular prism and a rectangular pyramid, each with congruent bases and equal heights. What is the relationship between the volume of the prism and the volume of the pyramid?

Figure 11.45

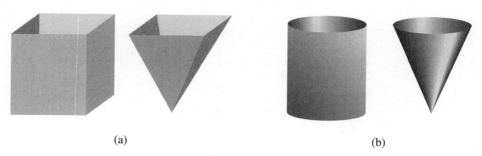

(a)   (b)

The simplest way of examining the relationship between the two volumes would be to compare their actual measures. One could fill the pyramid with water and then empty the contents into the prism. Repeating this process reveals that it will take three full rectangular pyramids to fill the rectangular prism. This leads to the conclusion that the volume of the pyramid is $\frac{1}{3}$ the volume of the prism with a congruent base and height.

The same relationship holds between a cylinder and a cone (Figure 11.45b). If you wish to demonstrate this to yourself, take an empty coffee can. Construct a paper cone of equal height and with equal base circumference. Fill the paper cone with rice and pour it into the coffee can. You will see that his can be done three times until the coffee can is full. This suggests the following valid generalizations.

Formula: Volume of a Pyramid.   The volume V of a pyramid whose base has an area A_b and whose height is h is

$$V = \tfrac{1}{3} A_b h$$

Formula: Volume of a Right Circular Cone.   The volume V of a cone whose base has an area A_b and whose height is h is

$$V = \tfrac{1}{3} A_b h = \tfrac{1}{3} \pi r^2 h$$

These solids are illustrated in Figure 11.46 (for a pyramid) and Figure 11.47 (for a right circular cone).

Figure 11.46   **Figure 11.47**

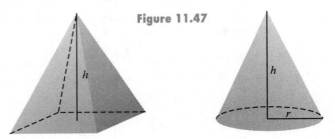

Spheres

We have delayed discussing spheres until this point because the volume and surface area formulas are closely related. The development of the volume formula for spheres is fairly complex. Therefore, we will present the volume formula of a sphere and use it to develop the surface area formula.

Formula: Volume of a Sphere.   The volume V of a sphere whose radius is r is

$$V = \tfrac{4}{3} \pi r^3$$

The sphere is shown in Figure 11.48.

Figure 11.48

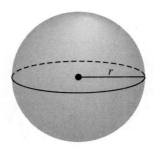

Consider a sphere that has been "cut up" as shown in Figure 11.49. Each of the figures that form the sphere closely resembles a pyramid. The apex of each pyramidlike solid is at the center of the sphere, and the base of the solid is on the surface of the sphere. The height of each pyramidlike solid is equal to the radius of the sphere.

Figure 11.49

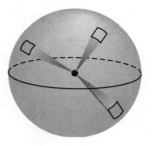

In Figure 11.49, notice that since the bases of the pyramidlike solids are on the surface of the sphere, each edge of a base is curved. Suppose the sphere were partitioned into a great number of these congruent pyramidlike solids. The larger the number of these solids, the closer the solids would resemble a pyramid. For the purposes of this exploration, let's accept the fact that with a large number of solids, the volume of a sphere can be determined by adding up the volumes of all of the "pyramids." We will use the notation A_n to denote the area of the base of the nth pyramid. Since the volume of a single pyramid is $\frac{1}{3}A_b h$ and the height is equal to the radius of the sphere, the volume of any pyramid will be equal to one-third times the product of the area of the base and the radius. The volume of the sphere can therefore be symbolized by

$$V = \tfrac{1}{3}A_1 r + \tfrac{1}{3}A_2 r + \tfrac{1}{3}A_3 r + \tfrac{1}{3}A_4 r + \tfrac{1}{3}A_5 r + \cdots + \tfrac{1}{3}A_n r$$

Since each term is multiplied by $\frac{1}{3}r$, the volume formula is equivalent to

$$V = \tfrac{1}{3}r(A_1 + A_2 + A_3 + A_4 + A_5 + \cdots + A_n)$$

The sum of the areas represented by $(A_1 + A_2 + A_3 + A_4 + A_5 + \cdots + A_n)$ is equal to the surface area, S, of the sphere. Therefore, we can substitute S for the sum in the above formula:

$$V = \tfrac{1}{3}rS$$

We already know the volume of a sphere to be $\frac{4}{3}\pi r^3$. Substituting, we get

$$\tfrac{4}{3}\pi r^3 = \tfrac{1}{3}rS$$

Multiplying both sides by $\frac{3}{r}$, we can now express the surface area of a sphere in terms of its radius as

$$S = 4\pi r^2$$

Figure 11.50a depicts a cross section of the sphere, which is a circle whose radius **great circle** is equal to the radius of the sphere. This cross section is called a **great circle** of a sphere. A sphere contains an infinite number of great circles, some of which are shown in Figure 11.50b.

Figure 11.50

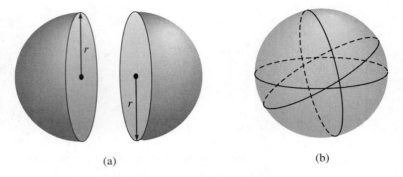

(a)   (b)

Investigation 22

An orange juice manufacturer wants to purchase oranges that yield the greatest amount of juice with the least amount of peel. Disposal of the peel is a costly operation. Is it better to purchase oranges with a diameter of 8 centimeters or oranges with a diameter of 12 centimeters, or is the size irrelevant?

Understand the Problem: To model this problem mathematically, we will assume that the shape of an orange approximates a sphere and that the amount of juice in an orange is a function of its volume. Therefore, this problem requires comparing volume and surface area for two different-sized spheres.

Devise a Plan: If the ratio of volume to surface area is the same in each case, then the manufacturer should simply purchase whichever oranges are less expensive, since there is no advantage to purchasing large oranges. Make a table to examine this problem situation.

Carry Out the Plan:

Diameter	Volume $(\frac{4}{3}\pi r^3)$	Surface Area $(4\pi r^2)$	$\dfrac{\text{Volume}}{\text{Surface Area}}$
8 cm	≈268 cm³	≈201 cm²	$\frac{268}{201} = \frac{4}{3}$
12 cm	≈905 cm³	≈452 cm²	$\frac{905}{452} \approx 2$

It appears that the larger the orange, the greater the volume to surface area ratio. Examine the ratio for a general case where r is the radius of the sphere:

$$\frac{\text{Volume}}{\text{Surface area}} = \frac{\frac{4}{3}\pi r^3}{4\pi r^2} = \frac{1}{3}r$$

The ratio of volume to surface area is a function of the radius. As the radius of the sphere increases, the ratio increases. This means that larger oranges contain more juice compared with the amount of peel that must be discarded. The juice manufacturer should purchase the largest oranges possible.

Look Back: How would price play a role in this problem? What if the larger oranges cost four times more than the smaller ones?

Temperature

To complete our study of measurable attributes, we will address the measurement of temperature in both the Fahrenheit and the Celsius scales. Both scales use the freezing and boiling points of water as reference points. Between these reference points, the Celsius scale spans 100 degrees, with 0° representing the temperature at which water freezes and 100° representing the temperature at which water boils. You will recall from our study of the metric system that the prefix "centi-" indicates a unit, 100 of which compose the basic unit. Since there are 100 divisions between the freezing and boiling temperatures in the Celsius scale, this scale is sometimes referred to as a centigrade scale.

The Fahrenheit scale spans 180 degrees between the freezing and boiling points of water: water freezes at 32° and boils at 212°. Since the Fahrenheit scale divides the same range of temperatures into a greater number of degrees than does the Celsius scale, a change in temperature of 1° F represents a smaller change than 1° C.

Figure 11.51 depicts the two scales and gives common temperature readings in each scale.

Figure 11.51

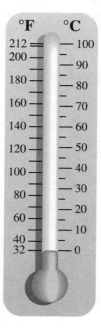

During our study of the metric system, we said that conversion between the English standard system and the metric system of measurement does not help you to become fluent in metric measurement. The same is true of conversion between the Fahrenheit and the Celsius scales. The best way to become comfortable with the Celsius scale is to equate the daily temperature with the reported number of degrees Celsius. However, at times it may be necessary to numerically convert from one system to the other. The following two formulas take into account that each system has a different temperature representing the freezing point of water and allows for the fact that 100 degrees in the Celsius scale covers the same change of temperature as 180 degrees in the Fahrenheit scale. This ratio of $\frac{100}{180}$ has been simplified to $\frac{5}{9}$ and is used in the following conversion formulas.

Let C represent the temperature in Celsius. Let F represent its associated reading in Fahrenheit.

To Convert from Fahrenheit to Celsius   **To Convert from Celsius to Fahrenheit**

$$C = \frac{5}{9}(F - 32) \qquad\qquad F = \frac{9}{5}C + 32$$

Investigation 23

Highway engineers must account for the fact that heat can cause roadways to expand. For this reason, many highways contain expansion joints at designated intervals to allow for such expansion. Without these joints, a very hot summer's day could cause a highway to buckle because of expansion of the roadway materials. A formula commonly used by highway engineers to determine the amount of expansion that a given roadway might need is stated here:

$$I = kL(T - t)$$

where I is the length of the expansion, T is the temperature in degrees Fahrenheit under consideration, t is the temperature at which the highway was built, and L is the length of the highway in question. The constant k for a two-lane highway is given as .000012 for temperatures reported in degrees Fahrenheit.

Suppose that a 1-mile stretch of two-lane highway was built on a day when the temperature reading was 12° C. What is the length of expansion in feet that would be expected on a hot day when the temperature reading is 35° C?

Since the constant k is stated for temperatures in the Fahrenheit scale, we must convert 12° C and 35° C into Fahrenheit equivalents. The formula $F = \frac{9}{5}C + 32$ can be used, along with a calculator, to determine the Fahrenheit temperatures, as shown here:

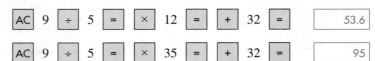

The roadway was built at 53.6° F, and the expansion temperature under consideration is 95° F.

The length of expansion that will result from a temperature of 95° F is small and should be reported in feet. This will require converting 1 mile to 5280 feet. The following formula and keystroke sequence can be used to determine the length of expansion:

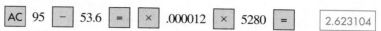

The 1-mile stretch of roadway will expand approximately 2.6 feet at a temperature of 95° F. The difference in temperature was entered into the calculator first to avoid using the memory key. An equivalent calculator solution is as follows:

Assessments for Section 11.3

1. Determine the metric equivalents of each of the following measures.
   - (a) 52 kg = _____ g
   - (b) 100 cg = _____ g
   - (c) 50 mg = _____ cg
   - (d) 5.5 cg = _____ mg
   - (e) .7 kg = _____ g
   - (f) 19.6 g = _____ cg
   - (g) 3000 g = _____ kg
   - (h) .035 kg = _____ g
   - (i) (5.2×10^3) cg = _____ kg
   - (j) (2.8×10^{-4}) kg = _____ g

2. A certain shipping company charges $5 per kilogram. Determine the shipping cost for each of the following weights.
   - (a) 16 kg
   - (b) 4.5 kg
   - (c) 800 g
   - (d) 2000 cg
   - (e) 10 items @ 50 g

3. Choose the most reasonable measurement for weight in each of the following instances.
   - (a) A small automobile: 100 kg   1000 kg   10,000 kg
   - (b) A newborn baby: .4 kg   40 kg   4 kg
   - (c) A box of rice: 9 g   90 g   900 g
   - (d) A candy bar: 1.5 kg   15 g   150 g
   - (e) An adult: 75 g   75 kg   180 kg

4. Estimate the weight of the following items in any appropriate metric measure.

   - (a) A small pumpkin
   - (b) A computer diskette
   - (c) A child's bicycle
   - (d) A motorcycle
   - (e) A packed suitcase

5. Determine the metric equivalents of each of the following measures.
   - (a) 32 kL = _____ L
   - (b) 1.5 mL = _____ cL
   - (c) 650 L = _____ cL
   - (d) 59 cL = _____ mL
   - (e) .3 kL = _____ L
   - (f) 2.56 L = _____ mL
   - (g) 6000 L = _____ kL
   - (h) 4.12 kL = _____ L
   - (i) (2.9×10^5) cL = _____ kL
   - (j) (4.1×10^{-5}) kL _____ L

6. Choose the most reasonable measurement for the volume of each of the following items.
   - (a) A coffee cup: 250 mL   25 mL   2500 mL
   - (b) A bathtub: 10 L   100 L   1000 L
   - (c) A contact lens case: 400 mL   .04 L   4 mL
   - (d) A bottle of shampoo: 90 cL   90 L   90 mL
   - (e) An orange juice can: 3.5 L   35 mL   355 mL

7. Estimate the volume of the following items in any appropriate metric measure.
   (a) A child's sandbox
   (b) The freezer portion of a refrigerator
   (c) The interior of a car
   (d) A water balloon
   (e) The rear portion of a moving van

8. A manufacturing plant packages cereal. As the boxes come off the assembly line, a highly precise scale is used to discard any boxes that are more than 2% underweight or 5% overweight. For a box of cereal weighing 400 g, what is the range of acceptable weights?

9. An assembly-line scale will reject any package that is more than 1.5% overweight. The plant manufactures three sizes of laundry detergent: small (2 kg), medium (5 kg), and large (12 kg). Would the following boxes be rejected or accepted? Explain your reasoning.
   (a) 2.05 kg small box
   (b) 2.01 kg small box
   (c) 5.75 kg medium box
   (d) 5.05 kg medium box
   (e) 12.18 kg large box
   (f) 12.08 kg large box

10. Three oranges weigh the same as two grapefruits. One grapefruit weighs the same as 21 grapes. How many grapes weigh the same as one orange?

11. Four bananas weigh the same as three grapefruits. Two grapefruits weigh the same as 16 cherries. How many cherries weigh the same as one banana?

12. Determine the volume of each of the following solids.
   (a) A rectangular prism whose length measures 15 cm, width measures 10 cm, and height measures 8 cm
   (b) A triangular prism whose height is 25 cm and whose bases are 30-cm, 40-cm, and 50-cm right triangles
   (c) A right circular cylinder whose height is 5 in. with a base radius of 5 in.
   (d) A right cone whose height is 5 in. with a base radius of 5 in.
   (e) A sphere whose radius is 10 cm

13. Determine the indicated measurement in each of the following solids.

(a) Surface area   (b) Volume   (c) Volume

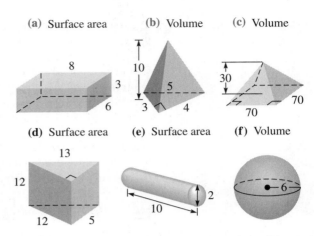

(d) Surface area   (e) Surface area   (f) Volume

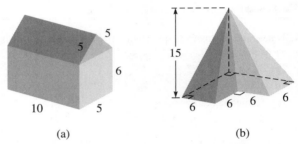

14. Determine the volume of each of the following solids.

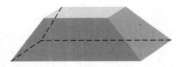

(a)   (b)

15. Explain two ways that the volume of the following solid might be determined.

16. How much potting soil is needed for a nursery that is going to plant seeds in 200 containers of the following shape and size?

Assume that each container is filled to the top with potting soil. These containers are in the shape of a frustum of a cone. The volume of a frustum of a cone is given by

$$V = \frac{1}{3}\pi h(R^2 + Rr + r^2)$$

where R and r are measures of the radii of the bases and h is the height.

17. A bundt pan is in the shape of a frustum of a cone. The dimensions of this bundt pan with a hollow tube in the center are shown here.

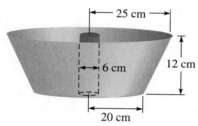

If it is recommended that the pan be filled to $\frac{3}{4}$ of its capacity to allow for the cake to rise, what is the maximum amount of batter that should be poured into the pan?

18. A certain ice cream parlor sells ice cream in two kinds of cones: a waffle cone and a sugar cone. The sugar cone is in the shape of a right circular cone, and the waffle cone is in the shape of a frustum of a cone, whose volume formula is given in Problem 16. Each cone is filled to capacity with ice cream and topped with a hemispherical ball of ice cream whose radius is the same as its holder, as shown here.

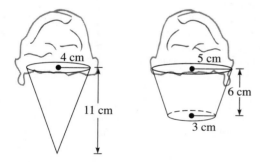

If both cones sell at the same price, which is a better buy?

19. An apple pie recipe calls for seven apples each with a diameter of 10 cm. The only apples you can get have a diameter of 8 cm. How many of the smaller apples do you need for the recipe? Estimate the solution first. (Assume the shape of an apple approximates a sphere.)

20. Find the volume of the following solid.

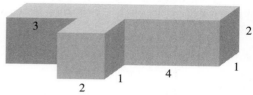

21. An in-ground swimming pool is rectangular on the surface, with dimensions 27 yds by 10 yds. A side view of the drop in depth is given in the following illustration.

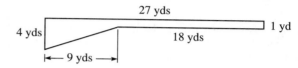

How much water completely fills this pool?

22. Two solid spherical objects are made of the same material. Their radii are in the ratio of $2:3$. What is the ratio of their volumes? What is the ratio of their surface areas?

23. A box is packed with spherical holiday ornaments. The box is in the shape of a rectangular prism with dimensions as shown in the illustration that follows. The diameter of each spherical ornament is $4\frac{3}{4}$ in. If 12 ornaments are packed in this box, what is the volume of packaging material that is needed to completely fill in around the ornaments? (Use $\pi \approx 3.14$.)

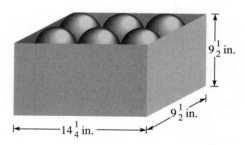

24. Mr. Johnson wishes to buy a waterbed for his second-floor bedroom. An engineer has informed him that the floor joists supporting the bed can hold only up to 1500 lb. The weight of a fully filled waterbed in the shape of a rectangular prism is computed by multiplying the volume of the bed times the density of water. The dimensions of the bed are 6 ft by 5 ft by $\frac{3}{4}$ ft. The density of water is 62.4 lb per cubic foot.

   (a) Can the bedroom floor support a waterbed of this size?

   (b) Can the bedroom floor support the waterbed with two people sleeping in it?

25. A contractor must lay a $\frac{1}{2}$-ft thick cement foundation for a garage. If she frames a trough to hold the cement as pictured in the diagram below, how many cubic feet of cement are needed?

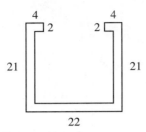

26. What is the weight in kilograms of the water contained within a child's rectangular wading pool that is completely filled with water and whose dimensions are 80 cm by 90 cm by 20 cm?

27. Estimate the Celsius temperature of the following situations.

   (a) A cup of freshly brewed coffee

   (b) A good day for ice skating

   (c) A healthy person's body temperature

   (d) The inside of your refrigerator

   (e) The inside of your freezer

   (f) A good day for a picnic

   (g) A good day for swimming

28. The Kelvin scale of temperature is often used in science. A temperature in degrees Kelvin is found by adding 273 to the temperature in degrees centigrade. Suppose an experiment requires a heat of 360° Kelvin. What is the Fahrenheit temperature equivalent?

29. The height of each of the figures in the illustration at the top of the right-hand column is 20 cm, and $P_1 \parallel P_2 \parallel P_3$. The areas of the cross sections X_1, X_2, and X_3 are all equal. The areas of the bases A_1, A_2, and A_3 are all equal. The base of the square pyramid has an edge that measures 10 cm.

   (a) What is the radius of the right circular cone?

   (b) What is the length of the edge of the base of the triangular pyramid, whose base is an equilateral triangle?

   (c) What is the volume of the right circular cone?

   (d) What is the volume of the triangular pyramid?

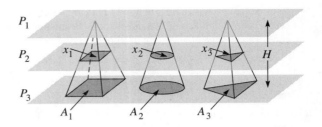

In Other Words

30. Explain the difference among volume, weight, and mass.

31. Explain how the metric system connects measurements of length, volume, and weight.

32. Explain how the volume of a cone can be derived from the volume of a pyramid.

33. Can two boxes of the same volume weigh different amounts? Can two boxes of the same weight have different volumes? Explain your answer.

34. In which scale, Celsius or Fahrenheit, would a temperature increase from 5° to 10° represent a greater rise in the temperature of the air? Explain your answer.

Cooperative Activity

35. Groups of two

Individual Accountability: Obtain an empty half-gallon juice or milk carton. This container is particularly good for this activity because its base is approximately 1 square decimeter. You will also need a 1-liter container (soda bottle) and an uninflated spherical balloon.

   Cut the folded top portion off the milk carton. Fill the liter bottle with water (not to the rim). Estimate the height that will be reached in the milk carton when the bottle of water is emptied into it. Pour the water into the carton. Measure the height. Compare the actual height with your estimate. Record your data.

   Refill the liter bottle with water. Estimate the radius of the sphere that will form when the balloon is filled with 1 liter of water. Fill the balloon with 1 liter of water. Measure the circumference of a great circle for this sphere. Record your data.

Group Goal: Work together to determine the radius of the sphere that was formed when the balloon was filled with 1 liter of water. Determine a way to relate the height h of the "cubeful" of water in the milk carton and the radius r of the sphere that held 1 liter of water. Determine a generalization that can be made that relates s and r when the volume of a sphere is equal to the volume of a cube.

Vocabulary for Chapter 11

acre

acute angle

alternate interior angles

altitude

angle arc

are

area

azimuth circle

central angles

circumference

complement

complementary angles

corresponding angles

cubic unit

degree

dihedral angle

endpoint

equilateral triangle

exterior angles

golden ratio (golden section)

great circle

hectare

isosceles triangle

mass

median

midpoint

oblique prism

obtuse angle

perimeter

perpendicular bisector

protractor

Pythagorean triples

ray

right angle

right circular cone

right circular cylinder

right prism

right rectangular prism

right regular pyramid

right triangle

scalene triangle

sectors

slant height

straight angle

straightedge

supplement

supplementary angles

surface area

transversal

vertex

vertical angles

volume

weight

Review for Chapter 11

1. Find the perimeter and area of each of the following figures.

(a)

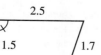

(b)

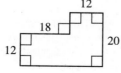

(c)

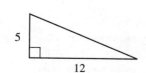

(d)

2. Offer possible dimensions of each polygon whose perimeter is given below.

(a) Rectangle: perimeter = 15 in.

(b) Square: perimeter = 7.5 cm

(c) Rhombus: perimeter = 22.25 cm

(d) Isosceles trapezoid: perimeter = 30 in.

(e) Regular hexagon: perimeter = 28.5 cm

(f) Regular pentagon: perimeter = $28\frac{1}{8}$ in.

3. Offer possible dimensions of each polygon whose area is given below.

(a) Rectangle: area = 28 ft^2

(b) Square: area = 2.25 m^2

(c) Square: area = 150 cm^2

(d) Right triangle: 172.5 cm^2

(e) Circle: 113.04 in^2 (Use $\pi = 3.14$.)

4. In each case below, a figure is formed by joining congruent sides of regular polygons. Determine the measure of angle A in each figure. Do not use a protractor. Explain your reasoning.

(a)

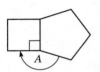

(b)

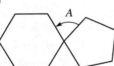

(c)

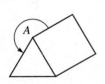

(d)

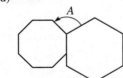

5. Two angles are supplementary. One angle is twice the measure of the other angle. Determine the measure of each angle.

6. Two angles are complementary. One angle is five more than four times the other. Determine the measure of each angle.

7. Use your protractor to draw angles of the following measures.

(a) 35°   (b) 100°   (c) 65°   (d) 180°   (e) 270°

8. Two angles are in the ratio of 1 : 1.5.

(a) Can the two angles be complementary angles? Explain your answer.

(b) Can the two angles be supplementary angles? Explain your answer.

(c) If the sum of the angles is less than 180°, can the smaller of the two angles be obtuse? Explain your answer.

(d) If the larger of the two angles is a right angle, what is the smaller angle?

(e) If the smaller angle is the complement of a 30° angle, what is the larger angle?

(f) If the larger angle is the supplement of a 105° angle, what is the smaller angle?

9. What are the measures of the interior angles in an isosceles right triangle? Explain your answer.

10. In an isosceles triangle, the base angles are twice the measure of the vertex angle. Determine the measure of each interior angle.

11. In the following diagram, $\overline{AB} \parallel \overline{CD}$, $\overline{GH} \perp \overline{AB}$, and $\overline{GH} \perp \overline{CD}$. The measure of $\angle X$ is 35°. Determine the measures of the angles labeled 1–13.

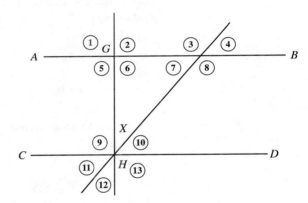

12. Perform the following constructions.

(a) Draw a segment that is 5 cm long. Bisect this segment.

(b) Draw a 50° angle. Copy this angle.

(c) Draw a 6-cm segment. Label C anywhere on the segment. Construct a perpendicular through point C.

(d) Draw line segment $\overline{AB}$. Construct a line CD that is parallel to $\overline{AB}$.

(e) Draw any triangle. Construct an altitude.

13. You have already determined that a regular hexagon can be partitioned in three different ways in order to determine its area: (a) two congruent trapezoids; (b) six congruent equilateral triangles; and (c) a rectangle and two congruent isosceles triangles. Using the dimensions pictured in the following figures, show that these three methods will result in the same area.

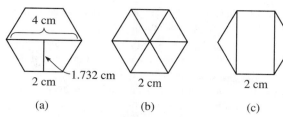

(a)	(b)	(c)

14. Determine the area and circumference of a circle whose dimensions are given here.

(a) Radius = 8 cm   (b) Diameter = 8 cm
(c) Radius = $1\frac{1}{2}$ in.   (d) Diameter = $\frac{1}{2}$ in.

15. Find the area of the shaded region in each of the following figures.

(a)

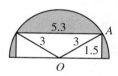

(b)

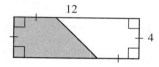

(c)

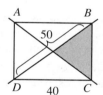

(d)

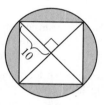

16. Determine the surface area and the volume of each of the following solids.

(a)

(b)

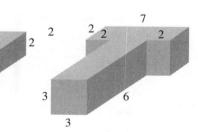

(c)

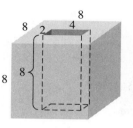

(d)

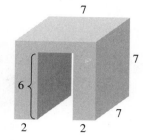

(e)

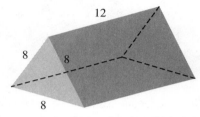

17. Determine the surface area and the volume of the following solid. Explain your methodology.

$\frac{1}{4}$ of a hemisphere whose radius is 10 units

18. (a) Two cones have the same height. Their base radii are in the ratio of $1:3$. What is the ratio of the volumes of these cones?

(b) Two cones have congruent bases. Their heights are in the ratio of $1:3$. What is the ratio of the volumes of these cones?

(c) Two cylinders have the same height. Their base radii are in the ratio of $1:3$. What is the ratio of the volumes of these cylinders?

(d) Two cylinders have congruent bases. Their heights are in the ratio of $1:3$. What is the ratio of their volumes?

19. Describe or illustrate two different ways that can be used to determine the volume of each of the following figures. Compute the volume using each method described.

(a)

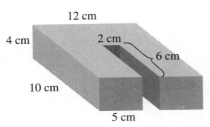

(b)

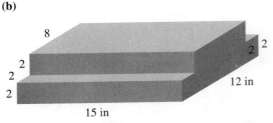

20. A cylindrical water pipe has an inside diameter of $1\frac{1}{2}"$. The pipe runs from a central water source along a straight path for a distance of 120 ft. How much water is contained within this length of pipe when it is full? (Use 3.14 for π.)

21. A bicycle wheel measures 65 cm in diameter. How many complete revolutions would the wheel make to cover a distance of 1 km?

22. A spherical balloon has a radius r and volume v. If you continue to blow up the balloon to a point where the volume is eight times its original volume, what is the length of the new radius?

23. Eight strips of adhesive tape, each 1.5 cm wide and 21 cm long, are used to completely cover the curved portion of a cylindrical juice can as illustrated below.

What is the volume of this juice can?

24. Use a compass to construct a semicircle. Label the endpoints of the diameter A and B, respectively. Inscribe three angles, ACB, ADB, and AEB, in the semicircle, with ver-

tices C, D, and E on the semicircle. Measure each of these angles. Make a generalization.

25. A muffin manufacturer bakes muffins in tins with cylindrical shells. The diameter of each of the cylindrical muffin shells is 6 cm, and the height is 5 cm.
   (a) If the tins are to be filled to $\frac{3}{4}$ capacity, what is the volume of batter per muffin?
   (b) What is the inside surface area of the paper disk that will be used for each muffin?

26. You are given the following rectangular prism.

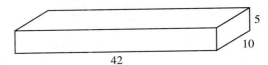

Cut this prism into three smaller rectangular prisms A, B, and C such that the ratio of the volumes of A to B to C is $1:2:3$. State the dimensions of the new prisms formed.

27. Examine the following irregular solid. Describe a way in which the volume of this solid can be computed. Use the dimensions to determine the actual volume.

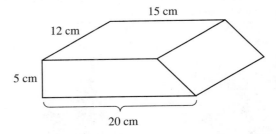

In Other Words

28. Define a dihedral angle. Give a real-world example.

29. Explain how the formula for the volume of a cylinder is derived from the formula of the volume of a prism.

30. Explain the relationship that exists in every circle between the diameter and its circumference.

31. If you know the volume of a rectangular prism and one of its dimensions, can you calculate the exact surface area? Explain your answer.

32. How do the properties of a rhombus relate to the geometric constructions covered in this chapter?

Cooperative Activity

33. Groups of four

Individual Accountability: Write and solve one application problem for each of the following topics.

(a) Volume

(b) Simultaneous equations

(c) Area

(d) Metric weight

Group Goal: Examine and solve all of the problems that have been created by the members of your group. Select one problem from each category that best assesses knowledge of that particular topic.

12

Making **G**eometric **C**onnections

Examine the photograph at the right.

Describe what you see.

Are all of the items identical?

On what basis can you make this decision?

What irregularities might be acceptable?

What might a mathematical description of this photograph contain?

Introduction

In their 1989 report *Curriculum and Evaluation Standards for School Mathematics*, the National Council of Teachers of Mathematics (NCTM) made the following statement concerning mathematical connections:

> The mathematics curriculum is generally viewed as consisting of several discrete strands. As a result, computation, geometry, measurement, and problem solving tend to be taught in isolation. It is important that children connect ideas both among and within areas of mathematics. . . . When mathematical ideas are also connected to everyday experiences, both in and out of school, children become aware of the usefulness of mathematics. (p. 32)

This chapter is about making geometric connections. We discuss both the ways in which geometry connects to other branches of mathematics and the ways in which the various topics of geometry relate to each other. Section 12.1 begins by examining the relationship between algebra and geometry. As the NCTM quote above says, geometry is too often taught in isolation. In this section, we integrate geometric and algebraic concepts so that you will see how both of these branches of mathematics include approaches to and methods of solving problems that will allow you to investigate problems from a broader base. Here we explore the Cartesian coordinate system and discuss how it can be used to plot points and measure distances on a plane, and then show how these geometric ideas can be translated into algebraic equations. We also discuss systems of equations and explain how they can be solved geometrically by using graphs, and algebraically by using the substitution method and the addition/subtraction method. We also cover equations of curves and work with the concepts of circumscribing and inscribing. Section 12.2 discusses similarity and congruence, two concepts vital to the process of indirect measurement. Properties necessary to establish both similarity and congruence are covered. Section 12.3 introduces LOGO, a computer programming language easy enough for elementary students to work with yet powerful enough to allow for sophisticated programming. After studying this chapter, your repertoire of problem-solving tools will have become even more extensive.

12.1   Coordinate Geometry: An Algebra/Geometry Connection

Recently, mathematics educators have expressed concern over the fact that students are taught algebra and geometry as two separate and distinct topics. This was the traditional approach at the secondary school level until the 1980s, when some states revamped their high school curricula to introduce an integrated approach to the study of algebra and geometry. This new view of secondary school mathematics focuses on ways in which both algebra and geometry are used as investigative tools. Students are encouraged to view problem situations from both an algebraic and a geometric vantage point. It is hoped that students will recognize that there is more than one way to solve a problem, and more than one branch of mathematics that can be called upon to model a problem situation.

The concept of an algebra/geometry connection is not new. In fact, the French mathematician and philosopher René Descartes (1596–1650) developed a branch of

analytic geometry

mathematics known as **analytic geometry**, in which geometric figures are viewed within an algebraic framework. The most widely studied component of analytic geometry at the elementary and secondary school levels is the **Cartesian coordinate system**.

Cartesian coordinate system

Here, geometric figures are examined in a system that allows them to be represented algebraically using the real number system and equations. The Cartesian coordinate system extends the concept of the number line by assigning numerical labels to all points in a plane. Two perpendicular number lines that intersect at the zero point on each axis form the basis of this view of mathematics. Traditionally, one line is horizontal and the

x-axis

other line is vertical. The horizontal line is known as the **x-axis** and the vertical line as

y-axis, quadrants

the **y-axis**. These axes divide the plane into four regions called **quadrants**. The top right-hand region is the first quadrant, and the remaining regions are labeled in counterclockwise order, as shown in Figure 12.1.

Figure 12.1

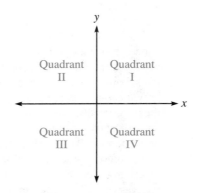

origin

The point of intersection of the x-axis and the y-axis is known as the **origin**. Each of the axes is divided into equal units. Positive numbers are found on the x-axis to the right of the origin, and negative numbers are found on the x-axis to the left of the origin. On the y-axis, positive numbers are found above the origin, and negative numbers are found below the origin. Every point of the plane is given a label that refers to its relative

coordinates

position from the origin. This label is an ordered pair of numbers known as the **coordinates** of a point in a plane and is symbolized by (x, y) where x represents the horizontal distance of the point from the origin and y represents the vertical distance of the point from the origin.

The order of the pair is extremely important, since $(4, -5)$ and $(-5, 4)$ represent two different points in the plane. It is standard notation that the x-coordinate, known as the

abscissa, ordinate

abscissa, is the first entry of the pair, and the y-coordinate, known as the **ordinate**, is the second entry. Therefore, the point $(4, -5)$ is located by moving four units to the right of the zero and then five units down. The point $(-5, 4)$ is located by moving five units to the left of zero and then four units up. Figure 12.2 depicts these points in the Cartesian plane.

Figure 12.2

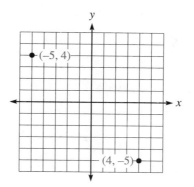

The process of locating a point in the plane when given its coordinates is called **plotting a point**.

Investigation 1

Plot the following points in the plane by using graph paper or the laminated card below: $A(-4, 0)$, $B(0, 4)$, $C(8, 5)$, $D(9, -8)$, and $E(6, 3)$. Connect the points A, B, C, D, E, and A in that order to create a closed figure. Name the figure that is formed. Justify your reasoning.

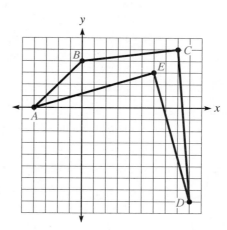

The figure formed is a nonconvex pentagon. For the figure to be convex, the line segment connecting any two interior points must lie wholly within the interior of the figure. It is easy to see that points $(3, 4)$ and $(8, 1)$ lie in the interior of the polygon. Because the line segment that connects these two interior points partially falls in the exterior of the polygon, as shown on page 572, this pentagon is nonconvex.

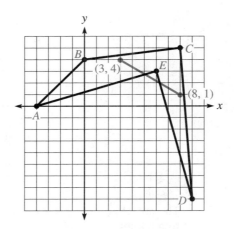

The line segments drawn in Investigation 1 were determined by the endpoints. Between these endpoints lie an infinite number of points that share a particular relationship. Listing all of the points is an impossible task. We therefore call upon an algebraic representation of the set of points by examining the characteristics the points have in common. All points that lie on the x-axis have the form $(a, 0)$ where a is any real number and indicates a location on the x-axis. Because each of these points has zero as its y-coordinate, this collection of points that forms the x-axis is algebraically characterized by the equation $y = 0$. Similarly, all points that lie on the y-axis have the form $(0, b)$ where b is any real number and indicates a location on the y-axis. Because each of these points has zero as its x-coordinate, this collection of points that forms the y-axis is algebraically characterized by the equation $x = 0$.

Investigation 2

Give both an algebraic and a geometric representation for each of the following sets of points.

(a) The set of points whose x-coordinates are -3.

(b) The set of points whose y-coordinates are 5.

(a) Each element of the set of points whose x-coordinate is -3 has the form $(-3, b)$. Some members of this set are $(-3, -2)$, $(-3, 0)$, and $(-3, 15)$. A geometric representation of this set is as follows.

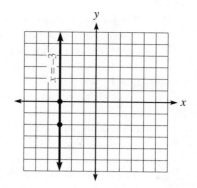

Because all points on this line are characterized as having an x-coordinate of -3, the algebraic representation of this set of points is given by $x = -3$.

(b) Each element of the set of points whose y-coordinate is 5 has the form $(a, 5)$. Some members of this set are $(-7, 5)$, $(0, 5)$, and $(13, 5)$. A geometric representation of this set is given here.

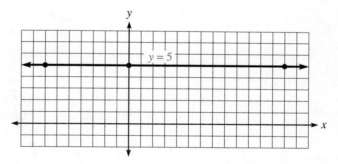

Because all points on this line are characterized as having a y-coordinate of 5, the algebraic representation of this set of points is given by $y = 5$.

Distance

The shortest distance between any two points in a plane is the length of the line segment that connects them. Examine two points in the plane in Figure 12.3.

Figure 12.3

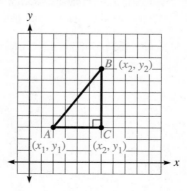

Point A has coordinates (x_1, y_1), and Point B has coordinates (x_2, y_2). For ease of representation, these points have been located in the first quadrant, where all values are positive. We now label and locate point C with coordinates (x_2, y_1). Notice that point C can be viewed as the vertex of triangle ABC, which is opposite side $\overline{AB}$, as shown in Figure 12.3.

The distance between points A and B is the length of the side $\overline{AB}$ of this triangle. Side $\overline{AC}$ is a horizontal line segment that is part of the line $y = y_1$. Side $\overline{BC}$ is a vertical line segment that is part of the line $x = x_2$. Horizontal and vertical line segments meet at right angles. Therefore, $\triangle ACB$ is a right triangle with $\angle C$ a right angle. Finding the distance between points A and B is now reduced to determining the length of the hypotenuse $\overline{AB}$ using the Pythagorean theorem. Recall that the Pythagorean theorem states that the square of the measure of the hypotenuse of a right triangle is equal to the sum of the squares of the measures of the sides that form the right angle. The length of side $\overline{AC}$ is the horizontal distance between points A and C. This can be symbolized by $|x_2 - x_1|$. The length of side $\overline{BC}$ is the vertical distance between points B and C. This can be symbolized by $|y_2 - y_1|$. Applying the Pythagorean theorem, we get

$$(AB)^2 = (AC)^2 + (BC)^2$$
$$(AB)^2 = |x_2 - x_1|^2 + |y_2 - y_1|^2$$
$$AB = \pm\sqrt{|x_2 - x_1|^2 + |y_2 - y_1|^2}$$

Because length is represented by a positive value, we choose

$$+\sqrt{|x_2 - x_1|^2 + |y_2 - y_1|^2}$$

as the symbolic representation of the length of $\overline{AB}$. In general, given two points (x_1, y_1) and (x_2, y_2), the distance, d, between these points is determined by

$$d = +\sqrt{|x_2 - x_1|^2 + |y_2 - y_1|^2}$$

Investigation 3

The vertices of a triangle are $A(-4, 5)$, $B(3, 2)$, and $C(3, -3)$. Determine the perimeter of this triangle in the units shown on the grid.

Understand the Problem: What is given? You are told the vertices of $\triangle ABC$. What is unknown? You are asked to determine the perimeter of $\triangle ABC$.

Devise a Plan: Locate the points on the Cartesian plane and construct the triangle ABC.

Carry Out the Plan:

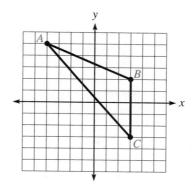

Use the graph above. A visual estimate might rely on the length of $\overline{BC}$. It can be seen that $\overline{BC}$ has a length of 5 units. $\overline{AC}$ appears to be roughly twice as long as $\overline{BC}$, and $\overline{AB}$ appears to be somewhat longer than $\overline{BC}$. Estimates of these lengths might be 10 units and 7 units, respectively. We can therefore estimate the perimeter as the sum $10 + 5 + 7$, or 22, units.

Since $\overline{BC}$ is a vertical segment, it is easy to see that its length is 5 units. We will have to use the distance formula to determine the lengths of the other two sides.

The following calculator keystroke sequences can be used to determine these lengths. Two versions are shown. The first will assume your calculator has parentheses keys $($ $)$. The second will assume your calculator does not have these keys.

The coordinates for side $\overline{AB}$ are $A(-4, 5)$ and $B(3, 2)$.

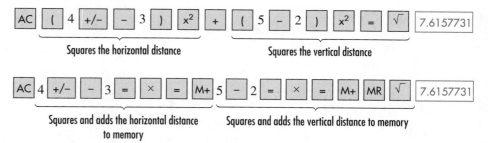

The length of side $\overline{AB}$ is approximately 7.6 units.

The length of side $\overline{AC}$ can be determined by using either of these two keystroke sequences for the points $A(-4, 5)$ and $C(3, -3)$. $\overline{AC}$ is approximately 10.6 units long.

The perimeter of $\triangle ABC$ is approximately $7.6 + 10.6 + 5$, or 23.2, units.

Look Back: Notice that this is close to our estimate of 22 units.

Midpoint of a Line Segment

Recall Construction 2 on page 503 in Chapter 11 that was used to bisect a line segment. The point of bisection of the line segment was identified as the midpoint of the line segment that partitions the segment into two congruent segments. We will now examine a way to determine the midpoint of a segment that has been drawn in the Cartesian plane.

For a point to be the midpoint of a segment, it must satisfy two conditions: (1) it must lie on the segment in question; and (2) it must be equidistant from the two endpoints. In Figure 12.4, you are given a line segment $\overline{AB}$ whose endpoints are A with coordinates (x_1, y_1), and B with coordinates (x_2, y_2). Suppose we assign the midpoint, M, of $\overline{AB}$ coordinates of $(\overline{x}, \overline{y})$. For illustrative purposes, segment $\overline{AB}$ is depicted as the hypotenuse of right triangle ACB, with C the vertex of the right angle, and having coordinates (x_2, y_1).

Figure 12.4

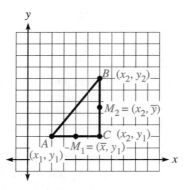

Examine the horizontal segment $\overline{AC}$ with its midpoint M_1 at $(\overline{x}, y_1)$. Since M_1 is the midpoint of $\overline{AC}$, it is equidistant from A and C; that is, the horizontal distance from A to M_1 is equal to the horizontal distance from M_1 to C. This can be symbolized as

$$(x_2 - \overline{x}) = (\overline{x} - x_1)$$

Solve for $\overline{x}$ in terms of x_1 and x_2.

$$x_2 - \overline{x} = \overline{x} - x_1$$
$$\underline{+ x_1 + \overline{x} = + \overline{x} + x_1}$$
$$x_2 + x_1 = 2\overline{x}$$
$$\tfrac{1}{2}(x_2 + x_1) = \overline{x}$$

Notice that the x-coordinate of the midpoint is half the sum of the x-coordinates of the two endpoints.

This line of reasoning can be extended to the midpoint M_2 on the vertical segment $\overline{CB}$. This midpoint has coordinates $(x_2, \overline{y})$. Since M_2 is the midpoint of $\overline{CB}$, it is equidistant from C and B. This can be symbolized as

$$(y_2 - \overline{y}) = (\overline{y} - y_1)$$

Solve for $\overline{y}$ in terms of y_1 and y_2.

$$y_2 - \overline{y} = \overline{y} - y_1$$
$$\underline{+ y_1 + \overline{y} = + \overline{y} + y_1}$$
$$y_2 + y_1 = 2\overline{y}$$
$$\tfrac{1}{2}(y_2 + y_1) = \overline{y}$$

The y-coordinate of the midpoint of the vertical segment is equal to half the sum of the y-coordinates of its endpoints.

Examine segment $\overline{AB}$ in Figure 12.5. It appears that the midpoint M can be expressed in terms of the coordinates x_1, x_2, y_1, and y_2.

Figure 12.5

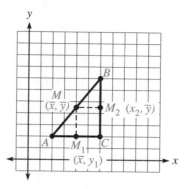

Thus, the midpoint M with coordinates $(\overline{x}, \overline{y})$ for any line segment $\overline{AB}$ whose endpoints are (x_1, y_1) and (x_2, y_2), respectively, can be expressed as

$$M\left(\frac{(x_1 + x_2)}{2}, \frac{(y_1 + y_2)}{2}\right)$$

We leave it to you to prove that point M with these coordinates is equidistant from the endpoints and that M lies on the segment in question. This proof will be addressed in the Problem 27 at the end of this section.

Investigation 4

A computerized sign is composed of a grid containing small squares that can be illuminated. The grid is 125 squares long and 75 squares high. How can a graphic artist locate the square that is at the center of this sign?

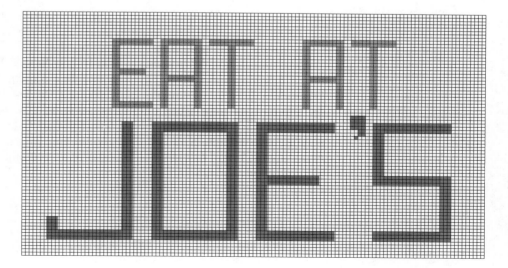

Understand the Problem: What is given? You are told the dimensions of a rectangle. What is unknown? You need to find the location of the square at the center of the rectangle.

Devise a Plan: The artist could use one of several methods to locate the center. Recall from our work with polygons that the diagonals of a rectangle bisect each other. Therefore, the point of bisection is the center of the rectangle. The artist might choose to stretch two strings from opposite diagonals to determine the point of intersection. If the sign is inaccessible, the grid might be modeled using a Cartesian coordinate system as follows.

Carry Out the Plan: Label each square using a row value (x) and column value (y), with the bottom left-hand square having coordinates (1, 1) and the top right-hand square having coordinates (125, 75). The problem is now reduced to locating the midpoint of the segment whose endpoints are (1, 1) and (125, 75) as follows:

$$\bar{x} = \frac{(1 + 125)}{2} \qquad \bar{y} = \frac{(1 + 75)}{2}$$

The midpoint is (63, 38). Therefore, the center of the sign can be located at the square that is in the 63rd column and 38th row.

Look Back: Now look back at the work you have done. Could you have solved this problem by folding a graphical model in half and half again along its diagonals?

Straight Lines

Examine the following set of ordered pairs:

$$(-7, -14)$$
$$(.5, 1)$$
$$(3, 6)$$
$$(0, 0)$$
$$\left(\tfrac{1}{4}, \tfrac{1}{2}\right)$$

What relationship holds between the x- and y-coordinates? In each case, the y-coordinate is twice the x-coordinate; or conversely, the x-coordinate is half the y-coordinate. Figure 12.6a depicts the location of these points in the Cartesian plane. In Figure 12.6b, the points have been connected, resulting in a visual pattern. Notice that the segments connecting these points lie on a single line. This line has been extended in both directions, passing through an infinite number of ordered pairs that are related to each other in the same fashion. The relationship between the x-coordinate and the y-coordinate can be symbolized as $y = 2x$, or $x = \tfrac{1}{2}y$.

Figure 12.6

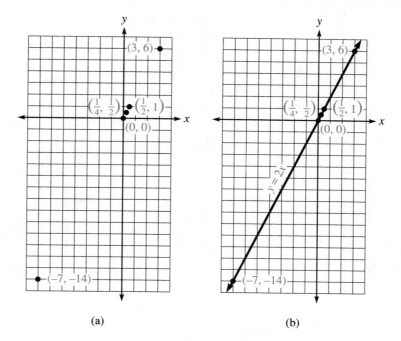

(a)   (b)

Examine the following presentations of two separate patterns among points in the Cartesian plane.

Verbal Description	**Verbal Description**
The y-coordinate is three more than twice the x-coordinate.	The y-coordinate is one less than twice the x-coordinate.

Ordered Pairs	**Ordered Pairs**
$(-4, -5)$, $(-2, -1)$, $(0, 3)$, $(.5, 4)$, $(3\frac{1}{4}, 9\frac{1}{2})$	$(-8, -17)$, $(-2.5, -6)$, $(0, -1)$, $(2\frac{1}{4}, 3\frac{1}{2})$, $(5, 9)$

Graphical Description (a)   *Graphical Description (b)*

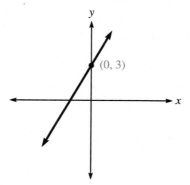
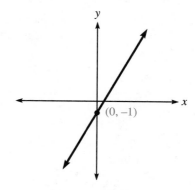

Algebraic Description   *Algebraic Description*

$$y = 2x + 3$$ $$y = 2x - 1$$

In Figure 12.7, the three graphs $y = 2x$, $y = 2x + 3$, and $y = 2x - 1$ have been plotted on the same set of axes.

Figure 12.7

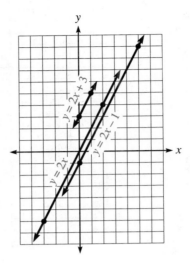

Notice the similarities among them:

The three lines appear to be parallel.

As you move from left to right, each line rises.

Each line intersects the y-axis.

These pieces of information were also embedded within each algebraic description. The line represented by $y = 2x$ crosses the y-axis at $(0, 0)$. The line represented by $y = 2x + 3$ crosses the y-axis at $(0, 3)$. The line represented by $y = 2x - 1$ crosses the y-axis at *y*-intercept $(0, -1)$. The point of intersection of the y-axis and a line is called the **y-intercept**. The coordinates of the y-intercept can be determined from the algebraic representation of a line. In each of these cases, the value that is added to or subtracted from the x term determines the y-intercept.

What is the significance of the similarity that each x has been multiplied by 2? This is related to the fact that the lines are parallel. Examine the vertical and horizontal differences between any two points on each line in Figure 12.8.

$$y = 2x$$
$$(1, 2) \quad (3, 6)$$

$$y = 2x + 3$$
$$(-4, -5) \quad (1, 5)$$

$$y = 2x - 1$$
$$(0, -1) \quad (4, 7)$$

Figure 12.8

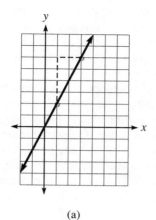
(a)

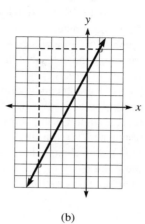
(b)

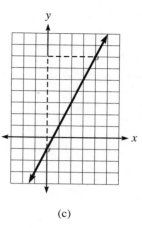
(c)

Set up the ratio of the vertical difference to horizontal difference in each case:

$$\frac{4}{2} \qquad \frac{10}{5} \qquad \frac{8}{4}$$

slope of a line   Each of these ratios can be simplified and expressed as $\frac{2}{1}$. This ratio is called the **slope of a line** and is interpreted as the ratio of the change in the y-coordinate to the change in the x-coordinate. The ratio can be generalized for any two points (x_1, y_1) and (x_2, y_2) as follows:

$$\text{Slope} = \frac{\text{Change in } y\text{-coordinate}}{\text{Change in } x\text{-coordinate}} = \frac{y_2 - y_1}{x_2 - x_1}$$

The slope of a line defines its inclination. Lines with the same slope will have the same inclination and therefore be parallel. Lines with a positive slope incline to the right, whereas lines with a negative slope incline to the left.

If the algebraic representation of a line is in the form $y = mx + b$, the value of b represents the y-intercept and the value of m represents the slope of the line. This represen-

slope-intercept equation of   tation is called the **slope-intercept equation of a line**.
a line

Investigation 5

Examine the algebraic representation of each of the following lines. Predict the slope and y-intercept. Determine three points that lie on each line. Plot and connect these points to confirm your predictions.

(a) $y = 3x - 2$

(b) $y = -2x + 1$

(c) $y = \frac{4}{3}x$

(a) $y = 3x - 2$

This algebraic representation tells us that the y-coordinate is two less than three times the x-coordinate. Some points that have this pattern are $(-2, -8)$, $(1, 1)$, and $(4, 10)$. The graph of the line will cross the y-axis at $(0, -2)$. The slope of the line is $\frac{3}{1}$, or 3. A positive slope indicates that the line inclines to the right; that is, as the x-values increase, the y-values increase.

The graph can be drawn in a number of ways. Each point can be plotted and then connected to form a straight line, or we can begin at any point and use the numerical representation of the slope to determine other points on the line. This method is illustrated here. Begin at $(-2, -8)$. Change the y-coordinate by three units (go up three units), then change the x-coordinate by one unit (go to the right one unit). We are now at the point $(-1, -5)$. This point is consistent with the pattern established, since two less than three times -1 is equal to -5. The process can be repeated again.

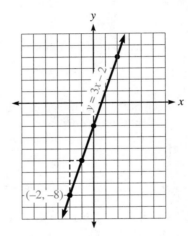

(b) $y = -2x + 1$

The slope of this line is $\frac{-2}{1}$. The coordinates of the y-intercept are $(0, 1)$. Some points that lie on the line are $(2, -3)$, $(1, -1)$, and $(4, -7)$. Since the slope is negative, the line inclines to the left; that is, as the x-values increase, the y-values decrease. The graph is shown below.

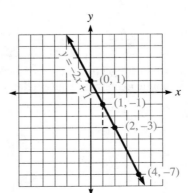

(c) $y = \frac{4}{3}x$

The slope of this line is positive. The line intersects the y-axis at (0, 0). From this point, a change of three units in the x-value is paired with a change of four units in the y-value. This results in the point (3, 4). By repeating this process, the points (6, 8) and (9, 12) can be determined. The graph is pictured here.

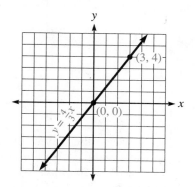

We will now investigate two special cases. Recall that the equation of a horizontal line passing through (0, b) is y = b. The equation of a vertical line passing through (a, 0) is x = a. We will now examine the slope of each line.

Choose any two points that lie on the horizontal line y = b (see Figure 12.9a on page 584). Let $(x_1, y_1) = (r, b)$ and $(x_2, y_2) = (s, b)$. Use the slope formula to determine a value for the slope as follows:

$$\text{Slope} = \frac{\text{Change in } y\text{-coordinate}}{\text{Change in } x\text{-coordinate}} = \frac{y_2 - y_1}{x_2 - x_1} = \frac{b - b}{s - r} = \frac{0}{s - r} = 0$$

Since the y-coordinates are the same for all points lying on this line, the numerical representation of the slope has a numerator of 0 and therefore a value of 0. The slope of any horizontal line is equal to 0.

Now choose any two points that lie on the vertical line x = a (Figure 12.9b). Let $(x_1, y_1) = (a, r)$ and $(x_2, y_2) = (a, s)$. Use the slope formula to determine a value for the slope as follows:

$$\text{Slope} = \frac{\text{Change in } y\text{-coordinate}}{\text{Change in } x\text{-coordinate}} = \frac{y_2 - y_1}{x_2 - x_1} = \frac{s - r}{a - a} = \frac{s - r}{0}$$

Since the x-coordinates are the same for all points lying on this line, the numerical representation of the slope has a denominator of 0. Division by 0 is undefined. Therefore, the slope of any vertical line is undefined. A vertical line has no slope.

Figure 12.9

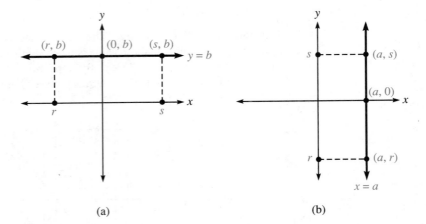

(a)   (b)

We have already seen that parallel lines have equal slopes. We will now focus on a special case of intersecting perpendicular lines. Figure 12.10 depicts rhombus *ABCD* with each side five units in length. Diagonals $\overline{AC}$ and $\overline{BD}$ are drawn. Recall that the diagonals of a rhombus are the perpendicular bisectors of each other. Let L_1 represent $\overline{AC}$, and L_2 represent $\overline{BD}$.

Figure 12.10

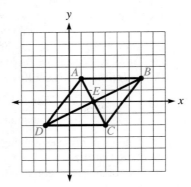

L_1 and L_2 intersect at $E(2, 0)$. The fact that these two lines are perpendicular could be verified by using the Pythagorean theorem to verify that the triangles formed at E are right triangles. The slope of L_1 is $\frac{(-2 - 2)}{(3 - 1)}$, or $\frac{-2}{1}$. The slope of L_2 is $\frac{2 - (-2)}{6 - (-2)}$, or $\frac{1}{2}$. Notice the relationship between the slopes of the perpendicular segments. They are the negative reciprocal of each other.

This relationship will hold for all pairs of perpendicular lines and line segments. Examine Investigation 6.

Investigation 6

You are given the equations of three pairs of lines. In each case, graph the pair on the same set of axes and measure the angle formed at the point of intersection. What visual and numerical patterns do you recognize?

$$y = 5x + 2 \qquad y = \frac{1}{4}x - 3 \qquad y = \frac{3}{5}x + 1$$

$$y = -\frac{1}{5}x - 1 \qquad y = -4x + 4 \qquad y = -\frac{5}{3}x - 2$$

For ease of reference, choose and label a point on each line. In addition, label the point of intersection of each line. The labeled graphs of each pair are shown here:

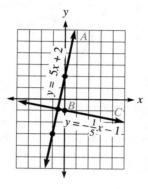 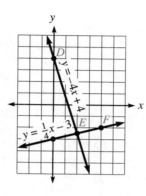 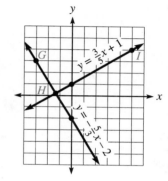

Use your protractor to verify that angles *ABC*, *DEF*, and *GHI* are right angles. Therefore, each pair of lines is perpendicular. Examine the equations of the lines. It appears in each case that the slopes are negative reciprocals of each other. In addition, notice the following similarity when the slopes of each pair are multiplied:

$$5 \times -\frac{1}{5} = -1 \qquad \frac{1}{4} \times (-4) = -1 \qquad \frac{3}{5} \times \left(-\frac{5}{3}\right) = -1$$

In general, the product of the slopes of perpendicular lines is equal to −1.

Investigation 7

Graph each of the four lines whose equations are given here:

$$L_1: \; y = \frac{1}{2}x + 2 \quad L_2: \; y = -\frac{3}{4}x + 2 \quad L_3: \; y = \frac{1}{2}x - 3 \quad L_4: \; y = -2x - 3$$

Label the points of intersection as follows:

$$A \rightarrow L_1 \cap L_2$$
$$B \rightarrow L_2 \cap L_3$$
$$C \rightarrow L_3 \cap L_4$$
$$D \rightarrow L_4 \cap L_1$$

Define figure *ABCD*. Justify your definition.

The four graphs are shown here:

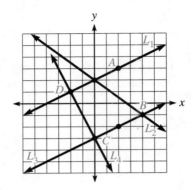

Figure $ABCD$ is formed by the intersections of these four graphs. $ABCD$ is a quadrilateral. Side $\overline{BC}$ is parallel to side $\overline{AD}$ since the slopes of the lines that form those sides are equal. Side $\overline{AD}$ is perpendicular to side $\overline{DC}$ since the product of their slopes equals -1. Side $\overline{BC}$ is perpendicular to side $\overline{DC}$ since the product of their slopes equals -1. Therefore, this quadrilateral contains two right angles and one pair of parallel sides. The figure is a right trapezoid.

Point-Slope Form of the Equation of a Line

We have seen that the slope of the line passing through points (x_1, y_1) and (x_2, y_2) is given as

$$m = \frac{y_2 - y_1}{x_2 - x_1}$$

Examine the line $y = 5x - 1$ whose graph is pictured in Figure 12.11.

Figure 12.11

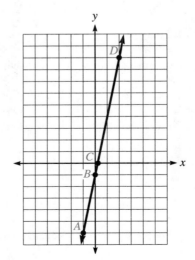

Let (x, y) represent any point on this line. Examine the representation of the slope of the line that passes through (x, y) and points A, B, C, and D.

Point on Line $y = 5x - 1$	Slope of the Line Through (x, y) and Given Point on $y = 5x - 1$
$A(-1, -6)$	$\dfrac{y - (-6)}{x - (-1)}$
$B(0, -1)$	$\dfrac{y - (-1)}{x - 0}$
$C(\frac{1}{5}, 0)$	$\dfrac{y - 0}{x - \frac{1}{5}}$
$D(2, 9)$	$\dfrac{y - 9}{x - 2}$

We know from the equation $y = 5x - 1$ that the slope of the line must be equal to 5. Therefore, each of the algebraic representations of the slope given in the table above must equal 5. Let (x_1, y_1) be any point E on $y = 5x - 1$. The algebraic representation of the slope is given as

$$\frac{y - y_1}{x - x_1} = m$$

Multiplying both sides of this equation by $(x - x_1)$ yields

$$(y - y_1) = m(x - x_1)$$

point-slope form   This is the **point-slope form** of the equation of a line passing through point (x_1, y_1) with slope m. The point-slope form is used when the slope of a line and a point on that line are known. For example, the point-slope form of the equation of a line with slope 5 passing through point $D(2, 9)$ would be written as

$$(y - 9) = 5(x - 2)$$

Simplifying, we get

$$y - 9 = 5x - 10$$
$$y = 5x - 1$$

This is consistent with the equation of the line pictured in Figure 12.11.

Systems of Equations

If two lines intersect, at the point of intersection is a single point that lies on both lines. Therefore, the point of intersection satisfies, or solves, each of the equations. Figure 12.12 on page 588 depicts the intersection of lines $y = -3x + 9$ and $y = 2x - 1$.

Figure 12.12

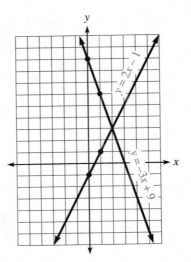

Notice that the lines intersect at (2, 3). These two equations are known as a system of equations. A **system of equations** is a set of two or more equations. The point of inter- section in this system is the point that simultaneously satisfies both equations. There- fore, this point is called a simultaneous solution of the system of equations.

system of equations

In a system of two equations, the lines need not always intersect. It is possible that a system contains two parallel lines or two lines that coincide. It would follow that two coinciding lines are equivalent, and every point satisfying the equation of one line also satisfies the equation of the other. It can be shown that two lines that coincide have the same algebraic representation. For example, examine the following system:

$$2y = 4x - 6$$
$$y - 2x = -3$$

These two equations appear dissimilar. Rewrite them in the slope-intercept form as follows:

$$2y = 4x - 6 \qquad y - 2x = -3$$
$$y = 2x - 3 \qquad \quad y = 2x - 3$$

Notice that the two equations in the system are equivalent.

Investigation 8

Ramon purchased eight tickets to a school play. Each adult's ticket cost $4. Each child's ticket cost $2. The total cost of the tickets was $22. How many of each type of ticket did Ramon buy?

Understand the Problem: What is known? You are told the number of tickets bought, the price of an adult's ticket, the price of a child's ticket, and the total cost of the purchase.

What is unknown? You are asked to determine the numbers of adults' and children's tickets purchased.

Devise a Plan: This problem can be solved in a number of ways. Perhaps the easiest way is to construct a table. Enter numbers of tickets whose sum is 8. Examine the cost.

Carry Out the Plan:

Number of Adults' Tickets	Number of Children's Tickets	Cost
0	8	$4 \times 0 + 2 \times 8 = 16$
1	7	$4 \times 1 + 2 \times 7 = 18$
2	6	$4 \times 2 + 2 \times 6 = 20$
3	5	$4 \times 3 + 2 \times 5 = 22$

The table shows that Ramon purchased three adults' tickets and five children's tickets.

This problem could also have been solved graphically. Let y represent the number of children's tickets and x the number of adults' tickets. Use these variables to interpret the problem algebraically:

Ramon purchased eight tickets to a school play. $x + y = 8$

Each child's ticket cost $2. Each adult's ticket cost $4.

The total cost of the tickets was $22. $4x + 2y = 22$

These algebraic representations are equations of straight lines and can therefore be viewed as a system. Graphing them and determining the point of intersection will yield the values that satisfy both equations.

$$x + y = 8 \quad \rightarrow \quad y = -x + 8 \quad \rightarrow \quad \text{slope: } -1 \quad y\text{-intercept } (0, 8)$$
$$4x + 2y = 22 \quad \rightarrow \quad y = -2x + 11 \quad \rightarrow \quad \text{slope: } -2 \quad y\text{-intercept } (0, 11)$$

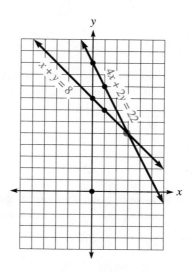

The point (3, 5) satisfies both equations and indicates that Ramon purchased three adults' tickets and five children's tickets.

Look Back: Verify your results by substituting the solution into both equations.

Although this graphing approach may appear laborious, new developments in graphing technology remove the tedium from the graphing process and make graphing systems of equations a useful problem-solving technique. These new developments include graphing software and graphics calculators (see Appendix).

The Substitution Method

The graphical approach to solving a system of equations relies on the notion that the point of intersection of two lines is easily read from the graph. Unfortunately, this is not always the case. You would be hard-pressed to distinguish $\left(\frac{2}{3}, \frac{3}{4}\right)$ from $\left(\frac{3}{5}, \frac{7}{10}\right)$ by examining a graph. Although it is true that systems can always be graphed, a graph is not always the best way to solve a system of equations. We turn to algebra for alternate methods.

Examine the following system.

$$y = 3x$$
$$y + 2x = -5$$

These two lines intersect at $(-1, -3)$, as shown on the graph in Figure 12.13.

Figure 12.13

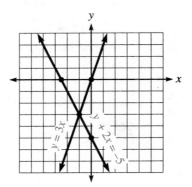

Notice in the first equation that $y = 3x$. We substitute $3x$ for y in the second equation to reduce the equation to one variable as follows:

$$y + 2x = -5$$
$$3x + 2x = -5$$
$$5x = -5$$
$$x = -1$$

We have now determined the x-coordinate of the point of intersection. By substituting $x = -1$ into either equation, the y-coordinate of the intersection can easily be determined. Since the first equation is already in the form "$y =$," it is simpler to substitute $x = -1$ into this equation.

$$y = 3x$$
$$y = 3(-1)$$
$$y = -3$$

The point of intersection is $(-1, -3)$. The last step in solving any mathematical problem is always to "look back." Here, it is necessary to check that the point $(-1, -3)$ indeed solves *both* equations, as shown here:

$$y = 3x \qquad\qquad y + 2x = -5$$
$$-3 = 3(-1) \qquad -3 + 2(-1) = -5$$
$$-3 = -3 \qquad\qquad -5 = -5$$

Since $(-1, -3)$ satisfies both equations, $y = 3x$ and $y + 2x = -5$ intersect at this point. This agrees with the graphical representation given in Figure 12.13.

The Addition/Subtraction Method

This method of solving a system of equations relies on manipulating equations through addition and subtraction. Three premises underlie this method:

1. The same number can be added to or subtracted from both sides of an equation without changing the equality.

2. Both sides of an equation can be multiplied and divided by the same nonzero number without changing the equality.

3. Equations can be added or subtracted, resulting in a new statement that is also an equation.

Examine the following system of equations:

$$2x + y = 10$$
$$-2x - 3y = -6$$

The goal of this method is to reduce the system of equations to a single equation with one variable. Notice that adding the terms on the left of the equal sign and the terms on the right of the equal sign of both equations eliminates the x term since $2x + (-2x) = 0$.

$$2x + y = 10 \qquad \text{Add both equations.}$$
$$\underline{-2x - 3y = -6}$$
$$0 - 2y = 4 \qquad \text{Solve for } y.$$
$$y = -2$$

Once a value for one of the variables has been obtained, this value can be substituted back into either of the two equations to determine the other variable as follows:

$$2x + y = 10 \qquad\qquad -2x - 3y = -6$$
$$2x + (-2) = 10 \qquad -2x - 3(-2) = -6$$
$$2x = 12 \qquad\qquad -2x + 6 = -6$$
$$x = 6 \qquad\qquad -2x = -12$$
$$x = 6$$

The point of intersection of these two lines is $(6, -2)$.

Sometimes, simple addition or subtraction of the equations in a system is not sufficient to eliminate one of the variables. For example, consider the following system:

$$7x + 3y = -2$$
$$3x + 2y = -3$$

Neither the x nor the y variable is easily eliminated by adding or subtracting the equations. We will need to manipulate these equations in order to eliminate one of the variables.

coefficients   The numerical parts of the terms $7x$, $3y$, $3x$, and $2y$ are called the **coefficients** of x and y, respectively. Focus on a single variable. Determine the least common multiple of the coefficients of that variable. For example, the least common multiple of the y-variable coefficients 3 and 2 is 6. If we multiply the first equation by 2 and the second equation by (-3), a new equivalent system results. When these two equations are added, the y term will easily be eliminated.

$$2 \times (7x + 3y = -2) \quad \rightarrow \quad 14x + 6y = -4$$
$$-3 \times (3x + 2y = -3) \quad \rightarrow \quad \underline{-9x - 6y = 9}$$
$$5x = 5$$
$$x = 1$$

Substituting $x = 1$ in either of the two original equations results in a y-value of -3. Therefore, the point of intersection of $7x + 3y = -2$ and $3x + 2y = -3$ is $(1, -3)$, as shown in Figure 12.14.

Figure 12.14

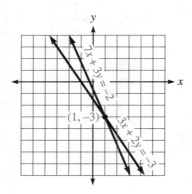

Investigation 9

Akira has a total of 18 coins, composed of only nickels and dimes. These coins have a total value of $1.45. How many of each coin does she have? Solve this problem in two different ways.

Understand the Problem: What is known? You are given the total number and total value of a set of coins consisting of nickels and dimes.
What is unknown? You must determine the number of each type of coin.

Devise a Plan: We will solve this problem by substitution and then by constructing a graph.

Carry Out the Plan: Let $x =$ the number of nickels and $y =$ the number of dimes.

Akira has a total of 18 coins.	$\rightarrow$	$x + y = 18$
These coins have a total value of $1.45.	$\rightarrow$	$.05x + .10y = 1.45$

$$.05x + .10y = 1.45$$
$$.05x + .10(-x + 18) = 1.45$$
$$.05x - .10x + 1.8 = 1.45$$
$$-.05x = -.35$$
$$x = 7$$

Substitute $x = 7$ into either of the two equations to determine that $y = 11$. This solution is consistent with the graphical solution shown here ($.05x + .10y = 1.45$ is equivalent to $y = -.5x + 14.5$). Both representations show that Akira has 7 nickels and 11 dimes.

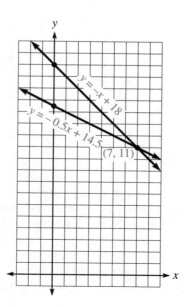

Look Back: This problem could also have been solved using the addition/subtraction method as follows:

$$x + y = 18$$
$$.05x + .10y = 1.45$$

Focus on the y variable. The least common multiple of 1 and .10 is 1. Multiply the second equation by -10 as follows:

$$x + y = 18 \qquad \rightarrow \qquad x + y = 18$$
$$-10 \times (.05x + .10y) = 1.45(-10) \qquad \rightarrow \qquad \underline{-.5x - y = -14.5}$$
$$.5x = 3.5$$
$$x = 7$$

Substitute $x = 7$ into either of the two equations. The result yields $y = 11$.

Each of these methods of solution is equally valid. Depending on the circumstances, one or the other may be more efficient.

Equations of Curves

So far in this section, we have focused on linear equations, that is, equations of straight lines. We can also represent nonlinear graphs in algebraic form.

One of the defining features of a straight line is its slope. The slope of a straight line is constant everywhere on that straight line. This can be verified by selecting any two pairs of points that lie on a straight line and computing the slope of the segment that joins them. This is not the case in a curve. Examine Figure 12.15.

Figure 12.15

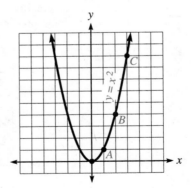

Points A, B, and C lie on the curve $y = x^2$. The y-coordinate of every point on this curve is the square of its x-coordinate. Begin at point A. To arrive at point B, you must change y by $+3$ units and change x by $+1$ unit. Now, continue from B to C. Here, the change in y is $+5$ units for each $+1$ unit change in x. The concept of slope as it relates to curves is thoroughly studied in calculus. For the purposes of this text, it is enough to know that the slope of a straight line is constant along its entire length.

It is important to recognize patterns that relate a graphical representation of a curve to its algebraic representation. Investigation 10 identifies such relationships.

Investigation 10

In Figure 12.15 you were given the equation of $y = x^2$. In the set below, you are given both the algebraic and graphical representation of curves that belong to the same "family" as $y = x^2$. Identify the algebraic characteristic that affects the graphical representation. If A is any real number, explain what the graph of $y = x^2 + A$ might look like.

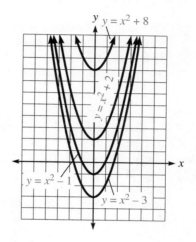

$$y = x^2 + 2$$

$$y = x^2 + 8$$

$$y = x^2 - 1$$

$$y = x^2 - 11$$

In the graph above the curve $y = x^2$ is shifted up or down along the y-axis depending on the value and sign of A. It appears that the curve $y = x^2 + A$ shifts the curve $y = x^2$ A units from the origin either up or down, depending on the sign of A.

The equation of one curve deserves special attention. Recall that the set of points equidistant from a fixed point is called a circle. Examine Figure 12.16.

Figure 12.16

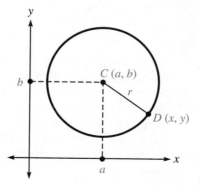

The point C with coordinates (a, b) is the center of the circle, and any point D on the circle has coordinates (x, y). The distance from C to D is a fixed number, r, and is determined by using the distance formula as shown on page 596.

$$\sqrt{(x-a)^2 + (y-b)^2} = r$$

$$(x-a)^2 + (y-b)^2 = r^2$$ The result of squaring both sides to remove the square root on the left of the distance representation

This is the algebraic representation of a circle. In general, if (a, b) is the center of a circle with radius r, the equation of this circle is given as

$$(x-a)^2 + (y-b)^2 = r^2$$

For example, the algebraic representation $(x-2)^2 + (y-3)^2 = 25$ defines a circle whose center is at $(2, 3)$ and whose radius is equal to 5 (since $5^2 = 25$). The algebraic representation $(x+2)^2 + (y+3)^2 = 25$ also defines a circle whose radius is 5 units, but whose center is at $(-2, -3)$. This can be seen by rewriting the equation as

$$[x-(-2)]^2 + [y-(-3)]^2 = 5^2$$

Examine Figure 12.17, which shows a circle whose radius is 5 units and whose center is at the origin. Notice that the axes form four angles whose vertices are at the **central angles**   center of the circle. These angles are called **central angles**. Within the circle itself, the sides of these angles are radii of the circle. The four central angles formed by the axes pictured in Figure 12.17 are right angles. (Central angles need not be right angles and need not be formed by the axes.) In Figure 12.18, the lines $y = 2x$ and $y = x$ have been drawn. Portions of these lines are radii of the circle and form central angles.

Figure 12.17
Figure 12.18

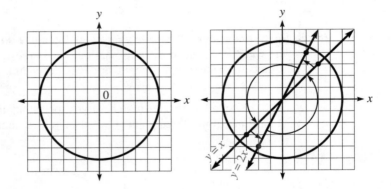

Angles can also be formed at points other than at the center of a circle. The segments and lines forming these angles have special names. In Figure 12.19a $\angle ABC$ is formed on the circle by diameter $\overline{AB}$ and line $\overleftrightarrow{BC}$. Notice that line $\overleftrightarrow{BC}$ intersects the circle at one and only one point, B. We call such a line a **tangent** to a circle. A tangent to a **tangent**   circle is perpendicular to the radius at the point of tangency. Therefore, since $\angle ABC$ is formed by a tangent and a radius of a circle, $\angle ABC$ is a right angle. In Figure 12.19b, an angle is formed on the circle by a chord and a tangent, and is not necessarily a right angle.

Suppose that the segment forming a chord of a circle is extended to form a line. **secant**   This line would intersect the circle at two points. Such a line is called a **secant** of a circle. In Figure 12.19c, two secants form an angle that is on the circle. In Figure 12.19d, two secants form angles that are within the circle.

Figure 12.19

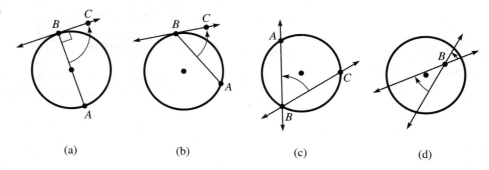

(a)   (b)   (c)   (d)

Investigation 11

A circle has the equation $(x - 4)^2 + (y - 3)^2 = 25$.

(a) Write the equations of two lines that will form central angles of this circle.

(b) Write the equation of a tangent to this circle at $(0, 0)$.

(c) Write the equation of any secant of this circle.

(a) Two lines that form central angles at $(4, 3)$ must themselves contain $(4, 3)$. Therefore, choose any two slopes, say, $m_1 = 2$ and $m_2 = 3$, and use the point-slope formula to determine the equations of the lines as shown here.

$$y - y_1 = m(x - x_1)$$

$m = 2$ $(x_1, y_1) = (4, 3)$ $\rightarrow$ $y - 3 = 2(x - 4)$ $\rightarrow$ $y = 2x - 5$

$m = 3$ $(x_1, y_1) = (4, 3)$ $\rightarrow$ $y - 3 = 3(x - 4)$ $\rightarrow$ $y = 3x - 9$

These lines are shown here:

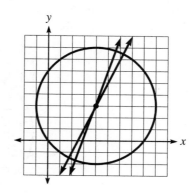

(b) Since a tangent to a circle is perpendicular to the radius at the point of tangency, we must first determine the slope of the line segment that joins (0, 0) and (4, 3). This segment is a radius of the circle. The slope is determined as follows:

$$\frac{(y_2 - y_1)}{(x_2 - x_1)} = \frac{(3 - 0)}{(4 - 0)} = \frac{3}{4}$$

Since the tangent is perpendicular to the radius at the point of tangency, it will have a slope of $-\frac{4}{3}$. Using this slope, point (0, 0), and the point-slope formula yields the equation

$$y = \frac{-4}{3}x$$

as pictured here:

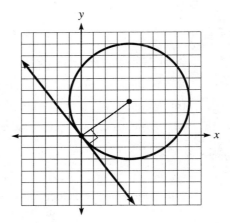

(c) A secant of a circle intersects the circle at two points. Choose any two points on the circle, say, (4, 8) and (8, 0). The slope of the line passing through both of these points is

$$\frac{0 - 8}{8 - 4} = -2$$

Using this slope, either of the two points, and the point-slope formula yields the equation $y = -2x + 16$. The graph of this secant is pictured here:

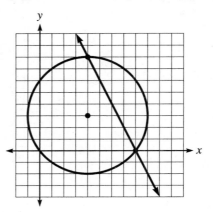

As you have seen here, the complementary tools of algebra and geometry lead to significant insights. Before closing this section we will examine the relationship between figures that are contained (inscribed) within a circle and figures that enclose (circumscribe) a circle.

Investigation 12

Square $ABCD$ has endpoints $A(-4, 4)$, $B(2, 4)$, $C(2, -2)$, and $D(-4, -2)$. Determine the equation of the largest circle that can be inscribed within this square.

Plot the four points on the coordinate axes and construct square $ABCD$.

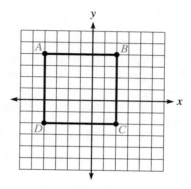

The largest circle that can be inscribed within the square would be tangent to each of the four sides of the square. Therefore, the center of the circle must be equidistant from each of the four sides of the square. To find this point, construct diagonals $\overline{AC}$ and $\overline{BD}$. These diagonals intersect at the center of the square, which is point E with coordinates $(-1, 1)$. By constructing a perpendicular line segment from point E to any side, it can be seen that the perpendicular distance from the center E to the sides of the square is equal to three units. This perpendicular distance represents the measure of the radius of the circle in question. The equation of a circle whose center is $(-1, 1)$ and whose radius equals three units is

$$[x - (-1)]^2 + (y - 1)^2 = 3^2$$
$$(x + 1)^2 + (y - 1)^2 = 9$$

This inscribed circle is pictured on page 600.

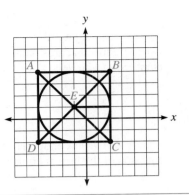

The study of circumscribed circles about triangles and inscribed circles within triangles can be approached from two different viewpoints. One view uses coordinate geometry as its basis, and the other uses Euclidean constructions.

Circumscribing a Circle about a Triangle

circumcenter
A circle can be circumscribed about any triangle with the three vertices of the triangle lying on the circle. The center of such a circle is called the **circumcenter**. The circumcenter lies at the intersection of the perpendicular bisectors of each of the sides. Here, we will examine three approaches that can be used to circumscribe a circle about a given triangle.

Examine the triangle in Figure 12.23, whose vertices are $A(0, 0)$, $B(-4, 8)$, and $C(-12, 0)$.

Figure 12.23

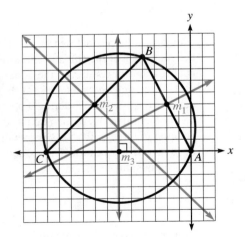

Coordinate Geometry Approach

1. Because the circumcenter lies at the intersection of the perpendicular bisectors, it is necessary to locate the midpoint of each side. Let m_1, m_2, and m_3 be the midpoints of sides $\overline{AB}$, $\overline{BC}$, and $\overline{CA}$, respectively. The coordinates of the midpoints are $m_1(-2, 4)$, $m_2(-8, 4)$, and $m_3(-6, 0)$. The slope of the perpendicular bisector of a line is the negative reciprocal of the slope of that line. Organize this information in the following way.

	Endpoint	Midpoint	Slope of Line Containing the Side	Slope of ⊥ Bisector
$\overline{AB}$	(0, 0) (−4, 8)	$m_1(-2, 4)$	−2	$\frac{1}{2}$
$\overline{BC}$	(−4, 8) (−12, 0)	$m_2 (-8, 4)$	1	−1
$\overline{CA}$	(−12, 0) (0, 0)	$m_3 (-6, 0)$	0 (horizontal line)	undefined (vertical line)

2. Begin at the midpoint of $\overline{AB}$, (−2, 4). The slope of the perpendicular bisector is $\frac{1}{2}$. Another point on the bisector can be found by changing the y-value by +1 and the x-value by +2. This yields the point (0, 5). Draw the line segment that passes through the points (−2, 4) and (0, 5).

3. Begin at the midpoint of $\overline{BC}$, (−8, 4). The slope of the perpendicular bisector is −1. Another point on the bisector can be found by changing the y-value by −1 and the x-value by +1. This yields the point (−7, 3). Draw the line segment that passes through the points (−8, 4) and (−7, 3).

4. Begin at the midpoint of $\overline{CA}$, (−6, 0). The slope of the perpendicular bisector is undefined. Draw a vertical line through (−6, 0).

5. The three lines intersect at (−6, 2). This is the circumcenter of the circle that can be circumscribed about △ ABC. It is the point which is equidistant from the vertices A, B, and C.

In Problem 29 at the end of this section, you will be asked to determine the equation of this circle.

Algebraic Approach

We know that the circumcenter lies at the point of interesection of the perpendicular bisectors of each side. If you know the equations of two of these bisectors it is sufficient to determine the circumcenter by solving them as a system.

We have already determined that the slope of the perpendicular bisector of $\overline{AB}$ is $\frac{1}{2}$, and that it passes through the midpoint of AB at (−2, 4). Therefore, its equation is

$$y - 4 = \tfrac{1}{2}(x - (-2))$$
$$y = \tfrac{1}{2}x + 5$$

The slope of the perpendicular bisector of $\overline{BC}$ is −1, and it passes through the midpoint of $\overline{BC}$ at (−8, 4). Therefore, its equation is

$$y - 4 = -[x - (-8)]$$
$$y = -x - 4$$

Set up and solve the system as follows:

$$\begin{array}{ccc}
y = \tfrac{1}{2}x + 5 & \rightarrow & y - \tfrac{1}{2}x = 5 \\
y = -x - 4 & \rightarrow & -(y + x) = -4 \\
\hline
 & & -\tfrac{3}{2}x = 9 \\
 & & x = -6
\end{array}$$

Substituting $x = -6$ into the second equation yields $y = 2$. Therefore, the circumcenter is at (−6, 2).

Euclidean Construction Approach

This approach is straightforward and relies solely on constructing perpendicular bisectors to each of the given segments (see Section 11.1), as shown in Figure 12.20:

Figure 12.20

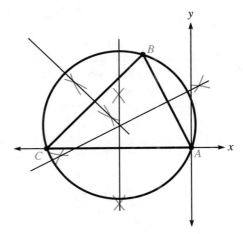

Notice that the circumcenter is located at the intersection of the perpendicular bisectors.

Inscribing a Circle Within a Triangle

incenter

The Euclidean construction approach will be followed to determine the center of a circle that is inscribed within a given triangle. This center is called the **incenter**. Although coordinate geometry can be used to find a circle's incenter, the process is long and complicated. Because of this, we present only the Euclidean construction approach.

The incenter of a circle is located at the point of intersection of the three angle bisectors. Figure 12.21 depicts the use of the construction that bisects an angle (see Section 11.1) within this context.

Figure 12.21

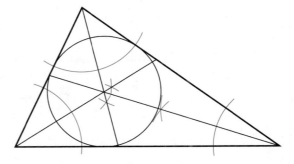

The radius of the circle is the distance from the incenter to the point at which the angle bisector meets the opposite side. Notice that the segments that form the sides of the triangle are each tangent to the inscribed circle.

Assessments for Section 12.1

1. Determine four points that satisfy each of the following equations.

   (a) $y = 2x - 5$

   (b) $6x + 3y = 12$

   (c) $y = -3$

   (d) $x = 11$

   (e) $y = x^3$

2. Determine if the given point falls on the line whose equation is stated here.

   (a) $(2, 3)$ $y = 2x - 1$

   (b) $(-2, 6)$ $y = -2x - 2$

   (c) $(0, -3)$ $y = 3x - 3$

   (d) $(\frac{1}{2}, 6)$ $y = 4x + 4$

   (e) $(-3, -1)$ $y = -x - 4$

   (f) $(4, 0)$ $y = \frac{1}{4}x - 1$

3. Write the equation of a line that passes through the given point.

   (a) $(1, 1)$

   (b) $(-1, 0)$

   (c) $(0, -11)$

   (d) $(-2, 3)$

   (e) $(6, 6)$

4. Determine the distance between each of the following points.

   (a) $(2, 1), (3, 5)$

   (b) $(0, 3), (4, 0)$

   (c) $(-1, 2), (-3, 5)$

   (d) $(0, 0), (-5, 3)$

   (e) $(-4, 1), (1, -4)$

5. You are given the coordinates of points A, B, C, and D. Determine if line $\overline{AB}$ is parallel to $\overline{CD}$.

   (a) $A(1, 3), B(4, 1), C(0, 0), D(4, -2)$

   (b) $A(-1, 3), B(1, -1), C(1, 4), D(3, -1)$

   (c) $A(1, 1), B(2, 1), C(-1, -1), D(3, -1)$

   (d) $A(0, 2), B(4, 0), C(0, 0), D(2, -2)$

   (e) $A(0, 2), B(4, 1), C(0, 0), D(4, -1)$

6. Write the equation of the line that passes through the given point with the given slope.

   (a) $(0, 2)$ $m = \frac{1}{2}$

   (b) $(4, -6)$ $m = \frac{-3}{4}$

   (c) $(1, 4)$ $m = \frac{1}{3}$

   (d) $(-1, 0)$ $m = 4$

   (e) $(5, 4)$ $m = 0$

   (f) $(-1, 7)$ m is undefined

   (g) $(3, 6)$ $m = -2$

   (h) $(-3, 5)$ $m = -1$

   (i) $(4, -10)$ $m = -3$

   (j) $(1, 1)$ $m = \frac{-1}{2}$

7. Despite the lack of coordinates, write an equation of a line whose graph appears in each of the following figures.

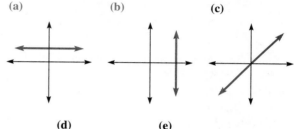

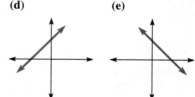

8. Determine the midpoint of the line segments whose endpoints are given below.

   (a) $(10, -3), (4, 3)$

   (b) $(2, 6), (-8, 4)$

   (c) $(-2, -6), (5, 9)$

   (d) $(5, 6), (-2, -4)$

   (e) $(-3, 9), (0, 0)$

9. Determine the coordinates of point D such that figure $ABCD$ is a rectangle, three of whose vertices have coordinates $A(-5, 2), B(-1, 5), C(3, 0)$.

10. Write the equation of the circle whose center and radius are given below.

    (a) $(-1, 2)$ $r = 5$

    (b) $(0, 0)$ $r = 2$

    (c) $(-3, -1)$ $r = 3.5$

    (d) $(0, -5)$ $r = 3$

    (e) $(-4, 3)$ $r = 2.25$

11. Despite the lack of coordinates, write an equation of a circle whose graph is pictured on each plane.

(a)   (b)   (c)

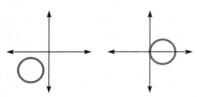

(d)   (e)

12. You are given the endpoints of a diameter of a circle. Write the equation of the circle.
    (a) (−2, −3), (4, 5)
    (b) (−1, 4), (−9, 4)
    (c) (3, 2), (3, −4)
    (d) (−1, −4), (−11, 0)
    (e) (5, −1), (7, 9)

13. You are given the coordinates of the vertices of a polygon. Determine the type of figure formed when the vertices are joined in the order presented.
    (a) $A(0, -2)$, $B(-2, 4)$, $C(2, 4)$, $D(0, 2)$
    (b) $A(-1, -5)$, $B(-5, -1)$, $C(1, 5)$, $D(5, 1)$
    (c) $A(6, -6)$, $B(-3, -3)$, $C(-4, 3)$ $D(5, 0)$
    (d) $A(1, -6)$, $B(1, 4)$, $C(7, 6)$, $D(8, 0)$
    (e) $A(-8, 1)$, $B(-1, -3)$, $C(-5, -5)$

14. Despite the lack of coordinates, write a system of equations for each of the following graphs.

(a)   (b)   (c)

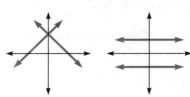

(d)   (e)

15. Find the point of intersection (if it exists) for each of the following pairs of equations.
    (a) $y = 2x - 1$ $y = x + 2$
    (b) $y = -x + 3$ $y = -3x + 5$
    (c) $y = \frac{1}{2}x - 1$ $y = x - 4$
    (d) $y + x = -2$ $2y = -2x + 6$

16. Determine five points on the circle whose center is at (2, −5) and radius is 13 units.

17. Plot the points $A(-3, 0)$, $B(-1, 6)$, and $C(3, -8)$ on the coordinate axis. Join the points to form $\triangle ABC$.
    (a) Construct three semicircles with diameters $\overline{AB}$, $\overline{BC}$, and $\overline{CA}$, respectively.
    (b) Determine the length of the radius of each semicircle.

18. Determine the coordinates of point D in each so that the figure $ABCD$ formed on the coordinate axes is the given polygon.
    (a) Rectangle $ABCD$: $A(-4, 4)$, $B(4, 4)$, $C(4, -3)$
    (b) Rectangle $ABCD$: $A(1, 8)$, $B(10, 2)$, $C(6, -4)$
    (c) Square $ABCD$: $A(-2, 2)$, $B(1, 5)$, $C(4, 2)$
    (d) Parallelogram $ABCD$: $A(-2, 3)$, $B(4, 3)$, $C(6, -1)$
    (e) Parallelogram $ABCD$: $A(-5, 3)$, $B(-2, 4)$, $C(6, 0)$
    (f) Rhombus $ABCD$: $A(-3, -1)$, $B(0, 3)$, $C(5, 3)$
    (g) Kite $ABCD$: $A(0, -6)$, $B(-2, 0)$, $C(0, 3)$
    (h) Isosceles trapezoid $ABCD$: $A(-2, 3)$, $B(3, 3)$, $C(7, -1)$

19. A collection of 12 coins consisting of only nickels and quarters has a value of $1.20. How many of each type of coin are in the collection?

20. A collection of nickels and dimes totals $1.40. The number of nickels is four less than twice the number of dimes. How many of each type of coin are in the collection?

21. The sum of two numbers is 5. The difference between the numbers is 11. What are the numbers? Solve this problem both algebraically and graphically.

22. The sum of two numbers is 10. The difference between the larger number and twice the smaller number is 1. What are the numbers? Solve this problem both algebraically and graphically.

23. The area of a circle is 28.26 units². The center of the circle is located at the point (1, 2). Write an equation of the circle. (Use $\pi \approx 3.14$.)

24. The circumference of a circle is 25.12 units. The center of the circle is located at (0, 4). Write an equation of this circle. (Use $\pi \approx 3.14$.)

25. The center of a circle is located at the intersection of the lines $y = x + 2$ and $y = -x + 6$. The radius of the circle is five units. Sketch this circle on the coordinate axes and write its equation.

26. The diagonals of a rectangle lie on the lines $y = 2x - 3$ and $y = -2x + 9$. List the vertices of one such possible rectangle.

27. The midpoint of the line segment that joins $A(x_1, y_1)$ and $B(x_2, y_2)$ can be expressed as

$$M\left(\frac{(x_1 + x_2)}{2}, \frac{(y_1 + y_2)}{2}\right).$$

(a) Show that M is equidistant from A and B.

(b) Show that M lies on the line that passes through A and B.

28. The coordinates of the vertices of an isosceles triangle are $A(-2, -2)$, $B(-4, 8)$, and $C(6, 6)$. Write the equation of the line that coincides with the segment that forms the altitude of the triangle from vertex B.

29. On page 601, you were given the vertices of $\triangle ABC$: $A(0, 0)$, $B(-4, 8)$, and $C(-12, 0)$. The circumcenter of the circle that can be circumscribed about ABC was located at $(-6, 2)$. Write the equation of this circle.

30. You are given the vertices of $\triangle DEF$: $D(-2, 0)$, $E(6, 8)$, and $F(8, 0)$.

(a) Draw $\triangle DEF$ on the coordinate axes.

(b) Determine the circumcenter of the circle that can be circumscribed about $\triangle DEF$.

(c) Determine the equation of the circle found in part (b).

(d) Draw $\triangle DEF$ on another set of axes. Use the geometric constructions to locate the circumcenter.

31. You are given $\triangle RST$ as shown here.

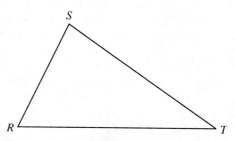

(a) Use a compass and a straightedge to construct a triangle XYZ that is congruent to $\triangle RST$.

(b) Circumscribe a circle about $\triangle RST$.

(c) Inscribe a circle within $\triangle RST$.

In Other Words

32. Define the concept of slope.

33. What is the difference between zero slope and no slope?

34. Describe how the distance formula relates to the Pythagorean theorem.

35. Explain the meaning of a solution to a system of equations. What is the graphical interpretation? What is the algebraic interpretation?

36. Describe how the letter and number coordinates of a map relate to the Cartesian system.

Cooperative Activity

37. Groups of two

Individual Accountability: On a sheet of graph paper, sketch four different figures whose perimeter is 48 units: a square, a rectangle, a trapezoid, and a kite.

Group Goal: Arrange the quadrilaterals in order from least to greatest area. Arrive at a generalization about the relationship between the perimeter and area of a polygon. Had the original list included an equilateral triangle whose perimeter is 48 units and a circle whose circumference is 48 units, predict where in the progression they would fall. Construct these two figures on the coordinate axes to verify your predictions.

12.2   Similarity and Congruence

In Chapter 11, we introduced geometry as measurement. Two types of measurement were covered in that chapter: direct and indirect. When the area of a polygon is calculated by covering or tiling, and when the volume of a solid is calculated by filling, direct measurement is being used. Even the ancient mathematicians of Alexandria found that direct measurement was an arduous task in many situations. The discovery of many formulas we use today is credited to these scholars.

When a formula is used to calculate the area or volume of a particular figure or to determine the measure of a side, indirect measurement is being used. The importance of indirect measurement should not be underestimated. The Alexandrians devised ways to measure the seemingly unmeasurable. For example, they were able to "measure" the radius of the earth, the sun, and the moon. They determined distances between stars and planets. The earliest mathematician to use indirect measurement to chart the skies was Hipparchus in the second century B.C. Hipparchus devised ingenious ways of measuring heights of mountains and distances from earth to heavenly bodies. The techniques of indirect measurement invented by Hipparchus are still used today in cartography, geography, surveying, and navigation.

In this section, we will introduce two concepts that play a role in indirect measurement: similarity and congruence. Informally, similar figures have the same shape, and congruent figures have the same size and the same shape.

Similarity

An example of the concepts of similarity and congruence can be found in the copies made by a photocopy machine. Many photocopiers have the capability of enlarging and reducing a figure. When an enlargement or a reduction of a figure is made, the "copy" has changed in size but not in shape. This, in essence, is the definition of similar figures. Two straight-line figures are said to be **similar figures** if they are the same shape but not necessarily the same size. When an exact copy of a figure is made, we see an example of congruence. The new figure has the same size and the same shape as the original. Congruence will be covered in the latter portion of this section, and viewed as a special case of similarity.

similar figures

Similar Polygons

Similar figures have an additional characteristic that can be seen by studying the enlargements and reductions made of polygon *ABCD* on a photocopy machine. Examine Figure 12.22.

The angle and side measurements of the five figures in Figure 12.22 are organized in the following table:

Figure	Length of Sides in Centimeters				Angle Measurement in Degrees			
	$\overline{AB}$	$\overline{BC}$	$\overline{CD}$	$\overline{DA}$	$m\angle A$	$m\angle B$	$m\angle C$	$m\angle D$
(a)	4.0	3.5	2.0	3.0	90	60	120	90
(b)	3.6	≈ 3.2	1.8	2.7	90	60	120	90
(c)	3.2	2.8	1.6	2.4	90	60	120	90
(d)	2.6	≈ 2.3	1.3	≈ 2.0	90	60	120	90
(e)	5.0	≈ 4.4	2.5	≈ 3.8	90	60	120	90

Figure 12.22

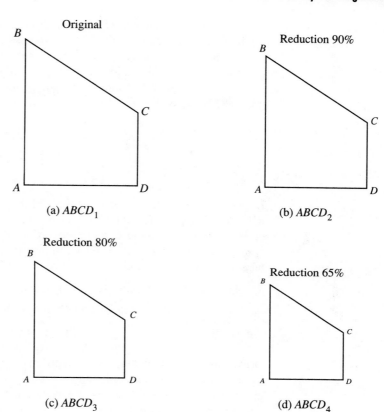

Original

(a) $ABCD_1$

Reduction 90%

(b) $ABCD_2$

Reduction 80%

(c) $ABCD_3$

Reduction 65%

(d) $ABCD_4$

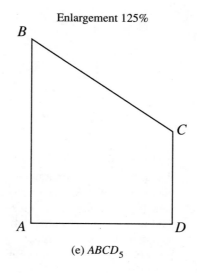

Enlargement 125%

(e) $ABCD_5$

We can immediately see that the angle measures of each polygon remain the same through the enlargement and reduction processes, which might lead you to expect that the reduction and enlargement uniformly affected all four sides of the figure. This can be verified by setting up ratios between the lengths in the original figure and the lengths in the altered version. Examine the lengths of the sides in both parts (c) and (e) of Figure 12.22, compared with part (a).

$$\frac{AB_3}{AB_1} = \frac{3.2}{4} = .8 \qquad \frac{BC_3}{BC_1} = \frac{2.8}{3.5} = .8 \qquad \frac{CD_3}{CD_1} = \frac{1.6}{2} = .8 \qquad \frac{DA_3}{DA_1} = \frac{2.4}{3} = .8$$

$$\frac{AB_5}{AB_1} = \frac{5}{4} = 1.25 \qquad \frac{BC_5}{BC_1} = \frac{4.4}{3.5} \approx 1.25 \qquad \frac{CD_5}{CD_1} = \frac{2.5}{2} = 1.25 \qquad \frac{DA_5}{DA_1} = \frac{3.8}{3} \approx 1.25$$

In each case, the ratio between the length of the altered side and the length of the original side is equal to the reduction or enlargement percentage. The uniformity of results clearly shows that the ratios are in proportion. The same results can be obtained when comparing any of the altered figures to the original. When similar polygons are compared, two characteristics can be observed:

1. The corresponding sides are in proportion.

2. The corresponding angle measurements are equal.

We use the symbol ~ to denote similarity. Therefore, $ABCD_1 \sim ABCD_5$.

 Although corresponding angles of two figures must be congruent to establish similarity, this congruence alone is not sufficient to establish similarity for figures with more than three sides. Examine the two polygons in Figure 12.23. Corresponding angles are congruent, and yet these figures are not similar since corresponding sides are not in proportion. For polygons to be similar, both the criteria mentioned above must be met.

Figure 12.23

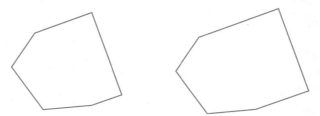

Similar Triangles

We now turn our attention to triangle similarity. Figure 12.24 depicts two similar triangles, *ABC* and *DEF*. The order of naming triangles for similarity is extremely important. If $\angle A$ corresponds to $\angle D$, $\angle B$ corresponds to $\angle E$, and $\angle C$ corresponds to $\angle F$, then it can be written that $\triangle ABC \sim \triangle DEF$. (Although $\triangle EFD$ is an alternate name for the latter triangle, it does not maintain the correct correspondence in the order of the letters.) In addition, the following proportion can be set up:

$$\frac{AC}{DF} = \frac{AB}{DE} = \frac{CB}{FE}$$

Figure 12.24

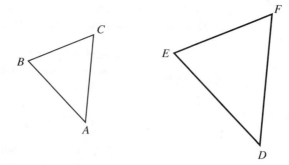

What is the minimum amount of information needed to prove that two triangles are similar? If the corresponding angles of two triangles are congruent, then the triangles are similar. The angle equality necessitates that the sides are in proportion. The proof of this fact will not be addressed here, but it can be informally verified by attempting to alter one or two sides of a triangle without changing the angles. This cannot be accomplished. Formally, this similarity property is called the angle-angle-angle property (AAA) and is stated as follows:

angle-angle-angle property of similarity (AAA ~ AAA)

Angle-Angle-Angle Property of Similarity (AAA ~ AAA). If the measures of corresponding angles of two triangles are equal, then the triangles are similar.

Although the AAA property assures you of similar triangles, it is not necessary to know that all three corresponding angles are congruent. Since the sum of the interior angles in every triangle is equal to 180°, it is sufficient to know that two corresponding pairs are congruent. For example, given triangles *ABC* and *DEF* above,

$$m\angle A + m\angle B + m\angle C = 180° = m\angle D + m\angle E + m\angle F$$

Now suppose that corresponding angles *A* and *D* are congruent, and corresponding angles *B* and *E* are congruent. The third angle in each triangle must necessarily correspond, and be congruent, as shown here.

$$
\begin{array}{rcl}
m\angle A + m\angle B + m\angle C &=& m\angle D + m\angle E + m\angle F \\
- m\angle A - m\angle B & & - m\angle A - m\angle B \\
\hline
m\angle C &=& m\angle F
\end{array}
$$

This leads to the following formalized triangle similarity property.

angle-angle property of similarity (AA ~ AA)

Angle-Angle Property of Similarity (AA ~ AA). If two angles of one triangle are congruent to two corresponding angles of another triangle, then the two triangles are similar.

Two more similarity properties are pertinent here.

side-side-side property of similarity (SSS)

Side-Side-Side Property of Similarity (SSS). If all corresponding sides of two triangles are in proportion, then the triangles are similar.

side-angle-side property of similarity (SAS)

Side-Angle-Side Property of Similarity (SAS). If two pairs of corresponding sides are in proportion and the angles included between them are congruent, then the triangles are similar.

The similarity properties can be summarized as follows: Two triangles are similar if and only if at least one of the properties, AA, SSS, or SAS, can be demonstrated as true.

The concept of similarity can also be used to further explore relationships within triangles. Examine the proportion that was set up for the similar triangles pictured in Figure 12.24.

$$\frac{AC}{DF} = \frac{AB}{DE} = \frac{CB}{FE}$$

Each ratio is formed by comparing a side of $\triangle ABC$ to a corresponding side of $\triangle DEF$. This is not the only proportion that is a consequence of triangle similarity. Examine the following algebraic manipulations.

$$\frac{AC}{DF} = \frac{AB}{DE}$$

$$\frac{DE}{AC} \cdot \frac{AC}{DF} = \frac{AB}{DE} \cdot \frac{DE}{AC}$$

$$\frac{DE}{DF} = \frac{AB}{AC}$$

Notice that a new proportion is created, setting up ratios of sides within each triangle itself. Many more of these ratios can be symbolized. The context of a situation will dictate which proportion to use.

Investigation 13 employs the concept of triangle similarity. The height of a tall structure can be approximated indirectly by modeling the situation as two similar triangles.

Investigation 13

Eye-level height is the distance from the ground to one's eyes. Suppose that a person's eye-level height is 1.75 meters. She places a mirror on the ground a distance of 15 meters from the base of a tree and moves away from the mirror until she can see the highest part of the tree reflected in the mirror. She marks this location on the ground and measures the distance from that point to the mirror. This distance is 2.2 meters. Use this information to determine an approximation for the height of the tree.

Understand the Problem: What is known? You are given the eye-level height, the distance from the base of the tree to the mirror, and the distance along the ground from the mirror to the person.

What is unknown? You are asked to determine the height of the tree.

Devise a Plan: The strategy of drawing a picture should help you understand this problem.

Carry Out the Plan:

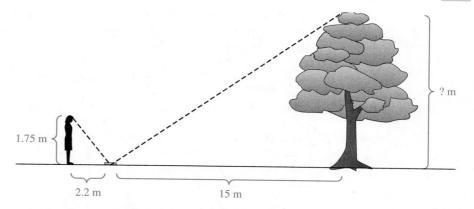

If the two triangles pictured here can be shown to be similar, then the height of the tree should be proportional to the height of the person. Through experimentation in physics, it has been shown that when light rays are reflected, two congruent angles are formed. In this simplified sketch, angle i is called the angle of incidence, and angle r is called the angle of reflection.

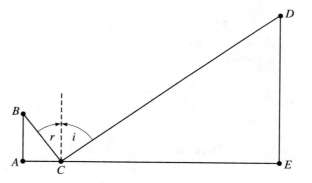

This information will help establish triangle similarity. The tree and the person are both perpendicular to the ground and are parallel to one another. Therefore, $\overline{AB} \perp \overline{AE}$, $\overline{DE} \perp \overline{AE}$, $\angle A \cong \angle E$, and $\overline{AB} \parallel \overline{DE}$. Construct another line that is parallel to $\overline{AB}$ and $\overline{DE}$ and passes through point C. The angles of incidence and reflection have been labeled in the diagram below.

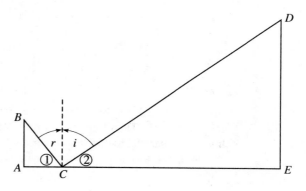

Since $m\angle i + m\angle 2 = 90° = m\angle r + m\angle 1$, it follows that $\angle 2$ must be congruent to $\angle 1$. Since two pairs of corresponding angles of the triangles are congruent, $\triangle ABC \sim EDC$. Let x represent the height of the tree. Since

$$\frac{DE}{CE} = \frac{BA}{CA}, \qquad \frac{x}{15} = \frac{1.75}{2.2}$$

Solving for x, we get $x \approx 11.93$ meters. The tree is about 12 meters tall.

Look Back: Since the distance from the mirror to the tree is approximately seven times the distance from the mirror to the person ($2.2 \times 7 = 15.4$), it is reasonable that the height of the tree be approximately seven times the eye-level height of the person ($1.75 \times 7 = 12.25$). ∎

Figure 12.25a depicts two similar triangles, ABC and DEF. Without altering the shapes, we will move $\triangle ABC$ inside $\triangle DEF$ so that $\angle C$ and $\angle F$ coincide (Figure 12.25b).

Figure 12.25

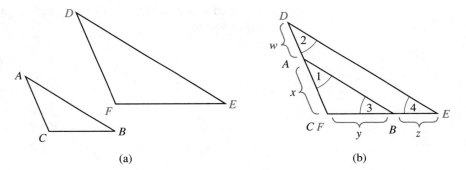

(a)   (b)

Since these triangles are similar, it is clear that

$$\frac{DF}{AC} = \frac{EF}{BC}$$

Replacing these segment names with the symbols representing their measures yields the following ratio:

$$\frac{x+w}{x} = \frac{y+z}{y}$$

$$\frac{x}{x} + \frac{w}{x} = \frac{y}{y} + \frac{z}{y}$$

$$1 + \frac{w}{x} = 1 + \frac{z}{y}$$

$$\frac{w}{x} = \frac{z}{y}$$

Since $\angle 1 = \angle 2$, these angles can be viewed as corresponding angles formed by the transversal $\overline{DF}$. Therefore, $\overline{DE} \parallel \overline{AB}$. We have made a very interesting discovery. A line that is parallel to one side of a triangle partitions the other two sides proportionally. We use this information to solve the problem in Investigation 14.

A bridge is 1 kilometer long. The toll plaza for the bridge is located .25 kilometer from the bank of the river. The bridge authority is considering constructing another span as illustrated in the figure below.

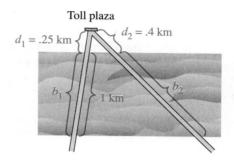

If the distance from the beginning of the new bridge to the toll plaza is to be .4 kilometer, and assuming that the river banks are parallel, what would be the length of the new span?

Understand the Problem: What is known? You are given the distance from the toll plaza to the bank of the river along two paths, as well as the length of the existing bridge. You also know that the river banks are parallel.

What is unknown? You must determine the length of the new bridge span.

Devise a Plan: Since the river banks are parallel, the bridges can be viewed as transversals that cut the parallel lines. Therefore, a proportion can be set up.

Carry Out the Plan:

$$\frac{b_1}{d_1} = \frac{b_2}{d_2}$$

$$\frac{1}{.25} = \frac{b_2}{.4}$$

$$1.6 = b_2$$

The length of the new span will be 1.6 kilometers.

Look Back: This solution is reasonable. The new toll plaza length is less than twice the original. It makes sense that the new span be less than twice the original bridge.

We will now apply the properties of triangle similarity to construct similar polygons. In Figure 12.26, on page 614, you are given polygon *ABCDEF*. Construct a similar polygon *RSTUVW* on side *RW* using the following five steps.

Figure 12.26

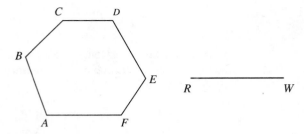

1. Select any vertex of the polygon in Figure 12.26. Here we will choose *A*. Draw all of the diagonals at *A* to create angles 1, 2, 3, and 4, as shown below.

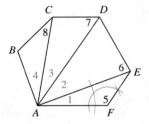

2. Copy ∠1 onto point *R* on $\overline{RW}$. Copy ∠5 onto point *W*. Draw Δ*RVW*. Δ*AEF* ~ Δ*RVW* by *AA* ~ *AA*.

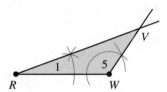

3. Copy ∠2 onto point *R* on $\overline{RV}$. Copy ∠6 onto point *V* on $\overline{RV}$. Draw Δ*RUV*. Δ*ADE* ~ Δ*RUV* by *AA* ~ *AA*.

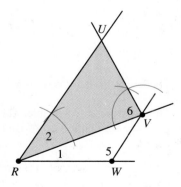

4. Copy ∠3 onto point R on $\overline{RU}$. Copy ∠7 onto point U on $\overline{RU}$. Draw $\triangle RTU$. $\triangle ACD \sim \triangle RTU$ by $AA \sim AA$.

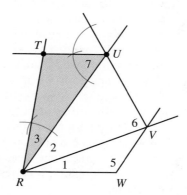

5. Copy ∠4 onto point R on RT. Copy ∠8 onto point T on RT. Draw $\triangle RST$. $\triangle ABC \sim \triangle RST$ by $AA \sim AA$.

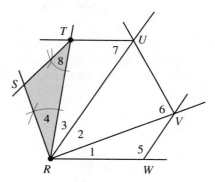

You have now constructed polygon *RSTUVW* (see Figure 12.27), which is similar to *ABCDEF*. All corresponding line segments that form the polygon (including the diagonals) are in proportion. The ratio of corresponding sides is known as the **ratio of similitude**. This ratio, when expressed as a percentage, can indicate the reduction and enlargement percentages displayed on a photocopy machine.

ratio of similitude

Figure 12.27

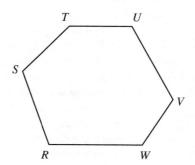

Congruence

We will continue the photocopy analogy to introduce the concept of congruence. Whereas the capability of enlarging and reducing is a useful feature of a copy machine, the function used most often is the production of a 100% copy. A 100% copy is an exact duplicate of the original; it is the same size and the same shape. The original and the copy can be considered to be similar figures, since corresponding angles are congruent and the corresponding sides are in proportion. However, the ratio of similitude will always be equal to 1. When similar figures have a ratio of similitude that is equal to 1, **congruent figures** they are said to be **congruent figures**. Two or more figures are congruent if they have the same size and the same shape. We use the symbol ≅ to denote congruence.

Verifying that two figures are congruent can be accomplished in a variety of ways. Informally, you can trace one of the figures. If that trace coincides with the second figure, then congruence has been established. Alternately, all sides and angles can be measured in both figures. If corresponding parts are found congruent, then the figures are congruent.

The remainder of this section will focus on triangle congruence. Again, we ask if there is a minimum amount of information needed that will establish congruence. Secondary school geometry emphasizes the rigors of proof in this area. For the purposes of this text, we will examine the minimum requirements for congruence via a construction approach. Proofs will be informal rather than formal.

1. If all corresponding sides of two triangles are congruent, is this sufficient information to establish congruence? Given $\triangle ABC$, construct $\triangle DEF$ such that $\triangle ABC \cong \triangle DEF$ by copying line segments only (see Figure 12.28.)

Figure 12.28

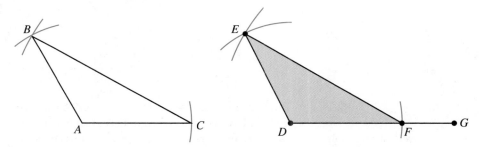

Begin by copying any of the three sides onto line segment $\overline{DG}$. Locate F on $\overline{DG}$. Copy line segment $\overline{AB}$. The opening of the compass can be viewed as the radius of some circle, all of whose points are at a distance of $\overline{AB}$ from A. Put the point of the compass at D and mark off an arc above segment $\overline{DF}$. The point E must lie somewhere on that arc. Now, repeat the process by copying $\overline{CB}$. The opening of the compass can be viewed as the radius of some circle, all of whose points are at a distance of CB from C. Put the point of the compass at E and mark off an arc above the segment $\overline{DF}$. The point E must lie somewhere on that arc. In fact, it will lie at the intersection of the two arcs. Triangle DEF is congruent to $\triangle ABC$.

Copying line segments assures you that $\overline{AB} \cong \overline{DE}$, $\overline{BC} \cong \overline{EF}$, and $\overline{AC} \cong \overline{DF}$. You can see that if the corresponding sides of two triangles are congruent, the triangles will be indeed be congruent.

This leads us to the first triangle congruence property.

side-side-side property of congruence (SSS ≅ SSS)

Side-Side-Side Property of Congruence (SSS ≅ SSS).   Two triangles are congruent if corresponding sides are congruent.

2. If two sides and the included angle of one triangle are congruent to their corresponding parts in a second triangle, is this sufficient information to establish congruence? Given $\triangle ABC$, construct $\triangle DEF$ such that $\triangle ABC \cong \triangle DEF$ by copying $\angle A$ and the segments $\overline{AB}$ and $\overline{AC}$. (See Figure 12.29.)

Figure 12.29

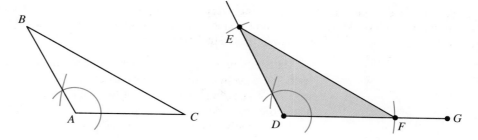

Begin by copying any of the three sides onto $\overline{DG}$. Here, we will copy $\overline{AC}$ so that A corresponds to D and C corresponds to F. Now, copy $\angle A$ so that $\angle A \cong \angle D$. Notice that the congruence of these angles is not dependent on the length of the rays forming the angle. We must now copy side $\overline{AB}$ so that A corresponds to D and B corresponds to E. Draw segment $\overline{EF}$. It is congruent to $\overline{BC}$. It appears that $\triangle DEF \cong \triangle ABC$, since copying two sides and their included angle determines the length and position of the third side.

This leads us to the second triangle congruence property.

side-angle-side property of congruence (SAS ≅ SAS)

Side-Angle-Side Property of Congruence (SAS ≅ SAS).   Two triangles are congruent if two sides and the included angle of one triangle are congruent to their corresponding parts in the other triangle.

3. If two angles and the side included between them in one triangle are congruent to their corresponding parts in a second triangle, is this sufficient information to establish congruence? Given $\triangle ABC$, construct $\triangle DEF$ such that $\triangle ABC \cong \triangle DEF$ by copying two angles and the side included between them. (See Figure 12.30.)

Figure 12.30

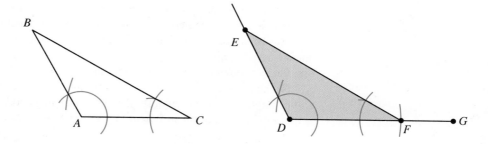

Begin by copying any of the three sides onto $\overline{DG}$. We will copy $\overline{AC}$ so that A corresponds to D and C corresponds to F. In order for $\overline{DF}$ to be an included side, we must construct angles at D and F. Copy $\angle A$ so that $\angle A \cong D$. Copy $\angle C$ so that $\angle C \cong \angle F$. Notice that the rays forming the sides meet at one point, E. It appears that $\triangle DEF \cong \triangle ABC$, since copying two angles and their included side determines the lengths and positions of the other two sides.

This leads us to the third triangle congruence property.

angle-side-angle property of congruence (ASA ≅ ASA)

Angle-Side-Angle Property of Congruence (ASA ≅ ASA).   Two triangles are congruent if two angles and the side included between them of one triangle are congruent to their corresponding parts in the other triangle.

In addition, if two angles and any side of one triangle are congruent to their corresponding parts in another triangle ($AAS \cong AAS$), congruence is also established. This is true, since knowing the measure of two angles dictates the measure of the third angle. Therefore, the side will necessarily become an included side. Establishing AAS congruence is equivalent to establishing ASA congruence.

4. If three angles of one triangle are congruent to their corresponding angles in a second triangle, is this sufficient information to establish congruence? Given $\triangle ABC$, construct $\triangle DEF$ such that $\triangle ABC \cong \triangle DEF$ by copying all angles. (See Figure 12.31.)

Figure 12.31

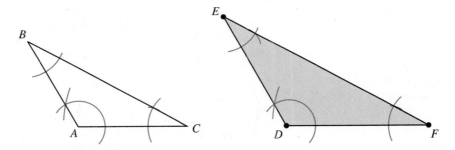

Notice that no congruence conditions are placed on the corresponding sides. Therefore, we can begin by copying angles onto a line segment of any length. If $\overline{AC}$ and $\overline{DF}$ are constructed so as to be corresponding and congruent, we will be unable to test if three angles alone are sufficient for congruency (since ASA assures us of congruent triangles). Line segment $\overline{DF}$ must therefore not equal the length of $\overline{AC}$. With this done, we need not go any further. Since $\overline{AC}$ corresponds to $\overline{DF}$, we have established that at least one pair of corresponding parts of the two triangles is not congruent. Therefore, the two triangles cannot be congruent.

You can see that triangles that have congruent corresponding angles may or may not be congruent, even though they will be similar. Therefore, although AAA does establish similarity, it is not sufficient for establishing congruence.

5. If two sides and a nonincluded angle of one triangle are congruent to their corresponding parts in another triangle, is this sufficient to establish congruence? Given $\triangle ABC$, construct $\triangle DEF$ such that $\triangle ABC \cong \triangle DEF$ by copying two sides and a nonincluded angle. (See Figure 12.32.)

Figure 12.32

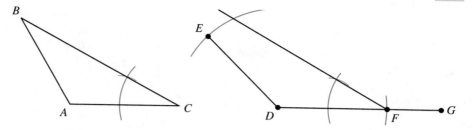

Begin by copying segment $\overline{AC}$ onto $\overline{DG}$ with A corresponding to D and C corresponding to F. Copy $\angle C$ onto $\overline{DF}$ so that $\angle C \cong \angle F$. Since $\overline{AB}$ is not adjacent to $\angle C$, copy $\overline{AB}$ so that A corresponds to D. Notice that no restriction is placed on this construction other than this correspondence. If you view segment $\overline{DE}$ as the radius of some circle whose center is at D, $\overline{DE}$ can be constructed in an infinite number of ways. Notice that in the orientation pictured in Figure 12.32, no single triangle is formed. As you can see, SSA does not establish congruence.

In summary, $\triangle ABC \cong \triangle DEF$ if and only if at least one of the following properties can be established: SSS $\cong$ SSS, SAS $\cong$ SAS, or ASA $\cong$ ASA (or AAS $\cong$ AAS).

Investigation 15

Suppose it is necessary to determine the distance across a body of water from A to B. How can triangle congruence be used to determine this length without actually crossing the water?

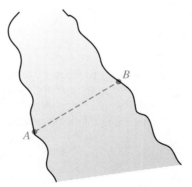

A transit is a device used by surveyors to locate and measure distances and determine angle measurements. This device in conjunction with a steel tape ruler or a trundle wheel (a "rolling ruler") can be used to solve this problem.

If a right triangle can be constructed with $\overline{AB}$ as its base, and a second right triangle that is congruent to the first is constructed on land the length of the side of the "land" triangle that corresponds to $\overline{AB}$ can be measured. Follow these six steps:

1. Standing at point A, locate point B using the eyepiece of the transit. Rotate the transit 90° in a counterclockwise direction.

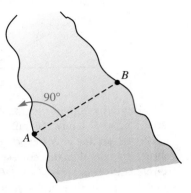

2. Mark off some point C, a fixed distance d from A so that $\triangle CAB$ is formed with, $m\angle A = 90°$, and $CA = d$.

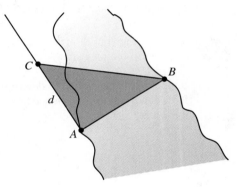

3. Continue to mark off a distance d past C. Label this point E. If the transit were placed at point E, the surveyor would see that points E, C, and A coincide; that is, they would lie on the same straight segment that is perpendicular to the segment representing the distance across the lake.

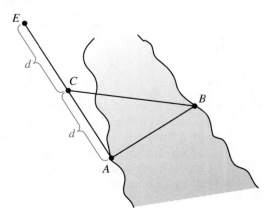

4. Position the transit at E. Focus the transit at point A. Turn it 90° clockwise. Mark off some point T in the distance.

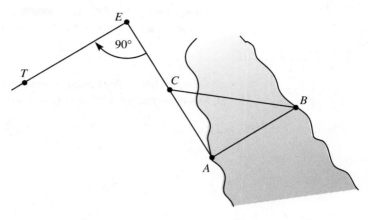

5. Relocate the transit at point C. Focus at point A. Turn the transit counterclockwise until point B is in sight. Record the measure of $\angle ACB$.

6. Focus the transit at point E. Turn the transit counterclockwise through an angle equal to the measure of $\angle ACB$. Locate a point R in the distance. Label the point of intersection of $\overline{CR}$ and $\overline{ET}$ point F.

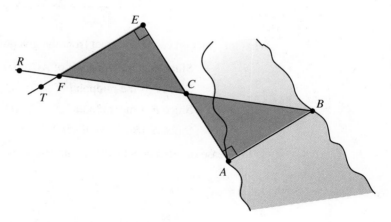

Notice that two right triangles have been formed.

$$\angle E = \angle A = 90°$$
$$EC = CA = d$$
$$\angle ECF = \angle ACB$$

Therefore, $\triangle ACB \cong \triangle ECF$ by ASA.

Since corresponding parts of congruent triangles are congruent, the length of $\overline{FE}$ must be equal to the length of $\overline{AB}$. It is easy to measure $\overline{FE}$ along the ground.

Investigation 16

Given equilateral triangle ABC, prove informally that the triangle formed by joining the midpoints of the sides is itself an equilateral triangle.

Understand the Problem: You are given an equilateral triangle ABC with midpoints of the sides D, E, and F. You must informally prove that the new triangle formed is equilateral.

Devise a Plan: Draw a diagram.

Carry Out the Plan:

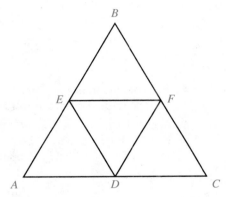

What information can you extract from the given information?

Since D is the midpoint of $\overline{AC}$, $\overline{AD} \cong \overline{DC}$.

Since E is the midpoint of $\overline{AB}$, $\overline{AE} \cong \overline{EB}$.

Since F is the midpoint of $\overline{BC}$, $\overline{BF} \cong \overline{FC}$.

Since $\triangle ABC$ is equilateral, $m\angle A = m\angle B = m\angle C = 60°$.

For ease of reference, label the four triangles with numbers, as below.

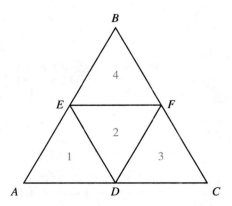

Try to prove that the three triangles formed at the vertices of $\triangle ABC$ are congruent.

$\triangle 1 \cong \triangle 3$ by SAS since $\overline{AD} \cong \overline{DC}$	(S)	Midpoint partitions a segment in half
$\angle A \cong \angle C$	(A)	Equilateral triangles are equiangular
$\overline{AE} \cong \overline{FC}$	(S)	Halves of congruent segments are congruent

Since these triangles are congruent, $\overline{ED} \cong \overline{DF}$ (corresponding parts of congruent triangles are congruent). We know that $\triangle 2$ is at least isosceles.

For the same reasons as above, $\triangle 3 \cong \triangle 4$ by SAS. Therefore, $\overline{DE} \cong \overline{EF} \cong \overline{FD}$. Triangle 2 is an equilateral triangle.

Look Back: How can you show that the area of $\triangle ABC$ is four times the area of one of the equilateral triangles?

In addition to what we have already covered, a special congruence property can be used for right triangles. Examine Investigation 17.

Investigation 17

A vertical flagpole is held up by two guy wires of equal length that are attached to the flagpole at the same height. Must the distances along the ground from the ends of the guy wires to the base of the flagpole necessarily be equal?

Understand the Problem: What is known? You are given two guy wires of equal length meeting a flagpole at the same height. The flagpole is vertical, so it forms right angles with the ground.

What is unknown? Are the distances from the base of the flagpole to the ends of the guy wires along the ground equal?

Devise a Plan: Draw a picture of this situation. Model the situation mathematically.

Carry Out the Plan:

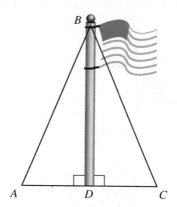

Since the flagpole is vertical, it meets the ground at right angles. Therefore, $\overline{BD} \perp \overline{AC}$. If it can be shown that $\triangle ADB \cong \triangle CDB$, then $\overline{AD}$ must be congruent to $\overline{DC}$ by the corresponding parts property. Since the guy wires are of equal length, $\overline{AB} \cong \overline{CB}$. The segment $\overline{BD}$ is a side of both triangles in question. We now have three corresponding parts that are congruent: $\overline{AB} \cong \overline{CB}$, $\overline{BD} \cong \overline{BD}$, and $\angle ADB \cong \angle CDB$. Unfortunately, this appears to be the SSA relation that was shown not to establish congruence. Perhaps another approach is necessary. A strategy we have used previously for finding the length of a side in a right triangle is the Pythagorean theorem.

$$(AB)^2 = \sqrt{(AD)^2 + (BD)^2} \qquad (BC)^2 = \sqrt{(CD)^2 + (BD)^2}$$

Since the guy wires are the same length, $AB = BC$. Therefore, $(AB)^2 = (BC)^2$, and

$$\sqrt{(AD)^2 + (BD)^2} = \sqrt{(CD)^2 + (BD)^2}$$

Square both sides to remove the square root sign and simplify.

$$\left(\sqrt{(AD)^2 + (BD)^2}\right)^2 = \left(\sqrt{(CD)^2 + (BD)^2}\right)^2$$

$$(AD)^2 + (BD)^2 = (CD)^2 + (BD)^2$$
$$- (BD)^2 \qquad\qquad - (BD)^2$$

$$(AD)^2 = (CD)^2$$

$$\overline{AD} \cong \overline{CD}$$

Therefore, the wires touch the ground at equal distances from the base of the flagpole.

Look Back: How could this situation have been modeled using geometric constructions?

We have shown that if two sides of a right triangle are congruent to corresponding sides of another right triangle, then the third pair of corresponding sides must also be congruent in length. Therefore, the SSA property can hold only for right triangles. We can generalize the following property.

If $\triangle ABC$ and $\triangle DEF$ are both right triangles, congruence can be established if the lengths of their corresponding hypotenuses and the lengths of one of the corresponding **hypotenuse-leg property of** legs are congruent. This property is called the **hypotenuse-leg property of congruence**
congruence (HL $\cong$ HL) and is symbolized by **HL $\cong$ HL**.

Assessments for Section 12.2

1. On a sheet of graph paper or the laminated card, draw a figure that is similar to the given figure with the stated ratio of similitude. The ratio of similitude represents the ratio of the lengths of the corresponding sides of the given figure to the newly constructed figure.

(a)

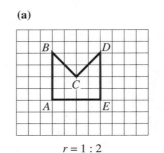

$r = 1 : 2$

(b)

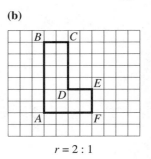

$r = 2 : 1$

(c)

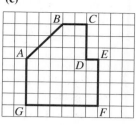

$r = 2 : 1$

(d)

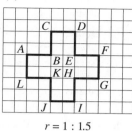

$r = 1 : 1.5$

(e)

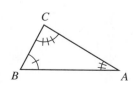

$r = 3 : 1$

(f)

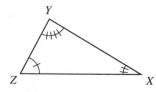

$r = 4 : 1$

2. Determine whether each of the following statements is true or false. Justify your answers.

(a) Any two squares are similar.

(b) Any two rectangles are similar.

(c) Any two equilateral triangles are similar.

(d) Any two right triangles are similar.

(e) Any two parallelograms are similar.

(f) Any two rhombi are similar.

(g) Any two congruent triangles are similar.

(h) Any two isosceles triangles are similar.

3. In each case, construct similar triangles *ABC* and *XYZ* based on the given information. Justify why these triangles are similar triangles.

(a) $m\angle A = 30° = m\angle X$, $m\angle B = 50° = m\angle Y$

(b) $m\angle A = 45° = m\angle X$, $m\angle C = m\angle Z$, $m\angle C = m\angle A$

(c) $m\angle A = 80°$, $m\angle X = 55°$, $m\angle B = 45°$, $m\angle Y = 45°$

4. You are given similar triangles *ABC* and *XYZ*. Corresponding congruent angles are indicated in the diagrams below. Find the length of the indicated side.

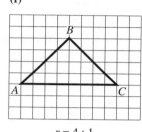

(a) $CA = 8$ cm, $YX = 6$ cm, $ZY = 4$ cm, $BC = ?$

(b) $AB = 2$ cm, $XZ = 3$ cm, $BC = 7$ cm, $ZY = ?$

(c) $BC = 1\frac{1}{4}$ in., $ZY = 4\frac{1}{2}$ in, $XY = 14\frac{5}{8}$ in., $AC = ?$

(d) $XZ = 12$ cm, $AB = 9$ cm, $XY = 6.5$ cm, $AC = ?$

(e) $AC = 11.25$ cm, $XZ = 9.75$ cm, $XY = 11.25$ cm, $AB = ?$

5. In each of the following cases, triangles *RST* and *UVW* are similar triangles with the stated ratio of similitude (r). Sketch a pair of triangles. Identify corresponding sides. Offer a set of lengths that would represent the sides of these two similar triangles.

(a) $\triangle RST: \triangle UVW \rightarrow r = 1$

(b) $\triangle RST: \triangle UVW \rightarrow r = \frac{1}{2}$

(c) $\triangle UVW: \triangle RST \rightarrow r = 2.5$

(d) $\triangle UVW: \triangle RST \rightarrow r = .15$

(e) $\triangle RST: \triangle UVW \rightarrow r = 2\frac{1}{8}$

6. In the following diagram, $\triangle WXY$ is a right triangle with $m\angle WXY = 90°$ and $m\angle XZW = 90°$.

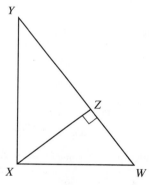

(a) If $m\angle W = 55°$, what is the measure of $\angle ZXW$?

(b) Explain why $m\angle W = m\angle YXZ$.

(c) Explain why $m\angle Y = m\angle WXZ$.

(d) Explain why $\triangle WXY$ cannot be an isosceles right triangle.

(e) Explain why $\triangle XZW \sim \triangle YXW$.

(f) Explain why $\triangle YZX \sim \triangle YXW$.

(g) Explain why $\triangle XZW \sim \triangle YZX$.

7. Recall your work in Chapter 5 with equivalence relations. A relation was said to be an equivalence relation if it was shown to be reflexive, symmetric, and transitive.

(a) Is the relation "is similar to" an equivalence relation?

(b) Is the relation "is congruent to" an equivalence relation?

8. Examine each of the following pairs of similar figures.

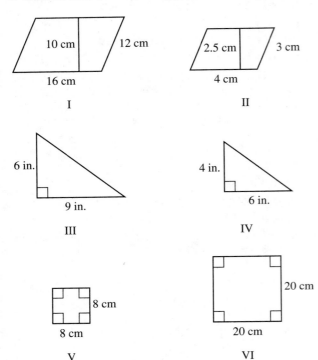

I   II

III   IV

V   VI

Complete the following tables.

Table 1

Figure	Perimeter	Area
I	(a)	(b)
II	(c)	(d)
III	(e)	(f)
IV	(g)	(h)
V	(i)	(j)
VI	(k)	(l)

Table 2

Similar Figures #:#	Ratio of Similitude	Ratio of Perimeters	Ratio of Areas
I : II	(m)	(n)	(o)
II : I	(p)	(q)	(r)
III : IV	(s)	(t)	(u)
IV : III	(v)	(w)	(x)
V : VI	(y)	(z)	(aa)
VI : V	(bb)	(cc)	(dd)

(ee) Make a generalization about the ratio of the perimeter of similar figures.

(ff) Make a generalization about the ratio of the areas of similar figures.

9. On a sunny afternoon, a person who is 5 feet tall casts a 4-foot-long shadow. How long a shadow would be cast by a tree that is 25 feet tall? Explain your reasoning.

10. A mirror is placed on the ground at a distance of 5 m from the base of a tree. A person can view the top of the tree in the mirror when she is standing .4 m away from the mirror. If the eye-level height of this person is 1.6 m, what is the height of the tree?

11. Right triangles *DEF* and *GHI* are similar to $m\angle E = m\angle H = 90°$ as shown here.

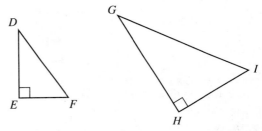

If *DF* = 41 cm, *EF* = 9 cm, and *GI* = 51.25 cm, find the measures of *GH* and *HI*. Explain an alternate way of solving this problem.

12. Trace the following figure. Construct a similar figure such that the ratio of similitude of the second figure to the first figure is 3 : 1.

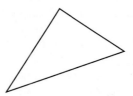

13. Trace the following figure. Construct a similar figure such that the ratio of similitude of the first figure to the second figure is 3 : 1.

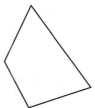

14. Given $\triangle RTS$ and $\triangle VTU$, with $\overline{UV} \parallel \overline{RS}$ and $\overline{US}$ intersecting $\overline{VR}$ at T, explain why $\triangle RTS$ and $\triangle VTU$ are similar triangles.

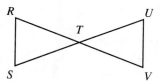

15. In the following pairs of figures, congruent parts of triangles are indicated with like hash marks. Determine whether or not the triangles are necessarily congruent. Explain your reasoning.

(a)

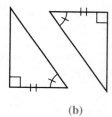

(b)

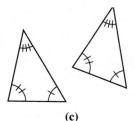

(c)

16. Figure $ABCD$ is a kite. How can the reflexive property be used to "prove" that $\triangle DAB \cong \triangle DCB$?

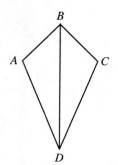

17. Given parallelograms $ABCD$ and $BEDF$, answer each of the following questions, which together will develop the proof that $\triangle DEC \cong \triangle BFA$.

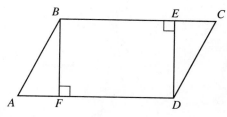

(a) Why is $\angle A \cong \angle C$?
(b) Why is $\angle CED \cong \angle EDA$?
(c) Why is $\angle EDA \cong \angle BFA$?
(d) Why is $\angle CED \cong \angle BFA$?
(e) Why is $\angle ABF \cong \angle CDE$?
(f) Why is $\overline{AB} \cong \overline{CD}$?
(g) Why is $\triangle DEC \cong \triangle BFA$?

18. Given nonconvex quadrilateral $QSZV$ with $\triangle QST \cong \triangle ZSR$ with R on $\overline{QS}$ and T on $\overline{ZS}$, answer each of the following questions, which together will develop a "proof" that $\triangle QVR \cong \triangle ZVT$.

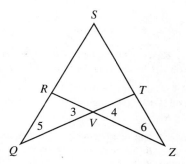

(a) Why is $\angle 3 \cong \angle 4$?
(b) Why is $\angle 5 \cong \angle 6$?
(c) Why is $\overline{QS} \cong \overline{ZS}$?
(d) Why is $\overline{RS} \cong \overline{TS}$?
(e) Why is $(\overline{QR} \cup \overline{RS}) \cong (\overline{ZT} \cup \overline{TS})$?
(f) Why is $\overline{QR} \cong \overline{ZT}$?
(g) Why is $\triangle QVR \cong \triangle ZVT$?

19. Given $\triangle AED$ with $\triangle AEC \cong \triangle DEB$, as shown in the figure at the top of page 628, describe how it follows that $\triangle AEB \cong \triangle DEC$. (*Hint:* List all of the congruences that follow as a consequence of the fact that $\triangle AEC \cong \triangle DEB$. Determine how these pieces of information can lead you to establish that $\triangle AEB \cong \triangle DEC$.)

20. You are given the following figure with $\overline{RS} \cong \overline{TS}$ and S is the midpoint of $\overline{QV}$. Describe how it follows that $\overline{QR} \cong \overline{TV}$.

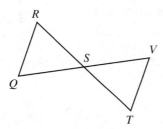

21. Given $\triangle XYZ$ and line segment $\overline{AB}$, construct a congruent triangle on $\overline{AB}$ by copying the three sides of $\triangle XYZ$.

22. Given $\triangle RST$ and line segment $\overline{AB}$, construct a congruent triangle on $\overline{AB}$ by copying only two sides and an included angle of $\triangle RST$.

23. Given $\triangle DEF$ and line segment $\overline{AB}$, construct a congruent triangle on $\overline{AB}$ by copying only two angles and an included side of $\triangle DEF$.

24. Given pentagon $CDEFG$ and line segment $\overline{AB}$ and using only a compass and a straightedge, construct a pentagon on $\overline{AB}$ that is congruent to $CDEFG$.

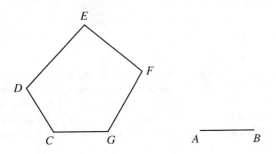

25. You are given quadrilaterals $ABCD$ and $EFGH$. You know that $\overline{AB} \cong \overline{EF}$, $\overline{BC} \cong \overline{FG}$, $\overline{CD} \cong \overline{GH}$, $\overline{DA} \cong \overline{HE}$, and $m\angle A = m\angle E = 90°$. Are $ABCD$ and $EFGH$ necessarily congruent?

In Other Words

26. Describe three real-world situations in which similarity plays an important role.

27. Describe three real-world situations in which congruence plays an important role.

28. It is said that geometry is a very "logical" subject. Explain how the logic studied in Chapter 1 relates to this section.

29. Are the following two statements true? Justify your answers.

(a) If two figures are congruent, then they are similar.

(b) If two figures are similar, then they are congruent.

30. Suppose you have four congruent triangles and six congruent rectangles cut out of paper. You are asked to construct two triangular prisms. Are these two prisms necessarily congruent?

Cooperative Activity

31. Groups of two

Individual Accountability: Each group member is to cut out eight congruent isosceles right triangles, four of one color and four of another color. Each group member is to arrange the eight triangles into at least three different square patchwork quilt designs. Keep a record of each design created. One such design is shown here:

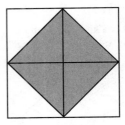

Group Goal: Each partner is to take turns verbally describing one of the patterns to the other partner. The pattern should not be visible to the partner. After a verbal description, congruence of the patterns should be visually verified. Make a list of the terms used to communicate the designs.

12.3   LOGO: A Technological Tool

logo

In the 1970s, under the direction of Seymour Papert, a group of researchers at the Massachusetts Institute of Technology developed a computer programming language called **LOGO**. This language grew out of their work with artificial intelligence. The researchers wanted to create a language that would make it easier for children to interact with computers. The language that allowed for this interaction is very simple and allows children to formulate and test ideas. Although easy to learn, LOGO is also powerful enough to allow for some very sophisticated programming.

Papert refers to LOGO as turtle geometry. Graphics are drawn on the screen by a cursor called "the turtle." Different types of LOGO display different turtles, ranging from an icon that resembles an actual turtle, to a simple triangle. The student directs the movement of the turtle on the screen through a series of commands, some of which we will outline in this section.

It is not the purpose of this text to introduce any one particular type of LOGO. The languages available for Apple and IBM computers are basically the same, with a few exceptions. We encourage those interested to read through a LOGO manual and adapt this section to the programs that are available to you.

Basic Discoveries

Turtle geometry is based on position and heading (the direction in which the turtle is facing). The position of the turtle can be likened to a location on the Cartesian plane. In some versions of LOGO, there is a command that allows the user to locate the turtle at a particular point on the screen that is defined by x- and y-coordinates.

All basic LOGO commands are referred to as *primitives*. The primitives used to change position and heading are shown in the following table.

Command	Abbreviation	Result
FORWARD #	FD #	Maintains the current heading and moves the turtle a certain number of spaces in a forward direction.
BACKWARD #	BK #	Maintains the current heading and moves the turtle a certain number of spaces in a backward direction.
RIGHT #	RT #	Maintains the current position and rotates the turtle a certain number of degrees to the right.
LEFT #	LT #	Maintains the current position and rotates the turtle a certain number of degrees to the left.
HOME	HOME	Returns the turtle to the center of the screen with a heading of 0°.

Any movement forward or backward will leave a trail on the screen in the form of a line segment. This is how turtle graphics are created. If, however, you wish to move the turtle from one position on the screen to another without displaying a line segment, the command PENUP (PU) should be entered. Once the turtle is located at the desired position, the command PENDOWN (PD) is used. [*Note*: The screen can be cleared at any time. A "clear" command is included in each version of LOGO. For example, in both Apple LOGO and IBM LOGO, the command is CLEARSCREEN (CS).]

The cursor can be located at any point on the screen and can be oriented in any direction. The direction is measured using 360°, as shown in Figure 12.33.

Figure 12.33

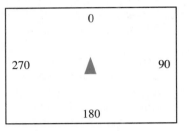

The heading labels are fixed. However, commanding the turtle to rotate 90° left or right (LT 90 or RT 90) will not always result in the turtle facing the 90° heading. The turtle will interpret a rotation command based on its present heading. For example, suppose the turtle is facing down as shown in Figure 12.34a. The turtle's heading is 180°. The command RT 90 will cause the turtle to rotate in a clockwise direction to the right 90°, resulting in a new heading of 270°, as shown in Figure 12.34b. The command RT 90 will cause the turtle to rotate to the right 90°, resulting in a new heading of 0°. In some versions of LOGO, the command PR HEADING (print heading) can be entered to display the heading of the turtle at any given time. If a particular heading is desired, some versions allow the command SETH # (set heading at #), which will set the heading to the desired fixed degree location.

Figure 12.34

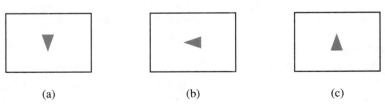

(a)   (b)   (c)

Investigation 18

The turtle is positioned on a blank screen in the HOME location (at the center). Its heading is 0°. Write the commands that will direct the turtle to draw a 50 by 30 rectangle with the present location forming the lower left vertex.

Commands can be entered individually or in sequence connected by spaces. For clarity, we will list commands individually.

Command	Interpretation	Display
FD 30	Moves forward 30 units	
RT 90	Turns right through 90°	
FD 50	Moves forward 50 units	
RT 90	Turns right through 90°	
FD 30	Moves forward 30 units	
RT 90	Turns right through 90°	
FD 50	Moves forward 50 units	
RT 90	Turns right through 90°	

Notice in Investigation 18 the sequence of commands **FD 30 RT 90 FD 50 RT 90** was repeated. In LOGO, it is possible to have the turtle duplicate actions a certain number of times by using the **REPEAT** command. This command takes the following form:

REPEAT #   [commands]

# of executions   commands to be repeated

The command for constructing a 50 by 30 rectangle could be written as

REPEAT 2 [FD 30 RT 90 FD 50 RT 90]

By determining the fewest number of commands that can be repeated, a variety of shapes can be efficiently drawn. Let's examine the repeat statement that would be used to construct an equilateral triangle, a square, and a pentagon, all of whose sides measure 60 units.

When trying to solve this problem, it is a good idea to trace the desired outcome on a sheet of paper. The segments and turns required to draw the equilateral triangle, the square, and the pentagon are depicted in Figure 12.35.

Figure 12.35

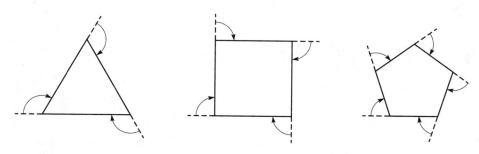

Notice that in each case, the turtle turns through an exterior angle that is formed when a side is extended. This exterior angle is the supplement of the interior angle. Recall that in regular polygons, the number of degrees in each interior angle is given by

$$\frac{180(n-2)}{n}$$

Let the measure of the exterior angle be represented by E, and let n represent the number of sides of the regular polygon. Since the exterior and interior angles are supplementary, we can write

$$E + \frac{180(n-2)}{n} = 180$$

$$E = 180 - \frac{180(n-2)}{n}$$

$$E = \frac{(180n - 180(n-2))}{n} = \frac{(180n - 180n + 360)}{n} = \frac{360}{n}$$

The turtle turns $\frac{360}{n}$ degrees and moves forward 60 units for a total of n times. The repeat commands for each figure in Figure 12.35 are written as follows:

Equilateral Triangle $\rightarrow$ REPEAT 3 [FD 60 RT 120]

Square $\rightarrow$ REPEAT 4 [FD 60 RT 90]

Pentagon $\rightarrow$ REPEAT 5 [FD 60 RT 72]

In general, if n is any positive integer greater than 2, representing the number of sides of a regular polygon, and d is the length of each side of the polygon, the LOGO command to display the polygon can be written as:

REPEAT n [FD d RT $\frac{360}{n}$]

Investigation 19

The following figure is composed of a regular hexagon, an equilateral triangle, and a square all of whose sides measure 40 units. Write the LOGO commands that will display this figure. (Assume the turtle starts at the indicated position with a heading of 0°.)

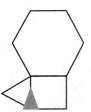

1. Trace this figure. Can it be drawn without any overlapping of lines? It appears that drawing the square first, then the triangle, and finally the hexagon will result in the figure above using the least number of commands.

2. Draw the square.

REPEAT 4 [FD 40 RT 90]

Notice that the turtle is back to its original position and heading.

3. Draw the equilateral triangle. Be careful! Simply using the **REPEAT** command just stated for an equilateral triangle will result in the following figure.

Here, the turtle has moved through an exterior angle of 120°. Although the equilateral triangle drawn is correct in size, it is incorrectly placed. In order for the triangle to be drawn correctly, it is necessary for the heading of the turtle at a vertex to be in the direction of the extension of a side. This can easily be accomplished if we use the **RT 180** (or **LT 180**) command to rotate the turtle. Notice that the turtle now has a heading of 180°.

Now the **REPEAT** command can be implemented:

$$\text{REPEAT 3 [RT 120 FD 40]}$$

This results in the following figure.

4. The turtle is back to its home location with a heading of 180°. In order to draw the hexagon, it is necessary that the turtle be located at a vertex of the hexagon with a heading in the direction of the extension of a side. This can easily be accomplished with the following commands:

$$\text{BK 40   RT 90}$$

The turtle moves backward 50 units over a previously drawn line segment. It then rotates 90° in a clockwise direction resulting in a heading of 270°. Finally, we use the command

$$\text{REPEAT 6 [RT 60 FD 40]}$$

to complete the desired figure.

Procedures

One of the advantages of LOGO is that its vocabulary of commands is limitless. Once the basic commands are learned, they can be joined together to form a procedure. A **procedure** is a set of commands that are executed by a user-defined command name. The method for setting up a procedure differs according to the particular version of LOGO you are using. In general, the user defines a procedure in the edit mode of the computer by first giving it a descriptive name, listing the commands that will result in a desired display, and closing the definition with the command END. The name of a procedure cannot be a LOGO primitive.

For example, suppose you wished to recall and use the configuration of square/triangle/hexagon, as presented in Investigation 18 a number of times. You could call this procedure INVEST19 and define it as shown here:

```
TO INVEST19
REPEAT 4 [FD 50 RT 90]
RT 180
REPEAT 3 [RT 120 FD 50]
BK 50 RT 90
REPEAT 6 [RT 60 FD 50]
END
```

This procedure can be saved to the disk and then loaded at any time in the future. By typing INVEST19, LOGO will execute the series of commands that display the square, triangle, and hexagon shown in Investigation 19.

Investigation 20

You are given pentagon *ABCDE*. Write a LOGO procedure that will draw a pentagon similar to *ABCDE*. The ratio of similitude between the new pentagon and *ABCDE* must be 1 : 5. Assume that the turtle is at the HOME location with the heading of 0°.

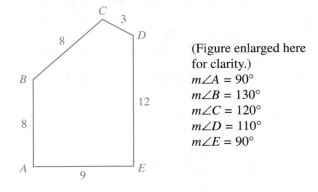

(Figure enlarged here for clarity.)
$m\angle A = 90°$
$m\angle B = 130°$
$m\angle C = 120°$
$m\angle D = 110°$
$m\angle E = 90°$

Recall our work with similar figures. Two figures are similar if corresponding angles are congruent and corresponding sides are in proportion. Therefore, you must develop a set of commands that will construct a figure in which the measure of each side is five times that of the corresponding side in *ABCDE*. In addition, each of the interior angles must be congruent to its corresponding angle in *ABCDE*. You are given the measures of angles *A*, *B*, *D*, and *E*. You must determine the measure of angle *C*.

The sum of the interior angles of any convex pentagon is 540°. Since

$$m\angle A + m\angle B + m\angle D + m\angle E = 420°$$

then $m\angle C$ must be 540° − 420°, or 120°. We now have enough information to write the procedure called **PENTAGON** as follows:

Procedure	Interpretation
TO PENTAGON	Defines a command called **PENTAGON** as a procedure
FD 40	Moves the turtle forward 40 units
RT 50	Rotates the turtle 50° to the right (180° − 130° = 50°)
FD 40	Moves the turtle forward 40 units
RT 60	Rotates the turtle 60° to the right (180° − 120° = 60°)
FD 15	Moves the turtle forward 15 units
RT 70	Rotates the turtle 70° to the right (180° − 110° = 70°)
FD 60	Moves the turtle forward 60 units
RT 90	Rotates the turtle 90° to the right (180° − 90° = 90°)
FD 45	Moves the turtle forward 45 units
END	Signals the end of the procedure **PENTAGON**

Exit from the edit mode using the commands necessary for the version of LOGO you are using. When you type **PENTAGON** and hit ENTER , the following figure will be displayed. This figure is similar to *ABCDE*.

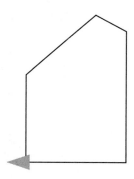

LOGO has the ability to set up and store variables. A variable in LOGO is the same concept as a variable in algebra. A variable represents a number or a set of numbers. In algebra, we restrict variable names to single letters, whereas in LOGO the name TOM could be a variable. In LOGO programming, it is preferable to use descriptive variable names. The variable LENGTH might be used to present the length of a rectangle, ANGLE could be used to represent the measure of an angle, and RATIO could be used to represent the ratio of similitude.

Examine the following LOGO procedure, which employs the variables LENGTH and WIDTH to draw rectangles of varying sizes.

```
TO RECTANGLE :LENGTH :WIDTH
REPEAT 2 [FD :WIDTH RT 90 FD :LENGTH RT 90]
END
```

The first line defines a procedure called RECTANGLE that contains the variables LENGTH and WIDTH. When variables are used in commands, the variable name is preceded by a colon. The second line of this procedure is a basic REPEAT command. Notice that the variables :WIDTH and :LENGTH take the place of any specific numerical value.

Once out of the edit mode, this procedure can be executed as follows. Some displays are given here.

RECTANGLE 20 20

RECTANGLE 30 60

RECTANGLE 100 200

Notice in RECTANGLE 100 200 that the variable :LENGTH is equal to 100, and the variable :WIDTH is equal to 200. This is why the width appears longer than the length in the rectangle in the resulting figure.

Investigation 21

In this investigation, LOGO will be used to strengthen your visualization and estimation skills. The problem under consideration is to determine the effect on the area of an equilateral triangle when the measure of each side is doubled, and when the measure of each side is tripled. Write a LOGO procedure that could be used to investigate this change in area. (*Note*: Although the area can be computed numerically, it is not the purpose of this activity to do so. Rather, you will be asked to visually estimate the change in area.)

A single procedure that uses a variable to draw equilateral triangles of various sizes can be written. The procedure is given here. Notice that the first command in the procedure rotates the turtle 30° to the right from the 0° heading. This command is included in the procedure so that the orientation of the equilateral triangle can be one in which the base is a horizontal line segment. The third command in the procedure reorients the heading of the turtle to 0° so that subsequent triangles will be drawn with the same orientation for comparison purposes.

```
TO TRIANGLE :SIDE
RT 30
REPEAT 3 [FD :SIDE RT 120]
HOME
END
```

Exiting from the edit mode and executing the following commands will result in this display:

TRIANGLE 20

TRIANGLE 40

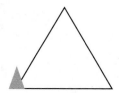

```
TRIANGLE 60
```

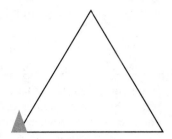

It appears that doubling the length of the sides of an equilateral triangle results in a triangle whose area is four times the original. Tripling the sides of an equilateral triangle results in a triangle whose area is nine times the original. The algebraic verification of this estimation will be left to you.

Recursion

recursive procedure

Finally, we will examine the effect of a procedure that calls upon itself during execution. This is called a **recursive procedure**. Examine the following two procedures.

```
TO SQUARE                          TO SQUARE
REPEAT 4 [FD 60 RT 90]             REPEAT 4 [FD 60 RT 90]
END                                SQUARE
                                   END
```

Both procedures will display the same square. The difference between the procedures is not in the display, but rather in the execution of the display. The first procedure executes the commands to draw a single square whose sides measure 60 units. Once the square is drawn, the procedure ends. In the second procedure, the square is drawn, and then the procedure is called up again. Another square is drawn over itself. This continues indefinitely, or until the user enters a particular command to stop the execution of a procedure. (This command varies. For example, in Apple LOGO, the user presses CTRL-G ; in IBM LOGO, the user presses CTRL-BREAK .) Obviously, using recursion in the way shown here makes little sense.

Recursion can, however, be used to construct interesting figures. Examine the following procedure and the resulting display, which is shown in Figure 12.36.

```
TO SQUARE
REPEAT 4 [FD 60 RT 90]
RT 10
SQUARE
END
```

Figure 12.36

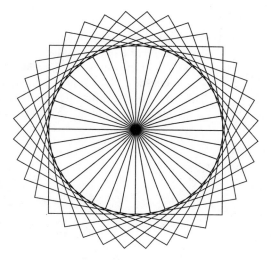

But how many squares are printed before overwriting occurs? To answer this question, it is necessary to first determine what causes the squares to "turn." Notice that an RT 10 is included in the procedure. After a square has been completely drawn, the turtle returns to its original heading. Had the RT 10 command not been included, overwriting would occur with the second square. The RT 10 command causes the turtle to change its heading by rotating 10° to the right, and then commence drawing the square. This causes a succession of squares to be drawn. Since the rotation is 10°, there are (360° ÷ 10), or 36, such squares drawn before the design overwrites.

Investigation 22

A pentagram is a five-pointed star. It can be formed by drawing the diagonals of a regular pentagon. One such pentagram is illustrated here.

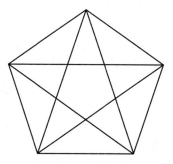

Write a LOGO procedure that uses recursion to construct the pentagram inside of a pentagon like the one above.

It is first necessary to determine some angle measures. You already know that each interior angle of a regular pentagon is 108°. We will use this information to determine the measures of the three vertex angles that partition each interior angle.

Examine △*BAE*. It is formed by two congruent sides of the pentagon and a diagonal. Angle *A*, the included angle between the pentagon's sides, is equal to 108° (since it is an interior angle of the regular pentagon).

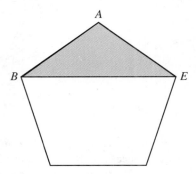

Triangle *BAE* is an isosceles triangle; therefore, the base angles, ∠*ABE* and ∠*AEB*, must be equal. Their measure is determined by subtracting 108° from 180°. This leaves 72° to be divided equally between the base angles. The measures of ∠*ABE* and ∠*AEB* are both 36°. This line of reasoning can be repeated five times. Each of the three angles that form the vertices of the pentagon will measure 36°.

The pentagram within the regular pentagon can be formed by five congruent isosceles triangles. Since the triangles are congruent, recursion can be used.

The following recursive procedure will draw the pentagram within the pentagon.

```
TO PENTAGRAM
RT 18
FD 95
RT 144
FD 95
RT 108
FD 60
RT 72
FD 60
RT 90
PENTAGRAM
END
```

Notice that the second command reorients the turtle 18° to the right before drawing the isosceles triangle. This is necessary so that the base of the first isosceles triangle drawn is horizontal. Examine the numbers associated with each command. Attempt to explain why such numbers were chosen.

Assessments for Section 12.3

In Problems 1–10, write the LOGO commands that will create the indicated figure.

1.

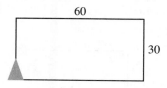

2.

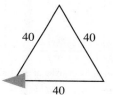

3.

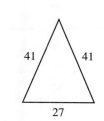

4.

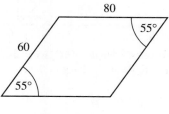

5.

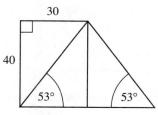

6.

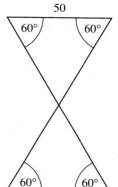

7.

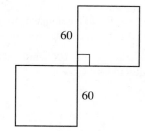

8.

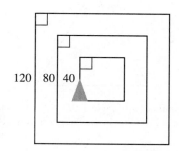

9.

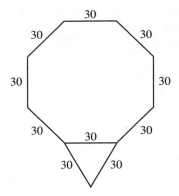

10.

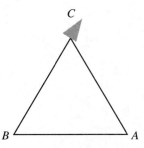

In Problems 11–20, the turtle is identified by a triangle facing in the direction shown. Determine the angle measure that would accompany the **RIGHT** command in order to turn the turtle toward point *A* in each. Explain your reasoning.

11. Given: equilateral triangle *ABC*; turtle at *C*, facing in the direction from *B* toward *C*.

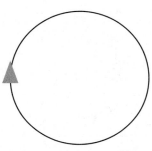

12. Given: equilateral triangle *CBD* with $\overline{AB}$ the bisector of ∠*B*; turtle at *B*, facing in the direction from *C* toward *B*.

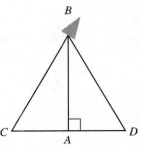

13. Given: square *ABCD*; turtle at *C*, facing in the direction from *B* toward *C*.

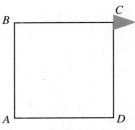

14. Given: square *ABCD*; turtle at *B*, facing in the direction from *D* toward *B*.

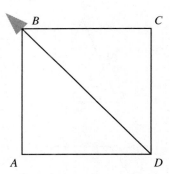

15. Given: isosceles triangle *ABC* with *m*∠*B* = 50° and $\overline{BC} \cong \overline{AC}$; turtle at *C*, facing in the direction from *B* toward *C*.

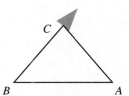

16. Given: regular pentagon *ABCDE*; turtle at *E*, facing in the direction from *D* toward *E*.

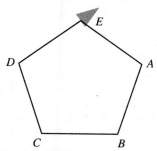

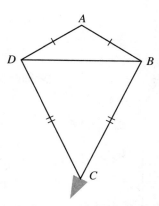

17. Given: parallelogram *ABCD* with $\overline{CA}$ a diagonal, $m\angle BAC = 30°$, and $m\angle CAD = 50°$; turtle at *C*, facing in the direction from *B* toward *C*.

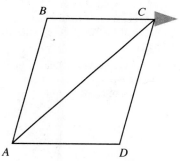

18. Given: trapezoid *ABCD* with segment $\overline{AC}$ a diagonal and $m\angle A = m\angle D = 90°$, $m\angle CAD = 55°$, $m\angle CAB = 35°$, and $m\angle ABC = 110°$; turtle at *C*, facing in the direction from *B* toward C.

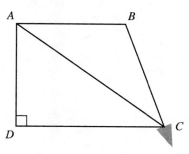

19. Given: kite *ABCD* with $\overline{BD}$ a diagonal, $m\angle A = 120°$ and $m\angle B = 85°$; turtle at *C*, facing in the direction from *B* toward *C*.

20. Given: regular hexagon *HBCDEF* and equilateral triangle *DCG*; turtle at *G*, facing in the direction from *B* to *G*.

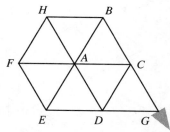

In problems 21–25 write the LOGO procedure that will output the following figures. All figures are polygons with the dimensions shown here.

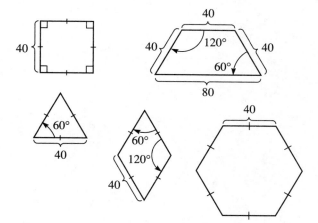

21.

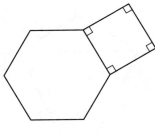

22.

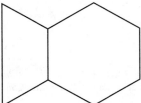

23.

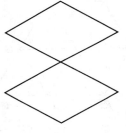

24.

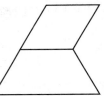

25.

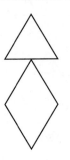

In LOGO, you can perform basic arithmetic operations. For example, the following commands illustrate the use of addition, subtraction, multiplication, and division operations: `FD (:X +20)`, `RT (:ANGLE −40)`, `BK :SIDE*2`, `LT :DEG/2`. Use this information where necessary to write the required LOGO procedures in problems 26–30.

26. Write a procedure that uses the variable `:ANGLE` to construct the angle bisector of the angle whose measure is stored in `:ANGLE`. Assume that the lengths of the segments that form the side of the angle and the length of the angle bisector segment are each 50 units in length.

27. Write a LOGO procedure that will construct a perpendicular bisector of length 160 units to a line of any given length (`:LEN`).

28. Write a LOGO procedure to construct a regular pentagon, the measure of whose side is stored in `:SIDE`. Within the same procedure, construct a similar pentagon such that the ratio of similitude of the first figure to the second figure is stored in `:RATIO`.

29. Construct a recursive procedure that will display 10 hexagons constructed about a fixed point before overwriting occurs. The display should look as follows:

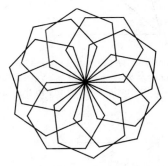

30. The following figure is composed of an octagon and an equilateral triangle.

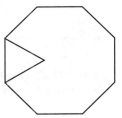

Write a recursive procedure that will create the following display before overwriting occurs.

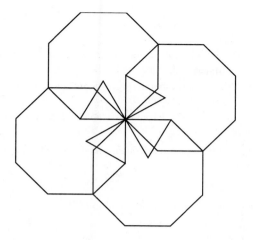

33. Explain the connection between programming in LOGO and if-then logic.

34. How can LOGO be used to illustrate the following statement: "As the number of sides of a regular polygon increases, the polygon resembles a circle"?

35. Seymour Papert maintains that learning to program a computer using LOGO will change the way children learn mathematics, and in fact, change the way they learn everything. Discuss this statement.

Cooperative Activity

36. Groups of two

Individual Accountability: Each group member must develop two procedures that employ variables. One procedure should display a nonconvex pentagon. The other procedure should display a nonconvex octagon.

Group Goal: The group is to develop a LOGO procedure that will verify that the four polygons are indeed nonconvex.

In Other Words

31. Explain recursion in a LOGO procedure.

32. We have used the phrase "defining a procedure." Exactly what does this mean?

Vocabulary for Chapter 12

abscissa

analytic geometry

angle-angle-angle property of similarity
    (AAA~AAA)

angle-angle property of similarity
    (AA~AA)

angle-side-angle property of congruence
    (ASA ≅ ASA)

Cartesian coordinate system

central angles

circumcenter

coefficients

congruent figures

coordinates

hypotenuse-leg property of congruence
    (HL ≅ HL)

incenter

LOGO

ordinate

origin

plotting a point

point-slope form

procedure

quadrants

ratio of similitude

recursive procedure

secant

side-angle-side property of congruence
    (SAS ≅ SAS)

side-angle-side property of similarity
    (SAS)

side-side-side property of congruence
    (SSS ≅ SSS)

side-side-side property of similarity (SSS)

similar figures

slope-intercept equation of a line

slope of a line

system of equations

tangent

x-axis

y-axis

y-intercept

Review for Chapter 12

1. Determine the length and midpoint of the segments whose endpoints are listed here.
   (a) $(-2, 4)$, $(5, 7)$
   (b) $(0, -4)$, $(9, -4)$
   (c) $(4, 6)$, $(-3, 2)$
   (d) $(1, 1)$, $(-6, 3)$
   (e) $(3, -8)$, $(3, 9)$

2. Write the equation of the line that passes through the points listed in each part of Problem 1.

3. A line $\overline{AB}$ passes through the points $A(0, -3)$ and $B(2, 3)$. Determine an equation of another line whose slope is 50% greater than the slope of $\overline{AB}$ and passes through point A.

4. What type of figure is formed when the following four points are joined in order:

   Point A: The y-intercept of $y = 2x - 1$
   Point B: The x-intercept of $y = x + 3$
   Point C: The y-intercept of $y = 1 + 5x$
   Point D: The x-intercept of $y = -5 + x$

   Justify your choice.

5. (a) Determine a point that lies on the circle

   $$(x - 1)^2 + (y - 1)^2 = 25$$

   (b) What is the center of this circle?
   (c) What is the length of the radius of this circle?
   (d) Use your answer from part (a) to write the equation of a line that passes through the center of this circle.

6. (a) Determine the coordinates of two points that are a distance of 13 units from each other.
   (b) Determine the coordinates of two points that are a distance of 6 units from each other.
   (c) What is the length of the line segment joining points A and B with coordinates $(-5, 2)$ and $(1, -8)$, respectively.
   (d) What is the length of the line segment joining the points C and D with coordinates $(4, -2)$ and $(7, -3)$, respectively.
   (e) Point E with coordinates $(3, 5)$ is an endpoint of a line segment that measures 5 units in length. Find the coordinates of the other endpoint.

7. The vertices of a quadrilateral have the following coordinates:

   $$R(-3, 4) \quad S(2, 5) \quad T(6, -3) \quad U(2, -4)$$

   (a) Draw this quadrilateral on graph paper. Determine the perimeter of this quadrilateral.
   (b) Use the upper bound/lower bound method to approximate the area of this figure.
   (c) What type of quadrilateral is $RSTU$? Justify your reasoning.

8. The vertices of a quadrilateral have the following coordinates:

   $$W(-3, 2) \quad X(1, 7) \quad Y(5, 2) \quad Z(1, -3)$$

   (a) What type of quadrilateral is $WXYZ$? Justify your reasoning.
   (b) Determine the length of each side.
   (c) Determine the lengths of diagonals $\overline{WY}$ and $\overline{XZ}$.
   (d) Determine the midpoint of the diagonals $\overline{WY}$ and $\overline{XZ}$.

9. Use your protractor and a straightedge to draw an equilateral triangle of any size. Label the vertices A, B, and C in clockwise order starting at any vertex. Find M_1 (the midpoint of $\overline{AB}$), M_2 (the midpoint of $\overline{BC}$), and M_3 (the midpoint of $\overline{CA}$). Connect M_1, M_2, and M_3 in that order. What new figure appears to have been drawn? How can you verify your claim?

10. Determine two equations that might be the algebraic representations of the lines pictured below.

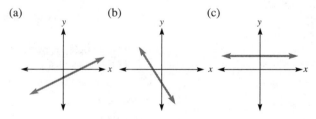

(a) (b) (c)

11. Solve each system.
    (a) $y = 2x - 6$
        $y = -x + 6$
    (b) $y = -3x - 5$
        $y = x + 3$
    (c) $y = 5 - 2x$
        $y = x - 4$

12. The vertices of a triangle are $A(-3, 0)$, $B(5, 0)$, and $C(3, 6)$.
    (a) Draw $\triangle ABC$ on the coordinate axes.
    (b) Determine the circumcenter of the circle that can be circumscribed about $\triangle ABC$.

13. Given: $\triangle EFG$ in which $m\angle E = 50°$, $EF = 5$ cm, and $GE = 6$ cm.
    (a) Construct $\triangle EFG$.
    (b) Inscribe a circle within $\triangle EFG$.

14. Determine the equation of a circle that might be the algebraic representation of the circle pictured in each graph.

(a)   (b)   (c)

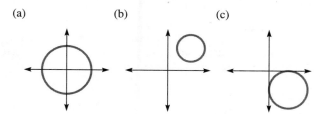

15. Given: $\triangle ABC$ with coordinates $A(-3, 4)$, $B(5, 2)$, and $C(1, -1)$. Determine the coordinates of any triangle EFG such that $\triangle ABC \cong \triangle EFG$.

16. A person has 30 coins in nickels and quarters. The total value of the coins is $3.10. How many of each type of coin does this person have?

17. Rachel's piggy bank contains 28 coins in dimes and pennies. The total value is $1.45. How many of each type of coin does Rachel have?

18. Given: pentagon $RSTUV$ with coordinates $R(-5, 1)$, $S(-4, 4)$, $T(-1, 5)$, $U(2, 3)$, and $V(1, -1)$. What are the coordinates of a pentagon that is congruent to pentagon $RSTUV$?

19. Given pentagon $ABCDE$ as shown here, trace $ABCDE$ and construct a pentagon that is congruent to pentagon $ABCDE$.

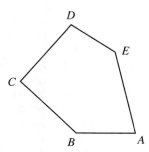

20. $\triangle DEF$ and $\triangle GHI$ are similar triangles. The ratio of similitude of $\triangle DEF$ to $\triangle GHI$ is $4:1$. The measure of side $\overline{FD}$ is 10 cm. What is the measure of its corresponding side in $\triangle GHI$?

21. The sides of a triangle measure 4 cm, 6 cm, and 4.5 cm. What is the perimeter of a similar triangle if the side corresponding to the 4.5-cm side measures 13.5 cm?

22. A 12-foot-high pole casts a shadow that is 9 feet long. At the same time, a tree casts a 24-foot shadow. What is the height of the tree?

23. Given: $\triangle UVW \sim \triangle XYZ$. The ratio of the lengths of corresponding sides is $3:1$. The perimeter of the larger triangle is 12 less than 5 times the perimeter of the smaller triangle. What is the perimeter of each triangle?

24. Given: parallelogram $QSUV$ with $\overline{VT} \perp \overline{US}$ and $\overline{VR} \perp \overline{SQ}$. Explain why $\triangle VUT \sim VQR$.

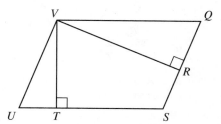

25. Given: nonconvex quadrilateral $DEFG$ with $\overline{DE} \cong \overline{EF}$, and $\overline{GE}$ bisecting $\angle E$. Explain why $\triangle DEG \cong \triangle FEG$.

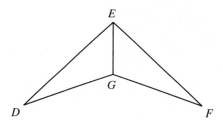

26. Two triangles are congruent. The measure of the longest side of the first triangle can be represented by $3x + 2$. The measure of the longest side of the second triangle can be represented by $8x - 13$. What is the measure of the longest side in each triangle?

27. Given: $\triangle FDG$ with $\overline{DF} \cong \overline{DG}$, $\overline{GE} \cong \overline{FH}$; $\overline{GE}$ bisects $\overline{FD}$ and $\overline{FH}$ bisects $\overline{DG}$. Explain why $\triangle FDH \cong \triangle GDE$.

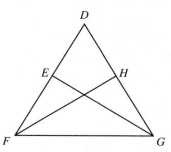

28. You are given isosceles triangles ACE, ABF, and GDE with $\overline{AC} \cong \overline{EC}$, $\overline{AB} \cong \overline{FB}$, and $\overline{GD} \cong \overline{ED}$, as shown on page 648. Explain why $\angle HFG \cong \angle HGF$.

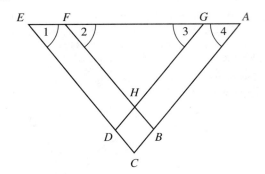

29. The following LOGO procedure will construct a rectangle with the given measurements.

```
TO RECTANGLE
REPEAT 2 [FD 50 RT 90 FD 120 RT 90]
END
```

Write a procedure that will display a rectangle similar to the one in the procedure **RECTANGLE** with any given ratio of similitude.

30. An isosceles trapezoid pictured here can be partitioned into two congruent right triangles and one rectangle.

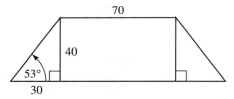

(a) Write three procedures. Two procedures draw the right triangles. One procedure draws the rectangle.

(b) Write a new procedure called **TRAP** that will display the isosceles trapezoid. This procedure should call upon the three procedures written in part (a).

31. Write a recursive LOGO procedure that will display each of the following figures.

(a) Eighteen equilateral triangles drawn about a fixed vertex.

(b) Twelve regular pentagons drawn about a fixed vertex.

In Other Words

32. Explain the following statement: Corresponding parts of similar triangles are in proportion.

33. Explain the following statement: Corresponding parts of congruent triangles are congruent.

34. Suppose that $\triangle ABC \cong \triangle DEF$, $\triangle DEF \sim \triangle GHI$, $\triangle GHI \sim \triangle JKL$, and $\triangle JKL \cong \triangle MNO$. Explain the relationship (if any) between $\triangle ABC$ and $\triangle MNO$.

35. What is the least amount of information you would need to know to state that two right triangles are congruent? Explain your answer.

36. Explain how an 18-sided regular polygon would be drawn in LOGO. Do not write the commands; just explain the movements and turns of the cursor.

Cooperative Activity

37. Groups of four

Individual Accountability: Group members are to read each of the following paragraphs. Based on the information given and his or her knowledge of the geometric terms used, each member is to sketch each figure.

(a) This figure contains 12 lines of symmetry. It also has rotational symmetry. Its opposite sides are congruent and parallel. All angles are congruent.

(b) This figure is a combination of three polygons. Two of the polygons are congruent right triangles. The third polygon is a rectangle. Position the rectangle so that the longer side is horizontal. The two congruent right triangles will be adjacent to the rectangle on opposite vertical sides. One triangle will point upward and the other will point downward. Construct the right triangles so that the vertex containing the right angle is formed at the midpoint of each of the vertical sides. The altitude of each triangle is equal in length to the vertical side of the rectangle and will therefore extend past the rectangle.

(c) This figure is composed of four similar nonoverlapping rectangles. Sketch a rectangle so that the longer side is horizontal. Partition the segment that forms the "top" side of the rectangle into three congruent segments. Construct a rectangle that is similar to the original rectangle. The leftmost third segment will form its longer side. Partition the segment that forms the right side of the original rectangle into two congruent segments. Construct a rectangle that is similar to the original rectangle. The top half will form its shorter side. Partition the base of the rectangle into four congruent segments. Construct a rectangle that is similar to the original rectangle. The three left-most fourths will form its longer side.

Group Goal: Compare each individual member's sketches with each other and with the solution given by your instructor. The goal of the group is to create an original sketch and a description to accompany it. Based on the preceding three examples, try to make your instructions as clear as possible. The goal is to have the other members of your class accurately reproduce your sketch.

13

Other **G**eometries

Examine the photograph at the right.

Describe what you see.

What mirror images do you see?

Describe the relationship between the tree and its reflection.

What might a mathematical description of this photograph contain?

Introduction

Chapters 10, 11, and 12 introduced a variety of shapes and solids. These shapes and solids were measured, dissected, compared, and constructed. Relationships between and among them were established. In this chapter, we will examine other geometrical viewpoints. In transformational geometry (Section 13.1), we examine motion on a set of points. In projective geometry, we examine a mathematics that grew out of the need of artists to represent three-dimensional reality on a two-dimensional canvas (Section 13.2). In topology, we examine an area of mathematics in which the rigidity of shapes is no longer a property of those shapes (Section 13.2).

There are many other ways of viewing geometry, too numerous and beyond the scope of this book to be included here. We have selected these three branches of mathematics because they provide many techniques for solving problems in nonroutine settings.

13.1   Transformational Geometry

transformational geometry

transformations

We have examined figures in terms of their size, shape, and position. **Transformational geometry** is a branch of mathematics in which the size, shape, and/or position of figures undergo a change. These changes are called **transformations**. Examine the shape depicted in Figure 13.1a. This shape can undergo a variety of transformations. Three such transformations are shown in parts (b), (c), and (d) of Figure 13.1.

Figure 13.1

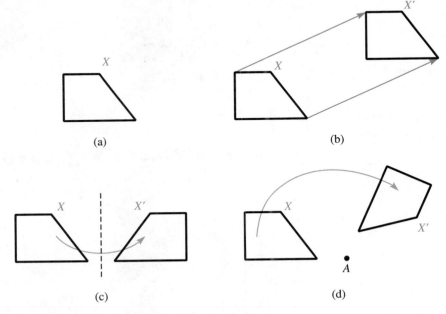

(a)

(b)

(c)

(d)

In Figure 13.1b, the trapezoid has been transformed by sliding it in the plane. In Figure 13.1c, the trapezoid has been transformed by flipping it over a line. In Figure 13.1d, the trapezoid has been transformed by turning it to the right around point A. In

invariant each of the transformations, we are concerned with those aspects of the figure that have changed and those aspects that have remained unchanged, or are **invariant**. You can see in parts (b), (c), and (d) of Figure 13.1 that only the position has changed. The size of the figures is invariant. These types of transformations are motions in a plane that are

rigid motions called **rigid motions**.

You can see that in each case, vertex X has been moved to a new location in the plane and labeled X'(read "X prime"). In a transformation, every point in the original

image figure corresponds to a unique point in the new figure, called the **image**. Since this point association between the original figure and the image is unique, the transformation is said to be a one-to-one correspondence between points of two geometric figures.

Translations

In Figure 13.1b, each point of the trapezoid has been shifted along the plane an equal distance and in the same direction to form the image. This transformation is called a

translation **translation**. The translation of the trapezoid in Figure 13.1b can best be examined by superimposing a grid, as shown in Figure 13.2.

Figure 13.2

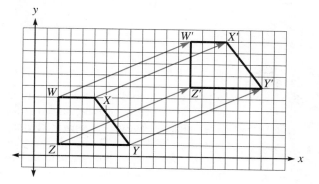

The translation shifts trapezoid $WXYZ$ to $W'X'Y'Z'$. Examine segments $\overline{WW'}$, $\overline{XX'}$, $\overline{YY'}$, and $\overline{ZZ'}$. Each of these segments has the same length and all are parallel. This can be verified using the tools of coordinate geometry. First, identify the coordinates. Then calculate the distance between the point and its image. Finally, determine the slope of the line segment that joins the point and its image. The following table helps to organize the data and allows you to easily verify that the translation shifts the vertices of the trapezoid the same distance and in the same direction.

Point	Image	Distance	Slope of Segment Joining Point and Image
$W(2, 5)$	$W'(13, 10)$	≈ 12	$\frac{5}{11}$
$X(5, 5)$	$X'(16, 10)$	≈ 12	$\frac{5}{11}$
$Y(8, 1)$	$Y'(19, 6)$	≈ 12	$\frac{5}{11}$
$Z(2, 1)$	$Z'(13, 6)$	≈ 12	$\frac{5}{11}$

Investigation 1

In designing a wallpaper pattern, graphic artists are concerned with regularity. Regularity can be ensured by using a translation. Suppose the pattern illustrated below is to be repeated on the wallpaper such that the image of point A will be located at $(7, 9)$. Describe the translation in question, and list the ordered pairs that define the vertices of the image.

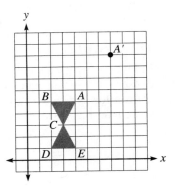

To shift from A to A', it is necessary to move four units up and then three units to the right. This movement can be viewed as forming a right triangle whose legs are four and three units, respectively. Using the Pythagorean theorem, the length of the hypotenuse is therefore five units. This means that the distance from A to A' is five units in length.

The slope of the line segment that forms the hypotenuse is $\frac{4}{3}$. Since a translation shifts every point the same distance in the same direction, each of the vertices must be shifted four units up and three units to the right. The line segment that can be drawn between every point and its image will be five units in length and have a slope of $\frac{4}{3}$.

The vertex points of the image are $A'(7, 9)$, $B'(5, 9)$, $C'(6, 7)$, $D'(5, 5)$, and $E'(7, 5)$.

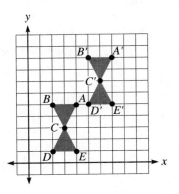

Reflection

In Figure 13.1c, the image of the trapezoid is no longer formed by a shift or a slide. It appears as if the image is a mirror image of the original trapezoid. If a mirror were placed along the dotted line, the image drawn would indeed appear as a reflection in the

reflection   mirror. For this reason, this type of transformation is called a reflection. A **reflection** is a transformation that "flips" a figure about a given line to form its reflection image.

In a translation, every point of the image is the same distance and direction from its corresponding point in the original figure. This is not the case in a reflection. Examine Figure 13.3.

Figure 13.3

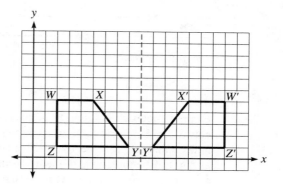

Trapezoid *WXYZ* has been reflected, or flipped, about the line $x = 9$. Connecting each vertex point with its image shows that a reflection does not move each point the same distance. It is obvious that $\overline{YY'}$ has a length of two units, whereas $\overline{XX'}$ has a length of eight units. However, a special relationship does exist between the points and their images, and the line of reflection.

The midpoints of the segments that connect each point with its image will lie on the line of reflection. In addition, the line of reflection will be perpendicular to each of these segments. This relationship is highlighted in Figure 13.4. It is not necessary to determine the slopes of the lines to show perpendicularity since the lines in question are vertical and horizontal.

Figure 13.4

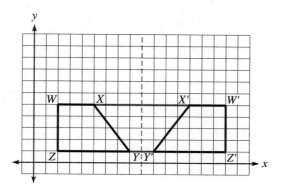

Investigation 2

Many musical compositions consist of translations and reflections of musical notes. Examine the following simplified piece of music. Identify those notes (numbered here for ease of reference) that illustrate translations and reflections. How might the properties of translations and reflections be verified?

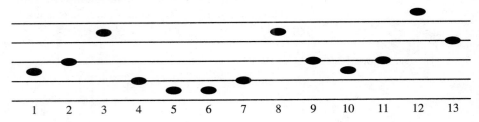

Examine notes 2, 3, 4, and 5. It appears that a vertical line of symmetry can be drawn between notes 5 and 6. Notes 6 through 9 can then be viewed as reflection images of notes 5 through 2, respectively. This reflection could be verified by viewing the notes as points. The midpoints of the horizontal segments joining points 5 to 6, 4 to 7, 3 to 8, and 2 to 9 would lie on the vertical line of reflection.

Notes 10, 11, 12, and 13 follow the same pattern as notes 6, 7, 8, and 9. Notes 10 through 13 can be viewed as a translation of notes 6 through 9. This transformation can be verified by drawing segments to connect points 6 to 10, 7 to 11, 8 to 12, and 9 to 13. These segments will be parallel and of equal length.

When musicians transpose music from one key to another, the transposed music can be seen as a translation of the original piece of music.

Investigation 3

Use only a compass and a straightedge to construct the reflection image of figure *ABCDE* about line *l*.

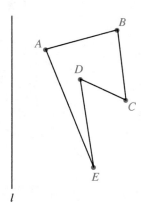

To construct the reflection image of *ABCDE*, you must recognize that the line of reflection is the perpendicular bisector of the segment that joins a point and its image. View each vertex of *ABCDE* as a point off line *l*. Construct a perpendicular to the line from each vertex.

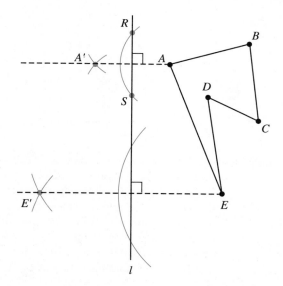

In the figure above, two perpendiculars have been constructed. Recall this construction, which was outlined in Section 11.1. Its justification was based on the fact that the diagonals of a rhombus are perpendicular bisectors of each other. Points *R*, *A*, *S*, and *A'* can be viewed as forming the vertices of a rhombus. Therefore, the perpendicular distances from *A* and *A'* to the line of reflection are congruent. For the same reason, this will hold true for all other vertices and their images. Figure *A'B'C'D'E'* below, is the reflection image of *ABCDE* since the line of reflection is the perpendicular bisector of the segments that join each point to its image.

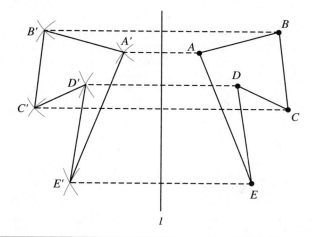

Rotation

In Figure 13.15, the image containing X' is neither a translation nor a reflection. The trapezoid appears to have been turned around some fixed point A.

Figure 13.5

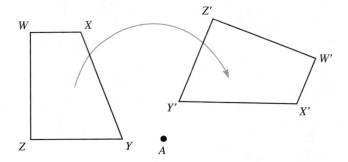

rotation   This type of transformation is called a **rotation**. In a rotation, a center of rotation is necessary. The image is formed by rotating the original figure in a clockwise or counterclockwise motion about the center of rotation. In a rotational transformation, the distance from a point to the center of rotation is the same as the distance of the image of that point to the center of rotation. In addition, the angle formed at the center of rotation by any point X with its image X' is constant. For example, in Figure 13.5, it is easy to verify that $m\angle WAW' = m\angle XAX' = m\angle YAY' = m\angle ZAZ' = 120°$ using a protractor. It can also be verified that $WA = W'A$, $XA = X'A$, $YA = Y'A$, and $ZA = Z'A$ using a ruler.

Investigation 4

The length of the minute hand on an analog clock is 9 centimeters. The length of the hour hand is 6 centimeters. Suppose that a triangle is formed by these two hands at exactly 7 o'clock. What time is it when the hands form a triangle that has been rotated 95 degrees in a clockwise direction?

Understand the Problem: What is known? You are given the length of two sides of a triangle formed by two hands of a clock showing 7 o'clock.
What is unknown? You must determine the position of the triangle when it is rotated 95° in a clockwise direction.

Devise a Plan: Draw a diagram to illustrate this situation.

Carry Out the Plan:

The figure above shows the clock in question at 7 o'clock. The center of the clock will act as the center of rotation for this transformation. The "points" at the end of the hour hand and at the end of the minute hand must sweep through 95 degrees in a clockwise direction, as shown in the figure below. The image of $\triangle HCM$ is $\triangle H'CM'$. Triangle $H'CM'$ is formed at approximately 10:16.

Look Back: Since the movement of 95° is equivalent to a movement through a little more than $\frac{1}{4}$ of the clock face, the minute hand pointing to the 12 will now point just past the 3 (3 hours is $\frac{1}{4}$ of 12 hours). For the same reason, the hand pointing to the 7 will now point just past the 10.

It is important to examine the three transformations—translations, reflections, and rotations—in terms of the properties of figures that change and those that remain invariant. In a translation, the only attribute that changes is the position of the figure, since a translation is a linear shift only. In a reflection, position also changes, but relative direction between segments and between angles can also change. A segment that is to the left of another segment in the original may not continue to be so in the reflection image. The relative position change also occurs in a rotation. A vertical line in the original figure may not be vertical in the rotation image. However, in all three of these transformations, the size of the figure is invariant.

Glide Reflections

It is possible to perform a transformation by combining two transformations. Once again, let's examine the trapezoid pictured in Figure 13.1a. Here, we will superimpose a grid so we can easily verify the transformations.

In Figure 13.6a, trapezoid *WXYZ* has been translated by adding six units to every *x*-coordinate and zero units to every *y*-coordinate to form *W'X'Y'Z'*. In Figure 13.6b, the translation image *W'X'Y'Z'* is then reflected about the *x*-axis to form the reflection **glide reflection** *W"X"Y"Z"* (*"* is read as "double prime"). In a **glide reflection**, a translation of a figure first occurs. Next, a line of reflection is established, which is parallel to the translation. The translation image is then reflected over this line to produce the glide reflection image of the original figure.

Figure 13.6

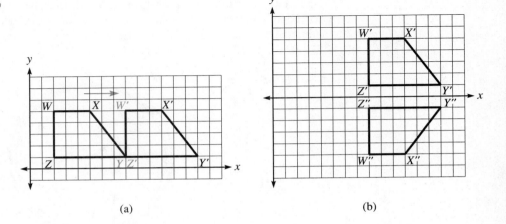

(a)   (b)

Investigation 5

Examine the following logo.

Explain how the logo was formed using a glide reflection.

Superimpose a grid over the logo as shown here.

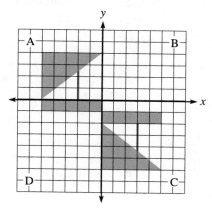

The logo can be divided into four quadrants (*A*, *B*, *C*, and *D*). We can show that the figure in quadrant *C* is the glide reflection image of the figure in quadrant *A* as follows.

First, translate the figure in quadrant *A* by adding five units to every *x*-coordinate and leaving the *y*-coordinates unchanged. The translation segments that can be drawn between points on the original figure and their images are all of equal length (five units) and are all parallel (horizontal segments).

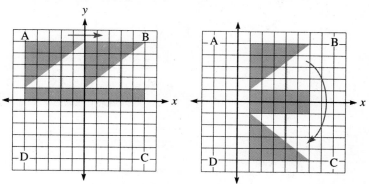

Second, let the *x*-axis be viewed as a line of reflection for this glide since it meets the condition that the line of reflection be parallel to the translation. Reflect the translation image from quadrant *B* over the *x*-axis into quadrant *C*. This reflection can be verified by establishing that the midpoints of the vertical segments joining the points in the figure in quadrant *B* with their respective images in quadrant *C* all lie on the *x*-axis (the line of reflection). Therefore, the logo is formed by a figure and its glide reflection image.

Isometries on a Coordinate Plane

You have been introduced to the properties of translations, reflections, rotations, and glide reflections. It should be clear that each point in the original figure (henceforth preimage   called the **preimage**) corresponds to a unique point in the image for each of these transformations. In each case, the lengths of the line segments composing the preimage are congruent to the lengths of the corresponding line segments composing the image. Therefore, length is invariant in these transformations. Any transformation that pre-

isometry   serves length is called an **isometry**. In an isometry, the preimage and the image are congruent. Later on in this section, we will introduce transformations that do not preserve length and are therefore not isometries.

On the coordinate plane, the one-to-one correspondence between the points of the preimage and the corresponding points of the translation image can be viewed as a relation and symbolized as $(x, y) \to (x', y')$. In other words, each ordered pair of the preimage is related in the same way to a unique ordered pair in the translation image. Since a translation is a shift in a plane, x' and y' can be expressed in terms of a shift in x and y. For example, Figure 13.7 depicts parallelogram $ABCD$ and its translation image $A'B'C'D'$. By examing the vertices of both the preimage and the image, a relation can be established.

$$A(-11, 5) \quad A'(2, 7)$$
$$B(-7, 7) \quad B'(6, 9)$$
$$C(-4, 5) \quad C'(9, 7)$$
$$D(-8, 3) \quad D'(5, 5)$$

Figure 13.7

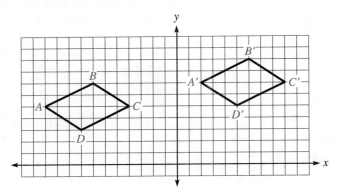

The translation can be expressed as $(x, y) \to (x + 13, y + 2)$.

Can a reflection be expressed as a relation in terms of x and y? For the purposes of this text, we will examine only reflections on the coordinate plane whose line of reflection is horizontal or vertical. Let's first examine a situation in which the line of reflection is vertical.

In Figure 13.8, the triangle ABC has been reflected about the line $x = -2$. The coordinates of the preimage and image vertices are listed here.

$$A(-9, 4) \quad A'(5, 4)$$
$$B(-12, 8) \quad B'(8, 8)$$
$$C(-7, 6) \quad C'(3, 6)$$

Figure 13.8

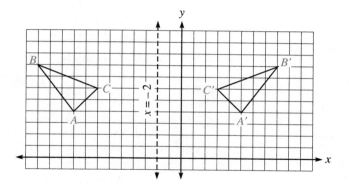

By examing the vertices, it appears that a reflection about a vertical line preserves the value of the y-coordinate. The x-coordinate is neither preserved nor changed by a constant value (as was the case in a translation). Notice that the horizontal distance from a point in the preimage to the line of reflection is equal to the horizontal distance from a corresponding point in the image to the line of reflection. The distances are listed in the table below.

Preimage	Horizontal Distance to $x = -2$	Image	Horizontal Distance to $x = -2$
$A(-9, 4)$	$|-9 - (-2)| = 7$	$A'(5, 4)$	$|5 - (-2)| = 7$
$B(-12, 8)$	$|-12 - (-2)| = 10$	$B'(8, 8)$	$|8 - (-2)| = 10$
$C(-7, 6)$	$|-7 - (-2)| = 5$	$C'(3, 6)$	$|3 - (-2)| = 5$

The distance from the x-coordinate of the image to its corresponding preimage x-value is equal to twice the horizontal distance from the point to $x = -2$. With this knowledge, it is possible to develop a generalization that will represent a relation for a vertical reflection. Suppose that a point (x_1, y_1) is to be reflected about the line $x = a$. Then

$$2(x_1 - a) = x_1 - x_1'$$
$$x_1' = x_1 - 2(x_1 - a)$$
$$= x_1 - 2x_1 + 2a$$
$$= 2a - x_1$$

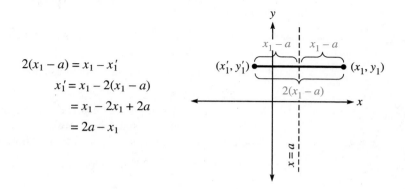

Therefore, the reflection about any line $x = a$ can be symbolized by $(x, y) \rightarrow (2a - x, y)$. In the case presented in the figure above, when $a = -2$, then

$$(x, y) \rightarrow (2a - x, y)$$
$$(-9, 4) \rightarrow ((2 \times (-2) - (-9), 4) = (-4 - (-9), 4) = (5, 4))$$
$$(-12, 8) \rightarrow ((2 \times (-2) - (-12), 8) = (-4 - (-12), 8) = (8, 8))$$
$$(-7, 6) \rightarrow ((2 \times (-2) - (-7), 6) = (-4 - (-7), 6) = (3, 6))$$

It will be left to you in Problem 20 at the end of this section to develop a similar generalization for a reflection about a horizontal line in a coordinate plane.

Can a rotation be expressed as a relation in terms of x and y? To answer this question, you must clearly understand the nature of a rotation. For every rotation, it is necessary to know the number of degrees of the rotation, the direction of the rotation, and the center of rotation. Unlike translation and reflection, the numerical values needed here (degrees, direction) are not linear measures. Therefore, it seems that the coordinates of points of the rotation image cannot be expressed as a linear relation.

In one instance, a recognizable relation can be established on the coordinate plane. Examine what happens to the point (3, 5) when it is rotated in a clockwise direction 90°, 180°, and 270° about the center of rotation at the origin, as shown in Figure 13.9.

Figure 13.9

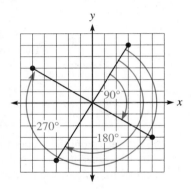

- Under a rotation of 90° in a clockwise direction with the origin as center,
  $(3, 5) \rightarrow (5, -3)$

- Under a rotation of 180° in a clockwise direction with the origin as center,
  $(3, 5) \rightarrow (-3, -5)$

- Under a rotation of 270° in a clockwise direction with the origin as center,
  $(3, 5) \rightarrow (-5, 3)$

Notice that these rotations create perpendicular lines that appear to be a "new set of axes." A pattern can be established between the coordinates of the preimage and those of the corresponding image. In general, the following relations hold:

- Under a rotation of 90° in a clockwise direction with the origin as center,
  $(x, y) \rightarrow (y, -x)$

- Under a rotation of 180° in a clockwise direction with the origin as center,
  $(x, y) \rightarrow (-x, -y)$

- Under a rotation of 270° in a clockwise direction with the origin as center,
  $(x, y) \rightarrow (-y, x)$

We are now ready to determine which isometries or combinations of isometries are used to attain a particular image. Examine Investigation 6.

Investigation 6

You are given $\triangle ABC$ and its image $A'B'C'$. The image can be the result of one or more isometries. Determine the transformation(s) that were used to obtain the image of $\triangle ABC$.

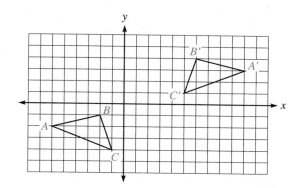

Understand the Problem: What is known? You are given the location of the image and the preimage.

What is unknown? You must determine the transformations that effected the change from the preimage to the image.

Devise a Plan: To solve this problem, we will use the problem-solving strategy of working backward.

Carry Out the Plan: Notice in $\triangle A'B'C'$ that B' is above and to the left of A' and above and to the right of C'. In the preimage, B is above and to the right of A and above and to the left of C. In a translation, relative position is preserved. Therefore, the transformation used could not have been only a translation. It appears that the image is a result of more than one transformation.

Since the image of vertices A and C appear from left to right as C' and A', it is possible that $\triangle A'B'C'$ is the result of a reflection. There are an infinite number of possible lines of reflection that could be tested. A horizontal line of reflection would locate B' below both C' and A'. Since this is not the case in the corresponding points of the preimage, we will try a vertical line of reflection. Select any vertical line that does not intersect the interior of $\triangle A'B'C'$. We will use $x = 3$. We have already established that a reflection about a horizontal line $x = 3$ will take the form

$$(x, y) \rightarrow (2 \times 3 - x, y)$$

We can use algebra to determine each of the points of the preimage as follows on page 664. For $A'(10, 3)$,

$$(x, y) \rightarrow (2 \times 3 - x, y)$$
$$(x, y) \rightarrow (10, 3)$$

Therefore,

$$(2 \times 3 - x, y) = (10, 3)$$
$$6 - x = 10 \quad \text{and} \quad y = 3$$
$$x = -4 \quad \text{and} \quad y = 3$$

The point $A''(-4, 3)$ is the preimage that corresponds to the reflection image point $(10, 3)$ about line $x = 3$.

For $B'(6, 4)$,

$$(x, y) \rightarrow (2 \times 3 - x, y)$$
$$(x, y) \rightarrow (6, 4)$$

Therefore

$$(2 \times 3 - x, y) = (6, 4)$$
$$6 - x = 6 \quad \text{and} \quad y = 4$$
$$x = 0 \quad \text{and} \quad y = 4$$

The point $B''(0, 4)$ is the preimage that corresponds to the reflection image point $(6, 4)$ about line $x = 3$.

For $C'(5, 1)$,

$$(x, y) \rightarrow (2 \times 3 - x, y)$$
$$(x, y) \rightarrow (5, 1)$$

Therefore

$$(2 \times 3 - x, y) = (5, 1)$$
$$6 - x = 5 \quad \text{and} \quad y = 1$$
$$x = 1 \quad \text{and} \quad y = 1$$

The point $(1, 1)$ is the preimage that corresponds to the reflection image point $(5, 1)$ about the line $x = 3$.

We now have the following figures:

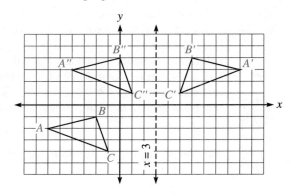

$\Delta A''B''C''$ is in the same relative position as ΔABC. What translation could therefore have been used to transform ΔABC to $\Delta A''B''C''$?

We have already seen that a translation can be symbolized as $(x, y) \rightarrow (x + c, y + d)$. The values of c and d can be determined in the following manner:

$$A(-6, -2) \rightarrow A''(-4, 3)$$

Since $(-4, 3) = (-6 + c, -2 + d)$ under some translation, $c = 2$ and $d = 5$.

$$B(-2, -1) \rightarrow B''(0, 4)$$

Since $(0, 4) = (-2 + c, -1 + d)$ under some translation, $c = 2$ and $d = 5$.

$$C(-1, -4) \rightarrow C''(1, 1)$$

Since $(1, 1) = (-1 + c, -4 + d)$ under some translation, $c = 2$ and $d = 5$.

Therefore, the translation in question is $(x, y) \rightarrow (x + 2, y + 5)$.

Look Back:
composition

Working progressively, we see that $\Delta A'B'C'$ is the result of a translation and then a reflection. This is known as a **composition**. We can symbolize the composition as follows:

$$(x, y) \rightarrow (x + 2, y + 5) \rightarrow (2 \times 3 - x, y)$$

Any combination of transformations, such as a glide reflection, can be viewed as a composition of isometries. As you have seen in this investigation, the image from the original translation becomes the preimage of the reflection.

This image could also have been formed by a reflection about the line $x = 2$, followed by a translation of $y + 5$.

Symmetry

In Chapter 10, we introduced the concepts of point and line symmetry within the context of spatial visualization. Symmetry can also be viewed in a transformational context. Recall that a figure was said to have line symmetry if there exists a line that divides the figure into two congruent halves. A figure is said to have rotational symmetry if there exists a point around which the figure can be rotated less than one complete turn in order to result in an identical figure.

Notice the connection between symmetry and transformations, as illustrated on page 666. In Figure 13.10, figure $ABCD$ is reflected about three different lines. In parts (a) and (b) of Figure 13.10, the reflection image is located in a different position than the preimage. In Figure 13.10c, a line of reflection is chosen so that the reflection image about the line is the preimage itself. In such a case, when the image and preimage are taken together, the line of reflection is called a **line of symmetry**, and the figure will have line symmetry. It is for this reason that line symmetry is sometimes known as **reflectional symmetry**.

line of symmetry

reflectional symmetry

Figure 13.10

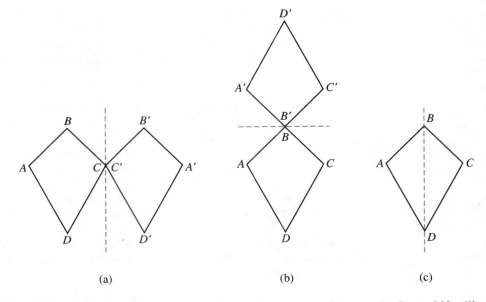

(a) (b) (c)

In Figure 13.11, the center of rotation is located at *A*. Rotating the figure 90° will result in an image that is exactly the same as the preimage. A figure is said to have **point symmetry** if it can be rotated about a point onto itself. Of course, all figures have point symmetry if they are rotated one complete turn. The condition that the image matches the preimage in size, shape, and position before one complete turn must hold in order that a shape have point symmetry. It is for this reason that point symmetry is sometimes known as **rotational symmetry**. Notice that after four turns about the center of rotation, the figure returns to its original position. Such a figure is said to have rotational symmetry of order 4. In general, the **order of rotational symmetry** of a figure is the number of turns necessary to bring the figure back to its original position, with the stipulation that each turn results in an image that matches the preimage.

point symmetry

rotational symmetry

**order of rotational
symmetry**

Figure 13.11

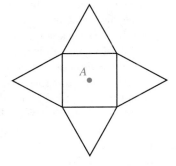

Symmetry can be used to examine figures and combinations of figures that cover a plane. Recall that the term *covering* was used when area was introduced. At that point, we were concerned with completely covering a closed figure with squares. The number of square units that covered a closed figure was said to be the measurement of the area of that shape.

Other basic units could be used to cover closed figures (see Figure 13.12). Notice that in each of these cases, a single figure completely covers a shape without leaving any gaps, and without any overlapping.

Figure 13.12

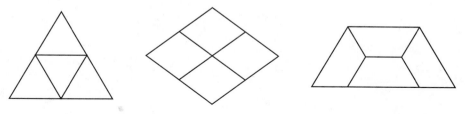

tessellation   We will extend this concept to the complete covering of a plane. A **tessellation** of a plane is the covering of the plane with figures such that no figures overlap and there are no gaps between the figures. What characteristics must a figure have for it to completely tessellate the plane?

Consider the simplest tessellations, those involving regular pentagon. Figure 13.13 depicts three such tessellations.

Figure 13.13

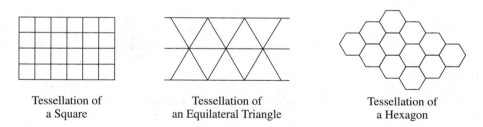

| Tessellation of a Square | Tessellation of an Equilateral Triangle | Tessellation of a Hexagon |

Using the problem-solving strategy of looking for a pattern, try to determine why these three regular polygons completely tessellate the plane, whereas a regular pentagon or octagon does not. Stop reading for a moment and think about this question.

Focus on a single vertex point in each of the three tessellations. Four squares meet at each vertex, six equilateral triangles meet at each vertex, and three hexagons meet at each vertex. Since a full rotation about each vertex point contains 360°, you might expect that the measure of an interior angle of any of these regular polygons is a factor of 360. In fact, this is the case. The interior angles of a square each measure 90° (90 | 360), the interior angles of an equilateral triangle each measure 60° (60 | 360), and the interior angles of a regular hexagon each measure 120° (120 | 360).

Consider the measure of an interior angle of a regular pentagon. Each angle measures 108°. Since 108 does not divide 360, regular pentagons, by themselves, do not tessellate the plane. Such is also the case with octagons. In general, the only regular polygons that tessellate the plane by themselves are those with three sides, four sides, and six sides.

Regular polygons, however, are not the only figures that tessellate the plane. Examine the quadrilateral in Figure 13.14.

Figure 13.14

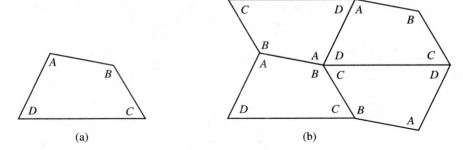

(a)   (b)

Since the sum of the four interior angles of any convex quadrilateral is 360°, four congruent copies of the quadrilateral would tessellate if a different vertex angle of each copy met at a single point. The figure in Figure 13.14b can be constructed using a transformation as follows.

1. Locate the midpoint of each of the sides. Label it *E*, *F*, *G*, and *H*, respectively.

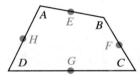

2. Begin with $\overline{AB}$. Use the midpoint of that side, *E*, as the center of rotation. Rotate the quadrilateral 180° in a clockwise direction. The image and the preimage will share a common side, $\overline{AB}$.

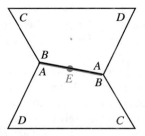

3. Using the midpoint of side $\overline{AD}$, point *H*, as the center of rotation, rotate the quadrilateral 180° in a clockwise direction. The image and the preimage will share the common side $\overline{AD}$.

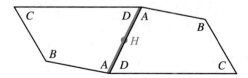

4. Using the midpoint of side $\overline{CD}$, point G, as the center of rotation, rotate the quadrilateral 180° in a clockwise direction. The image and the preimage will share the common side $\overline{CD}$.

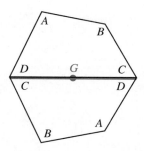

Notice that the figure shown in Figure 13.14b is a tessellation formed by quadrilateral *ABCD*. The center "vertex of the tessellation" is formed by the four vertices of the quadrilateral, $\angle A$, $\angle B$, $\angle C$, and $\angle D$. Since the sum of the measures of these four angles is equal to 360°, shape *ABCD* tessellates. It will be left to you in Problem 28 of this section to show how any triangle can be made to tessellate a plane.

Some irregular shapes can also tessellate the plane. They can be constructed using the transformations we have covered in this section.

Creating a Tessellating Figure by Translation

Begin with square *ABCD* as shown in Figure 13.15a. Alter side $\overline{CD}$ by "bumping" into the interior of the square as shown in Figure 13.15b. The vertex points that define the alteration of side $\overline{CD}$ are labeled *E*, *F*, *G*, *H*, and *I*. Vertically translate the segments joining the points *C*, *E*, *F*, *G*, *H*, *I*, and *D* so that *B* is the image of *C* and *A* is the image of *D*. The translation images of these line segments are shown in Figure 13.15c.

Figure 13.15

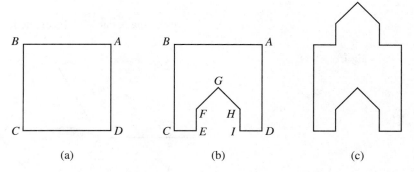

(a)   (b)   (c)

A tessellation can now be created by translating the new figure vertically and horizontally to cover the plane. The tessellation is depicted in Figure 13.16 on page 670.

Figure 13.16

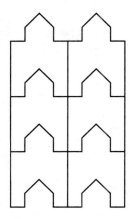

Creating a Tessellating Figure by Rotation

Begin with equilateral triangle ABC as shown in Figure 13.17a. Alter side $\overline{AC}$ in any way. Figure 13.17b depicts a curved alteration of side $\overline{AC}$. Rotate the curve AC 60° in a clockwise direction with C as the center of rotation. This rotation will cause B to become the image of A. The image of the curved side AC will now be found on the side BC, as shown in Figure 13.17c.

Figure 13.17

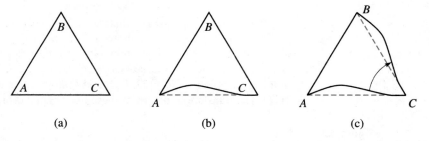

(a) (b) (c)

A tessellation of the plane can now be created, as shown in Figure 13.18.

Figure 13.18

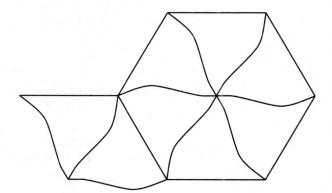

Tessellations have become very popular in the graphic arts media. Many corporate logos are tessellating figures. Perhaps the most famous tessellations are those that were created by Dutch artist M. C. Escher (1898–1972). An Escher tessellation is shown in Figure 13.19.

Figure 13.19

©1938 M. C. Escher/Cordon Art-Baarn-Holland

You and your classmates will be given the opportunity to explore Escher tessellations in the Cooperative Activity at the end of the assessments following this section.

Nonisometric Transformations

The enlarging and reducing capabilities of a photocopying machine were used in Chapter 11 to introduce the characteristics necessary to establish similarity. The enlargement or reduction of a figure can be viewed as a transformation. This type of transformation **dilation** is known as a **dilation**. Examine quadrilateral $ABCD$ in Figure 13.20. $ABCD$ is to be di-
constant of dilation lated so that point X is the center of dilation and the scale factor, or **constant of dilation**, is 3. The process is outlined below and graphically portrayed in Figure 13.21 on page 672.

Figure 13.20

1. Using X as the center of dilation, draw rays extending from X that pass through the vertices $ABCD$.

2. Since the scale factor is 3, the images A', B', C', and D' will be located along their respective rays such that $XA' = 3 \cdot XA$, $XB' = 3 \cdot XB$, $XC' = 3 \cdot XC$, and $XD' = 3 \cdot XD$.

3. Connect the images A', B', C', and D' forming the quadrilateral $A'B'C'D'$, which is the dilation image of $ABCD$.

Figure 13.21

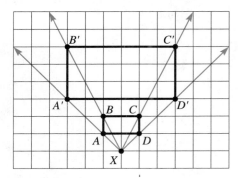

Formula: In general, a dilation with constant of dilation c (where c is a positive number) is a transformation such that the image of the center of dilation, X, is X itself; and for any point A in the preimage with A' as its dilation image, $\overrightarrow{XA}$ and $\overrightarrow{XA'}$ name the same ray with $XA' = c \cdot XA$.

As you can see, a dilation is not an isometry. All isometries preserve length. This is not the case in a dilation. Notice that the lengths of the sides of quadrilateral $ABCD$ in Figure 13.20 are not equal to the lengths of their corresponding sides in the dilation image.

Investigation 7 examines a dilation on the coordinate axes. For the purpose of this text, all such dilations will have the point $(0, 0)$ as the center of dilation.

Investigation 7

Given quadrilateral $ABCD$, draw quadrilateral $A'B'C'D'$, which is the image of $ABCD$ under a dilation with a constant of dilation 2. On the same set of axes, draw quadrilateral $A''B''C''D''$, which is the image of $ABCD$ under a dilation with a constant of dilation $\frac{1}{2}$.

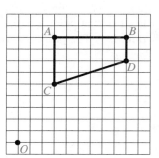

Draw and extend rays $\overrightarrow{OA}$, $\overrightarrow{OB}$, $\overrightarrow{OC}$, and $\overrightarrow{OD}$. Mark off point A' on $\overrightarrow{OA}$ such that $OA' = 2 \cdot OA$, B' on $\overrightarrow{OB}$ such that $OB' = 2 \cdot OB$, C' on $\overrightarrow{OC}$ such that $OC' = 2 \cdot OC$, and

D' on $\overrightarrow{OD}$ such that $OD' = 2 \cdot OD$. Connect points A', B', C', and D' to form the dilation image of $ABCD$ with a constant of dilation 2.

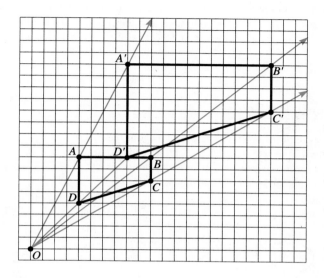

Locate A'' on ray $\overrightarrow{OA}$ such that $OA'' = \frac{1}{2} \cdot OA$, B'' on ray $\overrightarrow{OB}$ such that $OB'' = \frac{1}{2} \cdot OB$, C'' on ray $\overrightarrow{OC}$ such that $OC'' = \frac{1}{2} \cdot OC$, and D'' on ray $\overrightarrow{OD}$ such that $OD'' = \frac{1}{2} \cdot OD$. The resulting figure $A''B''C''D''$ is the dilation image of $ABCD$ under a dilation with a constant of dilation $\frac{1}{2}$, as pictured below.

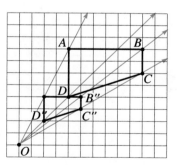

A dilation can be represented as a linear relation in terms of x and y as follows. Let c be the constant of dilation. Then the dilation relation on the coordinate axis can be represented as

$$(x, y) \rightarrow (c \cdot x, c \cdot y)$$

Any transformation that is an isometry produces an image that is congruent to the preimage. Such transformations are translations, reflections, rotations, and glide reflections. These transformations are commonly known as **congruence transformations**.

congruence transformations

Since a dilation is not an isometry, a congruent image is not produced. In a dilation, the preimage and the image form similar figures with a ratio of similitude equal to the constant of dilation.

Assessments for Section 13.1

1. On the laminated card or grid paper, copy each of the following figures. Translate each figure in the direction of $\overrightarrow{AB}$ so that the distance between every point in the preimage and the corresponding image point is equal to the length of AB.

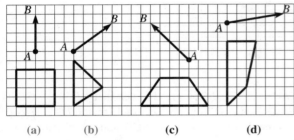

    (a)   (b)   (c)   (d)

2. Copy each figure on a sheet of paper. Rotate the figure about O in a clockwise direction the given number of degrees to produce the rotation image.

  (a) 45°   (b) 90°   (c) 100°

  (d) 180°   (e) 270°

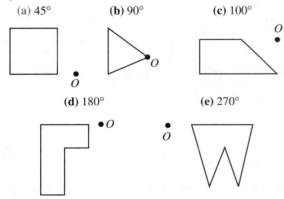

3. Copy each figure on the laminated card or grid paper. Reflect the figure about the indicated line of reflection to produce the image.

4. Draw a larger size version of each figure on a blank sheet of paper. Using only a compass and a straightedge, construct the reflection image about the indicated line of reflection.

    (a)   (b)   (c)

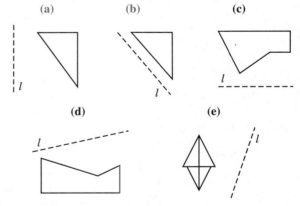

    (d)   (e)

5. On the laminated card, graph trapezoid *WXYZ* whose coordinates are *W*(2, 2), *X*(3, 5), *Y*(7, 5), and *Z*(8, 2). Graph the composition image *W″X″Y″Z″* of *WXYZ* under the indicated translation and then line of reflection.

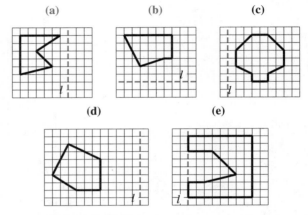

  (a)   (b)   (c)

  (d)   (e)

(a) Translation: $(x, y) \rightarrow (x - 5, y + 3)$
Line of reflection: $y = 3$

(b) Translation: $(x, y) \rightarrow (x, y - 7)$
Line of reflection: y-axis

(c) Translation: $(x, y) \rightarrow (x - 8, y - 7)$
Line of reflection: $y = -5$

(d) Translation: $(x, y) \rightarrow (x + 1, y + 1)$
Line of reflection: x-axis

6. Identify the figure formed by the union of the preimage and the reflection image in each of the following situations. Justify your reasoning.

(a) Equilateral triangle ABC reflected over one of its sides

(b) Square $ABCD$ reflected over one of its sides

(c) Parallelogram $ABCD$ reflected over the longer side

(d) Scalene triangle ABC reflected over its longest side

(e) Regular pentagon $ABCDE$ reflected about one of its sides

7. You are given right trapezoid $ABCD$. Identify the figure formed by the union of the preimage and the reflection image given each of the following lines of reflection. Justify your reasoning.

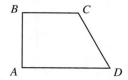

(a) $\overline{AB}$

(b) $\overline{BC}$

(c) $\overline{CD}$

(d) $\overline{DA}$

8. Begin with figure A in the following illustration. Explain the transformations that were used to change figure A to figure B, figure B to figure C, and so on to figure F.

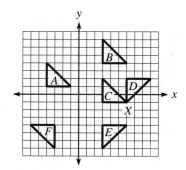

9. Begin with figure A in the illustration below. Explain the transformations that were used to change figure A to figure B, and so on to figure D.

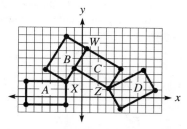

10. (a) Draw the line $y = x$ on a set of axes. Rotate the line $90°$ in a clockwise direction about $(0, 0)$. What is the equation of this rotation image?

(b) Draw the line $y = 2x + 1$ on a set of axes. Rotate the line $90°$ in a counterclockwise direction about $(0, 1)$. What is the equation of this rotation image?

(c) Draw the line $y = -x - 5$. Explain a rotation $(0, -5)$ that would produce an image with a positive x-intercept.

11. The line segment $\overline{AB}$ has $A(0, 3)$ and $B(4, 0)$ as endpoints. The segment is rotated about point B in a clockwise direction so that the image $A'B'$ is a vertical line. What are the coordinates of the image point A'?

12. Do each of the following figures have reflectional symmetry, rotational symmetry, neither, or both?

(a)

(b)

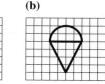

(c)

(d)

(e)

(f)

13. The coordinates of trapezoid $ABCD$ are $A(-6, 2)$, $B(-6, 4)$, $C(-2, 8)$, and $D(-2, 2)$. Determine the coordinates of the image of $ABCD$ in each of the following transformations.

(a) Reflect $ABCD$ about side $\overline{CD}$.

(b) Translate $ABCD$ so that the image of A is point D.

(c) Reflect $ABCD$ about the y-axis.

(d) Rotate $ABCD$ $90°$ in a clockwise direction about point D.

(e) $(x, y) \to (x - 1, y - 8)$, then reflect about the x-axis.

(f) $(x, y) \to (x - 1, y - 8)$, then reflect about the y-axis.

14. Examine the following equilateral triangle whose altitudes intersect at center O. Complete the following chart to identify the image points under each of the following rotations with O as the center of rotation.

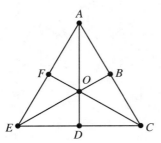

Rotation		A	B	C	D	E	F
(a)	120° counterclockwise						
(b)	120° clockwise						
(c)	240° counterclockwise						
(d)	360° counterclockwise						
(e)	240° clockwise						

15. Use the equilateral triangle pictured in Problem 14 for this problem. Complete the following chart to identify the image point under each of the following reflections.

Line of Reflection		A	B	C	D	E	F
(a)	$\overline{AD}$						
(b)	$\overline{EB}$						
(c)	$\overline{FC}$						

16. What constant of dilation would be used to enlarge this quilt pattern to cover an area that is four times as great? Sketch the dilation image to justify your answer.

17. Design a simple wallpaper pattern that is formed by

(a) Translation **(b)** Reflection

(c) Rotation **(d)** Glide reflection

18. Determine the constant of dilation in each of the following figures.

(a)

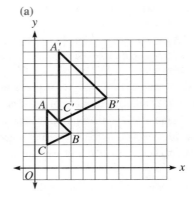

(b)

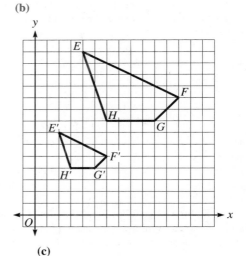

(c)

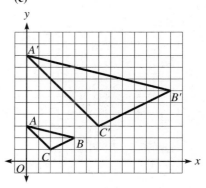

(d)

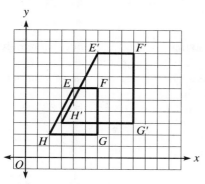

19. On the laminated card or grid paper, construct the dilation image for each of the following shapes with the given constant of dilation and a center of dilation at the origin.
    (a) Octagon *ABCDEFGH*: constant of dilation = 2
    (b) Triangle *ABC*: constant of dilation = $\frac{1}{2}$
    (c) Square *ABCD*: constant of dilation = 1.5

20. Suppose a point (x, y) that is below $y = b$ is to be reflected about the line $y = b$. If (x', y') is the reflection image, write an expression for the coordinates of the reflection image in terms of x, y, and/or b.

21. A half turn is a 180° turn in a clockwise or counterclockwise direction about a given point. You are given $\triangle ABC$ with coordinates $A(-4, 1)$, $B(-6, 5)$, and $C(-1, 3)$. Apply a half turn about the origin.
    (a) What are the coordinates of the half-turn image of $\triangle ABC$?
    (b) What are the slopes of the segments that form the sides of $\triangle ABC$?
    (c) What are the slopes of the segments that form the sides of $\triangle A'B'C'$?
    (d) What relationship, if any, exists between the slope of the segment that forms a side of $\triangle ABC$ and the slope of its corresponding image?

22. You are given $\triangle RST$ with coordinates $R(1, 3)$, $S(4, 4)$, and $T(3, 1)$.
    (a) Determine the coordinates of the dilation image with a constant of dilation of 2 and a center of dilation at the origin.
    (b) Find the slopes of the segments that form $\triangle RST$.

(c) Find the slopes of the segments that form $\triangle R'S'T'$.
(d) What conclusion might you draw concerning the relationship between the slope of a segment and the slope of its corresponding dilation image?

23. Suppose that point F has coordinates $(4, 2)$. The coordinate of its dilation image F' under a dilation whose center is at the origin is $(10, 5)$. What is the constant of dilation?

24. Construct a regular hexagon. Alter any three adjacent sides. Translate each alteration to the opposite side. Cut out a template and use this template to verify that the hexagon tessellates the plane.

25. From among the following figures—a rhombus, a hexagon, an octagon, an equilateral triangle, and a square—all of whose sides measure 1 inch, identify pairs of figures that together will tessellate the plane. Cut out templates and use these templates to verify your tessellations.

In Other Words

26. Define a translation, a rotation, a reflection, and a glide reflection.

27. What is an isometry?

28. Explain how any triangle can be made to tessellate the plane.

29. What purpose does the center of dilation serve in constructing a dilation image?

30. Explain the relationship between transformations and symmetry.

Cooperative Activity

31. **Groups of three**

Individual Accountability: One group member is responsible for reading and summarizing two journal articles about tessellations from *The Arithmetic Teacher*. The second group member is responsible for obtaining pictures or photographs of actual tessellations, such as quilts, tile floors, stained glass, and so on. The third group member is to develop a description and obtain several examples of tessellations by the artist M. C. Escher.

Group Goal: Working together, the group is to discuss commonalities among the various examples of tessellations in order to (a) create an original quilt design, and (b) create a model of an Escher-type tessellation.

13.2 Changing Your Point of View: Projective Geometry, Topology, and Networks

One of the more challenging problem-solving strategies is the one that requires **changing your point of view**. Many students find this strategy difficult, since there is no consistency from problem to problem concerning what you will change your point of view from or to. Just as with any problem-solving strategy, however, practice will help improve your understanding and performance. Examine Investigation 8.

Investigation 8

You are given six toothpicks of equal length. How can they be arranged to form only four congruent triangles? At this point, obtain six toothpicks (or six pencils of equal length) and attempt to solve this problem.

Understand the Problem: Arrange six congruent toothpicks to form four congruent triangles.

Devise a Plan: Various solutions are possible. Commonly, people begin by forming a square with four of the toothpicks and crossing the others in the form of two diagonals as shown below.

A weakness in this solution is that the toothpicks are not long enough to form diagonals. This can easily be verified since the hypotenuse of a right triangle must be longer than either of the two legs.

Another possible solution is to construct two parallel toothpicks and four transversal toothpicks:

A weakness in this solution is that without using a ruler, it is very difficult to lay out the toothpicks to ensure that the four triangles are congruent. This solution also results in the formation of an additional shape other than a triangle.

Another possible solution is shown here:

This solution shares some of the same weaknesses as the preceding solution. In addition, it contradicts the given information stating that *only* four congruent triangles are to be formed.

What do all of the above attempts have in common? Each attempt has assumed that the solution lies on a plane. However, the problem statement does not limit the solution to two dimensions. If you change your point of view and pursue a solution in three dimensions, it should occur to you that a regular tetrahedron consists of four congruent triangular faces, and can be constructed using toothpicks.

Carry Out the Plan: This is what the "solution" to the problem will look like:

Look Back: How can you verify that the triangles formed are congruent?

The problem in Investigation 8 is a simplified example of the dilemmas that face many mathematicians. Frequently, the solutions to these dilemmas are found by changing the assumptions that dictate a particular solution. This process is illustrated in the evolution of geometries other than Euclidean geometry, specifically, projective geometry and topology. In both of these cases, changing point of view resulted in an entirely new branch of mathematics.

Projective Geometry as It Relates to Perspective Drawing

A major revolution in the history of painting occurred as the Middle Ages gave way to the Renaissance. During the Middle Ages, artists paid little attention to the portrayal of reality as it was actually seen. Rather, symbolism dictated the composition of a painting. The most important figure in the painting was typically the largest figure, which served as the center of attention. The artist portrayed the scene as if it existed in two dimensions. Few attempts were made to develop a sense of depth (see Figure 13.22).

Figure 13.22

In the fifteenth and sixteenth centuries, a new view of painting began to take shape. Artists such as Leone Alberti (1404–1472), Leonardo da Vinci (1452–1519), and Albrecht Dürer (1427–1528), tackled the problem of representing the reality of a three-dimensional world on a two-dimensional canvas. Out of the labors of these artists/ mathematicians grew a branch of mathematics known as **projective geometry**. In this section, projective geometry as it relates to perspective drawing will be discussed. We will focus on the concepts of projection and section.

projective geometry

Renaissance artists viewed a canvas as if it were a glass screen. From the artist's eye, imaginary "viewing lines" passed through the glass screen and onto the scene that was to be painted. These lines are called **projection lines**. The points at which the projection lines pass through the screen form what is known as a **section**. When the points of a section are joined to portray a figure or scene, the section appears to be three-dimensional.

projection lines
section

In some cases, the concepts of section and projection were taken literally, as shown in two woodcuts, one by Albrecht Dürer, *Demonstration of Perspective* (Figure 13.23a), and one by Erhard Schön, *Underweissung der proportzion* (Figure 13.23b).

Figure 13.23

(a)   (b)

A classic illustration of perspective is found in a picture of railroad tracks as they appear to converge to a single point somewhere in the distance (see Figure 13.24).

Figure 13.24

The tracks are portrayed from the viewpoint of someone who is standing in the middle of the tracks. To this viewer's eye, the parallel rails meet at one point. The artist calls this point the principal vanishing point. In fact, the rails are perpendicular to the plane of the viewer. In a perspective drawing, any such perpendicular lines must meet at a single vanishing point, located on the horizon line. Notice how in a perspective drawing, the rules of Euclidean geometry can be violated. Parallel lines can appear to meet! But in actuality the wooden horizontal cross pieces that are parallel to one another remain parallel to the plane of the viewer.

In general, lines that are perpendicular to the plane of the viewer converge on the canvas at a single vanishing point that is located on the horizon line. Lines that are parallel to the plane of the viewer will remain as such on the canvas. We will use these facts to create a perspective drawing in Investigation 9.

Suppose you are standing in front of a long corridor. Your eye-level height is 5 feet. The entrance way is 4 feet wide by 8 feet high. Using the scale in which $\frac{1}{4}$ inch represents 1 foot, sketch a perspective drawing of the hallway.

First, draw the opening of the corridor to scale. This will measure 1 inch by 2 inches. Next, draw the horizon line. In this drawing, the horizon line should correspond to your eye-level height. Since your eye-level height is 5 feet, the horizon line should be located at a point that is $1\frac{1}{4}$ inches "above" the floor of the corridor. Locate a point V at the center of the horizon line, which will represent the principal vanishing point in the drawing.

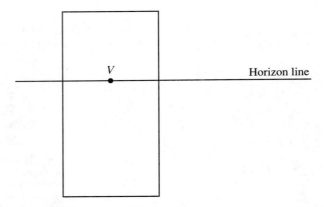

Since the edges formed by the walls and the ceiling, and the floor and the ceiling, are perpendicular to the plane of the viewer, they must meet at the vanishing point as shown here.

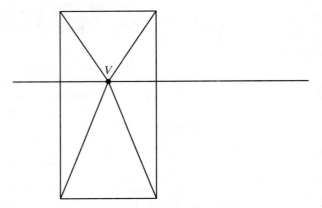

The sketch of a corridor in Investigation 9 would appear more realistic if some details, such as a tiled floor, were included. Suppose the floor at the entrance to the corridor was composed of two tiles, each 2 feet square, as shown in Figure 13.25.

Figure 13.25

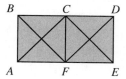

The appearance of the tiles in the perspective drawing will be dictated by the distance of the viewer from the principal vanishing point V. Let's assume that the distance from your eye to the vanishing point is 3 inches. (This close distance is dictated by the constraints of the size of this textbook page.)

A rule of perspective drawing is that parallel lines that are neither perpendicular nor parallel to the plane of the viewer must meet at some secondary vanishing points. These vanishing points lie on the horizon line and are located at a distance to the left and right of the principal vanishing point, which equals the distance from the viewer's eye to that principal vanishing point. Notice that in Figure 13.26, secondary vanishing points S_1 and S_2 have been located 3 inches from V.

Figure 13.26

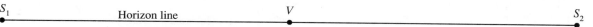

Return to the two squares of tile in Figure 13.25. The vertices have been labeled A through F for ease of reference. In actuality, the diagonals that are drawn intersect opposite corners. These diagonals will help us locate the opposite corners of the tiles in the perspective drawing. These diagonals are neither parallel to the plane of the viewer nor perpendicular to the plane of the viewer. They must therefore meet at the secondary vanishing points, as shown in Figure 13.27. It is now an easy task to locate the perspective drawing locations of the vertices of the square tiles.

Figure 13.27

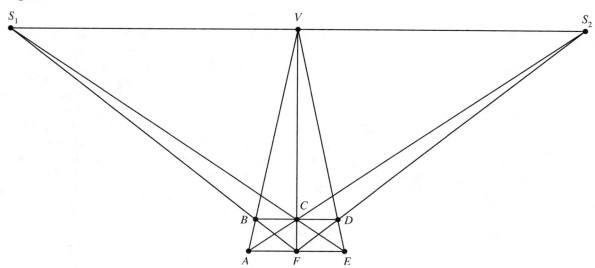

Investigation 10

A Red Cross symbol has the following dimensions:

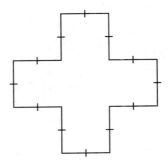

Sketch a perspective drawing of the "red cross."

 To better understand the location of the vertices of the figure in question, draw auxiliary lines as shown here. Intersection points are labeled for ease of reference.

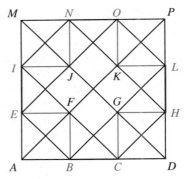

Now, we will begin to construct the perspective drawing. First, draw a horizon line across the top of the page. Locate the vanishing point at the center of the horizon line. We will use 3 inches to the left and right of the vanishing point as the two secondary vanishing points (S_1 and S_2). The line containing $\overline{BC}$ must be parallel to the horizon line. Since no eye-level height is stated, we will use 3 inches here as the distance from $\overline{BC}$ to the horizon line.

We will now draw square *AMPD*. This square will be used to locate the vertices of the figure in question. Position segment $\overline{AD}$ so that points *A* and *D* are equidistant from the vanishing point, and the measure of $\overline{AD}$ is $1\frac{1}{2}$ inches. The sides of the square, like the railroad tracks, must lie on segments that converge at the vanishing point. Draw segments $\overline{AV}$ and $\overline{DV}$.

In the original figure, $\overline{AP}$ and $\overline{DM}$ are diagonals of the square. These diagonals must be drawn to the secondary vanishing points. Segment $\overline{S_1D}$ intersects $\overline{AV}$ at M (the point that corresponds to the upper left corner of the square). Segment $\overline{S_2A}$ intersects $\overline{DV}$ at P (the point that corresponds to the upper right corner of the square). Connect A, D, P, M, and A in that order. This is the perspective drawing of the square that will enclose the "red cross." Locate points B and C on $\overline{AD}$. Draw segments $\overline{VB}$ and $\overline{VC}$.

The segment $\overline{VB}$ intersects $\overline{MP}$ at N. Notice in the original illustration that $\overline{BN}$ intersects $\overline{AP}$ at F, and $\overline{BN}$ intersects $\overline{DM}$ at J. Locate both F and J in the perspective drawing.

The segment $\overline{VC}$ intersects $\overline{MP}$ at O. Notice in the original illustration that $\overline{CO}$ intersects $\overline{DM}$ at G, and $\overline{CO}$ intersects $\overline{AP}$ at K. Locate both G and K in the perspective drawing.

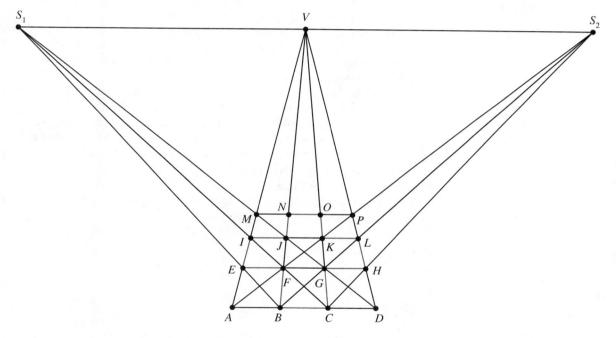

In the original illustration, segment, $\overline{BE}$ is the diagonal of square $AEFB$. In the perspective drawing, the line segment that contains segment $\overline{BE}$ must have the secondary vanishing point as one of its endpoints. The segment, $\overline{S_1B}$ intersects $\overline{AV}$ at point E. The segment $\overline{S_2C}$ intersects $\overline{DV}$ at H.

In the original illustration, segment $\overline{CI}$ is the diagonal of square $AIKC$. In the perspective drawing, the line segment that contains $\overline{CI}$ must have the secondary vanishing point as one of its endpoints. The segment $\overline{S_1B}$ intersects $\overline{AV}$ at point I. The segment $\overline{S_2B}$ intersects $\overline{DV}$ at L.

All of the vertices of the cross have now been located in the perspective drawing.

The field of projective geometry involves much more than simply creating perspective drawings. Like many other branches of mathematics, projective geometry was developed in order to make sense of the world. The Renaissance painters were faced with a problem—how to represent a three-dimensional world on a two-dimensional plane. Projective geometry grew out of their attempts to solve this problem.

In the assessments that follow this section, you will be asked to explore some interesting discoveries in projective geometry made by mathematicians Desargues (see Problems 6 and 7), Pascal (see Problem 8), and Brianchon (see Problem 9). Problem 10 will ask you to relate these theorems to the work we have done with perspective drawing.

Topology

topology We now turn to a branch of mathematics called topology. **Topology** is concerned with the structure of objects and figures. Geometric concepts we have previously addressed, such as the number of interior angles, the lengths of sides, the surface area, the volume, and the like, are not significant in topology. These characteristics of figures and objects focus on consistent and unchanging quantities. For this reason, Euclidean geometry is sometimes referred to as a "rigid" geometry.

In topology, however, we study the quality, or the makeup, of objects and shapes. For example, a doughnut is considered to be topologically equivalent to a drinking straw. This is because the doughnut can be transformed into the drinking straw without altering the basic structure of the doughnut. Imagine a doughnut made out of modeling clay. It could be rolled into the form of a drinking straw without "tearing" the center hole or creating a second hole. This characteristic allows these two objects to be considered equivalent. The frame of a pair of eyeglasses would be topologically different from the doughnut, since it contains two holes. A soup tureen with two handles would be topologically equivalent to the eyeglass frame.

Figure 13.28 contains three groups of objects that are considered topologically equivalent to each other.

Figure 13.28

In each case, the objects grouped together are considered topologically equivalent, since every item within a group can be transformed into every other item without adding or removing a hole.

Investigation 11 examines topological grouping from another point of view.

You are given the following 10 objects.

Examine each object. Determine the maximum number of cuts that can be made through the object starting at the exterior edge, so that the object still remains in one piece. Draw some conclusions based on your findings.

Understand the Problem: You are given 10 different objects. You are asked to examine the objects by focusing on ways of cutting the object without creating two or more pieces, as shown on page 688.

Devise a Plan: Use the problem-solving strategy of drawing a picture to solve this problem.

Carry Out the Plan: *Bowling Ball:* No cuts are possible that result in the object remaining in one piece. Any cut through the bowling ball will result in two distinct pieces.

Sock: No cuts are possible that result in the object remaining in one piece. Any cut through the sock will result in two distinct pieces, as shown on page 688.

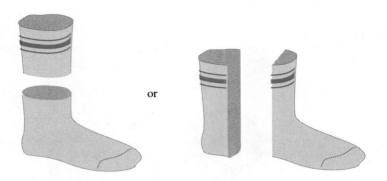

Looseleaf paper: Three cuts are possible, as shown here.

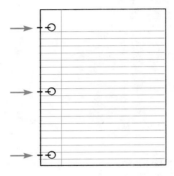

Compact disc: Only one cut is possible.

Scissors: Two cuts are possible.

Jacket: Two cuts are possible.

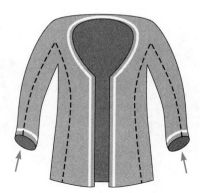

Light-switch plate: Three cuts are possible.

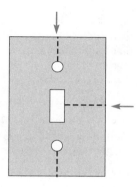

Pretzel: Three cuts are possible.

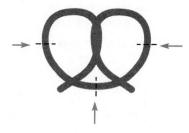

Mask: Two cuts are possible.

Ring: One cut is possible.

Look Back: These objects can be grouped according to the maximum number of cuts possible as follows:

> Zero cuts: bowling ball, sock
>
> One cut: compact disc, ring
>
> Two cuts: scissors, jacket, mask
>
> Three cuts: looseleaf paper, light-switch plate, pretzel

Notice that the number of cuts corresponds to the number of holes in the object. Since the number of holes in the object formed the basis of a topological grouping, it appears that topological equivalences can also be determined by the maximum number of cuts possible in an object that still allows the object to remain in one piece.

An interesting figure often studied in topology is called the Möbius strip. This surface was studied by and named after German mathematician and astronomer, August Möbius (1790–1868). To better understand the properties of a Möbius strip (see Figure 13.29), construct one as follows.

1. Cut out a rectangular strip of paper approximately 4 centimeters wide by 30 centimeters long. The actual dimensions of the strip may vary. These measurements are used for convenience.

2. Lay the strip flat on a tabletop. Lift one end of the strip. Twist it one half-turn in either a clockwise or a counterclockwise direction.

3. Tape the two ends together.

Figure 13.29

Once constructed, we can do a variety of explorations with the strip. Draw a large dot at any point on the strip. Starting at this point, begin tracing a line along the center of the strip. Eventually you will return to the point at which you began. Carefully examine the path you have traced. You will notice that the path traverses both "sides" of the strip. Therefore, a Möbius strip is said to have only one side.

Another interesting activity involves cutting a Möbius strip. Cut the strip along the path you have just traced. You must begin your cut on the line rather than at an edge. What will result? Predict the outcome before actually cutting the strip.

Repeat this procedure once again using the paper that resulted from the first cut. Predict the outcome before actually cutting the strip.

Networks

network   Another topological concept is that of a network. A **network** is a map, or diagram, that illustrates paths between a variety of points. The points on a network are called vertices. As with the origin of projective geometry, the study of networks grew out of a need to solve a real-world problem. Today, this problem is known as the Koenigsberg Bridge problem, and it represents how mathematics can be used to model an everyday situation.

There was a city in East Prussia called Koenigsberg. A modified map of the city is shown in Figure 13.30.

Figure 13.30

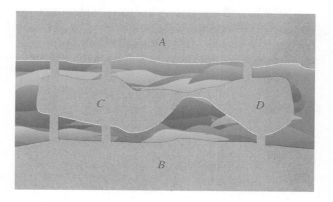

The city was divided into four regions by a river. The parts of the city labeled A and B in Figure 13.30 were on opposite banks of the river. Regions C and D were two islands. Seven bridges connected the four regions of Koenigsberg. It has been said that the citizens of that city used to enjoy taking long walks. A perplexing question arose. Was it possible to begin the walk at any location in the city, following a path that would take you to each of the four regions, while crossing each bridge once and only once?

This problem was solved by the Swiss mathematician and physicist Leonhard Euler (1707–1783), who used a network to model the situation. The network Euler used looked like Figure 13.31.

Figure 13.31

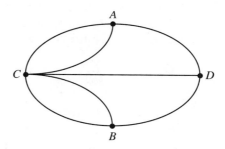

Each of the four regions was represented as a vertex on the network. Each path between any two regions represented a route a stroller might take to cross a single bridge. If a single route could be found in the network that covered each path once and only once, the network would be considered traversable.

Examine each of the vertices. Five paths meet at vertex C; three paths meet at vertex B; three paths meet at vertex A; and finally, three paths meet at vertex D. Euler studied the network carefully. He recognized that since five paths met at vertex A, a stroller could begin at A, leave, return, leave, return, and leave again without ever retracing any paths connected to A. In similar fashion, he noticed that A could also be a terminal point on the walk. The stroller could begin the walk at some other location, arrive at A, leave, arrive, leave, and finally arrive back at A again without ever retracing any path connected to A. Since three paths meet at each of the points B, C, and D, these points could also serve as starting or ending points.

Euler noticed that each of these vertices connected an odd number of paths. It is for this reason that he called them odd vertices. In addition, he found that a traversable network can contain exactly two odd vertices, or no odd vertices. Since the bridges of Koenigsberg were modeled by a network that contained four odd vertices, it was not traversable. Therefore, it was not possible for the citizens of Koenigsberg to complete a stroll that crossed each of the bridges once and only once without retracing any paths.

traversable   Networks are **traversable** if they contain only even vertices, or exactly two odd vertices (begin at one and end at the other). (See Figure 13.32.)

Figure 13.32

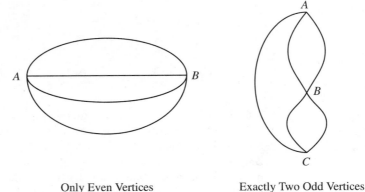

Only Even Vertices

Exactly Two Odd Vertices
A and C

Investigation 12

Children are often intrigued by the challenge of completely tracing the accompanying design without lifting their pencil or tracing over another line.

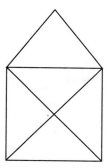

Examine the design from a topological viewpoint. Can the lines be traced in the manner described above?

This problem is analogous to determining whether the related network shown below is traversable.

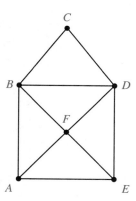

Determine if each of the vertices is odd or even.

Vertex	Number of Paths	Odd/Even
A	3	Odd
B	4	Even
C	2	Even
D	4	Even
E	3	Odd
F	4	Even

Using Euler's logic, a network containing exactly two odd vertices is traversable. This holds true for the network illustrated above. Therefore, it is possible to trace the design without retracing any lines in it. Either of the two odd vertices can be the starting points of the trace, as shown in the following diagrams.

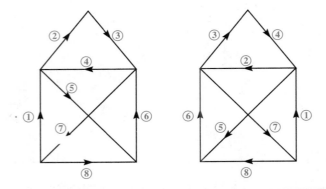

Investigation 13

A traveling salesperson must completely cover the territory along the New York State roads pictured in the map below.

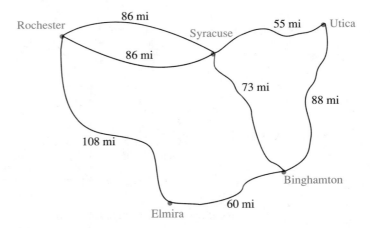

Since the total distance along these roads is approximately 556 miles, she will be reimbursed only for that mileage. She must rent a car in order to complete this trip. The drop-off charges for each of these cities are listed in the table below. In what city should the car be rented, and in what city should the car be returned in order to make the trip as economical as possible without retracing any routes?

		Pick-Up City			
		Rochester	**Syracuse**	**Utica**	**Elmira**	**Binghamton**
Drop-Off City	**Rochester**	$ 0	$60	$75	$40	$50
	Syracuse	70	0	40	65	50
	Utica	80	40	0	75	40
	Elmira	45	60	75	0	50
	Binghamton	65	50	45	50	0

Understand the Problem: What is known? The information you have consists of the cities that must be visited, their distances from each other, and the rate schedule for the rental car.

What is unknown? You must determine the most efficient order in which the cities should be visited.

Devise a Plan: This problem can be modeled using a network.

Carry Out the Plan:

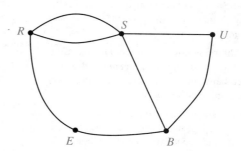

Since the problem stipulates that no routes be retraced, it is necessary to test the traversability of this network. To that end, determine the number of odd vertices. Notice that there are exactly two odd vertices, represented by the letters R and B. Therefore, the network is traversable, and the salesperson can travel without retracing any of the routes.

Since the odd vertices in the network provide the starting and ending points, your attention should be turned to the cities of Rochester and Binghamton. There are three routes leading from each of these cities. If you begin in one of these two cities, you cannot end in that city (leave, arrive, leave). According to network theory, if one odd vertex is the starting point, the other odd vertex is the terminal point. Examine the drop-off charge chart to determine if it is more economical to pick up the car in Binghamton and drop it off in Rochester, or vice versa. Clearly, the first choice is the solution. The salesperson should pick up the car in Binghamton and return it to Rochester. This will allow her to travel each of the roads only once and still make all of her stops.

Look Back: Trace some possible routes.

_____

This chapter has attempted to broaden your geometric point of view. In each of the three geometries presented, shapes or solids underwent some form of transformation. In transformational geometry, rotation, reflection, glide reflection, translation, and dilation transformations changed shapes in a plane. In projective geometry, the image of a projective transformation allowed the viewer to "see" a shape on a two-dimensional plane as if it were three-dimensional. In topology, topological transformations resulted in doughnuts becoming coffee cups and vice versa without changing the structure of the object itself.

There are other geometries with different points of view, and we venture to suppose there are geometries that have yet to be discovered. As a teacher of mathematics, it is important for you to realize that geometry, whatever form it takes, is an excellent tool for exploring and explaining real-world situations.

Assessments for Section 13.2

1. Draw a 4-cm by 4-cm square. Construct a perspective drawing of this square using any convenient measurement for the distance between the primary vanishing point and the secondary vanishing points.

2. Draw an isosceles right triangle with a horizontal base. Construct a perspective drawing using any convenient measurement for the distance between the primary vanishing point and the secondary vanishing points.

3. Draw a 3-cm by 3-cm square. Construct two perspective drawings. In the first drawing, use 3 cm as the distance between the primary and the secondary vanishing points. In the second drawing, use the longest length that the paper will allow as the distance between the primary and secondary vanishing points. Discuss the effect that the change in distance has on the perspective drawing.

4. Construct a perspective drawing for each of the following figures. The measurements given are in centimeters. Use any convenient length for the distance between the primary vanishing point and the secondary vanishing points.

(a)   (b)

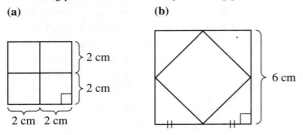

2 cm
2 cm
6 cm
2 cm   2 cm

(c)

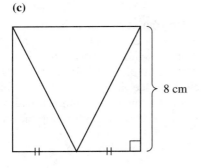

8 cm

5. Inscribe a circle within a 3 cm by 3 cm square. Construct a perspective drawing of the square. Sketch the circle in perspective within the square. Lay a sheet of paper over the perspective sketch of the circle. Trace this figure. Examine the trace. What shape does this figure appear to be?

6. Trace the following two triangles on a large sheet of paper. Beginning at vertex A, draw a line that extends through vertex D. Beginning at vertex B, draw a line that extends through vertex E. Beginning at vertex C, draw a line that extends through vertex F. Notice that the line segments that join corresponding vertices meet at a single point. Extend line segments $\overline{AC}$ and $\overline{DF}$ so that they meet at some point X. Extend line segments $\overline{AB}$ and $\overline{DE}$ so that they meet at some point Y. Extend line segments $\overline{BC}$ and $\overline{EF}$ so that they meet at some point Z. Examine the points X, Y, and Z. What conclusion might you draw? (This was a very important discovery in projective geometry made by French mathematician Gérard Desargues (1591–1661).

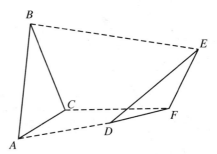

7. After completing Problem 6, draw two triangles such that the line segments joining their corresponding vertices meet at a single point. Test your hypothesis on this pair of triangles.

8. French mathematician and philosopher, Blaise Pascal (1623–1662) made a very important mathematical discovery as a teenager. He was able to offer an elegant proof of it, even at such a young age. Follow the steps outlined here. Draw a conclusion.

   1. Draw a circle of any radius.

2. Randomly mark any six points that lie on the circle at irregular intervals. Label them *A* through *F*, respectively. Connect the points in order.

3. Identify pairs of "opposite" sides. ($\overline{AB}$ will be "opposite" $\overline{DE}$, $\overline{BC}$ will be "opposite" $\overline{EF}$, and $\overline{CD}$ will be "opposite" $\overline{FA}$.)

4. Extend the opposite sides so that they meet at a point outside the circle. Label these points *X*, *Y*, and *Z*, respectively.

5. Connect points *X*, *Y*, and *Z*. Draw a conclusion about *X*, *Y*, and *Z*.

9. The French mathematician Charles Julien Brianchon (1785–1864) is known for his efforts in projective geometry. He discovered and proved a very famous theorem. Follow the steps outlined here.

1. Draw a circle of any radius.

2. Randomly select any six points that lie on the circle at irregular intervals. Label them *A* through *F*, respectively.

3. Draw and extend a line segment that passes through point *A* and is tangent to the circle at point *A*. Repeat this procedure for points *B* through *F*.

4. The tangents drawn should form six intersection points that serve as the vertices of a hexagon. Notice that the hexagon circumscribes the circle. Label the vertices *G* through *L* in order.

5. Connect opposite vertices (*G* to *J*, *H* to *K*, and *I* to *L*).

6. Draw a conclusion about the results.

Repeat the procedure on a different size circle with points at other locations on the circle to test your hypothesis.

10. Problems 6 through 9 illustrated some very important projective geometry concepts. What do these theorems and the work we have done with perspective drawing have in common?

11. Are the following statements true or false? Explain your answers.

(a) A pencil is topologically equivalent to a dinner plate.

(b) A hexagonal machine nut is topologically equivalent to a hexagonal machine bolt.

(c) A picture frame is topologically equivalent to a hula hoop.

(d) If rolled into a cylinder, a piece of modeling clay would have the same topological structure as a cardboard paper-towel tube.

(e) An uncapped tube of toothpaste is topologically equivalent to an opened jar of spaghetti sauce.

12. Suppose that the digits 0 through 9 have been molded out of modeling clay. Group the digits together according to their equivalent topological structures. Explain your reasoning.

13. Suppose the capital letters of the alphabet have been cut out of wood. Group the letters according to their equivalent topological structures. Explain your reasoning.

14. Construct a network that is *not* traversable. Explain your reasoning.

15. Construct a network that *is* traversable. Explain your reasoning.

16. Classify each of the following networks as traversable or not traversable. Explain your reasoning.

(a)   (b)   (c)

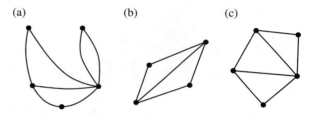

(d)   (e)

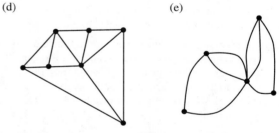

17. You are given a regular hexagon with all diagonals drawn. Vertices and points of intersection are labeled. Could this figure represent a traversable network? Explain your answer.

18. Suppose networks are drawn that take the following shapes. Any intersection points of sides or diagonals form the vertices of the network. Classify those networks as traversable or not traversable. Explain your reasoning.

(a) A rectangle with one diagonal

(b) A rectangle with two diagonals

(c) An equilateral triangle with medians drawn

(d) A hexagon with one diagonal drawn

(e) An isosceles trapezoid with the altitude drawn that forms the leg of a right triangle in the interior of the figure

19. Are the edges of the triangular pyramid shown here traversable? Explain your reasoning.

20. Are the edges of the triangular prism shown here traversable? Explain your reasoning.

21. Suppose the base of the pyramid from Problem 19 and the triangular face of the prism from Problem 20 were congruent and therefore glued together. Would the edges of the new figure formed be traversable? Explain your reasoning.

22. Suppose the base of the pyramid from Problem 19 is glued to the congruent base of the prism from Problem 20, and the congruent base of another pyramid from Problem 19 is glued to the other face of the prism as shown here. Would the edges of the new figure formed be traversable? Explain your reasoning.

In Other Words

23. Explain the definitions of projection and section as they apply to the early Renaissance painters.

24. Explain the nature of the lines and segments that converge to the primary vanishing point in a projective drawing; that is, what do their real-world counterparts have in common?

25. Why might the perspective drawing of an object be considered its image under a projective transformation?

26. Explain the notion of structural equivalence in topology.

27. What is a network? Name at least three examples where network drawings might be used to model real-life situations.

Cooperative Activity

28. Groups of two

Individual Accountability: Answer Problem 5 of this problem set if you have not done so already. Then cut out a circle with a radius of 3 cm from a sheet of construction paper.

Group Goal: You will need two large blank sheets of white paper, a flashlight, and the cutout of the circle you made above. Tape the paper to the wall.

(a) Focus the flashlight on the circle so that the shadow appears on the paper. Trace the shadow. Keep the circle fixed and move the flashlight to different locations. Trace the shadows formed.

(b) Place the flashlight on a desk so that it can be directly focused on the circle. Experiment with the shadows formed by tilting the white paper in a variety of ways. Trace the shadows.

These shadows can be thought of as projections of the circle. Discuss the projections formed. Can you draw any conclusions?

Vocabulary for Chapter 13

changing your point of view	projection lines
composition	projective geometry
congruence transformations	reflection
constant of dilation	reflectional symmetry
dilation	rigid motions
glide reflection	rotation
image	rotational symmetry
invariant	section
isometry	tessellation
line of symmetry	topology
network	transformational geometry
order of rotational symmetry	transformations
point symmetry	translation
preimage	traversable

Review for Chapter 13

1. You are given the endpoints of a line segment and the corresponding endpoints of its image under some transformation. Identify and explain the transformation.

   (a) $A(4, 4)$, $B(8, 8)$ $A'(4, 8)$, $B'(8, 12)$
   (b) $A(2, -3)$, $B(10, 1)$ $A'(-2, -3)$, $B'(-10, 1)$
   (c) $A(-4, 4)$, $B(4, 4)$ $A'(0, 8)$, $B'(0, 0)$
   (d) $A(1, -3)$, $B(4, -5)$ $A'(-1, 0)$, $B'(-4, -2)$
   (e) $A(1, 3)$, $B(3, 1)$ $A'(2, 6)$, $B'(6, 2)$

2. Examine the following figure.

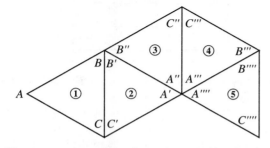

The construction of the figure began with triangle ABC. Four reflections were then performed to produce the images shown. Explain each of the reflections.

3. Copy each figure. Rotate the figure about O as indicated in each of the following figures.

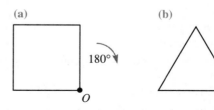

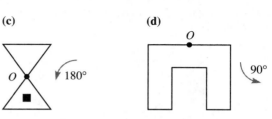

4. A solid of revolution is a calculus concept that concerns a three-dimensional figure that is formed by the rotation of a two-dimensional shape. For example, a cylinder can be formed by rotating a rectangle 360° about one of its sides as shown on page 700.

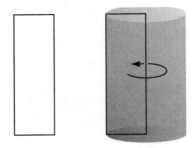

Determine the shape of the solid of revolution formed by each of the following rotations.

(a) A semicircle rotated 360° about its diameter

(b) A right triangle rotated 360° about one of its legs

(c) A circle rotated 180° about a diameter

(d) A right trapezoid rotated 360° about the side that is perpendicular to the bases

(e) A circle rotated 360° about some point that is in the exterior of the circle 2 cm away from a fixed point on the circle

5. You are given parallelogram $ABCD$ with vertices $A(4, 4)$, $B(8, 8)$, $C(12, 8)$, and $D(8, 4)$. Determine the coordinates of the image of $ABCD$ in each of the following transformations.

(a) A dilation with center at $(0, 0)$ and a constant of dilation of $\frac{1}{2}$

(b) A reflection about the y-axis

(c) A reflection about the x-axis

(d) A rotation of 90° in a clockwise direction about the origin

(e) A translation defined by $(x, y) \rightarrow (x - 2, y + 3)$

6. Examine the following square with O as the intersection of diagonals, midpoints of sides m_1, m_2, m_3, and m_4, and diagonals d_1, and d_2.

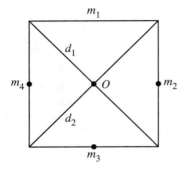

Complete the following table, which identifies the images of m_1, m_2, m_3, m_4, d_1, and d_2 under the given rotations with center at O.

Rotation	m_1	m_2	m_3	m_4	d_1	d_2
90° clockwise						
90° counterclockwise						
270° clockwise						
180° counterclockwise						
360° clockwise						

7. You are given triangle ABC with vertices $A(-12, -5)$, $B(-12, 6)$, and $C(-8, 0)$.

(a) Determine the coordinates of the image $\triangle A'B'C'$ when $\triangle ABC$ is reflected about $x = -6$.

(b) Determine the coordinates of the image $\triangle A''B''C''$ when $\triangle A'B'C'$ is reflected about the y-axis.

(c) Determine the coordinates of the image $\triangle A'''B'''C'''$ when $\triangle A''B''C''$ is reflected about $x = 4$.

(d) Under what single reflection could $\triangle A'''B'''C'''$ have been the reflection image of $\triangle ABC$?

8. Copy the square grid below on a sheet of graph paper. The grid is composed of nine squares, eight of which will be labeled with roman numerals as a result of some transformations. Examine the design in the center square.

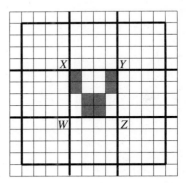

Fill in the remaining squares based on the transformations given here.

(a) The design in I is the image of the original pattern under a reflection about $\overline{YZ}$.

(b) The design in II is the image of the original pattern under a clockwise rotation of 180° about Z.

(c) The design in III is the image of the original pattern under a reflection about $\overline{WZ}$.

(d) The design in IV is the image of the design in III under a clockwise rotation of 90° about W.

(e) The design in V is the image of the design in III under a clockwise rotation of 180° about W.

(f) The design in VI is the image of the design in V under a translation that moves W to X.

(g) The design in VII is the image of the original design under a reflection about $\overline{XY}$.

(h) The design in VIII is the image of the original design under a counterclockwise rotation of 180° about Y.

9. Transformation A is $(x, y) \rightarrow (3x, 3y)$; B is $(x, y) \rightarrow (-x, y)$; C is $(x, y) \rightarrow (x, -y)$; and D is $(x, y) \rightarrow (y, x)$. You are given $\triangle XYZ$ with coordinates $X(0, 0)$, $Y(5, 8)$, and $Z(1, 4)$. Determine the coordinates of the vertices of the image under the following compositions of transformations.

(a) C then B

(b) A then D

(c) B then A

(d) A then B then C

(e) D then A then B

(f) D then D

(g) D then C then B then A

10. A triangle is first reflected about the x-axis, then the image is reflected about the y-axis. What single transformation can this composition of transformations be viewed as?

11. You are given right triangle ABC with $m\angle B = 90°$. Reflect $\triangle ABC$ about AB, forming $\triangle ABC'$. Reflect this image about side AC', forming $\triangle AB''C'$. Examine the figure formed by the three triangles that have been drawn. Could this figure represent a traversable network? Explain your answer.

12. Let relation R be defined as "has one or more factors (other than 1) in common with." Let set $B = \{2, 6, 7, 9, 15, 18\}$. Construct a network to represent the relation R on set B by letting each vertex of the network represent a single element of set B. Is this network traversable? Explain your answer.

13. Let relation Q be defined as "is a multiple of the same number (other than 1) as." Let set $A = \{12, 15, 21, 20, 25, 35, 49\}$. Construct a network to represent the relation Q on set A by letting each vertex of the network represent a single element of set A. Is this network traversable? Explain your answer.

14. Let relation W be defined as the relation "is not topologically equivalent to." Let set P contain the following elements: {doughnut, ruler, bagel, spoon, glove, colander}. Construct a network to represent the relation W on set P by letting each vertex of the network represent a single ele-

ment of P. Is this network traversable? Explain your answer.

15. Determine whether the edges of the following platonic solids are traversable. Explain your answer.

(a) Tetrahedron

(b) Octahedron

(c) Dodecahedron

(d) Cube

(e) Icosahedron

16. A single-story warehouse is separated into six storage areas that are connected by security doors, as illustrated in the following floor plan.

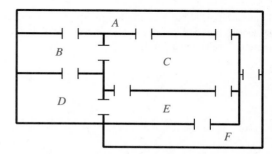

At night, each time the security guard makes the rounds, a door must be opened with a key and then locked behind the guard. Is it possible for the guard to walk through the entire warehouse by going through each door once and only once? If so, explain the path the guard might take.

17. Explain why a conveyor belt that turns two wheels might be attached in the form of a Möbius strip.

18. It is important to associate mathematical concepts with real-world situations whenever possible. Match the real-world situation to the associated mathematical concept. Explain your reasoning.

Real-World Situation	Mathematical Concept
Telephone system	Rotation
Hinged door	Translation
Overhead projector	Dilation
Kaleidoscope	Topological equivalence
Fun-house mirror	Network
Electric circuit	Reflection
Standard mirror	
Magnifying glass	
Sliding patio door	

19. Construct a perspective drawing of the following figure. Use any convenient measurement for the distance between the primary vanishing point and the secondary vanishing points.

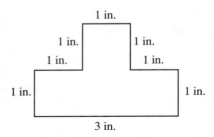

20. Draw a larger version of the figure below. Use the constructions outlined in Section 11.1 to construct a reflection image of the figure about line *l*.

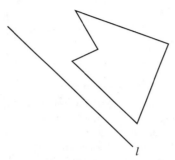

In Other Words

21. Explain why this chapter included the problem-solving strategy of changing your point of view.

22. Cite an example of a situation in which the image is the preimage under some transformation.

23. Suppose you are holding a mirrored holiday tree ornament. Explain why the laws of projective geometry are violated by the image you see.

24. Some people call topology "rubber-sheet geometry" by making references to figures drawn on a sheet of rubber. Attempt an explanation of this view of topology.

25. In a perspective drawing, we view a two-dimensional drawing and see it as if it were three-dimensional. When might a person view something that is three-dimensional and see it as if it were two-dimensional.

Cooperative Activity

26. **Groups of four**

Individual Accountability: Divide a sheet of paper into 15 irregular regions, such that no region is completely contained within another. Color the regions in such a way that no two adjoining regions are the same color. Regions that meet at a single point are not considered adjoining.

Group Goal: Examine the colored drawings. What conclusions might you draw about the minimum number of colors necessary such that no two adjoining regions share the same color. Test your hypothesis on a map that outlines the 48 contiguous states (excludes Alaska and Hawaii). What is the minimum number of colors needed to color such a map so that no two states that share a border are of the same color? We will agree that if two states meet at a single point, they do not share a border.

The results of this experiment form the basis of a very important topological problem that was solved in 1976.

Appendix A
More Investigations Using Technology: Computer Spreadsheets and Graphics Calculators

We begin this appendix with two quotes taken from reports issued by the National Council of Teachers of Mathematics. The first quote is from *Curriculum and Evaluation Standards for School Mathematics* (1989):

> Changes in technology and the broadening of the areas in which mathematics is applied have resulted in growth and changes in the discipline of mathematics itself. . . . The new technology not only has made calculations and graphing easier, it has changed the very nature of the problems important to mathematics and the methods mathematicians use to investigate them. Because technology is changing mathematics and its uses, we believe that
>
> - appropriate calculators should be available to all students at all times;
> - a computer should be available in every classroom for demonstration purposes;
> - every student should have access to a computer for individual and group work;
> - students should learn to use the computer as a tool for processing information and performing calculations to investigate and solve problems. (pp. 7–8)

The second quote is from *Professional Standards for Teaching Mathematics* (1991):

> In order to establish a discourse that is focused on exploring mathematical ideas, not just on reporting correct answers, the means of mathematical communication and approaches to mathematical reasoning must be broad and varied. . . . Teachers should . . . help students learn to use calculators, computers, and other technological devices as tools for mathematical discourse. (p. 52)

The National Council of Teachers of Mathematics highlights the importance of technology in both of these reports. We support these recommendations and feel that integrating technology into the elementary school curriculum is extremely important. We have purposefully shown how to solve problems using a calculator throughout this textbook. In the early 1980s, calculator usage in the elementary school classroom was supported by few and dismissed by many. Now in the 1990s, the calculator has become the most accessible piece of technology at all levels of the curriculum. Although a computer in every classroom is still a hope for the future, calculators in every classroom are rapidly becoming a reality. Many states have redesigned their standardized examinations, allowing for the use of a calculator. The power of the calculator as an investigative tool cannot be ignored.

This appendix will focus on two technological tools: the computer spreadsheet and the graphics calculator. Although many different spreadsheet programs and graphics calculators are available, it is not the purpose of this text to teach you the idiosyncrasies of any one particular software package. Rather, we offer you the opportunity to learn about two tools that are suitable for use at all levels, from elementary through graduate school.

A.1   Computer Spreadsheets

Years ago, accountants kept their records in a book called a ledger. This ledger would list debits and credits in organized columns and rows. It was the job of the accountant to do all of the mathematics necessary to make sense of the data recorded in the ledger. A **computer spreadsheet** is a technological tool that functions as an electronic "ledger." In its simplest role, a spreadsheet can be used as an advanced calculator to organize and make sense of a set of data. Mathematics educators are finding that the spreadsheet can be a rich source of problem solving at all levels.

computer spreadsheet

Let's begin by examining this display of an empty spreadsheet, as shown in Figure A.1.

Figure A.1

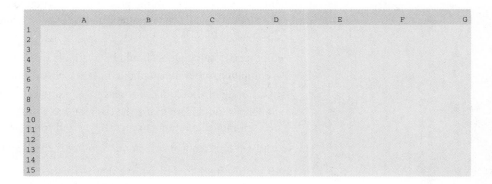

Notice that the rows are labeled using numbers and the columns are labeled using letters. A particular location on the spreadsheet is identified by its lettered column and numbered row. For example, C5 is the location that is at the intersection of column C and row 5. These locations are known as cells. A **cell** is a location on the spreadsheet where a column and a row intersect.

cell

A cell can contain three different types of information: a label, a value, or a formula. A **label** is a word or phrase that is used for identification purposes. It is often found as a column or row heading, or at some place in the display where an explanation of a calculated value is needed. A **value** is a number. The degree of accuracy of this number can be determined in the spreadsheet by defining the number of decimal places

label

value

that are to be used. If the spreadsheet is set for a degree of accuracy of 2, all entries will show two decimal places, and all calculations will be rounded to two decimal places. A **formula** is a rule or command that instructs the computer to perform some preprogrammed function. Formulas can be formed by using the standard arithmetic functions or other functions that are defined by the particular program being used.

formula

In Investigations 1–3, you will be given the initial spreadsheet display, along with the generic formulas that were used to create the spreadsheet. Be advised that spreadsheet programs do differ. If you are transferring the spreadsheets from this text to your own spreadsheet files, you must first "translate" the commands we have used into ones recognized by your software.

Why use spreadsheets? What can using this tool help you accomplish? Herein lies the answer:

> Spreadsheets allow the student to apply a variety of mathematics skills, both thinking and computing. A single spreadsheet can incorporate many mathematical topics and call on reasoning abilities that are rarely tapped in [elementary/secondary] textbook problems. Initially, students may use only the technique of random trial and error by entering values in certain cells and then hoping for the best. But, as work continues with spreadsheet programs, haphazard guesses may lead to the development of systematic trial-and-error skills. The student enters a value, examines the results, then chooses another value based on the newly calculated display. The immediacy of the result encourages students to systematize their plan of attack by affording them the opportunity to reflect, review, and retry.*

Investigation 1

A gourmet coffee shop offers its customers the opportunity to mix coffee beans to create their own blend to taste. Four different types of beans are used in the special mix. French Roast coffee costs $8.00 per pound. Mocha Java coffee costs $9.00 per pound. Colombian coffee costs $7.00 per pound. Hawaiian Kona coffee costs $10.00 per pound. Customers order each type of coffee in eighth-, quarter-, or half-pound quantities. The shop owner combines the desired types and amounts of beans, then grinds them.

Rich stumbled upon a particular mix of these beans that he thoroughly enjoyed. Unfortunately, he cannot remember the quantities of each type. His old sales receipt indicates that his last purchase was a 1.5 pound bag of the special mix, which cost him $12.00 before tax. Use the spreadsheet to determine a possible mix. Is your solution unique?

Understand the Problem: What is known? You are told that four types of coffee were used to make a 1.5-pound mixture at a total cost of $12.00.

*Richard Sgroi, "Systematizing Trial and Error Using Spreadsheets," *The Arithmetic Teacher* 39 (March 1992): 8–12.

What is unknown? You must determine quantities of each coffee type that together would cost $12.00 for a 1.5-pound bag.

Devise a Plan: Use a spreadsheet to model the situation and determine a solution.

Carry Out the Plan:

	A	B	C	D	E	F	G
1							
2							
3							
4							
5	COFFEE	COST PER	QUANTITY	AMOUNT			
6	TYPE	POUND					
7							
8	FRENCH ROAST	$8.00	0.000	0.000			
9	MOCHA JAVA	$9.00	0.000	0.000			
10	COLOMBIAN	$7.00	0.000	0.000			
11	KONA	$10.00	0.000	0.000			
12		TOTALS					
13							
14							
15							

Cells A5, A6, B5, B6, C5, D5, A8, A9, A10, A11, and B12 all contain labels. Notice that cells B8, B9, B10, and B11 contain particular values that represent the cost per pound of the individual types of coffee. A person using this spreadsheet would locate the cursor (sometimes represented as a blinking square to indicate the present position on the display) at cells C8, C9, C10, and C11. A quantity in pounds should be entered as a decimal. Keep in mind that the problem states that the quantities are restricted to eighths, quarters, and halves of a pound only. Upon a person entering these quantities, the spreadsheet has been set up to automatically calculate the total quantity purchased in pounds (cell C12), the price of the purchase for each type of coffee (cells D8, D9, D10, and D11), and the total price (before tax) of the purchase (cell D12). Some possible outputs after certain entries are made are depicted in the following four examples:

COFFEE TYPE	COST PER POUND	QUANTITY	AMOUNT
FRENCH ROAST	$8.00	0.125	1.000
MOCHA JAVA	$9.00	0.750	6.750
COLOMBIAN	$7.00	0.375	2.625
KONA	$10.00	0.250	2.500
TOTALS		1.500	12.875

COFFEE TYPE	COST PER POUND	QUANTITY	AMOUNT
FRENCH ROAST	$8.00	0.500	4.000
MOCHA JAVA	$9.00	0.375	3.375
COLOMBIAN	$7.00	0.125	0.875
KONA	$10.00	0.375	3.750
	TOTALS	1.375	12.000

COFFEE TYPE	COST PER POUND	QUANTITY	AMOUNT
FRENCH ROAST	$8.00	0.250	2.000
MOCHA JAVA	$9.00	0.250	2.250
COLOMBIAN	$7.00	0.750	5.250
KONA	$10.00	0.250	2.500
	TOTALS	1.500	12.000

COFFEE TYPE	COST PER POUND	QUANTITY	AMOUNT
FRENCH ROAST	$8.00	0.625	5.000
MOCHA JAVA	$9.00	0.250	2.250
COLOMBIAN	$7.00	0.500	3.500
KONA	$10.00	0.125	1.250
	TOTALS	1.500	12.000

In the first output, notice that the total quantity is the desired 1.5 pounds, but the price is approximately $12.88. Therefore, this could not be the mixture Rich had purchased. The second output displays a $12 purchase for a 1.375-pound bag of coffee. Again, this is not Rich's mixture. Both the third and fourth outputs show 1.5-pound mixtures costing $12. It appears that this combination of weight and price is not unique; in fact many more such mixtures are possible. Rich can purchase the mixtures described in the third and fourth outputs, taste the coffee produced, and then decide whether or not it suits his taste.

Look Back: Notice how the spreadsheet assisted in the problem-solving process. The most important part of the process is the trials that were made to determine the solution. How should the problem solver approach such situations? We contend that mere random guessing at numbers is inefficient and tedious. You must carefully examine any incorrect displays and decide how to modify the input in order to approach the desired outcome. This involves carefully considering a number of patterns and regularities. For example, if the price was correct but the poundage was too high, the quantities would have needed to be adjusted, which would have lowered the weight of the bag while maintaining the $12.00 price. Systematic trial and error will help you locate the correct solution(s).

Figure A.2 depicts the format of the spreadsheet. The formula SUM (cell:cell) finds the sum of the entries from the first cell name listed to the last cell name listed. The format of this command varies from software to software. Notice in Figure A.2 an equal sign appears before each formula. This is used to show that the contents in that cell are formulas rather than a value. This symbol varies from software to software. Consult your user's manual for the appropriate way to identify formulas in your particular software.

Figure A-2

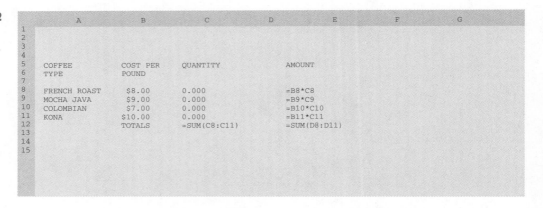

	A	B	C	D	E	F	G
1							
2							
3							
4							
5	COFFEE	COST PER	QUANTITY		AMOUNT		
6	TYPE	POUND					
7							
8	FRENCH ROAST	$8.00	0.000		=B8*C8		
9	MOCHA JAVA	$9.00	0.000		=B9*C9		
10	COLOMBIAN	$7.00	0.000		=B10*C10		
11	KONA	$10.00	0.000		=B11*C11		
12		TOTALS	=SUM(C8:C11)		=SUM(D8:D11)		
13							
14							
15							

Throughout this book, we have stressed that mathematicians search for relationships and try to establish patterns. Patterns can be found in both nature and in the human-made world. Once a pattern is determined, questions such as "Why does this happen?" and "How can we extend the pattern?" often arise. Looking for patterns and using patterns are problem-solving strategies that need to be developed, practiced, and applied. In Investigation 2 you are given the opportunity to do just that using a computer spreadsheet.

Investigation 2

There is a famous sequence in mathematics called the Fibonacci sequence. The Fibonacci sequence is often presented in the following form:

$$1, 1, 2, 3, 5, 8, 13, 21, \ldots$$

Once the pattern is determined, it is easy to find the subsequent terms of the sequence. (We won't tell you what the pattern is. We leave it up to you to discover it!)

The Fibonacci pattern can be applied to and extended from any two numbers. These numbers can be manipulated to form ratios, and the ratios can in turn be expressed as decimals. We will use the symbol X_n to denote the nth term of a particular Fibonacci sequence as follows:

$$X_1, X_2, X_3, X_4, \ldots, X_n, \ldots$$

Now examine the ratio formed by each term with the term that precedes it:

$$\left(\frac{X_{n+1}}{X_n}\right): \quad \frac{X_2}{X_1}, \frac{X_3}{X_2}, \frac{X_4}{X_3}, \frac{X_5}{X_4}, \ldots$$

(a) What is the pattern used to generate the Fibonacci sequence?

(b) What do you notice about the ratios after examining different Fibonacci sequences?

Understand the Problem: You are given a general form of a Fibonacci sequence and the general form of a new sequence that results by forming ratios of a term in the Fibonacci sequence with its preceding term. You are asked to identify the pattern that generates the Fibonacci sequence, as well as examine the terms in the sequence of ratios.

Devise a Plan: Use a spreadsheet to model this problem. Then experiment, analyze, and solve.

Carry Out the Plan: Examine the spreadsheet depicted below.

	A	B	C	D	E	F	G
1	Enter any two whole numbers with						
2	the lesser of the two in D2			1	1		
3							
4	The first ten terms of the Fibonacci sequence						
5	beginning with			1	are:		
6							
7	SEQUENCE			RATIOS			
8	1						
9	1			1			
10	2			2			
11	3			1.5			
12	5			1.6666667			
13	8			1.6			
14	13			1.625			
15	21			1.6153846			
16	34			1.6190476			
17	55			1.6176471			

We began the sequence by entering any two whole numbers. If one number is less than the other, enter the lesser of the two in cell D2 and the other number in cell E2. No other entries are needed. The Fibonacci sequence beginning with the two entries is displayed in column A from cells A8 to A17. The ratios are displayed in column D. The first ratio appears in cell D9. This is the ratio of the second term to the first term. The ratio in cell D10 is the ratio of the third term to the second term, and so on. Examine the results displayed by the spreadsheet. The following four outputs show this procedure repeated for four other Fibonacci sequences. What conclusions can you draw?

```
Enter any two whole numbers with
the lesser of the two in D2                          1          2

The first ten terms of the Fibonacci sequence
beginning with                                       1          are:

SEQUENCE                              RATIOS
      1
      2                                   2
      3                                 1.5
      5                           1.6666667
      8                                 1.6
     13                               1.625
     21                           1.6153846
     34                           1.6190476
     55                           1.6176471
     89                           1.6181818
```

```
Enter any two whole numbers with
the lesser of the two in D2                          3          5

The first ten terms of the Fibonacci sequence
beginning with                                       3          are:

SEQUENCE                              RATIOS
      3
      5                           1.6666667
      8                                 1.6
     13                               1.625
     21                           1.6153846
     34                           1.6190476
     55                           1.6176471
     89                           1.6181818
    144                           1.6179775
    233                           1.6180556
```

```
Enter any two whole numbers with
the lesser of the two in D2                         13         21

The first ten terms of the Fibonacci sequence
beginning with                                      13          are:

SEQUENCE                              RATIOS
     13
     21                           1.6153846
     34                           1.6190476
     55                           1.6176471
     89                           1.6181818
    144                           1.6179775
    233                           1.6180556
    377                           1.6180258
    610                           1.6180371
    987                           1.6180328
```

```
Enter any two whole numbers with
the lesser of the two in D2                    125           1952

The first ten terms of the Fibonacci sequence
beginning with                                 125           are:

SEQUENCE                           RATIOS
    125
   1952                            15.616
   2077                            1.0640369
   4029                            1.939817
   6106                            1.5155125
  10135                            1.6598428
  16241                            1.6024667
  26376                            1.6240379
  42617                            1.6157492
  68993                            1.6189079
```

Compare the four sequences. Look for a pattern.

- **First sequence:** 1, 2, 3, 5, 8, 13, 21, 34, 55, 89
- **Second sequence:** 3, 5, 8, 13, 21, 34, 55, 89, 144, 233
- **Third sequence:** 13, 21, 34, 55, 89, 144, 233, 377, 610, 987
- **Fourth sequence:** 125, 1952, 2077, 4029, 6106, 10135, 16241, 26376, 42617, 68993

Taking the difference between a term and its preceding term should uncover the pattern. Stop here and discover the regularity.

You should have determined that beginning with the third term, each term is the sum of the two terms preceding it. Now examine the ratios. The first three sequences appear to share some of the same terms. At some point, the numbers and the ratios in all three are similar. This is not the case with the fourth sequence. Notice that it does not have any terms in common with the other three sequences, and yet the ratios appear to be very similar.

In the two sequences below, we have taken the last two terms of the third sequence above and the last two terms of the fourth sequence above and treated them as the beginning terms of a new sequence. In this way, we can see the next eight terms of each sequence. Examine the following spreadsheet results. They are quite surprising. Stop here before continuing your reading. What do you notice about the ratios?

```
Enter any two whole numbers with
the lesser of the two in D2                    610           987

The first ten terms of the Fibonacci sequence
beginning with                                 610           are:

SEQUENCE                           RATIOS
    610
    987                            1.6180328
   1597                            1.6180344
   2584                            1.6180338
   4181                            1.6180341
   6765                            1.618034
  10946                            1.618034
  17711                            1.618034
  28657                            1.618034
  46368                            1.618034
```

```
Enter any two whole numbers with
the lesser of the two in D2                    42617        68993

The first ten terms of the Fibonacci sequence
beginning with                                 42617        are:

SEQUENCE                          RATIOS
   42617
   68993                        1.6189079
  111610                        1.6177003
  180603                        1.6181615
  292213                        1.6179853
  472816                        1.6180526
  765029                        1.6180269
 1237845                        1.6180367
 2002874                        1.618033
 3240719                        1.6180344
```

In both cases, the ratios approach 1.618034. Where have you seen this number before? This is the golden ratio we studied in Chapter 11. It is sometimes expressed as $\frac{1}{2}(\sqrt{5}+1)$. The ratio of a term with its preceding term in all Fibonacci sequences appears to approach the golden ratio as the number of terms increase.

Look Back: Try to answer the following questions. Would this relationship also be true with a Fibonacci sequence of decimal numbers? What would be the characteristics of the numbers chosen that approach the golden ratio more rapidly than other pairs of beginning numbers?

The following illustration depicts the formulas used to create this spreadsheet.

	A	B	C	D	E	F	G
1	Enter any two whole numbers with						
2	the lesser of the two in D2			1	1		
3							
4	The first ten terms of the Fibonacci sequence						
5	beginning with			=D2	are:		
6							
7	SEQUENCE			RATIOS			
8	=D2						
9	=E2			=E2/D2			
10	=D2+E2			=B10/E2			
11	=E2+B10			=B11/B10			
12	=B10+B11			=B12/B11			
13	=B11+B12			=B13/B12			
14	=B12+B13			=B14/B13			
15	=B13+B14			=B15/B14			
16	=B14+B15			=B16/B15			
17	=B15+B16			=B17/B16			

Investigation 2 could also have been accomplished with just a calculator if spreadsheet software had been unavailable. The spreadsheet outline given in this investigation can be used to organize your work. First, establish the pattern that is used to generate any Fibonacci sequence. Once established, choose any two whole numbers as the first two terms of your sequence. Generate the remaining eight terms. Set up the nine ratios $\left(\frac{\text{Term}}{\text{Preceding term}}\right)$, and express each ratio as an equivalent decimal. Examine the results. Repeat this procedure for at least three other Fibonacci sequences. What conclusions can you draw?

Investigation 3

A discount clothing store has the following pricing policy: When an item arrives from the manufacturer, it is listed at the full price for 3 weeks from the day of arrival. At the end of the 3 weeks, the item is listed for three-fourths of the full price for the next 4 weeks. At the end of this 4-week period, the item is listed at one-half of the full price for the next 5 weeks. Finally, the item is listed at one-third of its full price, and it remains at this price until removed from the selling floor by the owners.

A shipment of 600 coats arrived at the store on January 2. The warehouse owner paid $120 per coat. The owner marked each coat's full price at $1\frac{1}{3}$ times the amount he paid for it.

Over the next few months, a number of coats were sold at the full price and at each of the reduced prices. All remaining coats were sold at the final sale price. The total gross receipts for the coat sales were $64,000.

The following ratios were reported:

- The number of coats sold at $\frac{3}{4}$ of full price to the number of coats sold at $\frac{1}{2}$ of full price: $2:3$

- The number of coats sold at full price to the number of coats sold at $\frac{3}{4}$ of full price: $2:1$

(a) What is the full price for a single coat?
(b) How many coats were sold at each of the prices?
(c) Did the owner make a profit?

Understand the Problem: You are given information about the pricing policy and sales of a particular clothing store. You are asked to use the information to determine the full price of a coat, the number of sales for each of the prices, and the owner's profit.

Devise a Plan: Use a spreadsheet to model this situation. Then experiment, analyze, and solve.

Carry Out the Plan: Examine the following spreadsheet.

	A	B	C	D	E	F	G
1							
2	600 COATS		PRICE PER COAT		0		
3							
4							
5	FRACTION		NUMBER		GROSS		
6	OF PRICE		SOLD		RECEIPTS		
7							
8	FULL PRICE		0		0		
9	3/4 PRICE		0		0		
10	1/2 PRICE		0		0		
11	1/3 PRICE		0		0		
12		TOTAL		TOTAL			
13		SOLD:	0	GROSS:	0		
14	--						
15							
16		NUMBER		AMOUNT			
17		REMAINING:	600	REMAINING	64000		
18							

Enter a unit coat price in cell E2 (this is $1\frac{1}{3}$ times \$120, or \$160). Enter the number sold at each price in cells C8–C11. The gross receipts at each price will be calculated for you in cells E8–E11. The total number of coats sold will appear in cell C13, and the total gross receipts in cell E13. The rows below row 15 report updated information on the numbers of coats yet to be accounted for and the total income yet to be accounted for.

Output for the three spreadsheet displays follows:

```
600 COATS                PRICE PER COAT                      160


FRACTION                 NUMBER                   GROSS
OF PRICE                 SOLD                     RECEIPTS

FULL PRICE                        160                       25600
3/4 PRICE                          80                        9600
1/2 PRICE                         120                        9600
1/3 PRICE                         240                       12800
              TOTAL                      TOTAL
              SOLD:               600  GROSS:               57600
-------------------------------------------------------------------

              NUMBER                     AMOUNT
              REMAINING:          0  REMAINING              6400
```

```
600 COATS                PRICE PER COAT                      160


FRACTION                 NUMBER                   GROSS
OF PRICE                 SOLD                     RECEIPTS

FULL PRICE                        220                       35200
3/4 PRICE                         110                       13200
1/2 PRICE                         165                       13200
1/3 PRICE                          45                        2400
              TOTAL                      TOTAL
              SOLD:               540  GROSS:               64000
-------------------------------------------------------------------

              NUMBER                     AMOUNT
              REMAINING:         60  REMAINING                 0
```

```
600 COATS                PRICE PER COAT                      160


FRACTION                 NUMBER                   GROSS
OF PRICE                 SOLD                     RECEIPTS

FULL PRICE                        200                       32000
3/4 PRICE                         100                       12000
1/2 PRICE                         150                       12000
1/3 PRICE                         150                        8000
              TOTAL                      TOTAL
              SOLD:               600  GROSS:               64000
-------------------------------------------------------------------

              NUMBER                     AMOUNT
              REMAINING:          0  REMAINING                 0
```

In the first output, notice that 600 coats are accounted for and the ratios stated are correct, but the total gross sales are not equal to $64,000. In the second output, the ratios are again correct and the total gross sales equal the desired amount, but only 540 coats are sold. Finally, the third output depicts a solution that does not contradict any of the given information. The ratios are correct, and the gross is $64,000 for a total sale of 600 coats.

You can see that the owner lost money on this deal. The total purchase price of the coats was $120 times 600, or $72,000. The gross receipts for the sale of the 600 coats were $64,000. The owner lost $8000 on this deal.

Look Back: Is the answer we found unique? Use your spreadsheet or calculator to answer this question. To assist you, the formulas used to create the spreadsheet for this investigation are given here.

	A	B	C	D	E	F	G
1							
2	600 COATS		PRICE PER COAT		160		
3							
4							
5	FRACTION		NUMBER		GROSS		
6	OF PRICE		SOLD		RECEIPTS		
7							
8	FULL PRICE		0		=E2*C8		
9	3/4 PRICE		0		=0.75*(E2*C9)		
10	1/2 PRICE		0		=0.5*(E2*C10)		
11	1/3 PRICE		0		=(E2/3)*C11		
12		TOTAL		TOTAL			
13		SOLD:	=SUM(C8:C11)	GROSS:	=SUM(E8:E11)		
14	--
15							
16		NUMBER		AMOUNT			
17		REMAINING:	=600-C13	REMAINING	=64000-E13		
18							

A.2   **G**raphics Calculators

graphics calculator The **graphics calculator** is an innovative educational tool. Although few elementary schools currently have the luxury of owning and using a graphics calculator, subsequent price decreases may change this. Ignoring its potential would be a big mistake. Those who ignored the potential of computers and calculators in the 1970s and early 1980s soon found themselves scrambling to keep up with those who recognized the powerful effect these tools would have on mathematics and learned how to use them.

The graphics calculator is a tool that can be used at a variety of mathematical levels. For the purposes of this overview, we will examine how it can be used as an investigative tool for mathematics teachers. A variety of graphics calculators are available (including models for overhead projection), and as time progresses more will be on the market. We will examine the TI-81 graphics calculator in this section. The keys and key sequences that are referred to here can be found on and used with most graphics calculators.

You will notice that a graphics calculator includes many keys that are not found on the standard four-function calculator, as shown in Figure A.3.

Figure A.3

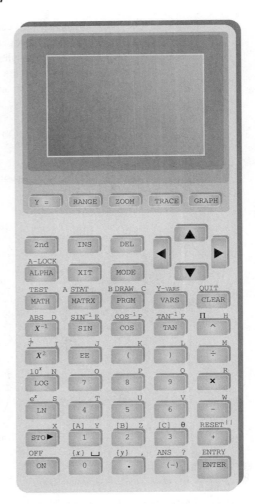

The graphics calculator has a large screen that not only displays graphs, but can also display many lines of commands.

It is not the purpose of this overview to teach you how to use all of the features on the TI-81 graphics calculator. Rather, we want to introduce you to the wide range of capabilities such a tool has. We hope you will become interested enough in its use to further your studies with this tool.

The Graphics Calculator as a Computerized "Scratchpad"

The graphics calculator has the capability of allowing expressions to be keyed in as they would be written. Take, for example, the expression

$$-4 - 7(18 - 3 + 4^2) + 11$$

The keystroke sequence for this expression is as follows:

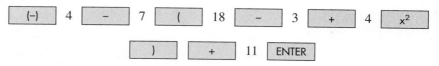

On the TI-81, the negation key $\boxed{(-)}$ is different from the subtraction key $\boxed{-}$. Also notice that it is not necessary to include a multiplication key between the 7 and the left parenthesis key.

The TI-81 follows the standard order of operations. Complex fractions can be keyed in and are evaluated following the logic of this order of operations. For example, to simplify

$$\frac{7}{3 - \frac{4}{5}}$$

we view the complex fraction in its equivalent "division" form:

$$\frac{7}{3 - \frac{4}{5}} = 7 \div (3 - \tfrac{4}{5}).$$

The following keystroke sequence can be used to simplify this complex fraction:

The TI-81 calculator has the capability of "remembering and recalling" the solution to the last calculation. This solution can be used in the very next calculation. For example, suppose you wanted to find the total price and the sales tax on a $2500 item with an $8\frac{1}{4}\%$ sales tax rate. You can first calculate the tax by multiplying 2500 by .0825. When $\boxed{\text{ENTER}}$ is pressed, the display reads 206.25. This amount must be added to 2500 to yield the total price. Rather than keying in the computed tax, pressing $\boxed{+}$ will display

$$\text{ANS} +$$

This indicates that the number you key in to follow the + symbol will be added to the previous answer of 206.25. The display will look as shown in Figure A.4.

Figure A.4

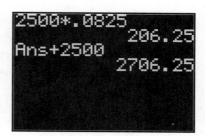

The final display, 2706.25, is the total price including the tax.

Examine the following keystroke sequence. Interpret the final display.

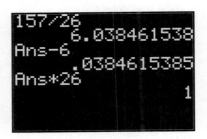

It is clear that 6.038461538 is the quotient of 157 and 26. In the next line, the whole number part of the quotient is subtracted, leaving only the decimal part of the quotient. This decimal is then multiplied by the divisor, 26, resulting in a product of 1.

Notice that $26 \times 6 = 156$, and $157 - 156 = 1$. This is not a coincidence. The quotient of 157 and 26 can be expressed as 6 plus a remainder of 1. In fractional form, this remainder would be written as $\frac{1}{26}$. But $\frac{1}{26} = 1 \div 26 = .0384615385$ (this $=$ is used loosely here since the calculator only reports a certain number of decimal places).

$$\frac{1}{26} = .0384615385$$

Multiply both sides by 26:

$$26 \times \frac{1}{26} = .0384615385 \times 26$$

$$1 = .0384615385 \times 26$$

The whole number remainder can be determined by multiplying the decimal portion of a quotient by the divisor.

Menus

The TI-81 is "menu driven." This means you can have a list of options appear on the display screen. By highlighting any of the options, a command or series of commands can be activated. Some of the menus are shown in Figure A.5.

Figure A.5

Statistics Menu

Draw Menu

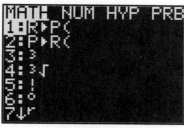

Math Menu

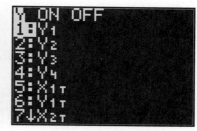

Y-Variables Menu

Test Menu

Variables

Algebraic expressions can be easily evaluated using variables. To store a value in a variable it is necessary to use the $\boxed{\text{STO►}}$ key. The $\boxed{\text{STO►}}$ key is used in conjunction with a numerical value and a letter of the alphabet. A number is entered, $\boxed{\text{STO►}}$ is pressed, and the calculator responds with an arrow and a blinking letter "A." This "A" indicates that the calculator has temporarily shifted into "alphabetic" mode, awaiting the user's entry of a letter. The letters A through Z can be found on the calculator and are just 26 of the possible entries that can be made at this point. For example, Figure A.6 depicts the display that indicates that 2 has been stored in the variable A, –2 has been stored in the variable B, and .25 has been stored in the variable C.

Figure A.6

Figure A.7 shows the keystroke and the display for the evaluation of

$$\frac{A^2 - 2C}{4B}$$

In order to activate the "alpha" mode, it is necessary to press the [ALPHA] key before each letter.

[( ] [ALPHA] A [x²] [−] 2 [ALPHA] C [ )] [÷]

4 [ALPHA] B [ENTER]

The display reads −.4375

Figure A.7

Now suppose you wish to evaluate the algebraic expression for different values of A, B, and C. One way is to store new values in A, B, and C, and then key in the expression again. There is an alternative. The TI-81 has the capability of allowing you to store four such expressions. Pressing [Y=] will display the screen shown in Figure A.8.

Figure A.8

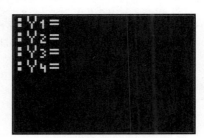

Four variables, Y_1, Y_2, Y_3, and Y_4, are available for input. Position the cursor next to Y_1, and enter the algebraic expressions as shown in Figure A.9.

Figure A.9

Return to the "work" screen by pressing [2nd] [CLEAR]. Any numerical values can now be stored in A, B, and C. We will use 10, 20, and 30, respectively. Once these values are stored, it is necessary to call up the Y_1 variable to the work screen. This is done by the following keystroke sequence

10 [STO▶] A 20 [STO▶] B 30 [STO▶] C [2nd] [Y-VARS] [ENTER] [ENTER]

The displays are pictured in Figure A.10.

Figure A.10

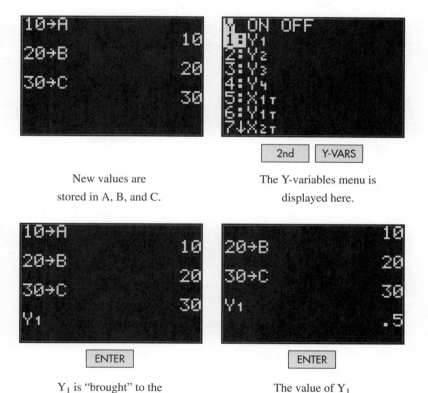

New values are
stored in A, B, and C.

The Y-variables menu is
displayed here.

[2nd] [Y-VARS]

Y_1 is "brought" to the
work screen for use there.

[ENTER]

The value of Y_1
is displayed.

[ENTER]

You can change the values of A, B, and C as often as you like, then repeat the sequence above to display the effect that it has on the algebraic expression stored in Y_1. The power of this feature is illustrated in Investigation 5.

Investigation 5

In many parts of the country, meteorologists report both the actual temperature and the wind chill temperature on very cold and windy days. The wind chill temperature is the temperature that it *feels* like outside because of the wind. The wind chill temperature can be calculated by the following formula:

$$\text{Wind chill in } °F = 91.4 - (.288 \cdot \sqrt{V} + .45 - .019 \cdot V) \cdot (91.4 - T)$$

where V is the velocity of the wind in miles per hour, and T is the actual air temperature in degrees Fahrenheit.

Suppose that at 6:00 P.M., the outside air temperature was 30°F and the wind velocity was 10 miles per hour. Each hour for 4 hours, the temperature dropped an average of 5 degrees and the wind velocity increased an average of 5 miles per hour. What was the wind chill temperature at 7:00 P.M., 8:00 P.M., 9:00 P.M., and 10:00 P.M.?

Understand the Problem: You are given a formula that is used to determine the wind chill temperature. You are also given information about the change in temperature and wind velocity over a 4-hour period. You must determine the hourly wind chill temperatures.

Devise a Plan: We will use the graphics calculator to create a table of temperatures.

Carry Out the Plan: Turn on the calculator. Press $\boxed{\text{Y=}}$. Clear any formula in Y_1 by locating the cursor on the line to be cleared and pressing $\boxed{\text{CLEAR}}$. The following keystroke sequence will result in the display shown at the top of page A-21.

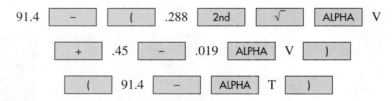

Now press [2nd] [CLEAR] to return to the work space.

To determine the wind chill when the temperature is 30° F with a wind velocity of 10 miles per hour, you must first store 30 in *T* and 10 in *V* as shown here:

$$30 \quad \boxed{\text{STO►}} \quad T$$

$$10 \quad \boxed{\text{STO►}} \quad V$$

These values will be used in the evaluation of the wind chill temperature formula that has been stored in the variable Y_1. The procedure is shown in the following sequence.

Displays the Y-variables menu.

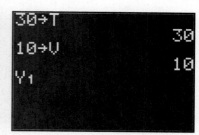

"Brings" the Y_1 variable to the workspace.

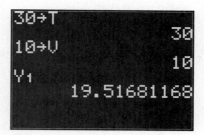

Evaluates Y_1.

The display reads 19.51681168. When it is 30°, a 10-mile-per-hour wind makes it feel as if it is approximately 20°.

The following table summarizes the values and keystrokes that are necessary to answer this question.

Keystrokes			V	T	Approximate Wind Chill Temperature	Time
30	STO▶	T				
10	STO▶	V	10	30	19.5°	6:00 P.M.
25	STO▶	T				
15	STO▶	V	1⁀	25	6.4°	7:00 P.M.
20	STO▶	T				
20	STO▶	V	20	20	−5.6°	8:00 P.M.
15	STO▶	T				
25	STO▶	V	25	15	−16.7°	9:00 P.M.
10	STO▶	T				
30	STO▶	V	30	10	−27.2°	10:00 P.M.

Look Back: What is the wind chill when the temperature is 35° with a wind velocity of 2 miles per hour? Examine your result. Is it reasonable? What might this lead you to believe about the wind chill formula?

Graphing

One of the most powerful features of the graphics calculator is, of course, its graphics. We will examine a few of the many capabilities of this tool as it relates to graphing.

The TI-81 has a viewing rectangle that graphs functions on the coordinate axes from −10 to 10. This range can easily be changed depending on the specificity the user desires. Pressing RANGE results in the display shown in Figure A.11.

Figure A.11

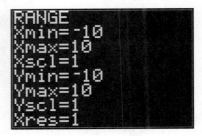

We will examine only the Xmin, Xmax, Ymin, Ymax, Xscl, and Yscl entries. A complete description of all of these variables can be found in the user's manual. The first four variables set the minimum and maximum values on the *x*- and *y*-axes. Notice that the standard range of −10 to 10 on each axis is depicted in Figure A.11. These can be changed to any desired values by entering a new number next to the variable name. The Xscl and Yscl (x- and y-scales) variables control the placement of the tick marks on the x- and y-axes. The increment between any two tick marks on the x-axis is determined by the Xscl value, and the increment between any two tick marks on the y-axis is determined by the Yscl value.

We are now ready to examine a simple function. Press [Y=] and then [CLEAR]. The Y_1 variable is ready for input. Let's graph the function $y = x$. Here, every y-value on the line is exactly the same as its x-value. Enter x by pressing [X|T]. Once the function is keyed in, press [GRAPH]. The display is shown in Figure A.12.

Figure A.12

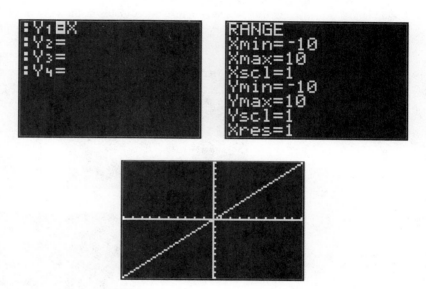

To obtain a different viewing rectangle, you can change the range. Figure A.13 shows the graph of $y = x$ when the range has been changed so that Xmin = 0, Xmax = 100, Ymin = 0, and Ymax = 100. Notice that only the first quadrant is shown in the display.

Figure A.13

Figure A.13 continued

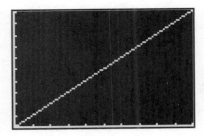

You may move around the rectangle by pressing the arrow keys, or you may move the cursor along the function by first pressing TRACE and then the arrow keys. You will now see *x*- and *y*-coordinates at the bottom of the viewing screen. As you move along the curve, the coordinates on the curve are displayed. Figure A.14 depicts the cursor location on the line $y = x$ as $x = 62.105263$ and $y = 62.105263$.

Figure A.14

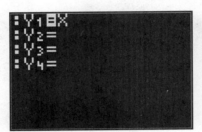 

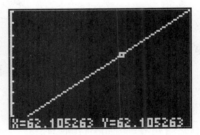

It is often unnecessary to have a degree of accuracy to six decimal places as pictured in Figure A.14. Many times, it is easier to interpret graphs when integers are used as inputs. This can be accomplished by changing the range to the following settings:

$$\text{Xmin} = -48$$
$$\text{Xmax} = 47$$
$$\text{Ymin} = -32$$
$$\text{Ymax} = 31$$

Pressing GRAPH and TRACE will result in only integer values of X used as inputs. The graph appears in Figure A.15.

Figure A.15

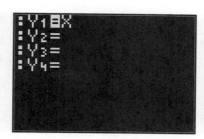 

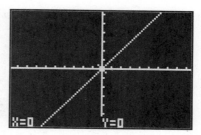

There are many range settings that will result in an integer viewing rectangle. For our purposes here, it is enough to know that in order to get such a rectangle the following range formulas must be used:

$$\text{Xmax} - \text{Xmin} = 95$$

$$\text{Ymax} - \text{Ymin} = 63$$

Figure A.16 depicts three different integer viewing rectangles of the function $y = x$.

Figure A.16

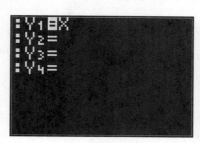 

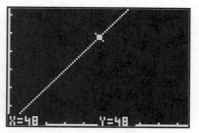

Figure A.16 continued

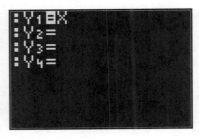

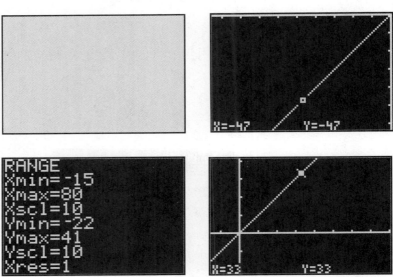

What do all of these settings have in common? We will explore the common elements of these settings in Investigation 6. But first, let's consider another way we can alter the viewing window.

We have shown that changing the range allows you to change the viewing window. You can alter this window in another way by using the $\boxed{\text{ZOOM}}$ commands. One such command is explained here to illustrate the power of this graphing utility.

Suppose we want to determine the point(s) of intersection of the graphs $y = x^3$ and $y = -(x - .5)(x - 2)$. These graphs are entered into the calculator via the $\boxed{\text{Y=}}$ mode as shown in Figure A.17.

Figure A.17

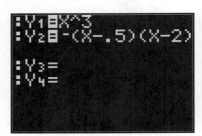 

The graph of the two functions appears to depict a single point of intersection, as shown in Figure A.18.

Figure A.18

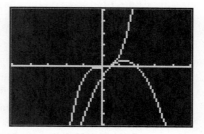

We will use the ZOOM box command to enclose a rectangular region that we wish to zoom in on. Notice that zooming in on the region boxed reveals that the two graphs do not share a point of intersection, as illustrated in Figure A.19.

Figure A.19

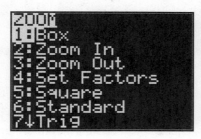

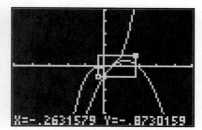

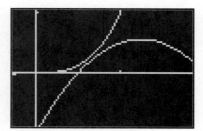

Investigation 6

You have already seen that the equation of a line can be expressed as $y = mx + b$. Investigate what happens in each of the following cases:

(a) b remains fixed, and the slope m is increased.

(b) b remains fixed, and the slope m is decreased.

(c) b remains fixed, and the slope is multiplied by -1.

(d) b remains fixed, and the slope is changed to its negative reciprocal.

Understand the Problem: You are asked to explore the effects that a variety of changes in the values of m have on the equation of a straight line.

Devise a Plan: Use specific cases and the graphics calculator for these explorations.

Carry Out the Plan: We will use the integer viewing rectangle in which Xmin = −48, Xmax = 47, Ymin = −32, and Ymax = 31. We will also use the equation $y = 2x + 10$ as a specific case.

The graphics calculator will display the following graph of $y = 2x + 10$ in the desired integer viewing rectangle.

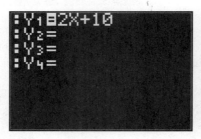
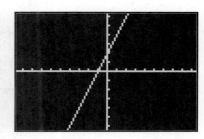

(a) $b = 10$ remains fixed, and the slope, 2, is increased.

We will use the equation $y = 4x + 10$, in which the slope has been doubled. Press ┃ Y= ┃ and enter the new equation in Y_2. When ┃ GRAPH ┃ is pressed, both the original and the new equation will be shown as follows:

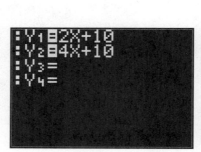
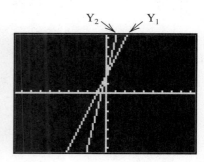

The second graph drawn was $y = 4x + 10$. It intersects the y-axis at $y = 10$, and it is slanted "to the right"; that is, as you move along the line from left to right, the y-values increase. This line appears to have a much steeper slope than $y = 2x + 10$.

(b) b remains fixed, and the slope m is decreased.

We will use the equation $y = x + 10$, in which the slope is half that of the original equation. Press ┃ Y= ┃ and enter the new equation in Y_2. When ┃ GRAPH ┃ is pressed, both the original and the new equation will be shown as follows:

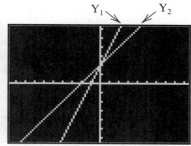

The slope of the second graph is not as steep as that of the original graph. The line $y = x + 10$ intersects the y-axis at 10 but has a more gradual rise to the right than does the original equation.

(c) b remains fixed, and the slope is multiplied by -1.

We will use the equation $y = -2x + 10$. Press [Y=] and enter the new equation in Y_2. When [GRAPH] is pressed, both the original and the new equation will be shown as follows:

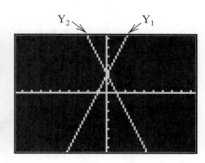

The new graph intersects the y-axis at 10. This graph "slants to the left"; that is, as you move along the line from left to right, the y-values decrease.

(d) b remains fixed, and the slope is changed to its negative reciprocal.

We will use the line $y = -\frac{1}{2}x + 10$. Press [Y=] and enter the new equation in Y_2. When [GRAPH] is pressed, both the original and the new equation will be shown as follows:

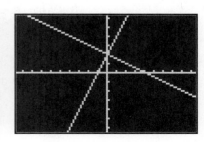

Recall your work from the geometry chapters, Chapters 10–13. Perpendicular lines have slopes that are the negative reciprocal of one another. It is difficult to see from the display that right angles are formed at the point of intersection. This is because the viewing rectangle is just that—a rectangle, not a square. We can compensate for this by pressing the keys | ZOOM | | 5 |, which will regraph both lines as if they were graphed on square-grid graph paper. The new graphs are pictured below.

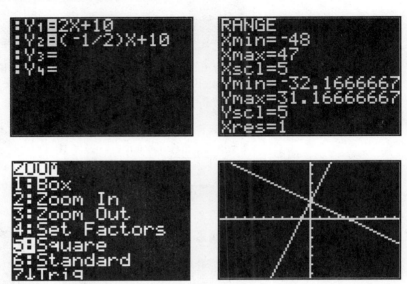

Look Back: Repeat parts (a)–(d) with a variety of other lines. Make some generalizations about the effect that changes in slope have on the graph of a line.

Investigation 7

Examine the general form of a quadratic equation:

$$y = ax^2 + bx + c$$

(a) Describe the graph of quadratics whose a terms are positive.

(b) Describe the graph of quadratics whose a terms are negative.

(c) What conclusions might you draw from these graphs.

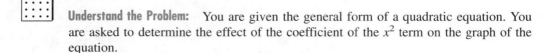

Understand the Problem: You are given the general form of a quadratic equation. You are asked to determine the effect of the coefficient of the x^2 term on the graph of the equation.

Devise a Plan: We will examine some cases by using the graphics calculator.

Carry Out the Plan: The following figure depicts three equations whose a terms are positive.

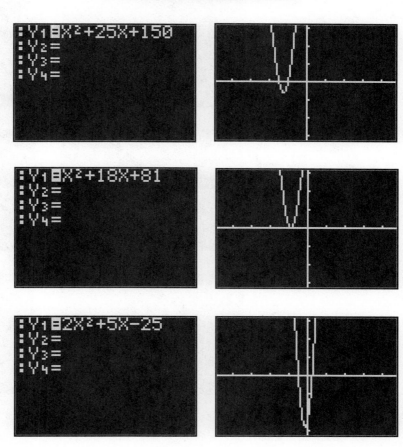

This next figure depicts three equations whose *a* terms are negative.

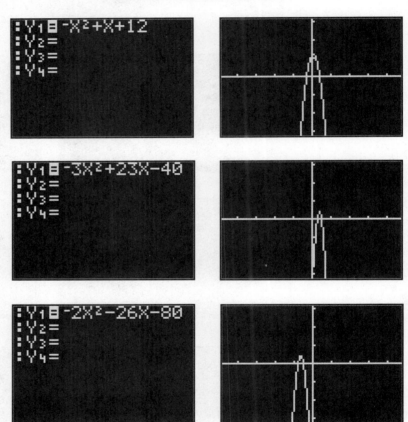

It appears that quadratic equations in which $a > 0$ "open upward," and have a minimum value, and quadratic equations in which $a < 0$ "open downward," and have a maximum value.

Look Back: What is the effect on the graph if $a = 0$?

Investigation 8

Determine a quadratic and a linear equation for each of the following situations:

(a) The graphs intersect at two points.

(b) The graphs intersect at one point.

(c) The graphs do not intersect.

Understand the Problem: You must find values of a, b, and c in $y = ax^2 + bx + c$, and values of m and b in $y = mx + b$, such that the graphs intersect in zero, one, and two points.

Devise a Plan: Use the strategy of trial and error and the graphics calculator to investigate the possibilities.

Carry Out the Plan: Perhaps the easiest situation is that of no points of intersection (c). You have already seen that a quadratic whose a term is positive "opens upward." Therefore, any horizontal line that falls below the minimum value of this quadratic will not intersect it. A similar reasoning can be used for a quadratic that "opens downward." Any horizontal line that is drawn above the maximum value of the quadratic will not intersect it. Some examples follow.

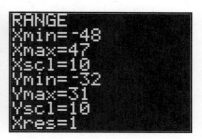

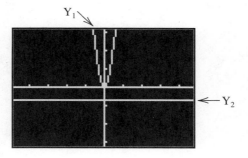

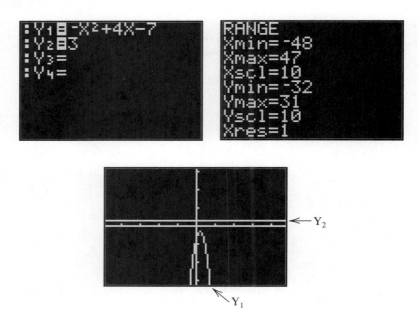

A vertical line will intersect a quadratic at one and only one point. But a vertical line is not a function, since for each x-value there are an infinite number of y-values. This cannot be pictured on the graphics calculator in the way we have described here. Some possibilities (without the aid of the calculator) are shown here.

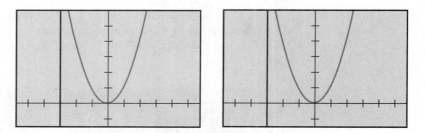

Finally, by trial and error, a variety of linear and quadratic equations can be found whose intersection points are displayed on the graphics calculator view screen. Some examples are given here.

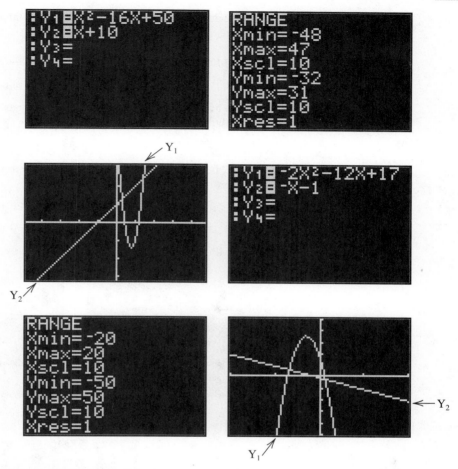

Look Back: Repeat this investigation using two quadratics rather than one quadratic and one linear equation. Find pairs of quadratics that intersect at zero, one, and two points.

Finally, we will examine a graphical approach to a problem that might traditionally have been solved algebraically.

Investigation 10

Julia has 38 dimes and quarters whose value is $6.50. Determine the number of each coin.

Understand the Problem: You are given a number of coins in two denominations and a total value for these coins. You are asked to find the number of each denomination of coin.

Devise a Plan: We will use a variable to set up linear equations and then graph these equations using a graphics calculator.

Carry Out the Plan: Let x represent the number of dimes. Let y represent the number of quarters.

$$x + y = 38 \quad \text{(total number of coins)}$$

The value of all of the coins is $6.50. This is equal to the sum of the values of the dimes and the quarters and can be expressed as

$$.10x + .25y = 6.5$$

In order to use the graphics calculator, it is necessary to write each equation in the form $y =$, as follows:

$$y = -x + 38 \quad \text{and} \quad .25y = -.10x + 6.5$$
$$y = -.4x + 26$$

The following illustrations depict the graphs of these two lines.

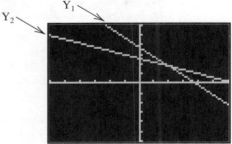

The intersection of these two lines occurs at (20, 18). Therefore, there are 20 dimes and 18 quarters.

Look Back: We leave it to you to solve this algebraically as a system of equations to verify the solution.

This brief introduction to the use of the graphics calculator was meant to arouse your interest. We hope you realize what a powerful tool it really is. The presentation here merely scratched the surface of this calculator's capabilities. Many manuals and workbooks are available for use with graphics calculators. As time goes on, we envision that this tool will become an accepted and welcomed part of mathematics instruction.

Vocabulary for Appendix A

cell	graphics calculator
computer spreadsheet	label
formula	value

Assessments for Appendix A

Each of the following problems can be solved by using the given spreadsheet or a calculator.

1. Suppose you have a total of 100 coins consisting of pennies, nickels, dimes, quarters, and half dollars. The total value of the coins is $13.02. Determine the amount of each type of coin. Is your solution unique? An empty spreadsheet and a spreadsheet with the formulas are given here:

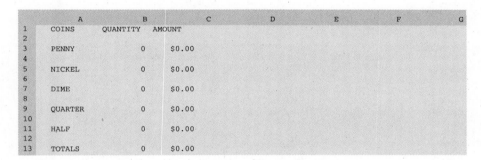

	A	B	C	D	E	F	G
1	COINS	QUANTITY	AMOUNT				
2							
3	PENNY	0	$0.00				
4							
5	NICKEL	0	$0.00				
6							
7	DIME	0	$0.00				
8							
9	QUARTER	0	$0.00				
10							
11	HALF	0	$0.00				
12							
13	TOTALS	0	$0.00				

	A	B	C	D	E	F	G
1	COINS	QUANTITY	AMOUNT				
2							
3	PENNY	0	=0.01*B3				
4							
5	NICKEL	0	=0.05*B5				
6							
7	DIME	0	=0.1*B7				
8							
9	QUARTER	0	=0.25*B9				
10							
11	HALF	0	=0.5*B11				
12							
13	TOTALS	=SUM(B3:B11)	=SUM(C3:C11)				

2. Find a four-digit number that has a remainder of 70 when divided by 99 and a remainder of 7 when divided by 101. An empty spreadsheet and a spreadsheet with formulas are given here:

	A	B	C	D	E	F	G
1							
2							
3							
4	ENTER THE DIGITS UNDER THE APPROPRIATE PLACE VALUE LABLES						
5							
6	THOUSANDS		HUNDREDS		TENS	ONES	
7	0		0		0	0	
8							
9	YOUR NUMBER IS;		0				
10							
11							
12	DIVISORS;			99	101		
13	WHOLE NUMBER PART OF QUOTIENT;			0	0		
14	REMAINDERS;			0	0		
15							
16							
17							
18							

	A	B	C	D	E	F	G
1							
2							
3							
4	ENTER THE DIGITS UNDER THE APPROPRIATE PLACE VALUE LABLES						
5							
6	THOUSANDS		HUNDREDS		TENS	ONES	
7	0		0		0	0	
8							
9	YOUR NUMBER IS;		=(1000*A7)+(100*C7)+(10*E7)+G7				
10							
11							
12	DIVISORS;			99	101		
13	WHOLE NUMBER PART OF QUOTIENT;=INT(C9/D12)				=INT(C9/E12)		
14	REMAINDERS;		=C9-(D13*D12)		=C9-(E13*E12)		
15							
16							
17							
18							

3. Find a six-digit number whose first digit is 1, such that if this 1 is moved to the end of the number, the number is tripled. An empty spreadsheet and a spreadsheet with formulas are given here.

	A	B	C	D	E	F	G
1	FIND A SIX-DIGIT NUMBER WHOSE FIRST DIGIT IS 1,						
2	SUCH THAT IF THIS 1 IS MOVED TO THE						
3	END OF THE NUMBER, THE NUMBER IS TRIPLED.						
4							
5							
6		0	0	0	0	0	0
7							
8	YOUR NUMBER IS;		0				
9							
10	THE REARRANGED NUMBER IS;				0		
11							
12	THE REARRANGED NUMBER IS NOW;			0 TIMES		0	

	A	B	C	D	E	F	G
1	FIND A SIX-DIGIT NUMBER WHOSE FIRST DIGIT IS 1,						
2	SUCH THAT IF THIS 1 IS MOVED TO THE						
3	END OF THE NUMBER, THE NUMBER IS TRIPLED.						
4							
5							
6			0	0	0	0	0	0
7							
8	YOUR NUMBER IS;		=(100000*B6)+(10000*C6)+(1000*D6)+(100*E6)+(10*F6)				
9							
10	THE REARRANGED NUMBER IS;		=(100000*C6)+(10000*D6)+(1000*E6)+(100*F)				
11							
12	THE REARRANGED NUMBER IS NOW: =D10/C8			TIMES	=C8		

4. Determine three three-digit numbers that use all of the digits 1 through 9 only once. The second number must be twice the first number. The third number must be three times the first number. The following spreadsheet sets up ratios between the numbers. The decimal result of these ratios in C13 and G13 will assist you in determining the desired three-digit numbers. A spreadsheet with formulas is also given. (*Note:* Ones have been entered in the first spreadsheet to avoid a division-by-zero error.)

	A	B	C	D	E	F	G
1							
2							
3			HUNDREDS		TENS		ONES
4	FIRST NUMBER		1		1		1
5	SECOND NUMBER		1		1		1
6	THIRD NUMBER		1		1		1
7							
8			FIRST NUMBER		111		
9			SECOND NUMBER		111		
10			THIRD NUMBER		111		
11							
12							
13							
14							
15	FIRST #	111			FIRST #	111	
16	--------	--------- =	1		--------	---------- =	1
17	SECOND #	111			THIRD #	111	

	A	B	C	D	E	F	G
1							
2							
3			HUNDREDS		TENS		ONES
4	FIRST NUMBER		1		1		1
5	SECOND NUMBER		1		1		1
6	THIRD NUMBER		1		1		1
7							
8			FIRST NUMBER		=(100*C4)+(10*E4)+(G4)		
9			SECOND NUMBER		=(100*C5)+(10*E5)+(G5)		
10			THIRD NUMBER		=(100*C6)+(10*E6)+(G6)		
11							
12							
13							
14							
15	FIRST #	=E8			FIRST #	=E8	
16	--------	---------- =	=E8/E9		--------	---------- =	=E8/E10
17	SECOND #	=E9			THIRD #	=E10	

Appendix **B**
Summary of the NCTM
Standards

In 1989, the National Council of Teachers of Mathematics (NCTM) published *The Curriculum and Evaluation Standards for School Mathematics*. This document articulates a philosophy of mathematics education and specifically addresses both curricular and evaluative issues in each of three areas: Grades K–4, Grades 5–8, and Grades 9–12.

The Standards begin by listing five general goals for all students as they study school mathematics. After reading the goals outlined by the NCTM, think about what your goals are for your future students. Are they similar to the five goals contained within *The Standards*?*

1. Students should learn to value mathematics.

2. Students should become confident in their ability to do mathematics.

3. Students should become mathematical problem solvers.

4. Students should learn to communicate mathematically.

5. Students should learn to reason mathematically.

You may have noticed that these goals do not focus on narrow, specific skills, but rather on broad dispositions toward learning mathematics. The aim of these goals is for students to learn to *think* mathematically instead of to learn to perform certain computations. One reason this ability is desirable is the increasing number of powerful and affordable calculators and computers accessible to students today. As students and schools are able to devote less time to purely mechanical tasks, the school mathematics curriculum can be broadened to pay greater attention to such topics as logic, problem solving, number theory, patterns, geometry, measurement, statistics, and probability.

In the 1950s, the mathematics taught in schools and the mathematics needed by professionals were almost one and the same. This is no longer true. The breadth and depth of mathematics needed in the workplace far surpasses what has been previously required. Corporations seek employees who can solve problems both as individuals and in group situations. Nurturing problem-solving abilities must be a primary goal in mathematics education at all levels.

*p. 5, NCTM *Standards*

It is for these and other reasons that the NCTM has included a "Summary of Changes in Content and Emphasis" in K–4 and 5–8 mathematics. These changes can be found on pages 20–21 and 70–73 of *The Standards*. We include them here to highlight the vision of the NCTM as it looks to the future of elementary school education.

The NCTM recognizes that if we are to set new standards in school mathematics, we must also examine the standards we hold for those who are learning to become teachers of mathematics. To this end, in March 1991, the NCTM published *Professional Standards for Teaching Mathematics*. This document focuses on the following five major changes in mathematics education:

1. Toward classrooms as mathematical communities—away from classrooms as simply a collection of individuals.

2. Toward logic and mathematical evidence as verification—away from the teacher as the sole authority for right answers.

3. Toward mathematical reasoning—away from merely memorizing procedures.

4. Toward conjecturing, inventing, and problem solving—away from an emphasis on mechanistic answer-finding.

5. Toward connecting mathematics, its ideas, and its applications—away from treating mathematics as a body of isolated concepts and procedures.[*]

As you enter the ranks of teachers of mathematics, it is our hope that you will carry the spirit of the *Curriculum Standards* and the *Professional Standards* with you.

Summary of Changes in Content and Emphasis in K–4 Mathematics

Increased Attention

Number

- Number sense
- Place-value concepts
- Meaning of fractions and decimals
- Estimation of quantities

Operations and Computation

- Meaning of operations
- Operation sense
- Mental computation
- Estimation and the reasonableness of answers
- Selection of an appropriate computational method

[*]p. 3, NCTM *Standards*

- Use of calculators for complex computation
- Thinking strategies for basic facts

Geometry and Measurement

- Properties of geometric figures
- Geometric relationships
- Spatial sense
- Process of measuring
- Concepts related to units of measurement
- Actual measuring
- Estimation of measurements
- Use of measurement and geometry ideas throughout the curriculum

Probability and Statistics

- Collection and organization of data
- Exploration of chance

Patterns and Relationships

- Pattern recognition and description
- Use of variables to express relationships

Problem Solving

- Word problems with a variety of structures
- Use of everyday problems
- Applications
- Study of patterns and relationships
- Problem-solving strategies

Instructional Practices

- Use of manipulative materials
- Cooperative work
- Discussion of mathematics
- Questioning
- Justification of thinking
- Writing about mathematics
- Problem-solving approach to instruction
- Content integration
- Use of calculators and computers

Decreased Attention

Number

- Early attention to reading, writing, and ordering numbers symbolically

Operations and Computation

- Complex paper-and-pencil computations
- Isolated treatment of paper-and-pencil computations
- Addition and subtraction without renaming
- Isolated treatment of division facts
- Long division
- Long division without remainders
- Paper-and-pencil fraction computation
- Use of rounding to estimate

Geometry and Measurement

- Primary focus on naming geometric figures
- Memorization of equivalencies between units of measurement

Problem Solving

- Use of clue words to determine which operation to use

Instructional Practices

- Rote practice
- Rote memorization of rules
- One answer and one method
- Use of worksheets
- Written practice
- Teaching by telling

Summary of Changes in Content and Emphasis in 5–8 Mathematics

Increased Attention

Problem Solving

- Pursuing open-ended problems and extended problem-solving projects
- Investigating and formulating questions from problem situations
- Representing situations verbally, numerically, graphically, geometrically, or symbolically

Communication

- Discussing, writing, reading, and listening to mathematical ideas

Reasoning

- Reasoning in spatial contexts
- Reasoning with proportions
- Reasoning from graphs
- Reasoning inductively and deductively

Connections

- Connecting mathematics to other subjects and to the world outside the classroom
- Connecting topics within mathematics
- Applying mathematics

Number/Operations/Computation

- Developing number sense
- Developing operation sense
- Creating algorithms and procedures
- Using estimation both in solving problems and in checking the reasonableness of results
- Exploring relationships among representations of, and operations on, whole numbers, fractions, decimals, integers, and rational numbers
- Developing an understanding of ratio, proportion, and percent

Patterns and Functions

- Identifying and using functional relationships
- Developing and using tables, graphs, and rules to describe situations
- Interpreting among different mathematical representations

Algebra

- Developing an understanding of variables, expressions, and equations
- Using a variety of methods to solve linear equations and informally investigate inequalities and nonlinear equations

Statistics

- Using statistical methods to describe, analyze, evaluate, and make decisions

Probability

- Creating experimental and theoretical models of situations involving probabilities

Geometry

- Developing an understanding of geometric objects and relationships
- Using geometry in solving problems

Measurement

- Estimating and using measurement to solve problems

Instructional Practices

- Actively involving students individually and in groups in exploring, conjecturing, analyzing, and applying mathematics in both a mathematical and a real-world context
- Using appropriate technology for computation and exploration
- Using concrete materials
- Being a facilitator of learning
- Assessing learning as an integral part of instruction

Decreased Attention

Problem Solving

- Practicing routine, one-step problems
- Practicing problems categorized by types (e.g., coin problems, age problems)

Communication

- Doing fill-in-the-blank worksheets
- Answering questions that require only yes, no, or a number as responses

Reasoning

- Relying on outside authority (teacher or an answer key)

Connections

- Learning isolated topics
- Developing skills out of context

Number/Operations/Computation

- Memorizing rules and algorithms
- Practicing tedious paper-and-pencil computations
- Finding exact forms of answers
- Memorizing procedures, such as cross-multiplication, without understanding
- Practicing rounding numbers out of context

Patterns and Functions

- Topics seldom in the current curriculum

Algebra

- Manipulating symbols
- Memorizing procedures and drilling on equation solving

Statistics

- Memorizing formulas

Probability

- Memorizing formulas

Geometry

- Memorizing geometric vocabulary
- Memorizing facts and relationships

Measurement

- Memorizing and manipulating formulas
- Converting within and between measurement systems

Instructional Practices

- Teaching computations out of context
- Drilling on paper-and-pencil algorithms
- Teaching topics in isolation
- Stressing memorization
- Being the dispenser of knowledge
- Testing for the sole purpose of assigning grades

Answers to Selected Assessments

CHAPTER 1
SECTION 1.1 Patterns (p. 11)

1. (a)   (b)

2. (a)   (b) ♀ ♀
                              ♀ ♀

3. (a) Ш (b)

4. Answers will vary.

5. Answers will vary.

7. Answers will vary. Some possibilities are Georgetown, Galveston, or Gainesville.

9. (a) E N T

11. (b), (d), and (e)

14. Answers will vary. Some possibilities are *ABC*, *DBE*, *ECF*, and *GDH*.

17. (a) B, C, D, E, H, I, K, O, X
    (b) A, H, I, M, O, T, U, V, W, X, Y

19. (a) Vertical, rotational, horizontal, diagonal
    (b) Vertical
    (c) Vertical, horizontal, rotational

20. (a) Horizontal, vertical, rotational
    (b) Asymmetric

22. (a)

23. (d)

25. (e)

27. (c)

29. (e)

33. (c)

35. (b)

37. (b)

39. (a)

SECTION 1.2 Identifying Relationships: The Study of Sets (p. 22)

1. Some answers will vary.
   (a) {Alabama, Alaska, Arizona, Arkansas}
   (b) {red, yellow, blue}

2. (a) School subjects
   (b) Seasons of the year

3. (a) Ø, {a, b, c}, {a}, {b}, {c}, {a, b}, {a, c}, {b, c}
   (b) Ø, {100, 200, 300, 400}, {100}, {200}, {300}, {400}, {100, 200}, {100, 300}, {100, 400}, {200, 300}, {200, 400}, {300, 400}, {100, 200, 300}, {100, 200, 400}, {200, 300, 400}, {100, 300, 400}

4. Answers will vary.
   (a) Set of border states, set of southern states, set of states in the central time zone

5. (a) {2, 4, 6, 8, 10, 12, 14}
   (b) {0, 2, 4, 6, 8, 10, 12, 14, 16, 18}
   (c) {0, 2, 4, 6, 8, 10, 12, 14, 16, 18}
   (g) {0, 12, 14, 16, 18}

6. (a)   (b)
   (c)   (g)

7. *A* = {Florida, Georgia, South Carolina, North Carolina, Virginia, New Jersey, New York, Connecticut, Rhode Island, Massachusetts, New Hampshire, Maine, Alabama, Mississippi, Louisiana, Texas, California, Oregon, Washington, Maryland, Delaware}

   B = {Washington, Idaho, Montana, North Dakota, Minnesota, Wisconsin, Michigan, Ohio, Pennsylvania, New York, Vermont, New Hampshire, Maine, Indiana, Illinois}

C = {Pennsylvania, New York, Delaware, Connecticut, Virginia, Massachusetts, New Hampshire, Maryland, New Jersey, Georgia, North Carolina, South Carolina, Rhode Island}

(a) {Florida, South Carolina, North Carolina, Virginia, New Jersey, New York, Connecticut, Rhode Island, Massachusetts, New Hampshire, Maine, Alabama, Mississippi, Louisiana, Texas, California, Oregon, Washington, Idaho, Montana, North Dakota, Minnesota, Wisconsin, Michigan, Ohio, Pennsylvania, Vermont, Georgia, Maryland, Delaware, Illinois, Indiana}

(b) {Florida, South Carolina, North Carolina, Virginia, New Jersey, New York, Connecticut, Rhode Island, Massachusetts, New Hampshire, Maine, Alabama, Mississippi, Louisiana, Texas, California, Oregon, Washington, Pennsylvania, Delaware, Maryland, Georgia}

(c) {Washington, Idaho, Montana, North Dakota, Minnesota, Wisconsin, Michigan, Ohio, Pennsylvania, New York, Vermont, New Hampshire, Maine, Delaware, Connecticut, Virginia, Massachusetts, New Hampshire, Maryland, New Jersey, Georgia, North Carolina, South Carolina, Rhode Island, Illinois, Indiana}

(g) {Pennsylvania}

8. (a) **(b)**

(c) **(g)**

9. (a) {h, i, j}
(b) {$a, c, e, f, g, h, i, j, l, m, n$}
(c) {$a, b, c, d, e, f, g, h, i, j$}

10. (a) **(b)**

(c)

11. Answers will vary. Some possibilities follow.
(a) A = {a, b, d} B = {a, b, e} C = {c}
(b) A = {d, e} B = {f} C = {g}

13. 1: Only CD
2: Only CD and stereo
3: Only stereo
4: Only CD and VCR
5: All three
6: Only stereo and VCR
7: Only VCR

SECTION 1.3 Elementary Logic (p. 38)
1. (a) ($\sim q$)
(b) ($\sim p$)
(c) ($p \rightarrow q$)

2. (a) $\sim r$ **(b)** $\sim q$ **(c)** $p \land q$

3. (a) $p \land q$
(c) $q \rightarrow p$
(e) $\sim q$
(h) $(q \land p) \rightarrow q$

4. (a) $p \land q$ **(c)** $\sim p$ **(e)** $(p \land r) \rightarrow q$

5. (a) You cannot ride the A train.
(c) You can ride the A train and you have a token.
(f) If you do not have a token, then you cannot ride the A train.

6. (a) You hire a typist for your paper.
(c) You purchase a computer and you purchase word processing software.
(f) If you do not purchase word processing software, then you do not purchase a computer.

8. (a) If it is Friday evening, then the phone answering machine is on. It is Friday evening. Then, the phone answering machine is on. $[(p \rightarrow q) \land p] \rightarrow q$
(b) If it is Friday evening, then the phone answering machine is on. The phone answering machine is not on. Then, it is not Friday evening. $[(p \rightarrow q) \land \sim q] \rightarrow \sim p$
(c) If it is Friday evening, then the phone answering machine is on. If the phone answering machine is on, then he is at the airport. Then, if it is Friday evening, he is at the airport. $[(p \rightarrow q) \land (q \rightarrow r)] \rightarrow (p \rightarrow r)$

10. (b)

p	q	$\sim q$	$p \to \sim q$
T	T	F	F
T	F	T	T
F	T	F	T
F	F	T	T

(d)

p	q	$\sim p$	$\sim q$	$p \wedge \sim q$	$q \wedge \sim p$	$(p \wedge \sim q) \vee (q \wedge \sim p)$
T	T	F	F	F	F	F
T	F	F	T	T	F	T
F	T	T	F	F	T	T
F	F	T	T	F	F	F

12.

p	q	$\sim p$	$\sim q$	$p \vee q$	$(p \vee q) \wedge \sim q$	$[(p \vee q) \wedge \sim q] \to p$
T	T	F	F	T	F	T
T	F	F	T	T	T	T
F	T	T	F	T	F	T
F	F	T	T	F	F	T

The compound sentence is a tautology.

14. (a) Valid   **(b)** Valid   **(c)** Valid

16. (a) I will type the report.

17. (a) Danielle will go to the doctor's office.

    (b) There is money in Laura's checking account.

CHAPTER 1 Review (p. 41)

1. (a)   **(b)**

2. (a) ◈ □ ◈   **(b)** P

3. (a) ◇   **(b)** ◖

4. (a)   **(b)** ○—▢

5. (a) *ABHG*, *BCDH*, *DEGH*, *FEGA*

    (b) *ABFE*, *BCGF*, *CDHG*, etc.

7. Answers will vary.

12. (a) POUT   **(d)**

13. (a) ✕   **(b)** ✡

14. (a) b   **(b)** a

15. (a) {10, 15, 20, 25, 30, 35, 40, 45, 50, 55, 60, 65}

    (c) {5, 10, 15, 20, 25, 30, 35, 40, 45, 50, 55, 60, 65}

    (e) {15, 25, 35, 45, 55, 65}

16. (a)   **(c)**

$A \cup B$ $B \cup C$

    (e)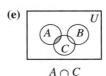

$A \cap C$

17. (b) {$R, T, W, G, B, D, C, E, F$}

    (d) {R, T, G}

    (e) {G, B, D}

21. (a) Exclusive "or"   **(b)** Inclusive "or"

22.

	Converse	*Inverse*	*Contrapositive*
(a)	$\sim q \to p$	$\sim p \to q$	$q \to \sim p$
(b)	$p \to q$	$\sim q \to \sim p$	$\sim p \to \sim q$

25. (a) The number 246829856 cannot be displayed on my calculator.

    (b) No conclusion can be drawn.

    (c) Jesse does not go to the movies with Ally.

CHAPTER 2

SECTION 2.1 Numeration Systems (p. 58)

1.

	Egyptian	*Roman*	*Hindu-Arabic*
(a)	‖‖ ∩ 99 ⌒⌒ / 99 ⌒⌒	$\overline{\text{XX}}$CDXV	20,415
(b)	‖‖ ∩∩∩∩∩ 999 / ∩∩∩∩ 99	DXCV	595

2. (a) *Egyptian*

, then

Roman
$\overline{\text{CDXXX}}\overline{\text{V}}\text{CCXVI}$

Hindu-Arabic
435,216

3. (a) >   **(b)** <

4. (a) 25,025   **(b)** 617,033,200

5. (a) Seven hundred ninety-seven

   (b) One thousand, three hundred twenty-six

6. (a) Twenty million, ten thousand, six

   (b) Thirty-four billion, seven hundred eight million, two hundred ninety-six thousand, fifteen

9. $\text{CXVI}(116)$, $\text{CXIV}(114)$, $\text{XCVI}(96)$, $\text{XCIV}(94)$, $\overline{\text{C}}\text{XVI}(100,016)$, $\overline{\text{CX}}\text{VI}(110,006)$, $\overline{\text{CXV}}\text{I}(115,001)$, $\overline{\text{CXVI}}(116,000)$, $\overline{\text{CXI}}\text{V}(100,014)$, $\overline{\text{CXI}}\text{V}(110,004)$, $\overline{\text{CXI}}\text{V}(111,005)$, $\overline{\text{CXIV}}(114,000)$, $\overline{\text{X}}\text{CVI}(10,106)$, $\overline{\text{XC}}\text{VI}(90,006)$, $\overline{\text{XCV}}\text{I}(95,001)$, $\overline{\text{XCVI}}(96,000)$, $\overline{\text{X}}\text{CIV}(10,104)$, $\overline{\text{XC}}\text{IV}(90,004)$, $\overline{\text{XCI}}\text{V}(91,005)$, $\overline{\text{XCIV}}(94,000)$.

11. (a) 7   **(b)** 23

12. (a)

Red	White	Blue
•	•	
•	•	

(b)

Red	White	Blue
	•	
	•	
	•	

(c)

Green	Red	White	Blue
•			•

(d)

Red	White	Blue
•	•	•
•	•	•
		•

14. (a)

Green	Red	White	Blue
•	•	•	•
•			

15. (a) $(2 \times 10^3) + (7 \times 10^1) + (5 \times 10^0)$
      $(2 \times 1000) + (7 \times 10) + (5 \times 1)$

   (b) $(3 \times 10^2) + (6 \times 10^0)$
      $(3 \times 100) + (6 \times 1)$

16. (a) $(3 \times 10^3) + (4 \times 10^1) + (2 \times 10^0)$
      $(3 \times 1000) + (4 \times 10) + (2 \times 1)$

   (b) $(1 \times 10^4) + (8 \times 10^3) + (1 \times 10^0)$
      $(1 \times 10,000) + (8 \times 1000) + (1)$

17. (a) 3062   **(b)** 5788

18. (a) 493   **(b)** 10,871

20. Answer for first part is: 25×10^7. Answer for second part is: $(n + 18) \times 10^n$ for $n = 0, 1, 2, 3, \ldots$

23. Answers will vary. One possibility is 321,123.

SECTION 2.2   The Calculator as an Instructional Tool (p. 68)

1. (a) Yes   **(b)** Yes

2. (a) No   **(b)** Yes

3. (a) | AC | 6 | + | 5 | = | = | = | = | = |

   (b) | AC | 3 | × | 2 | = | = | = | = | = |

4. (a) | AC | 2 | × | 8 | = | = | = | = | = |

   (b) | AC | 307 | – | 10 | = | = | = | = | = |

5. (a) | AC | 52 | × | 43 | = | 2236

   (b) | AC | 432 | × | 5 | = | 2160

6. (a) | 96 | × | 87 | = | 8352

   (b) | 96 | + | 87 | = | 183

7. (a) Yes   **(b)** Yes

10. | AC | 100 | – | 10 | = | = | = | = | – | 1
   | = | = | (14 keys)

12. 1188, 2277, 3366, 4455, 5544 $99 \times 89 = 8811$

15. (a) | AC | 321 | + | 50 | = |

   (b) | AC | 1095 | – | 50 | = |

(c) [AC] 5715 [−] 710 [=]

(d) [AC] 8463 [−] 4000 [+] 400 [=]

(or [AC] 8463 [−] 3600 [=])

(e) [AC] 10825 [+] 8000 [−] 800 [=]

(or [AC] 10825 [+] 7200 [=])

18. (a) 10042_{five} **(b)** 3031_{five}

19. (a) 1001000_{two} **(b)** 11010_{three}

20. (a) 145_{eight} **(b)** 101101_{two}

23. (a) 77   **(b)** 84   **(c)** 77   **(d)** 2123   **(e)** 6126

26. 4320_{five} (585), 4032_{five} (517)

CHAPTER 2 Review (p. 71)

1.

| | *Egyptian* | *Roman* | *Hindu-Arabic* |

(a) ‖‖‖‖‖ ‖‖‖‖ 𓏢𓏢𓏢𓏢𓏢𓏢 𓂆 $\overline{\text{XV}}\text{IIX}$ 16,009

(b) ‖‖‖‖ ‖‖‖‖ ∩∩∩ 999 𓏢𓏢𓏢𓏢 $\overline{\text{IV}}\text{CCCXXXVIII}$ 4338

2. (a) CMI   CMIX   CMXI   MCI   MCIX   MCXI

3. (a) True   **(b)** True

4. (a) Nine hundred twenty-one

(b) Eleven thousand, one hundred eleven

6. (a) 16

7. (a) 28: three reds, zero whites, and one blue

8. (a)

Orange	Green	Red	White	Blue
		• •		

(b)

Orange	Green	Red	White	Blue
	•			

9. (a) $(8 \times 10^2) + (2 \times 10^1) + (1 \times 10^0)$
$(8 \times 100) + (2 \times 10) + (1 \times 1)$

(b) $(2 \times 10^3) + (5 \times 10^2) + (4 \times 10^1) + (3 \times 10^0)$
$(2 \times 1000) + (5 \times 100) + (4 \times 10) + (3 \times 1)$

10. (a) 84,213   **(b)** 6,040,209

12. (a) 64   **(b)** 43

14. (a) Yes   **(b)** No   **(c)** Yes   **(d)** No   **(e)** No

15. (a) [AC] 3 [×] [=] [=] [=]

(b) [AC] 2 [×] [=] [=] [=] [=] [=]

17. (a) [AC] 5 [×] 8 [−] 7 [+] 6 [=]

(b) [AC] 7 [+] 8 [=] [−] 5 [=] [×] 6 [=]

20. (a) 5 [×] 4 [−] 6

(b) 900 [÷] 3 [+] 100

22. 36

25. (a) Answers will vary.

(b) 18 correct, 5 wrong, 2 left blank = 64 points

CHAPTER 3

SECTION 3.1 Models and Properties of Whole Number Addition and Subtraction (p. 83)

1. (a) 9   **(b)** 4   **(f)** 4

2. (a) 9   **(d)** 9   **(h)** 5

3. (a) No   **(b)** Yes

5. (a)

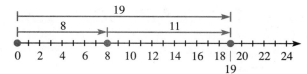

(b)

6. (a) No   **(b)** No

7. (a) Commutative   **(d)** Identity

8. Answers will vary using the commutative and associative properties.

9. (a)

(b)
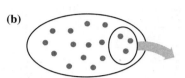

10. (a)
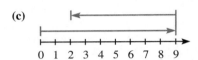

(c)
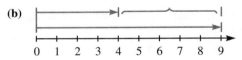

11. (a)
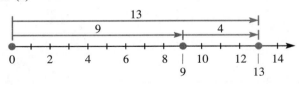

(b)
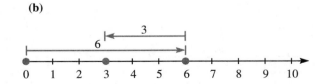

12. (a)

(b)
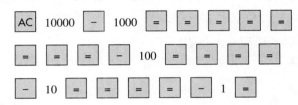

(c)

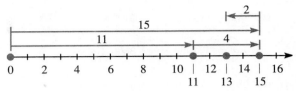

15. Answers may vary.

2	7	6
9	5	1
4	3	8

17. Answers may vary. One possibility is

| AC | 10000 | − | 1000 | = | = | = | = | = |

| = | = | = | − | 100 | = | = | = | = |

| − | 10 | = | = | = | = | = | − | 1 | = |

20. 47, 13

22. (a) 915   **(b)** 795   **(c)** 359
    (d) 4508   **(e)** 34,650

23. (a) 795   **(b)** 1320   **(c)** 2429   **(d)** 1758
    (e) 1132   **(f)** 1313   **(g)** 270   **(h)** 370

25. (a) No
    (b) After the first term, each term is the sum of the two preceding terms.
    (c) The differences after the first two terms generate the sequence itself.

SECTION 3.2 Algorithms for Whole Number Addition and Subtraction (p. 103)

1. Estimates will vary. Actual sums are
    (a) 281   **(b)** 247

2. Estimates will vary. Actual sums are
    (a) 1821   **(b)** 1372

3. Estimates will vary. Actual sums are
    (a) 13,652   **(b)** 16,928

4. Estimates will vary. Actual differences are
   (a) 2459   **(b)** 2535

7. (a) $263 =$ $200 + 60 + 3$
   $\underline{+ 1894} = 1000 +\ \ 800 +\ \ 90 + 4$
   $\qquad\qquad 1000 + 1000 + 150 + 7 = 2157$

   (b) $1742 = 1000 +\ \ 700 +\ \ 40 + 2$
   $\underline{+\ \ 695} =$ $600 +\ \ 90 + 5$
   $\qquad\qquad 1000 + 1300 + 130 + 7 = 2437$

8. (a)
```
    3  8  4
 +  2  9  7
  ⁰⁄5 ¹⁄7 ¹⁄1
    6  8  1
```
   (b)
```
    1  6  1  7
       2  6  3
 +     4  8  9
  ⁰⁄1 ¹⁄2 ¹⁄5 ¹⁄9
    2  3  6  9
```

9. (a)
```
     324
 +   789
      13
     100
 +  1000
    1113
```
   (b)
```
     677
 +   342
       9
     110
 +   900
    1019
```

10. (a)
```
   7 ¹2 ¹1 ¹3
 - 2  6  7  5
   3  7  8
   4  5  3  8
```
   (b)
```
   2 ¹3  9 ¹1
 - 1  5  8  5
      2  9
         8  0  6
```

11. (a)
```
    1583
 -  1296
       4
     200
 +    83
     287
```
   (b)
```
     743
 -   165
       5
      30
     500
 +    43
     578
```

12. Answers will vary.

13. (a) 28, 36, 45
   (b) 13, 21, 34

15. $A = 0, B = 2, C = 3, D = 6$

18. Answers will vary. Some possibilities are:

$$9 \div 9 + \frac{9}{9} \qquad \text{or} \qquad \frac{9}{9} + \frac{9}{9}$$

20. (a) If a base six number ends in a 2, 4, or 0, it has an even base ten equivalent.
   (b) If the sum of the base three digits are even base ten numbers, the number has an even base ten equivalent.

23. (a) When adding 6 and 8, the student puts the tens digit down and regroups with the ones digit (4). The student then adds 4 + 2 + 1 to get 7 in the tens place of the answer.

24. (a) The student subtracts the minuend from the subtrahend in the ones place.

26. (a) Four applicants will be called back.
   (b) Three failed both tests.
   (c) Thirteen females are not willing to relocate.

28. (a) 11000_{two} **(b)** 10121_{three}

29. (a) 1110_{two} **(b)** 1120_{three}

CHAPTER 3 Review (p. 107)

1. (a) $3 + 4 = 7$
   (c) $7 - 3 = 4$

2. (a) 8   **(f)** 3   **(i)** 8

3. (a) 5   **(e)** 4   **(h)** 3   **(k)** 18

5. Answers will vary. Since the sets are disjoint, the number of elements in the union of the sets is equal to the sum of the number of elements in each of the sets.

7. Set X is closed under addition since all sums are in X. Set X is not commutative since the order of the addends affects the sum. Set X is not associative since changing the groups changes the sum.

9. (a)

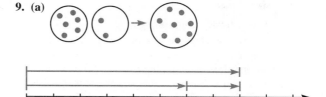

   (h)

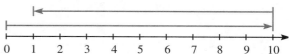

11. Answers will vary. Some possibilities are
   (a) $289 - 189$
   (c) $20 - 10 - 10$
   (e) $2 + 4 + 6$

19.

40	5	30
15	25	35
20	45	10

22. 3, 7, 11, 12, 15, 16, 20, 21, 25, 30

25. $A = 6, B = 7, C = 2$

29. 14, 15, 16, 17, 18

31. $A = 2, B = 9, C = 7, D = 8, E = 3, F = 0, G = 1, H = 2$

32. Erin is 12, Sara is 16, and Ally is 18.

CHAPTER 4

SECTION 4.1 Models and Properties of Whole Number Multiplication and Division (p. 123)

2. (c) Closed   **(f)** Closed   **(i)** Open

4. Answers may vary. Some possibilities follow.
  (a) $(70 + 9) \times 3 = (70 \times 3) + (9 \times 3)$
  (c) $(10 + 6) \times 35 = (10 \times 35) + (6 \times 35)$

6. (a) 0   **(b)** 1

8. 4,764,954,699. You also could have multiplied 95,301 × 50,000 and then subtracted 95,301.

10. Answers will vary. Some possibilities follow.
  (a) Twenty-four cookies need to be shared equally among six children.

12. Answers will vary. Some possibilities follow.
  (a) A popular rock group was having a concert. The tickets were going on sale May 5. One hundred twenty-five people camped out in line on May 2. Each day for the next 3 days, the total number of people in line was double the number from the previous day. How many people were waiting in line when the tickets went on sale May 5?
  (b) Three hundred students are to be interviewed for admission into a special program. They are separated equally among five large waiting areas. Students are called for the interview in groups of five. How many interview calls will there be per waiting area?

14. (a) True
  (b) False: $2 + (3 \cdot 4) \neq (2 + 3) \cdot (2 + 4)$
  (c) True

16. (a) 43,441,281   **(b)** 17,294,403   **(f)** 6   **(h)** 14

17. (a) 16,380   **(d)** 9372

19. Five bookcases containing three shelves, six bookcases containing four shelves, and eight bookcases containing five shelves.

SECTION 4.2 Algorithms for Whole Number Multiplication and Division (p. 136)

1. The actual products follow.
  (a) 92,520
  (b) 5,929,560

2. (a) 21   **(b)** 15

3. (a) 56   **(b)** 159

4. (a) 21   **(b)** 74

5. (a) 6154

6.

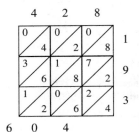

  (a) 82,604

7.

27	34
13	68
~~6~~	~~136~~
3	272
1	+ 544
	918

  (a) 918

8.

23	1 √
46	2 √
92	4
184	8 √
253	11

  (a) 11

9.

$$
42 \overline{)\,21{,}252} \qquad 500
$$
$$
\underline{-21{,}000}
$$
$$
252 \qquad 5
$$
$$
\underline{-210}
$$
$$
42 \qquad 1
$$
$$
\underline{-42} \qquad +
$$
$$
0 \qquad 506
$$

  (a) 506

11. 1444 and 1446

13. (a)

$$
\begin{array}{r}
327 \\
\times\,918 \\
\hline
2616 \\
327 \\
2943 \\
\hline
300186
\end{array}
$$

15. No pencils will be left over.

   (a) Division by 4 could be done manually, and the final 0 in the quotient deleted.

   (b) $[632,675,000 + 280] \div 40 = [(632,675 \times 1000) \div 40] + [280 \div 40] = 15,816,882$ boxes

17. (a)

   (b) Yes,

19. $A = 2, B = 3, C = 5, D = 0$

SECTION 4.3 Number Theory in the Context of Multiplication and Division: Primes, Composites, and Divisibility (p. 153)

1. (a) Divides, is a factor of, is not a multiple of, is not divisible by

   (b) Is a multiple of, is divisible by, is not a factor of, does not divide

   (c) Same as part (b)

   (d) Is not a factor of, is not a multiple of, does not divide, is not divisible by

2. Nine different arrangements are possible:

   $$1 \times 36 \quad 36 \times 1 \quad 2 \times 18 \quad 18 \times 2 \quad 3 \times 12$$
   $$12 \times 3 \quad 4 \times 9 \quad 9 \times 4 \quad 6 \times 6$$

   Factors: 1, 2, 3, 4, 6, 9, 12, 18, 36

4. (a) $60 = 2^2 \times 3 \times 5$

   (b) $144 = 2^4 \times 3^2$

5. (a) $2^2 \times 3 \times 5^2 = 300$

   (b) $2 \times 3^4 \times 7^2 = 7938$

6. (a) $A = 5, B = 3$

7. (a) $\{1, 2, 3, 5, 6, 10, 15, 30\}$

   (b) $\{1, 19\}$

8. (a) 720   **(b)** 2700

9. (a) Y^8 **(b)** A^{14} **(c)** B^9

10. (a) 243   **(b)** 1024

11. (a) 2, 4, 5, 8, 10

   (b) None

12. (a) Divisible by 7   **(b)** Not divisible by 7

13. (a) Not divisible by 11   **(b)** Not divisible by 11

14. Since $15 = 3 \times 5$, the number must have a 5 or 0 in the ones place, and the sum of the digits must be divisible by 3.

   (a) Divisible by 15   **(b)** Divisible by 15

15. (a) $101^{10201}\left((n + 1)^{(n + 1)^2}\right)$ for $n = 100$

   (b) 39,916,800. Multiply the first term by 3 to get the second term; multiply the second term by 4 to get the third term; multiply the third term by 5 to get the fourth term; and so on.

17. (a) $A \cap B = \{10, 20, 30, 40, 50\}$

   $A \cup B = \{5, 10, 15, 20, 25, 30, 35, 40, 45, 50, 60, 70, 80, 90\}$

   (b) $A \cap B = \{6, 12\}$

   $A \cup B = \{2, 3, 4, 6, 8, 9, 10, 12, 14, 15, 16, 18\}$

   (e) $A \cap B = \{2^2, 2^4, 2^6, 2^8, 2^{10}\}$

   $A \cup B = \{2^1, 2^2, 2^3, \ldots, 2^{10}, 4^3, \ldots, 4^{10}\}$

19. (a) No, since 15 evens = even, 3 odds = odd, even + odd = odd.

   (b) Yes, since 8 evens = even, 8 odds = even, even + even = even.

21. 144, 240, 246, 342, 348, 444, 540, 546, 642, 648, 744, 840, 942, 948

23. Since $0 + 1 + 2 + 3 + 4 + 5 + 6 + 7 + 8 + 9 = 45$, $3 \mid 45$ and $9 \mid 45$, the number is divisible by 3 and 9 and therefore not prime.

25. Two possibilities are 264 and 624.

27. $26,400

SECTION 4.4 Making Connections: Relations and Relationships (p. 172)

1. (a) {(Chou, Chou), (Chou, Toscano), (Chou, Gerver), (Chou, Trolio), (Toscano, Toscano), (Toscano, Chou), (Toscano, Gerver), (Toscano, Trolio), (Gerver, Gerver), (Gerver, Chou), (Gerver, Toscano), (Gerver, Trolio), (Trolio, Trolio), (Trolio, Chou), (Trolio, Toscano), (Trolio, Gerver)}

   (b) {(201, 101), (301, 201), (202, 102), (302, 202), (203, 103), (303, 203), (204, 104), (304, 204)}

2. (a) R = "is three times" {(54, 18), (18, 6), (6, 2)}

   (b) R = "is a factor of" {(3, 24), (3, 12), (4, 24), (4, 12), (12, 24)}

3. Answers may vary. Ordered pairs are listed below.

   (a) $\{(A, B), (A, C), (A, D)\}$

4. (a) {(3, 6), (3, 9), (3, 21), (7, 21), (11, 22)}

   (b) {(3, 6), (3, 9), (3, 21), (4, 16), (4, 20), (7, 21), (11, 22)}

5. (b), (c) are symmetric.

6. Answers will vary. Some possibilities follow.

"lives in the same neighborhood as"
"is the same age as"
"sits at the same table as"
"is paid the same hourly wage as"

9. Answers will vary. One possibile trace is $E \to C \to F \to A \to D \to B$.

10. Factors of 36 = {1, 2, 3, 4, 6, 9, 12, 18, 36}

{(36, 36), (36, 18), (36, 12), (36, 9), (36, 6), (36, 4), (36, 3), (36, 2), (36, 1),
(18, 18), (18, 9), (18, 6), (18, 3), (18, 2), (18, 1),
(12, 12), (12, 6), (12, 4), (12, 3), (12, 2), (12, 1),
(9, 9), (9, 3), (9, 1),
(6, 6), (6, 3), (6, 2), (6, 1),
(4, 4), (4, 2), (4, 1),
(3, 3), (3, 1),
(2, 2), (2, 1),
(1, 1)}

This is not an equivalence relation. The symmetric property does not hold.

13. (a) a is four times b

(b) a is one more than twice b

14. (a) Function: "is eight more than" or "decreased by eight is"

(b) Domain: 16, 6, 66

17. {(0, 36), (1, 35), (2, 32), (3, 27), (4, 20), (5, 11), (6, 0)}

19. (a) A number is multiplied by 5, then the output is decreased by 5.

(b) A number is decreased by 5, and the output is multiplied by 5.

(c) A number is decreased by 5, and the output is multiplied by 5.

(d) A number is multiplied by 5, and the output is decreased by 5.

(e) 45

20. (a) F raised the input to the fifth power. G takes the output of F and squares it. [$(G \circ F)(4)$]

21. (a) 109   (b) 119

22. (a) Answers will vary. $G(x) = 6x$

23. (a) 9   (b) 5

24. (a) 5   (b) 10

25. (a) $B = 1$

27. (a)

+	0	1	2	3	4	5
0	0	1	2	3	4	5
1	1	2	3	4	5	0
2	2	3	4	5	0	1
3	3	4	5	0	1	2
4	4	5	0	1	2	3
5	5	0	1	2	3	4

(b) Yes

(c) 0

CHAPTER 4 Review (p. 177)

1. (a) Answers will vary.

(b) It must be the product of 2 and 3, or 7 and 8.

2. (a)

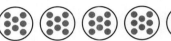

3. (a)

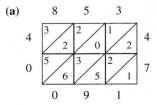

6. Answers will vary.

(a) $(90 - 1) \cdot 5 = (90 \cdot 5) - (1 \cdot 5)$
$(80 + 9) \cdot 5 = (80 \cdot 5) + (9 \cdot 5)$

(b) $(100 + 73) \cdot 42 = (100 \cdot 42) + (73 \cdot 42)$
$(200 - 27) \cdot 42 = (200 \cdot 42) - (27 \cdot 42)$

8. $A = 4, B = 2, C = 9, D = 3, E = 8$

9. Answers will vary.

(a) A restaurant has an early-bird special for customers who come in before 6:00 P.M. A fixed-price meal of $24 per person is discounted by $3 per person. What was the cost of the meal before tax and tip for a party of three arriving at 5:00 P.M.?

10. Answers will vary. Some possibilities follow.

(a) A car can rent for $27 per day. Approximately how much does the car rental company make per year if the car is rented every day?

11.

(a)

```
        8       5       3
    ┌───────┬───────┬───────┐
    │3     /│2     /│1     /│
 4  │    /  │    /  │    /  │ 4
    │  / 2  │  / 0  │  / 2  │
    ├─/─────┼─/─────┼─/─────┤
    │5     /│3     /│2     /│
 0  │    /  │    /  │    /  │ 7
    │  / 6  │  / 5  │  / 1  │
    └─/─────┴─/─────┴─/─────┘
        0       9       1
```

40,091

(b) 29   75

~~14~~   ~~150~~

7   300

3   600

1   1200
─────
          2175

13. $2520 = 2^3 \cdot 3^2 \cdot 5 \cdot 7$. There are 48 factors.

15. (a) 2^{18} **(b)** 2^2

17. $128 \times 15{,}625 = 2{,}000{,}000$

19. $67^2 = 4489$, $667^2 = 444{,}889$, $6667^2 = 44{,}448{,}889$, . . . , $666{,}666{,}667^2 = 444{,}444{,}444{,}888{,}888{,}889$

21. 38,888,888,885

23. eenie   meanie   minie   mo

     0   1   2   3

     2   1   1   3

26. (a) 1. All powers of 7 leave a remainder of 1 when divided by 6.

27. 13, 31; 37, 73; 79, 97

28. Answers will vary. Some possibilities follow.

(a) $17 + 19$ **(b)** $13 + 29$

29. Answers will vary. Some possibilities follow.

(a) $5 + 7 + 11$ **(b)** $23 + 31 + 5$

31. 1694

33. (a) {(12, 6), (1, 7), (2, 8), (3, 9), (4, 10), (5, 11), (6, 12), (7, 1), (8, 2), (9, 3), (10, 4), (11, 5)}
This is not an equivalence relation.

(b) {(1, 7), (2, 8), (3, 9), (6, 12)}
This is not an equivalence relation.

(c) {(1, 1), (1, 2), (1, 3), (1, 4), (1, 5), (1, 6), (1, 7), (1, 8), (1, 9), (2, 1), (2, 2), (2, 3), (2, 4), (2, 5), (2, 6), (2, 7), (2, 8), (2, 9), (3, 1), (3, 2), (3, 3), (3, 4), (3, 5), (3, 6), (3, 7), (3, 8), (3, 9), (4, 1), (4, 2), (4, 3), (4, 4), (4, 5), (4, 6), (4, 7), (4, 8), (4, 9), (5, 1), (5, 2), (5, 3), (5, 4), (5, 5), (5, 6), (5, 7), (5, 8), (5, 9), (6, 1), (6, 2), (6, 3), (6, 4), (6, 5), (6, 6), (6, 7), (6, 8), (6, 9), (7, 1), (7, 2), (7, 3), (7, 4), (7, 5), (7, 6), (7, 7), (7, 8), (7, 9), (8, 1), (8, 2), (8, 3), (8, 4), (8, 5), (8, 6), (8, 7), (8, 8), (8, 9), (9, 1), (9, 2), (9, 3), (9, 4), (9, 5), (9, 6), (9, 7), (9, 8), (9, 9), (10, 10), (10, 11), (10, 12), (11, 10), (11, 11), (11, 12), (12, 10), (12, 11), (12, 12)} This is an equivalence relation.

34. (a) Yes, this is closed under multiplication.

(b) Each element in the subset is of the form $(3^A, 3^B)$ where $A \geq B$.

(c) Yes.

(d) Each element in the subset is of the form $(3^A, 3^B)$ where $A \leq B$.

(e) Yes

37. (a) Yes, it is a function. For each element in set A there is a unique element in set B under the relation W.

(b) No, it is not a function. For each element in set A, there is not a unique element in set B under the relation M.

39. (a) The output will be four times the input.

(b) The output will be the input divided by 4.

41. Answers may vary. One possibility is $F(x) = 3x$ and $G(x) = x^2$.

43.

+	0	1	2	3	4
0	0	1	2	3	4
1	1	2	3	4	0
2	2	3	4	0	1
3	3	4	0	1	2
4	4	0	1	2	3

The relation is not reflexive since each nonzero number is not the additive inverse of itself. The relation is symmetric, since if a is the additive inverse of b, b is the additive inverse of a.

CHAPTER 5

SECTION 5.1 Extending the Number Line: Integer Addition and Subtraction (p. 191)

1. (a)

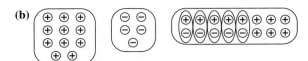

(b)

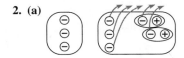

2. (a)

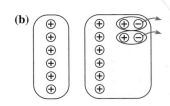

(b)

4. (a) −5 − (−2)

(b) +3 + (−2)

5. (a)

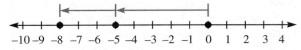

The solution is −8.

(b)

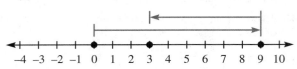

The solution is 3.

6. (a)

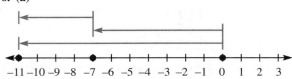

The solution is −4.

(b)

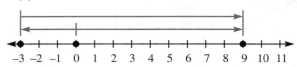

The solution is 12.

8. (a) +5 + (−4)

(b) −2 − (−3)

9. (a) −35 + (−56) = −91

(b) 93 + 27 = 120

10. (a) −90 − 45

(b) 45 − 34

11. (a) AC 9 +/− − 4 +/− =

AC 9 +/− + 4 =

12. (a) [−3 + (−8)] + (+2) = − 9

(b) −7 + [+2 + (−2)] = −7   or   −7 + [−2 + (+2)] = −7

(c) −231 − (−32) = −199

13. (a) −23 + [(+35) + (−48)] + (−29 + 83)

−23 + (−13) + 54

−36 + 54 = 18

15. −16 + (+34) = 18 feet above sea level

17. (a) 8   **(b)** −164

21. 38°

23. Reflexive: no; symmetric: yes; transitive: does not apply.

SECTION 5.2 Models and Properties of Integer Multiplication and Division (p. 205)

1. (a)

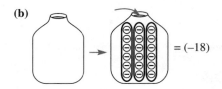

= (−28)

(b)

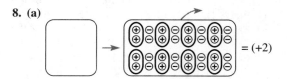

= (−18)

2. (a) 276   **(b)** −504

3. (a) 9   **(b)** −125

4. (a) +; −; +; −

5. (a) Negative even integer

(b) Positive odd integer

(c) Positive odd integer

7. [+5 · (−8)] ÷ (−4)} + [−6 · (−3)] = 28

The answer is not unique. Another possibility is

[−5 · (+8)] ÷ (−4)} + [+6 · (+3)] = 28

8. (a)

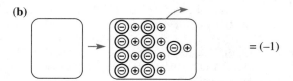

= (+2)

(b)

= (−1)

9. (a) +11   **(b)** −36

11. Answers will vary. The exact quotients and products are given here.

(a) 1357   **(b)** −858

12. Answers will vary. Rounded answers follow.
  (a) −45   **(b)** −5

14. **(a)** Yes   **(b)** No

15. −100. You lost $100.

17. **(a)** −9   **(b)** −972

18. **(a)** −8   **(b)** −28

20. **(a)** 128   **(b)** −750

21. **(a)** −2   **(b)** −155

24. **(a)** 30   **(b)** 30

25. **(a)** Yes. The absolute value of a product is equal to the product of the factors.

SECTION 5.3 Introduction to Algebra: Equations and Inequalities (p. 219)

1. **(a)** $3n + 7$
  (b) $(45 \div 9) - 5$

2. **(a)** 38
  (b) 32

3. **(a)** 8
  (b) 15

4. **(a)** $21 \geq -4$
  (b) $21 > 2$

5. **(a)** $32 > 35$; false
  (b) $-2 \leq 5$; true

6. **(a)** $x = 22$
  (b) $x = 30$

7. **(a)** $x = -8$
  (b) $x = 5$

8. **(a)** $x > -3$ **(b)** $x < -4$

9. **(a)** $x = \{2\}$
  (b) $x = \{-1, -2, -3\}$

10. 7

13. $370

15. Answers will vary. One possibility is $x = 12$.

17. $x = 2$ and $x = 6$

20. 113, 114, 115, 116

22. $x > 7$

24. 4 hours

CHAPTER 5 Review (p. 222)

2. **(a)** 4   **(b)** 4

4. 21

7. **(a)**   **(b)**

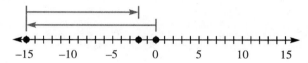

8. **(a)**

9. **(a)** $-5 \leq 12$; true

10. **(a)** −2   **(b)** 17

12. 6

14. **(a)** $x \geq 12$
  (b) $x < -8$

16. Answers will vary. Some possibilities follow.
  (a) $x = 0$
  (b) $\{\ \ \}$

18. **(a)** Let x = the number sold by Alex. $(100 - x)$ = the number sold by Barbara.
  (b) Alex = 67; Barbara = 33

20. **(a)** 81
  (b) 113
  (c) Answers will vary. One possibility is "double."
  (d) Answers will vary. One possibility is "code."

21. **(a)** 3   **(b)** 1

23. **(a)** $-b < a < b$ **(b)** $a > b$ or $a < -b$

25. $x = -5, y = -3, z = -2$

CHAPTER 6

SECTION 6.1 Number Theory Within the Context of Fractions (p. 238)

1. Answers will vary. Some possibilities follow.
  (a) $\frac{1}{2} = \frac{4}{8} = \frac{5}{10} = \frac{6}{12}$
  (e) $\frac{8}{11} = \frac{16}{22} = \frac{24}{33} = \frac{32}{44}$

2. Answers will vary. Some possibilities follow.

(a) $\frac{4}{3} = \frac{8}{6} = \frac{16}{12} = \frac{32}{24}$

(c) $\frac{7}{2} = \frac{14}{4} = \frac{21}{6} = \frac{28}{8}$

(e) $\frac{19}{5} = \frac{38}{10} = \frac{57}{15} = \frac{76}{20}$

3. (a)  **(b)**

4. (a)

(b)

5. (a) $\frac{2}{3}$ **(c)** $\frac{27}{44}$ **(e)** $\frac{4}{7}$

6. (a) 24 **(b)** 12

7. (a) Yes **(b)** No

8. (a) 180

11. Yes, he improved, since $\frac{80}{144} < \frac{96}{144} < \frac{108}{144}$.

13. Piece $a = \frac{1}{4}$ Piece $e = \frac{1}{16}$

Piece $b = \frac{1}{4}$ Piece $f = \frac{1}{8}$

Piece $c = \frac{1}{16}$ Piece $g = \frac{1}{8}$

Piece $d = \frac{1}{8}$

14. Park, school, restaurant, service station

16. $\frac{1}{8}, \frac{1}{6}, \frac{1}{4}, \frac{1}{3}, \frac{1}{2}$ As the denominator decreases, the value of the unit fraction increases.

19. $\frac{50}{195} = \frac{10}{39}$

21. Yes

23. 3289

SECTION 6.2 Models, Properties, and Algorithms of Rational Number Addition and Subtraction (p. 250)

1. Answers will vary. Some possibilities follow.

(a) 1 (c) $\frac{1}{2}$ (e) $2\frac{1}{2}$

2. Answers will vary. The actual answers follow.

(a) $1\frac{1}{14}$ (b) $\frac{3}{10}$

3. (a) $1\frac{13}{20}$ **(d)** $3\frac{6}{7}$ **(f)** $2\frac{23}{60}$

4. Answers will vary. Some possibilities follow.

(a) $\frac{1}{6}$ (c) $\frac{7}{24}$ (g) $\frac{1}{2}, \frac{1}{16}, \frac{1}{16}$

5. Answers will vary. Some possibilities follow.

(a) 4, 2 (c) 7, 7

6. $\frac{7}{8} + \frac{2}{4} = 1\frac{3}{8}$

8. (a) $\frac{1}{3} + \frac{1}{3} = \frac{2}{3}$

9. (a) $\frac{3}{4} - \frac{1}{3} = \frac{5}{12}$

12. (a) $\frac{1}{24}$ **(e)** $2\frac{7}{24}$

13. (a) $\frac{1}{7} = \frac{1}{14} + \frac{1}{14}$

(b) $\frac{1}{15} = \frac{1}{30} + \frac{1}{30}$

14. (a) $\frac{1}{3} = \frac{1}{4} + \frac{1}{12}$

(b) $\frac{1}{7} = \frac{1}{8} + \frac{1}{56}$

15. (a) $\frac{1}{3} + \frac{1}{15}$ **(b)** $\frac{1}{4} + \frac{1}{28}$

17. (c) $19\frac{7}{8}$

18. Answers will vary. Some possibilities follow.

(a) Two quarter-cups and two third-cups

19. (a) $\frac{4}{1} + \frac{3}{2}$

20. (a) $\frac{199}{200}$ nth term $= \frac{2n-1}{2n}$

(b) $\frac{10}{59,049}$ nth term $= \frac{n}{3^n}$

21. Answers will vary. Possible solutions follow.

(a) $\frac{5}{8}$

SECTION 6.3 Models, Properties, and Algorithms of Rational Number Multiplication and Division (p. 266)

1. Answers will vary. Some possibilities follow.

(a) 120 (b) $2\frac{1}{2}$

2. Answers will vary. Some possibilities follow.

(a) 14 (b) 7

3. (a) $\frac{2}{5}$ **(d)** $2\frac{8}{9}$ **(i)** 7 **(j)** $10\frac{6}{25}$

5. $\frac{9}{8}$

10. (a) $\frac{3}{4} \times \frac{1}{3}$ or $\frac{1}{3} \times \frac{3}{4}$

12. The markup was $10. One radio sells for $60.

14. Yes, the library will reorder books.

16. Freshmen: 130 sophomores: 143 juniors: 195 seniors: 182

18. Three education majors are seniors. Of the total class, $\frac{3}{40}$ are senior education majors.

20. (a) $\frac{1}{6}$

21. (a) $\frac{11}{31}$

24. 7

26. $1\frac{5}{8}$

27. Eight pieces with a $1\frac{1}{2}$-yard remnant

SECTION 6.4 Fractions in Context: Linear Measurement, Ratios, Proportions, Rates, and Dimensional Analysis (p. 280)

1. Answers will vary. Some possibilities follow.
   (a) Length, width, height
   (b) Weight, size, cost

2. Answers will vary. Some possibilities follow.
   (a) Hands, stick
   (b) Hands, ball

3. (a) $2, 2\frac{1}{2}, 2\frac{1}{4}, 2\frac{2}{8}$

4. (a) $2\frac{8}{16}$

5. $AB = \frac{8}{16}$ $CD = 1\frac{1}{4}"$ $EF = 2\frac{1}{2}"$ $GH = 1\frac{3}{4}"$ $IJ = 2"$
   (a) $1\frac{3}{4}"$ (c) $2"$ (e) $4\frac{1}{2}"$

7. Answers will vary. Some possibilities follow.
   (a) $12:13$ $12:25$ $13:25$

9. (a) 200 mi   (d) $4\frac{3}{4}"$

10. (a) 255 mi   (d) $6\frac{1}{2}"$

11. Answers are approximate.
   (a) $6\frac{3}{10}$ mi   (b) 12 mi

12. Answers are approximate.
   (a) $\frac{1}{2}$ mi   (b) $\frac{1}{2}$ mi

13. (a) 8   (c) 39   (g) 400   (i) 267

14. (a) $\frac{16}{24} = \frac{30}{45} = \frac{2}{3}$

16. (a) $6:1$

18. 99

20. (a) 45 days

22. 352 yds/min

24. 25 cents/min

CHAPTER 6 Review (p. 285)

1. (a) $\frac{2}{7}$ (b) $\frac{2}{3}$ (d) $\frac{3}{4}$

2. Answers can vary. Some possibilities follow.
   (a) $\frac{6}{9}$ $\frac{16}{24}$ $\frac{10}{15}$ (b) $\frac{14}{18}$ $\frac{21}{27}$ $\frac{28}{36}$

3. (a) $\frac{5}{15}$ (b) $\frac{36}{42}$

4. (a) $\frac{1}{2} \times \frac{1}{2}$ (c) $\left[2 \times \left(\frac{5}{6} + \frac{3}{4}\right)\right] \div \frac{1}{2}$

5. (a) $\frac{1}{4}$ $\frac{3}{10}$ $\frac{3}{8}$ $\frac{2}{5}$

6. (a) $\frac{4}{5}$ $\frac{5}{7}$ $\frac{7}{10}$ $\frac{1}{2}$ $\frac{17}{35}$

7. (a) $\frac{1}{6}$ (b) $1\frac{9}{10}$

8. (a) $\frac{11}{14}$ (e) $18\frac{2}{3}$ (f) $\frac{21}{40}$
   (j) $1\frac{11}{24}$ (k) $\frac{3}{8}$ (m) $7\frac{7}{12}$
   (o) $2\frac{1}{2}$ (p) 9   (s) $1\frac{1}{2}$

9. (a) 1   (c) 10

12. $4\frac{19}{24}$ characters

15. (a) $2\frac{3}{4}$ mi   (b) $2\frac{1}{2}$ mi

17. 63,360 ft/hr is faster. Convert one to the other and compare.

19. 12

21. No. The ratios of the children's ages of $3:3$ and $3:6$ do not form a proportion.

23. (a) $\frac{1}{7 \times 8}$

24. (a) $5\frac{17}{60}$
   (b) nth term $= 1 + \dfrac{1}{n+1}$

26. Five pieces with a remnant of $7\frac{1}{2}$ ft (which is $\frac{3}{32}$ of the roll)

CHAPTER 7

SECTION 7.1 Decimals: Modeling, Ordering, Comparing, and Estimating (p. 298)

1. (a) True   (b) False

2. (a) $<$ (c) $=$ (e) $=$ (h) $=$

3. (a) .38   (b) .005   (c) .0123

5. (a)    (b)

6. (a) 3.5   (d) 8.07   (g) 86.8

7. (a) 1.02

8. (a) .015, .178, .34, .6, .912
   (b) 2.035, 2.0355, 2.305, 2.35

9. (a) .76, .72, .532, .5, .03
   (b) 5.34, 5.314, 5.3, 5.034, 5

10. Answers will vary. Some possibilities follow.
   (a) .54, .55   (b) .27, .28

11. (a) +$1.63   **(b)** −$2.50

12. (a) 3.9   **(b)** 1.0   **(c)** 2.35   **(d)** 35

13. (a) .035; terminating since $200 = 2^3 \times 5^2$

   (b) .2125; terminating since $80 = 2^4 \times 5$

15. $\frac{4}{5} = .8$ hr per meter

17. (a) $\frac{5}{10} = .5$ **(b)** $\frac{7}{8} = .875$

18. (a) $\frac{15}{100} = .15$ **(c)** $\frac{439}{1000} = .439$

20. (b), (c), and (e) are defective

21. (a) 1.5

SECTION 7.2 Operations with Decimals (p. 309)

1. (a) 9.058   **(b)** 23.03   **(c)** 2.25

2. (a) 9.175   **(b)** 24.315   **(c)** .98

3. (a) 42.5   **(b)** .00001

4. (a) 1.25   **(b)** 12.4

6. (a) .714   **(b)** .111

7. (a) 10.85   **(b)** .1125   **(c)** 3.25   **(d)** 9.25

8. (a) $.\overline{2}$ **(b)** $.\overline{285714}$

9. (a) $\frac{15}{99}$ **(b)** $\frac{2}{99}$

11. 29 items at $.29 each

12. Answers may vary. One possibility is given for each.

   (a) 3.1, 2.5   **(b)** 3.1, 2.1   **(c)** 2.4, 2.4

   (d) 2.1, 2.5   **(e)** 2.2, 2.3

14. .308

16. Dolores

18. Answers may vary. Some possibilities follow.

   (a) 4.8 + .372 + 1.7 + .8

   (b) 3.7 × 87.3

20. (a) 1.8 g

   (b) 2.4 : 270

SECTION 7.3 Percents (p. 318)

1. (a) Twenty-five hundredths of the 28 students were absent on March 16. How many students were absent? (The answer is seven students).

2. (a) 10.44   **(b)** 7.8   **(e)** 180

   (h) 50   **(j)** 10%

4. (a) $72   **(b)** $168

7. 1.98 kg to 2.02 kg

9. 22% increase

11. 75 g

13. $2110

16. $8282.45

19. 150 seats

SECTION 7.4 Decimals in Context: Linear Metric Measurement (p. 328)

1. (a) 2.5 m   **(b)** 7 cm   **(c)** 8 m

2. (a) 10,000   **(b)** .010   **(c)** 35   **(h)** 50

3. Answers will vary. Some possibilities follow.

   (a) 16 cm   **(b)** 17 cm   **(c)** 75 cm

   (d) 30 m   **(e)** 2 m

4. 247.5 km   247,500 m

7. No

8. (a) 1.25 m

10. 4.05 m by 4.7 m

12. Approximately $3\frac{1}{4}$ hours

14. (a) 1.7 cm   **(b)** 3.7 cm

16. (a) 4.26×10^7 **(b)** 1.10×10^{12}

18. (a) $(5.37 \times 10^{11} + 6.73 \times 10^8) = 5.38 \times 10^{11}$

   (b) $8.95 \times 10^8 - 8.71 \times 10^4 = 8.95 \times 10^8$

   (c) $1.02 \times 10^8 \div 7.41 \times 10^4 = 1.38 \times 10^3$

19. $3.0 \times 10^{10} \times 1.3 = 3.9 \times 10^{10}$ cm $= 3.9 \times 10^5$ km

SECTION 7.5 The Bigger Picture: Rational Numbers, Irrational Numbers, and Real Numbers (p. 340)

1. Answers will vary. Some possibilities follow.

   (a) $\frac{12}{5}$ **(b)** $\frac{509}{100}$ **(c)** $\frac{875}{1000}$

2. Answers will vary. Some possibilities follow.

   (a) 1.21 and 1.201   **(b)** $\frac{41}{60}$ and $\frac{81}{120}$

   (c) $-\frac{21}{24}$ and $-\frac{41}{48}$

3. Answers will vary. Some possibilities follow.

   (a) Between $\frac{1}{2}$ and $\frac{3}{4}$

   (b) Between $\frac{5}{8}$ and $\frac{3}{4}$

5. Answers will vary. Some possibilities follow.

   (a) The difference between the numerator and the denominator alternates between 1, −1, 1, −1. . . . The numerators follow the pattern 2 2 4 4 6 6 8 8 . . . and the denominators follow the pattern 1 3 3 5 5 7 7 9 9. . . .

   (b) $\frac{10}{9}, \frac{10}{11}, \frac{12}{11}$

6. (a) Four times the sum of the alternating positive/negative unit fractions whose denominators are consecutive odd numbers.

(b) $\frac{1}{15} + \frac{1}{17} - \frac{1}{19}$

7. Answers will vary. Square roots correct to three decimal places are given here.

   (a) 3.873   **(b)** 5.385

9. (a) {0, 1, 2, 3}

10. (a) $\frac{\sqrt{5}}{2}, \frac{7}{5}, 1.41, 1\frac{2}{3}, \sqrt{3}$

11. (a) $\sqrt{5}, 1\frac{2}{5}, .\overline{1}, -1.04, -\sqrt{5}$

12. (a) Always yields a rational number

   (b) Always yields an irrational number

13. Answers will vary. Some possibilities follow.

   (a) $\pi \div \pi = 1$

14. (a) $\sqrt{2}, \sqrt{3}$

17. (a) 71.7 km

CHAPTER 7 Review (p. 343)

1. (a) $.108, \frac{1}{9}, .1\overline{2}, .125, \sqrt{3}$

2. (a) $(1.3 \times 10^{-2}), -\frac{1}{100}, -\sqrt{4}, -2.\overline{2}, -\sqrt{5}$

3. Answers will vary. Some possibilities follow.

   (a) 75   **(c)** 9   **(e)** 25

5. (a) 2.37×10^5 **(b)** 2.06×10^{-3}

6. (a) 4, 4.123   **(b)** 10, 9.644

7. Answers will vary. Actual square roots to nearest hundredths are given here.

   (a) 10.82   **(b)** 4.80

8. Answers will vary.

   (a) $\frac{351}{100}$ **(b)** $\frac{8}{9}$

9. (a) 2500   **(b)** 65

10. (a) 33.3%   **(b)** 46.0%

11. (a) .35   **(b)** .01

13. (a) $184.68   **(b)** $153.90

16. $948.09

17. 7.32 cm by 13.18 cm

19. 12.96%

22. 49 people

CHAPTER 8

SECTION 8.1 Looking for Trends: Organizing and Displaying Data (p. 362)

1. (a) 85

   (b) 17

   (c) 2–12, 13–23, 24–34, 35–45, 46–56, 57–67, 68–78, 79–89

(d) 0–21, 22–43, 44–65, 66–87

(e) 0–14, 15–29, 30–44, 45–59, 60–74, 75–89

(f) 0–8   3

   9–17   7

   18–26   8

   27–35   6

   36–44   5

   45–53   6

   54–62   4

   63–71   0

   72–80   0

   81–89   1

3. (a) Answers will vary. One possible set is 4, 5, 7, 12, 13, 13, 19, 20, 21, 28.

   (b) 9

5. (a)

Stems	Leaves
0	5 6 7 3 3
1	0 1 9 0 7 8 9
2	5 8 7 6 4 0 2 7 8
3	5 2 9 7 2 0 2
4	9 2 6
5	1 1 1
6	1 3

   (b) Histogram

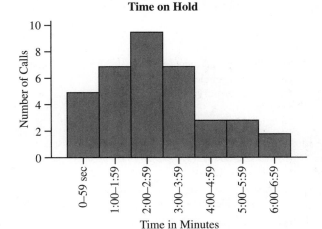

Time on Hold

(c) The histogram resembles the stem-and-leaf plot turned counterclockwise on its side.

7. (a) Washington

   (b) Newark

(c) Boston/Baltimore/Buffalo

(d) Philadelphia/Bridgeport

(e) Newark

9. (a) It appears that the number of complaints rose slightly but were consistently small.

(b) It appears that there was a sharp increase in the number of complaints as the year progressed.

(c) The dealership might use this graph to boast of a low complaint record.

(d) A consumer advocate group might use this graph to complain about the worsening record of the dealership.

(e) Each graph illustrates the same data. Neither is incorrect, yet both can be interpreted in ways that take completely opposite points of view.

11. (a) Bar graph

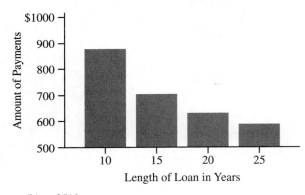

Amount of Monthly Payments

(b) ≈ $510

13. The bar graph accentuates the differences in land areas better than the circle graph does.
Northwest Territory: ≈34%
Quebec: ≈15%
Ontario: ≈11%

15. (a) 42

(b) 80–85, 86–91, 92–97, 98–103, 104–109, 110–115, 116–121, 122–127

(c) Answers will vary. One possibility is the weight of boxes mailed on a given day at a particular post office.

19. (a) 12.5 sq cm   (b) 6.25 sq cm

(c) 16 hours awake, 8 hours asleep. Since B represents half of A, and the total of A and B represents 24 hours, you can solve the equation $x + .5x = 24$ where x represents the number of hours represented by A.

SECTION 8.2 Analyzing and Summarizing Data (p. 386)

1. (a)

Duration (in minutes)	Number of Calls	Cumulative Frequency	Relative Frequency	Relative Cumulative Frequency
0–4	2	2	.055	.055
5–9	4	6	.111	.166
10–14	8	14	.222	.388
15–19	10	24	.278	.666
20–24	6	30	.167	.833
25–29	6	36	.167	1.000

(b) Approximately 17% of the calls lasted 20–24 minutes.

3. A: 12   B: 50   C: 110   D: 20   E: 8

5. (a) 8.845 hrs   (b) 9.175 hrs   (c) 9.5 hrs

7. 97

9. Answers will vary. One possible set is 83, 84, 84, 85, and 89.

11. (a) A ≈ 26.4   B ≈ 27.6   (b) 28.67   53.39

(c) enrollments are more dispersed about $\bar{x}$.

13.

Stems	Leaves
5	4 9
6	0 4 5 6 6 7
7	1 1 2 3 4 7 9 9
8	1 3 5 5 5 8 8 9
9	0 0 1 2 4 4 8 9 9

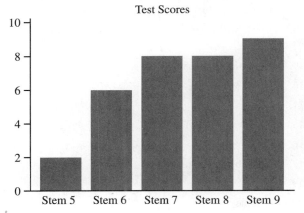

Test Scores

15. (a) 287

(b) Box-and-whisker plot

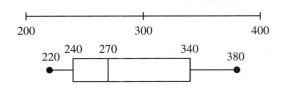

19. ≈3.85

21. (a) The mean is increased by 5.

   (b) The median is increased by 5.

   (c) The mode is increased by 5.

   (d) The standard deviation remains unchanged.

   (e) Q_3 is increased by 5.

   (f) Q_1 is increased by 5.

   (g) The interquartile range remains unchanged.

23. (a) Mean: 1 g   median: 1 g   mode: 0 g

   (b) 1

CHAPTER 8 Review (p. 390)

1. (a)

Interval	Frequency	Relative Frequency	Cumulative Frequency	Relative Cumulative Frequency
10–15	2	.067	2	.067
16–21	5	.167	7	.233
22–27	6	.200	13	.433
28–33	5	.167	18	.600
34–39	4	.133	22	.733
40–45	6	.200	28	.933
46–51	2	.067	30	1.000

(b)

Stems	Leaves
1	8 0 9 6 8 3 9
2	5 2 2 9 8 2 7 2
3	5 0 6 5 1 7 3
4	5 5 3 3 9 1 2
5	0

3.

Interval	Frequency	Relative Frequency	Cumulative Frequency	Relative Cumulative Frequency
70–74	2	.050	2	.050
75–79	5	.125	7	.175
80–84	4	.100	11	.275
85–89	12	.300	23	.575
90–94	5	.125	28	.700
95–99	8	.200	36	.900
100–104	4	.100	40	1.000

5.

Interval	Frequency	Cumulative Frequency	Relative Frequency	Relative Cumulative Frequency
1	10	10	.132	.132
2	4	14	.053	.184
3	8	22	.105	.289
4	14	36	.184	.474
5	12	48	.158	.632
6	6	54	.079	.711
7	18	72	.237	.947
8	4	76	.053	1.000

7. (a) 40 no-shows   **(b)** 25 no-shows   **(c)** 25

   (d) 30   **(e)** Bar graph

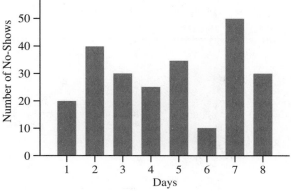

Number of "No Shows" at a Particular Hotel

9. Estimates for (a) and (b) will vary.

   (a) 1992: ≈45 calls per day

   (b) 1993: ≈30 calls per day

   (c) 1992: Day 3 to Day 4

11. Mean: 350,000 barrels; median: 325,000 barrels

13. Stacked bar graph

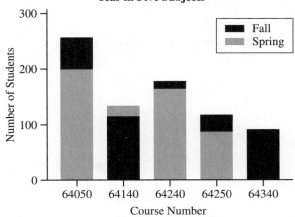

Course Enrollment for an Academic Year in Five Subjects

15. (a) Section   01: ≈ 7.25   02: ≈ .2   03: 0   04: ≈ −.474
   05: −.75. Section 01, Section 02, Section 03, Section 04,
   Section 05.

   (b) The smaller the standard deviation, the less variable
   the scores in the class will be. The section with the
   smaller standard deviation had scores that tended to
   cluster about the mean (more so than the other section).

17. **(a)** 77 to 90

   (b) $\approx -.538$

   (c) 73.75

   (d) ≈ 34

19. $A = 60$ $B = 86, 87,$ or 88 $C = 89, 90,$ or 91

21. **(a)** Class 1: 45.6   Class 2: 42.75   Class 3: 45.5

   (b)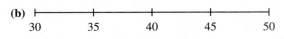

   Class 1

   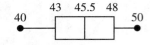

   Class 2

   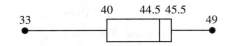

   Class 3

   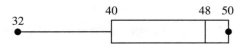

   (c) In Class 1, 45 is slightly below the median. In Class 2, 45 is above the median. In Class 3, 45 is below the median.

CHAPTER 9

SECTION 9.1 Properties of Simple Probability (p. 406)

1. **(a)** {H, T}   **(b)** {1, 2, 3, 4, 5, 6}

2. **(a)** $\frac{1}{8}$ **(b)** $\frac{7}{8}$

3. **(a)** $\frac{1}{8}$ **(b)** $\frac{4}{8}$ **(c)** $\frac{4}{8}$

   (d) 0   **(e)** $\frac{4}{8}$ **(f)** $\frac{5}{8}$

   (g) 4 : 4 or 1:1   **(h)** 4 : 4 or 1:1   **(i)** 1

7. **(a)** $A:\ \frac{5}{50} = \frac{1}{10}$ $B:\ \frac{13}{50}$ $C:\ \frac{18}{50} = \frac{9}{25}$ $D:\ \frac{11}{50}$

   $E:\ \frac{2}{50} = \frac{1}{25}$ $F:\ \frac{1}{50}$

   (b) Region C is most likely the largest.

9. **(a)** $\frac{1}{10}$ **(b)** 1 : 9

10. Answers will vary. Some possibilities follow.

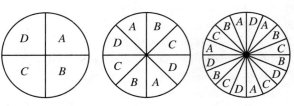

13. **(a)** (1, 1)   (1, 2)   (1, 3)   (1, 4)   (1, 5)   (1, 6)
   (2, 1)   (2, 2)   (2, 3)   (2, 4)   (2, 5)   (2, 6)
   (3, 1)   (3, 2)   (3, 3)   (3, 4)   (3, 5)   (3, 6)
   (4, 1)   (4, 2)   (4, 3)   (4, 4)   (4, 5)   (4, 6)
   (5, 1)   (5, 2)   (5, 3)   (5, 4)   (5, 5)   (5, 6)
   (6, 1)   (6, 2)   (6, 3)   (6, 4)   (6, 5)   (6, 6)

   (c) $\frac{6}{36} = \frac{1}{6}$

   (e) $\frac{6}{36} = \frac{1}{6}$

15. $4 : 26 = 2 : 13$

17. **(a)** .6   **(b)** $P(A \cap B)$

19. .35

21. $1 : 2$

SECTION 9.2 Picturing Probabilistic Situations (p. 425)

1. **(a)** $\frac{1}{2500}$ **(b)** $\frac{1}{2500}$ **(c)** $\frac{50}{2500} = \frac{1}{50}$

3. **(b)** $\frac{76}{80} = \frac{19}{20}$ **(c)** $\frac{1}{2}$ **(d)** $\frac{1}{20}$ **(e)** $\frac{1}{2}$

5. **(a)**

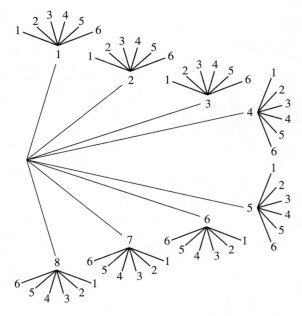

(b) $8 \times 6 = 48$

7. (a)

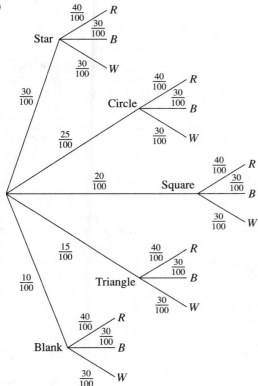

(b) $\frac{750}{10,000} = \frac{3}{40}$

9. Answers will vary. A possible set is two blue and three pink.

11. $\frac{1}{4}$

13. (a) $\frac{275}{1035}$ **(b)** $\frac{210}{735}$

15. .7056

17. (a) \$8.22   **(b)** +\$3.22 on average

19. –\$125

21. (a)

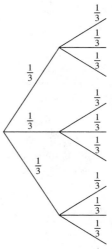

(b) The expected value = \$4. The owner will break even.

23. (a) The expected value is not affected by the price of playing the game, but here the expected value of a win is now – \$1.90.

(b) The expected value is not affected by the price of playing the game, but here the expected value of a win is now – \$.40.

SECTION 9.3 Counting Techniques: Pascal's Triangle, Permutations, and Combinations (p. 437)

1. (a) 4 paths   **(b)** 8 paths

2. (a) 1 7 21 35 35 21 7 1

(b) 1 9 36 84 126 126 84 36 9 1

3. (a) 36

(b) 28

4. (a) 128

(b) $\frac{6}{64} = \frac{3}{32}$

5. (a) $\frac{1}{2}$

(b) $\frac{10}{32} = \frac{5}{16}$

6. (a) $X = 24$ **(c)** $X = 6$ **(e)** $X = 8$

9. 5040

11. (a) 270,725   **(b)** $\frac{1}{270,725}$ **(c)** $\frac{1225}{270,725}$

(d) $\frac{49}{270,725}$ **(e)** $\frac{269,500}{270,725}$

13. 9×10^6

15. (a) 120   **(b)** 24   **(c)** 6   **(d)** $\frac{1}{120}$

17. (a) $\frac{1}{91}$ **(b)** 90 : 1   **(c)** 2184

19. (a) 210   **(b)** 90

CHAPTER 9 Review (p. 440)

1. (a) {1, 2, 3, 4, 5, 6, 8, 9, 10, 12, 15, 16, 18, 20, 24, 25, 30, 36}

(b) {3, 4, 5, 6, 7, 8, 9, 10, 11, 12, 13, 14, 15, 16, 17, 18}

3. (a) $P(A) = \frac{20}{150}$ $P(B) = \frac{25}{150}$ $P(C) = \frac{10}{150}$

$P(D) = \frac{40}{150}$ $P(E) = \frac{20}{150}$ $P(F) = \frac{35}{150}$

(b) Answers will vary. One possibility follows.

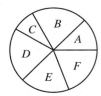

5. (a) $\frac{1}{2}$ **(b)** $\frac{5}{6}$

7. (a) $\frac{4}{52}$ **(b)** $\frac{1}{4}$ **(c)** $\frac{1}{2}$ **(d)** $\frac{12}{52}$ **(e)** $\frac{1}{52}$

9. (a) $\frac{751}{2361}$ **(b)** $\frac{418}{2361}$

11. 120

13. (a) $\frac{5}{121}$ **(b)** $\frac{5}{121}$ **(c)** $\frac{25}{121}$

15. (a) $\frac{2}{64}$ **(b)** $\frac{1}{16}$ **(c)** $\frac{25}{64}$

17. (a) $\frac{70}{150}$ **(b)** $\frac{25}{75}$ **(c)** $\frac{55}{75}$

19. (a) $P(A|B) \approx .091$ $P(B|A) = .125$ $P(A \cup B) = .9$

(b) .228

(c) .4

21. (a) $\frac{1}{6}$ **(b)** $\frac{1}{2}$

22. (a) 40,320   **(b)** 840   **(c)** 9900

(e) 56   **(g)** 100!

25. (a) 1,712,304

(b) $\frac{1}{48}$

27. $2.625 \approx $2.63

29. (a) $\frac{1}{64}$ **(b)** $\frac{1}{64}$ **(c)** $\frac{6}{64}$

CHAPTER 10

SECTION 10.1 Observing, Describing, and Classifying in Two Dimensions (p. 463)

1. Answers will vary. One set of possibilities for each part follows.

(a) E, J, B

(b) A, F, G

(c) $\overline{FH}, \overline{GJ}$

(d) $\overline{DJ}, \overline{JI}$, share point J

(e) $\overline{FH}, \overline{IH}, \overline{BH}$, share point H

3. (a) Convex   **(b)** Nonconvex

A line segment connecting the two points in shapes (a) and (c) will lie entirely within the shapes, and line segments in (b), (d), and (e) will not necessarily lie entirely within their shapes.

5. Answers will vary. Some possibilities follow.

(a) $\overline{GI}, \overline{EK}$

(b) $\overline{GE}, \overline{EI}$

(c) $\overline{HI}, \overline{HK}$

(d) GHK

(e) GIK

12. 1: Triangle, square, rectangle, kite, trapezoid, parallelogram, any polygon

2: Rectangle, pentagon, any polygon with five or more sides, trapezoid

3: Trapezoid, pentagon, any polygon with five or more sides

4: Trapezoid

13. Answers will vary. Some possibilities follow.

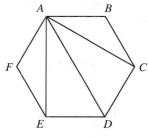

(a) $\triangle ABC, \triangle ACD, \triangle ADE, \triangle AEF$

(b) $\triangle AFE \cong \triangle ABC, \triangle AED \cong \triangle ACD$

15. A "misshape" is an n-sided polygon with an $(n - 1)$-sided polygon contained within it. Therefore, the shape in question *is* a "misshape."

17. (a) 30

(b) A 1×1 square has 1 square.
A 2×2 square has $1 + 4$ squares.

A 3 × 3 square has 1 + 4 + 9 squares.

A 4 × 4 square has 1 + 4 + 9 + 16 squares. Therefore, a 10 × 10 square has 1 + 4 + 9 + 16 + 25 + 36 + 49 + 64 + 81 + 100, or 385, squares.

19. (a) $\overline{BD}$ **(b)** $\overline{CE}$

22. (a) Convex trapezoid   **(b)** Convex trapezoid

SECTION 10.2 Exploring Three-Dimensional Figures (p. 477)

1. (a) Convex   **(b)** Convex   **(c)** Nonconvex
(d) Nonconvex   **(e)** Convex

3. 18 edges, 12 vertices, 8 faces

5. 12 edges, 7 vertices, 7 faces

7. (a) 8   **(b)** 10

8. (a) Yes   **(b)** No

9. (a) Yes   **(b)** No

11. (a) 3   **(b)** 4   **(c)** 1   **(d)** 2

13. (a) Rectangle

15. (a) Circle

16. (a) Triangle   **(b)** Triangle

18. (a) Circle

19. Answers will vary. One possibility for each follows.
(a) Pentagon   **(b)** Cone on a cylinder

21. Lower portion: 7 faces, 15 edges, 10 vertices
Top portion: 6 faces, 10 edges, 6 vertices
Both resulting solids are polyhedra.

CHAPTER 10 Review (p. 482)

1. Many answers are possible. One possible set for each part follows.
(a) $\overline{LD}$ **(b)** $\overline{KJ}, \overline{KQ}$
(c) $\overline{DK}, \overline{KQ}$ **(d)** $NQKJDA$

2. Answers will vary. One possible set for each part follows.
(a) G, K, I
(b) L, K, R
(c) $\overline{JK}, \overline{SR}, \overline{BC}, \overline{KB}$
(d) $\overline{RK}, \overline{PK}, \overline{NK}, \overline{LK}$ share point K

6. Answers will vary. Some possibilities follow.

(a)   **(b)**

7. Answers will vary.

9. Pyramid with a seven-sided polygon as its base (heptagonal pyramid)

11. 11 faces, 20 edges, 11 vertices. Yes, this is a polyhedral solid.

13. (a) Yes (triangular pyramid)
(b) No

14. Answers will vary. Some possibilities follow.
(a) Perpendicular to the base, through the apex.
(b) Parallel to the base.

16. Answers will vary. Some possibilities follow.
(a) Slice off one vertex of the rectangular prism.
(b) Make a horizontal slice from the bottom of the rectangular prism.
(c) Make a diagonal slice from the top of the pyramid.
(d) Cut through five faces of the solid.

17. (a) $\overline{BD}$ **(b)** $\{B\}$

18. Answers will vary. Some possibilities follow.

(a)   **(b)**

21. (a) Yes
(b) No

22. (a) Regular hexagon
(b) Square

24. Answers may vary. Some possibilities follow.

(a)

CHAPTER 11

SECTION 11.1 Tools of Geometry (p. 515)

1. (a) 90°   **(b)** 180°   **(c)** 270°
(d) 45°   **(e)** 60°

2. (a) Acute   **(c)** Right   **(f)** Obtuse

3. (a) 125°   **(b)** 30°

4. (a) $40°$ **(c)** $95°$

5. (a) $30°, 60°$
   (b) $44.5°, 45.5°$
   (c) $20°, 70°$

7. Answers may vary. Several possible true statements follow.
   $m\angle 4 + m\angle 3 = m\angle 2 + m\angle 1$
   $m\angle 1 + m\angle 2 + m\angle 3 + m\angle 4 + m\angle 5 + m\angle 6 = 360$
   The figure is a kite.

9. (a) $540°$ **(b)** $360°$ **(c)** $900°$

11. $720°(\angle 8 = 45°, \angle 7 = 120°, \angle 5 = 270°, \angle 3 = 150°$

13. Use a construction to drop perpendiculars to both end-points. Bisect each $90°$ angle formed at the endpoints. The point of intersection of the angle bisectors is the third ver-tex of the triangle.

15. Construction

19. Since diagonals of a rhombus bisect the vertices, $m\angle CBA = m\angle CBD + m\angle DBA = 80°$. Therefore, $m\angle CBD = m\angle DBA = 40°$.

23. $130°$. Because the north and south routes are parallel, the second road can be viewed as a transversal. The sum of the interior angles on the same side of the transversal is $180°$.

SECTION 11.2 Perimeter, Circumference, Area, and Surface Area (p. 542)

1. (a) 14 cm   **(b)** $23\frac{1}{4}$ in.

2. (a) 4.75 cm   **(b)** 28.3 cm

3. $\sqrt{48} = 4\sqrt{3}$

5. $\sqrt{20,000} \approx 141.4$

7. 52 cm

9. (a) The area is quadrupled.

10. (a) $1:4$

11. (a) Lower bound $= 9$ Upper bound $= 24$
      Estimate (average) $= 16.5$
   (b) Lower bound $= 18$ Upper bound $= 31$
      Estimate (average) $= 24.5$

13. (a) 15 square units   **(b)** 15 square units

15. 3

17. (a) $150\sqrt{3}S$
   (b) $\dfrac{3S^2}{2}\sqrt{3}$

20. (a) 4 cm^2 **(b)** ≈ 56.52 cm^2

21. Hour hand travels ≈ 31.4 cm
   Minute hand travels ≈ 50.24 cm
   Second hand travels ≈ 56.52 cm

25. Two possible answers are $20 \times 5 \times 4$ and $10 \times 10 \times 4$. The answers are not unique.

27. (a) 374 circles   **(b)** 20.1 in^2

29. 144 ft^2

31. 256 cm^2

33. $\dfrac{2(r+h)}{r + \sqrt{h^2 + r^2}}$

35. ≈ 1.2 m^2

SECTION 11.3 Measuring Weight, Volume, and Temperature (p. 559)

1. (a) $52,000$ g   **(c)** 5 cg   **(e)** 700 g
   (g) 3 kg   **(i)** $.052$ kg

3. (a) 1000 kg   **(c)** 900 g

5. (a) $32,000$ L   **(c)** $65,000$ cL   **(e)** 300 L
   (g) 6 kL   **(i)** 2.9kL

6. (a) 250 mL   **(b)** 100 L

9. (a) Rejected   **(b)** Accepted   **(c)** Rejected

11. 6 cherries

12. (a) 1200 cm^3 **(b)** $15,000$ cm^3

13. (a) 180 units^2 **(b)** 20 cubic units
   (c) $49,000$ cubic units

17. $\approx 14,118$ cm^3

19. 14 apples

21. 405 yds^3

23. 613 in^3

25. 64 ft^3

27. (a) $80°$ C   **(b)** $-2°$ C   **(c)** $37°$ C   **(d)** $5°$ C
   (e) $-5°$ C   **(f)** $20°$ C   **(g)** $28°$ C

29. (a) $r \approx 5.6$ cm
   (b) $s \approx 15.2$ cm

CHAPTER 11 Review (p. 563)

1. (a) Perimeter $= 8.4$ units
      Area $= 3.75$ units^2
   (b) Perimeter $= 100$ units
      Area $= 456$ units^2

3. Answers will vary. Some possibilities follow.

(a) $4' \times 7'$ (b) 1.5 m per side

(c) ≈ 12.25 cm per side   (d) 30 cm $\times$ 11.5 cm

(e) $r = 6''$

5. $60°$, $120°$

7. (a)   (b)   (c)

(d)   (e)

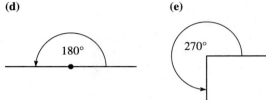

9. $90°$, $45°$, $45°$

11. $\angle 1 = 90°$ $\angle 2 = 90°$ $\angle 3 = 125°$ $\angle 4 = 55°$ $\angle 5 = 90°$ $\angle 6 = 90°$ $\angle 7 = 55°$ $\angle 8 = 125°$ $\angle 9 = 90°$ $\angle 10 = 55°$ $\angle 11 = 55°$ $\angle 12 = 35°$ $\angle 13 = 90°$

13. In each case, the area equals ≈ 10.392 cm^2.

15. (a) ≈ 6.19 square units

(b) 24 square units

17. $SA = 100\pi$

$V = \dfrac{1000\pi}{3}$

19. (a) Methods will vary. $V = 432$ cm^3

21. Approximately 490 revolutions

23. $V \approx 421$ cm^3

25. (a) $V \approx 106$ cm^3

27. $V = 1050$ cm^3

CHAPTER 12

SECTION 12.1 Coordinate Geometry: An Algebra/Geometry Connection (p. 603)

1. Answers will vary. Some possible solutions follow.

(a) $(3, 1), (4, 3), (5, 5), (6, 7)$

(b) $(1, 2), (2, 0), (3, -2), (4, -4)$

2. (a) Yes   (b) No   (c) Yes

3. Answers will vary. Some possible solutions follow.

(a) $y = x$ (b) $y = x + 1$

4. (a) $\approx \sqrt{17}$ units   (b) ≈ 5 units

5. (a) No   (b) No

6. (a) $y = \frac{1}{2}x + 2$

(b) $y = \frac{-3}{4}x - 3$

(c) $y = \frac{1}{3}x + \frac{11}{3}$

(d) $y = 4x + 4$

7. Answers will vary. Some possibilities follow.

(a) $y = 5$ (b) $x = 7$

8. (a) $(7, 0)$ (b) $(-3, 5)$

10. (a) $(x + 1)^2 + (y - 2)^2 = 25$

(b) $x^2 + y^2 = 4$

11. Answers will vary. Some possibilities follow.

(a) $x^2 + y^2 = 16$

(c) $(x + 6)^2 + (y - 4)^2 = 2$

13. (a) Nonconvex quadrilateral   (b) Rectangle

14. Answers will vary. Some possibilities follow.

(a) $y = x, y = -x$ (b) $y = 3x + 2, y = 3x + 8$

15. (a) $(3, 5)$ (b) $(1, 2)$

17. (a) Construction

(b) Diameter $\overline{AB}$ radius $= \sqrt{10}$ units
Diameter $\overline{BC}$ radius $= \sqrt{53}$ units
Diameter $\overline{CA}$ radius $= 5$ units

18. (a) $(-4, -3)$

(b) $(-3, 2)$

(c) $(1, -1)$

19. 9 nickels and 3 quarters

21. 8 and -3

23. $(x - 1)^2 + (y - 2)^2 = 9$

25. Center at $(2, 4)$; $(x - 2)^2 + (y - 4)^2 = 25$

29. $(x + 6)^2 + (y - 2)^2 = 40$

31. Construction

SECTION 12.2 Similarity and Congruence (p. 624)

2. (a) True

(b) False

(c) True

(d) False

3. (a) AAA

4. (a) $5\frac{1}{3}$ cm   **(b)** 10.5 cm

5. Answers will vary. Some possibilities follow.

   (a) $RS = 2$ $ST = 5$ $TR = 9$
          $UV = 2$ $VW = 5$ $WU = 9$

   (b) $RS = 2$ $ST = 5$ $TR = 9$
          $UV = 4$ $VW = 10$ $WU = 18$

6. (a) 35°

   (b) These are complementary angles; complements of congruent angles are equal to each other.

9. 20-ft shadow. Similar triangles by AA.

11. $GH = 50$, $HI = 11.25$

15. (a) Congruent

   (b) Congruent

17. (a) Opposite angles in a parallelogram are congruent.

   (b) Alternate interior angles are congruent.

19. Corresponding parts of congruent triangles are themselves congruent. ($\angle A \cong \angle D$).

   Corresponding parts of congruent triangles are themselves congruent ($\angle EBD \cong \angle ECA$).

   Supplements of congruent angles are congruent ($\angle EBA \cong \angle ECD$).

   Corresponding parts of congruent triangles are themselves congruent ($\overline{ED} \cong \overline{EC}$).

   AAS (or ASA)

21. Construction

25. Not necessarily. Here is a counterexample:

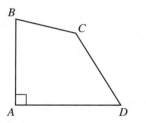 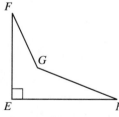

SECTION 12.3 LOGO: A Technological Tool (p. 641)

1. REPEAT 2 [FD 30 RT 90 FD 60 RT 90]

3. RT 20 FD 41 RT 140 FD 41 RT 110 FD 27

5. FD 40 RT 90 FD 30 RT 90 FD 40 RT 90 FD 30
   RT 127 FD 50 RT 106 FD 50 RT 127 FD 30

9. REPEAT 8 [FD 30 RT 45]
   RT 135 FD 30 LT 45 FD 30 RT 120 FD 30 RT 120 FD 30

11. RT 120

13. RT 135

15. RT 100

17. RT 130

19. RT 145

21. TO TWENTY1
   LT 30 REPEAT 6 [FD 40 RT 60]
   FD 40 RT 60 FD 40 RT 60 FD 40 RT 60 FD 40
   LT 90 FD 40 LT 90 FD 40 LT 90 FD 40
   END

23. TO TWENTY3
   LT 60 FD 40 RT 120 FD 80 LT 120 FD 40
   LT 60 FD 40
   LT 120 FD 80 RT 120 FD 40
   END

25. TO TWENTY5
   RT 30 FD 40
   RT 120 FD 40 RT 60 FD 40 RT 120 FD 40
   RT 60 FD 40
   LT 120 FD 20 RT 120 FD 40 RT 120 FD 40
   RT 120 FD 20
   END

27. TO PBISECTOR :LEN
   RT 90 FD :LEN BK :LEN/2
   LT 90 FD 80 BK 160
   END

29. TO HEXAGON
   REPEAT 6 [FD 30 RT 60]
   RT 36 HEXAGON
   END

CHAPTER 12 Review (p. 646)

1.   *Length*   *Midpoint*
   (a) $\sqrt{58}$ $\left(\frac{3}{2}, \frac{11}{2}\right)$
   (b)   9 $\left(\frac{9}{2}, -4\right)$

3. $y = \frac{9}{2}x - 3$

5. (b) (1, 1)   **(c)** $r = 5$

7. (a) $P \approx 27.5$ units

   (b) $A \approx 39.5$ units^2

9. The new figure is an equilateral triangle, which can be verified with a protractor and a ruler.

11. (a) (4, 2)   **(b)** (−2, 1)

15. Answers will vary. One possibility is $E(-3, -2)$, $F(5, -4)$, and $G(1, -7)$.

17. 13 dimes and 15 pennies

18. Answers will vary. One possibility is $A(1, 5)$, $B(2, 8)$, $C(5, 9)$, $D(8, 7)$, and $E(7, 3)$.

21. 43.5 cm

23. Perimeter of $\Delta 1 = 6$ units; perimeter of $\Delta 2 = 18$ units

25. SAS $\cong$ SAS

27. SSS $\cong$ SSS or SAS $\cong$ SAS (congruence).

29. TO RECTANGLE :RATIO
    REPEAT 2 [FD 50*:RATIO RT 90 FD120*
    : RATIO RT 90]
    END

CHAPTER 13

SECTION 13.1 Transformational Geometry (p. 674)

1. Answers will vary. Some possibilities follow.
   (a) Vertical shift up four units
   (b) Vertical shift up three units, then horizontal shift right four units

2. (a)   **(b)**

$\bullet$
O

3. (a)   **(b)**

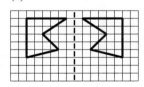 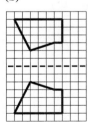

4. Constructions

5. (a) $W''(-3, 1)$, $X''(-2, -2)$, $Y''(2, -2)$, $Z''(3, 1)$
   (b) $W''(-2, -5)$, $X''(-3, -2)$, $Y''(-7, -2)$, $Z''(-8, -5)$

6. (a) Rhombus   **(b)** Rectangle

7. (a) Isosceles trapezoid   **(b)** Nonconvex pentagon

9. $A \to B$ rotation 120° clockwise about point X.
   $B \to C$ rotation 90° counterclockwise about point W.
   $C \to D$ rotation 120° clockwise about point Z.

11. $(4, 5)$

13. (a) $A'(2, 2)$, $B'(2, 4)$, $C'(-2, 8)$, $D'(-2, 2)$
   (b) $A'(-2, 2)$, $B'(-2, 4)$, $C'(2, 8)$, $D'(2, 2)$
   (c) $A'(6, 2)$, $B'(6, 4)$, $C'(2, 8)$, $D'(2, 2)$

15.

Line of Reflection	A	B	C	D	E	F
(a) $\overline{AD}$	A	F	E	D	C	B
(b) $\overline{EB}$	C	B	A	F	E	D
(c) $\overline{FC}$	E	D	C	B	A	F

18. (a) 2   **(b)** $\frac{1}{2}$

19. Answers will vary. Some possibilities follow.
   (a)

(graph with points A', B', H', G', F', E', and H, G, A, B, F, E, C, D, C', D')

21. (a) $A'(4, -1)$, $B'(6, -5)$, $C'(1, -3)$
   (b) Slope $\overline{AB} \to \frac{-2}{1}$, Slope $\overline{BC} \to \frac{-2}{5}$, Slope $\overline{CA} \to \frac{2}{3}$

23. 2.5

SECTION 13.2 Change Your Point of View: Projective Geometry, Topology, and Networks (p. 696)

1. Answers will vary. One possibility is

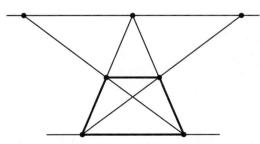

3. The change in distance affects the "height" of the perspective drawing.

5. Ellipse

9. The diagonals intersect at a single point.

11. **(a)** True   **(b)** False   **(c)** True

13. {A, D, O, P, R, Q}, {B}, {C, E, F, G, H, I, J, K, L, M, N, S, T, U, V, W, X, Y, Z}

15. Answers will vary. One possibility is

17. No, there are more than two odd vertices.

19. No

21. No

CHAPTER 13 Review (p. 699)

1. **(a)** Translation $(x, y) \rightarrow (x, y + 4)$

  (b) Reflection about the y–axis

3. **(a)**   **(b)**

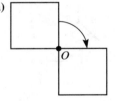

5. **(a)** $A'(2, 2), B'(4, 4), C'(6, 4), D'(4, 2)$

  (b) $A'(-4, 4), B'(-8, 8), C'(-12, 8), D'(-8, 4)$

  (c) $A'(4, -4), B'(8, -8), C'(12, -8), D'(8, -4)$

  (d) $A'(4, -4), B'(8, -8), C'(8, -12), D'(4, -8)$

  (e) $A'(2, 7), B'(6, 11), C'(10, 11), D'(6, 7)$

7. **(a)** $A'(0, -5), B'(0, 6), C'(-4, 0)$

  (b) $A''(0, -5), B''(0, 6), C''(4, 0)$

9.

	X	Y	Z
(a)	(0, 0)	(−5, −8)	(−1, −4)
(b)	(0, 0)	(24, 15)	(12, 3)
(c)	(0, 0)	(−15, 24)	(−3, 12)
(d)	(0, 0)	(−15, −24)	(−3, −12)

11. Yes, there are only two odd vertices.

13.

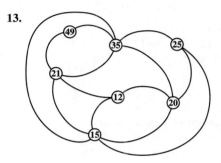

Not traversable

15. **(a)** Not traversable   **(b)** Traversable

17. Both sides will wear out uniformly.

APPENDIX A (p. A-37)

Answers may vary.

1. 27 pennies, 32 nickels, 14 dimes, 15 quarters, and 12 half dollars

2. 8188

3. 142,857

4. 219, 438, 657

Index